Religion in Iran

Religion in Iran
From Zoroaster to Baha'ullah

by

Alessandro Bausani

Translated by
J. M. Marchesi

Bibliotheca Persica Press
New York

©2000 Bibliotheca Persica Press
All rights reserved

Published by Bibliotheca Persica Press, New York

Distributed by:
Eisenbrauns, Inc
P.O. Box 275
Winona Lake, Indiana 46590
Fax: (219)269-6788

Library of Congress Cataloging-in-Publication Data

Bausani, Alessandro, 1921–
    [Persia relgiosa da Zaratustra a Bahâ'u'llah. English]
    Religion in Iran : from Zoroaster to Baha'ullah / translated
    by J. M. Marchesi.
      p. cm.
    Includes bibliographical references and index.
    ISBN 0-933273-26-6
      1. Iran—Religion.   I. Title.

BL2270 .B2813 2000
200'.955—dc21
                                      00-036102

Contents

Publishers' Note and Acknowledgments

The present volume is a translation of *Persia Religiosa* (Milan, 1959) by the late Alessandro Bausani (1921–1988), professor of Islamic Studies at the University of Rome and a scholar of noted erudition. It is the only work in a Western language which treats the history of religions in Persia in a comprehensive fashion. The author's vast knowledge of Middle Eastern and a number of South and Southeast Asian languages as well as the history, religion, and culture of their speakers gave Professor Bausani exceptional qualification to treat the religious history of Persia in a comparative perspective.

The first part of the book, which deals with pre-Islamic Iranian religions, was reviewed by Dr. Jamsheed Choksy, Associate Professor of ancient Iranian studies at the University of Indiana, and the post-Islamic period by Dr. Juan Cole, Professor of history at the University of Michigan, who also edited the volume. Both scholars added bibliographical notes to bring the references up to date. Their assistance is greatly appreciated.

The transcription system of the author has been kept unchanged. It will be noted that the two letters *hamza* and *'ain* are both rendered by a raised apostrophe.

The Publishers would like to express their gratitude to Mrs. Elsa Bausani for assisting the project and obtaining a waiver of the copyright for the English translation; Ms. Marchesi for her competent translation of the book; Prof. Scarcia-Amoretti, of the University of Naples, for her graciously agreeing to provide the volume with a biography of the author as well as an introductory description of *Religion in Iran*; Dr. Jalal Matini, editor of *Iranshenasi Journal*, for authorizing the reprinting of Prof. Dick Davis' review of two memorial volumes for Prof. Bausani; Prof. Heshmat Moayyad, of University of Chicago, for furnishing a selected bibliography (books only) of Prof. Bausani and Dr. Frank Lewis, of Emory University, Atlanta, for carefully and conscientiously reading and correcting the final proofs of the book at short notice, and Ms. Diane Dustin of ISIS-1 Corporation, for her meticulous work on the layout of the book and for cleaning and refining the illustrations.

The Publishers wish also to thank the Taslimi Foundation of Los Angeles for their much appreciated support of the project.

About the Author

Alessandro Bausani was born in Rome in 1921. He started studying Arabic at an early age. His Arabic studies led to his linguistic interest in the Near and Middle Eastern area. He attended the Faculty of Arts of Rome University (La Sapienza) under the guidance of well-known scholars such as Michelangelo Guidi, Ettore Rossi, and Francesco Gabrieli. He obtained his degree in 1943, producing a thesis on "The Historical Development of Neo-Persian syntax." He taught Persian language and literature in Rome from 1944 to 1956 and then, as full professor, in Naples, at the Istituto Universitario Orientale, where he gave courses also in Indonesian, Urdu, and religions and philosophies of the Middle and Far East. From 1955 to the early 1980s he traveled throughout the Muslim world from Morocco to Indonesia giving lectures in the languages of the countries he visited. In 1971, he moved back to Rome where he held the Chair of Islamic Studies until his death in 1988. He was a member of many academic and orientalist associations such as the prestigious Accademia Nazionale dei Lincei, of which he was "corresponding" member from 1967 and national member from 1983. He received many awards both in Italy and abroad, especially in Pakistan. He forsook an earlier interest in Marxism (which, in an Italian context, denoted opposition to Fascism) to embrace the Baha'i faith in 1949 and was an active member of the small Italian Baha'i community.

Bausani had a wide range of interests, from linguistics—taken in its broad sense (grammar and syntax's problems; origins of language and languages; 'Islamic' languages; invented languages, etc.) to the history of sciences in Islam, in particular, astronomy and mathematics. In order to give an idea of Bausani's primary contribution, I should like to briefly review two main aspects of his scholarly output.

The first concerns the study of religions and more specifically Islam, with a particular reference to its shi'ite and sufi variations; Jalâl-al-Dîn Rûmî was one of Bausani's beloved authors, and Isma'ilism one of his main topics. In this respect, the translation of the Qur'an which I have mentioned in the Foreword and *Persia Religiosa* itself, are, perhaps, his most important books. Analyzing Islam, he viewed it as a part of the comprehensive phenomenon of monotheism ("Note per una tipologia del monoteismo," in *Studi e Materiali di Storia della*

Religioni, XXVIII, 1957, pp. 67–88) pertaining to Western civilization ("Islam as an essential part of Western culture," in *Studies on Islam*, Amsterdam-London, 1974, pp. 19–36). In Islam's evolution he distinguished three phases: first, a very early stage in which Muhammad's absolute monotheism brought about an integration of the Arabs ethnically (*Maometto. I protagonisti della Storia Universale*, no. 90, Milan, 1967, p. 28; "L'Islam: integrazione o sincretismo religioso?" in *Incontro di religioni in Asia tra il III e il X secolo D.C.*, Florence, 1984, pp. 99–114); second, a classical phase, during which Islam absorbed and elaborated in an original manner both Greek philosophy and science and the Gnostic and other cultural legacies of the Near and Middle East, especially in the scientific field ("Religion in the Saljuq Period," in *Cambridge History of Iran*, V, Cambridge, 1968, pp. 283–302; "Religion under the Mongols," in *Cambridge History of Iran*, V, Cambridge, 1968, pp. 538–49; "Biruni between 'Scientia' and 'Sapientia,'" in *Mélanges d'Islamologie dédiés à la mémoire de M. Abel*, Leiden, 1974, pp. 58–68; "Al-Biruni, un grande pensatore del Medioevo islamico nel millenario della nascita," in *Rivista degli Studi Orientali*, XLVIII, 1974, pp. 75–97; *Un filosofo 'laico' del medioevo musulmano: Abu Bakr Muhammad Zakariyya' Razi* (Rome, 1981); "Aspetti scientifici delle Epistole dei 'Fratelli della purità,'" in *Atti del 'Convegno sugli Ikhwan as-Safa,'* Accademia Nazionale dei Lincei, (Rome, 1979 [1981]), pp. 27–47: one among the many articles he devoted to the Ikhwan as-Safa; "Le Scienze," in *Il Califfato di Baghdad* (Rome, 1968), pp. 181–208, etc.

In its third phase, Islam presented itself in its universal dimension and adapted to the cultures which welcomed it, like those of India, Indonesia, and Africa ("L'Islam non arabo," in *Storia della religioni*, T. Ventura, G. Castellani, eds., Turin, 1970–71, V, pp. 179–211; "Sopravvivenze pagane nell'Islam o integrazione islamica?" in *Studi e Materiali di Storia delle Religioni*," 1973, p. 27). He also devoted studies to contemporary Islam, with particular reference to India and Pakistan ("Note su Shah Waliullah di Delhi," in *Annali dell'Istituto Universitario Orientale di Napoli*, n.s., X, 1960, pp. 93–147; "Sir Sayyid Ahmad Khan (1817–1916) e il moto della terra" in *Rivista degli Studi Orientali*, XXX, 1955, pp. 55–102; *Muhammad Iqbal. Il poema celeste*, tr. and annot. Bari, 1965, p. 326, etc.)

A second major area of activity for Bausani concerned Persian literature in its classical phase and then in India, where Persian culture flourished in part because it was carried by Muslim dynasties such as the Mughals. In the *Storia della letteratura persiana* (History of Persian Literature) (Milan, 1960), the Islamic section by him covers 772 pages (see Foreword). Here, Bausani begins with the history of Persian language, goes on with the definition of literary genres of Islamic literatures, and proposes the first systematic index of literary motifs and symbols through which Persian literature structured the poetic conventions of Islamic civilization. Similar works include surveys of Pakistani and Malaysian literature: *Storia della letterature del Pakistan, Urdu, Pangiabi, Sindhi, Beluchi, Pashtu, Bengali, Pakistana* (Milan, 1958); *Malesia. Poesie e leggende* (Milan, 1963); "Note sulla struttura della 'hikayat' classica malese," in *Annali del'Istituto Universitario Orientale di Napoli*," n.s., XII, 1962. At one time or another Bausani devoted studies to or translated from almost all the great Persian poets, along with some Arab ones, producing works such as: an Italian translation of Umar Khayyam's Ruba'iyyat entitled *Quartine* (Turin, 1956); *L'Opera poetica di Ibn Sina* (Venice, 1956); "Il Libro della Barba" of Ubayd Zakani, in *A Francesco Gabrieli. Studi orientalistici offerti nel sessantesimo compleanno dai suoi collegi e discepoli* (Rome, 1964); *Le sette principesse* of Nizâmî of Ganjeh (Bari, 1967); *Poesie mistiche of Jalal al-Din Rumi* (Milan, 1980).

According to many scholars Bausani's fundamental contribution to the history of Persian literature was his pioneering works on "Indian style" of Persian poetry and its practitioners. His publications in this field include: "Contributo a una definizione dello 'stile indiano' nella poesia persiana," in *Annali dell'Istituto Universitario Orientale di Napoli*, n.s., VII, 1957, pp. 167–78; "Note su Mirza Bedil (1644–1721)," in *Annali dell'Ist. [ituto] Univ. [ersita] Or. [ientale] di Napoli*, n.s. VI, 1954–1956, pp. 163–199; "The position of Ghalib (1796–1869) in the history of Urdu and Indo-Persian poetry," in *Islam*, XXXIV, 1958, pp. 99–127; "La poesia di Ghalib," in *Orientalia Romana*, 3. Ghalib, Rome, 1969, pp. 97–167; "L'opera di Mirza Abdul Qadir Bedil nel panorama letterario culturale dell'Afghanistan," in *Il Veltro*, XVI/5–6, 1972, pp. 447–53; "Indian elements in the Indo-Persian poetry: the style of Ghanimat Kunjahi," in *Orientalia Hispanica sive studia F. M. Pareja octogenario dicata*, I, Leiden, 1974, pp. 105–19.

The first systematic bibliography of Bausani's publications appeared in *La Bisaccia dello Shaikh* (Venice, 1981), a book presented to him by his closest pupils on his sixtieth birthday (pp. 7–16). This bibliography (329 items) has been revised in Yad-nama. In memoria di Alessandro Bausani, B. Scarcia Amoretti, L. Rostagno, eds., Rome, 1991, I, *Islamistica*, pp. XIII-XXVII, but it is still incomplete. In particular, two posthumous works, *Saggi sulla fede Baha'i* (Rome, 1991), and the translation from Greek into Roman dialect of the Gospel according to Matthew (Rome, 1992), must be added.

Bausani's academic work was founded not only on the methods and ideas of the Western tradition of academic study of the Middle East but also on the contributions of contemporary Muslim academics themselves on these subjects. Being so attuned to the writings produced by colleagues in Africa and

About the Author

Asia was rare among Orientalists in the 1950s, when Bausani began to be internationally known, and his role in such intellectual cross-fertilization helps account for the wide impact of some of his research discoveries and theories (however controversial) not only in Europe but in the Muslim world itself.

Bianca Scarcia-Amoretti

About the Book

by Bianca Scarcia-Amoretti

Persia Religiosa was published in Milan in 1959 by Il Saggiatore, an important publishing house in the cultural panorama of the period, which took an active part in freeing Italy from the persisting tendency to intellectual provincialism bequeathed to it by the fascist regime. The book took its place alongside famous works of anthropology, literary theory, etc., by Italian and foreign authors but it was the only one devoted to an extra-European civilization. The subtitle "From Zarathustra to Baha'ullah" is significant in that it expresses the overall sense of what the author intended to achieve: giving pride of place to continuity as the key to reading the religious history of Persia However, this orientation is not a one-way process. In European, Iranist and Islamicist circles, Henry Corbin's vision of the uniqueness of Persia and the way in which Islam was altered so as to naturalize it on Persian soil was beginning to enjoy credibility. This vision, though drastically reworked, continues to be influential in Europe and the United States.

Between 1954, when Corbin's *Avicenna and the Visionary Recital* was published, and 1959, the French scholar expressed himself mainly through a prestigious Jungian periodical, *Eranos Jahrbuch*, which accepted many of his works on Sufism and Ismailism with particular reference to Persia. Corbin, too, maintained that there was no dividing line in Persia between pre- and post-Islamization, but his idea of continuity was antithetical to that formulated by Alessandro Bausani. Corbin, as we know, held that Persia's religious identity involved a faithfulness to that country's intrinsic destiny as the indisputable seat of Gnostic and metaphysical concerns which run through all the religious phenomena to which Persia has given birth. True Persian religion, in his perspective, belongs necessarily to a metahistorical and elitist dimension and is, consequently, poles apart from Islam, particularly if Islam is interpreted in the most common way, as a rational and legalistic religion, little inclined to philosophical speculation and hostile to even moderate forms of esotericism. Hence, according to Corbin, Persian religion progressively domesticated Islam, with a dual result. The first, strictly religious, was Shi'ism, which modified Islam by introducing into it the Persian patrimony of symbols, myths, and cults. The second, on a more general plane, was a coherent set of philosophical works that have often been described as Islamic, but in fact, were Persian.

Bausani, on the contrary, does not renounce history, setting the religious processes he is dealing with in their historical framework. He starts from the assumption that Persia is not bound to continuity, but that the particular phenomena that have constantly refashioned religion in Persia do demonstrate continuities. In this sense, an exceptional role can be attributed to Persia in relation to both the Near and Middle East and Western culture in general. It was not by chance that Bausani adhered to the Baha'i faith, to which the last part of the book is devoted. Bausani highlights the debt of the new religion to Shi'ism and in particular to the "schools" that were born and developed in Persia: the School of Isfahan, which reached back to the Ishrâqî or Neoplatonic illuminationist theory of Suhravardî, and the Shaykhî school, which reformulated the Shi'ite need for an active and ever-present intermediary between God and men. According to the author, these schools were an indispensable platform for negotiating the passage toward a more universalistic and ecumenical religious conception that, in particular, restores to religion the lost congruency with the present historical period. And Persia was the right place for it.

The capacity to update the tradition when it appears worn out and inadequate is not the only factor of continuity. There is a second one which we could call syncretism—even though the term is not entirely satisfying—which characterizes all the significant moments of Persian religious history. Over the period stretching from Zarathustra to Baha'ullah Persia was at the crossroads between many cultures; some coming from the East, others from the West. From the East, there were Indian influences and Central Asian ones which mediated more or less indirect Chinese influences; from the West, the Judeo-Christian and Greek Hellenistic heritages—until both were absorbed first into the Islamic message, then into the colonial dimension.

The dynamics of contact and penetration were not always the same. At times, Persia was the victim of invasions such as the emblematic one of Alexander the Macedonian (4th century B.C.) or that of the Mongols (13th century); at times Persia itself launched the invasions, such as the conquest of Babylon (6th century B.C.) with its Syro-Palestinian offshoots, the fateful clash with Athens (5th century B.C.), or the penetration into Yemen on the eve of Islam. Sometimes the contact was less traumatic and passed through more normal cultural routes. On the whole, however, Persia was the interlocutor and oriental rival of the West, whether it was represented by Greece, Rome, or Byzantium. On the other hand, it was the natural Western outpost towards India and China.

Bausani traced a historical profile of this kind of clash/encounter in a text written a few years later, *I Persiani* (Florence, 1962, English translation *The Persians*, London, 1971), which he presented as complementary to Persia Religiosa and in which he followed the same line of interpretation. Significantly, the title of the chapter on the cultural foundation of modern Persia is

"Muhammad or Darius?" In *Persia Religiosa*, Bausani analyzes only the religious phenomena. He starts with the presentation of Mazdaism and its original reprocessing of archaic material which led to a sort of proto-monotheism or, better, to a specific type of monotheism in which the figure of Zarathustra, as reformer-prophet, is indissolubly linked to the world-renewing function that characterized prophetic action. In fact, the prophet always represents the instrument that makes the syncretism we mentioned above possible. Every new prophet corresponds to a new intention and exigency requiring the integration of new and/or external elements, which connect back to a well-known conceptual and ritual typology.

Thus, for Mani, the founder of Manicheism, which Bausani defines as "an extreme heresy, of a Gnostic type, of Zoroastrianism," or Mazdak, who championed—always in Bausani's words—"a religious social reform . . . of clear Manichaean derivation." But the prophetic role emerges even more emphatically when Islam is involved because of the Baha'i religion since, for Bausani, the Baha'i faith is the beginning of the new prophetic cycle after the conclusion of the Muhammadan one which had grown barren and had exhausted any possibility to regenerate itself.

We must remember that, when Bausani wrote *Persia Religiosa*, he had already translated the Qur'an (Florence, 1955) and published a number of articles, including "Postille a Corano" II, 248, XXXIX, 23, XX, 15, in *Studi orientalistici in onore di Giorgio Levi Della Vida*, Rome, 1956 in which he questioned (p. 51) the conventional reading of Muhammad as khâtam al-anbiyâ' (seal of the prophets, which most Muslims took to mean the last of them), maintaining that in the cyclic conception characteristic of Islam, the expression simply indicates that he was the "seal of the prophets" of his time. This concept of the prophetic function is also valid for the period between the arrival of Islam on the Persian plateau in 651 and the appearance of the new religion during the first half of the 19th century. The author devotes what may at first seem disproportionate space to Isma'ilism (inasmuch as it is a particular kind of Shi'ism born of Arab initiative and in Arab circles but which found fertile ground in Persia to develop, to Avicenna (980–1037) in its Gnostic aspect, and to Sufism in the figures of Suhravardî (12th century) and Rûmî (13th century). On the other hand, comparatively little space is devoted to mainstream Islam of any sort, to such vast and diverse traditions of thought as scholastic theology, or to law in either their Sunni or Shi'ite forms. As Bausani sees it, Isma'ilism, Avicennian Gnosis, the Illuminationist Sufism of Suhravardî and the protesting Sufism of Rûmî, have in common an insistence on the renewal of the prophetic message, rediscovered through the Imam or the initiatory Master.

According to the author, there are two ways of proving that this attitude is Persian in the true sense of the term. The first is a substantial proof and consists in the never-abandoned reference to angelic metaphysics, otherwise defined as angelized Platonism, which Persian Islam inherited from ancient Persia. Such a constant return to ancient religious forms, which Bausani calls "re-archaicization" in the sense that it involves a conscious reference to the inheritance of the past, occurs, according to him, also in the political history of Persia each time it needs to redefine its own identity. The second is a formal proof and consists in the use of a symbology which certainly belongs to the Islamic literary code but is nourished on pre-Islamic Persian mythology, reintroduced into Muslim Persia by Firdausî (11th century) and which is woven into the entire fabric of Persian literature.

Hence, the author's narrative technique which leads us to enjoy *Persia Religiosa* on a number of different levels. The technique consists of entrusting the exposition of a philosophical theory or concept to a work of great literary import. Mazdak, for example, is recounted for us by Firdausî, Ismailism by Nâsir-i Khusrau (11th century), Neo-Platonizing Gnosticism by Avicenna's "Treatise of the Birds" (Risâlat al-Tayr), "the Eastern Wisdom" (Hikmat al-ishrâq) and "Crimson Intellect" ('Aql-i surkh) by Suhravardî , and so forth. The texts document a train of thought in which the poetic language becomes functional, as with the accurately decoded symbolism in Avicenna's commentary. Again, the chronology of Bausani's writing projects eloquently indicates the nature of this consistency. In 1957 he published a translation of *Zoroastrian Religious Texts* (Texti Religiosi Zoroastriani) and many articles which served as prelude to his fundamental works, Storia della letterature persiana (*History of Persian Literature*, Milan, 1960), in which the section on the Islamic period complements the contribution of another Persianist scholar, A. Pagliaro, devoted to pre-Islamic Persian literatures.

Many years have passed since 1959. The events that have profoundly changed the face of contemporary Persia in the course of these last forty years have provoked often radical revisions of the various approaches to the history of the country, and in particular to its religious history. Not only have changing political conditions affected intellectual fashions and historiographical currents, but even the rarefied atmosphere of Persian studies has been enriched by new, valuable works and real philological discoveries. Thus recent scholars have been able to draw on a great deal of material that was inconceivable when *Persia Religiosa* was written. Besides, the author himself did not present the book when it appeared as a systematic handbook or summary of the literature then known. In fact, he gave clear priority to utilizing the primary sources and used specialized criteria in his references to the secondary literature, which, even then, some people considered arbitrary.

In any case, the book has remained relevant. In a way, the fact that it has only now become available to the English-speaking public could be considered an added merit, providing the occasion for a more balanced evaluation of that new trend in European Oriental studies which produced its first important results—among them *Persia Religiosa*—precisely in the 1950s, at a time when the colonial empires were past or fading, and which were characterized by fewer guilt feelings toward "the Other" less likely to be viewed as "alien." At any events, the value of the book lies elsewhere. On the one hand its originality remains intact and it objectively fills a gap since no other history of Persian religiosity in these terms has been produced. It continues to be convincing and plausible, to bring up to date, and a follow-up chapter on what occurred in the twentieth century has been added. Furthermore, the book carries a message of interest not only to Persianist scholars but also to all Persians and, more generally, to all Muslims: by focusing on Persia as an important component—perhaps the most important—of the history of Islam, *Religion in Iran* highlights the nationalistic and sectarian risks implicit in every ahistorical reading of both Persia and Islam.

Rome, July 1998

Bausani and His Work: an Overview

The following is a review by Dick Davis, professor of Persian Literature at Ohio State University at Columbus, of two memorial volumes published in honor of Professor Alessandro Bausani in Naples (1995)[1] and Venice (1996)[2]. The review, which presents an overview of Professor Bausani's corpus, sheds further light on his erudition and his vast knowledge of Islamic culture and its development world-wide.

To students of Persian literature and cultural history Alessandro Bausani is best known as the author of two surveys, *Persia Religiosa, da Zaratustra a Baha'u'llah* (Milan, 1959) and *Letteratura Persiana* (Milan, 1960) as well as a number of articles, some of which, like *Muhammad or Darius? The Elements and Basis of Iranian Culture* (*Islamic and Cultural Change in the Middle Ages*, ed. Speros Vryonis, Wiesbaden, 1975, pp. 43–58), have had a wide influence on shaping recent Western views of Persian civilization. The word "surveys," though strictly accurate, does not of course do justice to the immense erudition, and often startingly original analyses, to be found in the two volumes devoted to religion and literature. He is certainly—with Browne, Nicholson, Berthels and Rypka—one of the greatest of non-Iranian scholars of Persian literature, and among Western commentators he stands alone in the breadth of his knowledge of Persian religious life. Most of us, if we could leave such a splendid legacy, would consider our time to have been well and productively spent, but what is immediately apparent from the memorial Festschrift for Bausani and his work (*Ricordo Che Non Si Spegne: Scritti di docenti e collaboratori dell' Istituto Universitario Orientale di Napoli in memoria di Alessandro Bausani*, Naples, 1995), is that although Persian was his major scholarly interest, it was by no means his only one. He had a lively interest in Arabic and Turkish, which is perhaps not a surprise; he wrote on the cultures of India and Pakistan, and such an activity is plausible, even if his interest in

---

[1] *Ricordo Che Non Si Spegne: Scritti di docenti e collaboratori dell'Istituto Universitario Orientale di Napoli in memoria di Alessandro Bausani.*
[2] *Annali di Ca' Foscari: Rivista della Facolta di Lingue e Letterature Straniere Dell' Universita Ca Foscari Di Venezia, XXXV, 3.*

Tamil seems a little off the beaten track for a Persianist. But how many of us who admire his writings on Iran also know of his work on Malay (about which he wrote two books), on Indonesian culture (the study of which he initiated in Italy), on Native American languages, on the history of codes and secret languages, or that he found time to compile a dictionary of the language of Fiji?

The Festschrift opens with a number of essays of personal reminiscence, and the portrait that emerges is remarkably homogenous from one writer to another; all mention his wide-ranging and insatiable intellectual curiosity (one calls it "una curiosita leonardesca"), many allude to his quite staggering linguistic capability (one contributor estimates that he could read comfortably in "about thirty languages"), virtually everyone invokes his profound humanity, his kindness and good humored friendship (one description refers to his "*agape* abbondate e raffinata insieme"). It may be true that, as Dr. Johnson said of writing epitaphs, scholars are hardly on oath when contributing to a volume of this nature, nevertheless, the portrait that emerges is of someone possessed of an extraordinary intellectual energy and insight, and able to inspire among his colleagues and students great loyalty and affection. The topics covered here, all of which were of interest to Bausani and on most of which he made scholarly contributions himself, include, among others, medieval Islamic philosophy, "classical" Arab geography and literature, the modern Arab world, pre-Islamic Iran, Indian Moghul history, the Hebrew drama, Manicheism, Hindu devotional religion, and Persian loan words in Circassian. Indonesian culture, the Muslims of the former Yugoslavia, and the origins of the Basque language, as well as the to be expected Persian literature, historiography and religion. The remark of the editor Adriano Rossi that "Bausani was the last of the pioneering generation of great Orientalists able to cover a number of disciplines" seems as much a comment on Bausani's own quite incredible energy and range of interests as it is on the general development of scholarship. "Leonardesca" seems an understatement.

About one third of the thirty-five essays deal with Persian or Persian-related topics, and a number of others are concerned with subjects of interest to many Persianists (e.g., the Moghul courts, the presence of Persian lexical items in other languages, medieval Islamic philosophical speculation). Of those directly concerned with Persian subjects, among the most interesting, in this reviewer's estimation, are those by Gnoli (a brilliantly argued piece on the origin and meaning of the epithet "Anushirvān," attached to the Sasanian monarch Khosrow 1), Piemontese (on a thirteenth-century account of Mani and his doctrines), Bernardini (on Khwāndamir's account of the Roman empire in the *Habib al-Siyar*), and D'Erme (on recurrent topoi in Hafez's poetry). Of considerable interest, too, is Maria Fontana's persuasive essay on a miniature contained in an early 15th century anthology dedicated to Iskandar ibn Shýh Rokh, which she interprets as a work of Shi'i inspiration, probably based on a Western Adoration of the Magi. Bruno Genito's contribution is a thorough survey of the problem as to why the civilization of the Medes should figure so prominently in ancient sources when archeologists have been able to find so little irrefutable material evidence of their presence. A. V. Rossi provides an elaborately argued article on the probable meaning of certain nouns of familial relationship in Achaemenid inscriptions. Tocci's essay on the analogies between Corbin's views of Persian religious thoughts and the speculations of Jung concerning the collective unconscious will excite some, though my own, perhaps too empirically Anglo-Saxon, skepticism as to the work of both Corbin and Jung means that I find myself in the role of one who has never been admitted to the sacred mysteries, and who suspects they might be largely hocus pocus.

Most Persianists will probably find the articles on Moghul civilization of interest: Iqtida Hasan draws attention to what appears to be an extraordinary autobiography (in Persian, but according to Hasan only available in an Urdu translation), by a late 18th-century Moghul prince (Ali Bakht Mohammad Zahiru'd-din Azfari). The account of his escape from the Red Fort sounds as daring and suspenseful as Casanova's from the Doge's palace (and roughly contemporary): an edition of the Persian text would seem to be very desirable. Umberto Scerrato's essay on the *hammam*s of the imperial Moghuls necessarily lacks the human interest of Hasan's piece, but it more than makes up for this with a wealth of documentation, including plans of the discussed monuments. Tangential to Persian, but worth any Persianist's attention both for itself and for its references to Jewish diaspora culture in Iran, is Gabriella Steindler's paper on the development of the Esther story as a vehicle for farce in Hebrew. For anyone with a scintilla of Bausani's own apparently endless intellectual curiosity, there are a number of papers here which have nothing to do with Persian but which make for fascinating reading; I found Vincenzo Valeri's piece on the probable origins of the Basque language, and Claudio Lo Jacono's essay on the characteristics of "Jinn" especially fascinating.

This is then a very various, informative volume, which is something of an omnium gatherum but which maintains a generally high standard of scholarship (despite one or two rather slight pieces). It is also in the main, as Bausani would certainly have wished it to be, a very enjoyable collection: the majority of the contributors are Italian, and most Italian scholars (there are exceptions) have not yet adopted the puritanical tone of so much scholarship in English, German and French, which can imply that language indicating one actually likes the material one studies is evidence of rank amateurism. Bausani's own immense oeuvre is itself a monument to the ways in which sheer intellectual pleasure can be a great stimulus to first-rate scholarly work, and this collection does him honor by providing so much potential pleasure to its readers.

The *Annali di Ca' Foscari* of 1996 (XXXV, 3) also contains a couple of articles of interest to Persianists. Ricardo Zipoli's "Elementi osceni nella lessicographia neo-persiana" discusses the incidence and meaning of particular obscene terms in the work of some twenty-five poets, providing a tabulated statistical analysis, as is Zipoli's wont. The essay complements and expands on work in this area by Paul Sprachman; given Zipoli's great thoroughness it is a little surprising that Noland and Warren (1981, "Iranian Values as Depicted in Farsi Terms of Abuse, Curses, Threats, and Exclamations," in *Maledicta*, V.1–2, pp. 229–41) which records a number of the same terms as Zipoli, providing evidence of their continued contemporary usage. Aldo Ferrari contributes a largely descriptive but very informative essay on Tsar Peter the Great's "Persian Expedition" (1722–23), the part played in this by Armenian notables, and the resulting loss to Iran of areas west of the Caspian, including Baku.

Bausani's Selected Bibliography
(books only)

Il Corano, Florence, 1955. Italian translation of the *Qur'an*, with an introduction, and followed by a commentary and analytical index.

Poesie di Muhammad Iqbal, Parma, 1956. Translation of Sir Muhammad Iqbal's Persian and Urdu poems, with an introduction and notes.

Quartine di 'Umar Khayyam, Turin, 1956. The ruba'iyyat of 'Umar Khayyam.

Opera Poetica di Ibn Sina, Venice, 1956. Translation of Avicenna's Arabic and Persian poems, with an introduction and notes.

Testi religiosi Zoroastriani, Rome, 1957. Zoroastrian texts translated from Pahlavi, with notes.

Storia delle Letterature del Pakistan, Milan, 1958. Urdu, Punjabi, Sindhi, Baluchi, Pashto, and Bengali literatures; reprinted in 1968.

Persia Religiosa, Milan, 1959. A religious history of Iran. Translated as *Religion in Iran* (New York, 1999).

Storia della Letteratura Persiana, Milan, 1960. A history of Persian literature, with a contribution by Antonio Pagliaro on the pre-Islamic literatures of Iran; reprinted in 1968.

I Persiani, Florence, 1962. A brief survey of Persian history with critical remarks and observations; translated into English (*The Persians*, London, 1971), German (*Die Perser*, Stuttgart, 1965), and Persian (*Iranian*).

Malesia: Poesie e Leggende, Milan, 1963. Malaysian poems and legends.

Il Poema Celeste, Bari, 1965. Translation from the Persian original of Mohammad Iqbal's *Javidan-nameh* or the Book of Eternity and other poems, with commentary and notes.

Le sette principesse, Bari, 1967. Translation from Persian of Nezami's masterpiece *Haft paykar*.

Le letterature del Sudest Asiatico, Florence and Milan, 1970. Literatures of Burma, Siam, Laos, Cambodia, Vietnam, Java, Malesian Indonesia, and the Philippines.

Storia delle Letterature del Sud-Est Asiatico, Milan, 1971. History of Southeast Asian literatures.

Buddha, Chiasso, 1973. On Buddha's life and religion.

Le Lingue Inventate, Rome, 1974. Invented languages. Translated into German as *Geheim und Universalsprachen* (Stuttgart, 1976).

Appunti di Astronomia e Astrologia arabo islamiche, Venice, 1977. Notes on Arabic-Islamic astronomy and astrology.

L'Enciclopedia dei Fratelli della Purita, Naples, 1978. Translation with introduction and brief commentary of 52 treatises and epistles of the *Ikhwýn al-Sùafý* or the Brethren of the Purity.

L'Islam, Milan, 1980. An introduction to Islam.

Gialal ad-din Rumi, Poesie Mistiche, Milan, 1980. Mystical poems of Rumi, with introduction and critical notes.

Posthumously published

Saggi sulla Fede Baha'i, Rome, 1991. Articles and lectures on the Baha'i faith.

La Bbona Notizzia. Vangelo di Matteo nella Versione Romanesca, Milan, 1992. Good tidings. Matthew's gospel in Roman version.

Introduction

Western knowledge of oriental thought is mostly limited to the religious thought of the Far East—the area that stretches roughly from India in the west to Japan in the east (I speak here of knowledge among educated readers, not of specialized scientific knowledge). In cultivated circles it is easy to find people who are passionately interested in Buddhism, Taoism, etc., while these same circles rarely produce a person who has freed himself of the old medieval prejudices toward Islam and toward Muslim religious thought, or anyone who has approached the religious world of the near East—let us say from Egypt to Persia—with the lively interest and passion that makes knowledge useful. One of the main purposes of this book is the "circulation" of the fundamental aspects of Persian religious thinking among educated Westerners. For the eventful history of the region (Persia or Iran) in which it developed, traversed as it was by the most varied currents and influences, offers us some insights into the religious world-views of a number of peoples in the Near and Middle East.

The three great invasions that overran Persia in the course of its millennia of history—i.e., those of Alexander of Macedonia (fourth century B.C.), the Muslim Arabs (seventh century A.D.) and the Mongols and Turks (thirteenth through fifteenth centuries A.D.)—divide the course of the religious and cultural history of Iran into several long periods. These include the period of the ancient religion, with the related question of the formation of the doctrine of Zarathustra (seventh through fourth centuries B.C. [or, according to recent scholarship, as early as the thirteenth century, B.C.-ed.]); that of the Mazdean medieval religion, with its heresies and theological problems (fourth century B.C. through seventh centuries [or even ninth century] A.D.); that of early Persian Islam, which was Sunni among the masses but which contained considerable infiltrations of "heretical" religious ideas for which the vestiges of ancient popular Iranian religiosity must have been partly responsible (eighth through fifteenth centuries A.D.); the modern period during which Persia—by now Shi'ite through the political influence of the Turkic Safavid dynasty—cut itself off from the surrounding "orthodox" Muslim world and nurtured religious and emotional tendencies that perpetuated, through mysterious channels, those of the preceding period and which gave rise—well into the nineteenth century—to a new religion, the Babi-Baha'i.

1

Is it right, the reader may ask, to give Persia and the religious thought of such disparate and widely separated periods a common denominator that may at first sight seem purely geographical? Or, in other words, is there a religious continuity between ancient, pre-Islamic, and modern, Islamic, Persia? This problem has engaged the minds of orientalists for a long time. First, some wanted to consider every slight deviation from a hypothetical Sunni "Semitic" Islam attributable to an "Aryan" Persian element.

This book is an attempt to answer this problem, a problem that I personally feel has been badly formulated. To begin with, "Aryan" and "Semitic" are terms that we should eliminate or at least use extremely cautiously and only in the sense of "abbreviations" of far more complex cultural phenomena, with no racist undertones. And we have continued using them occasionally in this sense in the present book. "Semitic" sometimes is synonymous with essentially monotheistic and prophetic religious thought and "Aryan" with monistic ideas and those with a tendency to pantheism. It must also be remembered that Semitic elements have been present in Persian culture since pre-Islamic times when first Assyrian-Babylonian and later Aramaic were the diplomatic and court languages. If a general characteristic of "Iranian culture" exists, this seems to me to be precisely suppleness, an aptitude for the synthesis of heterogeneous elements, the permanent composite nature of Iranian culture. In this sense a more concrete answer should be given to the query as to whether there is a continuity between pre-Islamic and Islamic Iran. If continuity is understood as direct continuity, then it does not exist, despite the attempts of Corbin and his enthusiastic Persian students to demonstrate it. But if one bears in mind that Iranian culture was, both before and after Islam, amply influenced by Mesopotamian syncretism—which embraces Iranian elements—we find this unity, though in a different perspective. The unitary aspect is bestowed by common contributions (even if in successive phases of development) to Iranian religious thought by the world that could be broadly defined as "gnostic"-Mesopotamian. It must be remembered that Mesopotamia was a part—and the most culturally advanced part—of the Persian empire from the sixth century B.C. onward and, subsequently, of the Muslim empire of the caliphs. Only relatively recently has there existed an Iran politically distinct from Mesopotamia or Iraq (where even now are located the most important spiritual centers of Twelver Shi'ism, which has been the official religion of Persia since the sixteenth century).

Consequently Persian "purist" nationalism is based (as are all nationalisms in fact) on an illusion and—in this particular instance—on an illusion to the creation of which certain European orientalists have contributed greatly. The "unity" throughout Persian thought, which we will attempt to demonstrate in this book, is not a unity to which only Persians have contributed. Still less is it a unity expressed only in the Persian language, since the Greeks, the Syrians, the Mesopotamians, the Turks, the Iranians and the Arabs have contributed to it. The latter have given it, through the splendid Arabic language, an unparalleled means of philosophical and theological expression, for we must not forget that Arabic is still studied in Persian middle schools as we study Latin, and abolishing it would, in my opinion, have disastrous effects on Iranian culture. But the unitary religious culture we have attempted to reconstruct spread its influence over a constantly expanding area. It included the whole of Muslim India, for India—though this is often forgotten—received state unity above all from Islam and was culturally Islamicized from the thirteenth to the nineteenth century, with Persian as her official language. All the vast areas of the former Ottoman Empire, the entire area forming present-day Afghanistan, Central Asia, Chinese Xinjiang and—only slightly exaggerating—the whole Muslim world, have been steeped in it to the marrow. And this unity—once declarations of *unicuique suum* have duly been made—became accessible to the general public, "universalized," especially through masterpieces of the Persian language. It too, one must not forget, is composite, and with half its vocabulary made up of Arab words—and this is a considerable testament to Persian prowess that should be enough to excite intelligent Iranians—certainly far more than sterile racial purisms.

It follows that ancient Iran and modern Iran assume an aspect of concrete historical continuity only if we look at the two phases from a geographical perspective located west of the territory now known as the Iranian plateau. This is the central theory of this book. It appears to me to confirm both of the traditional theories that dominated the study of premodern Iran—the "Aryan" and the "Islamic"—and is the only justification for a unitary religious panorama of Persia such as the one this book proposes to present. The reader, and the specialized reader in particular, will, I hope, consider the book the pioneer work it is meant to be and make allowances for certain defects. First among these is the neglect, out of necessity, of certain aspects of religious Iran such as the whole of Persian Sunnism (which includes a theologian of the calibre of al-Ghazzâlî, to mention only one name), many personalities and aspects of Sufism, certain tendencies or sects that involve Iranian culture in one way or another (i.e., the Yazidis), and a fuller study of modern Shi'ite popular religiosity (religious folklore). For to include a study of Persian Sunnism would obviously have implied a regular treatise on Islamics, since Persian Sunnism does not differ substantially from any other Sunnism, while the indispensable basic studies for the treatment of Sunni popular religion are still lacking, as we will show in the course of this work. In this regard I must point out that I had to presume in my readers a more specific knowledge of Islamics than is common, for otherwise the labor involved would have been doubled. But I have been careful to indicate some fundamental works that are easily accessible to the general reader. [English-speaking readers should see the updated bibliographies at the end of each chapter.-ed.]

I have quoted only a few works in European languages in the brief bibliographies at the end of each chapter, limiting the indications concerning technical articles—with siglas and abbreviations—to the text itself or to footnotes.

Some readers may find the contents of the book too "abstract": i.e., the theological and philosophical aspect of the religious problems may appear too marked and the cultural and ritual ones overshadowed. But the great originality of Iranian religions lies precisely in their "religious thought" and philosophical theology, rather than in their rituals. And besides, where Persia and almost all the religious East is concerned, the indispensable preliminary studies on the economic and social substratum of cultural phenomena are so limited [in 1957] that it would have been impossible to examine the culture specifically from a social point of view. And so we are left with a history and profile of religious "ideas" that however seem to me to have been collected for the first time in a unitary fashion. To liven the otherwise rather arid subject matter, I have employed many direct translations of texts so that the book is also a religious anthology of Persian thought. In fact, as far as I know, some of these texts (e.g., the "Crimson Intellect" that gives its name to part II) have never before been translated into any European language. All, or almost all, have been translated into Italian for the first time from Arabic, from Persian (modern, medieval and ancient) and from Turkish—a multiplicity of languages that highlights what we have said above. [For more recent English translations of some of these texts, see the bibliographical updates.-ed.]

And while we are speaking of "Crimson Intellect," I should like to mention that the rather strange titles of the three parts are intended to characterize different aspects of Persian religiosity. "The Cycle and the Angel" signifies two religious concepts—Cyclic Time and angelized Platonism that is also typical of the ancient religion, and continue to hold (always in the form of "Gnostic" concepts) an important place in the whole of the religious history of Iran. "Crimson Intellect," the picturesque title of a small mystical treatise by Suhravardi, refers to the world of symbols that is so typical of the Iranian philosophy and theology discussed in the middle chapters of the book. "The God who Changes" indicates the central characteristic of the arbitrary and personal Islamic God who became a Persian citizen after the Arab conquest and who is always ready to send new prophets and create new religions in his world. One of these—the most recent—is discussed in Chapter Eight.

Having had to renounce a rigorously scientific method for the transcription of the names, I have chosen a middle way: English consonants and Italian vowels, with the long vowels marked with a circumflex accent. As for the tonic accent, the reader should bear in mind that in modern Persian one rarely goes wrong if one places the accent on the last syllable.

For the photographic documentation my thanks go especially to my friend Professor G. R. Scarcia and to the late Professor Tucci, President of the Istituto Italiano per il Medio e Estremo Oriente, who have granted me access to the Institute's rich collection of photographs.

Part One

The Cycle and the Angel

Chapter One

The Problem of the
Mazdean Religion

Introduction

From the point of view of the history of religion, Mazdaism [or Zoroastrianism] is undoubtedly one of the more important higher religions, and its many aspects are extremely interesting, whether historical, philosophical, theological, comparative, or linguistic. Historically speaking, Mazdaism is a collection of real enigmas. Many observers [once] doubted, not without reason, the historical existence of the founder, the famous and mysterious Zarathustra (the Zoroaster of the Greeks), while others placed his existence from as early as two millennia before Christ up to a very few centuries before our era. Some have him born in the west of the Iranian territory, in present day Azerbaijan, and others in the diametrically opposite area. Some place the rise of the doctrine—later called Zoroastrianism—in ancestral antiquity and see in it the "oriental idea" that is said to have influenced Plato. Others, with possibly equally good reason, postpone it to as late as the first and second century before Christ, seeing it as a Persian echo of Platonism or rather of neo-Platonism. And again, from a philosophical and religious point of view, the various doctrines stemming from different sources and origins and known as Mazdean doctrines present, as we shall see, an extremely interesting historical and religious case upon which to reflect. For it never enters into really rational theology and philosophy but is based on material that remains substantially mythological, even though it is free of the complicated, teeming naturism typical of its Indian sister mythology.

From a comparative point of view, one can say without exaggerating that Zoroastrianism has supplied the material for the construction of the eschatological legends of all the great religions of the civilized world: Islam, late Judaism, and—through mysterious channels (perhaps via contact with Persianized Near-Eastern Christians) medieval Christianity of which the legends including those of the Christianized Nordic Sagas, which undoubtedly owe their angelic and eschatological visions to Iranian religiosity. Finally, from a linguistic point of view the Zoroastrian religious texts present at times insurmountable difficulties; but for this very reason they are a challenge to the interest and ingenuity of those scholars who cultivate Iranian philology (which some observers have characterized as the most difficult of all philologies). The texts most likely to be the authentic work of Zarathustra, the Gâthâs ("hymns"), are written in the most archaic Avestan language. This language presents such problems that one scholar [of the previous generation] frankly admitted that half these hymns were still all but incomprehensible. Further, the medieval Pahlavi language used to comment upon and explain the Avesta, in which we also have important summaries of the missing parts of the Mazdean sacred book, offers difficulties that at times surpass those of the texts it is explaining. These difficulties arise especially because of its singular system of orthography, in which Aramaic words mingle inextricably, like ideograms, with purely Iranian ones and the whole thing is in cursive writing with variously polyvalent signs. But this is not all. The most recent studies have progressively complicated the religious panorama of pre-Islamic Iran, showing that we are not dealing—as some believed when these studies started in Europe—with one Iranian religion, but with various "religions" or types of religiosity characteristic of one or another branch of the Iranian family. These religions and types of religiosity are being reconstructed with difficulty from fragments such as inscriptions, archaeological iconography and isolated texts later incorporated into the vaster and more unitary trend of Mazdaism.

The Texts

In a well known passage (I, 136) Herodotus says that the Persians "taught their children only three things from the age of five to the age of twenty: to ride horseback, draw a bow and tell the truth." If we compare a document of this kind with the following passage from the Annals of the Assyrian King Assurbanipal (V x R, I, 30 and foll.) we shall see that the Semitic king learned to ride horseback (and drive a chariot), draw a bow and "the wisdom of Nabu and the entire art of writing according to the traditions of the masters." The two declarations illustrate very clearly the difference between an Aryan civilization and a Semitic "scribal" civilization.[1]

Little by little, the Aryan civilization of ancient Iran, however, produced its "sacred book." In Iranian religious history we can clearly follow the process by which an Indo-European religion based on oral tradition entered into the "culture of books and scribes" typical of the Mediterranean, Middle Eastern region, moving, possibly with some hesitation, into a written tradition. The hesitations are well documented, for example, in an insistent motif that presents writing as the work and the invention of demons. According to a Sasanian tradition preserved, among others, by Firdausî (Vullers ed., p. 20 and foll.), one of the first mythical kings of humankind, Tahmûrath, succeeded in shackling the demons (*dêv*) after a bitter struggle, and this is why he is called *Dêvband*, "the shackler of devils." They asked his forgiveness and promised to teach him a new art—the art of writing—and not only one kind of writing but about thirty (seven according to another tradition, with considerable variations).[2]

And so the art of writing had something satanic about it (and as we shall see, for the ancient Persians "satanic" was often equivalent to "non-Iranian" (*anêrân*)). In fact the forms of writing used by the Persians throughout their religious and literary history were of non-Aryan origin—first cuneiform writing and, in the Median Persian period, Aramaic. On the other hand, the Avesta, the Bible of the Zoroastrian religion, assumed in time—and as a written text—such sacrality that its various parts are dedicated to the different Angels. Its paragraphs, passages and chapters (*hâti*) have a very strong sacral value and the priest "sacrifices" to one or another chapter of the Avesta as to a living being. The text itself is almost sacrally personified, as we shall see later too.

And here, at the very beginning of our study and while we are still concerned with the introductory theme of the meaning of the texts, we are faced with a contrast that will follow us throughout the book. This is the contradiction between, and the not always successful fusion of, two kinds of religiosity that could very approximately be called prophecy and nature. The former is represented here by the idea of sacred book given by a prophet, the latter by the idea of the demonic nature of the written sign.

Before going more deeply into the problem of the elements of the Iranian religion, we must examine the texts this religion in particular offers us, as well as their documentary value. These texts consist principally in the Avesta and the post-Avestan tradition in the Pahlavî language. To further exemplify the problems and intricacies involved in the study of everything connected with ancient Iranian religion, we would like to point out that (as of the first edition of this book), scholars specializing in the field did not agree either on the meaning of the name Avesta, or on the time of its composition, the number of books of which it was composed, the date of the written record of this fundamental text, the language in which it was written, the translation of the various parts, especially the earlier ones—in fact, practically speaking, on anything (though some progress has been made in the past thirty years). Since this is the case the best thing we can do is to turn to the Zoroastrian tradition itself to know at least something of what the venerators of the Avesta thought of their book.[3]

According to this tradition Kai Vishtâsp, the royal patron of the prophet Zarathustra (his followers place him traditionally in the sixth century), wrote or ordered the writing of the Avesta and the Zand (commentary) on 12,000 ox skins, depositing them in the royal treasury of Shîz (Media, near the lake of Urmia), while a copy was sent to the other archive of Stakhr (near Persepolis, in the Pârs area). The same tradition attributes an identical undertaking to a Darius son of Darius. The Stakhr copy was destroyed by fire during Alexander's conquest but the Shîz one was translated into Greek. A first attempt at restoration was carried out by the Arsacid king Valkash (Vologese, but there is more than one; possibly this is Vologese I, 51–75 A.D.), who had the surviving written and oral fragments searched for and put together again. Later Ardashîr Pâpakân, the founder of the Sasanian orthodox dynasty (226–241 A.D.), summoned the high priest (*môbadan-môbad*) Tansar to court and ordered him to reconstruct and *complete* the dispersed fragments, thus officially authorizing his work. But this was not the end of the story, for it seems that Ardashîr's son and successor, Shâhpûr (Sapore I, 241–272), had the secular documents concerning medicine, astronomy, geography, philosophy, etc., which had been dispersed among the Hindus, the Greeks and elsewhere, searched for and incorporated into the Avesta, and had a copy deposited in the treasury of Shîz. Finally, Shâhpûr II (310–379 A.D.) organized a general and public debate to end the struggle between sects that was tearing apart the "pure Mazdean religion": the priest Adhurpat, son of Maraspand, subjected himself to trial by fire (molten metal poured onto his chest), came through victorious and made additions of a liturgical nature to the Avesta. This tradition presents various interesting points:[4]

1. It attributes a written record of the Avesta to a period—that of Vishtâsp and Zarathustra—in which writing probably did not yet exist in Iran. Consequently this part must be considered legendary. Some recent scholars (Wikander) explained the two copies of Stakhr and Shîz by a fascinating hypothesis (though in my opinion without offering decisive proof) according to which the Avesta (Pahl. *apastâk*) indicated the whole of the religious traditions of the priests of the Pârs, while the *Zand* (so far understood in general terms as "commentary" on a "basic text," the *apastâk*) was the written record of the tradition, *meda*, of the magi of Shîz. The Median dynasty was in greater contact with the civilization of scribes of Asia Minor.

2. The existence of a copy of a Greek translation of the Avesta appears unlikely, despite Pliny's report that Hermippus (third century B.C.) speaks of the presence in the Alexandrian library of *twenty* sections of Zoroaster's sacred writings, each one 100,000 lines long. The original Avesta is traditionally indicated as divided into twenty one *nask*s ("sheafs"). But without the original Hermippian text it is very difficult to come to a decision.

3. The restoration of the older sacred texts is, in itself, far from improbable, but this raises the legitimate doubt that we are dealing with a recasting or even

a re-creation. How far, in fact, can we trust the presumed "tradition" and memory of the "priests"? Scholars have already expressed this doubt where other traditions are concerned (e.g., the famous *discovery* of the Hebrew Law tablets under Joshua). We are speaking now not of *discovery* but of out and out *reconstruction*, admitted even by tradition. Excessively radical scholars such as Darmesteter[5] have come to the conclusion that the Avesta must have been formed in the post-Alexandrian, Arsacid period, with Sasanian additions. Tradition itself admits that the priest Tansar completed and gave the finishing touches to the Avesta, that is, made out and out additions, in the third century A.D., and this is important because traditional sources generally tend to avoid diminishing the antiquity—which is the same as the sacrality—of their ancient texts.

In 1927 Nau carried Darmesteter's skepticism even further and tried to show that the Mazdean sacred texts were transmitted orally until towards the end of the seventh century and that the Zoroastrians did not possess any religious books before the last years of the Sasanian period.[6] Nau's theory, based exclusively on not entirely reliable Christian Syriac texts and unsupported by sufficient knowledge of Iranian sources, has been almost universally rejected by scholars. We quote it however to show the extent of the problems involved in every subject treated in this chapter.

4. The mention of secular Indian and Greek material supposedly incorporated into the Avesta in the period of Shâhpûr I (241–272 A.D.) (to which our earlier observation on the conservatism of traditions lends weight) is important. It is true that we are dealing with material considered part of the ancient Greek translation of the Avesta and "retranslated," but there is a growing suspicion that this has resulted in the addition of extraneous and recent elements (at least in their formulation).

To conclude, Zoroastrian tradition itself (even admitting to the legendary antiquity of the Avesta as a written document) gives us cause to suspect a possibly relatively recent origin of its holy Book, as well as information that confirms this suspicion. The certainty remains that the definitive written record of the Avesta (and its relatively recent system of writing) does not go back further than the fourth century A.D.[7]

In favor of a pre-Alexandrian origin we have on the one hand the (rather vague) information from Greek sources on Zoroaster and his writings[8], and on the other the markedly archaic character of the language of at least that part of the Avesta generally attributed by scholars to Zarathustra—the so-called Gâthâs (or "hymns," of which there are five), as well as the similarly archaic nature of certain mythical and religious concepts contained in them. Against this—besides the preceding observations—we have the fact too that the Avesta completely ignores a unitary Achaemenid type of "Persian empire"; the possibility that the usurper Alexander the Great is mentioned in the Avesta;[9] and the presence in it of conceptual material of a very late and neo-Platonizing nature. But these are merely conjectures that, in either case, can easily be answered. One can criticize the arguments in favour of the Avesta being pre-Alexandrian by saying that Greek information on a real Avestan text is unreliable and contradictory. As for the archaic character of the language, one could say that these texts could easily have been written by priests in a deliberately archaic language (and this partial inability to understand *on the part of the writer himself* would explain many strange singularities of the mysterious Avestan Gâthic language). On the other hand, the lack of reference to the Achaemenid Empire might lead one to believe that the Avesta reflects a social condition that even antedates the Achaemenids, while both the "Keresâni question" and that of the neo-Platonizing and gnostically oriented flavor of a great deal of Avestan material remains possibly rather too vague. An intermediate hypothesis seems more probable. While we can admit a very late written record of the Avesta and many conceptual additions and interpolations, we can identify two kinds of older nuclei in it. The first is the Zarathustrian Gâthâs—handed down it is not clear how or how faithfully—which present the opinions of the Reformer. The second is the archaic mythical material scattered throughout the *Yasht*s, which are wrongly called "recent Avesta," the whole thing being developed by someone who may have already had more or less vague neo-Platonic notions and tendencies. (One must not forget the strong and archaeologically-documented Hellenism of the Arsacid period.)

This discussion has led us almost imperceptibly to take a stand on the question of "content." Before continuing, however, these notes on the "texts" should be completed. On one point, at least, scholars seem to agree. The language of the Avesta is a northeastern, old-Iranian dialect. Consequently, despite attempts based on traditional material to have Zarathustra come from the Atropatene region, or present-day Azerbaijan (for tradition speaks of a *Median* origin), he came in all likelihood from the north-eastern area of the Iranian territory [and possibly from areas to the east of modern Iran.-ed.].

Further, the present Avesta is not the entire Sasanian Avesta. The catastrophe marked by Alexander's conquest was followed, after the Sasanian restoration, by an even more dreadful one—the Arab conquest. The parts of the Avesta still in our possession are, specifically, those most useful *for liturgical purposes* and therefore of a rather special kind. Of the twenty–one books (*nask*s) of the Avesta only one whole volume has come down to us, originally the nineteenth, the so-called *Vendidâd* (the inexact modern Pârsî pronunciation of the Pahl. *Vidêvdât*, Avest. *vidaêvo-dhâto*: "The anti-demonic law"). The sections of the present–day Avesta are: the *Yasna*, a book of liturgical hymns of which the oldest and most important part is made up of the five Gâthâs of Zoroaster; the

Vispered, a brief appendix to the Yasna consisting in "all the *ratu*" (we will speak later of the concept of *ratu*); the above-mentioned *Vendidâd*, containing a great deal of legal and ritual material as well as interesting legends and cosmographical descriptions; the *Yasht*, sacrificial songs in honor of the individual "divinities" (*yazata*, Pahl. *îzad or yazad*) who presided over the various days of the month, containing very ancient mythical material, and finally the *Khorda Avesta* or "little avesta," a kind of handbook of prayers for laymen, written partly in *pâzand* (Pahlavî in the clearer Avestan characters).

But the Avesta remains hard to understand without the Pahlavî texts (Pahlavî is the middle-Persian language of the Arsacid-Sasanian period) and the reader will find it useful to have an idea of the titles and contents of the most important works. These were almost all written around the ninth century A.D. in the period after the Arab conquest, at the beginning of the "Iranizing" caliphate of the Abbasids—which witnessed a remarkable rebirth of studies among surviving Iranian Zoroastrians. Their authors, learned priests, were able to consult older texts that have since been lost. They therefore represent a tradition that is certainly older than the period in which they were written. We will not provide information here about all the Pahlavî religious texts that have come down to us, nor about a few secular ones of no great importance or particular artistic beauty.[10] In all events there are not very many of them. We will, however, mention the *Dênkart* ("The acts of religion" or "The dogma of Faith"). This was composed in the ninth century of our era, in nine (incomplete) parts, and apparently continued to be modified until 932 A.D. It is extremely valuable because it contains a summary of all the lost books of the Avesta except for one that was already lost at the time, as well as various legends about Zarathustra. Unfortunately the style is so confused and ungainly and the probability of copyist errors so great that it can be considered one of the most difficult texts of Pahlavî literature. It has been translated only in part by European scholars (the English translation by the Pârsîs—loving custodians and interpreters of their texts—is not very reliable).

Possibly, after the *Dênkart*, the *Bundahishn* ("the primordial creation") is the next most important book of the Pahlavî texts from a religious point of view. This cosmogonic book was also composed in the ninth century. We have two versions of it: a shorter Indian version and a Persian one known as "The Greater Bundahishn." It describes the whole great cycle from the Creation to the Resurrection, with various legends concerning the ideas of the ancient Iranian people on geography, astronomy, etc., though in an unfortunately contorted and difficult style that leaves many philological and historical–cum–religious problems open.

There are also a number of short moral pieces and others explaining various religious questions, the catechisms, etc. Among these the so-called *Dâtistân i*

Mênôk i Khrat "The decisions of the spirit of Reason" (or "of Transcendent Wisdom") are worth noting for a very rare quality in Pahlavî literature, i.e. simplicity and at times a pleasant fluidity of style. This too is quite a late composition (subsequent to the Islamic conquest) and is a quite organic and ample exposition of religious questions in dialogue form between a wise and faithful follower of Mazdaism and personified Transcendent Reason who courteously answers all his questions (not only concerning morals but also quasi-mythology, theology, etc.). The "Book of the Advice of Zarathustra" (*Pandnâmak i Zartusht*, from the name of a priest and not to be confused with the founder of the religion [which is also known as *Chidag Handarz i Poryotkeshân*, "Select Counsels of the Ancient Sages"]), is simply a catechism and very useful as a general introduction to the Mazdean doctrine.

Among other important Pahlavi religious texts, of particular interest is the *Dâtistân i Dênîk* "Religious decisions (or sentences)" by a Manûchihr son of Yûvân Yam, high priest of Pârs and Kirmân in Persia after the Islamic conquest (second half of the ninth century). It consists of answers to questions on various religious, juridical, and moral subjects (which are extremely intricate and hard to decipher). The polemic work *Shkand-gumânîk Vichâr*, "The Explanation that routs doubts," is also very interesting. It, too, was probably written in the second half of the ninth century. It was intended as a refutation, from the Mazdean point of view, of the religious and philosophical ideas of atheists, materialists, Muslims, Jews, Christians and Manichaeans, insisting particularly that the Mazdean dualistic concept is religiously more "logical"; it is, relatively speaking, the most "philosophical" of the Zoroastrian books. Treating legendary material and written in a very plodding style, the *Artâ Vîrâf Nâmak* or "Book of Artâ Virâf" is significant because some scholars (Blochet) have seen in it the origin of the material that, later and enriched from other sources, became a part of Dante's *Divine Comedy*. It tells the story of a pious Mazdean's journey into after-life (after taking narcotics), apparently at the time of the Sasanian king Khusrau Kavâtân (531–578 A.D.), with the description of the torments of hell and the bliss of heaven. The "Epistles of Manûchihr," son of Yûvân Yam ([or Juwanjam]), whom we have already mentioned as the author of the *Dâtistân i Dênîk*), are also important for the study of Mazdean rituals. He considers questions of ritual purity in them, in opposition to the cultural innovations of his brother Zâtspram. They were written around 881 and give important information on the state of the Zoroastrian communities of Persia after the Arab conquest. We also have a miscellany known as "Anthology of Zâtspram" (*Vichîtakîhâ i Zâtspram*) by Zâtspram himself which contains cosmogonic, legendary and apocalyptic material. Apocalyptic texts such as the *Bahman Yasht*, which presents itself as a prophetic work (Ohrmazd tells Zarathustra what will happen to the Iranian nation and the Mazdean religion in the future), and "The memoirs of Zhamâsp" (*Abhyâtkâr i Zhamâspîk*)—similar in contents—are even more interesting. The former was based on Sasanian sources and was written possibly around the twelfth century A.D. The latter dates more or less from the same period, since it already tells of the Turkish invasions of Islamized Iran.

There is no point mentioning a number of other Pahlavî works here even though they might provide precious information—for example, the *Rivâyât* ("traditions"—an Arabic word) written at a much later date in Pahlavî or in Pârsî (Pahlavî transcribed into Arabic characters)—because an arid list of names would only bore the reader. We will provide information on some of them as the need to quote them arises.

Problems of the Content

An organic outline of the contents of the texts mentioned above would require writing a treatise on the Mazdean religion and we do not intend to do this here. However we do intend to point out problems that arise from a reading of the Mazdean texts and, while not attempting a unitary solution, we want at least to mention the more likely solutions that specialists are proposing. If we consider the liturgical hymns of the Avesta (*Yasna*) and especially the parts written in more archaic language (the Gâthâs), we witness the emergence of the distinct and marked personality of a prophet-reformer, Zarathustra, appointed by a supreme god, Ahura Mazdâ ("wise lord" [or "lord of wisdom"]), to speak to men through revelation. At the beginning of the world two spirits existed, an evil one who *chose* evil, a good one who *chose* good. The first good step to take is to follow the word of the Wise Lord (*Ahura Mazdâ*) and his laws as revealed by Zarathustra. The Wise Lord acts and speaks through archangelic powers with names such as Rectitude, Good Thought, Holy Docility, Elected Kingdom, Integrity, and Immortality. Taking care of the cattle and tilling the fields is supremely good work; bloody sacrifice and the ritual use of *Haôma* (inebriating drink) is deplored.

The good and the bad will be rewarded and punished according to their works, until the achievement of a total and future renovation of the world (though the future may be close at hand), an apocatastasis, a purification through molten bronze, towards which the hopes of the world tend. "Good" and "bad" often have a national or natural implication (a good nature is eternal) in our texts (the Iranians are good, the *anêrân*, the "non-Iranians," are demonic; a *dêv* or demon is often a man of non-Iranian race). But, in the Gâthâs, the religion Zarathustra preached is a religion to be accepted or rejected and even a Turanian can be saved, as a Gâthic passage explicitly states (cf. Y.46.12).

The prophet complains of the persecutions he suffers at the hands of certain priestly castes and his hopes for the triumph of Law and Good lie in securing the help of a King (who is mentioned and is Vishtâspa). When all is said and done he is the typical figure of a prophet fighting against a hostile environment, in defense of a divine revelation and moral concepts and, above all, anti-magical ideas (wizards are demonic beings).

Elsewhere (*Yasht*, passim) Zarathustra appears on transcendent planes, in conversation with genii who are transparent mythological and natural symbols, and sacrifices, as priest, to *Haôma* (the Sacred Beverage personified as a god), to *Anâhita* (the female goddess of the waters, of Babylonian [or other] origin), to the (god of justice and later) sun-god *Mithra*, etc. *Haôma* (and not Ahura Mazdâ) reveals myths of an ancient past rather than moral laws. Zarathustra appears more as a traditional priest than a reformer or prophet here. In the lost parts of the Avesta summarized in the *Dênkart*, Zarathustra is a being surrounded by miracles who lives in a far more "transcendent" atmosphere than any other "idealized" historical prophet. Jesus and the Muhammad of the legend are "historical" figures if we compare them to the Zarathustra of the tradition of the Pahlavi books and of many parts of the Avesta (where he already seems a demigod with only very slight ties with the real world).

If we move from the person of the alleged author to other aspects of the contents of the Mazdean texts we will have further surprises. Let us take *Haôma* (middle Persian *Hôm*): as we already said, in the Gâthâs Zarathustra appears to oppose its ritual use as a pagan custom (Y.48.10–32.14), but in the *Yasna*, of which the Gâthâs are ritually a part, there is a hymn called *Hôm Yasht*. Here Haôma appears as a youth with a beautiful body who speaks to Zarathustra and is invoked as destroyer of the magic-Ahrimanic powers from which he too stems. In the *Yasht*, dedicated to her, there is a visual description of the goddess *Ardvî Sûra Anâhita* (the goddess of the waters we have already mentioned) that can only have derived from the contemplation of a statue of the goddess: she stands erect, wrapped in a golden mantle, in the form of a slim, tall, splendid young girl, holding the *baresman*[11] in her hand, a necklace around her throat, tightly belted at the waist to enhance her breasts, and wearing a gilded crown with a hundred stars and eight rays from which hang small flags and so forth.

This mythical world is also present in the Gâthâs themselves: in *Gâthâ Ahunavaiti* "the soul of the primal ox" complains to the creator and the archangels about the suffering imposed on him by the evil ones. The Wise Lord is called "creator of the Primal Ox." Zarathustra says that "his" soul, adoring Ahura, "will go towards the cow Azi. . ." the symbol of advantages and prosperity, not only on earth but also in the world of the hereafter. The hymn (*Yasht*, 10) dedicated to the sun god Mithra is an inextricable combination of moral concepts (Mithra is first of all the god of Truth and of Keeping Faith) and of mytho-logical and natural symbology: Mithra, the lord of the vast lands has a thou-sand ears, is physically handsome, has ten thousand eyes, is tall. . . The warrior sacrifices to him on horseback . . . The first of the heavenly gods, he passes over mount *Hara Berezaiti*, in front of the immortal sun with its swift steeds (it should be noted how the god is clearly distinct here from the sun). While this Aryan God is deeply venerated in the Avesta and in all the Zarathustrian texts, other gods who are famous and venerated in the Aryan pantheon are in the lists of demons, for example *Indra, Sarva, and Nâsatya*. The name that in India (as well as in many Indo-European languages) indicates "god," *daêva* (Mid. Pers. *dêv*), is used in the Avesta and in the whole of Iranian tradition for "demon," while Ahura, which in the Indian pantheon tends at least to indicate infernal gods (*asura*, in the Sanskrit form) is used here as the name of the supreme god of Light, Ahura Mazdâ, "the Wise Lord." Where the Amesha Spenta—the arch-angels of the Gâthâs, Good Thought, Holy Docility, etc.—are concerned, it is hard to decide whether to translate their names, in the Gâthâs, with the corre-sponding moral terms of our languages or leave the original terms intact as "personal names," since their ethical and theological function is so transparent. In the other parts of the Avesta, and even more in the later Pahlavî documents, they are so clearly personified as to be practically speaking on the same plane as personal figures of gods like Anâhita or Mithra. And in the Gâthâs Ahura Mazdâ is spoken of as father of Spenta Armaiti ("Holy Docility") and as her spouse. There is also mention in several passages of the Avesta of a "body" of this supreme and spiritual god, this apparently abstract "Wise Lord!" A Pahlavî commentary to Yasna I.I. describes him "With well proportioned limbs." In the Gâthâs the "body of Ohrmazd" is fire and light, (e.g., in *Yasna Haptanhâiti* II,I).

But let us continue pointing out these contrasts through examples. Passages in the Pahlavî tradition mention Ahura Mazdâ as "pregnant with the world" (*Rivâyat Dât. i Dênîk* Chap. 46:3, p. 128). In the *Bundahishn* (chap. I) he is "father and mother" of creation, mother of creation in its transcendent state (which is described as developing like a foetus in an egg), father of creation as it is realized in the material world. And the concept of Ahura Mazdâ as father is to be found, as we have seen, in the Gâthâs too. He is generally called creator (*dâtâr*) and on several occasions the creation is described in a thoroughly "bib-lical" style.

As for the wicked god Ahriman, in some of our texts he seems to have an only slightly more accentuated function than our own "devil," but in others he appears in the form of a real, totally independent God, and this dualism is generalized to the point of distinguishing animals, plants and stars, as *ôhrmazdic* beings and phenomena, and *ahrimanic* animals, plants and stars, etc. In still other passages, Time (*Zurvan, Zamân*) is given greater metaphysical importance than the two gods and traditions (though mostly not of Mazdean origin) that have come down to us by which both Ohrmazd and Ahriman were sons of Zurvan.

The two "creations" of Ohrmazd and Ahriman, however, do not—as readers familiar with certain Christian or, rather, Gnostic concepts might deduce—correspond to the sky and the world or to the sky and the flesh. The material world too is the creation of the good God and Ahriman, who, with his counter-creation, has only temporarily contaminated it. But the moral dualism described above is linked in the Avesta (though less clearly in the Gâthâs), and even more in the Pahlavî texts, to a metaphysical dualism between *mênôk* and *gêtîk*, i.e. the "transcendent world" and the "terrestrial world." Everything exists in a transcendent state too: a transcendent earth and a visible, material earth exist, both created by Ohrmazd who is himself both transcendent and terrestrial. Both transcendent and earthly gods exist, the first of the latter being called Zarathustra.

Zoroastrian literature offers us a great many terms and concepts concerning the soul: the soul as vital breath (*vyâna*, Pahl. *gyân*) or vital force (*ushtâna*), the soul—as opposite element to the body—which continues living even after death (*urvân* Pahl. *ruvân*), the more rationalist term *khratu* ("intellect, reason") and still other variants of soul in senses that are also present in other religious cycles. But the two concepts of *fravashi* and *daêna* are unique and original to the Iranian religion. A *fravashi* is something between a person's "guardian angel" and his transcendent "double." The *fravashi* of just men or saints are venerated as important protecting divinities. The idea of *daêna* has a typically theological aspect: on the one hand it means "religion" but it also signifies the celestial maiden incarnating man's good works.

Where further eschatological and apocalyptic concepts are concerned, the religion described in our texts is presented on the one hand as entirely centered on the future and on Death, Judgment, Heaven and Hell (unlike Greek or Indian "archaic" religions). A "sacred history" exists, time has a positive value (and in fact is an instrument for the defeat of Ahriman), and so do the world and the flesh that will rise again, perfect, after the final apocatastasis (*frashô-kereti*). This perfected flesh is the "future body" (*tan î pasên*) of the Pahlavî texts. The agents of *frashô-kereti* (Pahl. *frashkart*) will be, in succession, three great future Saviours, the third of which (*Saôshyant*, Pahl. *Sôshans*) will be the greatest of all, and the expectation of their coming is very strong in the Mazdean spirituality that shows through in our texts. Here bliss is placed in the future, so that the beginning of bliss presents itself at the historical coming of a prophet whose future sons will save the world, redeeming it from all traces of Ahrimanic "counter-creation." But side by the side with this optimistic tendency there is also—inextricably connected with it—the pessimistic traditional tendency by which heaven was, on the contrary, "at the beginning," with an abundance of allusions to the happy period of the first sacred sovereigns. Where man's ultimate end is concerned, both the idea of the immortality of the soul and of the resurrection of the flesh seem to be present. After the individual death of the body, the soul of the just man, assisted by a number of psychic emissaries, suffers the "torment of the three nights" inflicted on it by diabolical beings and finally enters, through various trials, into the light-song of the *Garôdmâna* ("dwelling of the hymns") where it will contemplate Ahura Mazdâ. But at the end of the world, at the time of the *frashôkereti*, all men will take back their bodies that by then will have been purified.

Our texts are full of myths: specific myths deriving from the Aryan heritage having to do with nature, side by the side with other typically Zarathustrian and theological and allegorical ones. Already in the Avesta the mythical motifs concerning nature undergo a partial process of Evemerisation that continues in the Pahlavî texts, while the creation of new myths out of theological elements is also evident in the Avesta: thus, to mention only a border-line case, sacrifices are offered to this or that verse of the Avesta (personified book). In the Pahlavî texts (*Bund.* XXX, 28) the Gâthâs (personified!) *dress the souls* in the sky. The idea is based on the Avestan praise of the Gâthâs (Y.55.2) according to which the sacred hymns are "divine nourishment and, for our soul, clothing." Unusual mythical figures such as the holy Three-Legged Donkey (with purifying functions), the King *Gôpêt* (*Gôpêtshâh*) (a kind of beneficent minotaur who pours holy water into the sea to prevent the demonic animals of the sea—who have been absorbed by the clouds together with the water vapor—from raining down on the world), the fish *Kar* (who swims around the plant that will provide the white Haôma, producer of the "future body"), and many others, originated in Iran or were remodelled in a Zoroastrian sense. There has always been a tendency to give a theological explanation of all or almost all the myths (especially in the medieval Pahlavî texts).

Where rites and the priesthood are concerned we have already seen how Zarathustra is presented as struggling against priestly castes such as the *kavi* and the *karapan* (more or less identified as wizards), but at the same time professional remuneration for priests is mentioned as an established fact even in the Gâthâs. The bloody sacrifice of the ox is a horrible sin but at the same time the renewal of the Body of the world will be carried out also through the magic action of the fat of the sacrificial bull. In the general tradition of our texts the funeral ritual is based on exposing corpses to be devoured by birds in order to avoid contaminating the sacred elements (earth, water, fire). But though the rite of burial in tombs is documented for the Achaemenid kings and there are documents (extraneous to our texts) that speak of the burning of corpses, some passages in the Gâthâs mention a return of the corpse to mother earth (Y.34.10: the earth is a "place of rest for the just").

The ritual based on the libation of the sacred Haôma that—as we mentioned— seems to be discouraged in the Gâthâs, is nevertheless one of the central rites of the very complex and detailed Zoroastrian liturgy. Traces of prehistoric human sacrifice can be distinguished in some passages and Herodotus confirms this when he speaks of Xerxes immolating human victims. Fire, water and the various elements symbolized by their angels (*Amesha Spenta*, "the immortal saints") are objects of adoration, while formularies for confession in Pahlavî document the fact that regular confession of sins to the priest was practiced. The priests were divided into classes according to their functions: while the *zaôtar* (Ind. *hôtár*) and the *athravan* (Ind. *atharvan*) had their more or less precise equivalents in priestly functions and classes of the common Indo-Iranian heritage, other categories (such as *kavi*, *vifra* etc.) were, for the Avesta, magician-witch-doctors. Finally, the magi (*maghavan*) priests of fire and bearers of the sacred branches (*baresman*, Pahl. *barsôm*) and the *aêthrapati* (Pahl. *hêrbadh*) appear to be a purely Iranian priesthood; however, according to Herodotus, the Magi were at the same time a Median tribe. Herodotus also tells us that the Persians did not use altars or temples or images. But the Achaemenid bas-reliefs of Behistûn depict a fire altar and visible symbols of the supreme God. We have already seen how the Avestan description of the goddess *Anâhita* shows the existence of her effigies and the middle Persian texts speak of pyraeus, fire altars and regular temples.

Attempts at Interpretation

We deliberately presented the material in the preceding section—which we mentioned as being simply an anthology of facts—in a rather disorderly fashion. I think this will give the reader who has not read the Avesta or later Zoroastrian texts a rather . . . clear idea of the inextricable confusion of the motifs and currents and of the religious "facts" contained in our texts. This confusion is further increased by documents extraneous to the above-mentioned texts (Achaemenid historical inscriptions, Arsacid and Sasanian inscriptions, Manichaean books, Greek sources): for example, the Achaemenid inscriptions show that the royal family adored a supreme God called Ahura Mazdâ but other gods are mentioned too. These gods are later called *baga*, an Iranian term that is however completely extraneous to the Avesta. The Achaemenids buried their corpses and (may or may not have known) about Zoroaster.

There are two ways of bringing order into the untidy collection of all these facts, i.e. through a historical interpretation or through a theological interpretation. The historical interpretation belongs to modern scholars, the theological one to the Pârsî priests. We will start by examining the attempts at a historical interpretation of the raw undigested mass (*rudis indigestaque moles*) we have presented here in all its crude factuality. The first thing to strike even a lay reader of the preceding section is that one must inevitably suppose the existence—as the first step towards explaining the contradictions presented by this kind of structure—of two layers of traditions belonging to different classes, extraction or cultures that in time have merged, even if not too organically.

To these two religious groups or types or tendencies another factor— Zarathustra's personality—must be added. For though some texts make him appear a legendary figure he certainly was a vigorous and active reformer (both his very personal and unsymbolic name and the tone of the Gâthâs indicate this) in a period that cannot be determined at this point of our enquiry. Here then is a first attempt to bring order into the chaos: two groups of religious traditions, and one truly great religious personality.

But first we should examine some of the principal contradictions we have mentioned above in a more orderly and detailed manner and see what possible solutions there are for each one.

Zarathustra and His Legend

The history of religions abounds in examples of historical founders who, in time, through the natural veneration of their followers, have been transformed into gods. Even in anti-idolatrous Islam some currents arrived at a real quasi-deification of the Founder or of some of his supporters, especially, as we shall see later on, in Persia (see chapters III and IV). In the case in point we are faced with the fact that there is very little historical information on Zarathustra and what is there is extremely vague, being little more than what has been preserved in the Gâthâs.

The persecuted prophet's cry of pain, preserved for us in the *Gâthâ Ushtavaiti*, (Y.46.I and foll.) is too sincere and personal to be attributed to an extra-historical abstraction:

> To what land to escape, where must I go to escape? I am rejected by my own race and my companion, the community shows me no favour, nor do the leaders of the country, followers of Untruth. How can I, o Mazdâ, find your grace? I know, of Mazdâ, why I have no strength. I have only a few flocks and I dispose of few men. I complain to you; watch over us well, O Lord, giving us support such as a friend gives to a friend. Communicate to me, since you are Order, the power of Good Thought.
>
> When, O Mazdâ, will the resplendent dawns of the days come when the designs of the Saviours (will impose themselves) with efficacious phrases so that the world may take Order as its own? Who are those whom Good Thought will help? Me, since by you I have been chosen for the fulfillment. . . (From a translation into Italian by A. Pagliaro).

A little further on Zarathustra's relatives are mentioned, and their names have nothing mythological or symbolic about them. In fact the general picture suggests a historical reality. But once this has been admitted it cannot be denied that the declarations concerning Zarathustra contained in the Avesta itself and in the whole of later tradition lead to the conclusion that after being "the first of the earthly gods" in the Avesta he must very soon have assumed a mythical, semi-divine nature.

One of the late forms of the legend of Zarathustra ([possibly] based on much older material, however, and, basically, on the Zarathustrian section of the *Dênkart*) is contained in the interesting little new-Persian poem *Zarâtusht-nâmeh*, written by an Iranian Pârsî, Zarâtusht-i Bahrâm son of Pazhdû, in the thirteenth century. The miracles are inextricably interwoven into the "history" but we will see later what kind of miracles are involved. As an example, here is a passage that tells of Zarathustra'a enchanted arrival in Iran: the *Dênkart* says at one point, significantly, "then Zarathustra entered into the material world (*akhv i astômand*), in Sakastâna" (today Sîstân, on the border between Persia and Afghanistan), almost as if the preceding part of the story had taken place in immaterial, celestial areas.

> When Zarathustra was thirty years old and everything had been accomplished according to the decree of God, his soul felt a desire for the country of Iran. And so he left from there [from where? Corbin rightly speaks of a "land of the visions," the *Erânvêj* of tradition] with a few men, and their women too joined them to accompany them on the expedition. When he arrived with his retinue on the bank of a great river (or sea) he saw neither a boat nor a raft with which to cross it. Then Zarathustra's heart was saddened because of the women: he wished to find a passage, there, without making them cross in that way. . . because it is not suitable for women to bare themselves, especially in front of strangers. He wept to the Omnipotent Creator and begged him to give him passage across the water of the sea, and since he prayed with his whole soul with fear and trembling, the Holy God granted his wish. Zarathustra got up and, entering the water, ordered the people to follow him unhesitatingly. Everyone hurried towards the river without even removing their clothes and as ships glide on the moving billows thus they walked on the surface of the water. It seemed as if there were a bridge over the water and on that bridge Zarathustra swiftly crossed the river. It was the end of the month of *Esfandarmaz*, the day that is called *anêrân*. On that day Zarathustra, the Man of the Pure Law, reached the frontiers of Iran. It was a festival day and great and noble men from all over the country, numbering more than a thousand, were going to the place of the feast, passing by merrily and full of joy. When night fell, putting out the torches of the world, Zarathustra too wished to go to the feast. Alone, he passed through the dark night on the way, but his soul had Wisdom as a companion. . . After resting and being gladdened for a short while in that festive place that was similar to gentle

Paradise, Zarathustra left the feast and came to the bank of a river. When half of the month of *Urdibehesht* had passed and the earth became similar to Paradise, on the day of *Daibamihr* (Pahl. *dadhv pat Mihr*, the 15th day of the month, therefore May 5th) in the hour when the sun shows its face, he reached the bank of a river, an immense and bottomless river: in the Avesta it is called *Dâiti*, and its bed was never empty. According to tradition the water of that river was divided into four parts. The holy Zarathustra went into the water without any fear in his heart. The water of the first part came up to his calves, that of the second came above his knees, that of the third reached his belt, that of the fourth covered him up to his neck. But let not what I am telling you of the actions of the Provident God surprise you: this means that in nine thousand years the Law will be renewed four times. The first time Zarathustra Spitama will bring the good law from God, then *Hôshêdâr* will receive the Law, the third time *Hôshêdâr-mâh* will be a prophet, the fourth *Soshars*, the well-created, will make the earth as pure as Paradise. Therefore, as I have said, the Victorious God showed Zarathustra the passage across the river. His body was painlessly purified by the water: like gold whose value increases when it is refined by fire. Zarathustra washed his head and his body as he had washed his heart, with his loins girded in the service of God. Putting his foot on the (other) bank of the deep river, he put on a musk scented robe.

The historians who try to identify the sites of Zarathustra's legendary life (here, too, we are only giving a significant example) are constantly faced with dilemmas of the kind presented, for example, by this "river" (*daryâ*, also sea): it is placed in a historical tale and in a geographical landscape but at the same time it is openly declared symbolic. The world of the Beyond is separated from concrete Iran by a sea-river: Zarathustra's arrival coincides with the feast of the New Year. Once he has reached Iran another sacred river, the *Dâiti*, is the symbol of the unfolding of the sacred story. Water has an important role in Zarathustrian symbolism: the most important transcendent-mythical beings are, as we shall see, in the depth of the Waters. Faced with this broad complex of images of "vision" all efforts at geographical identification seem to me vain.

In order to understand the divinization of Zarathustra one must also bear in mind on the one hand that he probably was an "ecstatic" (we will this develop later) and on the other the possibility that as a historical person he has been idealized through the process—typical of the entire Mazdean tradition—of considering the phenomena of nature, things, persons, as angelic theophanies. Zarathustra, as we have seen, is called the "first of the earthly *yazata*"; following the "angelism" of his own doctrine, tradition soon identified him with his angelic prototype. Just as there is a "transcendent earth" that explains the earthly earth, so Zarathustra the angel-god comes *first* (a logical and metaphysical first that soon becomes a historical first) followed by Zarathustra the man. The man is a symbol of the angel, rather than vice versa. But we will expand on this later.

We have called Zarathustra an "ecstatic." In fact if we examine the many miracles of the Zoroastrian legend we will notice that many of them have a characteristic in common, i.e., that of appearing as "visions" or of being very easily explainable as visionary illusionist tricks. Even if these traditions are late ones they are indicative of an ancient *tendency*. In the case of Jesus, for example, the tendency is a thaumaturgical and medical one (in Islam Jesus is first of all a great healer). In the case of Zoroaster the tendency is decidedly "visionary." "Dreams" abound: the dreams of Zarathustra's mother before his birth; Zarathustra's own frequent dreams—openly declared as such. But the "play of light" element is central to the rest of the Zarathustrian miracles too. The prophet is born laughing and his laughter creates light in the palace (*Zarâtusht-nâmeh*): repeated visions of the angel *Bahman* (*vohu-manah-*"Good Thought") bring him revelation; God grants Zarathustra to *see* and *hear* the holy Archangels (*Amesha Spenta*). He is subjected to trial by fire (which plays an important role, as we shall see, in the Iranian tradition) in places of vision and comes through unscathed. Coming back to earth, he shatters the visible corporeal forms of the demons. Some miracles are curious cases of illusionism: for example the miracle of king Vishtâsp's favorite black horse that everyone saw one day, in the stable, without his four legs and reduced to a large stump resting on the ground. His four legs grew again one by one through Zarathustra's prayers while the king promised to comply with four conditions. Then the Archangels appeared in the form of four horsemen to King Vishtâsp and the king was convinced. Zarathustra had the vision of the tree with seven branches, the symbol of the history of the world, etc.

Amazing visionary miracles are attributed to him even after death in the *Dênkart*. The one closest to the phenomena of modern "spiritualist séances" (the idea is not mine) but of the Pârsî publisher Sanjana) is that of the double chariot of Srêt, the mysterious "chariot without a rider" (guided by the soul of a dead man) that appears in the sky: visible to all, the soul of king Vishtâsp (who is still alive) goes to meet him in another chariot. But he is not even mentioned in these post-Zarathustrian miracles (attributed to an effect of the Prophet) for this seems to be an ecstatic method the Prophet left as an inheritance to his followers. But there is still more: tradition tells us quite clearly what this method consists of. *Zarâtusht-nâmeh* tells of the first consecration of the sacred agape *darûn* (*drôn*, see following pages) by the Prophet in the presence of king Vishtâsp. When the wine, the incense, the milk and the pomegranate were consecrated through the recitation of formulas of the Avesta, the "king tasted of the blessed wine and became joyous over it; having drunk it he all of a sudden acquired knowledge. For three days his body remained immersed in sleep, like that of a drunken man, but his soul flew to adore God in the invisible world." Magic effects are also obtained through the other three elements of the sacred *drôn*: milk makes one forget death, the blessed perfume reveals the future, the pomegranate gives invulnerability. In a meeting with God (*Zarâtusht-nameh*, published by Rosenberg, p. 65) Zarathustra receives something similar to honey from the hands of Ohrmazd. After swallowing it he has phantasmagorical visions of heavens and hells: and the same trait appears— as we have seen—in the brief eschatological treatise *Artâ Virâf-namak*, in which the visionary prepares for his visions by taking *bang* (hashish)[12]. Seen in this light, some facts, which are generally not seen in this perspective, become quite logically explicable. It is a known fact, for example, that one phenomenon produced by a "shamanic" type of ecstasy (as well as the pseudo-ecstasies of drug addicts) is the perception of sound as light and of light as sound. And it is not a coincidence that a significant set of facts of this kind can be found in the Zoroastrian tradition. The supreme paradise of visions—which is above all the dwelling of *light* and described as such—is also called "house of the songs" or "of the hymns" (Av. *garô-demâna*, Pahl. *Garodman*) in the Gâthâs. In this sense the Gâthic passage Y.30.3, is very important though difficult to interpret: *at tâ mainyû paouruyê yâ Yema xvafnâ asrvâtem*, "the two Primordial Spirits who in (deep) Sleep were *heard* as Twins."[13] Here the ecstatic identification of the sense of hearing with that of vision is quite evident[14]. In the Mazdean catechism *Pandnâmak i Zartusht* the author brings blindness close to spiritual deafness on the Ahrimanic level: "because it is clear that this is why the sun gives orders to man here in the world three times a day (the ethical and religious orders of the sun follow here). . . Since it is in fact clear (i.e., "appears by revelation") that, as *the light* of the sun reaches the earth so *his word* comes down to earth." The ethical re-interpretation of the ecstatic phenomenon should be noted here. And the passage of the Pahlavî apocalyptic book *Zhamâspîk* ([or *Jamaspig*]; Messina ed. pp. 34 and 85) in which it is said "What has always been is the voice of Ohrmazd in the light, and the (preceding) light from Ohrmazd is the light that evokes Ohrmazd"[15] is even more striking because it could lead to transposition of the shamanic method to Ohrmazd himself.

Several considerations tend to confirm our conviction that the figure of Zarathustra should be defined as a magician-shaman with a strong ethical sense. We must remember the well-known, frequent, use of *dûgh-i vahdat* (the playful name the Persian mystics gave to hashish: "yoghurt producing union with God!") throughout Islamic Persia to produce ecstatic states; the several symptomatic declarations in the Gâthâs that attribute priestly-magical functions to Zarathustra; and, in addition, the phenomenon of shamanism and its ecstasy-producing techniques that are widespread throughout Central Asia, relevant given Zarathustra's likely origin in the northeast. One fact that, perhaps only apparently, may seem a proof to the contrary, which is to say the strong antipathy for wizards and magi in the Gâthâs, could well be explained by professional jealousy of the various categories of magicians-shamans. Zarathustra's ethical sense clearly distinguishes him from ordinary *yatu* and contributes to creating his hatred for them. But this ethos must not be mistaken, as it sometimes is, for ethics in the modern sense. It is an ethos that remains charged with "primitive" elements.

Specialists have interpreted Zarathustra's figure and works in extremely varied ways: some have considered him a great reformer (Widengren, Dumézil), or the author of a truly moralizing revolution (Dumézil); others (Nyberg) declare that there is no trace of the "reformer" in him, others still compare him to a revolutionary prophet of classic monotheism (Pettazzoni). Others again (Nyberg) consider him a professional priest-bard, an ecstatic, a kind of archaic theosopher and the prototype of future Persian "dervishes," the first apocalyptic thinker, and *mahdi*, the prototype of the Perfect Man. For some people (Pagliaro) he was a real philosopher, for others a religious reformer (Henning), etc. Two points should always be remembered when judging him. Firstly, as Christensen rightly says (*Iran sous les Sassanides* 1944 ed., p. 33), "the Iranian people of those times were not primitive." Secondly, that Zarathustra, as with every human being whether ancient or modern, had a complex personality and not an abstract "monochrome" character. Originally a professional priest-ecstatic of a special clerical caste, he was born between 1000 and 600 B.C. [or perhaps as early as 1200 B.C. according to recent work by Mary Boyce-ed.]. He grew up in a pro-shaman environment in the area of Khwârazm (Henning) or Bactria (Moulton and others), or Soghdia (Nyberg), [or Sistan (Gudi), or Kazakhstan (Boyce)] and he "used" his visions to produce a polytheistic and pantheistic ethical reform of his environment. [In the first edition of this book Bausani speculated that Zarathustra had these visions "probably under the influence of Median concepts, for this region had more contact with the ancient "Semitic" civilizations of Mesopotamia. The fact that tradition has him connected with Media and the Median tribe of the magi may also stem from real contacts (in the person of the founder himself whom we are led to believe was a "wandering priest") between the two areas of civilization." But this now seems unlikely.-ed.][17]

As with all religious reformers (e.g., Muhammad, who was far more in the limelight of history) it is not easy to define what was "new" in his doctrine. What was essentially new—when compared to the anonymous tradition of the past—was his "personality," which revived elements drawn from earlier, and at times contrasting, phases and cultures, reliving them in a genuine form. Analyzing this many centuries later we see the contrasts clearly, but it must not be forgotten that these contrasts grew faint and almost disappeared in the logic of the living person within the reformer. An "ecstatic" synthesis occurred in Zarathustra (which our modern logical thinking may possibly consider confusion, though religious thinking saw it differently) between mythical and natural elements and intellectual, abstract religious experience. We will now study the manner and development of this synthesis through an examination of the following points.

Gods or Demons?

The most frequent solution scholars have proposed for the problem of the gods (or "[spirits] worthy of worship," *yazata*) of Mazdaism is that, roughly speaking, two types of religiosity already existed in ancient Iran. One was centered on an omniscient celestial god, Mâzdâ—a more or less exact counterpart of the Indian Varuna, god of the sky, though Zarathustra accentuated his monotheistic and moralistic aspect. (Pettazzoni showed us how easy it is for the celestial supreme God to adopt ethical traits.) The other type, more polytheistic and nature-based, centered on the god Mithra, who was accompanied by other nature deities. Apparently the tendency toward monotheism and theology in Zarathustra, the prophet of Mazdâ, was unable to definitively defeat this Mithraic type of "naturism" and the Zoroastrian priests had to give in little by little to popular pressure, recognizing, along with the Zoroastrian angels, the gods of the "Mithraic" pantheon.[18] But this apparently attractive and convincing historical reconstruction seems to me to neglect one important point: i.e., the personality of the Founder of the Faith, which was human and consequently—we insist on this—full of contrasts. It was the personality of a man of religion, drawn to types of reasoning and to concepts very different from the more or less abstract reconstructions of logicians and historians. The main basis for asserting the "reformer's" later condemnation of the traditional ritual, sacrificial rites and use of inebriating Haôma lies in a few minor Gâthic passages. But there are also mythologizing elements in the Gâthâs and allusions to Zarathustra as a professional priest. Besides, we know nothing of what Zarathustra could have said or thought beyond the Gâthâs. Therefore, while maintaining the hypothesis of the evolution of the ancient Zoroastrian religion outlined above, we must bear in mind that the synthesis attributed to later priests may in fact have been initiated by the Founder. The Gâthâs may have been his supreme sermons, his Sermon on the Mount, but it may also be that, in the course of his life, his ethical tendency invested some of the figures of traditional religion with moral, "Mazdean," values. Though the hymns to Mithra, to Anâhita, and others, of the "Younger" Avesta were not sung to Zarathustra, they have their specific form because of the influence of his personality as moral reformer. And rather than abolishing the ritual of Haôma, which became central in later Zoroastrianism, he may well have purified it.

Here we come up against the important problem that the unusual name of *daêva* [which originally meant "gods"] is given to "demons" in the Gâthâs and in the whole Iranian religious tradition. Pettazzoni and others primarily relied on this transposition in depicting Zarathustra as a revolutionary monotheistic prophet—so revolutionary that, sweeping away a solid linguistic-religious tradition that was the common heritage of the Aryans, he moved the gods of the Indo-Aryan pantheon to the rank of devils both linguistically and religiously. There were of course already two categories of gods, *ahura* (Ind. *àsura*) and *daêva* (Ind. *deva*) both in Iran and in India. In India the *àsura* were evil and the *deva* good gods, while in Iran the opposite was true. Recent scholars do not all agree on attributing their transformation to Zarathustra, for it is more unusual for "god" to take on the meaning of "demon" than demon god. Avestan expressions such as *daêvaisca martyaisca* appear to give *daêva* a generically but not strictly diabolical sense of "demons"—"genii" in the sense of Arab jinn.[19] Pahlavî has inherited this same expression, where it certainly can no longer be thought of in the sense of "god" (*dêvân u martomân*, "demons and men"). In fact everything leads us to believe that already in ancient Iran the expression *daêva* signified *not so much god become demon* as an ambivalent "daimon," a development to which the personality of the Founder, Zarathustra, or to which the guild of priests, may have contributed—though all this cannot be proved with absolute certainty. Besides, the tendency to demonize gods is not absolutely original to Iran or to this particular historical period. We find some singular examples in nearby India too, though in later periods. In the *Ramâyana* of Tulsi-dâs (sixteenth century A.D.)—a fine example of *bhakti* or devotion to Rama—we find that the goddess Sarasvatî herself describes the gods as "miserable beings. Their dwelling is high, their conduct low: they cannot bear the prosperity of others!" and Indra, the powerful god of the Vedic pantheon, is compared to a dog, while the gods in general are "the vile horde of the gods."[20] Here apparently we should understand *dêv* in the Iranian sense! And in Tulsî-dâs the phenomenon is connected with the glorification of the earthly god Râma, with the creation of a personalistic incarnationist semi-monotheism, and with the non-moral action of the classic *deva*. This parallel may indicate the origin of the *deva*-demon metamorphosis in ancient Iran if we consider that it might have originated in a religious environment concerned with the study of the action of the gods and fate. In later Pahlavî treatises Ahura Mazdâ protests both against those who attribute the creation of evil to him and against those who want to have him appear a *dêv*! I do not believe, however, that the more specific metamorphosis of *dêv* into demon has a monotheistic origin in this case (i.e. in the presence of the Only True One all other gods are *deva*); if this were so there would be no explanation for the fact that only a few of the traditional gods went on to rank as devils. Consequently the process did not take place through a monotheistic reform, strictly speaking, but more probably through the introduction of a moralistic reflection that created this characteristic moral-classificatory dualism in Zarathustra's mind . The gods who remained gods (*yazata*, "venerated spirits" to whom sacrifice is offered, etc.) are in fact those who could best assume a moral character (the beneficent sun God Mithra, for example, the beautiful goddess of the fertile waters Anâhita, etc.) and were most open to the qualification of *spenta*, beneficent "producers of life."

The Archangels and Their Functions

The Archangelic figures with their transparently abstract names can only be the personal creations of a "theologian," i.e., Zarathustra himself (though the term "theologian" should be taken with a grain of salt). Where the Avesta is concerned, in the Gâthâs the terms Khshatra, Armaiti, Vohu Manah, Haurvatat, Ameretat, and Asha are used in a more abstract and theological form, while in the Younger Avesta, and even more in the Pahlavî tradition, they become progressively personified.

The phenomenon of abstract theological concepts becoming personal and concrete—a reverse form of mythicization—is typical of the singular Zoroastrian theism and can be explained by the persistent tendency, which gained strength after the founder's death, to give its originally rather bloodless moral and theological formulations the living personality common to other gods (good gods or *yazata*). This is how the "Angels"—the central concept of Zoroastrianism and all Iranian religious thought—were born.

The process by which these angels were linked to the natural elements is more complex. Good Thought (Vohu Manah) with Cattle, Rectitude (Asha, "Cosmic-moral Order") with Fire, the Reign (Khshatra) with Metal, Docility [or Piety] (Armaiti) with the Earth, Integrity (Haurvatat) with Water, Immortality (Ameretat) with Plants. Dumézil's solution,[21] which was enthusiastically taken up and developed by Widengren,[22] does not seem to me very convincing. According to this solution we are dealing with a sublimation of the gods of the common Indo-Aryan pantheon, distinguished according to Dumézil's well-known three-fold division of society into functions, that is, Mithra is concealed behind Vohu Manah, Varuna behind Asha (but Ahura Mazdâ himself is a sublimation of Varuna!), Indra (a demon!) behind Khshatra, Sarasvati behind Armaiti, two other demons, the Nâsatya, behind Haurvatat and Ameretat! But there is no really reliable documentation to substantiate this cleverly contrived theory, and it has something about it of a well-played game of solitaire. The whole problem arises basically because some follow an abstract evolutionist schema, in which what is simple, material, natural and concrete must perforce precede what is complex, supernatural, spiritual and abstract, and they are therefore surprised and stunned that abstract concepts can be used to represent natural elements or phenomena. This leads to the need to demonstrate that these abstract names must conceal nature divinities. The fact that Widengren chose these extremely original entities (which belong so typically to the less tradi-tional aspect of Zarathustra's thought) to support his idea of a "pantheistic" origin of the Iranian faith in one supreme god is very surprising.[23] In the *Amesha Spenta*s we are in the presence of the more reflective, less nature-oriented and therefore more monotheistic and prophetic tendencies of Zarathustra's very complex personality. The fact is that if we present the problem in terms of "abstract concepts transformed into" or "linked with," we cannot understand how they functioned in the mind of a personality who was so far from us and whose reasoning was so different from ours.

We are dealing with an inverse process to the one we mentioned earlier. If Zarathustra contributed to the moralization of those ancient gods who lent them-selves to it, his environment also led him to personalize the semi-theological creations of his thought and turn them into concrete and living symbols of natural "phenomena" (to which his visions gave a translucid divine reality). After him—through an accentuation of the two processes he himself had started—the *Yazata*s and *Amesha Spenta*s were in practice almost assimilated, and some Yazata were "promoted" to *Amesha Spenta*.[24] Anything else is mere conjecture rather than a hypothesis.

In fact, links already existed in Gâthic thinking and therefore probably also in Zarathustra between the *Amesha Spenta* and their "empires" in the king-doms of nature. *Ahunavaiti Gâthâ* 4.9 [Yasna 31.9] says of Armaiti (Docility [or Piety]): "Yours was Armaiti, yours the Intelligence that created the Ox when, O Ahura Mazdâ, you opened the way of the sky to man, according to which he is or is not a good farmer." Here Armaiti is already the "genius of the earth." And soon after: "And of the two he prefers the good farmer, the just teacher *who makes Vohu Manô increase*." Here Vohu Manô is already the symbolic representative of cattle, while a few lines further on he is also, clearly, "good Thought" and the following verse contains this perfectly theistic and creation-ist declaration: ". . . it is with your thought, O Mazdâ, that you originally formed us, and the World and Religion and the Intelligences, and that you placed life in the Body (of Gayomârt, Primordial Man, according to the Pahlavi annotation), that you created the Works and the Doctrine and that you inspire the desires of those who have this aspiration." Elsewhere (ibid. v. 21) it is said that Ahura Mazdâ gave the fullness of Integrity and Immortality and Rectitude, the Sover-eignty of the Kingdom and *the fat of Good Thought* to he who is his friend, etc.

Passages such as these show how risky Dumézil's correspondences are (Mithra is not principally the god of Cattle, nor Sarasvatî particularly that of the Earth etc.) and how, on the other hand, the archangel-elements are the first result of Zarathustra's personal speculation. In his attempt at primordial theosophy, Zarathustra—as the above-mentioned passage on creation shows—sees the world, religion, intelligences and cattle on the same plane, through a new and theistic way of developing earlier "pantheist-natural" elements. It was left to later speculation to make these correspondences more symmetrical and precise. Besides, the whole subject is incomprehensible without the concept of *menok* and of *gêtîk*, "transcendent world" and "earthly world," which we will be studying later on.

Vohu Manah is neither an abstract and philosophical Good Thought, nor Cattle, nor the Youth who appears as a divine messenger to Zarathustra in the theophanies, but a combination of all these things, i.e., he is an angel—a living symbol and not an allegory. This concept is connected, though not identified with, the other concept of the *ratu* of individual things, according to which each thing or being has a prototype that represents the qualities of the species better than anything else—a "lord of the species" as some Islamic Iranian speculations would call it later (see ahead, Chap. IV): Spenta Armaiti (Holy Docility or Piety) is first an angel and then the earth. From a historical, documentary point of view, the problem is more easily solved than one might think if one accepts, along with mythicization from below from nature, the possibility of a mythicization from above too, of which, as we shall see, there are examples in Iranian territory even in much later periods, under the influence of a new prophetic theism, Islam.

Our conclusion stems from a simple examination of the texts without hazarding too many conjectures, and is as follows. Zarathustra developed in his mind an abstract theology at a time before theological concepts could be transformed into philosophy, and it instead was reinvigorated by divine phenomena, versatile and alive, that belonged to a world that was still nature-oriented. Thus, Holy Docility came to represent the Earth, instead of being limited to an exclusively ethical concept. When all is said and done, we are witnessing a parallel process to the one that leads from the Gâthâs as sacred texts to the Gâthâs seen in visions as celestial, angelic persons who "dress" the souls of the good.

Ahura Mazdâ: Father or Creator?

In the previous passage we mentioned the "Creation" and quoted one of Zarathustra's obviously creationist passages. A little further on, in the same Gâthâ, we find another one in which Ahura Mazdâ is called "father of Vohu Manah" and of Armaiti. This paternity of Ahura Mazdâ is expressed in a very "pure" form in the Gâthâs and always in connection with the *Amesha Spenta*. Some passages in the late Pahlavi tradition still carry the idea of Ahura Mazdâ as father, and even, in one place, of Ahura Mazdâ as mother. I am referring here to a very late Pahlavi *rivâyat* (*Rivâyat Dâtistân i Dênîk*, chap. 46) in which is described the birth of Primitive Man, whose different limbs correspond to kingdoms of nature or phenomena of creation.[25] Further, a well-known passage of the *Bundahishn* speaks quite clearly of a symbolic position of Ahura Mazdâ as father and mother of the Cosmos (and explains this mystery very simply). It says, "the Creation of Ohrmazd was nourished in its spiritual (or transcendent) stage in such a way that (at first) it remained without thought, without a sense of touch, motionless, in a liquid stage similar to sperm. After the liquid stage came the mingling like that of sperm with blood; after the mingling came conception, like a foetus; after conception came diffusion, like hands and feet; after diffusion came the setting of eyes, ears, mouth; after the setting came movement, when it was born. Still now, on earth, men grow like this in their mothers' wombs and are born and nourished. Ohrmazd *assumes* both the paternity and the maternity of the act of creation (*u Ohrmazd pat dâm-dahishnîh mâtarîh u pitarîh i dahishn hast*; or rather "he is father and mother. . .") in the sense that, insofar as he nourished creation in its ideal form he acted as mother, and insofar as he created it materially he acted as father" (Bundahishn 1:58–59). This is evidently a relatively late and deeply felt symbolic representation of the creative process as conceived by Mazdaism, in its double sense of an "ideal" transcendent creation and its material realization. But do we not use the expression *to conceive* an idea too? Here, it is true, we are following a pattern that may have very ancient mythical models in order to better explain the *way* in which Ohrmazd created the world in its transcendent phase. Widengren used these two passages only (the first, a very late one that was possibly already influenced by the symbolism of Gnosis and the second, clearly and consciously explicative-symbolist) to construct a hypothesis according to which in ancient Iran the cosmos was seen as the body of the divinity. He thus confronted, with a theist and creationist concept represented by the Gâthâs and Zarathustra's thought, this ancient Iranian cosmological, pantheist concept (only documented however by these late passages and by a passage of the Pahlavi apocalypse, *Bahman Yasht* I. and foll., in which the course of the various ages of the world is symbolized by a tree with four branches;[26] *therefore* the cosmic tree is a symbol of God, the body of God!) . It is possible and even probable, as we have already said, that Zarathustra broke away from an ancient Indian pantheist and polytheist tendency. But the above-mentioned passages are not, in my opinion, proof of a Mazdean concept of pantheism and they appear very much like later elaborations stemming mainly from the central concept of Zoroastrian theology, which was already present, in kernel, in the Gâthâs and was highly developed later: i.e. that of the two worlds, *menôk* and *gêtîk*. This concept also explains the special position of the Archangels and many other aspects of Mazdean mentality.

The Two Dualisms

The Zoroastrian religion, traditionally, has been defined as dualism, and many people have seen in this dualism the principal characteristic of Iranian religiosity. But let us look at the sources more closely.

In the Gâthâs this dualism is based first of all on a moral, sacred, and social element, symbolized by the Ill-treated Ox. Since it is impossible for a good God to ill-treat the Ox, it must be that the Ox is ill-treated by demonic beings. Combining Zarathustra's monotheistic tendency with his social and sacred veneration for the Cow (an Indo-Aryan feature) and his tendency to visionary abstraction, we obtain an unusual picture. It is of a primordial dialogue that appears to take place in a World of Visions between the following characters: The Ox's Soul, Ahura Mazdâ, Asha, Vohu Manah and Zarathustra. The passage, from the *Gâthâ Ahunavaiti* (Y.29), deserves to be translated in full:

The Soul of the Ox was crying to you: "Why did you create me and who formed me? Here I am, a prey to the violent, to bandits, to those who tear me to pieces, who rob me. You are my only protector: make sure therefore that I have good pastures." Then the Creator of the Ox asked Rectitude: "What sacred prototype [*ratu*] have you given to Cattle, so that its masters, taking good care of it, may feed it and increase it? And what beneficent Lord have you established to repel the violence of evil beings from it? Rectitude well knew how to speak to the evil master who makes cattle suffer. He [the evil master] does not know of the brilliant [reward] that the just will receive: for he who answers the call immediately, in order to do good, is the most powerful of beings. The Wise [Lord] knows best how to calculate everything that is being done and will be done by men and demons. He is the sovereign arbiter, let us therefore do as he wishes. With my soul and my hands outstretched, adoring the [Wise] Lord among you, my soul will go with Azi the cow and I will solve my doubts with the Wise [Lord], since there is no death for the man who follows the right path, nor for the skilled worker: death exists only for the impious.

The Lord, who knows, himself indicated the means of salvation against destruction: but men did not take the material (*ahu*) and spiritual (*ratu*) Lord according to the Holy Law.

It is for the good farmer that your Creator fashioned you.

The Lord has pronounced this word of prosperity in accordance with Rectitude. The Sage has given fat to the cattle, and the Spirit of Good has instructed those who nourish themselves with it. Who is the man that, inspired by you, O Good Thought, will reveal your laws to men?

[Vohu Manah speaks]: "I have found a man who will listen to your instructions. He is Zarathustra the *Spitama*, who is in agreement with you, O Sage, and with Rectitude, who will sing what must be done and who will be given good abode for his word."

Then the soul of the Ox moaned over Zarathustra's powerlessness to give it joy and abundance, [it moaned] over the voice of the powerless man, "he whom I would wish [it said] lord of absolute power. When will he who will give him powerful assistance come? You therefore—Lord, Rectitude and Sovereignty—give them (i.e. Zarathustra and company) your help, come with Good Thought who will give them an excellent abode and joy. But it is from you, O Sage, that I expect them to receive everything, now."

(Zarathustra speaks): "Rectitude, Good Thought and Kingdom, where will you come to me? Oh Sage, do you recognize my high virtue? O Lord, it is our wish now to receive the generous gifts of a being like you!"[27]

Here the reader should note the idea of the sacred prototype (*ratu*), which in the case of cattle is the Primeval Ox, and the idea of evil understood mainly as active power of destruction, represented by the Ox's tormentors, by the bandits, by the subverters of Order. The lord of these evil beings is the Evil Spirit, "he who has chosen evil," while Ahura Mazdâ, from the very beginning, "has chosen good." Death and suffering "are not for the just," nor are they the work of the Creator of the Ox but of the Evil Spirit. It is interesting to note how Zarathustra gives the highest beneficent importance to this world, to cattle, to the earth, to agriculture—all elements that are optimistically considered good. Only the work of destruction of material and spiritual good is evil. Moral dualism is accentuated but not "metaphysical" dualism. Metaphysical dualism, or rather a distinction of planes, can be seen particularly in later speculation, by which, as in Platonic speculation, all things are understood to have their ideal transcendent prototype, *menôk*, as well as their visible form, *gêtîk*. Where does this second dualism (which is also devoid of any sense of contempt for matter) come from, since, in the radical and generalized form in which tradition presents it, it is not to be found in the Gâthâs?

Before turning to possible external influences we should see whether this dualism between ideas and terrestrial things is not a possible development of concepts that at one time were gâthic. On the one hand the Gâthâs already appear to contain the typical concept that everything has a *ratu*, a Spiritual Lord of the thing itself, which represents its quality in the most perfect way, a "lord of the species" (see ahead, chapter four). On the other, the idea seems to exist in kernel that God did not so much create the entire mass of beings but, rather, prototypes of the individual species. This is the sense of the Only Begotten Ox, *gaush aêvodâto*, (Y.31.9, etc.), the genius of animal nature, in which animal nature is, as it were, personified. And v. 4 of Y.30 (*Gâthâ Ahunavaiti*) too ("And the two Spirits met over what was Created First [*paiorim dazdê*], bringing life and death") seems to indicate a gradual creation, through metaphysical planes. Gayômart, who emblematically sums up the entire human species is the First Man, but he is a representation of Man rather than the first man in a *chronological* sense. We should also consider the Gâthic verse (Y.31.11): "It is with your thought that *originally*, O Mazdâ, you moulded us and the World and Religion and the Intelligences. . . that you created the Works and the Doctrine." One instinctively uses capital letters when translating.

In a list of the *ratu* of the different beings to be found in the later Avesta (Y.13.1 and foll.), women's *ratu* is the (Mazdean) Religion! Comparing this with the Gâthic phrase we have just read we see how this Religion (*daêna*, which we will come back to later) can easily be interpreted as a metaphysical, ideal, transcendent prototype. To this tendency we can add Zarathustra's keen visionary experience, which certainly made the religious ideas that inspired him appear extremely real and alive, even if they were not visible and present in the flesh. It is, therefore, not hard to conceive that the possibility already existed, of a speculative development along the lines that later led to the grandiose organization of the double plane of transcendent and earthly creatures, which characterizes the whole of Mazdean religion and gives it what at first sight appears to be a highly Platonizing character.

The following translations of several passages from the first chapter of the *Bundahishn* may give the reader a more immediate idea of this. I have generally followed Nyberg's interpretation ("Journal Asiatique," CCXIV, 1929), while bearing in mind some of Zaehner's corrections (*Zurvan*, p. 279 and foll.). They describe the creation of the world according to the Mazdean system that developed during the Sasanian period:

> . . . It is revealed doctrine that for the whole of Unlimited Time Ohrmazd was in the Supreme Height, surrounded by light, omniscient and good: That Light is the Throne (or Space) and the place of Ohrmazd and some people call it Uncreated Light. That omniscience and Goodness are Ohrmazd's garment, which some people call "Religion" (both are Religion: the definition is the same).[28] The Time of that garment is infinite like Ohrmazd and Goodness and Religion, are and will be for all the time that Ohrmazd lasts.
>
> Ahriman dwelt in the abysses, surrounded by darkness and provided with after-knowledge [*post-science?*] and thirst for blood. The thirst for blood is his garment and that darkness is his place: some people call it the Uncreated Darkness. . .
>
> I will now describe the creation of beings: first as it was in the transcendent stage, then as it was in the earthly stage. Before the creation Ohrmazd was not the Lord and after the creation he was the Lord who wished for goodness, who was wise, without suffering, manifest, providing all things, opulent, seeing all things. He then created the substance of the gods, to further improve the paradisiac condition of that transcendent world to which he himself was bound. When he planned the creation (since he obtained the dignity of Lord through the creation) Ohrmazd saw with his shining gaze that the Evil Spirit would never cease his wicked opposition, that opposition would not be destroyed unless it was through the creation of the world, that the Creation could start moving only through Time, and that the creation of Ahriman would also begin only after he had created Time. And so he created Time, in order to render the rebellion and the subsequent counter-creation ineffectual. . .
>
> Right after unlimited Time he created the Time of Long Dominion, which some people call Limited Time. Out of the time of Long Dominion he created Infinity, because nothing of Ohrmazd ever dies. Out of Infinity Eternal Damnation appeared,

since bliss never reaches the demons. Out of fatally destined Eternal Damnation the Loss of Consciousness of the Evil Spirit was born, since a thing of Ohrmazd, which he created, never changes from the beginning of creation. Out of the Passing to Another Stage of the Transcendent World (Evil) appeared the Perfect Will of the Creatures of the World. Righteousness is subject to the same rules as Creation. Ahriman, as a Dissident, has no relationship with Creation: an explanation of this is that Ahriman fought with Ohrmazd.

Ohrmazd's dominating Wisdom, Renown, Excellence, Eternity and the inefficiency of the Evil Within and Ahriman's lack of excellence (the after-essence of the Evil spirit) came to light when he created the created, the Time of Long Dominion being the first thing he created. At first Time was unlimited but after the mingling that struck Ohrmazd's Unity, limited time was created from this unlimited time. From the Primeval Creation, when he created the creatures, until the end of time, when the Evil Spirit will become ineffective, there is a period of twelve thousand years in which Time will be limited. After this it will again merge with Unlimitedness and then Ohrmazd's creatures will again be reunited with Ohrmazd. As it is said in Revealed Religion:

> Time is more Powerful than both creations
> Time is the unit for measuring the value of the Work
> Time is endowed with more treasures than those who are fortunate
> Time can judge better than wise judges
> The Time of our life runs out swiftly
> When the appointed Time comes even he who is splendidly adorned is destroyed
> The soul cannot save itself from [time] either when it moves upwards or when it

sinks into the abysses or when it descends beneath the universe into the place of cold waters.

Out of his very essence Ohrmazd created Earthly Light, out of Earthly Light the Form of his creatures. Then, in the form of fire—as is becoming to light—the Celestial Vault appeared. Those who are enemies of both creations say of this transcendent being:

"He is a Powerful Being, he is Time."

Next he created the form of the Good Wind, as is becoming to the atmosphere: some people call it the Breath of Long Dominion. Then he created the Earth in aid of the Wind of Long Dominion. Since he needed these three forces when he created the creatures.

The Evil Spirit created his creation out of Earthly Darkness, and according to another form—that of Black Fire—he created the evil monster as worthy of darkness as, for example, horrible poisonous animals. Then out of Earthly Evil Within he produced Lust, to guard the form (of evil creation), as befits Lust. Immediately after he created the substance of demons, so that the evil life of that ideal world from which the misfortune of Ohrmazd's creatures stemmed should become even more evil. Since he created Earthly Darkness out of Uncreated Darkness, Falsehood appeared out of Earthly Darkness. Out of Falsehood appeared the malice of the Evil Spirit, since he he himself was a part of the creation he had created. When he becomes powerless—since he created that body from Uncreated Darkness and his own creatures from this form—he will become powerless to complete his own creation.

Out of Earthly Light Ohrmazd created Truthfulness and out of it and of the Creator's overabundance the whole of creation appeared. Since he created Form Without a Beginning from Light Without a Beginning and all the creatures were within Form Without a Beginnning. Form Without a Beginning lies outside the flow of Time.

Out of Form Without a Beginning appeared the *ahuvar* verse, the transcendent *yathâhûvairyôk*[29] out of which Primeval Creation and the End of All Things are manifested. It is Religion, because Religion was created together with the creation. Out of the *ahuvar* appeared the Transcendent Year that now, in the mingling, lasts three hundred and sixty five days, half light and half dark, on which the determination of the Time of Long Dominion depends, and for which the struggle of the two Creations started. Since it is said that:

"The Creation of Ohrmazd dwelt, in the heights, in happiness, subject to a Lord, to ministers, to courts. The creation of the Evil Spirit dwelt, in the abysses, in disgrace, subject to a state of violence, oppression and sinfulness."

It was through the *Amesha Spenta* that Ohrmazd became able to fix destinies. When the *Amesha Spenta* were created, he created three Judges needed for the restoration of the world (at the end of time)—whose task it was, during the last period, to remove evil (from the world). And they sustain the transcendent creation in the transcendent state.

At first he created the earthly world in its transcendent state and then he transferred it to its earthly state. At first he created the *Amesha Spenta*, seven principles, then the rest: the seventh is Ohrmazd himself. Of the earthly creation in a transcendent state he first created six (forces): he himself was the seventh. For Ohrmazd both (states) are transcendent. The form of material existence derives in the first place from the *Amesha Spenta*, then from the Wind of Long Dominion.

At first he created *Vahuman*, who set Ohrmazd's creation in motion. The Evil Spirit at first created *Mîtôkht*, then *Akôman*. Out of the earthly form, Ohrmazd first created the sky, then out of *Vahuman's* specific goodness he created the earthly light that accompanies the Good Mazdean Religion. And this because he knew what would happen to the creation, until the end of time. Then he created *Urtvahisht*, then *Shathrêvar*, then *Spandarmat*, then *Hordât*, then *Amurdât*.[30] The seventh was Ohrmazd himself. The Eighth was Truthfulness, the ninth Pious Srôsh, the tenth Mânraspand, the eleventh Neriôsengh, the twelfth the high judge Rathfôk-birzait, the thirteenth Rashn the Just, the fourteenth Mithr lord of the vast pasture-lands, the fifteenth Arshvang the Good, the sixteenth Pârand, the seventeenth Sleep, the eighteenth the Wind, the nineteenth Juridical Organization, the twentieth Trial, Complaint and Defense, Peace, Prosperity, Grace.

In the earthly creation the Sky came first, then Water, and third the Earth, fourth, the Plant, fifth Cattle, sixth Man, seventh Ohrmazd himself. In order to help the Creation he created the Wind of Long Dominion, for when he created the Wind of Long Dominion, it became an instrument he needed for the creation of the world.

Of the demons with monstrous heads, the Evil Spirit, in his primeval hostility, first created *Akôman*, then *Indar*, then *Sâvul*, then *Nâhaidiâ*, then *Tarômat*, then *Tarîch* and *Zairîch*, then the remaining demons: he himself was the seventh. Never does he think, say, operate honorable things, and the beauty of Ohrmazd's creation does not befit him. No, the beauty of Ohrmazd's creation is not befitting to the whole of Ahriman's creation. Ohrmazd does not think of anything he cannot do. While the Evil Spirit (only) thinks of what he cannot do: "Let us fight together," (he says in fact).

Ohrmazd's creation was nourished, in its transcendent stage, in such a way that at first it remained without thought, without feeling, motionless, in a liquid stage similar to sperm. After the liquid stage, came the mingling, like that of sperm with blood; after the mingling came conception, like a foetus; after conception came diffusion, like hands and feet; after diffusion came the setting of eyes, ears, mouth; after the setting came movement, when it was born. Now too, on earth, men grow like this in their mothers' wombs and are born and nourished. With the act of creation, Ohrmazd assumed both its paternity and its maternity, in the sense that insofar as he nourished creation in its ideal form he acted as mother, and insofar as he created it materially, he acted as father. . .

Then the Evil Spirit was overthrown, then rendered powerless, as is written above, and thus he remained for three thousand years. While the Evil Spirit was powerless, Ohrmazd transported the creation to its earthly state. . .

The reader will have noted the singular Gnostic and neo-Platonic flavor of this *unique* system that lies between theology, philosophy and myth. But he will also have noted the profound sense of "order" (the creation was "subject to courts"), which was basically Zoroastrian (demonic beings were already the destroyers of an agricultural-social order in the Gâthâs), though here it has been transported onto a more juridical plane; and the sense of the positivity of earthly life, which—unlike what we find in Platonism and Gnosis—loses nothing through the *mênôk-gêtîk* metaphysical dualism. Here the fact of having transcendent prototypes does not seem to demean earthly things but, rather, makes them truer and more positive, "strengthening" and "helping" them, to use an Iranian expression. One should note how the *mênôk-gêtîk* relationship is presented in this passage of the *Shkand Gumânîk Vichâr* (ed. Menasce, pp. 92–94):

The *gêtîk* is the fruit (*bar*) of the *mênôk*; the *mênôk* is its root (*bun*), since the fruit is already present in the root. . . It is evident that the *gêtîk* is the fruit and the *mênôk* the root since every visible, tangible thing passes from invisibility to visibility. Since it is a known fact that man and other visible, tangible creatures stem from the invisible and intangible *mênôk*, in the same way the form (*kâlbut*), the species (*ainaa= adhvênak*), the height, the breadth, of a being are the same as those of the being who generated it; the bodies of men and of the other creatures, which now are manifest, were hidden and invisible in the semen that springs from the fathers, and the semen itself, which was in the loins of the fathers has moved on to the stage of manifestation, visibility and tangibility. One can therefore recognize, without risk and error, that this visible and tangible *gêtîk* was created out of an invisible and intangible *mênôk* and, in the same way, it will undoubtedly return from visibility and tangibility to the invisibility and intangibility of the *mênôk* itself.

This is an interesting passage because, while denying reincarnation, it maintains the pre-existence that is the necessary premise for a logical proof of immortality. However the *mênôk* world—root and active semen—differs from the world of Plato's ideas and is not a motionless prototype of it. Being far more protean than the ideal Platonic world, the *mênôk* indicates immortality of the *body*—though it is an insubstantial body—a *mênôk* body in fact.[31]

The problem of the reciprocal influence of the Gnostic neo-Platonic world and the Iranian world will probably remain unsolved, mainly because of the impossibility of dating the Iranian documents with any certainty. How far back does this passage, contained in an ninth century A.D. manuscript, in fact go?[32]

But the documents obviously prove that there is a link. Thus, to give only one example, the deification of Space that we find at the beginning of the passage from the *Bundahishn* exists also in the Gnostic Bardesane's speculation.[33] He considers space God's throne or support (this is easily explained by the double meaning of the Iranian word *gâtu*, *gâs*, "throne" and "space"). Zaehner points out that at least in this case, since we are in the presence of an Iranian linguistic phenomenon, the probabilities of a passage from Iran to Gnosis are many (op. cit., p. 202). The idea of Time and the Zurvanistic formulation of Mazdaism, which we will deal with shortly and which implicitly "explain" the dualism, seem, in particular, to be linked to Gnostic ideas.[34]

The discovery of the Dead Sea scrolls, which seems to have thrown considerable light on the Judaic-Gnostic sect of the Essenes and in general on the Gnosis of late Judaism, has given us a text as dualistic as "the struggle between the sons of darkness and the sons of light." The texts go back to the first century B.C., corresponding to the Parthian era that witnessed the peak of Hellenization in Iran and, in the West, the greatest diffusion of neo-Platonic Hellenism. Whatever the direction of these contacts, there were undoubtedly convergences between Iranian double dualism and Gnostic-Hellenistic dualism (the reader should remember the "Greek" material of the Avesta we mentioned above) and the entire history of the Mazdean tradition was—so to speak—more open towards the West than towards that India to which, from afar, certain primitive experiences of its religious life linked it.

To conclude, let us insist on remembering that Mazdaism never turned the "light-darkness" dualism into an "ideal world-material world" dualism. Mazdaism considered this identification the heresy par excellence, and Mani, who formulated it radically, the worst enemy. But we will speak more fully about dualism in the next section.

Zurvanism

A passage of the Avesta we quoted earlier speaks of Ohrmadz and Ahriman as two twin spirits (*yema*). Four different heresiographic and Christian polemic sources have left us a "Zoroastrian" myth that we reproduce here in the form in which the Armenian writer Eznik tells it. The four Christian authors appear to have had a common source—Theodore of Mopsuestia (d. 428)—though this is not certain.

> When nothing existed yet—they (the magi) say—neither the heavens, nor the earth, nor any other creature that inhabits the heavens or the earth, there existed a being called Zruan, which can be translated as "fate" or "fortune." For a thousand years he had offered sacrifice in order to have a son who would be called Ormizd and who would create the heavens and the earth and all they contain. And so for a thousand years he offered sacrifice, and then he started to reflect and said: "Of what use is the sacrifice I am offering? Will I really have a son called Ormizd? Or are my efforts in vain?" And while he was making these reflections Ormizd and Ahriman were conceived in the their mother's womb: Ormizd in virtue of the sacrifice offered and Ahriman in virtue of the above mentioned doubt. Realizing this, Zruan said: "There are two sons in that womb: I will make the first one who comes to me, whichever son it is, king." When Ormizd discovered his father's plan he revealed it to Ahriman saying: "Zruan, our father, has made this plan: whichever one of us goes fastest to him, he will make him king." When Ahriman heard this he bore a hole in his (mother's) womb and came out and presented himself to his father. When Zruan saw him, he did not know who he was and asked him: "Who are you?" And Ahriman answered: "I am your son." Zruan said to him: "My son is luminous and sweet smelling and you are stinking and obscure!" While they were exchanging these words, Ormidz was born too, and he was luminous and sweet smelling. He came forward and stood in front of Zruan. When Zruan saw him he knew that this was his son Ormizd for whom he had offered sacrifice. And taking the sticks he was holding, with which he was offering sacrifice, he gave them to Ormizd saying: "Until now it was I who offered sacrifice for you, from now on it shall be you who offer it for me." And while Zruan was giving Ormizd the sticks and blessing him, Ahriman drew close to Zruan and said: "Didn't you promise that you would make the first of your sons to come to you king?" And in order not to break his oath Zruan said to Ahriman: "Oh false and baleful being! You shall be granted the kingdom for nine thousand years and I have established Ormizd king over you, and after nine thousand years Ormidz will reign and everything he wishes to do he will do."
>
> Then Ormizd and Ahriman started making creatures. And everything Ormidz created was good and righteous, and what Ahriman made was wicked and contorted.

In the Zoroastrian Pahlavî texts (to give only one example, we refer the reader to the passage of the *Bundahishn* translated above) there are some passages that lead one to believe in a relatively late theological speculation, by which the dualism between Ahura Mazdâ and Ahriman, which was difficult to uphold philosophically, was resolved in some way with the postulation of Time as common principle, as well as common instrument, of the two supreme origins. In the Avesta (cf. Y.72.10, *Vendid.* 19.13, etc.) a "god" *Zurvan* is barely touched on among various of the other angel-deities we already mentioned: the fact that in *Vendid.* 19,29 *pathâm zrvô-dâtânam*, "paths created by time" are mentioned, along which men follow, after death towards the bridge *Chinvat*, does not appear to be a very convincing proof of a "Time" *deity*. And the forms *Za-ar-wa-an* or *Za-ar-wa* that were found in a twelfth century B.C. Nuzi tablet may not refer at all to the Iranian *Zurvan*. It must also be added that the supreme god of Manichaeism, the god of light as opposed to that of darkness, is not Ohrmazd (the Manichaeans gave this name to Primeval Man, *protos anthropos*) but *Zurvan*. The Buddhist works translated into Soghdian (a Central Asian Iranian language) use the name *Azrua*, a Soghdian form of Zurvan, for Brahma, while Ohrmazd is used to translate Indra (a demon in the Mazdean pandemonium!). The Manichaean formularies for confession contain, as one of the sins to confess, the declaration that Ohrmazd and Ahriman are brothers, that a single god created both good and evil. All these documents, which point to a Zurvanist form of Mazdaism, belong to the Sasanian era.[35] But how are we to interpret them?

Much is being written on the subject and "Zurvanic studies" may well be in the process of becoming an independent branch of "Iranian studies." An excellent and extremely valuable compendium of all the most recent knowledge on Zurvan, together with the original texts of the documents, is to be found in Zaehner (*Zurvan*, see the Bibliography). Anyone who reads the documents that have been collected on "Zurvanism" dispassionately, without preconceived theories, can, in my opinion, come to only one conclusion, i.e., that we are dealing with a theological school that differs greatly from Mazdean dualism and is more "philosophically" oriented. Its origins are late and at times it clearly shows the influence of ill-digested Hellenistic and Gnostic concepts. A theological school therefore and not a religion. The trend that sees a Zurvanist monism prior to Zoroastrian dualism seems to me nothing more than an interesting theory. To begin with the Avesta reveals no trace of the myth of the androgynous Zurvan that late non-Iranian and non-Mazdean authors speak of. I do not believe that one can reliably base any demonstration of the antiquity of this "pantheistic" concept (but is it?) on the Avestan *yema* (the two Principles of good and of evil can very well be called "twins" metaphorically) and on Indian phenomenological parallels (birth through sacrifice, androgynous divinities, etc.). The phenomenological resemblance can survive through long eras and unthought-of channels; Gnosis contains mythical concepts that are to be found in ancient India, but the deduction that they are equally old and primeval in

India and in the world in which Gnosis developed geographically does not necessarily follow. The fact that all or almost all the passages in Pahlavî texts that present the idea of Zurvan contain attempts at philosophical or paraphilosophical speculation and that they, as well as those from non-Christian sources, can at the most be dated not much earlier than the fourth century A.D. (cf. Henning, quoted in Zaehner) makes the opposite idea very probable, i.e., that when, with the advent of the Sasanians, the Zoroastrian clergy organized its sacred canon and started meditating theologically on the texts, some of them tried to "explain" the dualism and, at the same time, to unify moral and metaphysical dualism. In fact one of the principal characteristics of Zurvanist theology, as Zaehner points out clearly, is this greater tendency (but only a tendency) to consider the Good-Evil contrast identifiable with the "Spiritual World-Material World" contrast.

If we bear in mind that [Zoroastrians regarded the later religions of] Manichaeism and Mazdakism as heresies precisely because they fulfill this identification, considering Ahriman the creator of the world and of matter, and if we bear in mind that both these "heresies" arose in the Sasanian period (Manichaeism in the third century, and Mazdakism in the fifth through sixth) under the powerful influence of Gnostic syncretism, we can risk considering Zurvanism a semi-heretical tendency of people who were trying to find a philosophical explanation for the mystery of evil in the world without arriving at Manichaean radicalism. The fact that the Manichaeans chose Zurvan as the name of the supreme god (instead of Ohrmazd) when they wanted to adapt their system to Iranian religious terminology is not as strange as it might at first appear. The supreme and in some ways apathetic Zurvan of the Zurvanist currents was more suited to the inaccessibility of the supreme god of Manichaeism than the Ohrmazd who was the creator of matter and orthodoxy.

We must also bear in mind that the Zurvanistic fashion in vogue among European orientalists has led to some exaggerations in considering Zurvanism a well organized school or even an out and out religion on the one hand and, on the other, in giving Zurvanistic interpretations to what can be simply considered semi-philosophical Mazdean disquisitions. One should not analyze the texts too subtly and make too facile distinctions between Zurvanist and non-Zurvanist layers. At times the confusion stems from the minds of good Mazdean theologians (who were not well-versed in the Greek trend of philosophical reasoning that was coming in with the Sasanian era) rather than in the text. When, for example, three *dadhv*—Ohrmazd's assistant-"creators," Space, Time and Religion (*dên*)—are mentioned in Chapter III of the *Bundahishn*, or, as we have already seen in Chapter I of the same text, Time is ingeniously used as an instrument (just as the whole of material creation and men are instruments in the Mazdean mentality) in the struggle against Ahriman, I do not think that we should see a true organized school of Zurvanism in this "form of reasoning." Again, following the same trend, in the first chapter of the *Zâtspram, û-sh zamân bê ô adhyârîh Khvâst* the author says of Ohrmazd, "and He (Ohrmazd) asked help of Time," adding, "because he saw that Ahriman would not cease through the mediation of any other being of light. For Time is an excellent helper and straightener for both, and there is need of him." There is no trace here of any "superiority" of Time over Ohrmazd, as god. There is only—as in the whole of Mazdean theology—a very clear sense of Ohrmazd as an active and moral personal god who still has to act in something and with something (this sense is so clear that the Manichaeans, as we have seen, chose Ohrmazd not as supreme god but as proto-anthropus). This aspect of Ohrmazd gives rise to the apparent (though not moral) superiority of Space-Time, *within which* Ohrmazd exists and which helps him to create and act. Many misunderstandings would be avoided if Ohrmazd's marked personification were borne in mind. One of the incongruities of theologizing speculation is the fact that Time is an instrument of Ahriman's creativity too (*Zâtspram* chap. XXXIV), while on the other hand he appears as co-creator or at least instrument of Ohrmazd's creation (*Bundahishn*, III). But this incongruity will only surprise people who have no true experience of what a theology is. Nor is the myth of Ohrmazd "coloring Time" (*Dênkart*, Madan p. 21.15–24.5 par. 5), employing a good color for good Time and a bad color for bad Time (which explains the incongruity in the form of an image) as unique as Zaehner thinks. But is it really a myth? Or is it not, rather, a metaphorical expression that can be found in a similar form in other sacred books, for example in the Qur'an? (See chap. III of the present volume.)

And here is another supposedly Zurvanistic text: "Ohrmazd the Creator formed his creation and the *Amesha Spenta* and the Spirit of Wisdom (or learning or transcendent Reason) out of his own light and with the blessing of Infinite Time (*par âfrîn i zurvân i akanârak*): because Infinite Time is exempt from aging and death and pain and corruption and decadence and counter-creation and nobody will ever be able to violate him or deprive him of sovereignty in his sphere." Here too, despite praise for Time, can this lead one to deduce a real Zurvanist *religion* of which this text would be a fragment, a testimony—even though it has been made over as Mazdean? Objectively speaking, I do not think so. Nor do I believe that we should read much more than a theological consideration (similar to that which, for example, led in Islam to the concept of co-eternal attributes with God) into our texts (*Dênkart* and *Bundahishn*) where they mention other entities besides Time as being co-eternal with Ohrmazd. The fact that one text says that before the creation Ohrmazd was not lord (see above, *Bundahishn*) does not authorize deductions such as: "Therefore, since Time is co-eternal with Ohrmazd, before Ohrmazd the Lord, that is to say before the creation, the only lord, or god, *khvatây*, was Zurvan, consequently

Zurvan represents the true and only god for this text, etc." Theological discussions on the attribution of the title of "Lord" to God in the beginning, before the creation, are frequent elsewhere too, in passages that no one would dream of calling Zurvanist.

In fact very few documents that can, strictly speaking, be called Zurvanist in a religious sense have come down to us; and some—I mean those of the Christian controversialists—are of dubious documentary value. What remains, concretely, is the presence in the Avesta of a little stressed angelic time-destiny hypostasis called Zurvan, the assumption by the Manichaeans of Zurvan as the supreme god of light, the presence in various texts of evidence that in the Sasanian period a current had formed within Mazdaism to frustrate to some extent the excessively marked Ohrmazd-Ahriman dualism with speculation on the idea of Time. The corollaries of this current are on the one hand a lively interest in the problem of destiny and free will, with a tendency to favor destiny, and on the other an accentuated pessimism and a temptation (which was heretical for Mazdeans) to rediscover the dualism (born in Zarathustra's mind for ethical rather than metaphysical reasons) between the two personal gods Ohrmazd and Ahriman, in a metaphysical dualism of spirit and matter. Since this idea is decidedly extraneous to Iranian (Zoroastrian) religious spirituality it seems logical to look for its sources in the West, in neo-Platonism and Gnosis. The fact that Zurvanism seems to have been at its strongest in the Sasanian period; information on, for example, Agathias, who says that the Sasanian king Khusrau I (sixth century) studied Greek philosophy and was fascinated by Plato and Aristotle and that a Syrian by name of Uranus taught him philosophy, the presence in texts such as the *Dênkart*, the *Shkand-gumânîk Vichâr*, and others, of clumsily Aristotelian terms and forms of approach, the presence in fifth-century Iran of many Nestorians who had been expelled from the Empire, the traditions that speak of the presence in Iran (after Justinian had closed the Athens school in 529 B.C.) of Greek neo-Platonic "refugee" philosophers, the many parallels diligently noted by Zaehner between Gnosticism and Zurvanism, all lead me to believe that Zurvan was not an older god than Ohrmazd and Ahriman but, rather, more "modern" than they were, and that he was not a god but a semi-angelized concept born of the theological speculation of Mazdaism—a speculation that never succeeded in becoming entirely philosophical and constantly created myths and angels.

Where some Christian sources are concerned, they give the clear impression of confusing Manichaeism with Mazdaism, in particular Theodore Barkonaj (see M. Benveniste, *Le Témoignage de Theodore bar Konay sur le Zoroastrisme*, in "Mo," 1932), one of the authors who quotes the famous myth of the birth of Ohrmazd and Ahriman from Zurvan together with other very obscure myths containing Manichaean-oriented elements. We must also remember that the

Manichaeans themselves, in their syncretism, made Zarathustra the spokesman of their doctrines (cf. "Canto di Zarastustra," in Reitzenstein, *Die Hellenistischen Mysterienreligionen*, p. 126 and foll.). A Greek inscription in Cyrene (Christensen, *Iran sous les Sassanides*, p. 339, no.I) goes as far as attributing the Mazdakite communist doctrine to Zarathustra, possibly mistaking him for the homonymous founder of the Manichaean-oriented sect, better known under the name of Mazdakism (see Chapter II). These examples should suffice to put scholars on their guard against facile deductions based on non-Iranian sources.

The instinctive drawing back of European scientific minds—educated as they have been in the evolutionist tradition—from postulating the possibility that a speculation can create a god and myths can be born not only from nature but also in the minds of theologians, has been and is still the principal obstacle to a correct understanding of the historical rise of Zurvanism and, possibly, also of other phenomena in the religious history of Iran. The most systematic and complete Zurvanist text is also the most recent one (after thirteenth century A.D.): the famous *'Ulamâ-i-Islâm*—an account of a discussion between Muslim "'ulamâ" and Zoroastrian priests that occurred, as the text itself says, six hundred years after Yazdigird III approximately thirteenth century). This account states that, according to Zoroaster's religion, "Except for Time all things are created. Time is the creator and Time has no limits. . . He created Water and Fire and when he had put them together Ohrmazd appeared and simultaneously Time became the Creator and Lord with respect to the creation." We are in the presence here of the logical outcome (if the translation is exact; some people, Blochet for example, translate it differently) of the tendency we mentioned and Zurvan is openly declared the "creator of Ohrmazd" (and probably of Ahriman too, though this is not specified).

The Happiness of the Soul and the Body

Speculations on limited and unlimited time, combined with the typically Zarathustrian idea of the final redemption of the flesh and the traditional legends on the primordial origins, are extremely important because they both contribute to create the idea of "cycle," which is of the greatest significance in the Iranian religion. This idea also has its historical roots in an already ancient fusion between two types of religiosity in Iran. One is an "archaic" religiosity according to which happiness is *in illo tempore*, at the beginning (the beautiful time of the *poryôtkêshîh*, the primeval faith of the ancient heroes, the earthly paradise). The other is a personalistic one, of the prophetic type, according to which happiness is in the future, after the final trial by fire (the Gâthâs insist greatly on both a personal and an apocalyptic trial by fire) with the consequent resurrection of the flesh. Here too, as in many other cases, Zarathustra did not succeed in abolishing the "archaic" type of religiosity (nor, probably, did he wish to, since he himself was steeped in it). From the union of the mythical *in illo tempore* of the origins with the liveliness of the ethical but, as always, re-mythologized sense of the final apocatastasis an idea—the idea of "cycle" by which the Beginning was reconnected to the End and Time had a parabola that reabsorbed it into Eternity—was born and became more evident with the passage of time, gaining strength in Zurvanistic speculation.

It must however be borne in mind that not all scholars agree on attributing precise eschatological concepts to Zarathustra. There are in fact passages in the Gâthâs (Y.48.9–12; 45.11, etc., collected in Messina, *I Magi a Betlemme*, Rome, 1933) which would indicate that the "Saviour" was Zarathustra himself or, when the term is plural, Zarathustra with his helpers and collaborators. The eschatological idea of Saôshyant or rather of the three Saôshyants, born of Zarathustra'a semen and of the virgin who was to bathe in lake Kânsavya where the semen is miraculously preserved, is probably later (but not later than the fourth century A.D.) and, in the recent Avesta, it is connected with the myth of the origins and with the civilizing hero Yima in particular. The idea of the resurrection of the flesh, which is absent in the Gâthâs, is probably also post-Zarathustrian[36].

But scholars generally forget one aspect we mentioned above, i.e., they tend to systematize and consider the thought of Zarathustra and his followers from a logical point of view, forgetting the myth—producing atmosphere of Zarathustra's own environment—an atmosphere of vision and supra-reality in which the bard of the Gâthâs moved. Zarathustra undoubtedly felt that his work would find its realization in the future (*saôshyant* is, grammatically, a future participle); and it is most probable too that, in his vision, he projected himself and his collaborators into an ideal eschatological future. This leads to the possibility of an early split between him and the *future* saviour; but the unity is maintained with the later myth of Zarathustra's semen preserved in the lake and protected by *fravashi* (not *reincarnation!*).

This orientation of the historical evolution of Zoroastrianism also explains the possible contrast between the immortality of the soul of some texts and the resurrection of the flesh of others. In the first place, there is quite a clear distinction throughout Iranian tradition between the immortality of the soul until the day of final resurrection, and the immortality of bodies as well on the day of the final resurrection. Basically this approach is almost identical to the Christian and Islamic approach—and, more than any other, it effectively gives Iranian religiosity a singularly familiar, "Western" flavor. The two fates are clearly established in the *Bundahishn*. We read in Chapter III (ed. Anklesaria, quoted in Zaehner, *Zurvan*, p. 334):

> Man was created in five parts: body (*tan*), soul (*jân*), spirit (*ruvân*), prototype (*advênak*), and *fravashi*. The body is the material part; the soul is the part connected

with the wind, i.e. with inhaling and exhaling breath; it is the spirit that, together with conscience (awareness), hears, sees, speaks and knows, in the body; the prototype is what is situated in the station of the sun; the *fravashi* is she who is in the presence of Ohrmazd the Lord. This was created as it was because during the period of the Agressor's assault men die and their bodies are reunited to the earth, their souls to the wind, their prototypes to the sun, their spirits to their *fravashi*, so that the demons cannot destroy their spirits.

It is quite clear that this is how things were *during the period of the mingling and the assault*. But here is what will happen at the end of the world (cf. Messina, in *Orientalia*, 1935, p. 275):

At first the soul will see the body and question it on what it said. Men will have jointly only one voice and will offer high praise to Ohrmazd and the *Amesha Spenta*. At that time Ohrmazd will have completed (his work); the creation will be such that no work will need to be done within it, after the dead have been reconstructed (*rist vîrâst*). The Sôshans together with the helpers will offer up a sacrifice (*yazishn*) for the reconstruction of the dead, and the ox Hatâyôsh will be immolated in that sacrifice; with the fat of that ox and of the white *Hôm* they will compose ambrosia (*anôsh*), they will give it to all men and all men will be immortal until the perpetual course (of the world).

I don't see how anyone can find traces of pure "immortality of the soul" in the Iranian religion,[37] and even less of reincarnation, not even that of the Prophet Zarathustra.[38] The idea of the resurrection of the flesh is, I think, implicit in the direction religious speculation had taken in Zarathustra's own mind, i.e., the direction of ethical thought, however primitive.[39] The clear distinction between good and bad men has rightly been noted as characteristic, according to Zarathustra, of the after-death situation of human beings. "Those who accompany the follower of Rectitude will possess Splendor in the end, while the *daêna* (see ahead) of the followers of the *Druj* will lead them to an existence consisting in long darkness, filthy food and ill fame" (Y.31.20). Filthy food as the fate of evil souls and the notion itself of purification with molten metal at the end of time that was already current in Zoroastrian thought show how Zarathustra himself had a very plastic and physical concept of the soul. The escape of the spiritual soul from everything material, its total flight from matter (see for example Indian speculation, with its mystical and pantheistic tendencies, which contains a great deal of this) could not possibly satisfy Zarathustra's robust ethicism. Judgment, Glory, Punishment must take place in the form of concrete, temporal, well-being or discomfort. There are a number of consequences to the religious pursuit of these "primitive" concepts the positive value of Time, the rich and realistic apocalyptic and eschatological concepts, the complexity itself of the Mazdean notion of soul.

We have already seen how according to traditional Mazdean texts man is composed of five distinct parts: body, soul, spirit, prototype and *fravashi*. These are the "essential" souls, despite the many other designations that either represent semi-physical functions or are identifiable with one of these five.[40] Body, soul and spirit are quite common and understandable concepts. But *adhvênak* (prototype) and *fravashi* are more unusual. The non-Gâthic Avesta preserves the astro-biological concept, common to India too and not typically Iranian, of specimen souls preserved in the heavenly bodies. The moon is called *gaôcithra*, "having the race of the ox," (Y.1.11, Yt. VII etc.); the *Bundahishn* explains that when the Primeval Ox was killed by Ahriman his semen was taken to the moon and purified by the light of the heavenly body and from this various species of cattle were born (*Bund.* IV and IX). Later too the Persians of al-Bîrûnî's period (tenth century; cf. *Chronology*, p. 213) believed that the Moon's chariot was drawn by an ox of light. In Zarathustra's period, sacrifices offered to "increase the Moon's strength" were apparently still current, for he was irritated by those who sacrificed the Ox so that the averter of death (the Moon) might shine. In a parallel way, the recent Avesta (Yt. XII) places the souls of plants in the stars, while the specimen soul of man is linked, as we have seen, with the Sun. It is also significant that when the *Bundahishn* (chap. 1) speaks of the first Ox and the first Man, it refers to the former as "white and shining like the moon," and to Gayômart, the first man, as "brilliant like the sun." The Pahlavî *rivâyat* that accompanies the *Dâtistân i Dênîk* transparently preserves a myth very similar to the one of *Purusha*, in the Rig Veda (X, 90) of the slaying of primeval man whose various parts then form the cosmos. With *adhvenak* we are therefore in the presence of a prototypical soul linked with the astro-biological myth-rite and the idea of cosmic man that was alien to Zarathustrian preaching and probably "Zoroastrianized" later.

And now let us consider the *fravashi*. Though this concept is not present in the Gâthâs, in the rest of the Avesta it already has the characteristics it will maintain throughout the Pahlavi tradition. Even in passages such as Y.26.7, the *fravashi* is clearly distinct from the soul (*urvân*): "We sacrifice to the souls (*urvân*) of the dead from down here, to the *fravashi* of the saints" (*ashâunam*, those connected with Asha, divine "Rectitude" and "Order"). Apparently a distinction is made between the souls of the "common" dead and the (particularly powerful) *fravashi* of the saints. This offers us a good introduction to the heart of both the problem and the etymology of *fravashi*. Bailey's studies seem to confirm that the idea of *fravashi* is associated with "heroic defensive strength"[41] and originally indicated the protective and defensive strength that a Leader emanates, even when dead (cf. the proper names Fraortes, Fravartish, "eminent hero"). Klostermann[42] collected material that proves that the belief that a man's birth, especially the birth of great heroes, coincided with the appearance of a star, was widespread in antiquity. Now in the Pahlavî texts (cf. for example *Mênôk i Khrat*, XLIX) the *fravashi* are represented by the stars in the sky.[43]

This originally aristocratic notion must have slowly become more "democratic:" every man had his *fravashi*, which exercised its protective force not only for him but for the benefit of all those who invoked it. Rather like the "souls in purgatory" of the Catholic tradition except that in the Iranian concept, the living already have their *fravashi* in heaven. The *fravashi* of the just are situated so that they can protect the particularly sacred places of the Mazdean tradition. They guard the sky, they keep order in the world, they watch over the mythical *Vouru-kasha* sea or lake and the precious white Haôma that grows in it and will bring about the resurrection of the flesh at the end of time, over the North Star, over the body of the hero Keresâspa, over Zarathustra's sperm from which the future Saviour will be born, etc. As receivers of the souls of the just after death and entities undoubtedly connected with "warrior" functions they also remind one, as Dumézil noted, of the Germanic Walkyries. But the *fravashi* are more than this. An Avestan passage (Y.24.5) says: "We consecrate (these things) in sacrifice, prayer, joy and glory to the *fravashi* of the holy Zarathustra Spitama who, of the two worlds, loved holiness more; as also to all the *fravashi* of the saints, who are dead, of the saints who are alive and of the heroes who are as yet unborn, of the Saviours who will work towards the renewal of the world." The *fravashi* are therefore real transcendent "doubles" of men—past, present and future. The living too have their *fravashi*. These, in a sense (if we want to continue with analogies, which are always dangerous) come close to the concept of our "guardian angel," but it goes still further. We have seen that Zarathustra, the "earthly god," has his *fravashi*, and this is quite natural. What is more surprising is that even the *Amesha Spenta* (Yt. XIII, 82–84) and Ahura Mazdâ have *fravashi* (in *Vendid.* XIX, 46–48, Zarathustra is told to invoke Ahura Mazdâ's *fravashi*). This is a fascinating and profound concept (which has been brilliantly treated by Corbin)[44] but, as with many other singular and profound Mazdean concepts, it appears to have been formulated almost by chance and then simply allowed to drop out, in this curious religion that bore the seeds of so many inspired but undeveloped ideas.[45]

According to a typically Mazdean myth-theologoumenon, connected with the Gâthic idea of "choice" and preserved in the *Bundahishn*, at the beginning of the millenniums of the "Period of Mingling" Ahura Mazdâ offered the *fravashi* of the men (who had not yet become incarnate) a free choice that would determine their destiny. They could remain in the heavenly world, safe from Ahriman's assaults, or come down and become incarnate in material bodies in order to fight Ahriman in the earthly world. The *fravashi* answered "Yes" to coming down to earth. This gives rise to a split; the real man is his own *fravashi* now, in this earthly world, his angelic "I" that is both his Destiny and his more real transcendent double (though this must not be confused with the "proto-type" that goes back to a more nature-oriented world-view; here we are dealing with a choice, which is a moral concept).

So if an original pre-Zarathustrian concept of *fravashi* in the heroic-warrior sense existed, the further developments—which centered on the ethics of choice that suffuse Gâthic thought and on the mythicised theological "ideal" that, we saw, is typical of Zarathustra—were very different from what they might have been without the intervention of the personality of the Spitama prophet. Besides, though this term *fravashi* does not exist in the Gâthâs, another term explains the later developments of the warrior-chivalrous entity very well: the term *daêna*. Here are some Gâthic passages in which the term appears:

> He who wishes to deceive the Just One will end in lamentation, will dwell at length in darkness and will receive filthy food and words of insult. This is the world, O evil ones, to which your works and your *daêna* are leading you (Y.31.20).
>
> I will proclaim the two primeval spirits, of which the Good one said to the destructive Spirit: "No, neither our thoughts, nor our teachings, nor our intelligences, nor our vows, nor our words, nor our acts, nor our *daêna*, nor our souls agree. (Y.45.2).
>
> But their souls (the souls of the evil ones) and their *daêna* will groan when they reach the Chinvat bridge and will live for ever in the world of the *Druj* (Y.46.11).
>
> Tell me, O Ahura, of this Way of Upright Thought, where the Saviours' *daêna*, that is to say their good works (*yâ hukeretâ*) will savour the joy of his holiness . . . (Y.34.13).
>
> And the evil one and the pure one will render an exact account of their *daêna*, the evil one whose soul will groan in front of the Chinvat bridge, because with his deeds and his tongue he has destroyed the ways of [supreme] Good (Y.51.13).

A later text of the Avesta, the *Hadôkht Nask* (Yt. XXI-XXII) tells of the meeting of the just man's soul with his *daêna* in the form of a young girl (this is another example of the powerful myth-producing force of Iranian theological thought). Finally, in still later texts (*Vendid.* 10.18 and 5.21) *daêna* and *urvan* (spirit, soul) are almost synonymous.

Here is a Pahlavî summary (from the second chapter of the *Mênôk i Khrat*) of the soul's meeting after death with its *daêna* (which is not given this name here—and we will see why later—though the passage is a summary of the Avestan *Hadôkht Nask*):

> When the just man's soul passes over that bridge (*Chinvat*) it becomes as wide as a parasanga [an ancient Persian measure = about six kms], and the just man's soul passes accompanied by the pious Srôsh. Then the good works he has accomplished advance towards him in the form of a maiden who is more beautiful and good than any maiden in the world. The just man's soul says: "Who are you, for in all the world I never saw a more beautiful and better maiden than you?" The form of the maiden answers: "I am not a maiden, I am your righteous actions, O young man of

righteous thought, of righteous words, of righteous actions, of the righteous religion! For when—in the world—you saw someone sacrificing to the demon you, instead, started adoring God; and when you saw someone carrying out violence and robbery and afflicting and despising good men and gathering in their substance with evil actions you, instead, avoided treating creatures with violence and robbery; you took care of the just and welcomed them and gave them lodgings and gifts. Whether your wealth came from near or from afar, it was honorably acquired. And when you saw people give false judgments and allow themselves to be corrupted with money and commit perjury you, instead, undertook to tell the truth and speak righteously. I am your righteous thoughts, your righteous words, your righteous actions, thought, spoken, done by you. For, though I was already esteemed you made me even more esteemed, and though I was already honored, you made me even more honored, and though I was already splendid, you rendered me still more splendid."[46]

The problem of the *daêna* lies mainly in the fact that the term indicates more than this psychological element. It also indicates "religion" (Pahlavî, *dên*), i.e., the whole of religious good works too. Scholars have found this a particularly difficult problem, and it is true that it is hard for a twentieth century mentality to understand that one and the same word can mean "religion," the soul's "double," and a "maiden" who more or less represents both. Some (e.g., Nyberg) have explained this bivalency as a distinction between individual sense and collective sense (*primum* being "soul," the sum of souls being religion like "church;" but *daêna* does not primarily mean soul—it is clear from the texts that its primary meaning lies in the abstract sense of "religion" or "series of religious acts"). Others (Widengren) have made daring comparisons, seeing it as the "cow," or (Hertel) as the "heavenly light." More commonly the etymology is thought to go back to the root of "to see" (Nyberg, Duchesne-Guillemin). Duchesne-Guillemin very rightly says that the duality of the meaning of *daêna* must be considered in the same way as that of the entities that are both the personal virtues and the divine aspects of the *Amesha Spenta*; though he himself insists on explaining *daêna* with reference to nature, in its various contexts both as the "faculty to see" and the "object of the vision."

It seems to me that many of the difficulties disappear if we examine the texts (for example those quoted above) with simplicity and without preconceived ideas. In one of these (Y.51.13) we could substitute *ad lib.* the words "religion," "religious works" or "soul" for *daêna* in our languages too. In Y.31.20 the *daêna*—together with the works—leads towards heaven or hell and this seems to be a matter of "intimate religious stirring. "This holds good for Y.45.2 too. In Y.46.11 the soul and the *daêna* "groan." If we bear in mind how easily Zoroastrianism personifies Good Thought and Docility "angelically," turning them into symbolic and personal hypostasis of Cattle and the Earth, we should not be surprised that the sum of a man's religious good works—his "religion"—

can take the form of a maiden (it must not be forgotten that the *daêna* is the *ratu* of women!) and at the same time indicate a psychological hypostasis. Errors and difficulties stem from not wanting to admit this mythicization of the abstract, this priority of theologoumenon over myth that, as we have already seen, appears to characterize some aspects of Mazdaism. Another consideration that helps explain the meaning of *daêna* is that our modern abstract terms are abstract in an intellectualizing sense. To translate the term as "religion" does in fact sound too neutral. In the Pahlavî tradition the term *daêna* apparently also developed a cosmological value; according to the *Bundahishn* (chap. 1) Ohrmazd's omniscience and goodness are Religion. But many scholars do not seem to have noticed how much easier it is to understand this difficult passage if one translates "*his* religion" instead of *Religion* in an abstract form. Ohrmazd not only has a *fravashi*, but he also has a *daêna*, a religion, a sum of good religious works, i.e., goodness and omniscience. Therefore "good religious activity" remains a primary value in the meaning of *daêva*. This religious activity (like in the Indian karma, but in a different sense) creates a body around itself; for Ohrmazd this is represented by his Light-Garment and for man by his angel of light.

But there is still a further consideration. *Dên* (which has always been translated too univocally as "religion") has the far more active and personal value of "revelation" too. This is evident, for example, in a passage of the *Shkand Gumânîk Vichâr* (X, 20 and foll.):

> The creator's will cannot be known without the revelation (*dên*) of the Creator. There is no doubt over the fact that the revelation was decreed (*brihînît*) by the Creator. One must therefore conclude that God has decreed the *dên* (revelation) in order to make his will known; and the fact that he should make his will known in order to save (*bukhtârî*) souls manifests God's compassion and mercy. The fact that the *dên* (revelation) is salvific for the soul bears witness to the greatness and value of the *dên* itself.

The reader should note the varying meanings given to *dên*, which, however, fully maintains its sense of "revelation." God's psychological activity is revelation just as good, and bad works are *dên*, i.e., the "revelation" of man's soul. This passage can give us, if not a unitary explanation, at least a further contribution towards a better understanding of the tormented concept and its various stages of meaning.

It is this *daêna*—a personifiable and personified abstraction present in Zarathustra's thought—that modified the more warlike *fravashi* in a Zoroastrian sense. And it is the myth of the choice that, above all, gave Ahura Mazdâ a *fravashi*. How is Ahura Mazdâ similar to man, so that—like man—he has a *fravashi*? Simply because Ohrmazd too—the Gâthâs say—has chosen. Of the two spirits he chose the good one. It is very likely that linguistic similarities too (an etymology of *fravashi* or *fravarti* as "the one who chooses" is also possible) caused the warlike *fravashi* to be taken on in Zoroastrianism as the emblematic angel of the soul in its role of chooser between good and evil, while *daêna* is the very similar concept of (well) chosen religious works." It is therefore not surprising that *Daêna* (*dên*) does not appear among the powers of the soul in the Pahlavî texts and *fravashi* is the more usual term. Also, where the soul is concerned, Mazdean religious history presents a complex syncretistic process by which, on the one hand, mythical and nature concepts are spiritualized and, on the other, (apparently) abstract theologoumena are remythicised. In the case in question this gives rise to the singular figure that is simultaneously soul, angel, walkyrie and religion, which is one of the most original products of Zoroastrianism.

The Myth

Myths offer another example of this dual process. Mazdean texts are very rich in myths but, rather significantly (and I believe that one can never insist enough on this), they are never "told" *ex-professo*, but only "alluded to" in contexts whose main scope is not that of telling myths. And though this procedure is natural in the Pahlavî texts that summarize, translate or comment earlier texts, it would seem less natural in the Avesta. Here too the myths are set into liturgical hymns or legalistic texts as exemplifications and commentaries, just as in the Pahlavî texts they sometimes appear in the middle of a philosophical and theological disquisition. Once one has set aside the explanation that at first sight seems natural—i.e., that this is because only the most liturgical part of the Avesta was saved (though the *Vendidâd* is not basically liturgical and it is here that we find the most myths)—and also the one preferred by the "Myth and Ritual" school, according to which myths are always linked to rites, there still remains a further possible explanation. This explanation is that myths came relatively late into the Avesta and even when they had an ancient origin in nature they never had the freshness of nature myths but were used in the phase of rational-religious (theological) "explanation" and as examples or indications *in substantially religious contexts*. We spoke earlier on about "myths with an ancient origin in nature." A good example of this kind of Mazdean myth— which can be traced through comparison—is the myth of the slain dragon, of which a fragment exists in the *Abân Yasht* (Yt. 5.33. and foll), a hymn dedicated to the angel of the Ardvî Sûra Anâhita waters, containing a list of those who sacrificed to this angel-goddess in antiquity. The efficacy of the prayers and sacrifice to the goddess are explained as follows:

> Thraêtaôno, the heir (*visô-puthro*) of the powerful house of Athwya, in the four-cornered Varena (present day Gîlân), sacrificed to her: he offered her a hundred

stallions, a thousand oxen, ten thousand rams. And he implored her, saying: "Grant me this favour, O Good, beneficent Ardvî Sûra Anâhita, that I may crush Azhi Dahâka of the three throats, the three heads, the six eyes, the thousand senses, the enormously strong demonic Druj, who is grievously evil for the world; the strongest Druj Ahriman ever created against the world of bodies, for the destruction of the world of Good; and that I may save and free his women Savanhavach and Erenavach who are—in their bodies—the most beautiful among women and the wonder of the world." And Ardvî Sûra Ahâhita granted him this favour, as he brought his offerings, gave her gifts, sacrificed them, implored the gift of this grace.

A comparison with other cultures (particularly Indian culture, see the bibliography and other material in Widengren, *Stand*, pp. 51 and foll.) allows us to reconstruct a myth that was connected in the past with the feast of New Year and with rites whose purpose it was to defeat drought. Here, briefly, is the myth: a dragon rules the country and drought reigns supreme. A divine hero (in this case Thraêtaôna, Firdausî's Ferîdûn) conquers the fortress from where the dragon rules and defeats the monster. Thus the waters that were imprisoned in the fortress are freed, as well as the women the dragon held prisoners in his harem. Now rain that fertilizes the earth falls, while the young hero and liberator celebrates the *hieros gamos* with the freed women. One must not forget, however, that this is a "reconstruction" and that readers of the Avesta or listeners to it were probably no longer clearly aware of the original and truly "mythical-ritual" significance of the myth, which by then probably seemed merely a fine example of piety towards the angel-goddess and of the national heroism of king Thraêtaôna.

And I think it is even more dangerous to compare this particular myth with another, of a very different origin, which might be taken as an example of "theological" myth, i.e., the myth of Vishtâspa who frees the fettered Daêna. This is told (with the usual emblematic brevity) in *Farvardîn Yasht* (Yt. 12.99). For the most part this *Yasht* is an arid list of *fravashi*s of holy men to whom "sacrifice" is made. Some of their exploits are told in order to enhance the sacrificer's inspiration to sacrifice to his holy *fravashi*. This is what is said about the *fravashi* of Vishtâspa—the king who protected Zarathustra, accepted his religion (*daêna*) and spread it.

Let us sacrifice to the *fravashi* of the holy king Vishtâspa, who was strong and incarnated obedience, who wielded the club that stuns, who was sovereign and held his weapon ready and tried to make way for Rectitude (*Asha*) and was the arm and succor of this religion (*daêna*), the Religion of Ahura, of Zarathustra; who freed Holy Religion from her fetters when she was a prisoner and made her sit in the midst (of the people) governing from on high, quickly-spreading, holy, well provided with flocks and pastures in which she delighted.

Here, as opposed to the preceding case, we see the myth arise out of history. The mythicization is very advanced but the historical vestiges are still clearly evident. In the first place *daêna* means Religion-Revelation (as usual, as with the *Amesha Spenta* it is difficult to know whether to translate *daêna* with a proper name or as "Religion" with a capital *R*) and the episode is evidently connected with the assistance given by the pious king Vishtâspa to Zarathustra. The reader, however, should note that the attributes placed after his name *are the same as those of the angel Sraôsha* of whom Vishtâspa is the earthly symbol and emblem, just as Zarathustra is the earthly symbol-emblem of Ahura Mazdâ. This is an important moment in the journey from history to myth and in the unusual power the emblematic, transcendent, force of even concrete events had for the Mazdeans. This mythicization can mislead people who are struck by the mythical nature of these stories and refuse to accept this kind of transformation, insisting on considering this too a nature myth (insisting that *daêna* means "cow," Widengren quotes from the Rig-Veda; cf. *Stand*, p. 54). Further on we shall find more examples of this dual kind of procedure to demonstrate specific theological characteristics of Mazdaism. Here we need only note the historical aspect of the question. It is general opinion that the Zoroastrian reform that passed "like a meteor" (Duchesne-Guillemin) across ancient Iranian religious ground was unable to defeat the pre-existing traditional myths that re-emerged despite initial Zarathustrian opposition. This opinion has gained ground also because the (nature) myths have been taken out of their contexts and reconstructed and, of course, thus reconstructed, they take on a distinctly a-Zarathustrian aspect. But who is to say that fragments of myths have not been used already and transposed with an exemplifying-moralizing intent, if not by Zarathustra himself (though this is also probable), at least in the earliest Zarathustrian circles? For one often forgotten fact that Father G. Messina expresses well (in *I magi a Betlemme*, p. 16, no.1) is that "Zoroaster's doctrine, as it is expressed in the Gâthâs, does not constitute a religion; there is in fact no mention of a cult, a priestly class, sacred places, etc." In other words, we only have what tradition has handed down to us about Zarathustra, and Zarathustra may possibly have said a lot more in his preaching. This would help to explain the inextricable mythical unity of the recent Avesta. Therein, myth that is about to become moral example/history (in Firdausî Thraêtaôna becomes the historical king Ferîdûn) and history/theologoumenon that are about to become myth are balanced by means of an internal equilibrium that only those who cannot see beyond an external philology are able to deny.[47]

The Rite and the Cult

Here too, the Iranian religion presents problems that are extremely difficult to resolve. As we have seen, Zarathustra decidedly opposes the bloody sacrifice of the ox in the Gâthâs and, with rather less assurance, the inebriating rhythm of the *haôma*. In several places the *Yast* allude to bloody sacrifices and the eschatological representation of the end of the world and the resurrection of the flesh indicates the need for a bloody sacrifice of the ox; the *Saôshyant* will immolate the bull *Hatâyôsh*. But an essential fact must be borne in mind, i.e., that the sacrifices mentioned in the *Yasht* and the eschatological one mentioned in the *Bundahishn* are "performed outside of time" and are not a reality. They can be studied as a proof that, ancestrally, the Iranian people performed bloody sacrifice and that they preserved the sense of their efficacy in their subconscious tradition, but their presence in Zoroastrian texts ought not to surprise us, nor should we necessarily suppose that they were a penetration from other cultures. This is a contradiction only for those scholars who find it surprising that Mazdeans could disapprove of bloody sacrifice and at the same time make it the cause for the restoration of the world at the end of time. But the *Saôshyant* who will accomplish this and the ancient heroes or gods of the *Yasht* are not ordinary Mazdeans—they are on another plane of reality. There is no cause for astonishment or for great efforts to discover historical "strata" and different populations with which to explain these phenomena, even though it is true that some non-Persian historians have handed down information concerning animal and even human sacrifices in the Achaemenid (Herodotus, VII, 13, 114; Xenophon, *Anabasis* IV, 5, 35, etc.), Parthian and even Sasanian periods (Eghishe Vardapet, ed. Venezia, 1952, p. 21,5; Tabarî, 1,2, p. 819, AMS II, pp. 581 and foll.). Despite the untrustworthiness of some of these documents (real sacrifices are confused with killings, etc.) and the total absence of the mention of sacrifice in the Pahlavî religious texts that reflect the state of the religion in the late Sasanian period, the existence of bloody sacrifice as such in the royal Achaemenid warrior religion must be admitted. On the other hand the present-day Parsee ritual practice that—in view of its marked rigidity and conservative traditionalism goes back at least in part to the Sasanian period—shows absolutely no trace of sacrifice. It is a very complex set of rituals and its many different rites lead one to recall a common early Asian ritual heritage with complex purification rites, ritual meals, etc. Altogether the Parsee rites described in Modi's works (see the Bibliography) and Drower's very interesting *Water into Wine* (London, 1956) (the author witnessed rituals from which the profane and non-Zoroastrians in particular are generally excluded) have much more in common with Christian and Mandaean rites than with Indian cults. Practices such as the *Patît* (confession of sins) came later (in the post-Sasanian period in fact). In *Water into Wine* Drower has drawn on her detailed knowledge of Middle-Eastern rites to highlight the many coincidences between the Parsee and the Gnostic-Mandaean cults.

If we compare the description of human and animal sacrifices, which undoubtedly existed in the course of the history of the Persian reign, with these Parsee rites we lay our finger on the profound difference between a warrior religion with Indo-Aryan features and a priestly religion, which undoubtedly was influenced by near-Eastern cultures. In a well-known passage Herodotus (I, 131 and foll.) describes Persian rituals of the Achaemenid period:

> The following are certain Persian customs that I can describe from personal knowledge. The erection of statues, temples, and altars is not an accepted practice among them, and anyone who does such a thing is considered a fool. . . Zeus, in their system, is the whole circle of the heavens, and they sacrifice to him from the tops of mountains. They also worship the sun, moon, earth, fire, water and winds, which are their only original deities: it was later that they learned from the Assyrians and Arabians the cult of Uranian Aphrodite. The Assyrian name for Aphrodite is Mylitta, the Arabian Alolat, the Persian Mitra (sic). As for ceremonial, when they offer sacrifice to the deities I mentioned, they erect no altar and kindle no fire; the libation, the flute-music, the garlands, the sprinkled meal—all these things, familiar to us, they have no use for; but before a ceremony a man sticks a spray of leaves, usually myrtle leaves, into his headdress, takes his victim to some open pace and invokes the deity to whom he wishes to sacrifice. The actual worshipper is not permitted to pray for any personal or private blessing, but only for the king and for the general good of the community, of which he is himself a part. When he has cut up the animal and cooked it, he makes a little heap of the softest green-stuff he can find, preferably clover, and lays the meat upon it. This done, a Magus (a member of this caste is always present at sacrifices) utters an incantation over in a form of words that is supposed to recount the Birth of the Gods. Then after a short interval the worshipper removes the flesh and does what he pleases with it (trans. by Aubrey de Sélincourt, Penguin Books 1954, p.96).

Instead, this is how, roughly speaking, the priests and objects and places of ritual of the general bloodless Parsee sacrifice (Yasna) in honor of the whole complex of divinities are presented.[48]

The officiants are the two priests of modern Parseeism—the *zôti* and the *raspi*—instead of the eight of the Avesta(49). The special function of the former (see *zaôtar*, written "hotar") used to be to recite the Gâthâs, the latter (Av. *zathwishkar*) used to be in charge of mixing the sacred haôma with the milk.

Only hereditary priests (*môbad*) may celebrate the rite after complex ceremonies to attain ritual purity (*barashnûm*). The sacrifice proper is preceded by a preparatory introduction that present-day Parsees call *paragra* (an Indian term). This includes the preparation of the instruments and the offerings. These consist in: (1) the Barsôm (Av. *baresman*), bundles of twigs that now have been substituted with metal wires; (2) the Evanghîn (Av. *aywaônhanem*) or lace to tie the Barsôm twigs, made of a date leaf; (3) the Urvaram, a pomegranate twig that is pounded in the mortar with the Haôma; (4) the Jîv, or Jivam, i.e., milk, which now is goat's milk but probably used to be cow's milk; (5) the Zôhr (Av. *zaôthra*) or holy water; (6) the Hôm (Av. Haôma) a yellow plant that, dried, is imported from Iran; (7) the wood and the incense, *êsm-bôe* (Av. *aêsmo-bôidhi*) offered to the fire; (8) the Darûn, a small round non-leavened loaf: four or six are used depending on the cult they are destined to. Fruit, flowers, etc. are offered in other cults. The offering in general terms is called *myazada* (and now consists mainly of fruit and flowers).

The temple in which the cult takes place is usually divided into two essential sections: the room of the sacred fire (*adharân*) and the room in which the sacred ceremonies are celebrated (*îzishn-gâh*) The room of the fire is vaulted, to imitate the heavenly vault; the sacred fire is placed over a vase (*âtash-dân*) that is then situated on a stone platform called *adôsht* (the Pahlavî *atisht*), the throne of the fire. When the priest approaches the fire (as well as on other sacred occasions) he wears the typical *padân* (Av. *paitidâna*) over his face to prevent his breath from polluting the fire, and his hands are gloved. This, together with the white coats worn by the priests, makes Parsee celebrants look very much like surgeons in the operating theater. The faithful cannot enter this room, to the right of which is the *îzishngâh*, divided into various equal parts that are used at different moments, according to the different ceremonies. Here too there is a fire vase, but the fire that is placed in it only for the sacrifice "represents" the holy fire of the *adharân*. The sacrificial instruments are laid out on a stone called *urvis* next to which there is a basin of pure water. The *zôt*'s seat (chair) is in front of this. The mortar in which the haôma (*hâvan*) is pounded, the barsôm bound with the evanghîn and, resting on two mahrû or "half-moons" (two metal supports ending like an upward-turned half-moon), a dish with nine holes to filter the haôma, various vases, etc. are all placed on the *urvis*.

The ritual of the *Yasna* is remarkably long and complex and we cannot describe it fully here. We need only say that all 72 chapters of the Avesta known as Yasna are recited (in Darmsteter's translation they fill more than four hundred pages if we include the many notes). The sacramental meal, with its consumption of the darûn and the haôma mixed with milk, brings to mind Christian communion. It is hard to imagine two more different cults. While the first, described by Herodotus, has many Indo-Aryan references, this Parsee cult has only two definitely Aryan elements, i.e., the use of haôma (Sanskrit, *soma*) and the use of the twigs (*barsôm*), though this latter element is also present in a passage in Ezekiel (VIII, 16 and foll.).

The most logical explanation for this is the presence in ancient Iran of two traditions, noble-warrior and priestly, which is also confirmed by a number of other facts (cf. Zaehner, op. cit., p. 46, etc.; Christensen, *L'Iran sous les*

Sasanides, p. 116 and foll.): with the fall of the kingdom, the priestly tradition, naturally, remained sole guardian of the spiritual heritage of antiquity. The Armenian historian Eghishe Vardapet (op. cit., p. 43 and foll., quoted by Zaehner, op. cit., p. 47) describes the religion of the Sasanian sovereign Yazdigird II in the following terms: that he swore on the sun like all the Persian kings, that he ordered his subjects to adore the sun and serve fire, that he "multiplied sacrifices of white bulls and fleecy goats to fire." "He studied all the doctrines and examined the religion of the Magi and the Chaldeans and all the doctrines of the country." It appears, from this and other documents, that the Sasanians too kept up "noble" traditions against the priestly impositions, despite their fame for Mazdean orthodoxy. Bloody sacrifice is therefore a vestige of the religious class of the *arthêshtarân* (warriors).

The three most important fire temples or pyraei mentioned in the Sasanian tradition were dedicated to the three most important classes: the *farnbâgh* fire or priestly fire, the *gushnâsp* fire or royal fire, and the *burzênmihr* fire or farmers' fire—though scholars are not agreed on where they were located. Other pyraei were highly venerated too. It would be interesting (though we do not yet have sufficient material) to study the local traditions of these pyraei and see whether there are any links between these and the many sanctuaries of Islamic Persia called *imâmzâdeh*, for in fact we have proof that some of them rose in the selfsame places as the ancient fire temples.

The Sasanian feasts, too, often reveal characteristics of originally popular or rural festivals that were transformed or adapted by the priests. The Zoroastrian calendar was made up of twelve months bearing the names of the Amesha Spenta and other "gods." Each day of the month (30 days each, plus five intercalary or "gâthic" days added to the last month) had in its turn a name that was also the name of the Amesha Spenta and other divinities, but not in the same order as those of the months (the Babi calendar, which we will discuss in Chapter VIII, presents a singular parallel to this custom). The main festivities were: the six Gâhânbâr, each of which lasted five days—these were ancient seasonal feasts, the last of which fell in the five intercalary days and was apparently a feast of the dead during which, according to al-Bîrûnî (Chronol., pp. 237–38) provisions were deposited on the towers of the dead and beverages on the roofs of the houses to nourish the *fravashi* of the deceased. The most popular feast (then as still now in Islamic Iran) was the New Year or Naurûz—a typical Spring festival—as well as that of Mihragân, an Autumn festival, which was celebrated on the day of Mihr in the month of Mihr, i.e., the 16th of this month that corresponded more or less to the end of September or the beginning of October, and the feast of Sadhag (non-Persian *sadeh*), the feast of Fire *par excellence*, which was linked, as in fact many of the feasts were, with myths concerning the first cultural king-heroes. This popular, agricultural element holds an important place (though a difficult one to define) in the Sasanian religion.

The Problem of the Magi

Who were the priests, the "Magi," of whom Herodotus speaks racially as a "tribe from Media"? The scholars disagree on their origin. We will give two extreme examples of this. According to Moulton (*Early Zoroastrianism*, p. 182 and foll.) they may have been an aboriginal tribe of Elamite soothsayers and necromancers, neither Aryan nor Semitic, who were responsible for all the superstitious and pedantically ritualistic material of the Avesta (especially the *Vendidâd*) and the cause of the degeneration of Zarathustra's religion. Moulton thinks that they were responsible for introducing customs such as that of exposing corpses to the birds and of the *khvêtûkdâs* (marriage between very close relatives and even brothers and sisters) as well as for developing the well-known mechanical and systematic dualism of late Zoroastrianism. According to Father Messina (in *Ursprung der Magier*, see Bibliography) the Magi (he interprets the name *magavan* as "sharers in the gift," and the "gift" is Ahura Mazdâ's revelation to Zoroaster) were the Prophet's original disciples, the custodians of his doctrine, which was more a philosophy and theology than a religion proper. They were his missionaries and, after bringing the doctrine to the West, they formed a colony in Media from where they spread Zoroastrianism. In the more accurate Greek documents they were not famed as wizards and necromancers but were rather praised as philosophers and learned men.

More recent authors are inclined, rather, to confirm Herodotus's declaration according to which—in the non-Zoroastrian Mazdaism postulated by these scholars—the Magi were a priestly tribe from Media or a special class of Medians who had the privilege of priesthood (Christensen). When Zoroastrianism reached the Western countries, i.e., Media and Persia (in the strict sense of the word) the Magi became the spiritual leaders of the reformed religion. It is strange that the Avesta indicates the class of priests with the ancient Aryan term of *athravan*, while the ordinary name for "priest" under the Arsacids and Sasanians was *mogh*, wizard. The Magi continued to consider themselves a tribe and they were looked on as a category of people "who came from the same tribe and were consecrated to the service of the gods" (Ammianus Marcellinus, XXIII, 6,34).

For Nyberg too, the Magi were "an element of the organization according to classes of the ancient Median empire," a priesthood that developed from a cultural and social "guild" in an exclusively priestly direction. According to the Swedish school they were also responsible for keeping alive the Zurvanistic "religion," which was nothing other than a syncretist transformation of the ancient Median religion. The Magi began to emigrate westward from Iran during the reign of Xerxes. In the time of Xanthos of Lydia they were already established in that region and spread rapidly through Asia Minor. As their travels led them through Babylonia their religion was profoundly influenced by "Chaldean" ideas (especially astrological concepts, the idea of Cyclic Time, or the tendency to consider Time as a first Principle) and they used the international language of that time, Aramaic, though they probably remained in contact with their old Iranian siblings (Zaehner, *Zurvan*, with citations, p. 19). It is curious that—according to a famous Greek source (Plutarch, *De Is. et Osir.* 46)—for apotropaic reasons they sacrificed not only to Ohrmazd but also to Ahriman, "pounding *omomi* grass (the well-known haôma) in the mortar, invoking Hades (Ahriman) and darkness; then, having mixed the *omomi* with the blood of a sacrificed wolf they take it to a dark place where they throw it away."

It is true that a number of passages in the Pahlavî texts mention a real "religion of the devil," of *dêv-yasn* as opposed to *Mazdâ-yasn*. If one admits that the *dêv* were the ancient gods, it easily follows that the *dêv-yasn* were people who continued to sacrifice to the ancient gods. Some of the Magi did this (according to Zaehner who gets his information from Plutarch and Clement of Alexandria) and, with the suppression of the daevic cult that is attested in one of Xerxes's inscriptions (though he himself, according to a Greek document, acted very much like a daeva, sacrificing human beings!), they emigrated to Asia Minor, taking with them some of their distinctive doctrines.

In this confusion of contradictory information and theories some almost certain facts emerge: (1) The Magi were a real and true caste—if not a tribe—of Medians who, at a certain moment, accepted Zarathustra's religion (though he never mentions them). (2) There must have been a number of factions among the Magi themselves. Western sources only give us information on the already highly syncretist Magism of the Magi who emigrated towards Asia Minor through Babylonia, but this is worth just so much and, in my opinion, it should not be given the exaggerated documentary importance many scholars insist on giving it. (3) A non-Zoroastrian Mazdaism existed. This is the only solution to the problem raised by the adoration of Ahura Mazdâ by the Achaemenids and their contempt for the *daiva* that was accompanied by the total silence of Achaemenid sources on Zoroaster and by the anti-Zoroastrianism of some of their ritual practices. (4) The Magi who remained in Iran must have made some concessions to the faith of the warrior caste. The presence in the recent Avesta of non-Zoroastrian elements can be explained both with concessions of this kind (see Messina in *Ursprung*) and with the fact of the more extensive contacts of the Magi, who were Medes, with Mesopotamian culture and with the syncretism of their brothers who had emigrated to the West—a syncretism that, in the case of the Sasanian and post-Sasanian cult and ritual, must also have been enriched, as we have seen, with Mandaean and Christian elements.

Conclusion

The time has come to recompose the pieces of the highly intricate mosaic we have been examining. We do not, as we already said, have all the pieces, but those we have are possibly the most significant ones. Though we have had to set aside some problems for lack of space, one of the interesting "minor problems" that abound in the complicated field of the philology and religious history of pre-Islamic Iran should not be overlooked, i.e., that of the singular position of the seven planets in Mazdean theology.

In the more consistently orthodox Mazdean theology the seven planets (*apâkhtar*) are Ahrimanic beings, as opposed to the fixed stars that are, instead, Ohrmazdic. Strangely, though, their names are positive—Ohrmazdic. The inference is that the planets must have been demonized after they had acquired such full right to "good" citizenship in Mazdaism (or in Iran in general) that their names could no longer be changed. Some of their names, (for example, *Kêvân*, Saturn, of Babylonian origin) and their number, order, etc., together with the division into seven skies, show that we are dealing with a Babylonian loan. But among the names of the planets we find *Ohrmazd* for Jove, *Nâhîd* (*Anâhita*) for Venus, *Vahrâm* (*Verethraghna*) for Mars—names that indicate that the loan must have occurred at an advanced period of neo-Avestan syncretism—therefore from around the sixth century B.C. onwards. A rather late period for this demonization is confirmed by the presence of the concept of the evil planets of Mazdaism that, as we know, inherited Middle Eastern syncretist and Gnostic currents. This example is one of the many that confirm our idea of the considerable importance of the influence of Middle-Eastern syncretism on Mazdaism and of the late appearance of organized Mazdean theology. This theology offered two explanations for the contradiction of considering a celestial body with a name like Ohrmazd demonic. The first is mentioned in *Shkand Gumânîk Vichâr* (Menasce IV, 21) and in the late *'Ulamâ-i Islâm* with its Zurvanite tendencies, (Zaehner in *Zurvan*, p. 412). According to it, the planets were demons but in order to try to counter their Ahrimanic essence Ohrmazd dressed them in light and gave them Ohrmazdic names (the *'Ulamâ* has even preserved their demonic names, very evidently reconstructed later from those of the known *dêv* of the Mazdean pandemonium). The second, to some extent co-existing with the first, that the planets are not all bad—some are good and others bad. The good ones are "linked" with the eighth heaven (sky [the sky of the fixed stars]); the other three (Saturn, Mars and the ambiguous Mercury) are bad ones that have remained "unleashed." The myth of the linking of the planets is told in a late Persian *rivâyat* (Spiegel, *Die traditionellen Schriften*, p. 162 and foll.); the *Shkand Gumânîk Vichâr* speaks on the other hand of the linking of the five planets to the sun and the moon. It is interesting to see that the concept of the linking of the planets exists both in Manichaean and Mandaean (i.e., Gnostic); sources for this further confirm what we said above (cf. Zaehner, *Zurvan*, p. 161, no.3). This example of Mazdean syncretism is particularly important for us modern scholars because the concept of good planets and bad planets has come down to us in the horoscopes of our highly civilized daily newspapers![50]

To return to the reconstruction of our mosaic (for which this excursus on the planets can serve as an introduction) the first general impression we get from the facts and theories we have examined so far is the presence of a highly accentuated syncretism in the Mazdean religion and, more specifically, the confirmation of the working hypothesis we proposed at the beginning, i.e., the presence of a "dual" current in all, or almost all, its phenomena and facts. However the danger of generalizing this dual current into a single trend that I feel some scholars have succumbed to must be very carefully avoided. If, in other words, the Median stratum and the Persian stratum have to be introduced to explain certain phenomena, the warrior stratum and the priestly stratum to explain others, the Indo-Aryan stratum and the Zarathustrian or Iranian and Babylonian-Syncretist stratum to explain still others, and so forth, one must avoid introducing a systematic dualism between, let us say, a Median-Babylonizing-Zurvanist-Magi stratum and a Persian-Indianizing-dualist-warrior stratum or, worse still, bringing out vague concepts such as Aryan pantheism and Zarathustrian theism, etc. However paradoxical this may seem to those who lack a strong religious sense, our texts (which evolved from the seventh century B.C. to the ninth century A.D. through a complex syncretist process that it is still hard to decipher) present a grandiose and fascinating theological unity in their present final form. And Corbin's words (in "Terre céleste et corps de résurrection," *Eranos Jahb.*, XXII, p. 99)—which historians cannot but adopt after their research on strata and influences—seem to me to be correct: "A spiritual morphology that attempts to restore and enhance a truly lived devotion imposes a global vision of the canonical Avesta or at least what has come down to us of the Avesta (the Ritual—which centers around the Psalms [Gâthâs] of Zarathustra) as it is completed by Middle Persian (Pahlavî) and Persian commentaries and translations. Here too when the believer is reciting his bible or celebrating the liturgy, objections based on the pretext of historical stratifications may well appear to miss the point. By constantly asking ourselves 'where things come from' we end up running after inconclusive hypotheses. If we were to ask 'what does it tend to?' instead, the soul being questioned could at least irrefutably bear witness to what it yearned for." This penetrating and very erudite French scholar may sometimes ask the second question too exclusively in his highly stimulating works. Transposing historically such vivaciously theological conclusions and already seeing a unity of the kind we have mentioned in a historical Zarathustra can be dangerous. But it is equally dangerous to leave the inert corpse of the good Mazdean *Dên* on the operating table without even attempting to see it alive in the only possible way, i.e., in what remains of it in the active spirituality of its followers (after accurate [textual] analyses, though in the case of Iranian religion, unfortunately, these have had scant practical results.)

And so we could summarize our answer to the first question, "Where does it come from?" as follows. Towards the seventh or sixth century B.C. [or, as suggested above, perhaps much earlier, toward the thirteenth or even sixteenth century B.C.-ed.], in an unspecified area of the Eastern part of the Iranian territory, a group of priests with mystical and visionary tendencies, possibly influenced by Central Asian Shamanism, started a reform of Aryan paganism. This reform reduced the pagan gods (especially those representing phenomena of pure *power*) to powers of an inferior moral calibre, leaving pride of place to a god of Uranic origin, known as the "Sage" (Lord) *Mazdâ* (*Ahura*), God of light and vision. A great religious personality of whom we know little historically and who probably lived in the sixth century B.C. (or as much as a millennium earlier) continued this reform and stressed its ethical and eschatological nature. On the one hand, he endued the existing gods most suited to undergo this process with a moral meaning, and on the other he sketched—as the fruit of ecstatic visions—new figures of archangelic divine powers with "abstract" names. We know little of the rites of this reform. The first Zarathustrian circles may have preserved the common Aryan rites and a pre-Zarathustrian Mazdaism may have spread in Persia even before the advent of the Prophet. Having obtained the support of a king Vishtâspa of uncertain identity, the Prophet started spreading his doctrine. Either through his own wanderings (the legends confirm that Zarathustra travelled westward) or, later, through his "missionaries," the nucleus of his doctrine was assimilated by a caste of professional Median priests (who had also practiced rites that were hard to define, including pedantic ones of ritual purity, etc., and possibly necromancy and sacrifice to Cthonic powers). Little by little these priests were identified as the bearers of the Zarathustrian doctrine. During the Achaemenid period a non-Zarathustrian Mazdaism seems to have survived as state religion, while at the same time the Median Magi maintained their priestly prerogative, adapting themselves when necessary to "theological" situations that also displeased them, for obvious reasons.

Some of them emigrated westward (possibly after disagreeing with the principal group and after Xerxes's anti-Daevic edict). They assimilated many elements from local religions in Babylonia and Asia Minor including the concept of a millenary cosmic cycle, astrobiological ideas, the idea of a heavenly destiny, etc. With Alexander's Greek invasion and the extremely syncretist Parthian period that followed, all these religious tendencies mingled in proportions that are hard to evaluate and the main nucleus of the Avesta took shape. The religion of the Magi suffered further Gnostic and neo-Platonic influences. With the advent of the Sasanians the Magi gained considerable importance as the restorers of the ancient Achaemenid religion, in their own revised and corrected form. The theological schools took shape within this structure. They used borrowed though not always well digested instruments taken from Greek dialectics, the principal one being "Zurvanism"—a late, theologically-oriented formation in which the good-evil ethical dualism that had become more and more rigidly systematized in the theology of the Magi found a unitary and considerably more pessimistic explanation tending to blend with the heaven-earth dualism.

This identification was completed with the epitome of heresy in Mazdaism—Mani's doctrine, which identified metaphysical and moral dualism (with even more evident Gnostic, Christian, etc., influences). The Islamic conquest brought the social and political importance of Mazdaism and its rivals to an end, but it continued to be discussed and it revived exuberantly in the ninth century, when the most important Mazdean religious texts were composed in Pahlavî. A silent "reform" of Zoroastrianism tending to eliminate the more mythological doctrinal elements and the more "noble-warrior" ritualistic elements (e.g., the adoration of the sun and Mithra in the Armenian Eghishe's account of the religion of Yazdighird)[51] probably also occurred during the period following the fall of the Empire under the Arab blows, though we have no reliable documents to prove this (cf. Christensen, op. cit., pp. 143 and 436–38). And so the noble warrior caste—which at least on two occasions, as we shall see, (with Mani under Shâhpûr and Mazdak under Kavât) had profited from the religious discussions and favored even extreme forms of theological heresy in order to diminish the excessive power of the Magi—was definitively defeated.

Our answer to the second question: "Where does it lead to?" (which could also be formulated as: "What are the central spiritual values of Mazdean theology as we know it in its living form?") could be as follows.

Mazdaism (to which many people erroneously attribute the essential characteristic of "dualism") has three central themes: the idea of the Angel, the idea of the Salvation of Time, the idea of the logical, spiritual and moral precedence of the Invisible over the Visible. These three ideas are substantially closely interconnected, which I feel makes Zoroastrian Mazdaism a third type of religion that cannot be identified either with an "abstract and monolithic" kind of monotheism—to use Corbin's terms—or with a pan-psychological pantheism such as the Indians practised.

Time

In the description of the fight between Greeks and Trojans in Book XIII of the *Iliad* (E.V. Rieu translation, Penguin Press 1950) we read: "Peisander now made straight for the illustrious Menelaus. *(It was an evil fate that led him on this path*, with death at the end of it, death, Menelaus, in battle with you . . .)" A description of the battle in which Peisander appears at first to be winning follows. But there are no "surprises" left for the reader who already knows that fate has decided in favour of Menelaus.

This kind of narrative—the antithesis of what a modern writer of "thrillers" would produce—is often found in ancient literature. The archaic world had a horror of novelty; even from a literary point of view the description of an event was enjoyed more fully when the reader could discern the end in the beginning. I will not dwell on this concept that Eliade dealt with in a masterly fashion in his *Myth of the Eternal Return*. The sacred time of origins and myths must be restored, after its detour, and fall into our "time."

As we have already said, the Mazdean texts refer constantly to the restoration of the time of the beginning and the identity of the beginning with the end. We must also remember that the saviour *Astvat-ereta* will rise from lake Kânsavya with the "same weapon" with which Thraêtaôna defeated the dragon Dahâk at the very beginning of history (*Zamyâd Yasht* 19, 82–96); that many famous *kai* (primeval hero-kings) will contribute to final salvation; that the hero Sahm whose corpse is watched over to prevent its corruption by 99,999 *fravashi* of saints will wake up and fight for redemption; that after the resurrection Vishtâspa will reign again and the Saviour will restore the dignity of "first of the *môbad*s" to his father, Zarathustra, (Messina, *Magi a Betlemme*, p. 46, quoted by Markwart, *Naurôz*, in "Modi Mem." pp. 753–763). The concept of Zarathustra as the founder of a "new" religion is apparently avoided. The text mentions the concept of a "primordial" revelation (*poryôtkêshîh*) several times. The *Vendidâd* (F. II, I and foll.) states that before Zarathustra received the revelation Yima, who built his refuge in "the very beginning" as a protection from the cataclysms of the "end" (ibid.), received it in an imperfect form in primordial times. An emblematic part of the redemption seems to have been accomplished even through Gayômart, the first man, when he succeeded in imprisoning Ahriman, in primordial times (*'Ulamâ-i-Islâm*, in Zaehner, *Zurvan*, p. 411). And we could give many other examples. The unusual idea of Time that Mazdean theology developed takes its cue here to form the great cosmic drama: Time is an instrument for the struggle against evil, Time is an "angel." The cosmic drama is broken up rhythmically into three acts spread over twelve millenniums. The principal act is the "primordial creation" (*bundahishn*) introduced by three millenniums of prologue in which *mênôk* (subtle, celestial) creation is established, followed by three others during which creation is transferred to the earthly condition (*gêtîk*). Next comes the second act: the catastrophe. The Negator succeeds in penetrating into material Creation and turning it into desolation. This second act (of "Mingling") lasts for three millenniums, in the course of which Zarathustra appears as a prelude to the end. The three millenniums of the final act follow—each one inaugurated by the work of a Saviour and ending with the Transfiguration of the World (*frashkart*).

But "Unlimited Time" also dwells within Ohrmazd and beside Ohrmazd, as his "garment." It cannot be identified in an unqualified way with eternity, since this would signify the absurdity of the final resurrection of bodies. The Cycle moves from the Unlimited Time of the primordial Beginning through limited time, which serves as an instrument in the struggle, until the return to Unlimited Time. At all events the "Return to Unlimited Time" is not identical to "reabsorption into a-temporality" (in the sense of a Buddhist or Brahmanist nirvana). Just as Ohrmazd is God, with very marked personal traits, eternity is understood very plastically and concretely as "Unlimited Time." Limited time is its visible form—a luminous, light eyed, tall, vigorous fifteen–year–old youth (Nyberg, *Questions*, I, p. 231). And so Time is also an angel. Many of the scholars' infinite speculations on Zurvanism or non-Zurvanism could be simplified theologically, if not historically, by the inference (which is not immediately obvious to modern awareness) that "time is an angel" and not an empty receptacle without color or qualities. Unlike the archaic civilizations described by Mircea Eliade—of which Mazdaism has preserved many traits—Mazdean spirituality resolved the problem of time by admitting the concept of angelic time, present in the essence itself of God. There is no *fall in* Time; the *fravashi* choose Time for moral reasons. Time acquires a sacred value; history is sacred; happiness is in the future, but once it has been attained the future has the flavor of a very ancient ancestral home.

The Angel

We have already explained the historical reasons for the formation of the unusual Mazdean angelism. Instead of asking "What is Time?" "What is the Earth?" "What are the Waters?" a Mazdean (cf. Corbin, *Terre*, op. cit., p. 99) asks *"Who is Time?" "Who is the Earth?" "Who are the Waters?"*

The answers are the fifteen–year–old youth, docile *Sfandarmat* (Spenta Armaiti), beautiful Ardvî Sûra Anâhita. Bearing in mind the Prophet Zarathustra's original visionary experience, how *are* these images of visions what they represent?

They certainly are not angels in the Jewish, Christian and Islamic sense of God's messengers or his servants: Corbin rightly considers them closer to the God-Angels of Proclus. The *Zamyâd Yasht* (Yt. XIX, 15 and foll.) says:

> . . . the sovereigns with beneficent eyes, tall, swift, vigorous, supreme, everlasting, holy; who all seven (and note that the seventh is Ohrmazd himself) have the same thought, who all seven have the same word, who all seven have the same action. . . whose father and instructor is the same, the creator Ahura Mazdâ;[52] each watching the other's soul occupied in meditating good thoughts, in meditating good words, in meditating good actions, in meditating the Dwelling of the Hymns (Paradise), who have paths of light to follow to the liturgies in their honor, who have created and who govern the creatures of Ahura Mazdâ and who formed them and watch over them and look after them and preserve them! Who will create a new world free from old age and death, from decomposition and putrescence, eternally alive, eternally growing, sovereign and arbitrary, when the dead will rise again, when immortality will come to the living and the world will renew itself, when creatures will be released from death—the happy creatures of Good—and Deceit will fall and be destroyed.

The reader will observe how these creatures (who as we have seen "are" the Earth, the Metals, the Waters) transfigure the elements into moral values; and I think this is one of the greatest and most important novelties of Mazdaism.[53] They do not emanate the "dead" objects they symbolize, but are pre-existent to them in their dignity because, "they form them, watch over them, take care of them and contribute to the creation of new skies and new earth" from on high.

Mênôk-Gêtîk

Some observers have compared *mênôk-gêtîk* to Platonic cosmology but the differences are considerable. In the first place Mazdean cosmology does not admit "contrast" in this sense. *Mênôk* creation is a function of the *gêtîk* one and vice versa: the journey from the *mênôk* creation to the *gêtîk* creation, which occurred in the third, fourth and fifth millenniums of cosmic history, is not a deterioration but, morally speaking, can even be considered an improvement, since beings can validly fight the Ahrimanic powers only in the *gêtîk* form.[54]

At the same time it is a good thing that demons do not have a *gêtîk* body: the *shkastan i kâlbud*, "the splintering of the (visible) forms" of the demons (who were more able to fight in a visible form) is in fact one of the most important accomplishments of the traditional mythical Zarathustra. *Mênôk* does not mean "intelligible" as opposed to *gêtîk*, taken as "sensible," nor does the distinction correspond to corporeal-incorporeal (because the celestial powers too have slender bodies of light: the Yt. XI, 21–22 honors the *kehrpa*, "corporal form" of the angelic powers) but rather to a possibly transcendent and phenomenal relationship between invisible, celestial and earthly (though not in too philosophical a sense).[55]

Earthly things too were very different before the Ahrimanic invasion. Consequently matter is not considered evil as it is in Manichaeism and Gnosis, or in some way inferior, as in Platonism. The invisible is as real as the visible—a banal fact taken for granted by all religions but theorized here with considerable theological precision—and "forms a system"—together with the concepts we have already rapidly examined—in a grandiose spiritual synthesis. We should like to present this synthesis emblematically through a translation of the confession of Mazdean faith contained in the ancient *Yasna* XII of the Avesta and still repeated today by the believers in the "good religion":

> I declare that I am an adorer of Mazdâ, disciple of Zarathustra, enemy of the *daêva*, follower of the law of Ahura, praiser of the *Amesha Spenta* and offering sacrifice to them. I dedicate all the good things of the world to Ahura Mazdâ, the good God, of good measure, holy, brilliant, glorious, from whom all excellent things come, to him from whom the Ox comes, from whom Rectitude (*Asha*) comes, from whom Light comes, from whom Happiness united to Light comes!
>
> I choose the good Spenta Armaiti, may she be mine! May my praise keep the thief and the brigand far from the flock; may my praise keep desolation and disaster far from Mazdean villages. I give with all my soul to those who come (to the law) of their own will, to those who live of their own will, who live in the Ox on this earth. My praise calls down on them the goods things that Prayer brings to Holiness. May I never bring disaster and desolation down onto Mazdean villages, even if it were to save the body and this life. I abjure the empire of the evil *daêva*, who are extraneous to Good, who ignore the Law, who give Evil, the most maleficent of beings, the most sordid, the most extraneous to good; of the *daêva* and the adorers of the *daêva*, the magicians and witches, and of all evil beings, whatever they may be; of their thoughts and their words, of their actions, of their manifestations; I abjure the empire of all that is demonic and destructive. Just as Ahura Mazdâ taught Zarathustra in every meeting in which Ahura Mazdâ and Zarathustra came together; thus I too, adorer of Mazdâ, disciple of Zarathustra, reject the empire of the *daêva*, as the holy Zarathustra did.
>
> What the Waters love, what the Plants love, what the beneficent Ox loves, what Ahura Mazdâ the creator of the Bull , the creator of the just Man, loves; what Zarathustra has loved, what king Vishtâspa has loved, what Frashaôstra and Jamâspa have loved, what each of the Saviours, of the loyal workers and the Saints love, this is what I love, this is my Law. I am an adorer of Mazdâ. I declare myself to be an adorer of Mazdâ, disciple of Zarathustra, in praise and declaration.
>
> I praise the Good Thought, I praise the Good Word, I praise the Good Action, I praise the Good Revelation of Mazdâ, who rejects strife and orders that arms be laid aside, who follows the *hvaêtvadâtha*,[56] who is holy, who is the greatest, the best, the most beautiful of creatures present, past and future, who is a follower of Ahura, a follower of Zarathustra.
>
> I dedicate all good things to Ahura Mazdâ. This is the profession (*Astûitish*, "praise") of the religion of Mazdâ!

Notes

1. This confrontation is to be found in Widengren,"Stand und aufgaben der iranischen religiongeschichte," from *Numen* I and II, Leiden, 1955, p. 63.
2. Cf. the material gathered in Christensen, *Le premier homme et le premier roi,* Copenhagen 1918, vol. I, p. 190 and foll.
3. The term *Pârsî* indicates the Zoroastrians . . . who emigrated in successive waves to India where they now form a flourishing but small community of about 100,000 people. Their hereditary priests are the jealous custodians of the religious traditions of their ancient home. The tradition concerning the history of the Avestan text comes down to us from the ninth century A.D. Pahlavî book *Dênkart*, which we will be mentioning later (Cf. West, *Pahlavi Books*, in S.B.E., vol. XXXVII, pp. XXX-XXXI and 412–15). [This passage from the Denkart has most recently been translated by Shaul Shaked, *Dualism in Transformation* (London, 1994), pp. 99–102]. On the Avesta, the meaning of Abestag, and its date of writing down, now see Harold W. Bailey, "Apastak," *Acta Iranica* vol. 24 (Leiden, 1985), pp. 9–14; Mary Boyce, "Middle Persian Literature," *Handbuch der Orientalistik* 1.4.2.1 (Leiden, 1968), pp. 33–38; and Helmet Humbach, *The Gathas of Zarathustra and the Other Old Avestan Texts*, 2 vols. (Heidelberg, 1991), 1:49–67.-ed.]
4. Where this definitive transcriber of the Avestan text (whom Pârsî tradition holds in the greatest veneration) is concerned, it is interesting to note that he had a son called Zarathustra, who was the father of an Adhurpat, and four and a half centuries later his descendants (for the Zoroastrian priesthood is hereditary) still existed among the môbads. Both the name of his son and the circumstance of his definitive transcription of the Avesta have led some Persian Islamic authors to confuse him with Zarathustra, the (presumed) author of the Avesta itself. Cf. Mo'in, *Mazdâyasna va ta'sîr-i ân dar adabîyât-i fârsî*, Tehran, 1948, p. 105.
5. Cf. vol. III of his translation of the Avesta, Paris, 1893, pp.VII-CVII.
6. *Revue de l'Histoire des Religions*, t. XCV, 1927, pp. 149–199.
7. In favour of the existence of written Zoroastrian texts in the first Sasanian period we also have the important testimony of the "heretical" Mani (who lived between 215 and 277, see the foll. chap.). In *Kafelaia* (7, 27 and foll.) he says that "Zarades did not write books but after his death his disciples wrote—basing themselves on their memory—the books which they read today," while a Manichaean document by Turfan (Muller, HR II, p.94, 1916) speaks of a "Zoroastrian writing" (*zardushtagân nibhêgh*). However we are still in the Sasanian period here. [But for more recent findings see note 3 above.-ed.]
8. Collected by Clemen, *Die griechischen und lateinischen Nachriten uber die persische Religion*, Giessen, 1920.
9. The Keresâni of the *Hôm Yasht*. This is Darmsteter's hypothesis but the identification is based on rather weak proofs. However in the *Dênkart* there is in fact mention of Alexander in the Avesta (as the prophetic sacred text foresees) (Sanjana VII, 6, 6), but this may be a later interpretation.
10. Translated by A. Pagliaro, *Epica e Romanzo nel Medioevo persiano*, Florence 1927.
11. A small bunch of grass which the priest holds in his hand, especially during certain rites. In modern Pârsî usage this has been substituted with metal strands.

12. All the important texts of the legend of Zarathustra are indicated in Menasce, *Shkand Gumânik Vichâr*, p. 120, nos. 64–68.

13. Not everyone follows this translation though Widengren, among others, does. Darmesteter translates as follows: "les esprits primitifs ont eux mêmes proclamé leurs deux natures" I, p. 221. In order to "avoid complications" H. Humbach (in ZDMG, B. 107, H. 2 [Sonderheft] Aug. 1957, pp. 368–9) proposes: ". . . die Zwillinge, die als beiderlei Träume bekannt gaworden sing. . ." But (for us) this complication is precisely the most characteristic trait of the passage and is confirmed by the other examples we quote. [See now also Fereydun Vahman, *Arda Wiraz Namag: The Iranian 'Divina Commedia'* (London, 1986)-ed.]

14. Elsewhere (in *Studi e Mater. di St. delle Relig.*, vol. XXIV-XXV, 1953–54, 1955, and ibid. vol. XXVIII, 1957, pp. 145 and foll.) I have collected a set of texts (which could be enlarged upon) on the "word-light" mystical experience.

15. Zaehner (*Zurvan*, p. 382) says that evocation is a Manichean concept and gives a different translation, emending the text. But he appears to forget that Ohrmazd created light (religion) through the voice, i.e., with the recitation of the *ahuvar* formula, in the *Bundahishn* too (*Bund*. XII, 12–15).

16. Y.XXX (*Gâthâ Ahunavaiti*) v.5. is an indicative passage of the Gâthâs and useful because it shows how the remains of a nature-oriented concept of Ahura Mazdâ as celestial god (most people think of the Indo-Aryan Varuna who is in fact one of the *asura*s) are inextricably connected with moral elements "Of these two spirits the Evil Spirit has chosen to do evil; good has been chosen by the Beneficent Spirit *whose garment is the most solid stone (yê khraôzhdisteng asêno vastê)* (from the firmament)." This partial "materialism," this robust plastic sense of God remained, combined with moral values, until the latest theology. The *Dênkart* (IX, 30,7) comments this passage as follows: "Ohrmazd said: Mine are the good thoughts, the good words, the good deeds, O Evil Spirit! My garment is the sky which was created before this material world (*gêtîh*) of that Stone which is beyond all stones (here we have the "metaphysical stone" but it still remains a stone) encrusted with every precious stone; good thoughts, good words, good deeds are my *nourishment* etc." (See H. Reichelt, "Der steinerne Himmel," *Indog. Forschungen*, 32, 23–27) on the sky of stone which is a quite widespread motif in the Indo-European world).

17. In an article entitled "The fatherland of Zoroastrianism" (*Rodina zoroastrizma*, in "Sovetskoe Vostokovedenie,", V, Moscow-Leningrad, 1948, pp. 5–34) the Soviet orientalist V.V. Struve maintains that Zoroastrianism was born in the East of Iran, which was restless under Median feudalism (the tendency of the religion of the "magi," see ahead) and had nostalgic memories of its "tribal democracy"; it was born in fact as a social-political reaction to western influences. Struve also underlines "a strong democratic tendency" in Zarathustra's religion as opposed to that of the Median "magi" which represented a more aristocratic and authoritarian world. This is a social aspect of the infinite kinds of "contrasts" of the panorama of Zoroastrianism—an aspect which also deserves consideration.

18. An outline of this process, for ex. in Christensen *L'Iran sous les Sasanides*, p. 30 and foll. See also Widengren, *Stand und Aufgaben*, pp. 5 and foll.

19. Widegren uses this expression in support of the hypothesis of the existence of the word *daêva* in the sense of "god" in ancient Iran too. But the expression can also be under-

stood in the same sense as the identical and parallel Arab expression *ins wa jinn* "men and spirits" (generally elves, demonic non-human creatures)

20. Cf. *Le Lac Spirituel*, Vaudeville transl. Paris, 1955, pp. XVIII, XXIV.
21. *Naissance d'archanges*, Paris 1945, chaps. II-IV; *Tarpeia*, Paris, 1947, pp. 23–113.
22. Cf. *Stand und Aufgaben* p. 22 and foll. which presents a clear summary of the problem and of Dumézil's solution.
23. Widengren, op. cit., p. 8.
24. Cf. Menasce, "La promotion de Vahrâm" in *Rev. de l'Hist. des Rel.*, 1947, pp. 5–18, which deals precisely with one of the most important angel-gods, Vahrâm-Mars, the ancient Indo-Aryan Indra known with the epithet of Verethraghna.
25. In many Pahlavi texts, e.g., in *Shkand Gumânîk Vichâr*, I, 20 and foll. (ed. Menasce p. 25) there is a correspondence between the different limbs and the social conditions. Some people have compared this to the Indian image in the well-known *Purusasukta* (Rig-Veda X, 90). Menasce wisely points out the tardy nature of the Pahlavî texts on this subject and the fact that it is far more likely that we are dealing with *late* Indian or Greek material under the Sasanians (cf. *Dênkart*, ed. Madan, 429, 5–10) than with ancient myths.
26. The passage in *Shkand Gum. Vich.* I, 11 too, in which *Dên* (Religion) is imagined as a tree, is so transparently allegoristic and late that it tells us nothing in the sense of a hypothetical "pantheism." But the "tree" theme recurs when the prophet Zarathustra is compared to a tree (cf. *Dabistân-i Mazâhib* quoted in Rosenberg, *Zarâtusht-nâmeh* p. 8) and Vahman too, the First Intellect, is compared to a tree whose fruits are all the *mumkinât* (possibilities, contingencies). Daqîqî has taken up the theme (cf. chap. V). All this belongs to the typical late Gnostic-oriented speculations which have nothing to do with a primitive "pantheism."
27. In my translation I have followed Darmesteter's interpretation (op. cit). Though it is rather antiquated in some places, it has the advantage of reflecting the interpretative tradition of Zarathustra's followers better than some of the more recent conjectural reconstructions.
28. This is evidently an annotation inserted into the text.
29. A very well known prayer formula of the Avesta.
30. These are the Pahlavî names of the Archangels (the *Amesha Spenta*) which we know already in their Avestan form.
31. For further considerations, see Menasce, op. cit., p. 102 with the bibl. [On menog and getik see now Shaul Shaked, "The Notions of Menog and Getig in the Pahlavi Texts and their Relation to Eschatology," *Acta Orientalia* 33 (1971):59–107–ed.]
32. Where this is concerned, see Menasce's sensible observations, in a note to op. cit., p. 31 and passim.
33. Cf. Schaeder, in *Zeitschrift für kirchengeschichte*, LI, 1932, p. 50, Bidez-Cumont, *Mages*, I p. 62, note 4.
34. V. Widengren, *Religionens Värld*, chap. 10–11; Nyberg, *Religionen*, p. 409; as well as, Molé, in *Aiphos*, XII, 1952, pp. 289–324.
35. The inscription by Antioch I Commagene (69–34 b.C.) which speaks of *chronos apeiros* (an expression which seems to translate the Avestan *zurv akârana*, "Unlimited Time") belongs to the syncretist period of the Diadochi.
36. Lommel, on the contrary, (see *Die religion zaratustras*) finds an allusion to the resurrection of the body in two passages of the Gâthâs; but even if we do not consider any

passage in particular, the entire protean spirit of the Gâthâs (which gives concreteness to the spiritual images and personalizes and gives body to the concepts) is favorable to the idea.

37. Cf. Widengren, *Stand*, p. 44 and 63.

38. Cf. Widengren, ibid. p. 42. Nyberg, *Religionen*, pp. 30, 302, 391 and foll., 230 and foll., 305 and foll.

39. Cf. Widengren, ibid., p. 20.

40. Denominations collected in Widengren, op. cit. and Duchesne-Guillemin in *Anthropologie Religieuse*, Leiden 1955, pp. 93 and foll. See also Menasce, *ShGV*, p. 75. But one should add *vîr*, *hôsh*, *khrat*, etc.

41. The Pahlavî texts, on the other hand, generally relate the word with the root *parvar*, "to nourish," "to preserve," and the ShGV, VIII, 60, defines them as "preserving and nourishing powers."

42. *Handbuch zum Neuen Testament* bd. II, Tübingen, 1919, pp. 160–161.

43. On this, too, see Dupont-Sommier, "De l'immortalité astrale dans la "Sagesse de Salomon," in *Revue des ét. grecques*," LXII, 1949 pp. 80–87.

44. "Temps cyclique," in *Eranos Jahrb*, XX, p. 171.

45. Cf. Dhalla, "Ahura Mazdâ's fravashi" in *Indo-Iranian studies in honour of Sanjana*, pp. 115–116.

46. After reading these texts the impartial reader will realise that there is little sense in speaking, as Widengren does, of the "sich un die *daêna* konzentrierende erotische Element der zoroastrischen eschatologischen Schilderungen," *Stand*, p. 24.

47. Some myths have a Mesopotamian origin, for ex. the *Gaôkerena*, a plant at the bottom of the lake which will construct future immortality. In the Sumerian-Akkadian myth of Gilgamesh there is a plant at the bottom of the sea which gives eternal youth. One should not undervalue the Babylonian influence on ancient Iranian thought: the light-darkness dualism itself, for ex., which some people consider to be almost the symbol of Iranian thought, undoubtedly had a Babylonian origin. And the idea of heavenly models of things, which was so highly developed in Iran later, seems to be Sumerian.

48. This is the most complete of the many Parsee rites. For a description of them see (besides the above-mentioned works by Modi and Drower) the introduction to vol. I of Darmsteter's translation of the Avesta. [Also see now Firoze M. Kotwal and James W. Boyd, *A Persian Offering: The Yasna*, Cahiers de Studia Iranica 8 (Louvain: Peeters, 1991)-ed.]

49. This reduction seems to have occurred after the Arab conquest. "In these unhappy times," the *Bahman Yasht* says, "the sacrifice can be performed by two people so that the religion will not disappear." See *Darmsteter*, I, LXXI.

50. The inscription of the môbad Kartîr (the principal agent of Mazdean religious intolerance at the beginning of the Sasanian dynasty) found on the so-called "Kaaba of Zoroaster" at Persepolis and published in 1940 by B. Sprengling, gives us an authentic idea—coming as it does directly from their persecutor—of the mixture of non-Iranian religions present in Sasanian Iran in the third century: it speaks of the expulsion of Jews, Buddhists, Brahmans, Nazarenes and Christians, *mukta* (Indian mystics) and *zandîk* (Manicheans). Menasce (ShGV p. 244) wisely observes that when any Indian influence is found in Pahlavi books it is far more logical to think of late influences, from the Sasanian period, and "second hand" ones (of which we have seen an example above) rather than the *Rig-Veda* and the common Indo-Iranian ancestral past. [With

regard to Kartir's inscriptions, see now Philippe Gignoux, *Les quatre inscriptions du mage Kirdir: textes et concordances*, Cahiers de Studia Iranica 9 (Louvain: Peeters, 1991). on the religious sects mentioned in Kartir's inscription at the Ka'ba-yi Zardusht, particularly the sect of *Makataka (*mktky*), see Sir Harold Bailey, *Cambridge History of Iran*, III (2), pp. 907 f.-ed.]

51. In fact, information provided by non-Iranian authors on the Sasanian religion shows traces of naturalism and popular religion. From his studies on the calendar Nyberg shows that in the Sasanian period popular piety venerated three gods in particular (i.e. Adhur (Vahrâm), Mithra and *Dên*) besides Ohrmazd. Cf. Christensen, *L'Iran sous les Sasanides*, pp. 157 and foll.

52. Despite this orientation which places the *Amesha Spenta* on a level very similar to that of the persons in the Christian Trinity (though here they are seven) Mazdean theologians maintained in fact a far more theistic position. In a criticism of the Trinity in the *Dênkart* (Madan 31–33) a clear distinction is made between Vohuman the "First Created" (who later was understandably compared to Avicenna's Prime Intellect)—and Ohrmazd, and it is said that Vohuman knows what the Creator knew before his creation only inasfar as the Creator wishes him to know it: the contrary (which Christians maintain for their Trinity) would be absurd.

53. This singular cosmicizing of historical elements is repeated in the case of daivic elements too. The case of the "absolute prostitute," the *jeh* of the Pahlavî texts, is particularly curious and interesting. In *Zâtspram* XXXIV, 30 and foll., she is Ahriman's lover, the Primary Prostitute who attempts to sully Man, etc. In the *Bundahishn* (39, 11 and foll.) she is the enemy of Man, of the Ox. It has been suggested (Zaehner, *Zurvan*, p. 75) that she might be a survival of some female ctonic divinity reduced to the condition of demon. However it is more likely that here too we are dealing with the phenomenon (which the reader is well acquainted with by now) of "inverse" mythisation, of cosmicisation or angelic (in this case,rather, demonic) personification of ethical elements: so that Wikander's idea (*Der arische Männerbund*, Lund, 1938) according to which the *mairya* (cf. the Kurdish *mêr*, man, hero!) condemned by the Avesta were members of male secret societies often accompanied by "prostitutes" (*jahika*) may seem more plausible. (cf. Widengren, *Stand* p. 51 and, on the *jeh*, see also Christensen, *Premier Homme* v. I p. 15).

54. In the *Dênkart* (Madan 271) *gêtik* holds pride of place when considering the major or minor dignity of concepts such as *tani pasên* ("future body") *vahisht* ("paradise") and *gêtik* ("earthly world") since it is in the flesh and in the world that the fight against the demonic assault takes place and is possible! Therefore *mênôk* is not the static prototype of that which is but truly its ideal active principle. Good is not escaping from time (as in Buddhism and the various philosophies and mysticisms of India) but rather fighting within time, in the world, to become worthy of the Time and World which remain Time and World even though they are transcendent. The difference from Platonism is essential.

55. "Sight," for example, is considered *mênôk* in certain texts while "the eye" is *gêtîk*. This parallel offers a better explanation of the meaning of the two concepts, which must be understood if one is to understand Mazdaism.

56. Pahlavî *khvêtûkdâs*, the marriage between very close relatives.

Bibliography

Bailey, H. W. *Zoroastrian Problems in the Ninth Century Books.* Oxford, 1943.

Bartholomae, C. *Zarathustra. Leben und Lehre.* Heidelberg, 1924.

Bausani, A. *Testi religiosi zoroastriani.* Roma, 1957.

Benveniste, E. *The Persian Religion.* Paris, 1929.

Bianchi, U. *Zamân i Ohrmazd. Lo zoroastrismo nelle sue origini e nella sua essenza.* Roma, 1958.

Bidez, J. and F. Cumont. *Les Mages hellenisés.* Paris, 1938.

Casartelli, L. C. *The philosophy of the Mazdayasnian religion under the Sasanids.* Bombay, 1889.

Christensen, A. *Etudes sur le zoroastrisme de la Perse antique.* Copenhagen, 1928.

———. *L'Iran sous les Sasanides.* Copenhagen, 1944.

Darmesteter, J. *Le Zend Avesta. Traduction nouvelle avec commentaire historique et philologique,* "Annales du Musée Guimet," XXI, XXII, XXIV, (1892–1893), Paris.

Dhalla, M. N. *Zoroastrian Theology.* New York, 1914.

———. *History of Zoroastrianism.* New York 1938.

Duchesne-Guillemin, J. *Zoroastre: Etude critique avec traduction commentée des Gâthâs.* Paris, 1948.

———. *Ohrmazd et Ahriman.* Paris, 1953.

———. *The Western Response to Zoroaster.* Oxford, 1958.

Henri, V. *Le Parsisme.* Paris, 1905.

Jackson, A.V.V. *Zoroaster, the Prophet of Ancient Iran.* New York, 1899.

———. *Zoroastrian Studies.* New York, 1928.

Lommel, H. *Die Religion Zarathustras.* Tübingen, 1930.

Meillet, A. *Trois Conférences sur les Gâthâs de l'Avesta.* Paris, 1925.

Messina, G. *Der Ursprung der Magier und die zarathustriske Religion.* Roma, 1930.

———. "La Religione Persiana," in *Storia delle Religioni.* Ed. by P. Tacchi Venturi, Turin, Vol.I (1949), p.867 and foll.

Modi, J. J. *The religious ceremonies and customs of the Parsees.* Bombay, 1937.

Moulton, J.H. *Early Zoroastrianism.* London, 1926.

———. *The teaching of Zarathustra.* London, 1917.

Nyberg, H. S. *Die Religionen des alten Iran.* Leipzig, 1938.

Pettazoni, R. *La religione di Zarathustra nella storia religiosa dell'Iran.* Bologna, 1920.

Taraporevala, J. G. S. *Apologia del Parsismo.* Roma, 1928.

Von Wesendonk, O.G. *Das Wesen der Lehre des Zarathustra.* Leipzig, 1927.

———. *Das Weltbild der Iranier.* München, 1933.

Widengren, G. *Hochgottglaube im alten Iran.* Uppsala, 1938.

———. *The great Vohu Manah and the Apostle of God.* Uppsala, 1945.

———. "Stand und Aufgaben der iranischen Religionsgeschichte," *Numen,* Leiden, 1955.

Zaehner, R. C. *Zurvan.* Oxford 1955.

Additional Bibliography

Since Professor Bausani wrote this chapter on Zoroastrianism in the late 1950s, much fresh research on the subject has been published. In this note, I simply wish to refer the general reader to some recent books, mainly in English. The most important of these is the three-volume study by Mary Boyce, *A History of Zoroastrianism*, 3 vols. (Leiden, 1975–1991). This essential reference covers the ancient Aryan background, the Zoroastrian reform, the Achaemenid age, and the Hellenistic period. As noted above, Boyce now sees Zarathustra as having lived much earlier than the traditional date of the seventh century B.C., suggesting he may have lived in the thirteenth century B.C. Everything Boyce has written on the subject can be recommended, and some of her works are in paperback and more accessible than the three-volume survey. These include: *Zoroastrianism: its antiquity and constant vigour* (Costa Mesa, Ca., 1992) (pp. 27–45 summarizes her argument for Zoroaster's early date); *Zoroastrians, their religious beliefs and practices* (London, 1979); and *A Persian Stronghold of Zoroastrianism* (Oxford, 1977). Some scholars continue to argue for the traditional date of Zoroaster (7th-6th century) or somewhere between the 6th and 10th centuries B.C. See Ilya Gerschevitch, "Approaches to Zoroaster's Gathas," *Iran* 33 (1995):1–29.

For Zoroaster's Gathas, perhaps now a bit less opaque than they were in the 1950s, see Stanley Insler, *The Gathas of Zarathustra* (Leiden, 1975); Helmut Humbach, *The Gathas of Zarathustra and Other Old Avestan Texts*, 2 vols. (Heidelberg, 1991); and Jean Kellens and Eric Pirart, *Les textes vieil-avestiques*, 3 vols. (Wiesbaden, 1988–1991). For Pahlavî see Henrik S. Nyberg, *A Manual of Pahlevi*, 2 vols. (Wiesbaden, 1964); David N. MacKenzie, *A Concise Pahlavi Dictionary* (London, 1971); Bo Utas et al., *Frahang i Pahlavik* (Wiesbaden, 1988); and Christopher J. Brunner, *A Syntax of Western Middle Iranian* (Delmar, N.Y., 1977).

The subject of Iranian mythology, central to Bausani's concerns, is treated in John R. Hinnells, *Persian Mythology* (New York, rev. ed. 1985). For religious practices, Jamsheed K. Choksy, *Purity and Pollution in Zoroastrianism: triumph over evil* (Austin, Tx., 1989) is important. See also S.A. Nigosian, *The Zoroastrian Faith: tradition and modern research* (Montréal, 1993). For Zoroastrianism's influence outside Iran see James R. Russell, *Zoroastrianism in Armenia* (Cambridge, Mass., 1987). Important texts are assembled in Mary Boyce, ed. and trans., *Textual Sources for the Study of Zoroastrianism* (Chicago, 1984).

The subject of Mazdeanism or Zoroastrianism overlaps with the history of Iran in ancient and Hellenistic times. The standard reference work on that subject is now *The Cambridge History of Iran*, 7 vols. (Cambridge, 1968–1991), especially vols. 2 and 3. A general survey of the subject is Richard N. Frye, *The History of Ancient Iran* (Munich, 1984). For the Elamite civilization that influenced the invading Aryans, see Walther Hinz, *The Lost World of Elam, re-creation of a vanished civilization* (New York, 1973) and Elizabeth Carter, *Elam: surveys of political history and archaeology* (Berkeley, Ca.: University of California Press, 1984). See also the seminal works of M.A. Dandamaev: *The Culture and social institutions of ancient Iran* (Cambridge: Cambridge University Press, 1989); *A Political history of the Achaemenid empire* (Leiden:

E.J. Brill, 1989); and *Iranians in Achaemenid Babylonia* (Costa Mesa, Ca.: Mazda, 1992).

As for the conversion of Zoroastrian Iran to Sunni Islam, this is now thought to have been a slow process even among the urban population, with only 8 percent converted by A.D. 750, and about 80 percent converted by A.D. 870. The process must have been much slower in the countryside. See Richard W. Bulliet, *Conversion to Islam in the Medieval Period* (Cambridge, Mass., 1979); and Jamsheed K. Choksy, "Muslims and Zoroastrians in Eastern Iran during the Medieval Period," *Muslim World* 80 (1990): 217–230.

Chapter Two

Two Unsuccessful Prophets: Mani and Mazdak

Introduction

Setting a chapter on Manichaeism within a general panorama of Persian religiosity immediately presents a problem formulated by Scheftelowitz in 1924, i.e., "Is Manichaeism an Iranian Religion?"[1] I will start by saying that this seems to me, if anything, a pseudo-problem. If we decide to give special "spiritual" value to the founder's racial origins, the answer must be positive. We are now certain that Mani was of Iranian stock on both his father's and his mother's side (see below). If the question is whether Manichaean doctrine includes many elements of Iranian geographical origin (Mazdaism, Zurvanism, and possibly some elements of popular religion) the answer is positive too, as it is positive from a geographical and historical point of view, since Mani was a subject of the Sasanian empire, travelled throughout it and wrote at least one of his principal works in middle-Persian. More important still, at one point he apparently thought of having his new syncretic religion become *the* religion of the composite Sasanian empire. But if, on the other hand, we consider the essence of everything that Manichaeism is (without taking into account the origin of its individual parts) then I believe that the answer must clearly be negative. Manichaeism as a working system is typologically distinct from the only religious system connected with the Iranian world that we know much about—Mazdaism. Manichaeism is very evidently a form of Gnosis, and though Gnosis undoubtedly contains some Iranian elements,[2] this does not justify considering Gnosis an Iranian religion or type of religiosity.

In recent times studies and evaluations of the complex Gnostic phenomenon have considerably increased, possibly because of the present situation of pessimistic desperation and the growing need for "salvation" perceptible in our tormented modern world. In an interesting 1934–35 article the Gnosticism specialist Puech drew up an inventory of the hypotheses that had so far been proposed on the origins and characteristics of Gnosticism.[3] In the first period, Gnosis was considered a Christian heresy that had developed principally in the second century when Basilides, Valentinus, Marcion and Bardesane created their systems, and the result of the marked hellenization of Christianity that had been acceptable to Mother Church too in its more moderate forms (Harnack). After further studies and discoveries revealed a "pagan" Gnosis, Hermeticism, the Theosophy of the "Chaldean oracles" and Mandaeism, the initial phase was followed by a period in which a Bousset could write that Gnosticism was a phenomenon running parallel to Christianity, with which it had only very slight and purely exterior points of contact. According to this theory Gnosis was a pagan phenomenon, more or less impregnated with Iranian culture (rather more than less according to Reitzenstein), which started in Lower Mesopotamia, spreading to Asia Minor and Syria and, according to some scholars, to Egypt (Amelineau). A "Hebrew" layer was added to this first pagan layer and a later "Christian" one marked Gnosis only very superficially. According to Lietzmann and Bousset Gnosis was a regression from Christianity and not a progression; it was an attempt to orientalize Christianity and not to hellenize it. The next step in the history of the hypotheses on Gnosticism sees it not as the son or contemporary of Christianity but as its *father*! Believing the origin of the singular and still extant Gnostic sect of the Mandaeans to be very remote, Reitzenstein maintained that many Christian concepts could be explained by supposing that Christianity stemmed from the development of certain forms of pre-Christian Gnosticism imbued with Iranian and syncretic ideas (e.g., the concept of the "Son of Man" from the Iranian and Mandaean myth of primitive man).

Memorable discoveries of the last decades have greatly increased our knowledge of Gnosis (formerly known mainly through the works of anti-Gnostic controversialists). First, in 1931, came the discovery at Medinet Madi, near al-Fayyûm in Egypt, of an important collection of original Manichaean books translated into Coptic, which throw further light onto the doctrines of one of the most complex forms of Gnosis—Manichaeism. Second, in 1946 and also in Egypt, came the discovery at Nag Hammadi (about 50 kms. north of Luxor) of 44 books of a Gnostic sect of Sethians that had been translated into Coptic from the Greek. And the even later Dead Sea discoveries threw further light on the position and importance of Gnosticism.[4]

Since it is not our task to discuss Gnosticism in and of itself here, we will only mention what appear to be the fundamental results of these discoveries (I say "the general results" because the texts discovered obviously throw considerable light on our specific knowledge of the individual doctrines of the Gnostic "system"). These general results can be summed up in three points: (1) It has now been ascertained that Gnosis was a far vaster phenomenon than Harnack, for example, believed. It was a philosophical movement that preceded Christianity and was independent from it and, contrary to what a too narrow Biblicism led us to believe, it also spread in pre-Christian Jewish spheres. (2) From the doctrinal point of view, Mazdaism, Babylonian astrology, Semitic, Egyptian and other elements, all came together in Gnosis so that it is hard to consider any single element the "origin of Gnosis" rather than any other. (3) These elements merge into an integral way of functioning that is typologically different from Hellenistic philosophy and Indian pantheism on the one hand and Judeo-Christian monotheism on the other—a kind of third type, which made Quispel exclaim enthusiastically, "A new universal religion has been discovered!" (at the beginning of his interesting Zurich lectures, published in 1951 under the title of *Gnosis als Weltreligion*).

According to Quispel, three rivers, Gnosis, neo-Platonism and Christianity traversed the spiritual desert of the first century of our era. These currents were typologically different though united by a complex network of bridges and canals. But within the vast field of Gnosis that Quispel defined as being essentially "absolute knowledge that saves in itself, or, the theory of the attainment of Salvation through knowledge," what was the position of Manichaeism?

I would be inclined to say that while Manichaeism remained basically a Gnosis, it differed from other forms of Gnosis in that it was more clearly and specifically a "founder's" prophetic religion. In fact, once one admits the functional unity of Gnosis as "religion" that authors such as Quispel so enthusiastically propose, one is faced with an insoluble problem that makes this idea seem somewhat exaggerated, a result of the enthusiasm caused by recent discoveries. That is, if Gnosis is a "religion," who is its "founder?" For I believe that a true religion cannot be explained fully in terms of influences and counter-influences, of strata abstractly defined as "Babylonian," "Iranian" or "Hellenistic," etc. One has to be able to assume a creating personality and where Gnosis, taken in its general sense, is concerned there does not appear to be one. Manichaeism offers a personality of this kind and consequently many of its problems are clearer and more easily situated. We defined Mazdaism typologically (see my article quoted in Chapter I) as a "primary unsuccessful monotheism." Manichaeism presents itself with the characteristics of a "secondary (unsuccessful) monotheism." In other words—from a typological point of view in particular—the Manichaean-Mazdean relationship runs parallel to the Judeo-Christian one. Manichaeism appears as the fruit of the penetration, of a broad spectrum of syncretic and Gnostic currents into the heart of Zoroastrianism, just as Christianity was the fruit of the penetration of similar currents within Jewish monotheism. But both in pre-Christian Judaism (cf. the Dead Sea texts) and in Sasanian Zoroastrianism (with its Zurvanist tendency to pessimism and fatalism) the way had been prepared. I will not go into the considerable and obvious historical differences between the two processes here, the principal one being that while the founder of Christianity was an "orthodox" Jew (and the Dead Sea texts, or rather the deductions drawn from some of them, give credit to the old hypothesis by which Jesus was an "Essene"), Mani was *already* the son of a man who had been converted from Mazdaism to a Gnostic sect.

This notion of Manichaeism as the extreme Gnostic-oriented heresy of Zoroastrianism—confirmed to some extent by the ferocity of the "mother religion's" accusations and persecutions against the daughter religion—should of course be taken with a grain of salt and with all due historical specifications.

After this introduction we will now give an outline of the history of Mani and his doctrine and develop what we have only touched on briefly so far.

The History of Manichaeism

Our sources for the history and doctrine of Manichaeism were limited until about thirty years ago to the anti-Manichaean works of the Greek, Latin and Syrian fathers (of which the most important were Augustine's well-known refutation); some Islamic sources such as the Chronology of al-Birûnî (drawn up around the year 1000 A.D.), which quotes passages from Mani's autobiography; and the *Fihrist al-'ulûm* of an-Nadîm (composed in 988 A.D.), which includes Manichaean tales concerning the reformer's childhood and vocation and the story of the first leaders of his community, the *Acta Archelai*, composed in the second quarter of the fourth century by a man called Egemonius who tells the story—he says—of a discussion between Mani and the Christian bishop Archelaus of Kalkhar (Mesopotamia).

Other precious sources came to light later: the manuscripts in Iranian and Turkish discovered in Turfân (Central Asia) the first of which were published in 1904, and the Coptic Manichaean texts we have already mentioned, discovered at Fayyûm. The merit of these documents is that they were written by Manichaeans and not by enemies of the sect They offer precious information not only on the doctrine but also on historical details of the life of the religion and its founder. We know that Mani himself wrote seven fundamental books, or canons. These included the *Shâhbuhragân*, dedicated to the Sasanian emperor Shâhpûr I (the only one of the seven to be written in an Iranian language—Southwestern Pahlavî). In Eastern Aramaic he wrote the "Living Gospel," the "Treasure of Life," the "Pragmateia" (or Treatise), the "Book of Arcana," the "Book of Giants" and the "Letters." To these we must add an infinity of long and short treatises either attributed to the master (e.g., the *Kephalaia* or "discourses" found at al-Fayyûm) or the work of his followers' inspired efforts, homilies, ecclesiastical histories, formularies for confession, liturgical collections. The so-called "Manichaean Psalms" are particularly interesting from a literary point of view and some passages powerfully express the suffering of the soul that has fallen into the darkness of matter (Allberry published most of them on the basis of the Coptic finds at al-Fayyûm).

Drawing on studies of both the ancient texts and the newly discovered ones, we are now in a position to give an accurate outline of the Founder's life. I have followed Puech's clear summary and refer the reader to the ample critical notes of his precious little volume (quoted in the bibliography) for proofs and documentation.

According to our sources Mani was born on April 14, 216 (A.D.) in a city of Northern Babylonia—Mardûnû or Afrûnyâ. He was almost certainly born deformed, probably lame, and some scholars feel that this explains some aspects of his character and doctrine[5]. His father's name was Pâtek or Patig and he probably came from Hamadân (ancient Ecbatana). He was therefore Persian and belonged in fact to the royal family of the Parthian Arsacid kings. His mother, whose name was Maryam (Mary), was of the same noble origin. Mani's father exemplified the "spiritual crisis" that apparently tormented the last years of the Arsacid dynasty and the beginning of the Sasanian one.

At a certain point in his life a miraculous voice summoned him and commanded him not to eat meat or drink wine and to abstain from women. He went into the Mesenian desert and joined a probably Gnostic and possibly pre-Mandaean community of "baptizers" (Puech, pp. 39–40). Mani, who had been born in the meantime, spent his youth in this singular religious community but left it, repudiating baptism and the concept of baptism after two "revelations" for which we have reasonably precise dates; the first occurred when he was twelve or thirteen, the second when he was twenty–four. Apparently he received these two revelations from the King of the Paradise of Lights (the supreme god of Manichaeism) through an angel that the sources call "the Twin" or "the Companion." In the first of the revelations the angel told him to abandon the community he lived in because he was born for greater things; in the second, that the time had come for him to publicly reveal himself (cf. the "double" initial revelation recorded in a number of religions, including the recent Baha'ism—see also Chapter VIII). After the second revelation Mani started his apostleship with a journey to India, probably to the Indus valley that Shâpûr had conquered for the Sasanian empire in 241, and possibly during the same period as the Persian sovereign's conquest. At all events Mani certainly visited—among others—the regions of Makrân and Tûrân in the course of this first journey. The new Sasanian sovereign heard about the Prophet and his doctrines from some of his noblemen who had been fascinated by them, and summoned him to the capital, Gundêshâhpûr, in present day Khûzistân (between Persia and Iraq).

Mani hurried there and Pêrôz, the sovereign's brother, arranged an interview with Shâhpûr for him. Two disciples and his father accompanied him on 9th April 243 to this important meeting. The king came away favorably impressed and inspired and granted Mani's request that the missionaries of the new religion be allowed to preach undisturbed in all the provinces of the Empire. Little is known of Mani's career under the reign of king Shâpûr (241–273) except that—especially during the early years—the relationship between the two was excellent, Some scholars (Nyberg) even believe that the Sasanian sovereign was tempted for a while to adopt Manichaeism as the State religion. Mani became a member of Shâpûr's general staff during one of his military campaigns against the Roman Empire (probably the campaign of 256–260 against Valerian or possibly, ten years earlier, the campaign against Gordian III). It is a curious fact that, according to his biographer Porphyry, Plotinus participated in Gordian III's anti-Persian war of 242–244 out of curiosity about Persian and Indian philosophical ideas; the western man and the eastern man, both inspired by the *Nous*, on two opposing fronts! During Shâhpûr's reign Mani travelled as a missionary throughout the great Persian Empire; from a geographical point of view—we reiterate—the Manichaean religion is definitely an "Iranian" religion! It seems that Shâhpûr died towards the middle of April 273 and was succeeded, for barely a year, by his son Hormizd. The new *shâhânshâh* renewed the letters of protection Mani had obtained from his father and the authorization to go to Babylonia. When Hormizd was succeeded by his brother Bahrâm I (274–277) the prophet went to Susiana and from there tried to reach the country of the Kushân where we know that he had protectors and supporters. But the favor he had enjoyed at court had declined, mainly through the influence of the Magi, and he was prevented from fulfilling this plan. Returning to Mesopotamia he sailed up the Tigris as far as Ctesiphon where he met a local prince called Bat who had been converted to Manichaeism. Then after revisiting his birthplace during a last long pastoral journey (studied by Henning) he returned to the capital. The *môbad* Kartîr (the leader of the Magi and an inflexible innovator) was intolerant of Zoroastrianism and accused him of destroying Mazdaism and drawing the king's subjects away from the religious cult—a crime that, according to Sasanian law, was punishable with death. After a stormy interrogation in the presence of Bahrâm and Kartîr, the heretical leader was condemned. The king asked him, among other things: "Why was this revelation granted to you and not to Us, who are the sovereigns of the country?" Mani answered "Because this was God's will." He was led to prison in chains where he suffered his passion—his *staurosis*, *dârgirdêh*, "crucifixion" in the technical language of the Manichaeans (a term that they seem to have applied to any kind of death for one's faith). According to the most reliable sources Mani appears to have died not, as tradition has it, flayed, cut up into pieces, etc., but consumed by the weight of the great chains—three on his hands, three on his feet and one around his neck—which prevented him from any movement of limbs and head. His long agony lasted twenty six days; he died on Monday February 26, 277, at the age of sixty. The twenty six days of his "Passion" were filled with visits from his disciples and edifying episodes (or so Manichaeans believed). Just before his agony the prisoner prayed passionately (Allberry, Ps. CCXXVI and others). The prophet invoked all the heavenly entities, mentioning his works, commending his church to them and imploring supreme Liberation for himself. Three holy women closed his eyes and fled for fear of the king who ordered torches to be passed over the body to see whether he was really dead. The body may then have been handed over to the guards; according to Manichaean tradition it was beheaded, the head exposed on the city gate and the rest thrown to the dogs. His death marked the beginning of a very harsh repression ordered by Bahrâm. In 281–282, after an interregnum of five years, one of Mani's "vicars—Sisinnius [Mar Sinsin]— took over the direction of the Manichaean church. Though persecuted in Persia, Manichaeism spread with prodigious rapidity throughout a vast area and Mani's writings were translated into a great many languages. In the course of the fourth century this epitome of "heresy" spread westwards throughout the Roman Empire. In the East, Manichaeism held its own in Babylonia all through the Sasanian dominion and inspired, two centuries later, another formidable heresy (which we will consider shortly)—the heresy of Mazdak. After the Arab conquest, for some time the Umayyads (seventh through eighth centuries) were favorably disposed towards Manichaeism though this favor diminished with the Abbasids. The diaspora occurred in the tenth century and the supreme pontificate was transferred from Babylon to Samarkand (Central Asia), but the occult (or open) influence of the sect continued under the Abbasid Emperors. The famous *zindîq*s, the "free thinkers" of the Muslim world, were originally Manichaeans and the term *zandîk* already indicated in medieval Persian, and especially in the Sasanian period, the paradigmatic heretics, i.e., the Manichaeans. In the Far East, however, Manichaeism went through a triumphant period and by the end of the seventh century it had reached China through central Asia. In 763 the *qâghân* of the Uyghûr Turkish warriors was converted to this unwarlike and ascetic religion and (by an irony of fate!) Mani's otherworldly preaching became the state religion of a great Turkish empire from 763 to 840. Manichaeism came to an end in the East only in the twelfth century. In the West, there were still Manichaeans in North Africa in the eighth century but it is unlikely that the great heresies in medieval Europe of the Cathar-Albigensian type were of Manichaean, Oriental derivation.

His Doctrine

We must now try to explain two facts. On the one hand we have the singular and ferocious hatred of all organized religions for Manichaeism that, from this point of view, deserves the title of World Heresy far more than that of World Religion. On the other, we have its extraordinary "popular" diffusion despite its intellectually esoteric doctrine and its extreme asceticism and anti-worldliness.

Almost every religion and every philosophical school that came into contact with Manichaeism poured the most implacable hatred onto it. The Mazdeans appear to have considered it the paradigmatic heresy, and we well know what the Christians thought of it through the works of that familiar controversialist, Augustine.[6] When (as we shall see later) Mazdak, who was Manichaean-oriented, was condemned, a Christian bishop joined forces with his own persecutors, the Magi, against the unfortunate "heretic;" the Jews and the Muslims, who considered the *zindiq* the worst of heretics, did the same. Tradition had the Prophet say about the "seventy–two sects" into which his community would be divided in the future: "My community will be divided into seventy two sects. All will be saved except one: that of the Manichaeans!"

But, more singular still, even the Mandaeans (another Gnostic sect in many ways very similar to the Manichaeans) loathed Mani's religion, and Plotinus, whom many scholars consider responsible for (or at least one of the people responsible for) Gnosticism, expressed the same hatred—if not specifically against the Manichaeans, at least against the Gnostics.

Let us now examine what the Mazdeans say about the Manichaeans. The *Dênkart* (Madan, 216–18; see Menasce, ShGV, p. 228 and foll.) gives us a list of twelve propositions the "accursed trickster" Mani used to oppose the precepts of Adhurpat i Mahraspandân, the restorer of Zoroastrianism in the early Sasanian period. (I have generally followed Menasce's interpretation):

    I Envy and the other diabolical beings have man's body as their shelter [*gristak*] [i.e., man is evil of his very nature].
    II The rejection of agriculture, "the treasure of humanity."
    III The refusal to build oneself a house and a home.
    IV The refusal of marriage, for the elected.
    V The abolition of every juridical organization in the world.
    VI The danger that, with the abolition of agriculture, the cattle will be destroyed.
    VII Proclaiming that the origin of earthly things is the skin of the demon Kuni, thus giving a value of [evil] Principle to the corporeal world.
    VIII Attributing sinfulness to the longing for worldly things that, instead, are desired by God.
    IX Instead of attempting to draw the most possible elements of the spiritual world into oneself, considering them as harmful to the body and wishing to free one's own from them.
    X Man's body is a demon.
    XI God is not—as the Mazdeans believe—the guest of man's body. [see

> *Dênkart* 216, 15–16 "to receive the Angel in one's body is like making him
> the guest of the whole world." Contrarily: if we eliminate the *mênôk* from
> the body it is as if we eliminated it from the whole world].
> XII There will not be a restorer of the world, but the world will be destroyed
> forever by fire. [Mazdeans, on the contrary, had to contribute to perfect the
> world, in their bodies: "May we be the restorers of the World!" an Avestan
> prayer says].

These propositions, inflexibly opposed to the Mazdean doctrine, show us
two ways in which the Mazdeans considered Manichaeism particularly pernicious. The first is theoretical, for considering the flesh and matter demonic
meant, in fact, considering the Creator a demon, and this was an unpardonable
blasphemy (Mazdaism considered matter good and the creature of Ohrmazd
and it even had a heavenly prototype). The second is because the Manichaean
theoretical pessimism led, in practice, to an antinomianism, a denial and sub-
version of the laws, and this was particularly hateful to Mazdeans who were so
law-minded that they imagined laws and courts in heaven too . . . Fears felt by
Mazdeans concerning Manichaean social and practical antinomianism were in
the eyes of some of the former vindicated by upheavals caused by later movements they saw as offshoots of Manichaeism, which had what were depicted as
communist tendencies (see Mazdak).

In the section devoted to his refutation, the Zoroastrian apologia *Shkand
Gumânîk Vichâr* (which times) introduces the arch-heretic's doctrine in the
following words, which can also serve us as an introduction: "The beginning
of Mani's doctrine deals with the infinity of the two primordial Principles, the
middle with the Mingling (a term common to the Mazdeans too), the end with
the distinction of light from darkness." (*ShGV*, ed. by Menasce, pp. 252–3).[7]

A Manichaean fragment of the Turfân (Pelliot, in *JA* 1913, 114–16) defines
the rules for entering religion as follows:

First of all one must discern the two principles. He who asks to enter religion must
know that the two principles of Light and Darkness have completely distinct natures; if he does not discern this, how will he be able to put the doctrine into practice? Next, he must understand the three moments that are: (1) The anterior moment.
(2) The median moment. (3) The posterior moment. In the anterior moment the
skies and the earths do not yet exist; only Light and Darkness—separated one from
the other—exist. The nature of Light is Wisdom, the nature of Darkness is Stupidity.
No motion and no stillness exists in which these two (principles) do not oppose one
another. In the median moment, Darkness has invaded Light: Light hurls itself forwards to repel it—thus entering into obscurity—and tries at all costs to drive it out.
Through the 'great calamity' (the body) we acquire the disgust that spurs us on to
separate ourselves from the body; in the 'inflamed dwelling' (the world, compared
to a burning house one is trying to escape from) we take the vow with which we try

to escape. We tire the body to save luminous nature; thus the holy doctrine is firmly established. If we were to say that falsehood is true, who would dare to obey the orders received? We must carefully discern and seek for the causes that lead to liberation.

In the posterior moment, instruction and conversion are completed, truth and falsehood have both returned to their own roots; light has returned to the great Light, darkness, for its part, has returned to accumulated Darkness. The two principles are reconstituted: each one has returned what it held of the other.

Here already we can see how the essence of Manichaeism is the personal experience of the monstrosity of existence. This personal experience is projected (and this is the most unpalatable part for modern spirits) into myths, myths that have the particularly unpleasant characteristic of not being natural and of rising from below, or coming from above but not based on a wide-ranging religious sociality like the Zoroastrian ones, for they are almost the personal dreams of an exhausted and maniacal intellectual. As Puech appropriately says, "Throughout the Manichaean myth we run into the same hero and the same repeated situation: the Soul fallen into Matter and freed by his *nous*, by Intellect and Knowledge." And, even more appropriately, Origen, speaking of the Gnostics in general (*De Principiis*, IV, pp. 2,8) says: "They have given themselves up to imagination and have invented mythical hypotheses from which the visible world and certain invisible things too are derived which their soul has idolized ("moulded with great imaginativeness," *aneidolopóiesen*)."

And here is a summary of the Manichaean myth that was adapted to different cultural religious environments and languages, consequently the proper names often vary though the substance remains unchanged.

The Luminous Principle is called Father of Greatness (Srôshav, Zurvân). It has five "dwellings," which are at the same time hypostasis or luminous elements: intelligence, reason, thought, reflection, will. These are matched by five shadowy elements in the dominion of the King of Darkness: smoke, devastating fire, destructive wind, muddy water, darkness: the reader should note how light and darkness already appear as spirit-matter. The father of Greatness defends himself from the attack of the King of Darkness by producing the first Creation through "evocation:" the first to be evoked is the Mother of Life (or of the Living, *Ramratukh*) who evokes Primordial Man (Ohrmazd). We thus have the First Trinity (Father, Mother and Son; cf. Qur'an V, 116, which attributes the idea to the Christians. See ahead, too).

Next, Primordial Man produces five sons (*Mahraspand-Amesha-Spenta*— allusive terms that do not identify them with the Mazdean archangels). These are elements of Light as opposed to the five elements of Darkness, i.e., limpid aether, gentle wind, light, water, purifying fire. Armed with these five elements (who are also "persons-angels!") Primordial Man goes down to fight the King of Darkness who is armed with his five elements. Seeing that his adversary is stronger than he is, Primordial Man allows his five elements to be devoured by the shadowy elements so that they may become poison for them: and this is how our present five elements—which are both beneficent and harmful at the same time—were born. Then Primordial Man, in great distress, implores help of his Father seven times. His Father sends him a second evocation, the Friend of Lights (*Narisaf, Narishankh*) who evokes the Great *Ban* ("Builder") who in his turn evokes the Living Spirit (*Mihryazd*, Demiurge). We thus have a second Trinity. The Living Spirit generates five sons (I will spare the reader their names, though one is "Adam-Light") and—accompanied by them—he rushes to help Primordial Man, freeing him with a shriek as sharp as a sword. Naturally, the Calling Shriek (Ir. *khrôshtagh*) and Primordial Man's "answer" (*padvâkhtagh*) are "personified" too, like two gods! Then the Living Spirit has the King of Darkness's arcons killed and flayed by his sons and the Mother of Life forms the sky out of their skin, while their bodies are thrown onto the land of darkness where their flesh becomes "the earth," their bones the mountains, etc. This is a well known and very ancient myth, relived extremely "pessimistically" and intellectually. Thus the world is formed with the demons' filthy bodies and is composed of ten skies (each with twelve gates) and of eight earths. The Living Spirit then continues his work of redemption: stripping himself in front of the daughters of darkness (Theodore bar Khonai attributes a similar myth to the Zurvanist Zoroastrians!) he excites them sexually in order to make them drop part of the light they have absorbed. These liberated particles of light form the sun, the moon and the stars. In order to make his work of salvation and protection perfect, the Father produces a new evocation, the "Messenger" (or Third Envoy"; Iranian variants: *Rôshnsharhryazd, Narisâh, Mihryazd, Mishbaghê*). This "monad," together with the two preceding trinities, completes the divine septet. The Messenger generates twelve Virgins of Light with names like Regality, Victory, etc. (Later the Messenger too becomes three in Jesus, the Virgin of Light, and the Great Manvahmed, who is the Mazdean *Wahman, Vohu Manah*).

Taking up residence in the Sun, the Messenger sets the "vessels of light" in motion. The stars, the sun, the moon and the signs of the zodiac are like a machine for freeing the particles of light that climb up the column of light to the moon (which becomes full because of this) and little by little spill over onto the sun (new moon). As the Living Spirit did before him, the Messenger strips and appears as a woman to the male demons and as a man to the female demons: together with the semen they emit in the course of their sexual excitement, they free imprisoned light, but at the same time they let their "sin" fall down to earth. Part of this shadowy material that fell into the sea generates a monster, who is fought and defeated by Adam-Light; the other part, which fell on earth, generates five trees—the origin of all vegetation. The female demons, who were pregnant by nature, miscarry at the sight of the beauty of the Messenger or because of the revolutions of the zodiacal circle onto which they are tied. Their foetuses, *Mazan* and *Asreshtar*, who fall on earth and devour part of the luminous elements as they swallow plants, generate the animals. Thus they too, like the plants, are demonic and impure beings. And now we will see man's even worse origin: Matter, seeing the salvific work of the Third Envoy, fears that its imprisoned light will escape. Personified in *Az*, "Lust" (also the name of a well known Mazdean demon) it makes the abortive creatures described above copulate. Two demons, *Ashaqlûn* and *Namrâêl* take charge of the rest: *Ashaqlûn* (male) devours all the abortive children in order to concentrate as much light as possible, then he copulates with *Namrâêl* (female): from this union Adam and Eve (*Gêhmurd* and *Murdiyânagh* for Persian speaking Manichaeans) are born. The diabolical plan consists in keeping as much light as possible imprisoned in impure matter: and the reproduction of the species is extremely useful for this end. Next a Luminous Jesus, created by the angelic entities we mentioned earlier (for the Persians this saviour is Ohrmazd) is sent to Adam to awaken him from his deep sleep and "teach him" (the reader should note the typically Gnostic value given to "knowledge") his situation and nature. Adam "knew who he was" and his soul "which had become intelligent" came back to life. Adam was freed for ever.

This unique drama of liberation is sung in every possible form in the Manichaean "Psalms" and is possibly the theme in which the tragic sense of Manichaeism reaches its highest artistic expression (and still has something to say to us today). In a Psalm to Jesus, the "living I" evokes his sufferings in the prison of matter (Allberry, Ps. CCXLVI, p. 54, 11–23):

After entering into Darkness
I had to drink water that tasted bitter to me.
I carried a burden that was not mine.
I was in the midst of my enemies
the beasts surrounded me.
The burden I carried
was that of the Powers and Principalities.
They were inflamed with rage:
they rose up against me,
they rushed at me to seize me,
like a shepherdless sheep.
Matter and his sons
divided me up between them,
they burnt me in their fire
and gave me a bitter appearance.
The strangers among whom I was

did not know me.
They savored my gentleness
they wished to keep me with them.
And I was alive for them
but, for me, they were dead.

After this the story is nothing but the story of the constant spreading of evil, i.e., of the mingling of light and darkness due to successive generations of new men on the one hand and the progressive fulfillment of Salvation on the other. Wherever an active Power (creator, protector and revealing) and a passive Power, which is the Soul of the World, are present in the Universe, imprisoned light is suffering. This concept is sometimes assimilated to that of suffering Jesus (*Jesus Patibilis*), another aspect of which is the Luminous Jesus we have already seen. The cosmic Jesus is crucified in the world; the drama is an eternal one until the final liberation. Since a great deal of luminous matter is concentrated in trees the Manichaean Faustus was able to say to Augustine: "Jesus, the life and salvation of men, hangs crucified on every tree." The Psalms to Jesus, which make up a good part of the Manichaean Hymnary, are simply a tragic dialogue between the *Jesus Patibilis*, who sometimes takes on the voice of one or another man, and the Luminous Jesus *Yishô, zîmâ*.

> The joy, oh Lord, of your gentle cry, has made me forget life; the gentleness of your voice has made me remember my native city . . . O glorious *Nous*, fruit of Jesus, help me! I hurry to you, who quench the fear of death with your Victorious Cross! (Ps. LXXXV).

This passage, too, is beautiful[8]:

> May you free me from this nothingness
>> from the dark abyss that is all consumption
>> which is nothing but torture, wounded until death
>> and where there are no rescuers, friends.
>> Never will salvation be found here, never,
>> the shadows are everywhere . . .
>> There are prisons everywhere, with no way out
>> and those who come to them are sorely wounded.
>> Dryly arid, burnt, torrid winds,
>> and no greenery . . . never will any be found!
>> Who will free me from this, and from he who wounds,
>> who will save me from infernal anguish?
>> And I weep over myself: May I be freed from it
>> and from the creatures . . . who devour one another!
>> And the bodies of humans, the birds of space
>> and the fish down from the seas and the beasts and the demons . . .
>> who will free me from all this,

far from the infernal destroyers,
without flight or way out?

One could not find a better description of the "condition" of a person who feels that everything with a material being is filthy and demonic. One should compare this wish to be freed from everything generally considered the beauty of nature, to be freed from the filth of birds, fish, men, from horrible and squalid material life in all its forms, with Ohrmazd's hymns to good creation in Mazdaism and we will see of how different the two religions are!

In some hymns, however, as in this short song in Turkish discovered at Chotscho (Central Asia), published by Von Le Coq and translated by Bang (*Museon*, XXXVIIII, 1925, p. 4) we even find an unusual "sense of Nature" which is reflected in the beautiful and characteristic paintings of Manichaean documents and monuments:

1. The goddess Aurora has come in person,
     she, the goddess Aurora, has come!
     . . . .
     Arise all of you, Lords, Brothers
     let us sing hymns of praise to the goddess
   Aurora.
2. Clairvoyant divine Sun
   protect us!
     O divine Moon who (eternally new) show yourself,
   save us!
3. Goddess Aurora
     fragrant, balsamic,
     sparkling, light-giving!
   Goddess Aurora!

Aurora or Dawn, Sun and Moon appear all three to be symbols of Jesus, whom the Manichaeans also addressed with the feminine "Virgin of Light" (the Iranian Manichaeans also use the composite proper name *Vishô-bâm*, Jesus-Aurora). It has been rightly pointed out how this "practical Manichaeism"— the Manichaeism of hymns and refined paintings—offers the best explanation for the success of a religion that otherwise was so disagreeably ascetic.[9]

The slow salvation of light from darkness—obstructed by men's (mainly sexual) sin—will draw near to its conclusion when all men have adopted the methods of salvation proposed by Mani. This brings us to the third act of the drama. The apocalyptic trials the Manichaeans call "the great war" will be followed by the universal triumph of the Manichaean Church, the Last Judgement, the presence of souls before the *bêma*, Christ's "court of justice," the separation of good men from evil men. After a brief reign of Jesus, the Christ, the elect, the divinities will abandon the world. The terrestrial globe will burn for 1468 years and will be obliterated. The savable particles of light (some, in fact, will remain closed for ever in darkness) will be concentrated in the singular figure of the "Last Statue" (*istumên yazd*, "last God," in Iranian; *andriás* in Coptic) that will rise up to heaven, while the damned and the demons and all matter will be imprisoned in a kind of mass or globe, the *Bolos*, and lowered into a huge pit covered with a stone. The safety of the world of Light, which was problematic in the first act of the drama, will now be assured. This, possibly, is the scope of the great drama.

Manichaean morality is closely connected with this cosmological and dogmatic approach. Man's sphere is to separate, within himself, his divine being from his demonic being; to separate the new man, woken up by the call and conscious of his luminous qualities, from the flesh. Those who succeed in fulfilling this perfectly during their lifetime will enter into the kingdom of light immediately after death; those who do not succeed will be born again (this idea was probably originally Indian, though experts are still discussing the matter since it was not exactly a personal metempsychosis) in successive bodies of darkness, unless their sins were so grave that they are immediately damned and sent to Hell. But the Manichaeans well knew that perfect liberation, which implies very great sacrifices (complete abstinence from sexual acts, frequent fasts, a special vegetarian diet, etc.), could be attained only by the very few. Hence the organization of a hierarchy with five levels (from the lowest upwards: Hearers, Elect, Elders or Priests, Bishops, Teachers or Apostles and, at the very top, a kind of pope who was in charge of preserving, explaining and spreading the doctrine). Scholars are still discussing whether the Manichaeans had real sacraments. At all events their rites were rather simple (compared to the enormous complication of the rites of late Mazdaism). The imposition of hands admitted to the sect or led to higher grades; the elect consumed a daily meal together, which some people have compared to communion. Other characteristic Manichaean ritual gestures were the kiss of peace, the brotherly greeting, the handshake that was the symbol of the primordial handshake of the Living Spirit to draw Primordial Man out of darkness (see above). The essential activity of Manichaeans was directed towards publicizing and preaching this awakening of the "I." The liturgical life of the community was limited to prayers, singing, fasting. The main Manichaean feast was the one known as *Bêma* (throne, court of law), which celebrated both Mani's death and the last judgment; it centered around the Apostle's "empty throne" (*bêma*: this also was a relic of ancient Asiatic symbolism).

The Manichaeans also practised a kind of confession. The auditors confessed to the elect, and the elect confessed one another (every Monday), and there was a general confession of the whole community in front of the *Bêma*. Formularies for confession (*khvastûâneft*) that show the high moral tenor of Manichaeism have come down to us. It should be noted that, unlike many Gnostic sects, a "pneumatic"—an elected one—did not acquire perfection and faultlessness once and for all but could slip back into sin and lose his benefits as an elect. The auditor's morality was "easier" but still very high and codified in ten commandments. A kind of tithe had to be paid, too, for the needs of the community; prayer was preceded by ablutions with water or, if this was lacking, sand and accompanied by prostrations.

Because of the precision of its organization and the wide-ranging sociality of its morality, Manichaeism was, unlike other Gnostic sects, a true, independent, religion. Mani himself, at the beginning of his work in Pahlavî, *Shâhbuhragân*, says:

> Wisdom and good works have been carried in perfect sequence from one epoch to another by God's messengers. At one time they came to the region of India through a prophet called Buddha, at another, to the district of Persia through Zarâdusht , and at another still, to the West through Jesus. And, during this last period, the Revelation has come and the Prophecy has become manifest in Babylonia through me, Mani, the Messenger of the God of Truth.

The concept of consecutive revelations that is to be found in the Qur'an, too, is present, as we mentioned, in a more "legendary" and at first sight more primitive form in Mazdaism, from which Mani (who declares himself the "seal of the Prophets") probably inherited it.[10]

This brief outline will help the reader understand how all the controversies on the Christian, Hellenistic, Babylonian or Iranian "origins" of Manichaeism are based principally on the clear awareness in Mani and the Manichaeans that they were founding a universal religion valid (unlike the preceding ones) for all countries: "At first the earlier religions existed only in one region, in one language. But my religion is such that it will manifest itself in every region and in all languages and will be taught in the most distant countries" (T II D 126, "*SPAW*," 1933, p. 295).

Consequently, as we said, Mani and the Manichaeans willingly adapted the concepts and mythologemes of the various religions to their own system. Besides the Mazdean and Christian terms we have already come across, Manichaean texts speak freely of nirvâna, *samsâra*, *tao* etc., though of course it does not necessarily follow that Manichaeism had a Chinese or Indian origin. It may seem a truism, but the origin of Manichaeism lies mainly in the living personality of Mani—the misshapen prophet—and his spiritual "situation" in the decadent world of the Iranian-Babylonian frontier at the end of the Parthian Empire.

The principal hypotheses on the origins of Manichaeism (summarized by Widengren in *Mesopotamian Elements in Manichaeism*, Uppsala, 1946) can be reduced to three: (1) The ancient Mesopotamian hypothesis (Kessler, Wetter) which is partly justified by the unquestionably Mesopotamian elements Widengren recently discovered in Manichaeism (in particular the salvific myth of Tammûz, which probably remained part of popular Babylonian religiosity for a long time); (2) the Christian hypothesis (Burkitt, Harnack, Schaeder); 3. the Iranian hypothesis (Reitzenstein, Bousset, Widengren). Schaeder's observation, according to which the undoubtedly Iranian elements present in Manichaeism can be attributed to a "stylistic translation" (*Umstylisierung*) of Mani's doctrine for the East, just as we can speak of a Greek translation for the West, is particularly interesting. Other supporters of the Christian hypothesis consider the idea of the "saved Savior"—which is central, as we have seen, to Manichaeism—as a Gnostically-oriented interpretation of the basic concept of Christianity. We will understand the origins of Manichaeism more easily if we start from Schaeder's above-mentioned idea. From a Christian point of view, Mani's doctrines are a Christian "heresy," from a Mazdean point of view they are a Mazdean heresy, from a Buddhist point of view they could be a Buddhist heresy. But Mani the heretic had the privilege of being a martyr and being killed, and his persecutors had the (questionable) privilege of having "their" heretic. Since Mani was killed by the Mazdean Magi he probably deserves the title of "heretic of Mazdaism," at least where this external historical connection is concerned, as well as because, most likely, he wanted his religion to become the new faith of the Universal Persian Empire just as Christianity was to become that of the Roman Empire. One can therefore accept (even if rather superficially) Widengren's statement that Mani was, principally, the founder of a "reformed Iranian religion."

Mazdak's Heresy

But there were also far more practical reasons for the terror Manichaeism caused. Some sources allude to political and social aspects of Manichaeism (communistic tendencies, etc.) of which we know nothing where Manichaeism proper is concerned, but which, according to most of the texts, played a very important role in Mazdak's religious-social "reform." This reform seems directly derived from Manichaeism and it threw the reign of the Sasanian king Kavât (Ar. Qubâd) (488–531 A.D.) into great confusion. The best known Iranian "tale" of Mazdak is included in Firdausî's Shâhnâmeh ("Book of Kings;" ed. Macan III, 1611 and foll. I am translating from Forûghî's anthology, Tehran, 1323 s. pp. 48 and foll., number XV). Firdausî's tale is drawn from an "aristocratic" middle-Persian source, the *Khvatâi-nâmak*. We will discuss the reliability of the historical sources concerning Mazdak later and—faithful to our intention of allowing the original texts to speak for themselves as much as possible—reproduce Firdausî's tale, with a few abbreviations here and there.

And a man came, called Mazdak, an eloquent, wise intelligent and ambitious man.

He was a man of considerable stature and a vendor of wisdom and the valiant Qubâd leant him his ear.

He became a Minister (*dastûr*) of the sovereign, the keeper of the treasure he became, and the treasurer.

Now, because of a drought, there was less food in the world, for both nobles and plebeians.

The clouds disappeared from the sky and throughout Iran neither rain nor snow were seen.

All the great men of the world, at the court of Kai-Qubâd, asked for bread and wine, and Mazdak said to them: "Soon the king will show you a fruitful way."

Then he ran in front of the sovereign and said: "O virtuous king!

In this world I wish to ask you a question, asking you to answer it, to some degree!"

And Qubâd answered him in a singing voice: "Speak! May you renew, in this world, my dimmed honor!"

And Mazdak said: "If someone is bitten by a snake and his soul is flying away from his body, and another man possesses a powerful antidote, and he who was bitten does not have a part of that medicine, tell me, how should that man who possesses twenty drams of the medicine (and does not give it to the wounded man) be punished?"

The sovereign answered: "The man who owns the medicine is a murderer; to revenge the blood of the man who was bitten it is right that he should be slain at my court as soon as his adversary (the family of the dead man) has laid hands on him!".

Then Mazdak said: "O illustrious sovereign, suppose a man is tied with strong thongs and is denied food until he dies and gives up his soul and his desperate body; what would be the reward of a man who, possessing bread, yet still kept the chained man in indigence?

What reward? May the King tell me, and (he should know) that (chained) man was also wise and virtuous!"

The King answered: "He is a miserable creature and may the blood (of the dead man) fall on his head for the action he did not accomplish!"

Having heard these answers Mazdak kissed the ground and, bearing himself proudly, came away from Qubâd's presence; and, reaching the Gate of the palace he cried out to the great crowd: "Plunder all the granaries in the city where the wheat is hidden, one by one; let everyone take a share!"

Then all the famished people ran and plundered all the wheat, both in the city storehouses and in those of Qubâd, nor were they satisfied with only one grain of wheat! . . .

Then Qubâd had that eloquent man summoned and spoke to him at length of the plundering of the warehouses.

Mazdak answered: "May you be fortunate! May your words be the viaticum of wisdom!"

The words I heard from the Sovereign, I repeated them, humbly, to the people of Iran . . .

If you are a just judge, King, (you will admit) that neither the storehouses nor the wheat are of any use.

Hundreds of men have died of hunger and they have been killed by overfull warehouses!"

Mazdak's words afflicted Qubâd, and his mind was exalted by those words of justice.

From then on he asked a thousand questions and listened to many answers: he saw [Mazdak's] mind, and his soul, full of able words, full of what the Prophets and the just Magi and the Great men had already said, and he was completely changed by Mazdak's way of speaking; for his words overstepped all measure . . .

He said: "The rich and the powerful are equal to the poor whose hands are empty of possessions!

It is not right that some people should have superfluous riches: the rich are the warp and the poor the woof . . .

Women houses and possessions must be given as gifts! The indigent is one with the rich man! . . .

And God hates any servant of his who has another faith than this! . . .

He took away from one and gave to the other: so that the sages were dismayed.

But Qubâd heard him, entered his religion, and was happy in the world of his words . . .

And all the poor and those who earned their bread with their work gathered around him: his doctrine flourished around the world and no-one dared attack him . . .

Now it happened that one day Mazdak went out of his house at dawn and went to the king, and he spoke thus to the Sovereign of the World: "O you who are superior to all science and to all praise, you must know that Kisrâ (Chosroe)[11] is not of our faith; how can it be lawful for him to rebel against it? . . .

Five things make us deviate from rectitude, and the Sage can find nothing to add to them.

They are: wrath, hatred, envy, need and, fifth, to be overcome by Greed (âz).

If you succeed in being victorious over these five demons, the way of the Lord of the World will be manifest to you.

And because of these five we have women and possessions, so that the good religion (dîn-i beh) is in decadence in the world.

We must therefore place women and possessions in common, if you do not wish to see the Good Religion harmed, since Envy and Greed and Need, which secretly join Wrath and Hatred, stem from these two things, and then the demon corrupts the body of the wise men: therefore these two things must be placed in common!."

Having said this he took (the prince) Kisrâ by the arm, which greatly surprised the sovereign of Iran; the illustrious prince drew his hand back from him in anger and, irritated, he took his eyes off Mazdak . . .

Then the King asked Kisrâ: "For what reason do you draw away from our religion?"

And Kisrâ answered: "If I have the time to do so, I will prove that all this opinion is false."

Mazdak said to him: "How many days do you ask of the King who lights up the world?"

The prince answered: "I ask for five months, at the sixth I will explain everything to the sovereign!"

They agreed on this and each one went his way, and the haughty Sovereign entered his high palace.

In the meantime Cosroe sent men whom he knew to be wise and able to help (him) in every direction . . .

And these searchers of wisdom sat in council together and examined the question from all sides, and those sharp old sages communicated their words to Cosroe.

Having heard them, Cosroe went to Qubâd and spoke again of Mazdak saying: "The time has come for me to ask him for the Good Religion, and if he is right and Zarathustra's religion is fallacious, I will accept his holy faith and I will choose his rough habit with all my heart. But if what he says is false and he does not follow the way of the Most Pure One (God) then you must abhor the path of his religion and banish his ill-omened rite!

Entrust him and his followers to me, and may none of them remain alive!."

When, in the morning, the sun showed its (golden) crown and the earth became like an ivory sea, the son of the Sovereign of the World, the Eloquent One, rode out with priests and noblemen, and together they came to the King's palace, they came speaking words and seeking for a way . . .

And thus spoke a môbad to Mazdak in front of the assembly: "O man seeker of wisdom! You have introduced a new religion into the world, you have placed in common women and possessions; but how will the father know now who is his son, and the son, how will he know his father?

If men become equal in the world, and the lords are no longer distinguishable from the servants, who will ever choose to be a servant, and how will it be possible to exercise mastery?

Who will work for me and you? How will it be possible to distinguish good men from bad men?

And when someone dies, whom will his houses and possessions belong to, if the servant who is working is equal to the sovereign? . . .

If all are masters, who will be the servant? If all possess treasures who will be the treasurer?

None of the founders of religions ever spoke like this, you certainly have secretly worked like a demon (dîvânagî, also "madness").

You are leading men to hell, you do not condemn evil actions!"

When Qubâd hear the môbad's words, he was troubled, and admitted that they were right; the noble Cosroe joined him, and the heretic's heart was filled with anxiety . . .

The Lord of the World was sickened by that doctrine and his mind was filled with pain for what he had done.

> The king handed Mazdak over to Cosroe together with all those who observed his religion and doctrine.
> Among the nobles [Mazdak's] faith had three thousand adepts. And the King said to his son:
> "Act as you will with these princes and never speak to me again of Mazdak."
> Now Cosroe had a palace, a garden whose walls were higher than the mountain peaks; he had a moat dug around his walls and he distributed those men there.
> They planted them like trees, feet in the air and head down, buried deeply.
> Then Cosroe said to Mazdak: "Come, go into my magnificent garden!
> Since the seed you have sown in it during this period has produced fruit for you, o senseless one!
> You will see trees there that no-one has ever seen and no-one ever heard of even from the mouth of the ancient sages!"
> Mazdak went and opened the garden gate, hoping to find trees laden with fruit in the orchard, but when he saw what was there he fainted and let out a loud cry.
> Then Cosroe had a high gallows set up from which dangled a braided noose, and he had the unfortunate heretic hung alive, with his head downwards, and he killed him with a shower of arrows. If you have a healthy intellect, do not follow in Mazdak's footsteps!
> And so the nobles became secure in their possessions, and women, and children, and their rich treasures.

Firdausî's tale is only one of the sources we have for Mazdak's "revolt." It appears to have shaken the Sasanian society of the end of the fifth century to its very roots at a delicate moment in the life of the empire, after king Pêrôz's defeat in 484, during his expedition against the Ephtalites(?). Christensen has exhaustively approached the problem of Mazdakism from a historical point of view in a seminal work (see the Bibliography) in which he analyzes the various traditions concerning the heretic. He is in fact mentioned in contemporary Christian sources (the Syriac Pseudo-Stylite) and by the Byzantine historians Procopius and Agathias. We have some information from Pahlavî sources too (though these make a point of giving the blackest possible picture of the dangerous heretic) besides many Arab and Persian accounts (one of which is Firdausî's quoted above) whose source appears to be a Pahlavî noble-class chronicle, the *Khvatâi-nâmak*, in four different versions. There apparently also existed a "Romance of Mazdak" (*Mazdak-nâmak*) in Pahlavî, which can be partly reconstructed through Muslim sources (in particular Nizâmu'l-Mulk's twelfth-century *Siyâsat-nâmeh*).

To sum up what this source material reliably offers us, it appears that Mazdak himself was not the founder of the Mazdakite sect, but had a precursor, a Manichaean by name of Zarâdusht (the same name as the founder of the Mazdean religion, which is why the Mazdakites were also sometimes called *Zarâdushtakân*). In fact this homonymy explains the confusion that Western authors (Greek and Latin) have sometimes run into when speaking of Zoroaster's doctrine.

The sources (which, as we shall see, are confirmed by the doctrine) speak of the founder, who lived about two centuries before Mazdak, as a Manichaean.

The heretical leader's father was called Bâmdâd or Dawn[12] and Mazdak himself was probably born in Babylonia, in a city (Madaraya) on the banks of the Tigris. We also know that the Mazdakite doctrine was probably called *drust dên*, "right faith," by his followers. King Kavât joined a sect of communists chiefly because of the dynastic struggles among the nobles (in fact the sources indicate the presence of many high-born men among the Mazdakites). These struggles followed Pêrôz's disastrous reign and the grave political instability of Kavât's government even before he joined the Mazdakites, in the early years of his reign and before his imprisonment and flight from the Ephtalites. They were also caused by the ever present tension between the clergy and the warrior caste. And we must not forget that the noble castes that produced kings at that time and in those areas were not versed in the doctrine and knowledge of traditional religious rules (which were entrusted rather exclusively to the priests) and they were consequently an easy prey to clever preachers (just as Shâhpûr had been to Mani; and some sources consider Mazdak a "magus!"). These preachers may have been summoned to court out of sheer curiosity, to listen to theological disputes. Aside from the fact that the "communistic" social aspect of the doctrine on which authors later insisted does not seem to have held the central place in Mazdak's preaching that some people have attributed to it, the "communism of women," in particular, has been greatly exaggerated, for obvious reasons. Apparently, though, it was little more than a rather "free" form of marriage, and a break with the *khvêtûkdâs* (marriage between very close relatives) that was recommended as highly meritorious in Mazdean texts. The Mazdakites' reckless plan to impose their ideas concerning the succession to the throne on Kavât, i.e., to oppose the succession of Khusrau (the famous "Cosroe of the Immortal Soul" and one of the greatest Sasanian sovereigns) and prefer the king's eldest son, Kâûs, a convinced Mazdakite, was the last straw. According to Klìma's studies, the catastrophe occurred in 524 instead of the generally admitted 529 (528). Mazdak's disgrace was obtained through the method that had been applied to the other great heretic, Mani. That is, a theological conference was organized, as Firdausî confirms, in which Khusrau played an important role (which was natural considering his preoccupation with the succession). The finest Magi controversialists took part in the trial by the side of the Christian bishop Bazanes—who was the leader of the Christians in Iran. Like the Jews, the Christians sided with their Mazdean persecutors against Mazdak's unprecedented "communist" doctrines (which also proves convincingly that even if the socioeconomic element was not central to early Mazdakite religious preaching it must soon have become dominant; both Christians and Jews held vast possessions in Iran). The sources do not agree on how Mazdak was killed; probably as soon as the heretic's easy theological "defeat" was recognized, the soldiers of the king's guard threw themselves on him, killing him on the spot, and the persecution and massacre of his followers was unleashed. Apparently all of their religious books were burnt too.

The only information we have on Mazdak's doctrine from probably Mazdakite sources (though possibly seventh century ones, after the Arab conquest of Persia) is what has come down to us in the precious Arab heresiographical work by Shahrastânî (1076–1153 A.D.), a Persian Muslim from Khurâsân. We are translating it here because Christensen, the most learned scholar of Mazdakism, has used Haarbrücher's old and rather imperfect German translation (1850) and some details of his treatment of Mazdakite doctrine consequently need correcting.

> We are speaking of Mazdak, who appeared in the days of Qubâd, father of Nûshîrvân. He invited Qubâd to his religion, and the king accepted the invitation. But Nûshîrvân noticed his shame and his trickery and, calling him to court, he found him and killed him. Al-Warrâq[13] says that the Mazdakite doctrine concerning the two Worlds and the two Principles is the same as that of the greater part of the Manichaeans: the difference is that Mazdak said that Light works deliberately and chooses freely, while Darkness works blindly and at random. Light is learned and gifted with senses, while Darkness is ignorant and blind. He maintains that the mingling took place by chance and blindly and not deliberately and out of free choice. The same is true of salvation: it is fulfilled by chance, not through free choice. Mazdak forbad discord, hatred and mutual killing among men: and since these offences were caused mostly by women and by riches, he made (all) women licit and permitted men (to take) the riches (of the rich), making them share in all those things, as they share water, fire and fodder.[14]
>
> It is said of him that he also advocated suicide to save one's soul from Evil and from mingling with Darkness. His doctrine concerning the Principles and the Elements (*usûl-u-arkân*) was that they were three: that is to say Water, Fire and Earth. Their mingling produced the Orderer of Good and the Orderer of Evil , the former emerging from their limpid part, the latter from their turbidity (or else, "the first because of their limpidity, the second because of their turbidity"). It is also said of him that the object of his adoration sat on his throne in the upper world in the same way that the Cosroes (Emperors) did in the lower world and in front of him there were four Powers: those of Discernment (*tamyîz*), of Intellection (*fahm*), of Memory (*hifz*), of Joy (*surûr*) just as in front of Cosroe there were four dignitaries: the *môbadân-môbad* (head of the priests), the supreme *hîrbad* (another priest), the *sipahbud* (general), and the *râmishgar* (musician). These four powers governed created things through seven of their ministers: the *sâlâr* (general), the *pîshgâh* (antistes), the *bârwar* (bearer of a load, or *bânwar*?), the *parwân* (commissary), the *kârdân* (expert), the *dastûr* (counsellor) and the *kûdak* (slave). These seven powers circu-

lated in (*tadûrû fî*) twelve Spiritual Entities (*rûhâniyyîn*): *khvânanda* (he who calls), *dihanda* (he who gives), *sitânanda* (he who takes), *baranda* (he who bears away), *khvaranda* (he who eats), *davanda* (he who runs), *hizanda* (he who arises), *kushanda* (he who kills; or if it is read as *kashanda*, he who pulls), *zananda* (he who strikes), *kunanda* (he who does; or, if read as *kananda*, he who digs or tears), *âyanda* (he who comes), *shavanda* (he who goes), *pâyanda* (he who stays still). Every man in whom these four Powers and the Seven and the Twelve are gathered together becomes divine lord (*rabbânî*) in (this) inferior world and can do without any religious obligation. And he said that the Cosroe of the upper world governed through the Letters, the condensation of which (*majmû'uhâ*) is the Most Great Name, and the Supreme Arcanum was revealed to those who succeeded in imagining something of those letters, while those who could not remained in the blindness of ignorance, oblivion, dullness and sorrow in front of the four spiritual powers.

The Mazdakite sects are the Kûdakîya, the Abû-Muslimîya, the Mâhânîya, the Sapîd-jâmakîya. The Kûdakîya live in the areas of Ahwâz, Fârs and Shahrazûr, the others in the Soghdian area, in Samarkand, Shâsh and Ilaq.

This information contains several important points. In the first place the reference to the fortuitousness of "liberation." This is a feature that appears in other forms in the Islamic sects commonly called Malâmatîya (the "reprehensible ones," cf. chap. IV) and even in more distant cultural areas, such as that of the Far Eastern Zen Buddhism. The fortuitousness of "illumination" and liberation led to these sects giving little importance to ascetic exercises and traditional virtues: this could explain, up to a point, the rather "libertine" style of life the Mazdakites practised, which may easily have led to the exaggerations of the controversialists on the "communal position of women."

But the doctrine of the fortuitousness of the illumination brought with it another consequence, too, i.e., that "anyone," even a plebeian, might suddenly acquire it. On a metaphysical basis this was what justified the equality between nobles and plebeians that seems to have been one of the basic themes of Mazdakite preaching (and an extremely useful one for winning many adepts). The freed man, i.e., the man in whom—whoever he might be—the "luminous forces" had concentrated (the man in whom the four, the seven and the twelve had come together) no longer had need for exterior religious obligations. This point seems to have escaped Christensen's attention. Following Haarbrücker's erroneous interpretation, he translated this important passage in a both grammatically and logically unacceptable way, i.e.: "In each man all four forces are gathered together and the seven and the twelve have become lords in the lower world and their obligation has been lifted from them." For, what obligations could the Seven and the Twelve principles have? The sentence is in fact perfectly clear in Arabic. I also do not think that Christensen understood the passage concerning the two Orderers, of good and evil. They seem to have been born of the mingling of the elements, the Good Orderer from their limpid part, the Evil one from their muddy part. Here too we are in the presence of a rather "materialistic" casualism. The impersonality of the transcendent principles seems more accentuated in Manichaeism. For the official religions of the period, the advice to commit suicide (this is how one should interpret the *qatl al-anfus* of the text that Christensen translates as "killing of the souls," though this does not make sense) was also antinomian and scandalous. In view of the absolute dualistic premises involved we are still in the presence of a quite logically extremist position, though Manichaeism too (if we leave out the endura of its problematic western offshoots) seems to have rejected it.

Cabalism, which was to play an important role in many post-Islamic extremist movements, completes the picture. Together with a tendency to materialism, antinomianism, moral laxity and fortuitousness of the liberation, it forms a whole that is so reminiscent of certain Islamic heresies that one can legitimately suspect that Shahrastânî culled his information from a Mazdakite source—though a very late one. This suspicion is confirmed by the list of Mazdakite groups (given as actually existing in his time) that the heresiographer provides at the end of his information: the Abû-Muslimîya (i.e., the followers of Abû Muslim) and the Sapîd-jâmagân [the white-robed men] who are known, through other Islamic sources, to have been active in the great political and religious rebellions of the early times of the Abbasid Caliphate (see the next chapter) whose sources too give their origin as Mazdakite. So, though Shahrastânî gives us a fuller picture of the doctrine than anything we have from other authors, it is drawn from tardy sources and reflects aspects of late Mazdakism (which, however, probably has some continuity with its early period). If nothing else, Mazdak's name and tradition carried their weight since later revolutionaries felt the need to state that "Mazdak had become Shi'ite and urged men to avenge Abû Muslim," in order to win over a variety of anti-Abbasid elements to their propaganda (cf. *Siyâsat-nâmeh*, pp. 182–183, Schaefer transl., pp. 267–68).

Let us now see whether other sources offer any important variants to Mazdak's doctrine as outlined by Shahrastânî. Greek sources speak of Mazdakites as "Manichaeans" and all seem to agree on the sharing of women. The news spread as far as Cyrene where an inscription mentions Zarade (probably the Zarathustra who was the founder of Mazdakism and not the traditional Zoroaster) as advocating the community of goods and women[15].

The fact that the Mazdakites practised special abstinences is mentioned too. Bîrûnî and Ibn al-Athîr speak of their abstinence from the flesh of animals, while the Pahlavî commentary to a passage of the Avestan text of the *Vendidâd* in which "he who fights the heretic *ashemaôgha*, the impure one who abstains from eating" (4.49) is mentioned impersonally, also speaks of "he who fights the impure heretic who forces men through violence not to eat, like Mazdak son of Bâmdâd who . . . abandoned men to hunger and death."

According to some authors (Ibn al-Athîr) Mazdakites were only allowed to eat cheese, eggs, milk and butter. Eutichius, Tabarî, Firdausî himself, Tha'â-libî and others have Mazdak give highly esoteric and practical explanations (such as those we have seen in Firdausî) on the need for the community of possessions. Tabarî adds that—besides communism—Mazdak also preached mutual help among men as a particularly worthy act in God's eyes. The same author quotes among the prescriptions of the Mazdakite doctrine the exhortation to treat one's enemies mercifully and attributes king Kavât's excessive gentleness (a fact that does not appear to be historically demonstrable) to the fact that he was a heretic (*zandîk*), while the *Fihrist* tells us that the greatest hospitality was particularly recommended.

All this does not add much to Shahrastânî's more theologically precise information and we consequently have no means (and possibly never will have) of knowing when and how the later tendencies that undoubtedly appear in the Muslim heresiographer's text penetrated into Mazdak's Manichaean-oriented doctrine. They may belong to an ancient tradition and that the frequent allusions to a link between these heresies and Mazdakism by the heresiographers and historians of the first Islamic heresies on Persian soil may contain some solid elements of truth that go beyond the clearly "defamatory" dimension. It is hard to believe that a movement of such vast proportions, whose doctrines must have powerfully attracted vast strata of the underprivileged, can have ended suddenly with Khusrau Anûshîrvân's persecution.

Probably the first hotbeds of an anti-Abbasid rebellion—the first Persian heretics—were not, as some scholars maintain, the heirs of what remained of Mazdaism (we have indications that the Mazdean aristocracy adjusted quite quickly to the new state of things and the new "established" religion)[16] but rather of scattered Mazdakite and Manichaean centers that later were nourished conceptually and through broader channels by the renewal of Gnostic ideas that filtered through Muslim channels.

And so we have reached the heart of the problem of Persian Islam, to which the next chapters will be devoted.

Notes

1. An article in *Asia Major* I, 1924, pp. 460–490.
2. Cf. Widengren, "Der Iranische Hintergrund der Gnosis," *Zeit. f. Rel.*, 1952, 2, 98.
3. "Où est le problème du Gnosticisme?" in *Revue de l'Université de Bruxelles*, XXXIX, 1934–35, pp. 137 and foll. and 295 and foll.
4. [See now J.M. Robinson, et al., ed. and trans., *The Nag Hammadi Library in English*, (San Francisco, 3rd edn. 1988)-ed.]. An account in Italian is available in S. Moscati, *I*

manos critti ebraici del deserto di Giuda, Roma, 1955. On Nag Hammadi see J. Doresse, *Les livres secrets des gnostiques d'Egypte*, Paris, 1958.

5. Klima (O. Klima, "War Mani wirklich lahm?" in *Archiv Orientálni*, Prague, vol. 25, 1957, 3, pp. 384–387) has recently demonstrated how Mani's deformity is based on an emblematic "type" of "heretical demon" and probably has no historical consistency.

6. The author of the acts of the Christian martyrs of Karkha (quoted in Christensen, *L'Iran sous les Sasanides*, p. 200) speaks of Mani with . . . Christian forebearance as follows: "From the time of King Shapur, Mani, the den of all evil, vomited his satanic bile."

7. The initium, medium, finis of Augustine's *Contra Felicem*, II, 1, p. 828, 25, is almost literally reproduced.

8. Turfân, T II D, 178 in "Abh. d. Preuss. Ak. d. Wiss." 1926 IV, 112–13, from the Beneviste French translation reproduced in Puech, "La Gnose et le Temps," in *Eranos Jahrbuch* XX, p. 45.

9. L. Tl. Lefort, review of Allbery, "Manichaean Pslam-book," in *Muséon*, LI, 1938, p. 353.

10. *Shâhbuhragân*, Kessler p. 349. [A recent reconstruction of this text, with translation, is D.N. MacKenzie, "Mani's Shabuhragan I-II," *Bulletin of the School of Oriental and African Studies* 42 (1979):500–34 and volume 43 (1980):287–322–ed.]

11. King Qubâd's son and the hereditary prince.

12. The name is probably Manichaean. Bâm, "Aurora" or "Dawn," as we have already seen, is a divinity-symbol in Manichaeism that represents Jesus-light. *Bâm-dâd* means "creation of Aurora" or "creation of Dawn" [thus, Mazdak's father was, symbolically, the dawn of a new era-ed.].

13. He was a "Zoroastrian" who was converted to Islam.

14. A new source is introduced here.

15. Cf. W. Sherwood Fox, "Passages in Greek and Latin Literat. relating to Zoroaster and Zoroastrism," in *J. Cama Or. Inst.* no. 14, p. 118.

16. A passage in the above-mentioned treatise on the art of politics (*Siyâsat-nâmeh*) by Nizâmu'l-Mulk (the powerful eleventh century Seljuq minister and bitter enemy of every kind of "heretic") in which a Zoroastrian môbad foresees the coming of Muhammad and condemns Mazdak is typical of the harmony between Mazdeans and Muslims (who had been relentless enemies!) when it was a matter of condemning Mazdak. Obviously this is an apocryphal declaration, but it is interesting because it shows how the chain of the prophets "accepted" by Islam could include Zoroaster (and vice versa), but never "absolute" heretics like Mani or Mazdak.

Bibliography

On Manichaeism:
Peuch, H.-Ch. *Le Manichéisme. Son Fondateur. Sa Doctrine*. Paris, 1949. It includes, in the very complete notes, an extremely full bibliography.
Schaeder, H.H. *Studien zum antiken Synkretismus*. Leipzig-Berlin, 1926.
———. *Urform und Fortbildungen des manichäischen Systems*. Leipzig, 1927.
Widengren, G. *Mesopotamian Elements in Manichaeism*. Uppsala, 1949.

On Mazdakism:

Altheim, F. and R. Stichel. "Mazdak und Porphyrios." *La Nouvelle Clio* V (1953).

Bausani, A. "A proposito di un passo di Shahrastânî sulla dottrina mazdakita." *Rivista degli Studi Orientali* XXII (1947), pp. 74 and foll.

Christensen, A. "Le reigne du roi Kawadh I et le communisme mazdakite," in *Det Kgl. Danske Videnskab. Selsk. Hist.-Fil. Meddelelser.* IX, 6, Copenhagen, 1925

———. *L'Iran sous les Sasanides.* 1946.

Klima, O. "Mazdak und die Juden." *Arch. Or. Prague* XXIV (1956), 3, pp. 420 and foll.

———. "Uber das Datum von Mazdaks Tod." *Charisteria Orientalia* [in honour of J. Rypka]. Prague, 1956, pp. 135 and foll.

Nöldeke, Th. *Geschichte der Perser und Araber zur Zeit der Sasaniden.* Leiden, 1879.

Additional Bibliography

An accessible overview of Manichaeism's relationship to Gnosticism as currently understood may be found in Ioan P. Couliano, *The Tree of Gnosis*, trans. H. Wiesner and the author (San Francisco, 1992). Religion in Sasanian Iran is treated in Ehsan Yarshater, ed. *The Cambridge History of Iran, vol. 3: The Seleucid, Parthian and Sasanian Periods* (Cambridge, 1983). Book-length narrative accounts that have appeared in English since Bausani wrote include Geo Widengren, *Mani and Manichaeism* (London, 1965) and Samuel N.C. Lieu, *Manichaeism in the later Roman Empire and medieval China* (Tübingen, 2nd rev. edn. 1992); and Iain Gardner, *The Kephalaia of the Teacher: The Edited Coptic Manichaean Texts in Translation with Commentary* (Leiden, 1995). A further important Muslim treatment of Manichaeism has come to light, and is surveyed in Guy Monnot, *Penseurs musulmans et religions iraniennes* (Paris, 1974). Ludwig Koenen's discovery of the Cologne Mani Codex, a Greek text, demonstrated that Mani's father belonged to an Aramaic Christian sectarian milieu and so confirmed Bausani's insight that Manichaeism was only geographically Iranian, owing more to Gnosis and Christianity than to Zoroastrianism. Professor Koenen has informed me in conversation, however, that he does not think his discovery should cause scholars to ignore altogether the undeniable Iranian elements in Manichaeism. See A. Henrichs and Ludwig Koenen, *Der Kölner Mani-Kodex* (Opladen, 1988). For translations of Manichaean texts into English, see Jes Peter Asmussen, *Manichaean Literature: representative texts chiefly from Middle Persian and Parthian writings* (Delmar, N.Y., 1975) and Hans Joachim Klimkeit, *Gnosis on the Silk Road: Gnostic texts from Central Asia* (San Francisco, 1993). The issue of Manichaean elements in medieval European heresies is treated in Steven Runciman, *The Medieval Manichee: A Study of the Christian Dualist Heresy* (Cambridge, 1947).

For Mazdakism the major book-length treatment in a Western European language is Otakar Klima, *Beiträge zur Geschichte des Mazdakismus* (Prague, 1977); see also Patricia Crone, "Kavad's Heresy and Mazdak's Revolt," *Iran* 29 (1991):21–42.

Part Two

Crimson Intellect

Chapter Three

The Problem of Iranian Islam

Islam

This is not the place for a treatise on Islamics, nor for an outline of the historical and political phases of the Muslim conquest of Persia. The reader should however remember that after the battle of Nihâvand (641 A.D.) the successive occupations of Iran were almost always peaceful. The last Sasanian king, Yazdagird III, was robbed and killed by one of his subjects—a miller—in whose house he had taken refuge while fleeing from the Arabs in 651. The inhabitants of the country were forced to pay a "capitation tax" (*jizya*) and were incorporated into Islamic society as protected foreigners (*zimmî*). The local aristocracy—no longer backed by the central power and deprived of its privileged positions—tried to ensure the support of the new conquerors, provided the Arabs with counsellors, and some even embraced the new religion and enlisted in the Arab army. Very few cases of forced conversions have been recorded. The Arabs acted harshly only in cases of obstinate rebellion or resistance; Rhages (near present-day Tehran) and several other important cities suffered military conquest, with the consequent massacre of the male population. In Istakhr, the southern capital, 40,000 Persians were killed during a rebellion and the conqueror "swept away the greater part of the noble families" and the cavalry leaders who had sought refuge in the fortified city. But, as Minorsky (from whose "Storia dell'Iran Islamico," in *Civiltà dell'Oriente*, Roma, 1957, Vol. I, p. 462, this brief account is taken) says, "The country people seem to have lost little from this change of overlords and, in a sense, they have used the Arabs' relative naïveté to free themselves from hated masters. From a purely dogmatic point of view the conqueror's religion was much simpler than the ritualistic Zoroastrianism, which required the professional intervention of priests at every step. There was also a definite tendency in early Islam to eliminate racial inequalities and help the poor." However some particularly "sheltered" areas (the Caspian provinces and Tavaristân) only accepted the new faith definitively in the ninth century.

But what was this new faith? At the death of Muhammad (632)—the Prophet of Arabia, God's Envoy, the absolute leader the whole of the still small community, which was later to conquer half the world, venerated—a voice rose out of the general disarray and confusion. The voice of 'Umar, who was to become the second Caliph, thus announced the death of the Leader: "To those who believed in Muhammad I say: Muhammad is dead. To those who believe in God I say: He is the Eternal One who never dies," i.e., men are of no account—not even the Prophet—in the face of God's absolute eternal sovereignty, to whom they must give themselves, abandon themselves (this is the meaning of *islâm*). The unfathomable distance between God and man is absolute and is expressed in some texts in terms that could be *ante-litteram* Barth's or "Calvinist" concepts. God is the Lord, man the slave. According to the great Orientalist Goldziher, if any religion proves those who place the essence of religiosity in the feeling of dependence, *Abhängigkeitsgefuhl*, to be right, this religion is Islam. Within it God is entirely free and arbitrary. In order to guarantee God's arbitrary freedom orthodox Islamic theology even went as far as a certain indulgence towards voluntaristic anthropomorphism; God can change his mind, he can abrogate verses dictated to his Prophet at moments when they might have been useful, he reveals his law throughout time through successive prophets, he creates and destroys the universe at every instant without the help of secondary causes, *causae secundae*. Side by side with this absolute lack of dogma we find simple and primitive normative and organizational institutions for the benefit of this world, administered by God himself, in a kind of grandiose democratic theocracy that was suited to the primitive Arabian bedouin setting but was easily corruptible in the face of new exigencies. These institutions were a simple system of taxation, canonical prayer that must be repeated five times a day with easy ritual gestures, and the absence of priesthood and real temples. Verses 2–4 of the second chapter of the Qur'an give an excellent summary of Islam: " . . . the godfearing, who believe in the Unseen, and perform the Prayer, and who expend of that We have provided them; and who believe in what has been sent down to Thee and what has been sent down before thee and have faith in the Hereafter".[1]

Granted that the reader is familiar with a general outline of the Islamic religion we must now consider the religious reactions of the Zoroastrians to the new faith. We are very fortunate in having a Pahlavî text for this study—the frequently quoted *Shkand-gumânîk Vichâr*—written at the time of the ephemeral ninth century Zoroastrian renaissance and much of which is specifically devoted to the controversy with the Muslims who, however, are never named for reasons of prudence, though the school of the Mu'tazilites is mentioned.

This school sharpened its weapons of discussion on Greek dialectics in order to fight the "dualistic" tendencies that threatened early Islam, and it certainly influenced the style of the above-mentioned short Pahlavî treatise that we know was composed in the same century.

The Dênkart too contains a great deal of anti-Muslim controversial material; in fact the *Shkand-gumânîk Vichâr* draws its inspiration from the *Dênkart*.

It is interesting to note that Zoroastrian theologians were most disagreeably struck by two points in particular where Islam was concerned. These are synthetically summarized in a passage in the *Dênkart* that exemplifies them through two remarkably precise Qur'anic quotations.[2]

One point is expressed in the Qur'anic phrase according to which (Kor. LV, 29) "Each day He (God) is upon a new labour," which is translated very exactly from the Pahlavî *har rôc pat dakhshê*: That is, the completely free movement of the Qur'anic God who constantly changes his mind, alters, creates something new—identical in this, in fact, with the God of the Old Testament.

The other point, to which one can easily understand Mazdean dualism being particularly sensitive, is that of eschatology. That is, Mazdeans simply could not understand how, after duping Adam and Eve so ably, the God of the Qur'an could say with almost wicked satisfaction (Kor. XXXVIII, 84–85): "God said: This is the truth and the truth I say: I will fill Gehenna with thee (Satan) and with whosoever of them (men) follows thee, all together." The horrified Zoroastrian priests—who like all good priests, did not see some of the "primitive" aspects of their own religion but only those of others—had no trouble declaring that a God of this kind seemed more like Ahriman than God.

On the Muslim side, these criticisms (and we have a lot of information on disputes between Mazdeans and Muslims, especially at the court of the tolerant Abbasid caliph al-Ma'mûn, 813–833 A.D.) were answered with alacrity by the Mu'tazilites—the promoters, in Islam, of a dialectical dogmatic theology (*kalâm*, i.e., "speech"). The "dualist" danger was strongly felt by these early theologians though it is not clear what they effectively meant by dualism (*thânawiya, zandaqa*) and we have sufficient data to believe that they often confused Mazdaism and Manichaeism. The term *zandîk* (which already indicated heretics, and Manichaeans in particular, in Pahlavî) indicated the Manichaeans in its Arabized form of *zindîq*, and later became generally synonymous with free thinker, "libertine." M. Guidi edited a ninth-century treatise by al-Qâsim ibn Ibrâhîm in the Mu'tazilite style against the "Manichaeans".[3] Fundamentally it was an answer to the ex-convert Ibn al-Muqaffa's anti-Islamic objections that were very similar to those we have already seen in the *Dênkart* and in the *Shkand-gumânîk Vichâr*. According to some sources Ibn al-Muqaffa' was a Mazdean and not a Manichaean and he had been only superficially converted to Islam.[4]

Consequently, though some historians believe that Islam brought Persia nothing but the destruction of everything pre-Islamic and that the two worlds—Mazdean and Islamic—remained impenetrable, this view is overly simplified and should be corrected. For in the ninth century at least some Zoroastrian priests (e.g., the authors of the *Dênkart* and the *Shkand-gumârîk*) were certainly better acquainted with Muslim theology than our Western medieval and post-medieval scholars up to the beginning of the scientific age, and could quote the Qur'an correctly. On the other hand (though this was possibly rarer) some learned Muslims had a relatively good knowledge of certain points of Manichaean and Mazdean doctrine. But, however strange this may seem, these were not the first contacts between Iran and Islam. The Qur'an itself includes some Iranian material, despite the somewhat justified skepticism of some authors towards a too facile pan-Iranism. Without claiming to exhaust or definitively resolve the problem, we will study a few examples with a view to show how what the Qur'an and Islam brought to seventh century Persia was not as alien as would have been the case for, say, China or India. Persia in some ways had after all long been "Gnosticized" and "Semitized," and the reader should not forget that Semitic Aramaic was the court and international language.

We will start with the episode of man's primordial choice (Kor. VII, 172):

> And when thy Lord took the children of Adam, from their loins their seed, and made them testify touching themselves: "Am I not," he asked, "your Lord?" They said: "Yes, we testify!" Lest you should say on the Day of Resurrection: "As for us, we were heedless of this!"

In 1921 Nallino (Op. Compl., vol. II, p. 213) defined the verse we have just quoted as "this curious Qur'anic passage for which no scholar has as yet indicated a source." It has also remained unexplained in Blachère's recent accurate Qur'anic commentary (1944–1951), but there is nothing "curious" about it for an Iranist to whom, in fact, it must ring clearly familiar in some ways. Such as it is, it seems almost a *contaminatio* between the two passages we are about to quote: the first describes the well-known "choice" of the *fravashi* of the *Bundahishn* (quoted also in chap. I), and the second, in some ways more similar, deals with the Amesha Spenta's choice of Orhmazd as Lord and judge in answer to his specific question, recorded in the *Zhamâspîk*.

> And He (Ohrmazd) took counsel with man's conscience (*bôdh*) and his *fravashi* and instilled omniscient wisdom (*khrat*) into man and said: "What do you think is most useful, that I destine you to the material world and that you struggle, become one (*tan-kartîyâ*) with the *Druj* and destroy it and that we make you rise again at the end, whole and immortal, and create you anew in material form and that you be free from death for ever, and from old age, and from enemies, or that you remain eternally

preserved from the Aggression?" And the *fravashi* of men saw, with omniscient wisdom, the evil that would come to them from the *Druj* and from Ahriman in the material world, but, because of their preservation from the enmity of the adversary, and their being whole again and immortal at the time of the Future Body forever and ever, they accepted to go into the material world. [*Bundahishn*, chap. III, 21–22, ed. Zaehner].

And here is the passage from the *Zhamspîk* (ed. Messina, p. 37 text, p. 38 trans.)

(Ohrmazd) said: "Who should be the first lord and judge?" And the Amesha Spenta, and especially Artvahisht said: "May you, O Ohrmazd the creator, be that lord and judge for us, the only, eternal one, who always has been and ever will be; and be you our creator, you who have produced and created us with your own excellent sense." And they were agreeable to one another.

I feel sure that the inspiration for this Qur'anic passage does not come from the Persian texts we have quoted but from some source familiar with Iranian ideas that were held to be sacred. What can this source be? It is well-known that Iranian elements entered into the eschatology of later Judaism, but Midrashic Jewish literature offers an episode that is only partly similar, i.e., God showed Adam all his descendants with their leaders, sages and scribes, and on that occasion Adam asked and obtained from God that forty years should be taken from the millennium of life assigned to him and given to David to whom only three hours of life had been allotted.[5]

But the essence of the Qur'anic passage lies precisely in the concept of primordial choice that, as we have seen, is so typically Iranian. The Islamic tradition took this concept as its own and "improved" it with even more legendary details (cf. Ibn Qutaiba, *K. ta'wîl mukhtalif al-hadîth*, Cairo, 1326 H. pp. 104–107). Rubbing Adam's back, God made all his posterity come out in the likeness of ant's eggs (*dharr*) and made them acknowledge God's unity; on that occasion God also separated those predestined for heaven from those predestined for hell. That is, after creating Adam, he had one part of his future offspring—as white as silver—come out of his right hand and the other part of his descendants come out—as black as coal—from his left hand. God held them each "in a handful" and said: "Those will be in heaven and I will have no care for them, and these on the other hand will be in hell and I will have no care for them." The *hadîth*, which appears in various forms (cf. Ghazzâlî, *Durra* ed. Gauthier, Genève, 1878, pp. 3–4) is also quoted by Avicenna (*Metafisica*, IX, p. 6).

It is very strange that a passage originally so favorable, in a sense, to free choice is often quoted (deformed by the hadîth that accompany it) specifically in favor of predestination by Muslim theologians in later controversies over free-choice versus predestination. This is a further proof of how the absolutely clear concept of choice it contains remained extraneous, or at least secondary, to the Muslim mentality—thus proving the extra-Muslim source of the passage.

This passage is extremely important for another reason too. It was one of the first (and purely Qur'anic) sources for the penetration into the Islamic spiritual world of the concept of the pre-existence of the soul that later became widespread in Sufi currents but, as Nallino points out, (op. cit., p. 214) was already present before Sufism emerged, in hadîth that circulated towards the second half of the first century of the Hegira.

We have made an in-depth study of this Qur'anic passage because the concept of *rûz-i alast* the day of "'Is it not I?'" (your Lord) carries great weight in the whole of the Persian lyric-mystical tradition (see also Chapter V) of which it is one of the most widespread motifs, particularly in a predestinational sense.

Dumézil (in *Naissance d'Archanges*, Paris, 1945) provided further proof for De Lagarde's hypothesis according to which the two Qur'anic angels of magic, Hârût and Mârût, (Kor. II, 102) are—in name—a distant echo filtered through complex sources of the two Mazdean Amesha Spenta, Haurvatât and Ameretât (see ahead). These Qur'anic "angels-magicians" have little that is Iranian besides their name, but their "journey" from the Iranian highlands to the Arabian deserts, through Babylonia, offers us an important indication of the sources through which the Iranian material to be found in the Qur'an passed before finally reaching the Arabian prophet, that is, sources of Babylonian Gnostic-Manichaean syncretism.

The well-known Qur'anic allusions to shooting stars hurled at the demons who are trying to penetrate into the sky (Kor. XV, 17–18; XXXVII, 7–9; LXVII, 5; LXXII, 8–9) have their counterpart both in the Mazdean concept (cf. *Mênôkê Khrat*, chap. XLIX) particularly concerning the function of certain stars (Vanand and Haftôiring) "who guard the passages and gates" of heaven and hell, and in a fragment of myth preserved in the Zhamâspîk (op. cit., p. 41 of the text and 92 of the trans.) in which the shooting stars are demons.[6]

One of the favorite arguments in the Qur'an against those who deny the resurrection of the flesh is: "If God has already created all beings out of nothing will it not be even easier for him to re-mould the dead from their dust?" The idea is so frequent that it is hard to choose which passages to quote. Take, for example, Kor. XXIX, 19–20, which highlights the idea that this is "easy" for God. The very same arguments, also based on the "ease" of this recreation at the moment of the resurrection of the flesh, are to be found in Pahlavî texts such as Chapter XXXIV of the Zâtspram (ed. Zaehner in "BSOAS"; X pp. 377–398, cf. *Zurvan*, p. 343 text, 348 trans.). Here the dialogue is between Ohrmazd and Zarathustra. Ohrmazd answers the Prophet's questions concerning the possibility of the resurrection of the flesh of the dead that have been torn to pieces and dispersed (and this echoes—even in the choice of words—the almost identical questions the incredulous Arabs asked Muhammad) as follows: "When those creatures did not yet exist, I had the power to mould them;

and now that they have been and are dispersed, it [is still] easier [*hugartar*] to recompose them." There is a similar dialogue in a passage of the *Bundahishn* too (published by Father G. Messina in "Orientalia," 1935, p. 270).

In Kor. the II, 138 the unusual expression "God's color" recurs. "Here is God's color. And who can color better than God? He alone do we adore." Though the expression is poetically effective, it is not very clear; the oldest Muslim commentators (Tabarî, ad loc., vol. I, p. 423) either explain "color" in connection with the idea of "baptism" or "unction," or they identify it with the *fitra* (God's impressed nature, natural religion or *religio naturalis*) or else they identify the term "color" with that of *dîn* ("religion": medieval Persian *dên*). As far as I know the only other religious text in which this same image of God's "color" appears, though applied to a very different context, is the *Dênkart* (Madan, p. 21, quoted in Zaehner, *Zurvan*, p. 379 and 381) in the expression: "The Creator Ohrmazd colored Time." Is it too far-fetched—bearing in mind the *dên-zamân* (Religion as Time) identification of the *Bundahishn* (see chap. I, part I)—to compare the "time" of the Dênkart to the *dîn* of the Arab commentary to the Qur'an? And yet the remarkable likeness of the expressions remains.

In the Qur'an (LVI, 89) the blessed will have *rauh wa raihân* in heaven. *Rauh*, which means "peace" and "quiet," also can mean "pleasant fresh breeze," and *raihân* is "basil." The Pahlavî text *Mênôkê Khrat* (Chapter VII) says of the blessed in heaven that sweet-smelling wind and fragrance like that of basil constantly surround them (*har zamân vât i hubâd y bôd i sparmakân homânak ô pityârak âyêt*). The similarity seems too close to me to be accidental.

7. In an unusual passage of the Qur'an (VI, 38) we find: "No creature is there crawling on earth nor bird flying with its wings but they are nations like unto yourselves. We have neglected nothing in the Book: Then, to their Lord they shall be mustered." In Mazdaism we find the idea that every "community" of animals or even of things has a *ratu* (see Part I, Chapter I), just as Zarathustra is man's *ratu*.[7]

As we saw earlier, this idea "fits into the system" in Mazdean theology while it seems rather out of place in Semitic religiosity. The transmission from Mazdaism to the Qur'an is therefore very likely, and we also have the intermediate link of the Book of Enoch, a Judaic text of the post-exile period. For the Slavic Enoch (chap. 58) says in fact: "The Lord called all the beasts of the earth and all the wild animals . . . In this (world) not all the living souls will be judged, but only man. But for the souls of animals there will be, in the Great Aeon, a place and a home . . . ."

These brief notes certainly do not claim to exhaust the subject.[8] The number of five daily prayers in Islam, for example, appears to have a Mazdean origin. Even stronger links between Iranian culture and the Qur'an exist in the area of eschatological descriptions. The eschatological scales, even the details of the famous heavenly maidens (*hûrîs*) (angels dressed in green);[9] the levelling of the mountains at the end of the world,[10] the "fathers separated from their sons,"[11] the earth which "rejects its weights,"[12] are all elements the vivid Iranian fantasy developed for its final *frashkart*. Where the heavenly maidens are concerned, the following passage from a Soghdian Manichaean text from central Asia (published and translated by Henning, in *BSOAS* vol. XI, 1943–46, p. 476) is interesting. It shows that the concept of *daêna* (which we have already studied) was present and in fact amplified in Manichaean spirituality:

> . . . at whatever moment he dies eighty maiden angels will come to meet him with flowers . . . and a golden bedstead, and they will speak to him thus: Do not fear etc . . . . And his fruitful work, in the form of a wondrous divine princess, a virgin, will come before him, immortal, . . . with on his head a flowered . . . and she herself will guide him to heaven.

This Iranian idea also exists in some Christian legends.

The transmission to the Qur'anic world probably occurred in two directions: post-exile Judaism, which absorbed a great deal from Iran through Babylonia (the Midrashic texts are full of Iranian elements), and the Gnostic-Manichaean sects of the Arab frontier. The tithes, fasting and canonical prayer that are some of the "pillars" of Islam are to be found in very similar forms in the liturgical organization of the Manichaean church. Manichaean canonical prayer was preceded, as we mentioned, by ablutions or, if there was no water, by an "ablution" with sand; this was identical to the Islamic custom. And it was composed of prostrations and stations very similar to the typical prostration (*rak'a*) of Muslim canonical prayer. The Manichaean "heavenly virgins" too are mirrored, as we saw, in the Qur'anic houris, while some scholars attribute Manichaean origins to what is possibly the most important theological "dogma" of the Qur'an, the idea of the successive stations of God through the Prophets. The Manichaean (and Mandaean) list of apostles who preceded Mani include Shethel, Enoch and Abel who all play an important role as prophets in the Islamic tradition too. The Qur'an (V, 73, 116) mentions a singular trinity, composed of God the Father, Mary and Jesus—the idea being attributed to Christians in general—but scholars have found no trace of any Christian sect that specifically admitted this kind of trinity. It is apparently a Manichaean type of trinity since they identified the (female) Holy Spirit with the "Mother of Living Creatures" (cf. the preceding chapter).[13] The Qur'anic idea of Muhammad as the "seal" of the Prophets (this appears only once in Kor. XXXIII, 40)[14] seems also to be originally Manichaean. But setting aside specifically Manichaean influences the Qur'an evidently contains much that is more generically "Gnostic."

The Qur'an reworked and reconsidered material from various sources in such forcefully bare and demythologizing theistic forms that the Old Testament itself seems almost "polytheistic" in comparison! This must not, however, lead us to forget that nearly all the Jewish and Christian material in the Qur'an came from sources such as Midrashic literature and the Christian apocrypha, i.e., through strongly gnostically–oriented sources. Consequently it is mainly through Gnosis or the late-Jewish syncretic legends and Manichaeism that the Iranian element penetrated into the sacred book of Islam. And in some cases—in view of the fact that the ninth century Zoroastrian priests who were the authors of the most important Pahlavî treatises were better versed in the Qur'anic books than had been thought —some of the above-mentioned "coincidences" between the Qur'an and (late) true Mazdaism may easily have occurred in the opposite direction. We even have some recorded cases of the transmission of Qur'anic material to late Jewish sources; transmission from the Qur'an to the Pahlavî texts may have originated the coincidences described in paragraphs 4, 5 and 6.

Gnostic-Manichaean and, indirectly, Iranian material is obviously far more abundant in the immense body of the hadîths, or "traditions" attributed to the Prophet. We will give only a few examples. Among the less "sensational" we find the prohibition of silk—based purely on reasons of austerity in the Islamic tradition, it has its counterpart in the relative depreciation of this material in favor of "purer" cotton in Mazdean texts (such as *Mênôkê Khrat*, chap. XVI). In the Mazdean system the reason is obvious: silk is produced by a worm, a *khrafstr*—consequently an Ahrimanic creature—while cotton and wool come from far more sacred and pure sources. The Zoroastrian tradition carries a tale (cf. *Zardushtnâmeh* ed. Rosenberg, p. 31) of a miraculous purifying opening of the young Zarathustra's breast by the angels. Muhammad's Islamic tradition tells of an almost identical episode based on the slight and purely poetic and emotional Qur'anic evocation: "Have we not expanded thy breast for thee?" (Kor. XCIV, 1). Though this episode is to be found throughout vast cultural areas,[15] it does not appear to exist in Arab-Semitic ones. Both the Islamic and the Mazdean tradition forbid urinating standing up (cf., for example, for Mazdaism, *Mênôkê Khrat*, chap. II) and both traditions, strangely, forbid walking with one shoe (*Mênôkê Khrat*, ibid.);[16] this kind of walking is typical of Satan. The torment the angels inflicted on a dead person in his tomb (*adhâb al-qabr*) certainly has an Iranian origin. The Islamic tradition gives colorful and macabre details of this (based only on very slight Qur'anic allusions, as in VIII, 50) but it is nothing other than the famous torment of *sê-dôsh* (the three nights) so often described in the Mazdean texts. A distant Iranian influence can probably be attributed to the famous legend of Muhammad's ascension (*mi'râj*) to heaven, which was developed from very slight and purely symbolic-visionary Qur'anic passages such as XVII, 1, and LIII, 1–18. The theme of the heavenly journey that reached Islam through the brief Pahlavî treatise *Artâ Vîrâf* and from there, almost certainly by way of medieval Muslim legendary sources to Dante, is too vast a subject to be even briefly considered here.[17] According to tradition Muhammad had a special "seal of Prophecy" between his shoulders. The *Fihrist* has left us the Manichaean legend according to which Mani had something shining like a flame on his shoulders when he stood in front of King Shapur for the first time (Cf. Christensen, *L'Iran sous les Sasanides*, p. 196).

But we will close this necessarily rather arid and disorderly list of examples that I hope, however, has demonstrated two things to the reader: (1) The debt of rising Islam cannot be attributed in an overly simple manner to Christianity or Judaism (with discussions as to whether the debt is greater to the one or the other religion), but above all to certain special forms of Christianity and Judaism that were deeply imbued with Near Eastern Gnostic-Syncretic material, of which Mazdaism and Manichaeism were basic elements. (2) The Qur'an itself (which an overly "racist" and elementary form of criticism often presents as the most unpolished and primitive of sacred books) contains a great deal of material that still carries the symbolic fragrance of Gnosis and its author must have had a far wider knowledge of the earlier Asian religious world than we are apt to believe.[18]

The approach of certain Qur'anic tales based on the Bible or on Jewish and Christian apocrypha is removed completely from "history" and uses the material as allusion to religious experiences and the characters (Pharaoh, the Seven Sleepers of Ephesus, Joseph the Jew, etc.) as archetypes of religious-moral situations. This approach already presents, as Strothmann noted, an excellent reason for the clearly "Gnostic" interpretation of certain later sects (*Ismail Kor Komm*, Introd., p. 2).

Widengren (*Muhammand and his Ascension*) has shown how in the Qur'an some technical terms, too, which so far have aroused little interest—e.g., the adjective "rebel" which accompanies Satan in many Qur'anic passages, Vanity opposed methodically to Reality (*Haqq-Bâtil*), the habit of transposing commercial terms in a religious sense (commerce, *tijâra*; treasure, *khizâna*), the frequent use of ablutions, etc.—are derived from Gnostic sources if, of course, we also admit that many elements present in late Judaism and Christianity are Gnostic. But the most important fact is—as we said before—that Muhammad's personality in a way "de-gnosticized" this material and transposed it in an eschatological sense (and most Gnostic doctrines, except for Manichaeism, were lacking in eschatological spirit). Thus we again run up against the problem of a Manichaean influence on Muhammad; the paths this followed are not clear, though we should not forget that Manichaeism was propagandized in the Arab linguistic territory from the time of 'Amr ibn 'Adî (before 300 A.D.),[19] in al-Hîra, and that before Islam some *zindîq* (almost certainly Manichaeans) travelled as far as Mecca.[20]

The study of Iranian terms in the Qur'anic vocabulary leads to the same conclusions. That is, these words were not directly derived from any Iranian language but rather came in through Syriac or Hebrew mediation. One point must however be stressed. These "strange-sounding" and evocative Persian terms, which were noticed by Arab writers such as al-Kindî,[21] contributed a great deal to inspiring the "esoteric" and allegorical currents of the exegesis in the Sacred Book.

The First "Iranian" Religious Uprisings

In the preceding paragraph we have attempted to show how Islam and Iranian culture were not completely heterogeneous worlds but had points of real if indirect contact on the one hand, and points of "possible exchange" on the other. The real contact (Manichaeism) occurred indirectly (probably in both directions) at the time of the formation of the Qur'an and in some cases directly (from the Qur'an to Zoroastrian circles) immediately after the Islamic conquest of Persia. The possibility of further contact occurred later at the time of the first attempts at political and religious anti-Arab revolt that, however—because of this possibility—was not anti-Islamic.

In fact the first religious anti-governmental uprisings against the Caliphate (which started towards the end of Umayyad rule and continued actively during the first part of the Abbasid period) included cases of Zoroastrian "heretics" who took over part of the Islamic terminology and were opposed both by the orthodox Muslims and the orthodox Zoroastrians. The main cause for the "religious unrest" that characterized the second half of the eighth century and the beginning of the ninth was Abbasid propaganda, which attempted to undermine the power of the rival Umayyads through the exploitation of every form of discontent (in the ancient East political unrest always had a religious side to it). The discontent was especially vigorous in the peripheral regions of the vast territory of the Caliphate (and therefore in Persia and, in particular, eastern Persia, Khurasan, etc.). This was a key period in the religious history of Persia. "Iranian" and Islamic elements mingled almost imperceptibly, forming a non-Arab Islamic *quid* (Abbasid propaganda relied greatly on the mawâlî—non-Arab elements who were "clients" of the conquering Arab tribes) and this later, after the Abbasid "betrayal," was used against the old allies.

We will now examine some of the most important of these religious-political movements, starting with the more obviously extra-Islamic ones even if, chronologically, they come after the first "proto-Shi'ite" Islamic religious risings.

The Bihâfrîd uprising produced an example of what we mentioned above, i.e., the alliance between Muslims and orthodox Zoroastrians. Around 745 a man called Bihâfrîd (a typically Persian name, as was his father's, Mâh-fravardîn), whom the sources agree in calling a magus or Zoroastrian (*mâjûs*), presented himself as a prophet and innovator of Zoroastrianism at Nîshâpûr, in eastern Persia (Khurâsân). The sources (all Muslim) that mention him mingle the facts with many strange and possibly legendary elements: e.g., that he appeared on top of a high, stairless, inaccessible cupola so that the people wondered how he had gotten there. He answered questions concerning his identity with: "I am Bihâfrîd (also Bihzâd) the Magus and I have been sent by God to bring men to the religion of Zarathustra." Very soon 30,000 followers gathered around him and the Abbasid propagandist Abû Muslim fought bitterly against him.[22]

Other sources say that he travelled through China, returning with a vast cloth of such finely woven silk that it could be held in the palm of one hand. At one point he feigned death and remained for a year in his tomb, secretly assisted and fed by his wife. Then he "rose again" and presented the green cloth as a heavenly garment given him by God as a pledge during the year he spent in heavenly worlds. His doctrine included seven daily prayers, with the Sun as direction of prayer (*qibla*); inebriating and narcotic drinks were forbidden, as were *khvêtûkdâs* (marriage between close relatives), the adoration of fire, "murmuring" (*bâj*) the canonical books (a Mazdean custom that seems to have particularly struck the Muslims); altogether the tendency was to free Mazdaism from everything that might most provoke the Muslims. At the request of the local Zoroastrians (this was naturally much appreciated!) the well-known Abbasid propagandist Abû Muslim fought him and finally had him executed.[23]

Even more important than his doctrine as we know it from our sources was the fact that he presented himself under an aura of wonder, as a "prophet," using the classic form of the "I am!" As we shall see, these early stirrings of religious revolution were all linked with phenomena of prophetism or of the personality cult of the Founder, and there must have been an input of elements of popular religiosity of which we know nothing.

The work of Sindbâd, another "Zoroastrian" (though only in his name, which is strictly Iranian) who was active in the same area soon after Bîhâfrîd, appears to have been far more profoundly islamized. Sindbâd was also called Pêrôz Ispahbad, the "victorious general" or General Pîrûz. In his preaching, which turned out to be far more dangerous than Bihâfrîd's precisely because it was more "Islamic," "Abû Muslim's revenge" plays a central role. The great leader of Abbasid propaganda (who was too powerful and influential) was murdered in 755 A.D. by the same people who had exploited his by–then victorious deeds. The motif of this revenge appears almost constantly in many of the religious-political stirrings that occurred in this area and during this period. I provide below a summary of the passage on Sindbâd in Nizâmu'l-Mulk's *Siyâsat-nâmeh* (p.182 of the text, p. 266 and foll. of Schefer's translation). It must be remembered that the author was ferociously anti-heretical and his statements cannot be taken literally, but they contain interesting elements of truth. It appears that Sindbâd was a Zoroastrian (*gabr*) friend and collaborator of Abû Muslim, who had made him a general. At his commander's death he travelled from Khorâsân to Rayy (near present-day Tehran) and invited the "Zoroastrians" and "Mazdakites" of the neighboring regions (the area south of the Caspian sea, Iraq, etc.) to join him. After murdering the Abbasid governor of Rayy and seizing the abundant treasures Abû Muslim had left there, he publicly proclaimed that he would avenge Abû Muslim's blood and passed himself off as his "prophet" (*rasûl*). He spread the word that Abû Muslim had not really died but—shortly before succumbing to his assassin's blows—had invoked the "greatest name" (*ism-i a'zam*) of God and had changed into a white dove and flown to heaven. And he added that Abû Muslim was in the company of the Mahdî[24] and Mazdak in a copper castle and that all three would return. His preaching attracted people from various currents. When he was alone with Zoroastrians (*gabr*) he would say: "The reign of the Arabs is coming to an end: I found it written in a Sasanian book. I will not abandon the struggle until I have destroyed the Ka'ba set up (as a place of cult) in place of the Sun" (see ahead). When, on the other hand, he was alone with a Mazdakite he would say: "Mazdak was Shi'ite: I therefore invite you to join the Shi'ites and revenge Abû Muslim's blood." This passage is followed by some (not too exact) details on the military revolt. This revolt, which in fact also involved Dailamite "mountaineers" who had been only superficially "Islamized" (or not at all), developed mainly in the area between Rayy (Rhages) and Hamadân, and Sindbâd was killed after his defeat in the mountainous area of north-western Persia.

A few years later, in 767 or 768, Ustâd-Sîs' religious-political rebellion in the Khurâsân area (Eastern Persia), supported by the populations of Bâdghîs and the Sîstân and Tukhâristân areas, drew many followers though it was quelled by the then hereditary prince (later caliph), al-Mahdî. Ustâd-Sîs too was considered a "Zoroastrian" (though he was certainly a heretical one) and he also attracted the remnants of Bîhâfrîd's followers.[25]

He too declared that he was a "prophet" but the only thing the sources say about his doctrine is that he led an immoral life and ended his life killed as a highwayman.

The most important of these movements, and also possibly the most interesting from a religious point of view, was the one led by al-Muqanna', the "Veiled Prophet" of Khurâsân, celebrated by T. Moore in "Lalla Rookh." He appeared in those same regions little more than ten years later under al-Mahdî's caliphate. Since the events connected with this singular person's revolt are re-counted very vividly in the source material and present a "typical" picture of similar movements, we offer our readers a translation of these events (with only a few abbreviations) as they are told in a precious Persian source— Narshakhî's *Ta'rîkh-i Bukhârâ*. Its merit lies in the fact that the author (who lived in the tenth century in that same area) generally made use of still older material, closer to the events, which occurred around 779.[26]

Ahmad ibn Muhammad ibn Nasr relates that Muhammad Ja'far, in his book, has a chapter on this subject, but it is incomplete. Ibrâhîm, who is the one who gives news of Muqanna', and Muhammad ibn Jarîr at-Tabarî relate that Muqanna' was a man from the rural area of Marv, from a village called Kazeh and his real name was Hâshim ibn Hakîm (according to other sources 'Atâ) and that he started out as a laundryman. Later he devoted himself to scientific studies and learnt a little of everything, especially the science of sleight-of-hand, magic spells and talismans; and he became especially skilled in sleight of hand. He also claimed to be a Prophet and was annihilated by the (caliph) al-Mahdî, the son of Mansûr in the year 167 of the Hegira (A.H. 783). He was extremely skilled in the use of the magic arts, had read many books on the science of the ancients and had become a master in witchcraft. His father's name was Hakîm (which also means "sage," "doctor") and he was one of the generals of the governor of Khurâsân at the time of Abû Ja'far Dawâniqî and came from Balkh. He was called Muqanna because he kept his head and face covered (*Muqanna* means "veiled" in Arabic), being excessively ugly, bald and blind in one eye: thus he always wore a green veil to cover his head and face. This Muqanna was a general of Khurâsân at the time of Abû Muslim, the head of the (Abbasid) Propaganda, and he became vizir of 'Abdu'l-Jabbâr al-Azdî. Some time after he proclaimed himself Prophet, Abû Ja'far Dawâniqî had him brought from Marv to Baghdad and cast into prison. When, after a few years, he was freed he returned to Marv, called together the people and said to them: "Do you know who I am?" And they answered: "Yes, you are Hâshim ibn Hakîm!" But he replied: "You are mis-taken: I am your God and the God of the whole world" (dust on his mouth!)[27] and he added: "I can call myself by whatever name I wish: I am in fact he who showed himself to creation in the form of Adam, then (I appeared) in the form of Noah, then in the form of Abraham, then in the form of Moses, then in the form of Jesus, then in the form of Muhammad (May God pray for him and bless him!), then in the form of Abû Muslim, and finally in this form that you see." Those present said then: "Others have claimed to be prophets, but you actually claim to be God!." He answered: "They were psychic, I am pneumatic and I was within them. I possess the power to be able to show myself in whatever form I wish." He also wrote epistles to every country giving them to his missionaries (*dâ'î*) to deliver. The letters were formu-lated as follows: "In the name of God, clement and merciful. From me Hâshim ibn Hakîm, Lord of Lords, to So and So son of So and So. Praise is due to God, beyond whom there is no god, the god of Adam, of Noah, of Abraham, of Moses, of Jesus, of Muhammad, of Abû Muslim: and now the power and Sovereignty, the Majesty and Proof (belongs) to al-Muqanna. Believe in me and know that the Kingdom belongs to me (a curse on him!); the Glory and (quality of) Creator belong to me, there is no other God than I (dust on his mouth!) and whoever believes in me will have Heaven, whoever does not believe in me will have Hell!" While he was still at Marv he sent missionaries all over the place and led many people astray. An Arab at Marv by name of Abdullâh ibn'Amr believed in him and gave him one of his daughters in marriage. This Abdullâh crossed the Oxus and came to Nakhshab and to Kish, spreading propaganda everywhere in favor of this Muqanna (a curse on him!) and leading many people astray. The greater part (of Muqanna's followers) were at Kish and in the country around Kish. The first village to openly undergo mass conversion to Muqanna's religion was Sûbakh in the country near Kish and their leader (*mihtar*) was called 'Amr Sûbakhî. They rebelled and killed the mayor, a pious Arab: and so the greater part of the villages of Soghdiana followed this Muqanna'. Many of the villages of Bukhârâ too turned "unbelieving," publicly declaring their unbelief. Thus the disorder became immense and a serious calamity fell on the Muslims. Muqanna's (followers) assaulted caravans, sacked villages and caused great ruin. In the meantime Muqanna's fame spread throughout Khurâsân. The governor of the region, Humaid ibn Qahtaba, ordered Muqanna's arrest. But he fled from his village and hid until he heard that great masses had adhered openly to his religion in Transoxiana. And so he prepared to cross the Oxus. The governor of Khurâsân ordered that the banks of the Oxus be constantly watched by a hundred horsemen who rode up and down, ready to arrest him if he tried to cross the river. He reached the banks of the Oxus with thirty–six companions and succeeded in crossing by building some beams (? '-m-d): he reached Kish and the whole region delivered itself up to him and the people loved him. There was a strongly fortified castle on the mountain of Sâm (var. Siyâm, Sanâm) that enclosed running water and wooded areas and sown fields and, (within), a second even more powerful castle. He ordered that it be repaired and gathered a great mass of provisions and great riches there, and he placed guards to watch over it. Thus the "White-Clad Ones" multiplied and the Muslims were powerless to destroy them.[28]

A delegation brought this news to Baghdad: at that time al-Mahdî was the Caliph. He was greatly saddened and sent an army to fight against him. Then he himself went to Nîshâpûr to bring remedy to the scandal, in the fear that Islam might be destroyed and that Muqanna's religion might conquer the whole world. For Muqanna' had called the Turks too, declaring the blood and possessions of the Muslims theirs by right: already great armed bands were coming from Turkestan eager for plunder and they stripped a number of regions taking prisoners away with them and killing the sons and women of the Muslims . . ." (Here there is more detailed information on local struggles of the "White-Clad Ones" in and around Bukhârâ, and especially at Narshakh, the Author's native town. These struggles lasted for years with alternating success).

. . . Muhammad ibn Ja'far relates that 50,000 men of Muqanna's army, people from Transoxiana, Turks and others, gathered one day, prostrate and tearful, at the gates of the Veiled One's Castle and asked him to show himself. They obtained no reply. And so they insisted saying: "We will not go away until we have seen the face of our Lord!" Muqanna' had a page by the name of Hâjib to whom he said: "Go and tell my servants (dust on his mouth!) that Moses too asked Me once to show Myself to him, but I did not show Myself to him, because he could not have borne the sight of Me. In fact, anyone who gazes on Me is unable to bear it and dies immediately." But they so multiplied their supplications and prayers saying: "We want to see you, we even accept to die!" that he fixed an appointment for a given day when he would manifest himself to them. In his castle there were a hundred women, daughters of the *dihqân*s (small Iranian landed nobility) of Soghdiana, Kish and Nakhshab whom he kept with him. In fact he always had beautiful women pointed out to him and took them to the castle to keep them near him. In the castle there were only these women and his private page besides himself. For victuals he did as follows: once a day he would open the gate of the castle and there was a person outside entrusted with preparing whatever was needed. He would call his page to bring in the supplies. Then he would close the castle gate until the following day. But nobody saw his ugly face because he kept it covered with a green veil. Now he ordered those women to each take a mirror and climb onto the roof of the castle and hold them facing each other at the very moment the sun touched the earth. A great number of people had gathered together: when the sun struck those mirrors everything around was filled with light because of the reflection. At that very moment he said to his page: "Go and say to my servants: God is turning his face to you, look!" They looked and saw the world filled with light and they were filled with fear. Immediately they bowed down, crying out: "Lord! The power and the glory we have seen is sufficient; if we see more our livers will burst!" And so they remained, until Muqanna' ordered his page to say: "Raise your heads, your God is pleased with you and has forgiven you your sins." And the people raised their heads, full of fear, and he said to them: "I have made all regions yours by right. You may have the blood, the belongings and the sons of those who do not believe in me (dust on his mouth!). All those people went away from there to sack and they boasted and strutted in front of the others saying: "We have seen God!"

Muqanna's ruin occurred as follows. Sa'îd, who was the governor of Herât, besieged Muqanna's castle with a great army and had houses and baths built so that they could keep up the siege both in summer and winter. Inside the castle (as we said) there was a spring of water, trees and tilled fields and courtiers and generals with powerful armies. And within the castle there was another fortress too on top of the mountain that nobody was allowed to enter, and he lived there with his women. It was his habit to take food with those women and remain drinking wine with them. And everything continued this way for fourteen years. When the governor of Herât laid siege and dispersed his armies, (Muqanna's) general who was in the castle opened the gate and came out and surrendered, accepting Islam. Thus the Muslims conquered the castle: Muqanna' understood then that he would not be able to keep up the force within. Muhammad ibn Ja'far relates a tradition he heard from Abû 'Alî Muhammad ibn Hârûn, who was a dihqân of Kish. It runs as follows: My grandmother was one of the ladies of the castle whom Muqanna' had taken for himself and she told me that one day Muqanna' sat down at table as usual with his women to eat and drink, but he mixed some poison into the wine. He offered each woman a special goblet, saying: "When I drink from my goblet, you all must drink from yours." All drank, but I, instead of drinking, poured the contents of my goblet into my gown without him noticing. The women all fell down dead and I threw myself down among them pretending to be dead and still he did not notice. Then Muqanna' stood up, looked around and saw all the women lying dead, and he went to his page and unsheathing his sword beheaded him. Three days earlier he had ordered the oven to be lit: he went to the oven, took off his clothes and threw himself into the flames. Noticing the thick smoke that came out of it I approached the furnace but saw no trace of him. I was the only living creature in the castle. The reason for his throwing himself into the fire is this. He often said: "When my servants rebel against me, I will ascend to heaven; and then I will return with an army of angels to subjugate them." He burnt himself alive so that people would say that he had risen to heaven to fetch the angels who would help them to victory, so that his religion might remain in the world. That woman opened the castle gate and Sa'id Harashî entered and confiscated all the treasures within it.

According to Ahmad ibn Muhammad ibn Nasr, followers of Muqanna' still exist in the region of Kish, in Nakhshab and in some villages around Bukhârâ such as Kûshk, 'Umar Kûshk, Khûstuwân and Zarmaz. These people know nothing of Muqanna' but they follow his religion. Their doctrine is as follows: they do not recite the canonical prayers, they do not fast, they do not carry out the major ablutions, but they are honest people and they keep their conduct hidden from the Muslims, declaring themselves to be Muslims. It is also said that they consider their own wives to rightfully belong to others, in fact they maintain that a woman is like a rose, he who smells it does not take anything away from it. When a man goes alone to a woman he makes a sign on the door of the house so that when the husband arrives he may know that his wife is in the house with another man. Thus he can go away until the other man has finished and he is able to enter into his own house. They have a leader (ra'îs) in a village whom they obey.

The story also goes that they have one man in every village whose duty it is to deflower any virgin girl who goes as a bride to that village before handing her over to her husband. Ahmad ibn Muhammad ibn Nasr relates: "I asked the old country people what the meaning of this custom was and why they left all this grace of God to one person only, everyone else accepting to be deprived of it. They answered that it was their custom that every adolescent who reaches puberty satisfies his sexual needs through that man until the moment he marries: the penalty for this is that when he marries he leaves him his wife for the first night. When this man becomes old another one is appointed to take his place and the youths of the village use him constantly. The name of the individual who fulfills this function is thakâneh[29]. However I have not been able to verify the truth of these statements. This story was told me by the old country people and by the villagers (jamâ'at): may God save and free us from such things!"[30]

Another singular miracle performed by al-Muqanna' is the "moon of the well of Nakhshab," which is reported in other sources and which became so famous in the Islamic world that it is listed among the themes of traditional poetry. The veiled prophet, or rather God, is said to have made the moon come out of a well at Nakhshab (according to the incredulous Muslims again with the help of mirrors . . .) to the wonder of his artless followers. Besides the elements that the passage of Narshakhî's story translated above reveal of his doctrine, according to other sources he preached metempsychosis (Tabarî, Abû'l-Mahâsin) and only revealed his entire and complete doctrine to a circle of initiated people (Ibn al-Athîr).

Before examining these singular doctrines we will go on to study those of another "religious agitator" who lived a few decades after Muqanna', i.e., Pâpak (Ar. Bâbak)[31].

With Pâpak the theatre of religious revolutionary activity moved from the far eastern fringes of Iranian territory to the western ones, of Azerbaijan and Mesopotamia. Pâpak was probably the son of an Iraqi (the name, Abdullâh, could indicate a Muslim convert) from Ctesiphon (Madâ'in). In Azerbaijan, where he lived in poverty as a young man, he met a Khurramite leader whose doctrines he followed.

The rather vague term of Khurramite was used by a number of heresiographers to indicate generically almost all the movements we have studied so far. Some people think it is derived from the Persian *khurram* ("ribald"), i.e., those of the ribald religion, because they admitted the communal use of women, etc.) others from a place name. The Khurramite doctrines were summarized as follows by Mutahhar b. Tâhir (who wrote in 966 and knew some Khurramites personally) (ed. Huart, vol IV, p. 30 of the text, p. 29 of the trans.).

They are divided into various sects and classes, but they all agree on the doctrine of return (*raj'a*, not to be confused with transmigration!) and assert the change of name and of body. They claim that all the prophets (*rusul*), despite the differences between their laws and their religions, are inspired by a single Spirit, and that revelation (*wahy*) is never interrupted: according to them anyone who adheres to a religion is in the way of truth, as long as he hopes for the Reward and fears the Punishment, and therefore they cannot accept that he be offended or accused of bad actions (unless) he wants to deceive their community or destroy their religion. They refrain carefully from shedding blood, unless they are openly at war. They greatly esteem and venerate Abû Muslim (see above) and curse Abu Ja'far (i.e., the Abbasid caliph al-Mansûr) for having killed him and they multiply their blessings on Mahdî ibn Fîrûz, because he descends from Fâtima the daughter of Abû Muslim. They have leaders (*a'imma*) whom they turn to for judgements, and Apostles (*rusul*) who circulate among them and whom they call *firishtagân*. According to them nothing bears greater holy blessings than wine and (alcoholic) beverages. The foundation of their religion is the assertion of the (principles) of Light and Darkness. We found those we have seen personally in their villages, in Masabadân and Mihrijan Qadhaq, extremely solicitous over cleanliness and purity and over treating other people courteously through good works. We found that some of them admit the right to use women freely, as long as they are willing, and the lawfulness of everything that pleases and towards which human nature is inclined, as long as it damages nobody.

We ought not to consider too seriously the fact that some heresiographers call Pâpak a "Zoroastrian" on the basis of the light-darkness dualism of his doctrines (and it is surprising that some orientalists such as Spuler go along with this). Summarizing the little material available in the sources (all inimical) on his doctrine (besides the doctrines translated above described rather inaccurately and "journalistically" by Ibn Tâhir), Pâpak apparently admitted the adoration of Fire, marriage between very close relatives and transmigration even between men and animals (Ibn al-Athîr, VI, iii). The widow of his Khurramite master, Jâvêdân ibn Suhrak, declared that Papak was the incarnation of her husband's spirit (*rûh*, Tab. III, 1015, Athîr, loc. cit.) and the authoritative interpreter of his teachings. She later married him. Outwardly Pâpak remained attached to Islamic rites; but, besides describing his doctrines, the sources speak of specific Khurramite rites such as eating "bread" and drinking "wine" in the course of a ritual feast that also included a kiss of the hand and a confession of faith (*Fihrist*, 344). His adepts (like he himself in fact) were mostly of low social extraction and (as usual) the sources claim a Mazdakite derivation for his doctrine and practice.

Pâpak's movement endangered the Caliphate more than other similar ones and his subversive activity lasted from 816 to 838, with its geographical center in the fortress of al-Badhdh (or Badhdhain) on the border between Azerbaijan and Arrân. According to one source (*Fihrist*, 343) Pâpak had difficulty in making himself understood in Persian, at least when he was young, though this does not mean that he spoke Arabic or other languages but is simply an indication that he may have spoken in dialect and was of low social extraction, nor can it be taken (as some people have done) as sufficient proof of his non-Iranian origin. Pâpak's revolt was drowned in blood; after the fortress was stormed and Pâpak fled to Armenia he was betrayed, arrested, led to Baghdad and killed there in the throes of the most cruel torments that he bore stoically. His death did not mark the total suppression of the Khurramite movement (called *harramite* too in the sources, from the root *h-r-m*, "illicit"). Samâ'nî (56 r., see below) provided interesting information according to which Pâpak's followers met once a year to celebrate their founder's death with sexual orgies.

Is there any truth in the supposed connection between these movements and Mazdakism? Ibn al-Nadîm writes with great clarity and precision (*Fihrist*, ed. Flügel, p. 342):

The haramîya are of two categories: the first haramîya, known as the red-dressed ones (*muhammira*) are to be found in the region of al-Jibâl between Azerbaijan, Armenia and Dailam, at Hamadân and Dînâvar and between Isfahân and the area of

Ahwâz. These were originally Zoroastrian (mâjûs) then their religion was reformed: they are also known as *al-l-q-t-h* and their leader is Mazdak . . . Then there are the Pâpakite haramîya, whose leader is Pâpak . . . who claimed to be God and introduced killing, sacking, wars and cruel punishments into the haramite religion that were unknown to it before [see in fact the above-mentioned text].

The allusion to "reformed Zoroastrianism" is interesting: in a more acceptable historical form one might speak of a "popular" Iranian religion influenced by elements of Gnostic-Mesopotamian Syncretism.

A quick synopsis of these semi-Muslim if not entirely extra-Muslim movements of the eighth through ninth centuries will be useful at this point for an in-depth study of the different aspects of the problem.

Early Shi'ism

The material we have examined above raises the following questions:

1. These movements were born in two different geographical centers: one in the north-eastern Iranian territory (Khorâsân and Transoxiana); the other in the north-western area (Azerbaijan, Dailam, the Babylonian frontier). Must we attribute different origins to these two nuclei or are we dealing with germs transported from one to the other? (In this particular case from east to west, since the earliest movements appear to have had their origin in the east.)

2. All the movements under consideration appear to have an "incarnation" as their central doctrine or, if we remove all theological sense from the term, a concentration or representation or manifestation of the Divine in a given human person. Can this be called an "Iranian" doctrine?

3. In many of these movements, if not in all, the concepts of "reincarnation" (the sources use the two terms of *raj'a* and *tanâsukh*, which in fact have rather different meanings), of a succession of prophets or incarnations of the divinity (the last of which is regularly that of the founder of the sect), of a certain alleged sexual freedom, with a corresponding communism of the women or khvêtûkdâs, are recurrent. What is the origin of the three fundamental doctrines the heresiographers attribute to these movements?

4. In many cases the followers of these "founders" were low-ranking people or non-Arabs (in the case of Muqanna', Turks as well as Iranians), or else the remnants of preceding heresies that had been destroyed. Can one give a central "national" or "class" motif to these religious movements?

5. In many cases these movements showed a considerable interest in Muslim events, even though the heresiographers all agree that they were outside the pale of Islam (however it seems rash to me to place them, with Spuler, among the "Zoroastrians" without any qualification). But this holds good more for the facts than the doctrines; for example, the curious importance given to the person of the

Abbasid dynastic propagandist Abû Muslim (whose ideas cannot be proved historically to have been particularly "heretical"). How therefore are these movements related to Islam? Are they Islamic heresies or movements completely outside this religion? And what, in particular, is their relationship with the primitive Shi'ites?

It is not easy to answer these questions and they would remain completely incomprehensible to the profane reader if they were not preceded by a study of the primitive Shi'ites and their doctrines, which ran their course shortly before this period.[32]

We will begin by saying that European scholars have been susceptible to two kinds of tendencies against which we must be on our guard. The first, which could be termed "racist," consists in taking for granted an abstract, Arab "Semitism" which gave rise to Islam and which would have been constitutionally incapable of admitting ideas such as those of incarnation or emanation, and incapable of deep mythological symbolism, etc. According to these tendencies, the Qur'an contains none of these elements and is an unpolished and primitive book written by a half-ignorant bedouin with ill-digested ideas culled here and there from the Jews, the Christians or Christian sectarians. This is why these orientalists often prefer a more anthropomorphic and "Sunni" exegesis and tradition, considered more in keeping with the "original Semitic spirit" of Islam, and so forth.

The second—connected with the first —is the "Aryan" origin of all that is contrary to this abstract Semitic schema in the "heretical" Islamic doctrines. Here too some orientalists follow, more or less consciously, the traditionalist heresiographer Ibn Hazm's doctrine, concisely expressed in his own words (I, 35–36):

> The reason for which the greater part of these sects departed from the Islamic religion is the following. The Persians had such an extensive empire and such great power over all peoples and such an exalted concept of themselves that they called themselves "free," and "sons" while they considered the other peoples their servants. When they suffered the transfer of power from their hands to the Arabs, whom they considered the lowest ranking of all people, their situation became a difficult one and their misfortune seemed to them to be doubled . . .
>
> They felt that they would be most successful if they deceived Islam through cunning; therefore a certain number of them externally professed Islam and earned the favor of the Shi'ites, showing love for the Prophet's family and condemning the injustice perpetrated against 'Alî. Then they led them along different paths until they departed from Islam.

But as a reaction to this second tendency some scholars have exaggerated in the opposite direction, minimizing the spiritual and religious influence of the

Iranian world on Islam and referring everything back to Christian influences or even to a remodelling, under Christian or Christian-oriented guidance, of originally "Arab" concepts. This is the predominant tendency at present, though it has been counterbalanced by some cases of neo-Iranism, if we can call it that, which attempt to repropose, with fuller and more researched documentation, the "Iranian" theory of the early orientalists (this revival can be seen especially in Corbin's learned works).

As for the Islamic sources (which are almost the only ones extant on the oldest Shi'ites) on the one hand they have been discredited by an abstractly classificatory and anti-historic tendency based on one of Muhammad's apocryphal sayings, i.e., "My community will be divided into 73 sects, only one of which will be saved." This tendency led them to multiply the "-isms" (in Arab-*iyya*, which is even more abused than our-ism!), often without good cause, in order to reach the . . . established number of 72, on the other by the conviction that they alone possessed the truth and by the easy acceptance of irresponsible "rumors" concerning the "shameful" doctrines of the heretics. In this way cliches are created that can be applied indifferently to the most varied tendencies. Here I will anticipate what we are going to discuss further on and take the liberty of introducing a personal experience. In the course of a trip to Persia I was conversing pleasantly with one of my fellow travellers (a tailor, with little education) during the interminable stops the bus made in the *châikhâneh*s of the immense Iranian plateau, and I happened to mention the Baha'is (the most recent of the Persian "religions," born in the course of the last century and harshly persecuted for a long time: see Chapter VIII). My interlocutor (a pious Shi'ite) was deeply scandalized that I should know people of this kind and told me tales of their "marriages between brothers and sisters and between children and parents," of their sexual licence, etc., which exactly reproduced, almost word for word, certain cliches by Muslim heresiographers of many centuries ago on the various "extreme" sects of Islam. Where the Baha'is are concerned the untruth of these cliches can be experimentally checked in view of the availability of all their books and the fact that their founders lived in recent times. But we can legitimately suspect that these accusations may often, if not always, be false in the case of other older sects too. They are mainly based on three elements of doctrine "attributed" to the heretics (all three of which the good tailor falsely attributed to the present-day Baha'is), i.e., incarnation (*hulûl*), metempsychosis (*tanâsukh-i arvâh*), sexual licence, especially in the sense of marriage between very close relatives. Why these three points in particular rather than others?

But let us return to our study of the first "Shi'ite" movements (first in the sense that they began at is origins, at the end of the Umayyad period, 750 A.D.). We will take it for granted that the reader has at least a general knowledge of the early history of Islam and of what is meant by Shi'ism. At all events it should be remembered that by *shî'a* (implying 'Alî: 'Alî's "party") we intend the political movement that upheld the rights of 'Alî (the Prophet's son-in-law and father, through Hasan and Husain, of the only male descendants of Muhammad's family) to the Caliphate (a purely political-theocratic office of successor to the Prophet, not as prophet but as head of the Muslim community) or Imamate, as the Shi'ites later preferred to call it (from imâm, i.e., *praepositus*); rights that the Shi'ites considered had been usurped by the three first "elective" Caliphs, Abû Bakr, 'Umar and 'Uthmân. These struggles for succession took on vast proportions; great bloodshed occurred and Islam remained divided by it forever. At least in the early times political and religious Shi'ism remained distinct one from the other; the very first Shi'ites did not have special or heretical doctrines, nor, inversely, were all those who tended towards certain doctrines, known later as specifically Shi'ite, necessarily Shi'ite politically. Ibn Hazm's simple and very general definition of "Shi'ite" clearly indicates this: "He who agrees with the Shi'ites that 'Alî is the most excellent of men after the Prophet and that he and his descendants after him are more worthy of the Imamate than any other, is a Shi'ite, even if he does not agree with them in all their other doctrines." On the other hand, a few paragraphs further on Ibn Hazm maintains that there were doctrinal extremists (*ghulât*) among the Sunnis too and he quotes, among others, al-Hallâj (Friedlander, "Heterod.," pp. 32 and 34). Setting aside the purely political movements, the proto-Shi'ite religious movements can be reduced to the following (excluding minor currents and sub-sects).

We are told that already under 'Alî's Caliphate (656–661 A.D.) a man by name of 'Abdullâh ibn Sabâ, thought to be a southern Arabian Jew converted to Islam, venerated 'Alî too greatly and was exiled by him to Madâ'in (Ctesiphon) and said that 'Alî himself had some of his followers burned alive. Later, 'Abdullâh ibn Sabâ denied the Caliph's death, maintaining that a demon had been killed in his place and that he was hidden among the clouds. He preached his early return to guide the Arabs with his staff and bring justice on earth. The contradictions present in the sources concerning the events connected with this mysterious character and the prejudice that these ideas were incompatible with the "unpolished and primitive" period of early Islam have led some orientalists to deny the historical truth of this "'Abdullâh ibn Sabâ episode." In my opinion it is not at all impossible that these doctrines were already present in the early period. In the Qur'an we find both the divinization of founders of religions (Jesus, and also, for a mysterious and not better identified Jewish sect, Ezra, [cf. Kor. IX, 30]) and more or less eccentric Christian eschatological doctrines.

The following Qur'anic passage is interesting because it already reveals—in kernel—the Islamic criticism of this proto-*ghuluww* (religious extremism).

> "The Jews said: "Uzair is the son of God!" And the Christians said: "Christ is the son of God!" This they say with their mouths, imitating the way of speaking of those who opposed the faith. May God curse them! What grave error they have fallen into! They have taken their doctors (*ahbâr*) and their monks (*ruhbân*) and Christ the son of Mary as Lords (*arbâb*) in the place of God . . ."

There is an interesting allusion here to a "divinization" not only of Christ, but of priests, monks and leaders of sects as of something well known to Muhammad. There probably existed some *ghulât*—Jewish and Christian "extremists"—in Muhammad's time too among the Gnostic or semi-Gnostic sects that had spread in Arabia. There is nothing in fact in classical Judaic tradition that authorizes us to believe in any divinization of Esdra (if the problematic 'Uzair really is Esdra).

However our Jewish Muslim's sojourn in Madâ'in (Mesopotamia) is interesting as is the fact that, in kernel, his preaching contained the essential elements of the later Shi'ite doctrines. These included the idea of a specific sacredness or semi-divinity of the Leader, the idea of his "disappearance" and feigned death (*ghaiba*), the idea of his return "at the end" to put things in order and the persecution and death (facts rather than ideas) of the Leader himself.

After 'Alî's death and after the hated Umayyads had taken over the Caliphate, pro-'Alî revolts continued sporadically, always in Mesopotamia and especially around Kûfa. In 686–687 al-Mukhtâr[33] led a Shi'ite revolt that started in Kûfa and extended to the north of Mesopotamia. For those who deny the historicity of 'Abdullâh ibn Sabâ, it was the first Shi'ite rising with a specifically religious character. After Fâtima's sons (Hasan and Husain and their relative descendants), Al-Mukhtâr chose the younger branch as the legitimate descendant of 'Alî and pretender to the Imamate, i.e., Muhammad "son of the Hanafite" (Ibn al-Hanafîya), who turned out to care very little for this honor. Later, too, these discussions over the greater or lesser legitimacy of a succession, which was often taken as a pretext for subtle theological differences, were to be enormously important in the struggles between the Shi'ite sects. Al-Mukhtâr, who presented himself as a true prophet, preached specific religious elements at least one of which, the cult of the empty throne, had evidently an extra-Islamic origin. This cult involved the veneration of a so-called "throne of 'Alî" that was even used as an oracle. According to our sources, it was southern Arabian in origin (connected with the customs of Yemenite Jewish communities?), but it brings to mind the Manichaean *bêma* mentioned earlier on. Al-Mukhtâr's followers (whom the heresiographers knew as Kaysânites) placed particular importance on the person of the imâm, to whom they attributed occult lore (some people thought this was derived from his Fatimid step-brothers Hasan and Husain, though according to others he was the legitimate imâm after 'Alî, skipping his two more famous step-brothers) and semi-divine qualities. They also followed the doctrine known as *badâ*, which consisted in admitting that God could decide one thing first (for example to bestow the Imamate on a given person) and then "change his mind:" a concept that tallies with the atmosphere of the Qur'anic God. At Muhammad ibn al-Hanafîya's death the community split, as happened to almost all the Shi'ite sects, over questions of succession, the most interesting faction being the one that maintained that Muhammad ibn al-Hanafîya was not dead but had only disappeared and "was hidden" on the mountain of Radwa (seven days walk from Medina, in Arabia). This mysterious period of the disappeared imâm (who naturally was "to return at the end of time" to save his community and convert the world) is sung by the Kaisânite poets Kuthayyir and as-Sayyid. Here is a passage by as-Sayyid (quoted in Friedlander, "Heterodoxies," II, p. 37):

And years and months (have passed) . . . But He still can be seen at Radwa in a deep cavern among panthers and lions.
He dwells in flowering gardens while gazelles with shining black eyes and young ostriches wander together with ashen-grey goats, when the sun sets.
And wild beasts graze with them, and yet no-one assaults them to tear them to pieces with sharp claws.
By His grace they are safe from destruction and graze together without fear in the same pasture and drink at the same source.

Another source (Baghdâdî, quoted in Friedlander, op. cit., II, p. 35), describing the imâm's mysterious period at Radwa, says: "And near him there are a source of water and a source of honey from which he takes his nourishment. And on his right he has a lion and on his left a panther to protect him from his enemies." While the first description brings to mind the well-known passage in Isaiah (XI) the second brings to mind a rough icon representing a legendary Christian saint. If not the first person to introduce the idea of the mahdî, Mukhtâr was the first to give it a concrete form in a historical character—Muhammad ibn al-Hanafîya—and I don't believe we have to go too far to discover its origin, which lies evidently in a Christian or, more exactly, sectarian Christian idea. An important aspect of Mukhtâr's movement was that it relied (as all the sources agree) on non-Arab elements and tended towards social egalitarianism; but the non-Arabs (the so-called *mawâlî*, clients) of Iraq were not all necessarily Persian. A curious piece of information referred to in one of Ibn Hazm's manuscripts (Friedlander, op. cit., p. I, 78) relates that the Kaisânite poet as-Sayyid (from whom we quoted a passage above) answered the question: "Who shares these doctrines with you?" with "a shoemaker from Rayy." Is this an apocryphal tale to discredit the poet? Or a sarcastic answer to free himself from a bore? What is significant however is the allusion to the Persian city. The two

Kaisânite poets, and especially Kuthayyir, apparently believed in the transmigration of souls. The Kaisânites also followed another extreme doctrine preached by a member of the sect who declared, after Muhammad ibn al-Hanafîya's death, that he himself was both God and his prophet. This "doubling of the image" of the divine founder is very characteristic of the extreme sects and we run into it, with other names and under other aspects, even in modern Bâbism and Baha'ism (see Chapter VIII).

Other Kaisânites supported the Imamate of one of Muhammad ibn al-Hanafîya's sons, who died however without descendants, thus further complicating the confused picture of this ancient Shi'ite sect. According to the sources many of the sub-sects that grew out of this situation insisted that the divine spirit was incarnated in their own imâm. It is interesting to note that some of these Hâshimite sects (from Muhammad ibn al-Hanafîya's son, whose name was Abû Hâshim) maintained that at the death of their own imâm the Imamate could easily go out of 'Alî's family.

And here we have an interesting point: the "extreme" doctrines (the divinization of the imâm, etc.) were not necessarily linked with 'Alî's family during these early years of Shi'ism. In 745 a man called 'Abdullâh ibn Mu'âwiya (who was not one of 'Alî's direct descendants) rebelled against the Umayyads and rapidly became ruler of a state in Fârs (Persia). He was killed after two years by the Abbasid propagandist Abû Muslim with whom he had taken refuge. According to all the heresiographers his preaching included claiming the imâm's successive divine incarnations and his divinity, the negation of resurrection and future life (though this doctrinal point was frequently attributed to this kind of heresiarch), the allegorical interpretation of religious precepts and the nonfulfillment of the religious practices of Islam.

Among the followers of the Husaini pretenders to the Caliphate (i.e., the descendants of Husain son of 'Alî, who was killed at Karbalâ in 680) the movement of Mughîra ibn Sa'îd al-'Ijli stands out for its singular doctrines. He supported the Imamate of Husain's son, Muhammad al-Bâqir, apparently declaring him to be God himself and he (Muhammad) his prophet. He was killed at Kûfa in 737, about ten years before 'Abdullâh ibn Mu'âwiya's revolt. According to Ibn Hazm, Mughîra maintained that his God "had the form of a man with a crown (other sources add of "light") on his head and his limbs corresponded to the letters of the alphabet, the aleph (*alif*) corresponding, for example, to his thighs . . . ." He also maintained that his God, when he decided to create the world, "pronounced the supreme name, which fell on his crown. Then he wrote men's actions—both good and bad—with his finger, on the palm of his hand. But when he observed the bad actions he began to sweat (in fear) at their number. Two lakes grew out of this sweat, one brackish and dark, the other sweet tasting and luminous. Then he looked in the lake and contemplated his shadow. He tried to catch it but it fled from him. Finally he caught up with it and seized it. He gouged the eyes out of his shadow and, mincing them, created the sun with them and another sun. He created the infidels out of the brackish lake and the faithful out of the sweet tasting lake, with an ample mixture of both." (Friedlander, op. cit., I, 59–60).

Also in this case al-Mughîra's "god" (the Imâm al-Bâqir) seems to have had nothing to do with his revolt, and the "moderate" Shi'ites too execrated his doctrines (Friedlander, II, 80). Their Gnostic origin is evident: the crown plays an important role in the Jewish Cabbala, the man of light in Mandaeism, God formed by a body of letters is described by Irenaeus (Adv. Haer., XIV, 3) in connection with certain Gnostics and it is to be found in late Judaism too; the creation of the world through the pronunciation of the Most Great Name also belongs to Gnosticism (Irenaeus, ibid., XIV, 1, concerning Mark) and to Jewish cabalistic mysticism (cf. the Sefer Yetzîrâh). The fall of the Most Great Name onto the crown (according to other, better, versions of the myth, "on his head, like a crown") is to be found in the Cabbala too in the sense of the "Name inscribed on" the crown. The two lakes, the tears and the sweat are also present in the mythologies of certain Gnostic sects where—more logically and systematically in fact—one of the lakes is formed by the tears and the other by the sweat of "divine beings" and they correspond to the two waters—dark waters and luminous waters—of the Mandaeans.[34]

The curious idea of the god who looks at his reflection is, among other things, also Mandaean (Brandt, *Mandaïsche Schriften*, p. 184) and, in a slightly different form, the idea of the fleeing image is Gnostic too (Irenaeus, ibid., XIV, 1).

Without wasting time with minor movements we now come to the Khattâbîya movement, named after the founder Abû'l-Khattâb, who fomented a political and religious rebellion in the Kûfa area and was impaled in 755–6 in the early days of the Abbasid Caliphate. He followed the famous Imâm Ja'far as-Sâdiq (702–765) (another of Husain's direct descendants and therefore a descendant of the Prophet) who, even for the moderate Shi'ites, was one of the legitimate imâms of the Muslim community. Here too, Abû'l-Khattâb claimed the incarnation (*hulûl*) of the divinity in Ja'far, despite the latter's protests. The sect did not die out after his death and the defeat of his followers, who had trusted in his promise of certain victory and had fought against the lances and swords of the Caliph's army with stones, sticks and knives. They were supported by the usual belief in the founder's apparent death and his return, and over 150 years later there were still about 100,000 Khattâbites around Kûfa and in far-away Yemen. As for their doctrines, it seems that at one point Abû'l-Khattâb declared that he himself (and not Abû Ja'far) was the incarnation of God. This transfer occurred—in the same way that Shi'ite tradition described Muhammad's "nomination" of 'Alî as his legitimate "vicar"—through his explicit nomination by

Ja'far. It is more likely however that the relationship between Ja'far and Abû'l-Khattâb was that of God to Prophet (as it had been between Ibn al-Hanafîya and al-Mukhtâr). The heresiographers have emphasized the harshness of his doctrines against "infidel" enemies (i.e., all those who did not follow his ideas). Non-Khattâbites had to be killed and false testimony was obligatory. As usual the doctrine of metempsychosis and the abolition of the common Islamic law, rituals and morals has been attributed to them.

Summing up, we agree with Moscati's conclusions on the religious characteristics of the early Shi'ite movements, which are as follows:

1. Where these early Shi'ite movements are concerned the classic heresiographical three-fold division into a moderate, an intermediate and an extreme Shi'ism does not hold. Primitive religious Shi'ism was all more or less enthusiastic, pre-theological and tinged with doctrines that we will find later in the classic extreme Shi'ism and which the heresiographers called *ghuluww*, "exaggeration," above all an exaggeration in the divinization of the imâm.

2. This tendency towards *ghuluww* is not necessarily linked with the direct branch of 'Alî's descendants. On the contrary, the imâm-god was often either a member of the collateral branch of 'Alî's descendants or even someone who did not belong to the family at all but who arrogated to himself these charisms. Besides their importance in explaining the origin of the strange Yazîdî sect, the texts collected by Guidi and others[35] show how, after the fall of the Umayyad Caliphate, the "incarnationist" tendency also coagulated around people belonging to the party that opposed the Shi'ites, i.e., the Umayyads. In the best case the person whom the enthusiasts wished to consider God was almost always indifferent to this enthusiasm, in the worst, he had those who adored him massacred as madmen. The later case of the Abbasid Caliph al-Mansûr is a good example of this (besides those mentioned above). In 745–55 (according to other sources, in 759) he was besieged by a group of Râwandîya, the adepts of a sect from Khurâsân (eastern Persia), who professed that the divinity was incarnated in him and insisted on adoring him. Unable to persuade them of their mistake he ordered about two hundred of them to be thrown into prison. Their infuriated companions broke into the prison, freed them and hurled themselves against the Caliph, who barely escaped with his life! In this extreme case the person involved seems almost a pretext for triggering off a "personalist" religious enthusiasm.

3. All these movements considered the imâm a God or a Prophet, but in at least two cases a splitting of the image of the divine manifestation is documented. One of them is God, the other is his "apostle" (*rasûl*). Therefore either God is considered anthropomorphically or the prophet too is a hypostasis or divine emanation. The Apostle of Light, incarnated in Mani etc., appears to be the prototype of this concept, the last heir of the Iranian angelism that tended more and more to attribute to angels the material form of physical or historical persons.

4. They await the mahdî. The lost Imâm who will return at the end of the world.

5. Some believe in metempsychosis.

6. They interpret the precepts of canon law allegorically and therefore do not observe them, just as they do not believe in future life, interpreting the texts that concern it as allusions to the mahdî's future return to this earth; in some cases they do not observe the moral laws.

These movements have two other characteristics in addition to their doctrines: (a) the religious movements were normally supported by non-Arab elements (Jewish, Mesopotamian, Iranian, sometimes from the lower social classes). (b) They all originated in Mesopotamia, and more precisely in the city of Kûfa, and within this city the group (or tribe) of the Banû 'Ijl seems to have played a particularly important role in the "extremist" risings. Several of the agitators we have studied belonged to this tribe that was partly Christian but later was subjected to strong Iranian influences (art. "'Ijl" in *EI*): al-Mughîra, Abû Mansûr (who proclaimed himself imâm after Muhammad al-Baqîr, more or less during al-Mughîra's period), 'Umar ibn Bayân, a follower of Abû'l-Kattâb; and Abû Muslim—the famous Abbasid propagandist, who played a singular though involuntary role in the Khurramite type of risings—was a client of the Banû 'Ijl, too.

If we compare this data with the data on the Persian movements we studied earlier and which closely followed these first Shi'ite movements chronologically, certain facts will become clear to us:

In the first place the doctrines the heresiographers generally attributed to these movements are more or less the same. Above all else is, "incarnationism," from which in a sense all the others derive; metempsychosis derives from the idea, shared by many of these sects, of a return of the former imâm in the succeeding one; the ample use of allegorism and the disregard for the letter of canon law derive from the fact that these "incarnationist" eccentricities had to be justified with specific exegesis. Only a study of the original texts of these sects—if there were any—could prove the accuracy or falsity of the accusations brought against them by orthodoxy, but we do not possess them, and this is a serious handicap. A rather informal channel may however help us to partly overcome this and may offer some useful indications, i.e., a study and comparison of the texts of the later "extreme" sects—e.g., Ismailism and others—of which we luckily have the originals and which, both in their general tendencies and in the accusations brought against them by orthodoxy, resemble these older tendencies.

Now a study of these texts, which we will briefly anticipate here though they will be dealt with more fully in the next chapter, lead to the quite likely conclusion that the three principal orthodox accusations are only partly exact. With only a few exceptions, even the most excessive extreme sects did not accept the unqualified identification of God with the imâm—i.e., *hulûl*, literally "descent," a technical term to indicate the substantial unity of humanity with the divinity. The later sects which could draw on the "metaphysics of light" for their speculations often spoke of "place of apparition" (*mazhar*), identifying the imâm with a very pure mirror which reflects the light of a sun (God in his essence) but remains very far away from man and cannot be incarnated.

The Muslims considered metempsychosis (*tanâsukh*) particularly hateful and, in al-Bîrûnî's words, a typical characteristic of Indian idolatrous thinking. What could be better than to apply it to one's theological enemies even when it was not present, at least in its more specific form! What was common to various extreme sects however was the concept of the "return" of groups of qualities— the repetition of a cosmic and prophetic cycle—as if new actors were interpreting an ancient drama. *Tanâsukh* also implies the sense of the "ability to become incarnate" in various bodies of the only divine spirit, and al-Hujvîrî (in *Kashfu'l-mahjûb*) attributes *tanâsukh* to Christians too, "even if they do not want to admit it."

As for the accusation of libertinism, this may be due to two orders of facts. One is the scandal orthodox Muslims felt over a certain freedom the women may have enjoyed traditionally and for ethnological reasons in some social areas; it is well-known even today that in a number of Islamic countries peasant women who have to work and participate in public life are far freer than city women and easily (and unjustly) accused of licentiousness by the extremely easily scandalized Muslims. The second order of ideas is a theological and abstract one. In the Islamic tradition what little is still known about the ancient Mazdean religion includes information on the *khvêtûkdâs*. The ease with which the heresiographers attribute (erroneously) the qualification of *majûs*, "Mazdean," to many heretics, together with an instinctive linking of Mazdaism with the *khvêtûkdâs*, explains the accusations of incestuous marriages attributed—probably wrongly—to many of these ancient heresies.

Despite this necessary whittling down, all these movements still contain a nucleus of doctrines whose origin does not lie within Islam. What is their origin?

If we combine the fact of the presence of non-Arab and low ranking elements in these movements, if we add that their geographical center was invariably Mesopotamia, if we bear in mind that we have documentation on the presence in the western Mesopotamian area of the ex–Iranian empire of syncretist currents whose doctrines included various trends—Judaic, Christian, Gnostic, Zoroastrian, Manichaean, Mandaean—which combined towards the constitution of a complex patrimony of religious ideas current in the Mesopotamian region, then the answer is clear. And the answer also implies criticism of overly superficial dilemmas: Iranian origin, or Judeo-Christian origin? We have seen that the Judaism and Christianity that already influenced primitive Islam in its Arab cradle certainly were not a "pure ancient" Judaism or an orthodox Christianity but Judeo-Christian currents that had already been abundantly "gnosticized." Consequently we can speak of an "Iranian" element in early Shi'ism, but always bearing in mind the fact that the term "Iranian" must be taken in the sense of a mediated influence (older than Iranism) on the formation of Gnostic syncretism. Even in the most established cases, the semi-Islamic neo-Mazdakite movements of a Khurramite type, we are never speaking of a real "Mazdaism" but rather of Manichaean-Mazdakite currents of the Iranian religion. After their founders had been destroyed by Mazdean orthodoxy these currents had probably been transformed—together with elements of a popular Iranian religion all but inaccessible to us—into a kind of popular religious substratum, especially in certain marginal areas of the Iranian territory (Khurâsân, Transoxiana).

And here we come to the less strongly Islamic movements we spoke about earlier on. In view of the doctrinal similarities of these movements with those of the early Shi'ites and the fact that they exploded, generally speaking, a little later with the Umayyad crisis and the advent of the Abbasids, I think that we can reverse certain opinions that were current for some time and declare that the Mesopotamian proto-Shi'ite religious movements of the Umayyad period gave their cues to those of the various Bihâfrîds, Muqanna's and Pâpaks. We have already seen how the non-Muslim Persians under an Islamic regime were far better acquainted with Islam and its problems than the Muslims were with the problems and religious ideas of Mazdaism. We must also add that—because of their distance from the center—the Khurâsân area and the eastern regions of the Iranian territory in general always offered a favorite place of refuge to the followers of defeated sectarians and that the Khurâsân area was the center of Abbasid propaganda against the Umayyads. This proximity may have attracted all those who were discontented with the Umayyad régime, including the dispersed remnants of the followers of the proto-Shi'ite sectarians. But this does not mean that we exclude the possibility of doctrines that could be called popular or Mazdakite, since they contributed to these Iranian proto-Shi'ite movements. In fact the socialistic-libertine aspect seems to have been more accentuated in them. What I think we must exclude is a direct influence of Iranian thought on the "incarnationist" beliefs of these movements, and, all the more, an Indian influence as claimed by old Kremer (*Gesch. der herrsch. Idee.*, p. 12 and foll.). Iranian influence—let us repeat it—was only present in a mediated form, that is, the ancient Mazdean angelic concept contributed considerably to the creation of Manichaean angelism, with its incarnationist tendencies, and was probably also a very important element in some forms of Christian and Judaic Gnosis.

Conclusion

We will end this presentation on the question of the origins of a truly Iranian Islam by saying that we have no precise information concerning it in the early years. For the entire span of eight centuries, from the Arab conquest until about 1500, most of the inhabitants of Persia remained Sunni, i.e., orthodox Muslim. The greatest poets and men of letters—to mention only Firdausî (whose alleged Shi'ism is doubtful), Khayyâm, Nizâmî, Sa'dî, Rûmî, Hâfiz, and Jâmî—were Sunni, and some of them even pious Sunnis. The embryonic proto-Shi'ite movements and doctrines we have examined in this chapter were forming during the first centuries (eighth through ninth) of the religious history of Islam, especially in the western and far eastern regions of the former Iranian Empire. They were affected, even if in a mediated and distant form, by an influence that can be called Iranian (within the limits we have seen in Chapter II) because of the Iranian character of Manichaeism. I mean by this the tendency to mythologize from above, and the Qur'anic inflexible unity of God in angelic groups that were visible in one or another Man-Mirror of God. Once the political movement that accompanied them had been suffocated, some of these currents survived and fermented, contributing—as one of the many elements at stake—to form the immensely rich and complex world of Persian Sufism. The originally disorderly and enthusiastic tendency to venerate the house of 'Alî cooled down and became a part of the great "middle" or Imami Shi'ite theology developed by Arabs and Persians together (later on, this form of Shi'ism, under the Safavids in the fifteenth through the sixteenth centuries, became Persian by adoption). The extreme exponents of the 'Alid loyalist tendency developed their doctrines in depth and enriched them with the contribution of Hellenistic philosophy and some undoubtedly Iranian elements after the period of the great translations, thus flowing into the great river of Ismaili Gnosis, which, especially in the tenth through the twelfth centuries, played an important part in the formation of Persian religious thinking. The fact that stirrings of extremism or *ghuluww* survived in the substratum of Persian religiosity is proved by the periodical resurgence in the history of Persian religion of enthusiastic "incarnationist" movements such as Alamût's Ismailism, the first enthusiastic Shi'ism of the Shâh Ismâ'îl period, and nineteenth century Bâbism, besides those we have studied in this chapter. They involve a distant trend that goes back—beyond Islam—to Mazdakism and Manichaeism, in which elements of popular religiosity that will unfortunately remain unknown may have played a part. But despite all these movements Islam maintained its privileged position and the esteem of the Persian people. Contrary to what some observers have maintained, confusing Arab with Muslim and influenced by orthodox heresiographers, any Persian reaction there may have been was anti-Arab rather than anti-Islamic.

This is true in particular of the great Shu'ûbîya movement, which coincided with the period of the first Abbasids and with the more important role played by the Persians in public offices and in the cultural life of the Caliphal empire. This movement was accompanied by religious reactions such as those we studied above, but they were not organically linked to it (in the ninth century a temporary renewed interest in theological studies also occurred among the Zoroastrians) and the more refined and aristocratic Persians may in fact have looked on them disparagingly as explosions of contemptible populism. Besides, some Persians even took sides with the Arabs in the dispute!

Consequently Persian Islam must be taken in a very broad sense, and rather as a Persian contribution to Muslim religious culture than as a conscious polemic reaction to Islam.

Notes

1. For a better acquaintance with Islam and the history of the Islamic peoples, we advise *Islamologia* by Pareja-Bausani-Hertling, Rome, 1951.
2. I have tried to demonstrate this in my article "Due citazioni del Corano nel Dênkart," in *Scritti in onore di G. Furlani*, Rome, 1957, pp. 455 and foll.
3. M. Guidi, *La lotta tra l'Islam e il manicheismo. Un libro di Ibn al-Muqaffa' contro il Corano confutato da al-Qâsim b. Ibrâhîm*, Rome, 1927.
4. For the confutation of the dualism of a later century see H. S. Nyberg, *Réfut: d'Ibn ar-Râwendi*, Cairo, 1935.
5. G. Weil, *Biblische Legenden der Muselmanner*, Frankfurt a. M., p. 35, quoted in Nallino, op. cit., p. 213.
6. Frazer (*Golden Bough*, III, "The Dying God," London, 1912, p. 63) attributes to Muslims the belief that falling stars are jinn or demons driven out by the angels that fall in flames from the sky. Nallino ("Etimologia araba e significato di asub e di azimut" *RSO* VIII, p. 384, no.3) rightly points out that this is an error from a Qur'anic point of view: in the Qur'an the falling stars are not demons but are hurled against the demons. The Pahlavî text seems curiously to confirm Frazer's error (which possibly was based on folkloristic data more similar to the ancient Iranian myth).
7. Cf. *Vispered* I, 1, with a Pahlavî commentary; Y.13.1 and foll.; *Vidêvdât*, chap. XIII.
8. For this see Goldziher's old-fashioned but still useful "Islamisme et Parsisme", in *R.H.R.* See also Widengren, *Muhammad the Apostle of God and his Ascension*, Uppsala, 1955; especially chaps. VII-VIII.
9. Cf. *Zardushtnâmeh*, Rosenberg ed., p. 57.
10. In the *Bundahishn*. Cf. Messina, in *Orientalia*, p. 278.
11. Ibid., pp. 273–74.
12. Cf. Qur'an XCIX, 2 and *Zardushtnâmeh*, Rosenberg ed., v. 1399. Here the weights are the "hidden treasures" (see some of the Qur'anic commentators).
13. See also Ditlef Nielson, *Der dreieininge Gott in religions historischer Beleuchtung*, Copenhagen, 1922, in which an alleged "Semitic" idea of God the Father, God the Mother and God the Son is mentioned.

14. See however J. W. Sweetman, *Islam and Christian Theology*, Pt I, vol. 1, London, 1945, pp. 14–25, who maintains that even the biblical concept of the succession of different prophets is enough to explain this Qur'anic idea.

15. Cf. Schrieke, "Die Himmelsreise Muhammads," in *Der Islam*, VI, 1916, pp. 1 and foll. See Propp, *Le radici storiche dei racconti di fate*, Italian ed., Torino, 1949, pp. 151–58. The distant origin of this legend seems to lie in initiation rites.

16. For Islam, see the hadiths collected in Goldziher, *Abhandlungen zur arabischen Philologie*, I, Leiden, 1896, pp. 46 and foll.

17. Cf. E. Cerulli, *Il libro della Scala*, Città del Vaticano, 1949.

18. On this see my article "Postille a Cor. II, 248–XXXIX, 23–XX, 15," in *Studi Orientalistici in onore di G. Levi della Vida*, Roma, 1956, vol I, pp. 32 and foll. and ibid. (vol II, pp. 58 and foll.), I. Lichstenstadter, "Origin and interpretation of some qur'anic symbols."

19. Schaeder, in "Gnomon," 9/1933, p. 345.

20. Ibn Rustah, *Kitâb al-a'lâq an-nafîsa*, p. 217, 9–10, cf. T. Andrae, *Muhammad*, p. 146 and foll.

21. *Risâla* 95, quoted in Massignon, *Term Techn.* He quotes *istabrach, sundus, abâriq, namâriq*, which are to be found mainly in paradisiacal descriptions.

22. Salemann, *Mélanges asiatiques*, t. IX, p. 453 and foll. in Houtsma, "Bihafrid," *WZKM*, III, 1889, pp. 30 and foll.

23. On him and on other such movements see a bibliography of the sources in the works of B. Spuler, quoted in *Bibliografia*, pp. 196 and foll.

24. The awaited restorer of the world in Muslim eschatology.

25. Sources in Spuler, op. cit., p. 197.

26. For a discussion on the sources see Moscati, "Studi storici sul califfato di al-Mahdî," in *Orientalia* XIV (1945) pp. 333 and foll. Further sources in Spuler, op. cit., p. 109, note.

27. A short Muslim prayer used when something dreadful or a blasphemy is uttered.

28. As we have seen, the "white-clad ones" were apparently a sect with Mazdakite tendencies existed even before the appearance of the Veiled One.

29. Frye in *History of Bukhârâ*, Cambridge, Mass., 1954, p. 147 quotes a number of classic examples of sexual promiscuity and homosexuality in central Asia.

30. A text in *Description . . . de Boukhara par Muhammad Nerchakhy*, texte persan publié par Ch. Schefer, pp. 63 and foll. Frye (quoted in the previous note) has made a recent English translation of the book. On the veiled prophet and men's veils see A. Bombachi, "Gli Oghuz velati," in *Folklore*, Napoli, 1956. This article includes Turkish, Arab and Persian material on the veil, showing how the Turkish information is probably derived from Arab-Persian tales. According to Moscati, who quotes some cases of "veiled gods" in the Ancient East, the use of the sacred veil came from Syro-Mesopotamian centers. Spuler's hypothesis (*Iran in frühislamischer Zeit*, p. 198), according to which customs such as the veil of Muqanna' contributed to the representation of the veiled prophet Muhammad, are not convincing: if anything a previous tendency explains both things. In my opinion the two motifs—that of the fine knight of the stories who covered his face to avoid the evil eye and that of the "sacred" veil of the type Muqanna' wore— have two different origins.

On Muqanna's movement see the extremely useful comprehensive study by the Soviet orientalist A. Ju. Jakubovskij, "Vosstanie Mukanny, Dvizvenie ljudej v 'belyh odezdah'" (Muqanna's revolt and the movement of the "White-Clad Ones"), *Sovetskoe*

Vostokovedenie V, Moscow-Leningrad, 1948, pp. 35–54.
31. See D. Wright, in *Moslem World*, 1948.
32. For this see Moscati's excellent and lucid study, "Per una storia dell'antica si'a," in *RSO* XXX (1955), pp. 251 and foll. which we have referred to repeatedly. The volume also contains an important up-dated bibliography.
33. V. Van Gelder, *Mohtâr, de valsche profeet*, Leiden, 1888.
34. Ireneo, ibid., IV, 2; *Talmud Hagiga*, 13 b, *Bereshîth Rabba*, chap. LXXVIII; Brandt, *Mandäische Rel.*, pp. 30, 43, 51 etc.
35. "Sull'origine dei yazîdî" *RSO* XIII, 1932. See also Ch. Pellat, "Le culte de Mu'âwiya au II siècle de l'Hégire," *Studia Islamica*, VI (1956), pp. 53 and foll.

Bibliography

We have quoted our principal sources here and there in the text itself. The most important and recent general study on Iran (which includes a religious section) is B. Spuler, *Iran in frühislamischer Zeit*, Wiesbaden, 1952. It is difficult reading but it contains an ample bibliography.

Additional Bibliography

For further information on early heterodox Shi'ism, see Marshall G.S. Hodgson, "How did the early Shi'a become Sectarian?" *Journal of the American Oriental Society*, 75 (1955): 1–13; W. Montgomery Watt, *Islamic Philosophy and Theology* (Edinburgh, 1962); Elton L. Daniel, *The Political and Social History of Khurasan under Abbasid Rule, 747–820* (Minneapolis, 1979); Said Amir Arjomand, *The Shadow of God and the Hidden Imam*, (Chicago, 1984); and Moojan Momen, *An Introduction to Shi'i Islam* (New Haven, Conn. 1985).

Chapter Four

Ismailism, Falsafa (Philosophy), and Sufism

Introduction

In the preceding chapter we studied the origins of the teeming religious world generically called Shi'ism. Political Shi'ism—we repeat—must be clearly distinguished from religious Shi'ism; or rather, since Shi'ism is technically spoken of as a political–cum–religious movement, religious Shi'ism could be defined more exactly as a religious tendency focused on the imâm. For the imâm, the Religious Leader and source of authority, is at the center of the speculation and faith (in a political sense) of both Shi'ite and non-Shi'ite movements of this kind. Little by little they became systematized into a moderate, a middle and an extreme Shi'ism. Moderate Shi'ism or Zaidism (moderate because of the relatively lesser weight given to the imâm's sacred power) was on the whole of secondary importance in Iran, if we except the period after 864 A.D. in which a Zaidi state was created in the region south of the Caspian sea. This area had—significantly—remained resistant to Islamic religious penetration for almost two centuries after the conquest. The fundamental characteristic of middle Shi'ism (also called by the disagreeable and hybrid term of "Twelver Shi'ism") is that it asserts that the legitimate series of the imâms—'Alî's descendants—ended in the year 874, with the disappearance into the "well of Samarra" of the last one, the mysterious Muhammad. This current only imposed itself in the sixteenth century and it became the Persian religious current *par excellence* in the modern Islamic world, even though its origins were not linked with Iranian culture and Iran only gave it some interesting philosophers and great popular enthusiasm. We will study some of its aspects further in the following chapters.

There was also extreme Shi'ism—extreme in its veneration of, and the metaphysical and cosmological importance it gave to, the imâm. Its main current is best known as Ismailism, from the imâm Ismâ'îl, son of Ja'far as-Sâdiq, the sixth imâm (if we call 'Alî the first) who died prematurely shortly before 765 and whose son the "Ismailis" recognized as legitimate imâm instead of his brother Mûsâ Kâzim, whom the others (the "Twelvers") recognized. As usual, these dynastic questions were merely pretexts that masked deeper ideological divergences (we will see this more clearly later). Though Ismailism cannot be defined a purely Iranian movement, its doctrines include many more profoundly Iranian components than the more fortunate Twelver Imamism. The Iranian current of Ismailism soon produced religious literature in Persian using material that according to some scholars (Ivanow) goes back to the eighth century, and came to number among its ranks remarkable thinkers such as the poet Nâsir-i Khusrau (d. 1061).

In 909 Ismailism created a political empire for itself, the Fatimid state centered in Egypt. This state collapsed in 1130 with the death of the last Fatimid imâm, al-'Amir. In 1094 a schismatic group had already arisen that recognized Nizâr as legitimate imâm instead of his younger brother Musta'lî, whom their father apparently preferred and who had broken away from Fatimid Ismailism. These Nizârîs had been particularly fortunate in Persia, where they occupied the fortress of Alamût or "Eagle's Nest" in the mountains south of the Caspian Sea and created a chain of castles and a secret organization. They apparently posed a credible threat to the entire established power of the already crumbling Abbasid Empire until, in 1257, both the Ismailis of Alamût and their traditional enemies and persecutors, the Abbasid Caliphs, were destroyed by the Mongols.

In its early years Ismailism—as a religion—had been a basically Mesopotamian, esoteric, Imami gnosis with some traces of Iranian influence. With the great rage for translations from Greek and Syrian that marked the years 870–910, the Islamic world was penetrated by Greek thinking or, rather, by the combination of Aristotelianism and neo-Platonism that had filtered eastwards from Hellenistic Greece through Syria and had already been promulgated (before the translations) in a Hermetic and Pythagorean form in Islam by the pagan, star-worshipping Sabaean philosophers of Harrân.

Iran contributed prominent personalities to this Hellenized form of thinking—the so-called *falsafa*, an Arabized form of the Greek *philosophía*—among whom Avicenna (d. 1037) and Râzî (d. 1209) stand out. This Greek way of thinking was adopted and adapted by Ismailism. The Ismaili tendency was followed in the great hellenizing encyclopedia of the "Brothers of Purity" (Ikhwân as-Safâ), composed in the Basra region of lower Mesopotamia in the middle of the tenth century, though it was more neo-Platonic and Hermetic-Pythagorean than Aristotelian. And Ismailism at least partially influenced the son of an Ismaili, the young Avicenna.

Avicenna's philosophy or *falsafa* raised certain problems, among them the possibility of a mysticism based on a clearly Iranian "metaphysics of light" that also contained motifs with Ismaili tendencies. These problems were resolved by the great thinker Suhravardî the "Slain" (d. 1191)—one of the few representatives of the period and currents studied in this chapter who felt "consciously" Iranian and also consciously in debt to a Mazdean tradition. I say "also" because his thought was a remarkably profound and original synthesis of mysticism, Hellenism, Iranism and Imami Gnosis.

Thus, imperceptibly, we have moved into the field of mysticism, or Sufism, as Islamic mysticism is usually called. By now it has been demonstrated that early Sufism had nothing racially or religiously Iranian about it. On the contrary, born autonomously from the constant study of certain Qur'anic passages (and, besides, was not Muhammad himself a mystic at heart? Which of the "prophets" was not, to some extent?) it was enriched and grew in depth particularly through contact with neo-Platonism and Christianity. But it is also true that after the catastrophe that overcame Persian Ismailism at Alamût (1257) it began to dissolve into Sufism, tinging it to some extent with its theosophical vocabulary. Mystical poems by pious Sufis (who were sometimes Sunni, as well) and treatises on Sufism were interpreted in an Ismaili fashion, while the Ismailis consider one of the greatest Persian Sufis, 'Attâr (who died around 1230), one of their masters. This also explains the birth of legends (which possibly contain a grain of truth) such as the one by which Shams-i Tabrîz—the mysterious master and initiator of Jalâlu'd-Dîn Rûmî—was the son of Hasan III, one of the Grand Masters of Alamût and later an Ismaili imâm[1].

Persia gave some of its greatest philosopher-poets to Sufism: 'Attâr, Jalâlu'd-Dîn Rûmî, Jâmî, etc. and the whole of Persian classical poetry is steeped in Sufism (see the next chapter).

And so the ties that link these three great currents we will be dealing with now (extreme Imami Gnosis, Iranized Aristotelian-neo-Platonic-Pythagoric philosophy and Sufism) are inextricable. Though they stem from different ways of thinking, they form a composite atmosphere that imbued the whole Persian philosophical and religious world of the tenth through the sixteenth centuries that however remained, officially, mainly Sunni. The importance of these currents—which have lasted, basically, to the present day—is such that it justifies the greater length and range of this chapter as well as the long aesthetic-religious appendix that forms the next chapter. To make our task easier we have preferred to dwell on some of the very great personalities of the various currents, leaving others out. For often the description and exemplification of one vital and personal experience can give the layman a better idea of a movement than an overly general synthesis that assumes a knowledge of the details.

If we want to thoroughly understand the religious positions we are about to consider we must penetrate into the mind of a religious Muslim of the eighth through tenth centuries and reason more or less as follows. The Qur'an offers me four elements of revelation: (1) A supremely transcendent God, without intermediaries; (2) A God who also reveals himself to me as a living and active person; (3) A God who sends prophets to enlighten humanity which would remain in darkness if they did not periodically come into the world. (4) A God who is "light of heaven and earth." If—as is logical for our religious person— all authority comes from on high, from God, and if it is God's scope to guide humanity towards his goals through his prophets, then he cannot have left humanity, at the death of the last prophet, Muhammad, without an authoritative guide, as unique as he himself is, to convey divine orders from on high down to earth. Muhammad must have appointed someone to be "God's representative," possibly different from himself but with the same teaching authority as he had; the world cannot remain for one instant without an authoritative, infallible, religious leader. If this were not so God would have mocked humanity, and this idea is absurd. This view, generally speaking, characterizes the Shi'ites. It is almost impossible to conceive God's personality in absolute transcendence (this reasoning was especially valid after the introduction of Hellenistic philosophy): God's essence is, in its transcendence, unknowable, but it manifests itself on earth in different persons. The Religious Leader is the person of God, his limbs (His hand, His face) are God's limbs—those same limbs of God that are mentioned in the Qur'an. And, bearing in mind that though God is a person he is omnipresent light and creator, the person of Perfect Man is the Cosmos itself and his limbs and faculties are the heavens, the heavenly bodies and the earth. This is the extreme Ismaili position. And again, God's absolute personality can be driven so far that there is no room left for other real persons who are not God. This becomes a kind of extreme voluptuousness of self-negation and of the affirmation of God alone, which descends directly from the accentuation of God's transcendent rule and the absolute dependence of his "servant" (i.e., man)—an accentuation of the unity and unicity of God that leads to the affirmation that even man's autonomous existence is polytheism. And, finally, God's very transcendence is driven so far that only man's nothingness, the annihilation of all that is not God, can save it. Everything is one, because everything is transcendence. Here we have "pantheistic" Sufism, which could be more aptly called "theophanic" Sufism.

There are sufficient pretexts in the Qur'an to justify these positions: external influences have simply sharpened the contours, enriched the symbols and myths, outlined certain directions more clearly. Besides, already in ancient times, the most "Iranian" of these influences—the influence of the "metaphysics of light" and of "fire"—had travelled beyond the confines of Iran and fertilized the world of Mesopotamian syncretism.

The *Ummu'l-Kitâb* and the First Persian Ismailism

We will not describe and discuss the various theories proposed by orientalists on the origins of Ismailism here; the curious reader will find them listed in Lewis's *Origins of Ismailism* (Cambridge, 1940). We will only say that according to most recent studies it appears that the nucleus of the religious doctrines of early Ismailism stemmed from the Imâms al-Bâqir and Ja'far as-Sâdiq, mentioned in the last chapter, i.e., in Khattâbîya and Mughîrîya circles. Ivanow stresses the Khattâbîya contribution, considering Abû'l-Khattâb the undoubted founder of Ismailism. Though I believe that the adoration of al-Bâqir stressed in the al-Mughîra circles should not be overlooked.

Early Persian Ismailism presents us with a problem-book: the *Ummu'l-Kitâb*. Its title means "Mother of the Book," "Original Book." It was written in archaic Persian and isolated groups of Ismailis still living in the far away provinces of upper Oxus and Pamir in Central Asia consider it one of their most sacred texts. Russian scholars discovered it at the beginning of this century and the great Russian expert in Ismailism V. Ivanow made an in-depth study of it in 1932[2] and also brought out an edition of the Persian text.[3]

A first observation is necessary. Although, as we said, the Ismailis (or at least an isolated and therefore all the more "archaically oriented" group) consider the book sacred, it is never quoted in Ismaili literature and presents doctrines that differ in many points from the organized Ismaili theology of the two branches of the movement. This fact, besides a number of other peculiarities of style and contents, led Ivanow to believe that it was not an Ismaili but rather a proto-Ismaili work dating from a period of seething ideas and symbols prior to the theological systematization influenced by Greek thinking, and therefore going back to the tenth or eleventh century A.D..

At the beginning of the book an Abû'l-Khattâb is mentioned as semi-divine and the whole book fits into a framework-story that presents the Imâm al-Bâqir as a child accomplishing outstanding miracles and manifesting himself as divine theophany. If we add to this the fact that the context of the book indicates that the writer seemed most familiar with the regions of Mesopotamia and in particular southern Mesopotamia, we can at least agree with Ivanow that the work originated among proto-Shi'ite Mesopotamian sects (see the preceding chapter). If this is true, the book is extremely important because on the one hand it gives us a clearer picture of the theories these unfortunate heresiarchs followed and on the other it constitutes the missing link in the chain that unites them with Iranian Ismailism. For various reasons we find the attribution of the work to solely Khattâbîya circles less convincing. Firstly—according to heresiographical sources—Abû'l-Khattâb maintained the divinity of the Imâm

Ja'far as-Sâdiq and not that of al-Bâqir his father, while this book opens with the imaginative and fantastic tale of al-Bâqir's theophanies (thus pointing more towards al-Mughîra). Secondly, the book contains several unusual theories attributed to al-Mughîra (such as God seen as a macroanthropus with limbs corresponding to different parts of the cosmos (see the preceding chapter). Thirdly, the *Ummu'l-Kitâb* is full of unusual "Iranian" elements (including linguistic ones) that probably were extraneous to the Khattâbîya and Mughîrîya movements. In a later work Ivanow even went as far as to situate the book in the eighth century,[4] which seems excessive to us for a number of reasons. In fact, the very attribution of the entire book to the tenth century goes too far. The source material is not uniform; the oldest parts almost certainly go back to the eighth century, but there are a number of additions. The material was probably developed in southern Iraq in Khattâbîya and Mughîrîya circles and brought from there—through many vicissitudes that have not come down to us—as far as eastern Persia, where it certainly suffered Iranian-Manichaean additions. Elements in the language and doctrine would lead one to believe this.

We will start by observing the language from this point of view: the *Ummu'l-Kitâb* presents some singular surprises. It is the only post-Islamic Iranian text to repeatedly use the old Pahlavî and Avestan term *urvar*—plant—by the side of *nabâtât*, its Arabic synonym. Post-Islamic Persian had completely abandoned the old term. The only explanation for this is that these passages are translations of excerpts in a Middle Iranian language: Pahlavî? Manichaean Soghdian? I would opt rather for this second hypothesis, both because of where the text is preserved and the abundant Manichaean material it contains. Another singular linguistic term that appears twice in the *Ummu'l-Kitâb* is *kundû*. In one passage (Ivanow, pp. 4–104) we have the "unbelievers, who are of Ahriman's *kundû*." The many variations and the annotation "i.e., Satan's great earthenware vase" indicate that the word was no longer understood and sounded strange to the copyists (*kundû*—a term not used in Persian—is listed in some old dictionaries with this meaning of "vase"). The other passage in which we find the term brings us closer to its real meaning. Speaking of the creation of the world it says, among other things, that "these beasts and animals and the mountains and the hills and the *urvar* and the plants and the body (*kâlbud*) too, come from Ahriman's *kundû*." It ought not to be difficult to identify the mysterious *kundû* of the text. The Manichaean idea that the origin of all things was the "demon Kundag's skin" (*Kundag Druj*) is quoted in the "12 (Mazdean) precepts of Aturpat i Mahraspandân" (see Chapter II above) in the *Dênkart* (ed. Madan, p. 217; see the analysis of the passage in Menasce, ShGV, p. 231). The part of the Shkand Gumânîk Vichâr devoted to criticism of Manichaeism also says (ed. Menasce, pp. 252–3) that, according to the Manichaeans,

. . . heaven is made of the skin, the earth of the flesh, the mountains of the bones and the plants (*urvar*) of the hair of the demon Kunî (*Kunî Dêv*) . . . Kunî is Ahriman's general who at the beginning of the first battle, swallowed the light emanated by the God Ohrmazd. At the time of the second battle Kunî and many other *dêv* were taken and some were fixed to the Sphere, while Kunî was killed. The Macrocosm (*dâm-i* [b]**uzurg*) was thus taken and made by him[5].

This must therefore be a Manichaean myth, though Ivanow seems to have missed the point for he is surprised by this *kundû* (which should probably be read as Kundav, i.e., Kuni-dêv) and speaks of "Zoroastrianism" (in a note to *Notes*, p. 456). It is interesting to see that a Parthian text contains the proper name *'Kndg*—the name of a sinister character representing Ahriman in a story in the form of Jâtaka—while in Soghdian *kwntk* is a common name for "demon."

These unmistakably Iranian linguistic traces in the *Ummu'l*-Kitâb lead us to look for others in the present, late form (which is occasionally corrupted by the copyists). I will quote only two in order to avoid over-technical details. The first is *zaryûn* in the expression, on pp. 276–380, *dirakht sabz u zaryûn shud*: "the tree became green and fresh." Even though *zaryûn* is quoted in the classical Persian dictionaries that include unusual and Zoroastrian forms (see Steingass, p. 617) it is hardly ever used in common Persian (as is proved by the copyists' many variations) and corresponds exactly—both in meaning and form—to the Pahl. *zargôn*, *zargônak* (literally "golden color") used also to indicate how fresh and green plants are (Nyberg, Hilfsbuch, II, p. 253). The second adjective is *vash* in its sense of beautiful, good (often attributed to stars). This would indicate a really erroneous reading of the Pahlavî sign for *vêh* (good), which is almost identical to a *vash* (and *vash* itself is an erroneous reading of the sign registered in some dictionaries). All this appears to prove the existence of a Manichaean prototype in a middle-Iranian language for at least some parts of the *Ummu'l-Kitâb* and would also help us to understand some other "mysterious" terms (bungled by the copyists) in the book. For example, on pp. 29–79, where six stars symbolizing various faculties of the microcosm that recur at definite periods are mentioned, the words *naschîdarhâ*, *naschîdarmâh* and *nashîdar-tâbân* are at first sight inexplicable. But if we turn for a moment to Pahlavî writing, the names of the first two of the three final saviours (Oshêdar and Oshêdar-mâh) come almost naturally to our minds: in this form of writing Oshêdar can easily be read as Anshîdar. The closeness of Nashîdar to *nashîdarmâh* is too singular to be accidental and if we read the *Dênkart*, for example, (ed. Sanjana, Book VII, chaps. VIII, IX and the beginning of X) we find that Oshêdar and Oshêdar-mâh and the Saôshyant are connected when they appear at the end of the "rotation" (vartishnîh) of their respective cycles, with phenomena that easily assimilate them to heavenly bodies. With the advent of Oshêdar the sun stops in the sky for ten days, with the advent of Oshêdar-mâh it stops for twenty days and finally: "When the last rotation of the rotations of the era of Oshêdar-mâh will be completed that man, the Saôshyant, will be born, out of spiritual nourishment, out of the shape of the sun . . . who will look in every direction with six eyes." But a detailed examination of the Iranian elements in of the *Ummu'l-Kitâb* would lead us into technical byways inaccessible to our readers. We have already given sufficient proof that in all probability this text received a "loan" from texts written in a middle-Iranian language. Ivanow has rightly noted the many Manichaean doctrinal elements present in the book—though in a rather disorderly fashion and in a spirit strangely lacking in any understanding of esoterism. (This is an extraordinary fate for a scholar who devoted his entire life to the study of the most cabalistic and esoteric of the Islamic sects!) In many cases these elements find their precise and specific correspondences, i.e., the "trees of light" (*Notes*, p. 447), the "five [luminous] people" who form a group of five corresponding to the five members of the Manichaean Father of Greatness (and the use itself in this sense of the term "limbs" is Manichaean) (ibid. p. 448), the "sharp cry" of the Manichaean Living Spirit that corresponds to the cries and evocations in our text (p. 455), the transformation of the demons into animals, shells (p. 459), etc. Further study would easily reveal others; it is surprising, for example, that Ivanow missed the obvious Manichaean reference (cf. above, chap. II) in a passage in which (*Notes*, p. 460) Satan and his angels assume the form of a woman exciting the "dissidents" (*mu'tarizân*).

Now that we have established the probable origins and period of the text (which is in the form of a dialogue between the Imâm al-Bâqir and one of the faithful) let us consider the doctrine it contains. Two things in particular strike the reader. The first is the great freedom and sincerity with which the most "heretical" doctrines are proclaimed without even the slight "precautions" so often to be found in other Ismaili texts. The second is its considerably greater deviation from orthodox Islam than that of any other Ismaili text. The unknown author launches into mythological speculations with a wonderfully rich sense of color (all the colors of the rainbow appear in almost every line of the text); "psychological myth" reigns throughout it in the methodical search for correspondences between the limbs of the microcosm and the limbs of the macrocosm, so much so that an Indian influence might even be considered. Though the Gnostic-Mesopotamian-Manichaean origin of the ideas and contents of the book remains, the definitive version may have been written much later than Ivanow thought—possibly in India, from where the book (which may have been considered too dangerous by the more orthodox Ismailis) disappeared and was saved in the far-away and inaccessible Pamir valleys. But this problem will probably never be definitively resolved.[6]

I feel that the following doctrinal elements contained in this book (which does in fact deserve the name of "mysterious") are particularly important.

1. The central point (declared with disconcerting frankness) is that God has clearly defined and personal qualities and attributes, that God is "a person" (*shakhs*) and that, according to the Qur'an itself, he is "God in heaven and God on earth" (XLIII, 84), in the sense that the unknowable transcendent God is in heaven and the *déuteros theós*, the *ánthropos*, the *prótòktistos* personified in the Imâm is on earth[7]. But even before the creation God was a person of light (*shakhs-i nûrânî*) whose five parts—hearing, sight, smell, taste and word—were (or rather are, in as far as they are seen in history and on earth) Muhammad, 'Alî, Fâtima, Hasan and Husain. The various limbs of the luminous person of God have different colors; his right hand is the spirit of conservation and is the color of the sun, his left hand, which is violet, is the spirit of thought on whom depend the prosperity and length (*âbâdâni u dirâzî*, sic!) of all the spirits; the head, which is the Supreme Spirit, shines with a thousand colors.

2. This God with its various limbs can be considered from different aspects or planes; the one just described is the plane of divinity. The Sun is the same thing on the plane of luminosity (*mûrânîyat*), and the Soul sitting in the white sea that is the brain "the color of lightning, of cloud and of moon" (note the involuntary poetry of a dreadfully confused and formally arid text) is the same thing on the microcosmic plane. All the phenomena and manifestations are given a psychological explanation in the course of the book: the throne of God, the Ka'ba, the seven heavens and seven earths, etc., all are one of the limbs of the human body or one of the psychic faculties.

3. More specifically, God is 'Alî. At the beginning of the world God manifests himself in 'Alî; here too the adoration of this person produces a few involuntary flashes of poetry. As soon as 'Alî appeared in the sky, they all accepted him and the stars, the sun, the moon and the angels appeared. Then he appeared to the hills. The hills that accepted him were covered with flocks of sheep, fruit and good plants, and their wombs were full of minerals and gems. Those which did not accept him became arid rocks and peaks covered with thorns and wild animals, etc. This singular image of the creation is repeated for the other things of the world, including cities and jewels! But the story that forms the framework of the book shows how the Imâm al-Bâqir too was God. The five-year-old Bâqir is presented to us at school while he is answering the master's questions (on the cabalistic value of the letters of the alphabet) in such an amazing way that the Master bows down in adoration in front of his small but very great pupil and faints. When he recovers consciousness the Prophet himself is in front of him and not Bâqir; he faints repeatedly and sees further theophanies of Bâqir in 'Alî, Fâtima, Hasan and Husain. In the end al-Bâqir himself returns[8], thus completing a cycle of seven manifestations, the first and last of which are identical. Filled with enthusiasm, the master goes to the public square of the Mecca and proclaims Bâqir to be God. Bâqir himself and his father condemn him to death, even though they know that he told the truth; but the mystery must not be revealed.

4. The Creation is a luminous evocation. The descriptions are so realistic and vivid that they appear as phosphorescent sleights-of-hand and the author as a real visionary:

> In the first beginning which is the Eternal Lord (*Khudâvand-i jâvîd*) there was nothing else besides these five elected lights (*nûr-i khâss*) among which the Most High King (*malik ta'âlà*) manifested himself . . . What is now all these heavens and these earths was pure, limpid, thin, spiritual air (*havâ*). After these elect among the elect the five colors of the Judging Assembly (*Dîvân*) of the eternal Term of Terms (*ghâyatu'l-ghâyât*) appeared in 124,000 shadings of constantly changing color . . . Then the lofty King let out a cry (*âvâz*) to the right and let out a cry to the left and those two voices became rays and those two rays were all spirits which it is impossible to count, and each of these spirits was originally of seven colors, and each of these colors changed into thousands of shadings (Op. cit., pp. 81–82; 26–27).

In the same way that God emitted the creating cry (*âvâz-i âFarînish*), so the wicked angel created his creatures with a voice. Using other voices or cries God created other beings, "of which each articulation of their bodies emits seven flashes," and so forth. It is well known that the concept of creation through evocation is very frequent in Manichaean texts and the above example is a typical Mazdean presentation.

The many characters who collaborate in the creation are generally seen contemporaneously as angels and historical persons. We find Salmân (Muhammad's freedman who has an important place in the theological speculations of these sects) Miqdâd and Abû Zarr: according to "normal" Muslim tradition, these three people, for example, were among those who renewed their oath of fidelity to Muhammad under the "tree of Hudaibiya" at a particularly dangerous and important moment. This innocuous historical detail is transfigured in the speculations of the extreme sects and—as we shall see later—the simple Beduin tamarisk tree of an unknown Arab locality is transformed into a symbolic heavenly tree and the characters into angels, and the whole scene is transferred into the transcendent world or, rather, the transcendent fantasies in search of bodies in which to identify their ever growing "angelic personality" (an ancient Iranian tendency) find the most suitable place in which to manifest themselves within a historical Islamic person. And this is further proved by the fact we have repeatedly mentioned, that these identifications often irritated the "true" historical person who gave the incautious metaphysical speculator a rough time! Among these historical yet transcendental persons one of the "five lights"—Fâtima (Muhammad's daughter and 'Alî's wife)—has a particularly important place—and this is all the more striking in that she was a woman. Ivanow, with his twentieth century rationalist's attitude, considers it a "very strange story." We give it here because, on the contrary, it is not at all strange and is present in the Twelver Shi'ite tradition and in more recent texts (from Safavid Persia), besides appearing in an almost identical form in some of the sacred representations. This "very strange story" is a theophany of Fâtima (pp. 63–65) set in heaven after the creation of primeval men (very different from the traditional creation of only one couple because it involves many creatures; the forbidden tree is identified with sexual guilt, another characteristic that links our text to Manichaean tendencies).

> Then Gabriel, the Spirit of the Revelation brought them (men) immediately into Paradise and there they saw a form adorned with thousands and thousands of colors sitting on a throne with a crown on her head and two rings in her ears and a sword hanging on her bandoleer. The whole garden of Paradise emitted rays because of the apparition of that luminous form. The rebels[9] then wished to know who that Form was. The Spirit of Spirits (var. of "the Spirit of the Revelation") explained: "This form is one of the Judging Assembly (*dîvân*) of the eternal Term of Terms that has manifested itself in this Paradise from this Height that is above every Height. It is the form of Fâtima. Her crown is Muhammad, her ear-rings are Hasan and Husain and her sword is the prince of Believers 'Alî and her throne is the place of the power that is God's throne, may her Majesty be exalted!" Then all sang hymns of praise and glory to that Form.

It is strange that this female manifestation of the most holy divinity comes only a few lines before and after passages in which demons are incarnated in women, as the symbol of all evil. Often in fact Fâtima's name is masculinized and she is called *Fâtir* ("creator") in the texts of the extreme Islamic sects that glorified her most particularly, (this was true, for example, of the Nusairî). She is given both names in some passages and "Fâtima's creative form (*fâtir*)" is mentioned with reference to the transcendent Fâtima. We are naturally led to think of the Manichaean Mother of Life (*Emm d Hayyê, Mâdar-i Zindagân*, etc.)[10].

5. Transmigration is admitted very frankly but in a singular form that deserves special attention. In the first place *raj'at*, i.e., "return," is always mentioned and the Qur'anic passage "if we return to the city [Medina] the most powerful will drive out the most wretched" (LXIII, 8) quoted to support it. Now this passage refers to an ordinary historical episode that, as usual, has been transcendentalized and psychologized through a "symbolical interpretation" or *ta'wîl*. Each person's return is conditioned by his actions, his faith, the nation he belonged to, etc. The believer is reborn in this or that circumstance according to when he dies and according to the spirit (sensitive, spiritual, etc.) that dominates him. The fact that rebirth can occur in the time of Abraham or of Adam, during the period of Noah's Ark, etc. is a very curious aspect of this and is indicative of a special concept of Time.

6. The personalization of abstract concepts—a creative procedure involving a kind of remythologizing of purely mental elements or theologùmena—dominates the whole book, as it does all the speculations of the extreme Muslim sects. Thus Hasan and Husain *are* the day of the 'Ashûrâ (the 10th of Muharram, the day on which Husain was killed and, still earlier, the Jewish feast of fasting); "the spirit

of faith of the Throne of God" is Salmân, and so forth. Thus a mesocosm of personal hypostases that lies between the supreme world of the luminous hypostases and the Physical, earthly, psychological world is formed.

7. The ascetic and anti-worldly tendencies of the morality of the *Ummu'l-Kitâb* are striking and still show a very strong Manichaean influence. Every now and then there are words of contempt for the human body. Satan says that he has been created out of four foul liquids (including sperm); genital organs are a constant source of sin and rebellion and the source of all evils and vice; The Tree of Paradise is adultery. Salvation occurs through the ascent of the three highest spirits of the soul, the spirit of resistance (*mu'tariza*) the imprisoned spirit (*habsî*), the hopeful spirit (*muntariza*). Through various rebirths and experiences these spirits retrace the phases of the development of the world and the soul finally attains Salmân's level; its vices are expelled and God helps it to free itself from the sensible world (*hissî*) sending it a thousand "angels" who are identified with divine names or attributes.

But we have said enough about the text of this book. The doctrines it expresses are undoubtedly those of a Manichaean-type of Gnostic sect and, as we have seen, there is no reason not to believe the tradition that attributes, at least some of the older parts, to Khattâbîya and, I should like to add, Mughîrîya circles. The fact that the book is venerated by the Ismailis of a marginal and, in some ways, probably conservative region of the Ismaili territory supports the hypothesis according to which the earliest Ismailism started in these sects and only later took on the far more "Muslim" forms that we know through the great Arab and Persian Ismaili texts (which we will study in the following paragraph). The link between these doctrines and Ismailism is openly declared in a very important passage in the introduction to the *Ummu'l-Kitâb* (text in *Notes*, 428, no.1): "And the religion (*mazhab*) called *fida'î* or *tâlibî* in Syria is the one founded by Tâlib [sic!] and the Ismaili religion is the one founded by the sons of Abû'l-Khattâb, who sacrificed themselves for Ismâ'îl, the son of Ja'far as-Sâdiq, a religion that will last through the centuries." The text is vague but it establishes a very important relationship between the Khattâbîya-type sects and the Ismailis. Apparently after the unsuccessful deifying enthusiasm of the Mughîrîya and Khattâbîya for the persons of al-Bâqir and Ja'far who—as we said—persecuted their over-enthusiastic adorers, this enthusiasm was directed towards the figure of Ismâ'îl, whom the others did not consider legitimate, but who ended by giving his name to the sect. The absence of doctrines as "primitive" as those we have outlined above in the better known Fatimid Ismailism and the two Musta'lî and Nizârî branches can be explained in two ways: (a) because of a refinement due in particular to the introduction of Greek knowledge, or b) because of a concern to hide their teachings, which extended to their writings (and some Ismaili works are so colorless as to lead one to this conclusion).

While on this subject (since initiation and esoterism are basic to Ismailism) we will mention an ancient Ismaili treatise, discovered by Ivanow, which is valuable precisely because it provides us with what appears to be one of the most ancient initiation formularies.

This treatise, *Kitâbu'l'âlim wa 'l-ghulâm* ("The Book of the Wise Man and the Servant" or "of the Master and the Disciple"), is undated and anonymous but Ivanow, on the basis of a number of its characteristics, attributes it to a very early period, almost certainly prior to the Fatimid Empire and consequently to the end of the ninth century. The book is written in Arabic but takes place in Persia and is the possibly imaginary story of the conversion of a young man to Ismailism by a propagandist and his first steps in the career of an Ismaili propagandist (*dâ'î*). The book gives us a most vivid picture of the technique of Ismaili propaganda. In Fârs, the narrator tells us, there was a man who, in the midst of the general ignorance, attained true knowledge (i.e., became Ismaili). As his first task he embarked on long journeys to spread the word. One day, unobserved, he entered a distant city; he approached a group of people who were discussing religion and expressed great interest in what they were saying. Noticing his interest, they invited him to join the discussion and in this way he began to spread his message. His words struck the men but they then dispersed and each one went about his own business. But the missionary had made at least one good catch; one young man remained with him because he wanted to learn more. This already shows us the typically characteristic capillary and personal penetration used in Ismaili propaganda. As with the early Christians, the various Gnostic sects and, still now in Persia, with the Babi and the Baha'i (see Chapter VIII), the message was communicated personally to those who were ready to receive it. Besides the salvific value of the religious knowledge obtained in this way (which makes the purely political and religious propagandizing of the great masses as practised by ordinary Islam seem absurd)[11] there were also obvious reasons of practical prudence for this technique, in view of the persecutions against these communities. The intimate dialogue between the two is based entirely on the young man's desire to attain not only an exterior knowledge (*zâhir*) of matters of faith but also an inner (*bâtin*), esoteric, knowledge, and on the idea that a group of jurists whose opinions often differed could not give this kind of profound interpretation but only God himself from on high, through an authoritative person (the imâm or his missionary). And this, in fact, is the essence of all Shi'ism. The disciple starts his initiation by reciting an oath (*'ahd*) in words dictated by his Master—an oath that binds him in a "pact" (*'ahd*) with God. The pact with God, i.e., with the imâm or his authorized representative, is also a central concept of Ismailism. It gives a realistically visible and lively dimension of "transcendent" Qur'anic data. The oath centers around promising to maintain secrecy over the doctrine that will be revealed. The Master congratulates the disciple after the recitation of the formula: he has now entered into the confraternity of the "saints" or friends of God (*awliyâ' allâh*). Next the Master explains the longed–for "secret doctrine" (which Ivanow—setting himself up as usual as judge—defines as "disappointing" [sic]). In fact these doctrines are very similar to the rather primitive Gnostically-oriented doctrines in the *Ummu'l-Kitâb*, and could very well be Ismaili doctrine as it was organized before the introduction of Greek knowledge. (This is one of the best proofs of the antiquity of the book.) Literal cabalism has a place of great importance in it. It contains the usual doctrine of the Imamate but the technical terms used (in later Ismaili works too) to indicate the spiritual hierarchies seem more mobile and generic here. The imam is the Sun (a far more realistic symbol than we modern people might take it to be) veiled with veils of light to the eyes of the non-initiated. The Sun is the *zâhir* (external aspect) of the imâm. The prophets are given the usual Ismaili technical term of "speaking" (*nâtiq*), i.e., the enunciators of the laws and esoteric doctrine. Next to them we find the imâms (expounders of the esoteric aspect of the doctrine) who are accompanied by the *hujjat*s (literally, "proofs," "arguments." During the Fatimid period the *hujjat*s were real "bishops" residing in the various regions) and by the *bâb*s ("gates" to knowledge, initiators); by the *dâ'î*s, missionaries, and the *naqîb*s (dignitaries who, according to other texts, numbered twelve and accompanied the *Nâtiq*s) and by the "masters." The visible world and everything it contains is a set of symbols (*amthâl*) expressing the reality of the other world. The visible face of this two-sided unit is this world and its esoteric face the other world. This explains the apparently strange identifications we have found and will find in texts of this kind: the imâm is the sky and the twelve *naqîb*s of the *Nâtiq* are the twelve constellations of the zodiac, the *dâ'î*s are the stars. If the *Nâtiq* is alive, the earth is its *bâb*, if it is dead, it is its *vasî* (legitimate heir responsible for and depository of esoteric knowledge), and so forth.

The reader should note the double symbology implicit in this speculation. The physical sky is the symbol of an entity of the other world: but this entity is then called the imâm, who is also a person in this visible world. This leads us to the singular but extremely interesting conclusion that the "other world" indicates the world of persons-angels and not an abstract transcendent world. For those times this in itself would have been a sufficiently dangerous doctrine—to be carefully hidden—and it ought not to have struck Ivanow as "disappointing"! In this natural, psychological, angelic symbolism (which cannot be given in detail here) we also find—as in the *Ummu'l-Kitâb*—that Air is the supreme symbol, the greatest of the elements, the *zâhir* of God himself (a concept that may have penetrated Gnosis through Hellenistic speculations and moved from there into these circles for it is present, for example, even in eighteenth century Persian philosophers). But besides the *zâhir* and the *bâtin*, a super-bâtin, the *bâtin al-bâtin* exists. Animals only know the *zâhir*, men can know the *bâtin*, the angels know the *bâtin al-bâtin*, though this knowledge is also revealed to some men who are in fact angels. These concepts are inspired by a marked "aristocratic" sense. Only two kinds of men are worthy of being called men: the initiator-master and the initiated or those about to be initiated. Everyone else is ignorant rabble.

After all these discourses the disciple undergoes a further degree of initiation in the presence of a superior *dâ'î* or shaikh to whom he is led by his first teacher. This involves a kind of interrogation that we give here because it is one of the most ancient formulas of Ismaili initiation:[12]

> Shaikh: O Youth! You have been favored by a friend who was sent to you as a messenger, and you have been loved by a spiritual courier. What is your name?
>
> Youth: 'Ubaidu'llah ("God's little slave") the son of Abdullâh ("God's slave").
>
> Shaikh: This name describes your qualities, which we have already heard about. Are you free or are you a slave?
>
> Youth: I am a free man, the son of one of God's slaves.
>
> Shaikh: Who freed you from slavery, so that you became a free man?
>
> Youth: This master.
>
> Shaikh: But do you not see that he himself is a slave, and not the Lord? How can he have freed you?
>
> Youth: No, he could not free me.
>
> Shaikh: Then what is your name?
>
> Youth: (He does not know what to answer).
>
> Shaikh: Oh youth, how can one know something if it has no name, like a newborn infant?
>
> Youth: I have been born to you. You must give me a name!
>
> Shaikh: I will do so in seven days.
>
> Youth: Why this delay?
>
> Shaikh: For the good of the one who is newborn.
>
> Youth: And if the newborn one dies before these seven days come to pass?
>
> Shaikh: Nothing will happen to him, and he shall have his name when this period is over.
>
> Youth: And will the name you give me remain mine?
>
> Shaikh: Yes, if you become his slave.
>
> Youth: How can one speak in this way?
>
> Shaikh: The name is your lord and you his slave. Don't discuss this foolishly; go now until the established day.

As usual in Ismailism, the name is given a vividly concrete form. It is not— as we might believe—an "allegory," but the *bâtin* itself of the person who wears it: it is an angel-name. Ismailism as a whole and the religious thought in general dealt with in this chapter are incomprehensible if we do not consider them from the point of view of a personalist-angelic philosophy, which is "symbolic" in the most personal and real sense of the word and neither immanentist nor transcendentalist.

On the seventh day (see also the Sabaean ritual we will be discussing further on) the adept returns with his first teacher (who is called "his parent") He makes his ablutions, dons immaculate garments and again enters into the shaikh's presence. The two solemnly advance towards one another and when they are close the shaikh reveals the "mystery" to his disciple. The author of the book, who was also bound by his esoteric oath, naturally refused to write it down: these are matters that can only be communicated orally. The communication must however have focussed on the name of the living imâm who was being propagandized (*da'wa*). The nucleus of the revelation must have been: God *is* So and So (always giving the value of true symbol we have repeatedly mentioned to the is). After this revelation the text tells us that the youth was finally able to accomplish the pilgrimage to the Ka'ba in its true sense and, dressed in the sacred *ihrâm*, to walk around the House of God. The true pilgrimage (as pilgrimage to the imâm) is a frequent symbol both in Ismaili and Sufi texts. The young man, however, probably did not physically accomplish the rites around the visible imâm; these were merely symbolic. The newly initiated person's first duty was to immediately start teaching. The youth, accompanied by his spiritual father, returned to his city and converted his own father. It is interesting that these conversions are spoken of as "a coming away from one's own *milla*." *Milla*, in the Islamic sense, means "religious nation," Islamic religious community: consequently in those early days the Ismailis themselves, at least when they spoke together, appear to have felt that they belonged to a *religion* that was truly different from Islam, and this is highly significant.

This is confirmed in quotations from the discussions that followed between the neo-propagandist and the people he tried to convince and they are extremely interesting because they give us the "proofs" these first Persian Ismailis produced to convert the Sunni Muslims. In the first place they launched an attack against the reliability of the orthodox tradition, with the contradictory opinions of the different learned men and the various juridical schools. This was followed by an attack against the idea of God that was generally accepted by the Sunnis: a concentrated criticism of the idea of a God-person who is also transcendent (we have seen how the Ismailis retain and save the concept of God-person by attributing the "person" to the imâm and the most absolute transcendence to the unknowable essence of God). Their third line of attack (also very efficient when dealing with a religious man and a Muslim) was based on the fact that it was absurd that God should have sent prophets only at given moments in time, depriving other periods of his living grace. There followed the need for the people not to be abandoned to human doctors, interpreters of a book, between one Prophet (*nâtiq*) and another: they must have a constant living source of interpretative divine authority, the imâm, who knows the *ta'wîl*, i.e., the symbolic-angelic interpretation of the sacred Book. The idea the author of the book expresses at this point is extraordinary: i.e., that even God's revelation to Muhammad was not definitive and that another and last prophet will come after him—the seventh *Nâtiq*—whom the Muslims, who are as superstitious as the Jews were towards Christ, will refuse to recognize.

Successive Phases of Iranian Ismailism: Nâsir-i Khusrau

This first stratum of Persian Ismailism (see the preceding section) was followed by another that was deeply influenced by the Greek culture that had penetrated Islam through the famous "translation" period and had adapted itself to Ismailism in the famous Arabic encyclopedia of the "Brothers of Purity" composed in Basra, in southern Mesopotamia, in the second half of the tenth century A.D. Here, apparently, the enthusiastic Ismailism of the earlier "coloristic" Gnostic speculations subsided into forms that were both more orderly and, to some extent, closer to orthodoxy. Their excessively anthropomorphic approach to incarnation disappeared also and their distance from Islam and their representation of themselves as another religion was less emphasized. The sense of *ta'wîl*—the spiritual interpretation of texts—grew: while in Egypt Ismailism assumed government responsibilities, in Persia (especially after the Nizârî schism [1095] and the famous Hasan-i Sabbâh's conquest of Alamût [1090]) it presented itself more as a brotherhood of the initiated.

The *Rasâ'il* (epistles, treatises) of the "Brothers of Purity" offer an indicative and rather complete synthesis of the profane knowledge that was available at the time and was placed at the service of speculation with Gnostic tendencies that drew not only on the most famous Greek "philosophers" but eclectically on Hermes and Pythagoras too. These two sages (and, later, Socrates and Plato) were more highly esteemed than Aristotle who was considered to be mainly a logician and (as in the Middle Ages) the author of the *Liber de Pomo* and the Plotinian so-called "Theology of Aristotle." The nucleus of the doctrine contained in these epistles is the heavenly origin of the soul and salvation seen as a return to the original Homeland. The world was produced by God not so much through "creation" as through "emanation" (the Arabic verb *fâda* is used), just as the speaker emanates words and the sun emanates light. The epistles expound the well-known neo-Platonic doctrine of the intermediate degrees of emanation. Only the One can be born of the One. Universal Reason proceeds from Divine Unity (*'aql*), the Universal Soul (*nafs*) proceeds from Universal Reason, Prime Matter (*hayûlâ*, from the Greek *hyle*) proceeds from the Universal Soul, followed by nature, spatial matter, the world of spheres, the sublunar elements and finally the three kingdoms—animal, mineral and vegetable. The epistles, which also include short treatises on the natural sciences, advocate an evolutionist idea that is very interesting because it recurs in the whole of Sufi, Ismaili and philosophical tradition (though it is rather far fetched to label it, with Dieterici, as "tenth century Arab Darwinism").[13] The unknown author speaks also of links between the different reigns: palms are the link between the vegetable and animal reign, monkeys between the animal reign and man, and Saints between men and angels. The idea is a clearly edifying one: evolution must continue beyond man in angels and, higher still, reverse the way of downward emanation upwards, in the opposite direction. Man is thus the central point of the system of the universe.

In these treatises Greek philosophy combines with hermetic-Pythagorean speculations and, to use De Boer's term (in ERE, IX, p. 879), with the "older metaphysical emanational and redemptive influences."

Muslim literature holds traditionally that the "first" philosophy (Hermes, Agathodaimon, Asclepius, Pythagoras, Thales, Solon, Empedocles, Bâlînûs, i.e., Apollonius of Tyana) etc. penetrated into the Islamic world following a path that threaded its way from Alexandria through Antioch and the "Sabaean" city of Harrân. Until Islam was at its height, a pagan-gnostic community, which took the Qur'anic name of "Sabaean" to escape persecutions and pass for a "religion of the Book," had its center in this upper-Mesopotamian city. Thus a Hellenistic mysteriosophical community that combined elements of the Babylonian astral religion with Gnosis prospered there for centuries.

According to the Sabaeans the knowledge of the divine mysteries had been revealed by a triad: Urânî,[14] Agathodaimon and Hermes, who answered to the old idea of the Triple Hermes (cf. Martial V, 24: *Hermes omnia solus et ter unus*) identified in Biblical and Qur'anic terms as the prophets Seth and Idrîs. Sabaean eclecticism is evident in the names of the days of their week, which were sacred to different gods:[15] Sunday to Helios, Monday to Sin (the Babylonian god-moon), Tuesday to Ares, Wednesday to Nabu (another well-known god of the Babylonian pantheon), Thursday to Bal (Bâ'l, still another Syro-Babylonian god) Friday to Balthî (Bâ'l's paredra: "Lady") Saturday to Qrônôs. The much quoted *Fihrist* gives valuable information on their festivities and even a bad Arabic translation (possibly by an ex-Sabaean and so literal that it is almost incomprehensible) of an initiation rite: "The Five Mysteries" (*al-Asrâr al-Khamsa*). It contains at least one clearly Iranian word: *bughdârî* (in its sense of priests, initiated ones, participants in the God) from the Persian *bagh*, "God," and *dâr*, the root of "to have," to hold.

The initiation lasted seven days. The young men remained in the temple for seven days and must not be seen by any woman. There were ceremonies involving meals of bread and salt eaten together, consecrated bread, a beverage drunk from a mystical cup. Mas'ûdî (who died in 956) saw a Syriac inscription on the pediment of one of their temples[16] that was translated for him as follows: "He who knows himself becomes God" (*man 'arafa dhâtahu ta'allaha*). Light and illumination played an important part.

The fact that, whether they were authentic or not, the Sabaean theories were relatively widespread in Arabic—the international language of the time—is very important. Al-Kindî (who died soon after 870) already mentions this: according to the *Fihrist*, some of their books were translated into Arabic and their ideas quoted—even if in a more or less deformed and imaginative manner—by many Arab authors (see the ample anthology in Chwolssohn's *Sabier*). This provides us with an evident and tangible link between Islam and Hellenistic-Babylonian-Syrian syncretist Gnosis, though we lack a link between Islam and ancient religious Iran.[17] The philosophical ideas of the Sabaeans and Ikhwân as-Safâ penetrated vast cultivated areas of the Muslim world little by little and strongly influenced Muslim philosophy (*falsafa*) even when it drew far closer to Aristotelian Hellenism.

This introduction was necessary for a historical understanding of the fusion Nâsir-i Khusrau attempted between Greek philosophy and Ismaili theosophy within Persian Ismailism—a task that the presence of these intermediaries facilitated.

Nâsir-i Khusrau (who was also well known as a Persian poet and prose writer) was born in 1004 in Qobâdiyân, a village near Balkh (present day Afghanistan) in the eastern Iranian world and died between 1072 and 1077. His spiritual biography is entirely concentrated on his conversion to Ismailism, possibly from Sunnism (or Shi'ism?) but more probably from the religious indifference that is discreetly alluded to in his travel diary (*SaFar-nâmeh*) and mentioned more explicitly in a famous autobiographical ode.

One night (in the year A.H. 437 [A.D. 1045, he writes in his travel diary] I saw Someone in a dream who said to me: "For how long are you going to drink of this wine that annihilates wisdom in man? You would do better to come to your senses." I answered: The sages have been unable to invent anything better than this to lessen the preoccupations of our worldly life." But he replied: "Irresponsibility is not peace! One cannot give the name of sage to he who leads men towards irresponsibility, one should ask instead for something that increases awareness and wisdom." I asked him: "Where can I find this?" He answered: "He who seeks, finds," and pointing to the *qibla* he said no more. Waking from my sleep, this remained impressed in my memory and affected me deeply. I said to myself: "I have woken up from last night's sleep, now I must also wake up from the sleep of forty years." [Text in Schefer, *Sefernâmeh*].

Soon after this experience Nâsir started on the long journey that led him to the Egyptian Fatimid court and Mecca. It is probable (though not certain) that the dream itself has a symbolic value (his inebriation is ignorance of the true imâm, etc.) and that Nâsir became Ismaili, through a *dâ'î*, before leaving for the Fatimid reign that was the seat of the imâm at the time[18].

But the ode we will be reading shortly seems to confirm the traditional story that has him set out in search of God during that year and has his real conversion take place in Egypt. It is even more interesting as a study of his conversion and its spiritual causes. Since it is an authentic document on the personal religious experience of a great Persian Ismaili, a direct reading of a translation of the central part of the text will certainly be of use to the reader. In it he repeats the reasons for his conversion which centered on the need for a living presence of God, for a "certitude" that the tradition of the sages and jurists was unable to provide (and which was already present in the tale of the Master and the Disciple). The ode also provides important information on the possible historical setting for the religious influences that came to bear on Nâsir: unless he used rhetorical emphasis to indicate the range of his research before his definitive conversion he must have studied Indian, Greek, Hebrew, Manichaean, Sabaean and atheist-materialist (*dahrîya*) thought. In order to rectify the pan-Iranian enthusiasm of certain scholars the reader should note that Zoroastrian Mazdean thought is not mentioned. In other poems in fact Nâsir is harshly against it: in his *Raushanâ'î-nâmeh* Mazdeans are *gabr-i gumrâh*, "corrupted Zoroastrians" and he repeatedly speaks of them disparagingly in his "Collection of Lyrics"[19].

Three hundred and ninety four years after the Hegira my mother deposited me on this dusty center of the cosmos,

A being who grew, without knowledge, like a plant born of the black earth and a few drops of water.

And then, from being a plant, I reached the stage of beast, and for some time I remained like an unfledged bird.

And then, during the fourth stage, traces of Man entered into me when Reason penetrated into this turbid body.

Now when the sky-blue Cupola above me had completed forty two evolutions, my rational Soul began to seek for Wisdom.

I studied the order of the firmament and the passing of the days and the three Reigns of Nature, listening to lessons of the sages and reading.

And when I discovered that I was better than they all were I said to myself: "And yet there must be one who is better than all,

One who is like the Falcon among birds, and like the Camel among animals, like the Palm among plants, like the Ruby among jewels, like the Qur'an among books, like the Ka'ba among buildings, like the heart in the body and the Sun among the stars."[20]

And I tormented my sorrowful soul, and this thoughtful soul of mine began to ask questions of the thinkers;

I sought for a guide in Shâfi'î and Malik, in the words of Abû Hanîfa,[21] and I asked the sovereign judges of the world for their wisdom,

But when I asked How and Why, and wanted solid Proofs, they writhed in impotence, and one was deaf, and another blind.

One day I read the verse of the Oath of Fealty in the Qur'an [XLVIII, 10] in which God says that His "hand is over their hands" of the men such as Ja'far and Miqdâd, Salmân and Abû Dharr, who swore the oath under the Tree,

And I asked myself: "Where is that Tree now, where is that Holy Hand, where shall I seek that Hand and that Oath and that Sublime Assembly?" They said to me: "The Hand did not remain down here, the Tree did not remain, and now the hand is mutilated and that assembly dispersed;

Those were the Prophet's friends and now they are in heaven, especially those who swore the oath and the elect among the people."

I answered: "But it is clear in the Qur'an that Muhammad is the Nuncio and Admonisher, and the Illuminator and the Lamp,

And if the Unbeliever wants to put out that Lamp with the breath of his mouth, God will light it again above all the impious.

How can it be that none of them are left, as if the promise of the Sovereign Judge of the world were untrue?

Whose hand shall we take? Where shall we swear our oath to God? . . . What fault have we committed that we were not born in that Time? Why are we afflicted and deprived of the Prophet?"

And in my sorrow at my Ignorance my face became as yellow as a [faded] flower, and this cypress bent down prematurely in the shape of a circle,

Concerned and saddened by the fact that men are nothing but dust and plants and animals in the world . . .

The wise man is like musk that gives off wisdom like Perfume, or like a mine and the science within him is Gold,

And when perfume abandons the musk and gold the stone, the musk remains valueless and the stone false,

And so, since the perfume and the gold have [disappeared] from the musk and the stone, I will rise up and ask for knowledge of the Precious Casket!

And I rose up from where I was and set out on my journeying, and I had no memories of my house and garden and the familiar sights;

And I asked Persians and Arabs, Hindus and Turks and Sindhis and Greeks and Jews, all,

And philosophers and Manichaeans and Sabaeans and Dahrites and I asked endless questions on what I was eager to know.

Often the stones were my bed and my pillow, often the clouds were my tent and my pavilion.

Sometimes I descended into the deepest abysses and the Fish were my neighbors,[22] sometimes I went beyond the Sun and the Moon up the highest mountains;

Sometimes I crossed lands where water was as hard as marble, sometimes I wandered in a world where the earth was glowing embers.

Sometimes seas sometimes mountains, sometimes a roadless journeying, sometimes hills sometimes sand, sometimes ravines sometimes rivers,

Sometimes with a rope around my neck, like a camel, sometimes like a loaded mule,

And so I wandered from city to city asking and seeking, and I wandered and roamed from sea to land.

And they said to me: "The object of God's law cannot be discussed through reason, for Islam was established in the world through the sword!"

And I: "Why is Prayer not obligatory for children and madmen if Reason has no place in matters concerning God?"

I did not accept Tradition (taqlîd) and I did not hide my reasoning, because Reality (God) did not manifest itself through Tradition,

But when God wishes to open the gate of Mercy, what is difficult becomes easy, and what is easy, very difficult.

Thus, one day, I reached the gates of a city[23] that dominated the bodies of the firmament as well as the Horizons.

A city all gardens, full of fruit and flowers, and ornate with walls, whose earth was rich with green trees;

The surrounding countryside was encrusted with gems as if it were brocade, its waters were most pure honey like the water of the Kauthar,[24]

A city whose dwellings are only dwellings of Grace, a garden whose only pine tree is Reason,

A city in that the Wise are dressed in brocade, brocade not woven by men or women.

A city, finally, where Reason said to me: "Ask for what you need here, do not go beyond this dwelling!"

I went to the Gate-keeper and told him my story, and he answered: "Do not be saddened, your mine will be filled with gems:

The immense ocean, most precious pearls and most pure water are in this spiritual land; this is the Supreme Sphere, full of high stars and, moreover, it is a heaven filled with beautiful effigies."

When I heard him speak thus I thought he was Rizvân,[25] his profound words, his sweet language.

I said to him: "My soul (nafs) is weak and infirm: do not look at the [apparent] holiness of my body, and this rosy color!"

". . .Do not worry," he answered, "I am the Physician here, declare and explain this sickness of yours."

And I asked him about the First and the Last and then about the cause of the [Divine] Government (tadbîr) that is the origin of what is Governed (muddabar).

I asked him about the genus and operation of the form, and about the Preordainer and Destiny and the Destined.

"I know," I said, "that they are not distinct, how can it be then that one has precedence over the other?

About how this movement operated, and about day and night, and how the poor man becomes rich through him and the shadowy one shining,

About the prophets, and the contrasting questions, and the cause for the prohibition of blood and fermented wine."

And then I asked him about the Pillars (*arkân*) of the Law and why the five prayers were prescribed,

And about the fasting commanded for the ninth month of the year, and the tithe of the drachmas, and round gold . . .

And about the division of destinies (*qismat-i arzâq*) I asked him and I said: "How is it that the chaste man is sad and the tyrant joyous,

Or one chaste man is saddened and another glad, and one unbeliever is happy and another full of sorrow?

Why does one man have strength and sight while another is born blind and sick from his mother's womb?

Yes, it is true that God only operates justly, but reason is never satisfied at the sight of a blind man!

I see the day, and he is apparently all night, I want you to draw the sword out of this matter.

You say that a noble Stone[26] exists in a certain place and whoever comes to it— a pious pilgrim—is honored.

Azar[27] invites me to the idol and you invite me to a stone, therefore, for me today, you are truly an Azar . . . ."

He answered: "I will give you the medicine with proofs and arguments, but first I must place a solid seal on your lips."

And he, the Old Man of the many skills, called two Witnesses of the world of Nature and of the Psyche (*âfâq u anfus*), over my food and beverage.

I accepted, and he sealed my lips, and then, day by day, he gave me medicine by degrees.

When the sickness was annihilated and my tongue was loosened, and my cheek changed from yellow to rose-color again,

He transported me from the earth into the firmament, like a Ruby; if at first I was earth, today I am fragrant with amber;

And he placed my hand in the Prophet's hand, for the Oath under the lofty Tree surrounded by fertile shade . . .[28]

Sun is needed to turn a stone into a ruby . . . I am the ruby and my sun is that Man, through whose light this shadowy world becomes filled with shining light.

I will not name him in this poem for the sake of secrecy, I will only say that he is a being of such magnitude that Plato is his humble servant.

Teacher, Physician and One whom God has confirmed, he is a chosen symbol of science and wisdom. Happy the city that has him as its guardian! Happy the ship that has him as its anchor!

Oh you, whose Reason pondering Poetry is the measure of the Spirit, oh You whose Prose has fettered Wisdom to its rule, ...

I want a Greeting as motile and constant as the coloring of the moon[29] to reach you from me, your obedient servant,

Like the drop that has fallen from the narcissus and the anemone, like the fragrance that comes from the lily and jasmine,

Like the embrace of graceful and fascinating maidens, like the word of gentle eloquent fluent speakers,

Filled with grace and as fruitful as the March cloud that comes down the valley from the mountain like distilled musk,

As blessed and copious as Christ's miraculous breath, as lofty and adorned as the green cupola of the sky! . . .

This poem reveals why Nâsir set out on his spiritual search: there must be one Man in the world of men who is typical Man or—to use a Zoroastrian term that comes natural here—the *ratu* of men, as Zoroaster in the Avesta. The seeker wishes to repeat Hudaibiya's historical oath under the Tree hand in hand with this man, who is the imâm who guarantees the continuity of the presence of God in the world. When it is de-historicized, the event takes on an eternal salvific value and consequently it is impossible that there should be no-one in the world at present (and at all times) with whom to take the oath. This someone exists and he must be sought for. This personal and original search for truth is typical of all esoteric movements: Sunnism is criticized as the doctrine that admitted this search during the time of the Prophet but then prevented it with barriers of paper written by clergymen who confessed that they lacked inspiration and were purely human—a wall of non-divine tradition (*taqlîd*, "imitation") for non-prophetic times. This Ismaili rationalism, which accepted every rational and philosophical method in its search but then required absolute and total acceptance of the Master's teachings once this Master had been found, may seem strange. But it should not be forgotten that by search for truth in this angelic world we must always understand the search for the person who is truth. Once Nâsir has found him (in the Egypt that in this poem is transfigured into a holy land, a Qur'anic *balad al-amîn*, but which should not, because of this, be considered merely a symbol) he questions this Person-Truth. The questions he asks and the problems that torment him are very interesting: we find requests concerning legal questions (why five prayers, why is the blood of animals forbidden, etc.) placed on the same plane as abstruse metaphysical questions (why is a person born healthy or sick, etc.), almost as if to underline His omniscience. The initiation lies precisely in a true understanding of *ta'wîl* (the central concept of Ismailism) that is generally translated inexactly as "allegorical interpretation" though in fact—in view of the homology between the various planes of the cosmos, from the archangelical pleroma to the microcosm of the human person and the mesocosm of the men-angels—it ought to be more correctly and etymologically translated as "leading back to the upper plane," "seeing what is esoteric through what is exoteric." We will see examples of this soon through the answers to the questions asked in this poem. As Nâsir boldly says, without *ta'wîl*, the Black Stone that pious Muslims are encouraged to kiss in the Ka'ba would be undistinguishable from the idols of pre-Islamic paganism. Instruction is linked to an initiation that occurs in two stages and which seems to me to correspond perfectly to what we already know from the short treatise of "The Master and the Disciple": first there is the promise of secrecy, the sealing of the lips (connected possibly, through *ta'wîl*, with the biblical episode of the Dumb Zacharias in the Qur'an) then, in a given place on earth, which according to *ta'wîl* is Heaven, the *bai'a* (oath, *'ahd*, pact of fealty) is repeated in the hands of the living symbol of the Prophet and of God, the imâm.

In a way Nâsir's whole work is the explanation and answer to the central questions that tormented him in his search. We will consider some of them again when we look for the answers in his other works: though lack of space limits us to a few though significant (if rather disorderly) examples.[30]

1. In the thirteenth chapter of the *Jâmi'u'l-Hikmatain* on "the genus and the species" Nâsir starts—as is his custom in this text—by giving the answers offered by Greek philosophy. He has Aristotle, the "wise Greek" (*hakîm yûnânî*) and "lord of logic," (*khudâvand-i mantiq*), speak quietly in the first person. First I asked the names of the individual men: one was called Zaid, one 'Amr, one Ja'far, etc. But none of these names was applicable to any of the others. A further easy enquiry convinced me that the name "man" was applicable to all, indistinctly. Then I turned my eyes towards the world: I saw cows, donkeys, horses, etc. I found a name "animal" which could equally include both men and beasts. But I also saw things like plants and grasses in the world: to unite these to the rest I found a more general name, *afzâyandeh u rûyandeh* ("growing and vegetating"), *nâmî* in Arabic. A further observation of stones and minerals led me to come up with an even more general name: "body." But I also saw ethereal spirits in the world that, though they were not bodies, governed the bodies: the new name I thought up—again generalizing—in order to be able to unify "body" and "spirit" was *jauhar*, "substance." Since I saw nothing more I decided that substance was the "genus of genuses" (*jinsu'l-ajnâs*) and body and spirit its "species." But, in turn, the body, which is species in relation to substance, is genus in relation to the step immediately beneath it and so forth.

This was the Greek philosopher's answer. Now we will see the answer of the "people of the confirmation" (i.e., the Ismailis, who were "confirmed" through an authoritative revelation from above). Though they admitted that there was nothing wrong with the philosophers' statements, they added a distinction between world (*dunyâ*) and religious world (*dîn*). The world is made to exist through God's Intellect (*'aql*), the *dîn* through the Lord's *amr*. *Amr* is a Qur'anic term indicating a divine act (literally "order") parallel to the *khalq* (creation of the physical world) from which both man's soul and the entire cosmos of religious realities proceed. Man must have a preliminary philosophical knowledge of the *dunyâ*/world but his religious eye sees the *dîn*/spiritual world (by means of *ta'wîl*) through it[31]. The things of the world are symbols (*mithâl*) of a superior and truer cosmos, which is in fact organized along similar lines. The *jins* (genus) is called *asl* (roots-origin) here and the *nau'* (species) is called the *far'* (branch, derivation). In the cosmos of *dîn* the series Zaid-Man-Animal-Vegetable-Body-Substance corresponds to the following series that includes the grades of the sacred Ismaili hierarchy: Believers (Ismailis: *ahl-i da'vat*)-*dâ'î hujjat-imâm-rasûl-dîn*.

The reader should note that the last very general term is *dîn*, the cosmos of religion, and not God: God is, in a sense, even further.

But these figures of sacred dignitaries do not only correspond to the logical series of names. They also correspond to abstract religious entities of the pleroma (we mentioned this earlier and here we see the systematized genealogical tree). In the same order, from the lowest to the highest, we have: "those whose prayers have been granted" (*ahl-i istijâbat*)-*khayâl-fath-jadd*: universal soul-universal intellect-*dîn*.

Consequently the specification of the world of *dîn* produces two types of "branches"—one personal, the other metaphysical—(in the same direction in which the world of substance, as it becomes specified, produces the various subspecies). *Jadd*, *Fath* and *Khayâl*, which mean respectively Glory, Victory and Image, correspond to the angels Gabriel, Michael and Seraphiel of other traditions.

Here the *ta'wîl* consists in providing a theological interpretation to physical things. Historically speaking, this passage is particularly interesting for its use of the unusual terms of *Jadd*, *Fath* and *Khayâl*, which we identified above (with Corbin) as Gabriel, Michael and Seraphiel. In fact these terms are already present in a very interesting passage in question V of the early Manichaean-oriented *Ummu'l-Kitâb* (ed Ivanow, pp. 20–88 and foll.) in which we find successive and descending cosmic planes, each occupied by five persons-symbols-angels and each of a different color. Muhammad, 'Alî, Fâtima, Hasan and Husain, who are in the supreme pleroma (white), have their counterparts in five other unnamed entities in an inferior, red, world; still further down, in a flame-colored cosmos, whose light also derives from the higher planes, we find the angels Gabriel, Michael, Seraphiel (Isrâfîl), Azrael and Surâfîl; in the fourth, orange-colored, sphere the five eternal lights appear as five resplendent forms called *'aql* (intellect), *nafs* (soul), *fath* (victory), *jadd* (earnestness) and *khayâl* (imagination) in the human world (if the copyists have not changed the order these three ought to correspond here to Isrâfîl, Azrâ'îl and Surâfîl); next there is an emerald green world, with five other unnamed entities, a sixth violet-colored one that is traditional heaven and here the five lights are five unnamed houris[32]. A seventh world follows, the color of the sun, with its five lights, then an eighth the color of the moon and a ninth (called "this") that seems to be our sky blue (the heavenly sphere) where the five lights are the various imâms and dignitaries. The "five lights" that (in different forms) are always the same connect all the spheres vertically and are also identified with human faculties. But, to return to our *'aql*, *nafs*, *jadd*, *fath* and *khayâl*, these terms seem to correspond to the Manichaean "limbs of the Father of greatness," "reason, sense, intention, understanding and reflection." Corbin (despite the far more documentable Manichaean influence) daringly links *jadd* (literally, "intention") with the Aramaic word *gaddeh*—the ideographic form of the Pahlavi *farr* (Avestan *khvarena*)—and therefore with the Flaming Glory of the sovereigns of Iran, though this seems to me, to say the least, far-fetched (though attractive). According to this theory *fath* (Arabic for "victory," but also "opening," "position") is its victorious aspect (see ahead, on Suhravardî) and *khayâl* (imagination) an imaginative evocation of the image of glory (*imago gloriae*). With all due respect for Corbin's exegesis we prefer Strothman's (which Corbin quotes in his *Jâmi* (p. 92): he translates *jadd* with *énnoia*, fath as "unlocking of the meanings" (*Ausfschliessen des Sinnes*) and *khayâl* as "visionary idea" (*visionaire Vorstellung*). It seems more likely to us that these concepts and this pentad reached Nâsir through Manichaeism, mediated in its turn through texts such as the *Ummu'l-Kitâb*.

2. The *ta'wîl* we have just seen applied to something as apparently simple and innocuous as logic, and which has drawn us from the gender and the species to the colored and sparkling pleromas beyond the spheres and to unsuspected theosophical abysses, is, naturally, applied to "legal" questions too. The following is a brief example, taken from Chapter XX (on canonical prayer five times a day and the various numbers of prostrations each prayer entails) of our author's *Vajh-i Dîn* (see the note on his works). There are five obligatory daily Muslim prayers: at dawn, at midday, in the afternoon, at sundown and in the evening. Each one is composed of a slightly different number of *rak'at*s; the *rak'at* is a kind of unit of measurement for prayer composed of various gestures, prostrations, "stations" and bows accompanied by prayer formulas. Nâsir's *ta'wîl* is applied through the *dalîl ast bar* formula: i.e., this specific exterior thing indicates, is a sign or proof of, another specific, esoteric, "inner" thing. The *Vajh* (pp. 143 and foll.) begins by saying that prayer ("canonical" prayer, *namâz*, which should be distinguished from the heart's free invocation) indicates the *da'vat*, i.e., the invitation to God's Unity and an affectionate bond with the Saints. The dawn prayer is the symbol of the First (i.e., of the First Emanation that is the Intellect and the First Light as well as the *Nâtiq*, "speaker," i.e., the Prophet and founder of religious law, for example, Muhammad). This

is why it is said when the first Light appears in the sky. As the believer accomplishes this prayer, he must be grateful to God for having manifested the First Light (Muhammad, i.e., the Universal Intellect). The evening prayer, which is said at sunset, is the symbol of the Second (i.e., of 'Alî's Second Emanation, on a human plane, i.e., the vicar (*wasî*) of the Speaking Prophet, also called the "Silent One," and the repository of arcane knowledge) because the Second is the Waning of God's Light, while the First was its Dawn; for the Sun's light indicates Divine Unity. The following passage (p. 146) involving the *ta'wîl* of prayer is very interesting: "Tthe sunset prayer must consist in three *rak'at*s in the image of the Nâtiq/Speaker, because every light on this world rains down from those two angels (*firishteh*—the First and the Second) and three persons— *seh tan*—(to the surprise of the modern Persian commentator) receive it, i.e. *jadd*, *fath* and *khayâl*, who are subject to the Second" (that is, they follow him emanatively). Here we meet the same psychological and angelic triad we came across earlier (which disappears in later Ismaili texts) and again run into the personalizing or angelizing tendency that is so characteristic of Ismailism, with a further specification concerning the nature of the three entities: they are personal emanations of the Second (i.e., of the Universal Soul, *nafs*, or of 'Alî). The dawn and sunset are dealt with first because the two terms luminously symbolize the First and the Second. The midday and afternoon prayers come in between while the evening one is separate. This too is not fortuitous but is the symbol that indicates that Nâtiq/Speaker and Asâs/Foundation (another term for 'Alî)—which they represent—coexist in the same historical period while the imâm, symbolized by the evening prayer, is separate and consequently comes when their era is over. A further inner symbology of the number of the *rak'at* of each prayer teaches us that the soul of the Nâtiq/Speaker possesses all three persons-psychons, *jadd*/intention, *fath*/victory and *khayâl*/imagination, while the *asâs*/foundation does not share in the *jadd*/intention but only in the other two lights (as they are called now) of *fath*/victory and *khayâl*/imagination (and here the *nûr-i fath*, "light of the fath" brings to mind Suhravardî's "light of victory" [*lux victorialis*]). The imâm on the other hand only possesses the light of the *khayâl*/imagination. A further *ta'wîl* concerning the *rak'at* "reveals" that the Second, *furûd az khvîshtan* (as an emanation of itself, literally "under itself") sent six *nâtiq*s, i.e., legislating prophets: Adam, Noah, Abraham, Moses, Jesus and Muhammad.

The midday prayer indicates the Nâtiq/Speaker: its first two *rak'at*s state that he who does not accept the Nâtiq and the Asâs do not attain recognition (or knowledge) of the First and the Second. The Nâtiq is therefore the *qibla* (physical direction of the person praying that is spiritualized here in the *ta'wîl*) of the midday prayer. As the reader can easily anticipate, the qibla of the afternoon prayer is the Asâs/Foundation: this occurs in fact when the sun is beginning to pale, i.e., when the *zâhir* (the apparently exoteric aspect) of the Nâtiq begins to weaken and the period of the Asâs and the time of the appearance of the Qâ'im (Resurrector) begins. The function of the Asâs is the *ta'wîl*: without it they would have suffered the same fate as the Jews, Moses' religious-nation, and the Magi, Abraham's religious-nation, i.e., though they accepted their Nâtiq they did not follow or recognize their Asâs and are now reduced to their present condition. Here we find the old legend of Zarathustra's identification with Abraham. Through the *ta'wîl* of the Asâs the knowledge (and recognition) of all the other *hudûd* (the plural of *hadd*: an Ismaili technical term indicating the "hierarchies" we are examining here) can be attained.

The evening prayer symbolizes the imâm. The imâm operates in fact when the sun of the Prophecy and the interpretative vice-direction (Muhammad and 'Alî, the Nâtiq and the Asâs) has already set and we are in the night of the *da'va*—the "propaganda," "mission." In the heart of night, after the evening prayer, it is time for the supererogatory night prayer called *vitr*. This is considered more humble "legally" because it is not obligatory, but from the point of view of *ta'wîl* it is extremely important since it indicates the Qâ'im/Resurrector who will come at the end of time (or of the cosmic cycle) as seventh and last Nâtiq. He combines three dignities: those of Legislator Prophet (*Nabî*), Vice-director (*wasî*) and Resurrector (*Qâ'im*), in a concentration of Muhammad, 'Alî and "the future Christ," to use an exemplification that is not in the text. He will be son (descendant) of the Asâs (in the present case, 'Alî) and his *hujjat/* proof will precede him: his *hujjat* is identified according to the same system with the mysterious "Night of Destiny" mentioned in the Qur'an. The Qâ'im is the final scope and end of all the *hudûd*.

We needed to become acquainted with these meditations (which in some ways are so far from our modern mentality) in order to understand that they are not simply vague "poetical" aspects of Ismailism. But the *ta'wîl* method can lead to deeper and more interesting results where our awareness too is concerned . For example, interesting problems such as that of Time (which always caused Ismaili religious thinkers concern) are approached and resolved with remarkable insight in the short treatise *Gushâ'ish u Rahâ'ish*. One of the first questions it considers is whether the Creator came before the creation; and if he did precede it how can one explain the fact that an element of "time" exists in him? These meditations reveal, here and there, isolated ancient Iranian elements: in at least two points in the first questions of the *Gushâ'ish u Rahâ'ish* one conceptual and one formal element appear that bring to mind, for example, the *Bundahishn*. The reader will remember that in the first chapter of this Pahlavî text there is a discussion, among other things, on whether God (Ohrmazd) was or was not Lord and Sovereign before the creation: Nâsir brings up the same problem. *Formaliter*, the Ismaili writer repeatedly uses a rather singular expression, i.e., that of "creating something, an entity, in aid of another" (*bi-yârî-i*). In the Pahlavî of the *Bundahishn*, *pat adyârîh i* is an identical expression, used in an identical context. But we must not forget that the *Bundahishn* dates back to the ninth century A.D.

Earlier on we mentioned the concept of Qâ'im and we will never know whether Nâsir expected the arrival of the Qâ'im and the advent of the Resurrection as early as it was expected in the Ismaili circles of the Nizârî tradition of Alamût, with whose founder he appears to have been in contact. Hasan-i Sabbâh—the legendary "old man of the mountain" who conquered the eagle's nest and organized the *da'va* in Iran (dying at a very old age in 1124)—and his first successors never proclaimed themselves to be more than the *dâ'îs* of the imâm, who was alive but could only be known through them.

But on August 8, 1164, his descendant Hasan, who was known by the title of Maulânâ Hasan *'alâ dhikrihi's-salâm* ("our lord Hasan, may the mention of his name be a blessing") proclaimed himself, with great pomp, the promised Qâ'im, the descendant of the Imâm Nizâr (though there probably was no relationship between Hasan-i Sabbâh and the Fatimids, for Hasan seems to have been of Persian descent) and initiator of the new post-prophetic cycle of the Resurrection of Resurrections. We are fortunate enough to possess an Ismaili account of the event that also deserves to be quoted for its "ritual" interest. It has been preserved in the rather late anonymous Ismaili treatise *Kalâm-i Pîr*, "The Master's Discourses" (which Ivanow places in the Safavid period and which has been falsely attributed to Nâsir-i Khusrau). Further details are to be found in another text.[33] We have combined the two accounts here with a few adaptations and brief omissions indicated by dots.[34]

> On the seventeenth day of the blessed month of Ramadân of the year 559 (August 1164) at the hour of the constellation of the Virgin, the sun being in the sign of Cancer, He (i.e., Our Lord Hasan) ordered a *minbar* (pulpit) to be erected facing westward on the esplanade of Alamût. Four standards were raised up at the four corners of the minbar. The "companions" (*rafîq*, the other version uses the sufi term, *murîd*, the initiated) of the Khorâsân were placed on the right, the people of Persian Iraq on the left, and the Dailamites and "companions" of Rûdbâr faced the minbar. A chair was placed in the middle, opposite the minbar. He ordered the *faqîh* (jurisconsult) Muhammad Bustî to take his seat in the chair. Then He himself, the Lord of the thousands of worlds and of men, Our Lord Hasan (a blessing be on the mention of his name!) wearing white garments, his head swathed in a white turban, came down—at about noon—from the Castle and solemnly approached the right side of the minbar and ascended into it. He then gave the triple salute of peace (*salâm*) to the crowd, first to the Dailamites, then to those on the right and then to those on the left. He remained seated for a while in the minbar, then he rose again and, with the Sword in his hand, he said, very loudly: "Oh you dwellers of the Universe, Spirits, Men, Angels! Know that the Lord, the Sovereign of the Resurrection (*qâ'imu'l-*

qiyâma) (may there be adoration and glory be at the mention of his name!), is the Lord of all created things, is the Absolute Existent (*maujûd-i mutlaq*). He is in every way exterior to any negation of his existence[35] because He is exalted beyond that with which idolaters associate Him. Today he has opened wide the door of His mercy, and has raised everyone up from the dead with His generous grace. The obligation falls on everyone who knows to thank Him and glorify Him, even though He is infinitely exalted above these things, because He is Sovereign over His Time and alone knows His essence".[36]

After this he spoke the [well-known] speech of which the first words are: "It was mentioned: In what does the Resurrection consist . . ?" then he read a copy of the epistle that begins: "We, who are present, who exist . . ." and then again the First Predication (*khutba*). After this he sat down for a while and then, standing up again, recited the Second Predication. Then the *faqîh* Muhammad Bustî rose up on the chair turned towards the minbar and read and commented[37] the whole of that Predication and the Great Epistle. During this reading the Lord stood too. When the reading was over He came down from the minbar and accomplished two *rak'at*s of prayers, as is the custom on feast days.[38]

For the whole of that day the people exchanged congratulations and festive gifts and joy reigned, and the fetters and shackles of the law were removed from the necks of the servants of God. And the Lord ordered that on that same day there should be celebrations in Mu'minâbâd of Quhistân and everywhere.

This proclamation soon turned into disappointment, because nothing special occurred in the visible world after the Resurrection. In fact, less than a century later, in 1257, Persian Nizârî Ismailism was annihilated by the Mongols who conquered Alamût and the whole chain of fortresses connected with it. In secrecy at first, the Imamate continued, following the (genealogically rather doubtful) line of Hasan's descendants up to the last rather anglicized imâm, the famous present-day Aghâ Khân.

The later external vicissitudes of Nizârî Ismailism are of no interest to us. Today the sect exists mainly in India and Pakistan. It must be remembered, however, that after Ismailism lost its outward power it survived in Persia under cover of Sufism and it is extraordinary how much of the Ismaili metaphysical system and mental forms, *forma mentis*, are still present in Persia (all the more surprising since Ismailism was nothing but a persecuted and slandered sect in that country). It is not an exaggeration to say that most classical Persian poetry is deeply marked in form rather than in contents by Ismailism. "Extreme" ideas and those with Ismaili tendencies are evident at the outset of the Safavid religious reformation that imposed Twelver Shi'ism on the whole country, and made it the official religion up to the present day; Ismaili (or rather Sufi-oriented Ismaili) ideas enriched the whole movement of rebirth of Iranian religious thinking in the sixteenth through the eighteenth centuries and finally, in the last century, led to the creation of a new religion in Iran: the Babi-Baha'i movement whose affinity with Ismailism cannot be ignored. Nor should the much discussed "social" aspect of Nizârî Ismailism be ignored (though this book deals mainly with the history and phenomenology of ideas and pure thinking). It is indisputable that Ismailism was seen as a public menace by the dominant classes in tenth through thirteenth century Persia. Its theology did not only unhinge the Sunni Islamic system but also to some extent the conformist Shi'ite system, and the Ismailis (as the conversion of intellectuals like Nâsir-i Khusrau and the sympathy of Avicenna, for example, prove) powerfully attracted nonconformist spirits and, at times, even altogether anti-Muslim spirits or even ones with agnostic tendencies (this accusation comes from adverse sources but may be of some value). Some testimonies (which are however not entirely reliable, coming as they do from "orthodox" sources) state that Ismaili propaganda appealed especially to the poor classes,[39] while their deadly enemy Nizâmu'l-Mulk attributes the communal use of goods and women to them.[40] The Soviet scholar Bertels[41] interprets the Persian Ismaili movement, or the movement with those tendencies, as a system thought up by the great landowners to maintain their position against the "equalizing" influence of Sunni Islam after the Persian conquest, and the reader will have already noted how Ismaili theology in some ways lends itself admirably to an aristocratic social system. The fact remains, however, that the Ismaili threat endangered the spiritual and material structure of the far from progressive "Sunni" governments once they had taken over, and though every class felt threatened by a possible collapse, the lower ones were less exposed. This may be the most prudent opinion one can have concerning the social value of Ismailism.

Religious Aspects of Persian Falsafa. Avicenna.

We mentioned above that an Ismaili-oriented or, more broadly speaking, a mystically and gnostically oriented atmosphere dominated all or almost all the Persian intellectual circles of the period we are dealing with (tenth through thirteenth century). Only one great Muslim philosopher, Averroes (who does not interest us here, however, since he was possibly the least religious of them all and not Persian but Spanish), appears to have been almost immune to the influences of the neo-Platonic, Sabaean and Gnostic currents in Muslim philosophy in his attempt to retrace pure Aristotelianism. We have proof of this in the complex personality of the greatest of all Persian philosophers: Avicenna (980–1037). Cultivated Westerners are taught to think of Avicenna as "the great Arab philosopher." In fact Avicenna was neither Arab (both his father and mother were Persian and he never left Iranian territory in the course of his long peregrinations) nor, strictly speaking, only a philosopher, for, as we shall see, the parts of his work less known to the European public are imbued with mystical and Gnostic elements. We will open a parenthesis here to explain that the Arabic-Persian term of *fīlsūf*, *falâsifa* in the plural, i.e., a scholar of *falsafa* (corruptions of the well-known Greek words), implies a rather narrow concept of philosophy: only scholars of philosophy derived from Greek, Aristotelian, or neo-Platonic sources were called "philosophers." Personalities such as Nâsir-i Khusrau or Ghazzâli (another great Persian thinker who died in 1111 and whom space and the fact that there was nothing strictly "Iranian" about him prevent us from studying him here) would not be called "philosophers" according to Muslim tradition.

Abû 'Alî Ibn Sînâ is also called "Avicenna," a medieval Spanish corruption of Ibn Sînâ. He was born in the village of Kharmêthân (now Râmetân, near Bukhârâ in Uzbekistan) where his father, who came from Balkh (now Afghanistan), had been sent as a civil servant in the service of the prince of the local Samanid dynasty Nûh II ibn Mansûr (976–997). According to our sources, Avicenna's father was Ismaili and the youth must have listened to the discussions of his father's "propagandist" friends when they met in his home. But it is difficult to make out whether Avicenna himself was or was not Ismaili, and the problem may possibly be wrongly presented: for we are not looking for an "official" adherence but rather for subtle cultural influences. There are no traces of Ismaili doctrine in his truly philosophical works and this plays against the hypothesis of Avicenna's Ismailism, but some elements play in its favor: for instance his antipathy for the Ghaznavid Sunnis who tried in vain to capture him in the course of his adventurous life (for some time Avicenna was, rather unsuccessfully, also "prime minister" for a local potentate of Hamadân): the philosopher's flight from the Ghaznavids, during which he seems to have preferred the protection of small local princes who were Shi'ite or had Shi'ite tendencies, seems to be a *leitmotif* in his biography. Other points in favor of this theory can be found in his own works—not the great exoteric works but some of his so-called "mystical" short treatises and poems[42] for behind the "rational" philosopher we find the *'ârif*, the Gnostic, for whom the whole of philosophy is simply introductory to a self-realizing "vision" that is completely unknown to our modern philosophy and probably also to the purer Aristotelianism of a philosopher such as Averroes. Corbin's book *Avicenna and the Visionary Recital* (Princeton, 1960) is fundamental if we want to understand this aspect of Avicenna. But even before Corbin's fascinating studies the Soviet orientalist Bertels gave rather probative evidence (his important article is quoted above) in favor of Avicenna's adherence to the Ismaili Gnostic current, or at least of his marked tendency towards Shi'ism. What is certain, however, is that Avicenna belonged to the Shu'ûbîyâ, i.e., a partisan of the political, religious and literary tendencies that emerged in the eighth through ninth centuries and (in opposition to an Islam seen as a mainly Arab phenomenon) attempted to bring to the fore "national" (and especially the Persian) motifs of the culture of the Abbasid Empire. These were often strongly marked by religious "exaggeration" (*ghuluww*, extreme Shi'ism). His limited poetic production proves this tendency in quatrains such as the following (if it is authentic):

> The Most High Power has twice written 'Alî's holy name
> backwards on the sheet of man's face
> One *lâm* and two *'ain*s and two upside down *yâs*:
> his eyebrows and eyes and nose all most clearly written.

These lines tell us that the three letters that form 'Alî's name in Arabic resemble respectively a nose, an eye and an eyebrow. The idea that one of God's names is impressed on man's face (who, according to both the Qur'an and the Bible, was made in the image and likeness of God) in letters representing him is frequently found in extreme Shi'i religious circles, where "talismans" or symbols bearing two intertwined names of 'Alî are current. 'Alî, Man *par excellence*, is the Cosmic Anthropos who is simply a reflection of God (see above). Or the following theoretically more moderate but more emotional quatrain:

> Since the wine of love was poured into the primeval cup
> And the First Lover was filled with the fire of love,
> my soul and the love of 'Alî mingled for ever
> like sugar and milk.

If we also consider the Gnostic flavor of Avicenna's "visionary tales" and their resemblance to similar productions by followers of the "illuminative" philosophy of the Ishrâq (see ahead)—a current that certainly owes a great deal to Ismailism—this hypothesis grows more plausible. We cannot presume to resolve this possibly unresolvable problem and here will simply offer our readers some examples of the religious aspect of the great Iranian thinker's writings.

Avicenna's most eloquent religious works are a beautiful poem in Arabic—the ode to the Rational Soul—and the three epistles that Mehren, his first editor, wrongly described as "mystical."[43]

We will quote the entire ode to the Soul because it is very beautiful and because—according to recent studies—its authenticity appears certain, coming as it does from the oldest codices of his "Epistles" (which go back to the end of the twelfth century and which tradition has always attributed to him). The present translation was drawn from an Arabic text reproduced in a brief Persian commentary to the ode written in the seventh century of the Hegira (thirteenth century A.D.). It was edited by the Persian scholar, Professor 'Abbâs Iqbâl, and published for Avicenna's millenary festivities[44] in the periodical of the department of literature of the University of Tehran (year I, no. 4, 1954, pp. 14–29).

1. On you a glorious inaccessible saintly Dove has descended from the most high places.
2. To the eyes of all Sages she is veiled and yet shows herself uncovered, like a girl bereft of her veils.
3. She came to you against her will, but now would leave you with sorrow, even if she were tormented with suffering.
4. At first she shrank away uneasily, filled with shamed horror at your contact, but once she was united to you, little by little she grew used to the plains of this desolate desert.
5. And surely I believe that she has forgotten the time when she wafted in celestial gardens and the lovely abodes that, formerly, she was unwilling to leave.
6. Until finally, united to the D of her fatal Descent, detached from the C of her Center in the supreme lands.
7. The heavy W of her Weight clung to her and now she is among deserted tracks and ruins.
8. She weeps at the memory of the fresh dwellings of the sky with eyes that know no limit to tears.
9. And, like a cloud, she bathes in tears the traces of ancient abodes, cancelled by the fourfold breath of the constant winds.
10. For close-woven nets hold her and a cage prevents her from reaching the boundless Spring heights of the sky.
11. Until the day draws near for her journey towards the joyful meadows, and the time is close for her to leave for the vast plains,
12. And she prepares to leave every vestige of the world, and her Earthly Companion who by now is rejected and deserted,
13. She falls into a light sleep, and the veil is torn, and yet she sees what sleeping eyes never see,
14. And she chirps most gentle songs on the highest branch (for Knowledge purifies and raises up whoever is low).
15. But why did she descend from the heavenly peaks into this deep abyss at the foot of the mountain?
16. Her descent was certainly hard and binding law, so that she might listen to what she had never heard before,
17. And return to her homeland wise with every hidden secret of the cosmos, with her most pure garment unlacerated.
18. She is the one whose path was barred by Time, until she passed away into death without rising again to the world,
19. And she was as lightning, which flashes for an instant above the green meadow, and then vanishes as if nothing had flashed.

The western reader does not need a long explanation to understand the essence of this image. The Bird-Soul and its captivity in the net of the body is such a universal, archetypal image, it exists in our culture too (and takes a great deal from Hellenism and Gnosis). We need say little about it here, but the reader should see ahead. Where the form of expression is concerned, we will only note that the contrast between "desolate desert" and "green enclosures" was frequent in ancient Arabic poetry and is transposed here to indicate metaphysical realities. The expression in verses 6–7 (in which we have had to adapt the names of the letters to those of our alphabet) is not as strange and baroque as it may seem, if we consider the intense symbolical value of writing and its elements in all traditional civilizations and especially in esoteric Muslim circles. In verse 9 Avicenna uses—again as a metaphysical symbol—an image the Arab poets from the desert frequently used, i.e., the sadness caused by the sight of the ephemeral traces the abandoned encampments of the Beloved and her retinue left on the sand. Here the traces of abandoned abodes are the memory of the primitive celestial abode of the Soul and the "four winds" are the passions and preoccupations of the world. The whole ode is an echo of the redemptive-salvific theory of Gnosis that we have come across repeatedly.

Avicenna also developed the essential concepts expressed here in prose (a rather contorted Arabic prose, which however is occasionally lit up by precious images) in three short Gnostic rather than "mystical" treatises the titles of which are "Alive the Son of Awakened," "The Bird" and "Salâmân and Absâl." All three are expressions of the same tragic situation of the soul, torn between two poles and yearning for liberation, which purifies itself through its struggle and redeems itself through knowledge. This idea is also present in the Ismaili Epistles of the "brothers of Purity" that are imbued with Hermetic-neo-Platonic thought.

Because of the importance of these "visionary tales" (which may even have originated in the philosopher's genuine mental "visions," which were far more "plastic" than the purely intellectual ones of modern philosophers) as the first of a series of the symbolical tales that were to become very popular in the religious and literary history of Iran, we are presenting one of them—"The Bird"—in translation (with a few minor cuts). Logically it appears to occupy an intermediate position between the two others. The first—"Alive the Son of Awakened"—tells of the apparition to the Author "in his native dwelling" (i.e., when the soul is fulfilled in purifying concentration) of a young–looking Old Man (we will run into this motif again: see ahead) who, despite his age, greeted him first (cf. Beatrice's beatifying greeting). He answers the author's questions saying that his fatherland is Jerusalem (the celestial Jerusalem, the archangelic Pleroma) and his name is "Alive the son of Awakened" (Universal Intellect the son of God). He explains that the soul can only be freed from its evil companions through a long journey towards the "Orient." Next we have a "visionary geography" symbolizing psychic and metaphysical places: the journey starts with an ablution at the Murmuring Source that is near the spring of the Water of

Life. This ablution has levitating power and enables the traveller to go even beyond the *barzakh*. The source is beyond the Darkness that shrouds the Pole, in an immense expanse filled with Light. Beyond the physical Orient there are other symbolic lands where the Rising Sun, the *Dator Formarum*, rises (according to a singular expression to be found in Islamic tradition) "between the two Horns—or powers or peoples—of Satan" that are symbols of psychic faculties and tendencies. Some of these flying demons "do not limit themselves to a single species, but each individual has a strange and special form, composed of two, three or four natures, like a flying man, a snake with a swine's head, or half a man, or an isolated human foot, or a hand, or other similar living creatures." These are transparently symbols of mental images, as the author himself explains, adding: "And it is not an absurdity to believe that the composite images the painters draw are taken from this region." His journey continues in more and more distant lands, until the archangelic Pleroma and Its indescribable and elusive "Origin" are reached. The Young-Old Man leaves the Author with the desire to accomplish this journey.

In the "Epistle of the Bird" the Soul is temporarily admitted to this Orient, at the end of a heroic celestial ascension, for a secret interview with the Lord of the Pleroma. As in all these tales the Author speaks in the first person—in the form of a Bird here—and addresses the "brothers" (who are clearly the initiated). Elsewhere too (e.g., in the "Epistle of the Soul"[45] or in the treatise *al-Ishârât wa't-tanbîhât*)[46] the Author explicitly declares that he is revealing to the general public only the exoteric aspect of a far deeper esoteric doctrine that is alluded to symbolically for the benefit of the "brothers."

The Epistle of the Bird

> In the name of the clement and merciful God. I have no help other than in God; in Him do I trust, and He alone suffices me.
>
> Are any of my brothers[47] willing to give me some attention, to listen to my laments? They might keep me company, helping me to bear the burden. For, in fact, a friend will not be able to console his brother if he does not maintain his friendship immaculate, both in prosperity and in adversity. How can you be a faithful friend if you consider friendship as a business, something in which you seek refuge when a grievous event reminds you of your friend, and you neglect him when you can do without him? For we do not visit our companion unless misfortune visits us, and we remember our friend only when need brings him to mind! My God! Let this not occur among the brothers who are united through divine communion and have become companions through lofty proximity, who have contemplated the Supernal Truths with inner vision and have purified the intimate seat of their hearts from the impurities of doubt, united only by God's cry!
>
> Come now, oh brothers of Truth, share your secret thoughts and each of you

remove the veil from the intimate mystery of your heart, and contemplate one another and perfect yourselves for one another!

Come now, oh brothers of Truth, garb yourselves like porcupines in bristling armour, manifest your inner selves and veil your outer persons. In truth your secret will be exposed to the light and your visible aspect will be secret![48]

Come now, oh brothers of Truth, slip out of your skins with the agility of snakes, crawl as the worm crawls. And be scorpions, with armed tails, for Satan surely only assaults man from behind. Drink down poison and you will be safe, ardently desire death and you will live; fly high and do not seek refuge in nests, for it is in nests that birds are most often captured. And if you are prevented for lack of wings, rob them and you will triumph, for the sharpest look-out is he who flies with the greatest strength. Be ostriches who swallow boiling sands, snakes who know how to devour the hardest bones, salamanders who trustingly garb themselves in fire, bats who never show themselves to the day, for the bat is the best of all birds!

Come now, oh brothers of Truth! The richest man is he who dares in view of the Morrow, the laziest is he who remains on this side of his limits!

Come now, oh brothers of Truth! It is not surprising that Angels avoid evil, and that brutes commit foul deeds, but it is more than surprising that man should rebel against Divine Law, urged on by passions, even though it was through them that he lost his primeval form; and that he obeys these passions, even though his nature draws light from the intellect. The Lord knows it! The man who stands firmly and struggles against his desires and his foot does not slip in this struggle is similar to the Angels, and the man who is not strong enough to reject the invitation of lust is inferior to the brute.

But let us now come to the subject of our discourse:

A group of hunters went out to catch birds: they set their nets, they prepared their traps, they placed their bait and hid among the bushes while I was flying with a multitude of birds. When the hunters saw us, they started to whistle invitingly: I and my companions sensed an abundance of food and no doubt entered our hearts nor did suspicion prevent us from drawing close. We approached rapidly and all fell into the ambush of nets. And rings imprisoned our necks, and the thin meshes of the net caught our wings, and the ropes twined around our feet; and all our efforts to move only increased our suffering. We resigned ourselves to death and each bird's terror made him forget his brother's sorrow. For some time we studied every wile in order to escape, but then we forgot our true state: we grew accustomed to the nets and felt at home in the cages.

But one day, as I looked beyond the bars of my cage, I saw birds of our company who had succeeded in escaping and tearing themselves away from the nets, and now they were flying freely away from their cages: the rope around their feet still hampered them but did not prevent their safety and freedom.[49]

Seeing them reminded me of what I had forgotten and led me to loathe the conditions I had adapted to, and my sorrow and regret almost destroyed me and my heart wore itself out in laments. And from my cage I called to them to approach and teach me through what cunning they had escaped while long imprisonment still suffocated me; and I remembered the hunters' wiles. But they despised me all the more; then I invoked them, in the name of our old friendship and our strong bond of companionship and our well guarded pact, that their hearts should be trusting and that they should cast doubt from their bosoms.[50]

Then they came to me, and I questioned them on their condition; they reminded me that they had suffered the same misfortunes as I and that, in despair, they had grown used to these misfortunes. And they took care of me, and they loosened the bond around my neck and they freed my wing from the net, and the door of the cage was opened and I heard a voice say: "Take advantage of this to save yourself!" And I asked them to free my feet from the ring too but they answered: "If we had had the strength to do this we would have done it already and freed our own feet. How can he who is sick heal you?"

And I flew from the cage and they said: "Look, there is a vast expanse in front of you: we will be safe if we fly across it. Follow our tracks: we will save you and guide you along smooth paths."

And the whirr of our wings united us as we flew between two flanks of the highest mountain, which enclosed a valley that at times was fertile and grassy and at times desolate and arid. Finally we crossed it and arrived at the top of the mountain; and we found ourselves facing eight peaks[51] that were so high that the eye could not reach the top and we said to one another: "Let us see who can fly the fastest, for we will not be safe until we are beyond them!"

And we raced one another as fast as we could until, having flown over six, we came to the seventh.[52] Penetrating into those reaches we said: "Let us rest a while for we are exhausted: ample distance now separates us from our enemies." And thus we agreed to rest our tired bodies. (To pause in recollection is a better guide to safety than incessant movement).

And so we halted on that peak. And lo, there were cultivated fields and verdant gardens, fruitful with trees, running with rivers, whose coolness refreshes the eye in such shining and splendid forms that they almost awe the mind and amaze the marrow of one's heart. And our ears were gladdened by most gentle melodies and melancholy songs, and our nostrils bewitched by perfumes that surpassed the finest musk and the freshest amber. We ate of those fruits and drank of those streams and we stopped there only long enough to cast out our weariness, for we said one to the other: "Hurry, hurry, for there is no worse trap than a sense of security, nor better defended castle than diffidence of all things. We have stayed too long in this place, despite our remedy against sloth;[53] the enemy is pursuing us; he is following in our steps and spying on our every stop. Come now, let us go, let us abandon this land, sweet as it is. For the only sweet thing is salvation." We gathered together to depart.

We left that region and reached the eighth peak.[54] And it was very lofty, and its top was in the clouds, far up in the sky. Those slopes were inhabited by birds whose song was sweeter than any I have ever heard, whose colors were more beautiful and whose forms were more graceful than any I have ever seen. They were the gentlest birds I have ever met. Staying with them we discovered such things about their benevolence and sweetness and graciousness that we were saturate, nor would our hands ever be able to repay the debt even if we devoted our whole lives to doing so and asked for the help of a double life.

When we had established familiar intercourse we confided our misfortune to them. They expressed their participation and concern and told us that beyond the mountain there was a city where a Great King lived, and that any unjustly treated creature who asked for His help and confided in Him was relieved of all straits in virtue of His power and His help. Trusting in their indications we went towards the King's city until, arriving at the gate of the Court, we waited for permission.

The order granting the travellers access was finally issued, and we were ushered into his Castle. And we found ourselves in a great courtroom, vaster than words can describe, and when we had passed through it the curtain that separated us from the next room was lifted and we were in a hall so vast and splendid that the first one seemed to us narrow and wretched. And finally we reached the King's secret chamber, and when the curtains were lifted and our eye saw the Sovereign in all His beauty, our hearts remained prisoner of His fascination, and we were filled with venerating terror and were unable to express our complaint. Seeing our confusion, He affably gave us back our confidence and inspired us with the courage to speak to Him. And so we told our story and He said: "Only those who bound your feet have the power to loosen them.[55] I will now send them a Messenger with the order to do your will and free you from these thongs. Go then in happiness.

And so here we are, travelling with the Messenger.[56]

And my brothers turn to me asking me to tell them about the splendor of the King and to describe him in words both sufficient and concise. And I say: "He is a King whose description requires that you conceive in your heart all possible Beauty free of all Foulness, and every Perfection uncontaminated by any Defect. All royal perfection is His, and He lacks all defects, even if only imaginary ones. He is all beauty, in his Face, and all generous grace, in his Hand. He who serves Him has earned supreme fortune, and he who betrays Him has lost the world of Beyond and even this world."

But how many brothers, once they have heard my story, will say: "I think your mind has become deranged and madness has visited you! In God's truth, you have not flown—a bird—in the air but your mind has flown away; the hunters did not capture you one day but something has made your heart a prisoner. How could man ever fly or birds talk? Most certainly black Bile has overwhelmed the balance of your humors, and Aridity has invaded your brain.[57] The remedy [for your sickness] is to drink dodder tea, take baths in warm fresh water and inhale vapors of water-lily oil. You must be careful of your food and diet, choosing light viands, avoiding coitus, fleeing from insomnia and not thinking too much. For in the past we knew you as a judicious companion and a person of solid and acute intellect! God alone knows what we feel in our hearts: they are concerned and doleful for you, and our souls are saddened and perturbed over your soul's alienation!

How many useless and empty words they speak! For the worst discourse is the one that is uselessly lost.

But I ask God for help, and clear myself of all responsibility concerning the people of the world. He who believes differently is lost in this world and the next, "and the unjust will know what fate awaits them."[58]

The third "visionary tale"—about Salâmân and Absâl—has not come down to us in Avicenna's version but in a dry summary left us by the Ismaili philosopher Nasîru'd-Dîn Tûsî (d. in 1274). This proves, among other things, that whether Avicenna himself was an Ismaili or not, the Ismailis knew and appreciated his Gnostic works—possibly subjecting them to further esoteric interpretation or *ta'wîl*.

Salâmân and Absâl were two uterine brothers. Absâl was the younger and he grew in beauty and intelligence. Salâmân's wife fell wildly in love with him and tried to seduce him. Seeing her efforts vain, the woman proposed to her husband that he should marry his brother Absâl to his sister-in-law, i.e., her own sister. Then she proposed to her sister to allow her to spend the first night of their marriage with Absâl. A flash of lightning lit up the stormy sky and his bedmate's true identity was revealed through the darkness to the pious Absâl who repulsed her, left the room and determined to flee. Gathering a troop of soldiers together he conquered a good part of the world for his brother's kingdom. Returning home he thought that his sister-in-law had forgotten him, but this was not so. A war against dangerous enemies broke out: the wicked woman corrupted the high-ranking officers of Absâl's army and convinced them to abandon him. Grievously wounded, Absâl was left on the battlefield but a wild beast helped and nourished him: his wounds healed and he pursued his enemies and defeated them. Still not satisfied, the woman corrupted a cook and a steward, gave them a large sum of money and convinced them to poison Absâl, who died. His grieving brother renounced his kingdom and retired to a hermitage. A mysterious voice revealed the truth to him and he punished his wife, the cook and the steward, putting them to death.

This, in its aridity, is the plot of the symbolic tale that Corbin—using a rather arbitrary systematization to connect it to the other two—considers the symbol of the total belonging of the Human Soul (symbolized here by Absâl) to the Orient through death. According to Tûsî's more "philosophical" interpretation, Absâl was contemplative Intellect, the superior side of the soul, the terrestrial angel (terrestrial angels in this sense are also mentioned in "Alive the son of Awakened") whose vocation it was to become one with the Holy Spirit angel or Acting intellect. Salâmân was the rational human soul. Salâmân's wife was the lustful and irascible soul, the *nafs ammâra* (impulsive soul of the Qur'an, XII, 53). Her sister, on the other hand, was practical intellect and Tûsî also identifies her with the "soul at peace" mentioned in the Qur'an (LXXXIX, 27). These identifications (which were very common in our Middle Ages) are singularly distasteful to modern culture, but much of their unpalatability disappears if we bear in mind that they are not—as some Easterners, including Tûsî, have rather aridly and incorrectly interpreted them—"allegories." They are, rather, living, "angelic," "symbols" and, occasionally, polyvalent symbols like those that, once they have emerged from their creator's mind, become persons and almost take on a life of their own in the mesocosm of *mithâl* ("[imaginal] symbols"), a realm that all these currents accept but which the modern world has forgotten. The essential difference between allegory and symbol becomes clearer only if we see the first as a more or less artificial figuration of abstractions that can become known through other channels too, and the second as the annunciation and representation of something that cannot be expressed otherwise.

We mentioned above that Avicenna's tales form the first link in a chain of symbolic tales that spread throughout Persian literature, from this period until the nineteenth century. What is their origin? Here too we go back to Hellenistic-Gnostic sources. This origin is clearly documentable, at least for the story of Salâmân and Absâl, because another rather similar version exists from which this one was certainly taken. It was translated from the Greek by the well known translator Hunain ibn Ishâq (d. 873) (the original text has been lost, but it must have been widely read in Hellenist Hermetic circles) .

Besides, an interesting parallel exists in a strangely neglected Ismaili commentary on the Qur'an (edited by Strothmann)[59] with an unusual passage in the epistle "Alive the son of Awakened" concerning the strange flying creatures beyond the Orient composed of parts of different bodies. Speaking about the mysterious journey of Dhû'l-Qarnain (Alexander the Great of the legend) told in the Qur'an (XVIII, 83–98) the Ismaili commentator says that he found a people who "was scarcely able to understand speech" (Kor. ibid., 93) between the two great barriers at the confines of the world who had displaced limbs and contorted forms. These beings lacked various limbs and had been "punished" through a kind of deformation or transformation after death that was very similar to metempsychosis (though this subject requires further study). It is also interesting that the Ismaili *Ummu'l-Kitâb* mentions similar men deprived of their limbs, deformed, etc. If we accept that the *Ummu'l-Kitâb* was written in the tenth-eleventh century this means that about seven centuries elapsed before the Ismaili commentary, edited by Strothmann, was composed by a Yemeni, Musta'lî *dâ'î* (Diyâ'u'd-Dîn Ismâ'îl ibn Hibatu'llâh) who died in 1760. He probably drew on ancient traditional Ismaili sources. Since it is far more likely that this image was born in Gnostic *"Ummu'l-Kitâb*-style" circles rather than as the fruit of a philosophy (even an allegorical one), Avicenna probably drew on these sources and adapted them philosophically (in Avicenna's text the image is not of "punished" creatures but of separate mental forms, prior to their entry into consciousness): the inverse passage (Avicenna's personal philosophical allegory mythicized by Gnostics) seems to me very improbable.

The Hellenistic-Ismaili encyclopaedia of the "Brothers of Purity," (composed only shortly before the flowering of Avicenna's work) also contains symbolic tales. The origin of one of them, for example, which recalls the symbol of inebriation and lethargic sleep signifying religious ignorance (*Rasâ'il*, IV, pp. 212 and foll.) which we have already seen in the tale of the conversion of the Ismaili Nâsir-i Khusrau, can be traced back to the Buddhist novel *Barlaam and Josaphat* which penetrated into Islam through Hellenistic remakes (Cf. Corbin, *Jâmi'*, pp. 30–31, note 76).

Regardless of their origin, these Avicennian "symbols" considerably influenced the literary-religious history of Persia and of the Islamic world in general. The first—the symbol of "Alive the son of Awakened"—was developed in a very different form (which really only maintains the name of the protagonist) in the famous philosophical novel by the Spanish Arab Ibn Tufail, who died in 1185 and was a friend of his great fellow countryman Averroes. The characters of Salâmân and Absâl recur in different roles in it. In Sufi Persian literature the motif of the mystical journey that purifies the soul (also at the origin of Dante's *Divine Comedy*) was very widespread, starting with the poem "The journey of the Servants of God in the world of Return" (*Sairu'l-ibâd ilà'l-ma'âd*) by Sanâ'î (d. 1141) up to the poem *Misbâhu'l-arvâh* ("The lamp of the spirits") by the Sufi Auhadu'd-Dîn Kirmânî (d. 1237–38), in which the author, like Dante, has a guide (corresponding to Avicenna's Young-Old-Man) who is the Intellect. He too, however, like Virgil's guide, can lead him only to a given point in his journey. All this can be traced back to Artâ Vîrâf's prosaic visionary journey, written in Middle Persian. As usual, however, given the absence of some intermediate link, it is far more likely that we are dealing here with an Iranian influence on the Gnostic world from whence it "returned" to Islamic Iran. The motif of the mystical journey of the birds that we find in the second Avicennian epistle, is even more widespread in Persian literature. The best known poem of this type is Faridu'd-Dîn 'Attâr's famous "Language of the Birds" (*Mantiqu't-tair*) (d. 1221) that the curious reader will find in Ritter's very exhaustive descriptive-phenomenological volume (*Das Meer der Seele*, Leiden, 1955). The poem tells the tale of thirty birds (human souls) who fly across seven terrible valleys in search of their sovereign, the mythical Sîmurgh. Reaching the end of their journey they realize that Sîmurgh (a pun in Persian that can also mean "thirty birds") was simply themselves. The central Asian Turkish poet Mîr 'Alî Shêr Navâ'î (d. 1501) deals with a similar subject in his poem "The Tongue of the Birds," while the theme of the mystical journey across the various valleys (a fusion of elements from the two first Avicennian epistles) comes down to the twentieth century through Persian religious literature in the beautiful little prose poems *The Seven Valleys* and *The Four Valleys*, by the founder of the new Baha'i religion, Baha'ullah (d. 1892, see chap. VIII). And the lost epistle of Salâmân and Absâl is echoed, in a far more aesthetically refined form, in the poem of the same name by the last of the great Persian classic authors, 'Abdu'r-Rahmin Jâmî (d. 1492) who was also a great "mystic." Curiously in another poem, "The gift of the Free Men" (*Tuhfatu'l-ahrâr*), Jâmî himself, criticizing the purely superficial and loveless scientists, invites his readers "not to seek the light of the heart from Avicenna's eye, for his *Ishârât* [a short treatise that, by an irony of fate, Mehren calls "mystic"] is impious, his *Shifâ* [the "Book of Healing," a metaphysical treatise] mere sickness and his 'Salvation' [the title of another of his philosophical books], in fact imprisonment."[60]

The Persian mystics never felt very close to Avicenna. An important and possibly legendary tradition tells of a meeting between the proud philosopher (the authentic biographical data we have indicates him as having a proud and "difficult nature") and the great Persian saint Abû Sa'îd ibn Abî'l-Khair (d. 1048), one of the founders of the school of neo-Persian mystical poetry. After several days of private discussion the philosopher is reputed to have said about the saint: "What I know he sees"; while the saint said of the philosopher: "What I see he knows."

But Avicenna had an imitator who surpassed him in the great shaikh of Persian illuminative philosophy (*shaikhu'l-ishrâq*), Shihâbu'd-Dîn Suhravardî, "the slain" (*maqtûl*, d. 1191), who produced an abundance of similar epistles. And this leads us to a discussion of the problem of the differences between "mysticism," "ishrâq" and "Avicennism" as an introduction to the figure of the great Persian thinker.

The Ishrâqî Connection with Avicenna

According to Horten—an expert on Islamic falsafa (see his article "Falsafa" in *EI*[1])—what Arab (or rather Muslim), Peripateticism has over and above Aristotelianism is the idea of "contingency." Where things of the world are concerned, being and existence are radically distinct. Consequently existence must be granted to objects and be constantly preserved for them by a Being who necessarily exists. In Avicenna this theory has one shadowy aspect: the contingency of objects is given as a real difference between being and existence. Existence has to accede to being from the outside. But then being without existence is not real, it cannot become the substratum and receptive principle of a reality. And Avicenna's Peripatetic doctrine of "cognition" presented other problems that required the intermediary of an "active intellect" and its action on the soul, thus complicating the precise act of knowledge. In the twelfth century these problems were studied by a remarkable Persian thinker who carefully analyzed their peripatetic sense and transposed them in an "angelic" and "metaphysics of light" key, resolving them brilliantly by building a system that he himself termed Ishrâqî, "illuminative," around and beyond them. In an exposition of the broad lines of Persian religious thought Suhravardî's importance is considerable:

particularly because he was possibly the only post-Islamic thinker who—beyond literary reasons or heroic legends—had intuitions concerning certain central points of ancient Persian religious thought and consciously assumed the role of their reviver. It is true that he also assumed the role of reviver of Hermetic, Pythagorean and Empedoclean thought so that, as usual, it is difficult to discover any "direct loan" from ancient Persia that was not—very probably—mediated through Gnostic-Hellenistic syncretism.

As the great Italian Orientalist Nallino pointed out, Ishrâq means "radiating brilliance of a light" rather than "illumination," but it is commonly called the Suhravardian "illuminative" philosophy or, better, theosophy, and we will keep to this term for practical reasons: tradition also attributes a hikma *mashriqîya*, an "oriental wisdom" to Avicenna, and some people have erroneously understood this as *mushriqîya*, ("illuminating") (Nallino pointed this out too). It seems to us that he[61] was less to the point in his denial of any trace of esoterism in Avicenna, declaring him, as he did, free from the "eccentricities in the style of Proclus and Iamblicus" which he felt filled Suhravardî's works. There is an undoubtedly "esoteric" side to Avicenna's works and Corbin's important studies show us that Suhravardî's works contain more than "eccentricities." As he explicitly states (Cf. Corbin, Opera Metaph, Vol. I, p. 40), he considers himself an in-depth continuation of the "oriental" wisdom. Further acquaintance with the visionary tales of the two thinkers (which mention a "western exile" into matter and a journey towards the Orient into the luminous spiritual realities) allows us—beyond the philological trifles of *mushriqîya* or *mashriqîya*—to link up this "oriental wisdom" to the concept of "illuminative radiance," to a metaphysics of Light that had to be present in Avicenna—even if to a far more moderate degree—through the usual syncretist channels that influenced the whole of Muslim philosophy. One might even say that Suhravardî systematized and gave depth to the motifs, which in the far more "Peripatetic" Avicenna remained mere symbolical images that grew out of his restless researcher's soul in "moments of grace."

Having defined the problems concerning the name generally attributed to his philosophy we will now briefly consider his life in order to be able to situate his thought. Suhravardî was born at Suhravard, a small town (which no longer exists) in north-western Iran—ancient Media—in 1153. As a youth he studied at Marâgha under the same master as the great Fakhru'd-Dîn Râzî. After further studies at Isfahân he started his peregrinations and meditation, frequenting the Sufis (mystics). At the court of Salâhu'd-Dîn the Ayyubid—the Saladin of our medieval legend—he made friends with the sovereign's son who tried in vain to save him from the accusations of heresy hurled at him by the orthodox jurisprudents and theologians, who were terrified by some of his extremely bold theoretical statements and possibly even more by the Ismaili tendencies they discovered in his terminology (Saladin had recently defeated the Fatimid Ismailis, as an organized state). Suhravardî was only 38 years old when he was executed at Aleppo, on July 29, 1191. He was called "the slain one," *maqtûl*, to avoid calling him "martyr" (*shahîd*).

It is hard to "define" his work generically, though the term "mystic" is probably the closest we can get to reality; however the shrewd disquisitions on which he based and justified his theories, which form a real "system," distinguish him from purely emotional mystics. Besides—though this has not been studied sufficiently and we only mention it in passing—some passages in his works are close to certain Ismaili statements and his conscious "restoration" of a Hermetic, Pythagorean and Iranian "divine philosophy" or theosophy gives him an extremely original position among the great mass of the philosophers and mystics of Islam. We will start by examining this historically extremely interesting aspect.

With the frankness that was to cost him his life he says on page 111 of his work *Talvîhât* (62) (ed. Corbin, vol. I):

> . . . you must know that ever since wisdom was transmitted orally in ancient times the Sublime Sages (*al-hukamâ al-kibâr*), such a father of Sages, the Father of Fathers, Hermes, and before him Agathodaimon (note the strength of the Sabaean tradition) and again, like Pythagoras and Empedocles and the Prince of Sages, Plato, were far more estimable and lofty in stature than all those subtle "reasoners" we know among the Muslims . . .

In his *Mashâri' wa mutâharât*—in the classic style of the mystics who have their doctrines and practices go back in an almost uninterrupted chain (*isnâd*) to ancient teaching (these chains generally reached and stopped at 'Alî)—he offers us a far vaster and universalistic isnâd of esoteric doctrines: this is extremely interesting because of the accent he places on the Iranian element and also because of his special interpretation of certain famous mystics of Islam (the text is in Corbin, *Op. Metaph. et Myst.*, vol. I, p. 502 and foll).

> The last among the Greeks to have precise tidings concerning that Annihilating Light that leads to "minor death" was Plato, the Supreme Sage [elsewhere he even calls him "divine"]. And among the Great ones, Hermes consolidated himself, taking his lead from him [Plato], and his name remained in History. Among the Pahlavîs (*fahlaviyyîn*), the Possessor of Clay (*mâlik at-tîn' the First Man*), whose name was Gayômart (see ahead) and among those of his school (*shî'a!*) Ferîdûn and Kai-Khusrau. As for the lights of the Mystical Path (*sulûk*), in these more recent times the leaven fell into Akhî Akhmîn (the well known Egyptian mystic from Akhmîm, Dhû'n-Nûn, who died in 860) and descended from him into the Contemplative wayfarer (*sayyâr*) of Tustar (the tenth century Persian, Abû Sahl Tustarî) and into his school. While the leaven of the Khusrauânids, in the Mystical Path, descended into

the contemplative Wayfarer of Bistâm (Bâyazîd Bistâmi a Persian who died in 874) and after him into the Knight (*fatâ*) of Baidâ (the martyred mystic Mansûr al-Hallâj, who died in 922 and was a Mesopotamian of Iranian origin) and after them into the Contemplative Wayfarer of Amul and of Kharraqân (Abû'l-Hasan al-Kharraqânî, cf. Rûmî-Nicholson, VIII, p. 171).

As the reader can see for himself, the oldest Persian sages mentioned here do not appear to have had more marked personalities than a Hermes or an Agathodaimon. We know nothing of "mystical works" or mystical doctrines of a Gayômart and a Khusrau and consequently—so far at least—we are not dealing with an Iranian influence but rather (and this is substantially different) with the influence of a doctrine that considered semi-mythical Iranian characters among its prototypes: the Gnostic, Hellenistic, and Syncretist doctrine we have already outlined.

This aspect of Suhravardî's philosophy (which was not Iranian but Syncretist with Iranian elements is evident at the beginning of his *Hikmatu'l-Ishrâq* (Corbin, *Opera*, vol. II, pp. 10 and foll.):

> What I tell about the science of lights, its foundations and yet other things, will earn me the felicitations of anyone who follows the way of the Most High God. It was the *zauq*[63] of the prince and leader of philosophy, Plato, the possessor of confirmation and lights. Those who came before him, from the father of sages Hermes until his time, the great sages, pillars of wisdom, such as Empedocles, Pythagoras, and others, thought the same. The words of the ancients are symbolic (*marmûza*): the objections made against them, though they were directed against the external form of the words, do not touch their intentions: a symbol (*ramz*) cannot be disproved! And thus it is on this doctrine that the illuminative doctrine of light and of darkness which was that of the sages of Persia such as Jâmâsp, Frohâoshtr,[64] Buzurjmihr and their predecessors, was founded. It is not in this system that the impiety of the Magi and Mani's heresy consisted and, following it, we are not led to associate something with God. Besides, do not think that the sages, in this time which is close to us, profess a different doctrine. The world has never been deprived of wisdom, nor of an Individual who possesses it (*qâ'im bi-hâ*), in whom the proofs and foundations exist: he is the *khalîfa* (vicar) of God on earth.

We will stop to consider this extremely important passage. Suhravardî considered it a universal, esoteric doctrine (accessible to the "sages" who all professed it), and the common patrimony of an ancient tradition that was both Persian and Hellenistic-Egyptian. In this passage, in fact, he seems to say that the doctrine of the sages of Persia was based on that of the wise men of the Hermetic, Pythagorean and Platonic line of thought: and, as we already mentioned, this idea has more in its favor than it does against it. Generally, semi-legendary characters are indicated among the sages of Persia (Buzurjmihr is historical and Sasanian but we know very little about him and at all events he came very "late"). Giamâsp is also mentioned in Nâsir-i Khusrau's alleged autobiography translated by the Shi'ite Taqîyu'd-Dîn Muhammad Kâshi (d. 1539).[65] Wise apothegms are attributed to him, as well as works of natural science, alchemy and astrology. He probably was a sage of the Sasanian period—later confused with Jâmâsp, the brother of Zoroaster's father-in-law, (called Frashâoshtra in the Avesta). A reader of the Constantinople manuscript, which includes the *Hikmatu'l-Ishrâq* adds in a note: "Those of the Ishrâq are the sages of Persia who profess the two principles of light and darkness since they are the symbol of what is Necessary and what is Contingent." I don't think this statement should be given much consideration from a historical point of view: the distinction between light and darkness is not the whole of Iranian culture. What is important in this Suhravardian passage is, rather, the distinction he specifically makes between the Iranian religion as it was historically known to exist at the time (the "magi," the Zoroastrians, the "gabr," as they were contemptuously called), whom he (wrongfully) accused of absolute dualism and idolatry, and "the truer" Persian religion of the occult ancient illuminative tradition. Suhravardî also refuses to admit a possible Manichaean derivation. He rediscovers true Mazdaism and true Manichaeism through a personal *ta'wîl*, to which we reverently bow down but to which we cannot attribute, obviously, any historical value. The Ismaili-tinged term of *ta'wîl* comes almost instinctively, especially if we consider the final part of the passage which seems to have been written by an Ismaili: it speaks of the need for the "vicar of God on Earth" as most pure interpreter of occult tradition of wisdom, in a word, the imâm. We will see later the subtle difference between this character whom the mystics accepted—calling him, among other things, "pole"—and the imâm of Ismailism. For now, we need only indicate a common element. The Suhravardian *ta'wîl*, which makes him distinguish between historically visible and "true" dualistic Zoroastrianism and Manichaeism is admirably defined when he criticizes the foolishness of those who object to the Ancient Wise Men, taking their words ("one must not refute symbols!") literally.

This point introduces us to the core of the Suhravardian concept of the world and at the same time shows up one point (the only point in our opinion in which the martyr of Aleppo is truly heir to a genuinely Iranian cosmic vision, even if this reached him through indirect channels and was intuitively "restored" by him): his "angelic" concept of symbol. Already in the *Mutârahât*—which, at whatever stage it was written, was conceptually introductory to the *Hikmat al-ishrâq*—he approaches the problem of the *sâhib an-nau'* or *rabb an-nau'*, "The Lord of the Species," linking it with sure intuition to the Zoroastrian archangel and possibly also to the *ratu* of Mazdean metaphysics (Corbin, *Opera*, vol. I, p. 460):

This Lord of the Species of Fire is he whom the ancient Persians (*al-furs*) called Ardîbihist. For in fact the Persians exaggerated greatly concerning the "lords of the species" to such an extent that, for example, they even sanctified the lord of the species of the plant they called hôm, which enters into their rites, calling it hôm-îzad (="god Hôm"). As for Hermes, Agathodaimon and Plato, they do not present arguments to prove the existence of these lords of the species, but rather maintain that they have contemplated them. And if they have done so it is not up to us to argue the point against them.[66]

And, a little further on:

. . . and when you hear Empedocles and Agathodaimon and others speak of "lord of the species" try to understand their intention! And do not think that they mean that the Lord of the Species (idol) is a body, or bodily, or that he has a head or feet. And when you find Hermes saying: "A Spiritual Being instilled this knowledge into me and I asked him: Who are you? And he answered me: I am your perfect character (*tibâ'uka at-tâmma*, your truest "I," which the Iranians would call your *daêna*) do not believe that that being is like us.

The first thing to note in these passages is the precision of Suhravardî's intuition concerning what we ventured to define the essence of Iranian thought: i.e., "angelism"; on the other hand the modern reader must be on his guard against taking his declarations as declarations of "allegorical interpretation" which destroy the "existential reality" of these entities. No, this kind of world is different from both the purely intellective world and the physical world—it is an imaginative world, a world of symbols in which "angels" really exist and live while remaining different from both purely intellectual figures and living entities "like us."

This is how al-Ijî, (*Mawâqif*, quoted in Carra de Vaux, op. cit.) comments the idea of Suhravardian *rabb an-nau'*:

The philosopher of the doctrine of Illumination, according to which each of the species of the spheres, the stars, the simple elements and their compounds has its correspondent in a thing (it might be better to say a "person") of the world of the intellect—free from all matter, subsisting of its essence—which *governs* this species, instills its perfections into it and is such that its meaning embraces that of all individuals. It is what this philosopher calls the "lord of the species"—in the language of the (exoteric) "law," the "Angel": they say for example that there is an Angel of the mountains, an Angel of the seas, etc.

In an anonymous fourteenth century treatise on Platonic ideas this intermediate world (which should not be confused with the world of ideas, the main difference lying in the "personality" of the ghosts, ashbâh, who move in it) is clearly defined and Suhravardî is explicitly mentioned as being the first to speak about it from a philosophical point of view (text in Corbin, op. cit., I p. LII, no. 82): The first to explicitly admit its existence among the philosophers (*hukamâ*) was the philosopher of the Illumination (*sâhib al-ishrâq*, Suhravardî) who considered (*za'ama*, in the sense of considering wrongly), that the ancient wise men believed in their existence too." This is the world in which the images of the "visionary tales" move.

Before examining Suhravardî's tales we will briefly consider his philosophy (though this book is on religion, and philosophy in the strict sense does not take first place in it). This philosophy is entirely based on a metaphysics of light.

One of the foundations of illuminative philosophy is that the existence of the lowest possible implies [the existence] of the highest possible. If the Light of Lights were to determine, through the sense of unity, the existence of the darkest depths, no sense would remain in which it could decide the highest heights; if we suppose that this exists, a sense is needed to determine its existence, which must be higher than the one to be found in the Light of Lights, and this is absurd. We have proved the existence of "the governing pure lights [souls]" (*anwâr al-mujarrada al mudabbira*) which are in man. The Victorious, i.e. totally pure, Light (*an-nûr al-qâhir*: the celestial intelligence), is nobler than governing light, further away from dependence on darkness, therefore higher. Therefore its existence must precede. One must link what is highest and most noble to the closest light (*an-nûr al-aqrab*) to the victorious lights, to the governing spheres and lights, since this is possible. These lights are outside the world of contingencies (*'âlam al-ittifâqât*) and nothing forbids them what is most perfect for them.

Let us therefore consider the marvels of the order in the world of darkness and of bodies ["body" is *barzakh*]. Relationships between illustrious lights are more elevated than shadowy relationships and consequently they necessarily precede them. The Peripatetics recognized the wonders of the order in bodies (*barzakh*), while they limited intelligence to ten categories. Therefore, according to them, the world of bodies ought to be more brilliant, more admirable more excellent in its order, and wisdom more abundant. Now this is false. A clear-sighted intelligence considers that the wisdom, the elegance of order and the wonders of relationships are more abundant in the world of light than in the world of darkness. In fact, these are the shadow of those[67] and of the victorious lights, and the principle of everything is light. The essence of the idols (asnâm: the individuals of the physical world in which the lights are reflected, physical beings in whom Platonic ideas are realized), victorious lights, were seen by the pure when they came away from their temples [*hayâkil*, meaning bodies] a number of times (in ecstasy). Consequently they transmitted the proof of these things to various persons, and there is no person who is pure and gifted with vision (*mushahâda*) who does not profess this doctrine. The greater part of the teaching of the prophets and the pillars of wisdom follow this direction. Plato and his predecessors, like Socrates and his precursor, like Hermes, Agathadaimon and Empedocles, were all of this opinion and most of them stated explicitly that they were witnesses of this in the World of Light. Plato said of himself that he left the shadows and saw these things. The sages of India and Persia are equally emphatic concerning this. And if one gives credit to the observations of one or two people on astronomical matters, how could one refuse the words of these men, pillars of wisdom and prophesy, concerning what they saw in their spiritual observations?

The author of these lines was very far from the path of the Peripatetics who deny these things, being very strongly inclined towards them; and he would have embraced them even if he had not seen the Proof of his Lord. He who does not believe them or for whom the proofs are not sufficient should devote himself to ascetic exercises and put himself at the service of the masters of the vision; it may be that—enraptured—he will see the light irradiate in the world of the *jabarût*, and see the regal essences (*malakûtîya*) and the lights which Hermes and Plato saw and the celestial irradiations (*al-dawâ' al-mînuvîya*), sources of Glory (*khurra*) and Vision, of which Zoroaster spoke. The Just King, the blessed Kai Khusrau, was carried in rapture to them, and contemplated them. All the sages of Persia agree on this, so much so that, according to them, water had a lord of the image (archetypal person, *sâhib as-sanam*), in the world of the Kingdom, which they called Khurdâd, and the Trees too [whose angel] they called Murdâd and Fire whose angel was Ardîbihisht. These are the same lights Empedocles and the others mentioned. And do not believe that these great men of antiquity who were superior in strength and vision believed that humanity has an intellect ('aql), which is its universal form and exists identically in multiple individuals; for how is it possible for something which is not dependent on matter to be in matter, and consequently for something that is unique in its essence to be in multiple matters and in innumerable persons? Nor that they thought that the person who, for example is the archetype of man only exists because of what is beneath him, thus being passive, because they were the first to maintain emphatically that what is superior is not a result of what is inferior; if they had thought this they would have been forced to admit one type for another type, and so forth infinitely. Nor should we believe that they thought that these ideas are compound, so that they dissolve after a given lapse of time, but rather [they maintained] that they are luminous simple essences, even if their idols can only be imagined as compound; typological correspondence (*mumâthala*) in every respect does not condition Type.

The Peripatetics agree that humanity, in intelligence, covers a multiplicity of individuals; it is a type of what exists in reality, because it is pure while what exists in realities is not pure; it is not measurable or substantial, contrarily to what exists in reality, because it is pure while what exists in realities is not pure; it is not measurable or substantial, contrarily to what exists in reality, because total resemblance is not one of the conditions of the type. This does not oblige us to admit a type for animality, nor for the fact of being bipeds. But, in order to exist, everything needs something within it which places it in participation with Holiness [*al-quds*, the world of ideas, is given this name here]. There is not one archetype for the smell of musk and another for musk; but a Victorious Light in the world of pure Light has luminous dispositions (*hai'ât*) of irradiation, dispositions of love, of pleasure or of domination; and when its shadow falls on this world its Idol is musk with its smell, or sugar with its flavor, or the human form with the diversity of its limbs, according to the relationship we mentioned before.

People in ancient times often spoke in metaphors. They do not deny that possessed attributes (*mahmûlât*) are intellectual and that universals belong to intelligence. When they say that there is a universal man in the world of the intellect, they mean a victorious light, with varying irradiation according to the relationship, whose shadow, in numerable individuals, is the form of man; and this light is universal not in the sense that it is a possessed attribute, but in the sense that it has equal relationships of effusion in these numerable individuals. it is as if it were the universal, but it is rather the root (cf., for Mazdaism, chap. I). What we conceive the abstract sense of, without this preventing an association (multiplicity) from taking place in us, is not the universal. They admit that (the universal) has its own essence and that it knows its own essence: how then could it be an abstraction? When, for example—where spheres are concerned—they call on sphere universal and another specific, they do not indicate what is logically known as the universal; we know it.

As for the proof which some people invoke, i.e. that humanity as such is not multiple but unique, this is doubly false; because humanity in as far as it is humanity does not require either unity or multiplicity, but it can receive both epithets at the same time. If the unity were a condition of the concept of humanity, humanity could not be an attribute of multiple individuals. Therefore if we say that humanity does not require multiplicity, this does not mean that it requires unity; the contrary of multiplicity is non-multiplicity, and not asking for multiplicity does not mean that we are asking for non-multiplicity; the contrary of asking for multiplicity is simply not asking for multiplicity. The same can occur in the case of not asking for unity. Unique humanity, the predicate of the universal, is solely in the spirit and does not need the support of another form. Saying that individuals are mortal and the species is eternal does not oblige us to say that the latter is a self-subsisting universal thing. On the contrary, the adversary must agree that this permanence is a form in the intelligence . . . [Corbin, *Opera*, vol. I, pp. 154 and foll.].

An unusual term—barzakh—recurs in this long exposition. It means "barrier" in the Qur'an and is used in only three passages: twice in a purely physical sense of barrier which "divides two seas" (XXV, 53 and LV, 20), and once (XXIII, 100: "there, behind them, is a barrier until the day that they shall be raised up") where it seems to mean the insurmountable impediment to a return to life from the worlds of the beyond Influenced by the fascination of the passages in which the word recurs in the Sacred Text and by the fact that it is unusual and does not sound Arabic (it is Persian in origin), mystics and theologians have built up a great deal around it.

Thus *barzakh* has become "an intermediate wall between this and the other world," a kind of intermediate area only very slightly reminiscent of our own limbo in purgatory or, also, the dividing line between the physical world and the world of pure spirits. In some texts the body is a wall between this and real life. In the Ismaili text *Kalâm-i pîr* (ed. Ivanow, p. 113 of the text) a Persian verse is quoted that says: "There is no great distance between the world and the Beyond: But the way is barred by the wall (*dîvâr*) of your corporeal existence!" This seems to be the sense in which our author uses the term *barzakh*. Elsewhere he explicitly says, in *Hikmatu'l-Ishrâq*:

> The barzakh is the body . . . When light is taken away from some barzakh they remain shadowy . . . these barzakh are obscure substances . . . The nearest light (the first one produced, Bahman), seeing the majesty of the Light of Lights, considers itself to be shadow (*yastazlam nafsahu*) compared to it and this shadow is the highest barzakh, the all-embracing wall. (Corbin, op.cit., pp. 107 and foll.)

Another unusual technical term used in Suhravardî's metaphysics of light is *haikal*, "temple." It is of ancient Mesopotamian origin (Sumerian *ê* means "house," *qal* means "big") and has been very popular in the Islamic languages and religious philosophies of Persia up to the present day (see Chapter eight):

> The temple [we are again quoting Suhravardî himself] originally is the form, and the ancient sages believed that the stars were the shadows of the pure lights and their temples; they assigned each of the seven stars a talisman of the mineral kingdom, chosen at a fitting moment, and they placed these talismans in a house built at a suitable astronomical moment and in a suitable place; they celebrated the cult there at special hours, with suffumigations and other ceremonies specific to each heavenly body. They venerated these houses and called them "temples of light" (*hayâkil an-nûr* is in fact the title of one of Suhravardî's works) because they were the place of these talismans which were the temples of the superior lights.

Al-Ijî himself (*Mawâqif* quoted in Carra de Vaux, op. cit.) explains the passage temple-body: the temples—he declares—are also the planets themselves and since our bodies depend on the superior heavenly bodies they too, by analogy, are called the temples of our souls just as the heavenly bodies are the temples of the lights on which our souls depend. Here we see another of the principle "sources" (besides the Iranian source) of Suhravardî's metaphysics: i.e., astral Sabaeism in which these speculations and the idea of geometrical temples play an important part.

Sabaean-tinged technical terms are linked to the Iranian world through specific references. In addition to the terms we have already mentioned, it should be noted that Suhravardî also calls Victorious Light *nûr sipahbud*, using an Iranian word which means "general." Several times too he uses the traditional Iranian term of *khurra*, *farr*, the Avestan *khvarena*, the "flaming victory, the halo on the heads of Sovereigns and Saints (and this image has passed from

Iranian images into our own world). Towards the end of the *Mutâharât*, for example, he says that the influence of the heavenly bodies and their angels combined with that of the spiritual Pure Lights can either shed a khurra over the soul in which subjugating power predominates (we then have the victorious hero), or a light generating the more delicate aspects of love and affective inclinations (we then have the hero of beauty and wisdom), or, again, a wonderful equilibrium can predominate and then, and then only we have the *kayân khurra* ("glory of the Kai," the ancient mythical kings of Iran), the majestic and fortunate sovereign.

We saw above that the Iranian concept of "pre-existent 'I'" was attributed to Hermes. Hermes, who was central to Sabaean thought, is often quoted by our author and we find him in the following singular "episode," which introduces us to the visionary tales that interrupt the still Peripatetic aridity of his treatises (this was one of Suhravardî's typical procedures). These episodes are introduced as "effusions," *'arshî*, as opposed to *lauhî*: the first term (derived from *'arsh*, "God's Throne") indicates "inspired," directly experienced, the second (from *lauh*, the Celestial tablet), "derived from or studied in books." From *Talvîhât*, in *Opera* I, p. 108:

> Hermes rose up one night to pray by the Sun in the Temple of Light. And when the Columns of Dawn split, he saw an Earth that swallowed up cities that had angered God and gaping abysses opened in them. And he said: "My Father, save me from this place of evil neighbors!" And a voice reached him: "Cling to the rope of the Rays and ascend to the top of the Lofty See!" And he ascended, and beneath his feet he saw an earth and some skies.

The vision is transparently a symbolic representation of the body's triumph over night and the earth, with the help of victorious light. But here we also find terms (Pillars of Dawn, Father, See) that have a Manichaean ring about them and this is still another aspect of the extremely complex syncretist world that inspired Suhravardî. When discussing a passage on a Hermetic ecstasy towards the end of the *Hikmatu'l-Ishrâq*, his commentator Shahrazûrî deliberately introduces a long text specifically attributed to the "wise Mani" (Corbin, op. cit., I, p. XXXIII) and this is possibly the first time Mani is quoted respectfully in literature of this kind. Towards the end of the Psychology in Physics of the *Mutârahât*, soon after warning against "Mani's heresy" (which was probably a way of averting the suspicions of the non-initiated [Corbin, op. cit., I, p. 112 note] Suhravardî himself says:

> Among the symbols of some of the Orientals there is the [symbol] according to which Darkness surrounded Light and took it prisoner, then the Angels came to help it and were victorious over Ahriman, who is Darkness itself; but light gave darkness

a deferment until an established moment, and Darkness rose from Light through a lost thought [*li-fikra radiya*].

And he adds that the commentary (*ta'wîl*) is:

> ... that, as the *fahlaviyyîn* (ancient Persians) prove, the Soul is a luminous substance and Darkness the bodily forces; and the fortress is imprisonment, the dominion of such forces over it and their attraction of the soul to the lower world; and the help of the angels is the power that prepares the soul for illumination from above and motion upwards; and the deferment until an established moment is the persistence of these forces until death; and the lost thought (*fikra radiya*) the soul's inclination towards material things.

Suhravardî obviously was well-acquainted with the Manichaean myth. In fact, he seems to confuse it with the Mazdean Pahlavî doctrine that, as we demonstrated in earlier chapters, had no hatred for the body—a sort of confusion that is usual in these cases of presumed revivalism.

Corbin, with singular Aryan-Iranian "patriotism," reduces these Zoroastrian motifs to three in his rather fascinating short work *Les motifs zoroastriens dans la philosophie de Suhravardî* (from which we have already quoted). They are basically the three fundamental aspects of Zoroastrianism: angelogy, the *khvarena* and the pre-existent "I." I believe I have sufficiently demonstrated how both the "light-darkness" system and other apparently Iranian elements of Suhravardism are (at least in part) undoubtedly Iranian and, what is more important, consciously felt to be so by the author, but how in practice they also filtered through non-Iranian contributions (Hermetism, Pythagoreanism, Sabaeism, Gnosis). In Suhravardî the names of Hermes, Pythagoras, Agathodaimon and Empedocles are hardly ever severed from those of the (mythical) sages of ancient Persia. But I think it would be rash to call them "Zoroastrian" in an unqualified way and beyond the "veils of history," unless one has a very particular (theosophical) idea of "true Zoroastrianism."

Angelism, the *khvarena* and the pre-existent "I," as they "function" in Suhravardî, seem to me to do so in a Manichaean rather than a Zoroastrian style.

And the author's use of Arabic in his more important works ought to be sufficient to free his original quotations of "things Pahlavî" from any "national" sense of Iranian restoration. He does effect a restoration, it is true, but a restoration of "ancient traditions," and it is strange that Corbin should want to limit this to the Iranian "race" when other "races" such as Syro-Babylonian Semitism and Egyptian Hermetism as well as Greek neo-Platonism contributed to it equally.

We believe the reader will appreciate the publication of the translation of one of Suhravardî's Persian visionary tales at the end of this section.

200

Suhravardî wrote his many visionary tales in a style very similar to that of Avicenna. Besides "Crimson Intellect" . . . there are at least seven or eight other symbolic tales, often with fascinating titles: "The Rustle of Gabriel's Wing," "Western Exile," "The Language of Ants," "The Lovers' Relative ," "The Epistle on the condition of Infancy," "A day in the Sufi congregation," "The Bird" (translated from Avicenna's Arabic version with the same title), and "The Song of the Sîmurgh." Philosophically speaking, the most significant is possibly "Western Exile," which Corbin published in the second volume of his Suhravardian *editio princeps*. "The Language of Ants"—which refers distantly to the proverbial ants disputing in front of Solomon in the Qur'an (cf. Kor. XXII, 18–19)—is a rather simple collection of Sufi apothegms. "The Song of the Sîmurgh" deals with inner mystical experiences and often mentions the great Sufi martyr Mansûr al-Hallâj. All are dominated by the motif of the "redemption" of the soul from the thongs of the body and of the true homeland of the soul that is place-without-space, the *nâ-kujâ-âbâd*, the "Not-Where." The world of matter is always symbolized by the Maghrib, the West, leading back apparently to already Gnostic speculations[68].

These speculations in turn may stem from a spiritualized representation—a *ta'wîl*—of the biblical exodus from Egypt and Israel's return to its "homeland." And we must remember that Suhravardî does not conceive of the "return home," the union with God, as a union characterized by undifferentiated mingling with God, involving man's annihilation. The following important passage in the *Mutâharât* (Corbin, op. cit., I, pp. 500–501) proves Massignon's statement, according to which Suhravardî was the last non-Monist Muslim mystic:[69]

Pleasure (*lazza*) is not possible without conscious perception (*idrâk*). Some people have thought that by these "lights" we intended complete union of the soul (*ittihâd u ittisâl*) with the Originator (*mubdi'*), while it has been proved that the ittihâd is absurd, unless one sees it as a suitable spiritual condition (*hâla*) with separations (*talîqu bi 'l-mufâraqat*), and not as a bodily fusion (*ittisâl*) and the mingling (*imtizâj*) or the rendering vain of one of the two entities (*ibtâl*). And the idea of *hulûl* (incarnation) too is faulty. One might say, instead: given the very close relationship between the two, even if the soul is not in the body, it says, indicating the body, "I," so that many, forgetting their own souls, think that their individuality (*huwîya*) lies in their body. In the same sense one might say that so powerful a relationship of luminous, divine desire (*shauqîya nûrîya lahûtîya*) is reached between the soul and the principles (*mabâdi'*), that it is dominated by an instant and cancelling ray (*qayyûmî*) that annihilates all attention for other things, so that it indicates its Principle as "I" with a spiritual emphasis (*ishârâtan ruhânîyatan*).

This picture-framework (which is in fact the most beautiful part, for its central passages are weighed down by philosophical language) is an example of the nostalgic sense of "homecoming" we find in the story called "The Rustle of Gabriel's Wing." We have left out the doctrinal-symbolic passages that do not interest us here, since our purpose is to stress the style of the story. As in Avicenna's tale, it is characterized by the deliberate difficulty of a few rare words, strangely set in rather simple and dull Persian prose, as if to highlight the precious idiom and the sudden sparkle of almost "modern" images:[70]

> In the period when I succeeded in breaking out of the women's apartment and freeing myself from the belt and thongs with which children are habitually imprisoned, one night, when the copper-red twilight had vanished at the end of the azure sphere, and darkness, the brotherly ally of Nothingness, had spread to the confines of the lower world, oppressed with anguish I picked up a torch and went towards the people of my Mother's palace. That night, in despair over the onslaught of sleep, I wandered around the place until dawn. Then I was filled with the desire to penetrate into my Father's dwelling. It had two doors: one gave onto the city, the other onto the country and the garden. I entered and hermetically closed the door that gave onto the city. Then I opened the door onto the country. Unbolting it, I looked carefully: and lo, I saw ten Old Men with shining faces, in a row. Their aspect, their dignity, their majesty, their nobility and their splendor filled me with wonder, and in front of their grace, their beauty, their snowy locks and their bearing in general, I was again filled with such amazement that I lost the power of speech. Filled with terror and great fear I advanced one step and immediately moved one step back. I said to myself: "Come now, let me show courage and serve them, come what may!" I slowly advanced and prepared to greet the Old Man at the end of the row, when the extreme goodness of his nature made him forestall me, and he was the first to give me the greeting of peace, graciously adding such a smile that his teeth could be seen in the pupil of my eye. In spite of the affability of his ways and character, the respectful fear he inspired in me still prevailed. I said: "Tell me, O noble Lords, from which direction do you deign to come?" The old man at the end of the row answered: "We are a group of Pure Spirits and we come from Beyond Space (nâ-kujâ-âbâd)."

> . . . .

> Finally, when the beautiful day rose over my father's dwelling, the door that gave onto the quiet countryside closed and the one which gave onto the city opened. The first merchants passed on the way to their shops and the society of Old Men disappeared. I bit my fingers, so greatly did I long for their conversation. I burst into much lamenting and wailing. But all was in vain.

The strange, sad beauty of this picture that, among other things (the dawn with the first merchants, the first sounds of the awakening city) is singularly realistic, should be noted. Discovering whether Suhravardî really had visions would be a curious though obviously insoluble problem, but he certainly was remembered among the people as a magician. One tale, preserved in Turkish (Qirq Vezîr), describes him as performing sensational miracles at Saladin's court and give a strange "harem" justification for his death: there is also a scene, based on phantasmagoric visions, experienced when the inner windows of a pavilion closely resembling this framework for Suhravardî's epistle are opened.

And here is the translation of "Crimson Intellect" from the text Bayânî has left us.[71]

In the name of the clement and merciful God.

Praise be to the King who holds the Kingdom of both Worlds in his hand. The was of each person who was, came from His Was. The is of each person who is, comes from His Is. And from His shall be, the Shall be of each person who will be shall come.[72] He is the First and the Last, the Manifest and the Hidden, the Seer over all things.

And greetings and prayers be on His Messengers to men, especially on Muhammad the Elect, with whom the Prophecy ends, and on all his companions and the men who are learned in the religion of the gratification of God.

One of my dear friends asked me: "Do the birds understand one another's language?" I replied: Yes they do." And he said: "How is it that you know?" I answered: "At the beginning of life, when the [divine] Painter of Reality wished to manifest my nothingness, he evoked me in the form of a falcon. In the country in which I lived there were other falcons: we conversed together and understood one another." And my friend added: " How then did your condition change so greatly?" I answered: "One day the hunters of Destiny and Fate cast the nets of Predestination placing in them the grain of Desire and thus they made me a prisoner. Then they bore me away from that land that was my nest and brought me to another land, they sewed my eyes up, they bound my body with four enemy thongs and ten of them guarded me: five facing me and five with their backs to me. The five who faced me held me then in the world of stupefaction; to such an extent that I forgot my nest and that land and everything I knew, and I thought that I had always been as I was then.[73]

When some time had passed in this way they partly uncovered my eyes, so that I could look with the part that was unveiled, and I saw things I had never seen, and they filled me with wonder. And little by little, each day, they uncovered my eyes more and more, and I saw things that I marvelled at. Finally they opened my eyes completely and showed me the world as it is. And I looked at my thongs and my keepers and said to myself: "It seems that they will never free me from these four enemy thongs and that these keepers will never leave me so that I can open my wings; so that for an instant at least I can fly in the air and be free of shackles."

Now, after some time I noticed that my keepers were not watchful, and I said to myself: "I could not find a better occasion than this." I crept into a corner and, limping because of the thongs, I started off for the open country. There I met a man coming towards me; I greeted him when he was close and he answered very courteously. And looking attentively at that man I noticed that his face and beard were red. I thought he was young and said: "O youth, where do you come from?" He answered: "My son, you are addressing me wrongly: I am the First Son of Creation and you call me youth?"[74] I asked him then why his beard had not turned white. He said: "My beard is white and I am an old man of light; but he who caught you in the net and bound you with these enemy thongs and placed these keepers to watch over you also threw me into the Black Well a long time ago, and this red color you see on me is because of this. For otherwise I am white, and of light. But every white that depends on light seems red when it is mixed with black, like the first twilight of the evening or the last light of dawn, which is white when it is linked to the light of the sun; but one part is turned to the right, which is white, and the other part towards the left, which is black, but it seems red. Thus, even though the light of the body of the full moon is borrowed when it rises, it is defined as light, and one side is with the day and one side is with the night, and so it seems red. A lamp has this same quality, that beneath it is white and on top black because of the smoke and, between fire and smoke it seems red; and there are many similar and equal things to these."

Then I asked him: "O old man, where do you come from?" He answered: " From beyond the mountain of Qâf, for my dwelling is there and the nest you have forgotten was also there once upon a time."[75] I said: "And what did you do over there?" He answered: "I am a wayfarer and I wander around the world and see its wonders." I said: "And what wonders have you seen in the world?" "Seven things," he answered, "the first thing is the mountain of Qâf that is my country; the second is the Pearl that lights up the Night; the third is the Tûbâ Tree; the fourth is the Twelve Workshops; the fifth is the Davidic cuirass; the sixth the Balârak sword; the seventh the Source of Life."

"Tell me about them," I said. He answered: "In the first place the Mountain of Qâf that surrounds the whole world, and these are eleven mountains; and when you are freed from your thongs you will go there, because they took you from there and everything that is returns in the end to its first form." "And how shall I find the way to go to that place?" I asked. He answered "It is an arduous way. And before reaching it one has to go over two mountains—also those of Qâf—one hot and one cold, and their heat and cold are infinite." And then I said: "But it is easy. I will spend the winter on the hot one and the summer on the cold one." But he said: "You are mistaken. In no season is the air in that country propitious." I asked: "And how far are those mountains from here?" He answered: "However far you travel, in the end you will be able to return to the First Place; like the compass, one of whose points is on the center and the other on the circumference, and however much it turns it always end by coming back to the place it set out from." I asked: "And is it not possible to bore through these mountains and come out further, outside?" "No," he answered, "it is impossible to bore through them, but whoever has the ability can go beyond them even without boring through them, just like balsam oil: if you hold the palm of your hand in the sun until it is hot and dribble balsam oil onto it, the oil filters through your hand and comes out on the other side because of a special quality it possesses. Therefore if you obtain the specific ability to go beyond those mountains, you will do so in an instant." "And how," I asked him, "can one acquire this specific ability?" He said: "I will tell you now, in the course of our conversation, if you understand what I say." I asked him: "Once one has journeyed beyond these two mountains, will the rest be easy?" "Yes," he answered, "it will be easy, but if you know it. For some, in fact, remain prisoners for ever on these two mountains, others reach the third and stop there, others the fourth, the fifth, and so on until the eleventh: but the bird with the sharpest intellect will go the furthest."

Then I said: "Now that you have described the mountains of Qâf to me, tell me about the Pearl that lights up the Night." "The Pearl that lights up the Night," he said, "is also in the mountains of Qâf. But it is in the third mountain and, because of its presence, the dark night is lit up. But it does not always remain the same. Its light comes from the Tûbâ Tree.[76] Every time it is in front of the tree—from this same side you are on—it appears to be all light, like a brilliant round globe. When one side moves around and comes closer to the Tree, a little of its circle seems black, while the rest remains very luminous, and every time it draws closer to the Tree a part of its light turns black towards this side you are on. But towards the direction of the Tree, one half is luminous. When the whole of it is close to the Tûbâ Tree all the part that is turned towards you is black and the part turned towards the Tree is entirely luminous. Then, having gone beyond the Tree, it again grows luminous and as it moves away from the Tree the part towards you grows more and more luminous. It is not that the light progresses, but the body of the Pearl absorbs more light, and the blackness grows less and so forth until it again faces [the Tree]: then its entire body absorbs light. Let this comparison serve to make it clearer: make a hole in the middle of a ball and pass something through the hole. Then fill a tray with water and put the pierced ball on the tray, so that half of the ball is in the water. Now in an instant the water will have reached the entire contour of the ball. But if someone looks at the water from below, he will always see one half of the ball in the water. And if the observer who is looking from directly under the center of the tray looked a little beyond the center itself, he would not see one half of the ball in the water . . . and little by little, as he moves his observation point towards the edge of the tray he will see less and less of the ball in the water and more and more of the part of the ball that is empty of water. When he looks from precisely the edge of the tray he will see one half of the ball in the water and one half out of it. And again, if he looks from above the edge he will see less and less of it in the water and more and more out of it until, when [the eye] is precisely over the upper center of the tray he will see the whole ball, but the whole ball will be out of the water. And if anyone says to me that if he is under the tray he cannot see either the water or the ball, we will conjecture that he can: i.e. that the tray is of glass or something even more transparent: in the case of the ball and the tray the observer can see them by turning around them; in the case of the Pearl that Lights up the Night and the Tûbâ Tree it is (the Pearl itself) that, in the example, moves around the observer."[77]

Then I asked the Old Man: "Yes, and what is the Tûbâ Tree, and where is it?" He answered: The Tûbâ Tree is an immense tree, and whoever is destined to Paradise sees it there when he arrives. Among the eleven mountains we mentioned before there is one on which that Tree exists." "Does that Tree produce fruit?" I asked. "Every fruit you see in the world is on that Tree, and all these fruits you see in front of you are its products. If it were not for that Tree, you would not see either fruit, or trees, or sweet-scented grasses, or plants." "And what relationship," I asked, "do the fruit, the trees and the sweet-scented grasses have with it?" He answered: "The

Sîmurgh has its nest on the Tûbâ Tree. At dawn the Sîmurgh leaves its nest and spreads its feathers anew over the earth. It is through the effect of its feathers that fruit appears on the trees and plants of the earth."[78] I said to the Old Man: "I have heard that the Sîmurgh reared Zâl, and Rustam killed Isfandiyâr with the Sîmurgh's help.[79] The Old Man said: "Yes it is true." I asked: "And how did this happen?" He answered: "When Zâl was born of his mother his hair was white and his face was white. His father Sâm ordered him to be thrown into the desert. His mother had suffered greatly in giving him birth and when she saw that the child was uncomely, she accepted the order and threw Zâl into the desert. It was winter, and cold, and no-one imagined that the child would survive for long. A few days went by and the mother recovered from her deranged condition. Compassion for her son filled her heart and she said: "I will go into the desert and see how my son is." She went into the desert and saw that her son was alive and that the Sîmurgh held him under his wing. When Zâl's eyes fell on his mother, he smiled. His mother took him to her bosom and nursed him. She was about to bring him home but then she thought: "It is better that it should not be known how Zâl is and that he has survived for so many days. I had better not return home." And so she left Zâl in that same place under the Sîmurgh's wing and hid nearby. When night fell and the Sîmurgh left that desert, a gazelle came to Zâl and placed one of her udders into his mouth. When Zâl had finished drinking the milk, the gazelle lay down to sleep near the child, so that Zâl suffered no harm. The mother rose up, sent the gazelle away from near the child and brought him home." I asked the Old Man: "What is the secret (sense) of all this?" The Old Man answered: "I asked the Sîmurgh and the Sîmurgh said: 'Zâl came into the world in sight of the Tûbâ Tree and we did not allow him to perish. We placed the gazelle in the hands of the hunter again and instilled compassion for Zâl into her heart, so that at night she nursed and nurtured him, and during the day I myself kept him under my wings.'"[80]

"And how was it," I asked, "for Rustam and Isfandiyâr?" He answered: "It was so: Rustam came home exhausted after unsuccessfully trying to defeat Isfandiyâr. His father Zâl humbly beseeched the Sîmurgh: now the Sîmurgh had this particular quality that if a mirror or similar reflecting substance was held in front of him, every eye that looked in that mirror was blinded. Zâl made a perfectly polished iron suit of armour and dressed Rustam in it, he placed a most shining helmet on his head and tied limpid mirrors to his horse. Then he sent Rustam together with the Sîmurgh onto the battlefield. Isfandiyâr had to advance towards Rustam: when he was close to him the Sîmurgh's ray fell on the armour and the mirrors and the reflection reached Isfandiyâr's eyes, which were blinded. He thought he had been wounded in both eyes, because otherwise he would have been able to see. He fell from his horse and perished by Rustam's hand. It seems that the two *gaz* mentioned in the story were two of the Sîmurgh's feathers."[81]

I asked the Old Man: "So there has always been the same Sîmurgh in the world?" He answered: "He who does not know thinks in this way. But this is not so, in every period a Sîmurgh comes down to earth from the Tûbâ Tree and the one then on earth immediately disappears . . . While the one is coming down to earth the other goes towards the Twelve Workshops."

I asked: "What are the Twelve Workshops?"[82] "You must know, in the first place," he answered, "that when our King wished to render his kingdom prosperous and inhabited, he first filled our country with people; then he set to work and ordered that the Twelve Workshops be built, placing a number of apprentices (*shâgird*) in each one. Then he set those apprentices to work, until beneath those Twelve Workshops another workshop appeared and in this one he placed a Master (*ustâd*). Then he set that Master to work, until under that first workshop a second one appeared; then he set a second Master to work, so that under the second still another workshop and another master appeared, and so forth until there were seven workshops and for each workshop a Master was appointed. Then to each of those apprentices who were in the twelve houses he gave a garment of honor. Then he gave another one to the first Master and entrusted him with two of the upper workshops; and he gave a garment of honor to the second Master too, entrusting him with two more of the upper workshops. And he did the same for the third. To the fourth Master he gave a garment of honor more beautiful than all the others and entrusted him with one of the upper workshops, but he ordered him to watch over all twelve. To the fifth and sixth he gave the same as he had given to the first, second and third. When it was the turn of the seventh, only one of the twelve workshops was left and he entrusted it to him, but he did not give him a garment of honor. And the seventh master cried out: 'Each master has two workshops under him and I have only one and all have a garment of honor and I have none!' Then [the King] ordered two more workshops to be built under his workshop and set him in charge of directing them. Beneath all the workshops he placed, as their foundation, a sown field under two Bailiffs (*'âmil*) and this field too was entrusted to the seventh Master and it was decided that the splendid cloth of the garment of the fourth master should always provide a used garment for the seventh and that the fourth master should have a constantly renewed one, as we said of the Sîmurgh."

I asked: "O Old Man, what is woven in these workshops?" He answered: "For the most part brocade and all that is understandable to the human mind, as well as the Davidic Cuirass."[83]

"What is the Davidic Cuirass?" I asked. He answered: "The Davidic Cuirass consists in the various ties that were imposed on you." "And how is it made?" I asked. He answered: "In each of the three workshops of the twelve upper ones, a ring is made and, in all, four incomplete rings are made in the twelve workshops that are then presented to the seventh master to be perfected. When they reach the seventh master they are sent to the Tilled Field and they remain incomplete for a long time. Then the four rings are inserted into a ring and all threaded one into the other. They they take a Falcon like you prisoner and place this Cuirass on his neck, so that it completes his neck."

I asked the Old man: "How many rings are there in each cuirass?" He answered: "They could be counted only if one could say how many drops of water there are in the sea of Oman."

I asked: "How can one free oneself from this Cuirass?" "With the Balârak Sword,"[84] he answered. "And where is this Sword to be found?" I insisted. The Old Man said: "In our country there is an executioner and that Sword is in his hands, and it is established that when a Cuirass has lasted for some time, when that time is accomplished, the Executioner gives such a blow with the Balârak Sword that all its rings are separated." I asked: "Is there any difference in the damage caused to those who wear the Cuirass?" He answered: Yes, there is a difference. Some, in fact are so gravely damaged that if you lived for a hundred years and for all that time thought of nothing other than what could be the most terrible pain and imagined every possible torment, you never could succeed in imagining the damage caused by the Balârak Sword.[85] For some, on the other hand, it is easier."

"What must I do, O Old Man," I asked him "for this pain to be light?" He answered: "Go to the Source of Life and pour water from that Source onto your head, so that the Cuirass may come undone on your body and you may be preserved from the wound of the Sword. For that water tightens the Cuirass and when the Cuirass is tighter the Sword wound is lighter." I asked: "O Old Man, where is the Source of Life?" He answered: "In the Darkness. If you want to reach it, like Khizr,[86] tie on your sandals and take the way of Trust (*tawakkul*) until you reach the country of Darkness." I asked: "Where does this road pass?" He answered: "Wherever you go, if you [truly] go, you will find the way." I asked: "What is the sign of Darkness?" He answered: "Blackness. You are in darkness now, but you do not know it. When he who follows this way finds himself in darkness, he understands that he was in darkness before too, and that he never saw the light. Therefore this is the wayfarer's first step, and from here it is possible to advance further . . . He who wants to find the Source of Life will have to wander at length in Darkness: but if he is One of those who belong to the Source, in the end, after the Darkness, he will see the Light. Therefore it cannot be followed without that Light, for it is a Light that pours down from the sky over the Source of Life. If he finds the way and washes in that Source he will be safe from the wound of the Balârak Sword.

May you be slain by the Sword of Love to find
    Eternal Life,
so that no one can show the smallest living particle of you after that Sword thrust.

He who washes in that Source will suffer no further pollution. He who has discovered the sense of 'truth' (*haqîqat*) will reach that Source. And when he emerges from that Source he will obtain the same Ability as that of balsam oil, i.e. if you hold the palm of your hand in the sun and place a few drops of that oil on it, it will penetrate to the back of your hand. If you become a Khizr you will easily be able to go beyond the mountains of Qâf."

When I had finished telling my dear friend this adventure he said to me: "You are like he who is caught in the net and yet goes hunting; here I am, tie me to your saddle, for I am not a bad prey!"

I am the Falcon whom hunters of the world of
    all times need
My prey is the black eyed gazelles, who pour
    Wisdom from their eyes like tears.
Close to me, [men] are far distant even from
    words,
and then they give them [imaginary] meanings at
    my expense.[87]

Iranian Sufism: Maulânâ Jalâlu'd-Dîn Rûmî

The word Sufism, which is generally used to indicate Islamic mysticism and asceticism, comes from the Arabic *sûf*, "wool." A Sûfî is a person who dressed in the rough woollen robe worn by the first Arab mystics or ascetics that later became the typical monk's habit of the "religious orders" or mystical confraternities (*tarîqat*) that proliferated in Islamic territory from the twelfth century on. It had different names in the various regions and was called *khirqa* in Persia. Of all the currents we have studied so far mysticism (which from now on, to avoid confusion, we will call more specifically "Sufism") was the least specifically Iranian both in its origins and development. In spite of this almost all the great Persian poets were Sufi and, inversely, almost all the greatest Sufis were Persian. This is why we must say something more about Sufism, though we will limit our study to a very few eminent personalities to avoid useless repetitions of easily available material, since Sufism is possibly the most fascinating and popularized area of Muslim religious life besides being the most open to beautiful poetic translations (see *Islamologia*, pp. 507–8 and 531–2).

In the first place what is Sufism? We will have one of the earliest Persian Sufis—the tenth-century Abû Nasr as-Sarrâj from Tûs (Khurâsân)—speak for us. In his Arabic treatise *Kitâb al-luma'* (the Book of Flashes) he says:[88]

> As for Sufism, its characteristics and its essence, when Muhammad Ibn 'Alî al-Qassâb, the master of al-Junaid [a celebrated mystic who died in 910] was questioned on Sufism he answered: "Noble customs that appeared at a noble time from a man with a noble people." When Junaid himself was questioned about Sufism, he answered: "It is being with the Most High God, without intermediaries." Ruwaim ibn Ahmad defined it as follows: "To let oneself go to God, to abandon oneself to his will." When asked about Sufism, Summûn said: "It consists in possessing nothing and not allowing oneself to be possessed by anything." Abû Muhammad al-Jarîrî defined it as "entering into every high quality and coming away from every despicable quality." Amr ibn 'Uthmân al-Makkî pronounced himself as follows: "Sufism consists in this that the Servant (of God) behaves at every moment in the way most in keeping with that moment."

The reader can see for himself that the earliest phase of Sufism manifested itself in a primarily ethical doctrine involving— according to various sources— ascetic practices and voluntary poverty in particular.

What are the origins of this tendency? As we already mentioned, its earliest origins lie in ancient Islam itself: the sobriety of the Prophet's life, his emotive enthusiasm in his contact with the Divine and the Angel, some evocative Qur'anic expressions, all are elements that show how primitive Islam (at least as lived by some of its representatives) was already a form of "mysticism" as every religion is at its outset. Later Islamic insistence on the juridical aspect of religion (a typical characteristic of the two great Semitic religions—Judaism and Islam) led the spirits who attached greater importance to the early mystical experience to criticize the excessive externalism of legal practices and devote themselves to the mystical aspects of the Qur'an and of ancient tradition. The study and meditation of the following evocative Qur'anic passages would justify in itself the birth of a form of "mysticism."

The first is the "Verse of Light" (Kor. XXIV, 35):

> God is the Light of the heavens and the Earth; the likeness of His Light is as a niche wherein is a lamp (the lamp in a glass as it were a glittering star), kindled from a Blessed Tree, an olive that is neither of the East nor of the West whose oil well-nigh would shine, even if no fire touched it; Light upon Light; (God guides to His Light whom he will) (And God strikes similitudes for men, and God has knowledge of everything.)

Evidently the "metaphysics of Light" reached the Qur'an in kernel through late Christian sources (even though it may have had earlier Iranian origins), and the Qur'an already presents an imaginative kind of expression in parable form—presented in this particular instance as a very simple Christian church with its light in a niche in front of the altar (which the Arabian Prophet may have visited) which is the starting point for every mystical expression.

Another evocative passage concerns the "Day of *alast*" (Kor. VII, 172):

> And when thy Lord took from the Children of Adam, from their loins, their seed, and made them testify concerning themselves, "am I not your Lord?" They said, "Yes, we testify"—lest you should say on the day of Resurrection, 'as for us, we were heedless of this!"

Here (as we indicated above) we find the idea of the pre-existence of souls in a divine "pleroma," derived, in ways that are hard to identify, from Iranian sources. This Qur'anic idea made neo-Platonism—the royal road to every form of mysticism—appear familiar when it began to spread.

Two more passages were "combined" early on by tradition to form the Legend of *mi'râj* ("ascension"):

> Glory be to Him, who carried His servant by night from the Holy Mosque to the Furthest Mosque, from the precincts that We have blessed, that We might show him some of Our signs. He is the All-hearing, the All-seeing (Kor. XVII, 1).

and:

> By the Star when it plunges, your comrade is not astray, neither errs, nor speaks he out of caprice. This is naught but a revelation revealed, taught him by one terrible in

power, very strong; he stood poised being on the higher horizon, then drew near and suspended hung, two bows'-length away, or nearer, then revealed to his servant that he revealed. His heart lies not of what he saw; what, will you dispute with him what he sees? Indeed he saw him another time by the Lote-Tree of the Boundary nigh which is the Garden of the Refuge, when there covered the Lote-Tree that which covered; his eye swerved not, nor swept astray. Indeed, he saw one of the greatest signs of his Lord (Kor. LIII, 1–18).

Here, in these "dark-colored words" that subsequent centuries of meditation loaded with extremely rich symbolic meanings and experimental spirituality, the early Muslims too saw the religious experience of an ascension—whether spiritual or physical—toward those worlds from which the soul must have come. God-Light, the Pre-existence of souls in a primeval world in God's company, Ascension to that world: these three ideas can easily be culled from the Qur'an and are sufficient to empty of content the theories that declare all mysticism "impossible" against the "arid background" of Qur'anic Islam. In fact we have an example of how daily meditation, the "savoring" of the sacred text (to use Massignon's metaphor), is the way to mystical ascension. Before the middle of the ninth century A.H. Khawwas (quoted in Massignon, *Lexique technique*) said: "At first, to regain sweetness in reading the Qur'an I read it as if Muhammad were dictating it to me; then as if Gabriel were announcing it to Muhammad; then, finally, as if it were God himself: and all his sweetness was given me then" (in Sha'rani, *Tab.* I, 61).

For further "proof" of what we have just said we refer our readers to Massignon's major works. He was the chief upholder of the theory of the essential mysticality of ancient Islam (though his works are slightly confused in places by the fact that—a mystic himself—he entered possibly rather too personally into his subject). To this we must add what we said above about the logicality (also from a psychological point of view) of the birth of a mysticism that was independent from the absolute transcendence of God, and we will see that Sufism has nothing "Christian" or "Aryan" about it except for the Semitic Arabism of its early origins. However they undeniably influenced the course of its development, though most Orientalists now agree that these influences were at first Christian (from an ascetic point of view) and then (where theory was concerned) Christian-neo-Platonic and Gnostic. Contrary to what Horten maintained (even though he did so with considerable erudition and philosophical insight) the Indian influence was limited (and concerned only certain aspects of the Sufism of Indian Islam, which came very late). Are there any specifically Iranian influences? Apparently not, if we intend direct Iranian influences, though there was some indirect Iranian influence on the late Christian and Gnostic-Syncretic world. But exception must be made, as we have seen, for Suhravardî and the Ishrâqî school of Sufism, which was both Sufism and philosophy.

Here we must again warn the reader against making distinctions that are too clear-cut. The form of thought we are considering in this section of the book— i.e., philosophy, Ishrâq, Sufism, Ismaili Gnosis—takes its rhythm mainly from differences of "accentuation." If we were to try to define a special Sufi accentuation as compared to other movements I would describe it as a more immediate personal emotivity in religious experience. For a Sufi, practice is more important in religion than theory (as the above-quoted early definitions indicate) and, in contrast with the Ismaili concept of the unique teaching authority of the imâm, or the philosophical concept of the primacy of "reason" as guide to the spiritual, the average Sufi believes that everyone—through adequate guidance and discipline—can attain the deifying contact that the official Sunni religion reserved to the Prophet alone, the Shi'ite heretics of various tendencies to the imâm and certain aristocratic philosophers or ishrâqî to the perfect Sage. This also explains why the Sufis were less harshly persecuted by the Sunnis than by the Shi'ites, for whom anyone who placed himself, in the course of his theopathic experiences, in an identical position to that of their imâm was grievously blaspheming. But we have already seen how Persian Sufism, after the fall of Alamût and the dispersion of Ismailism, in many cases became a form of crypto-Ismailism—assisted by already existing tendencies in Sufism (i.e., the sense of "Saints" and the hierarchy of saints with the "Pole" at its top) that could easily be used to support the Imâm.

But Persia contributed an extremely important element to Sufism: its very agile poetic language. This language suited philosophical poetry, which we now find extremely difficult, if not impossible, to understand, and created universal masterpieces both in the form of long "poems" (*masnavî*) used for theoretical descriptions and in the agile quatrains (*rubâ'îyât*) used for the rapid annotation of theopathic experiences. Persian poets created, as well, a style and system of images that are so fundamental for an understanding of Persian spirituality that we will devote the next chapter to them. We find the mystical poetry of Iran spiritually more congenial than that of Arab Sufism, not because it is "Aryan" but rather because, possibly like Persian poetry, it is the result of a fusion of similar religious traditions. In comparison, the almost untranslatable products of Arab Sufism are generally more terse and emotionally charged, though (to our taste at least) more contorted and fragmentary from an artistic point of view.

We cannot present even a brief systematic history of the development of Persian Sufism here: even if we were only to give a historical outline and examples of its great exponents we would have to write a book within the book. We will therefore limit ourselves to a few explanatory notes before presenting the greatest Iranian Sufi, Maulânâ Jalâlu'd-Dîn Rûmî.

Earlier on we mentioned some vivid personal theopathic experiences: Bâyazîd of Bistâm (who lived as a hermit and died in 874 in his native town of Bistâm in Khurâsân) was one of the first, most characteristic, and possibly most extreme of the Iranian mystics. Of Zoroastrian descent (though this is of relative importance, since he occasionally speaks with little affection of the "Gabrs") he learnt (and this is more important) the most profound secrets of mysticism, including the theory of *fanâ* or annihilation, from an Indian Muslim, Abû 'Alî as-Sindî.[89] He has left us some *shathîyât*, i.e., phrases pronounced in a state of *shath*, ecstasy, in which the human and divine personality apparently become interchangeable, and he is reputed to have said: "Glory to Me, glory to Me! How great is my Majesty!" Another great Persian mystic, Farîdu'd-Dîn 'Attâr (who was over a hundred when he died around 1230),[90] wrote his "little flowers." The following is an example, which may serve as an introduction to the atmosphere of extreme Sufism:

> It is said that the shaikh often went walking near the cemetery. One night, returning from the cemetery, he met a local young nobleman who was playing a lute. When he approached Bâyazîd, the shaikh said: "There is no help and strength except in God!"[91] The young man was irritated and brought his lute down heavily onto the shaikh's head, breaking both the lute and the shaikh's head. That youth was drunk and he did not know who he was. Without a word, Bâyazîd returned to his cell. The next morning he called one of his companions and asked: "How much does a lute cost?" Having been told the price, he wrapped some coins in a piece of material and sent them, together with a piece of cake, to the young man with the following message: "Bâyazîd asks your forgiveness and sends word to say: Yesterday you broke your lute. I beg you to buy another one with this money. This cake is to remove any anger and bitterness you may have in your heart at having lost your lute."

And again:

> One day Bâyazîd said: "The yearning of the Country of Lovers has set up a throne of torture and detachment in that Country and has unsheathed a sword of terror of separation and has given a narcissus branch of Union into Hope's hand. Every instant a thousand heads are raised on top of those swords." And he added: "Seven thousand years have passed and that narcissus is still tender and fresh and the hand of no hope has been able to pick it."

We have quoted one of the actions and one (among many) of the sayings of the great and eccentric saint of Bistâm. The former shows us experimentally the mystic's identification with God's qualities (first among these the absolute generosity and love, which are at the origin of creation). The latter is an example of the creativity of images, which was specific to mystics as against what we have seen of the Ishrâq. Here the mystic's personal experience creates the (true) "ghosts" of a world, which, in order to reach it, led to thousands of heads falling (so far) unsuccessfully. And this reveals both the fascination and the limits of the position of pure mysticism, i.e., the constant danger, from an authentically religious point of view, of psychologism, of personal creations "not authorized from above" but rising from below—a danger that only recognition of an "imâm" can overcome.

Hallâj's head was one of the famous ones that fell to reach "that world" (in 922 in Baghdad). We must speak about him here because, though he was Persian only by birth and had forgotten his native language, he was of capital importance for the whole of Muslim mysticism and himself became the object of mystical meditation. He too had a secret link, which it is very difficult to analyze, with some form of extreme Shi'ism. Experts[92] have seen a connection between some of his doctrines and those of the Nusairîs a Syncretist Gnostic sect of which there are some small nuclei today in Syria and which used to also exist in Mesopotamia. The similarity lies mainly in the terminology and concept of incarnation, of union between *nâsût* (humanity) and *lâhût* (divinity)— terms identical to the analogical Christian ones (taken in fact from Syrian terminology) that, after Hallâj, were to disappear from the language of the Muslim mystics. In the tenth and eleventh centuries, Muslim authors noted a similarity between Hallâj's doctrine of *hulûl* (incarnation) and that of the heretic Ibn al-'Azâqîr. Bartold[93] quotes Sâbit (*Irshâd* I, 296), according to whom "Ibn al-'Azâqîr's appearance was Hallâj's own appearance," while according to the Persian philosopher, historian and moralist Ibn Miskawayh (d. 1030 A.D.), Ibn al-'Azâqîr spoke of God's incarnation within him in the same terms used by Hallâj concerning himself.

This Ibn al-'Azâqîr, whom Bartold studied in the above-mentioned article, was Hallâj's contemporary. He lived and wrote in Mesopotamia, professing the doctrines we studied in Chapter III. He can be considered a late echo (by then already influenced by the early Ismaili doctrines) of those heretics. One of his particularly interesting doctrines (because it is already present in Hallâj) is that God creates his own opposite in order the better to specify himself. In the beginning God became incarnate in Adam and at the same time in Satan.[94] Each one, precisely because they were opposites, "indicated" the other. The indication of Truth is better than Truth itself and its contrary is closer to the thing itself than what is similar to it. After Adam, God was incarnated in five other men and, correspondingly, in five satanic beings: what is Satanic is therefore a part of God and complete God is Satan plus Adam, in a constant dialectic process. Idrîs and his "Satan" come next and, after his death, "God's liquefaction" occurs in five other men. Next Noah, Sâlih, Abraham (his Satan is called by name: Nimrûd), Aaron (and respectively Pharaoh),[95] then David-Goliath, Solomon (his Satan is not given a name) and Jesus and his Satan (after their death their Satans are usually "dispersed" in their disciples and their Satans), then in 'Alî with his respective unnamed Satan (here too, as with Moses, the *sâmit*/silent one and not the *nâtiq*/speaker is mentioned as the incarnation) and finally in Ibn al-'Azâqîr himself, who added—and his doctrine had even more pantheistic tendencies than did that of the Ismailis—that God manifests himself in all things and all thoughts. An Idea (*khâtir*) rises out of the heart of every man within which what is hidden to him assumes a form in order that he may "see" it. This miraculous inner mirror is God, etc.

We have mentioned this unusual heretic (whose doctrines contain rather different shadings to those we have already studied) because he was a contemporary of the great Hallâj and also because his doctrine on Satan was to play a very important part in the speculations of the mystics. In fact these two doctrines of "incarnation" and "dialectics with Satan" were possibly Hallâj's most typical ones and we will therefore examine them briefly.

God created Adam "in his image" (*fî sûratihi*, according to the Qur'an) therefore Adam is God. Hallâj summarizes this in the verses: "Glory be to He who manifested His Humanity as the intimate aspect (*sirr*) of the glory of his sparkling divinity; then he manifested himself openly to the created in the form of one who eats and drinks until his creature can perceive him, like the glance of an eyelid on an eyelid" (*Tawâsîn*, p. 130). His terminology is entirely Christian, except that Christianity applies these terms only to Christ. The divine spirit (*rûh*) descends and is incarnated: he uses the word *hulûl*—a term hated not only by the orthodox Muslims, but by all, or almost all, the "heretics" who used, as we have seen and will see, images taken from the metaphysics of light to indicate the man-god contact. In a word, they all were Docetists. Hallâj instead was a complete "incarnationist"—a very rare phenomenon in the history of Islamic religious thought. This is how he describes "the incarnation," as theopathetically experienced in himself:

> You [God] flow between the membrane of the heart
> and the heart as tears flow beneath the eyelids
> and you descend (*tahullu*) into the intimate depths
> of a man's bosom (*fu'ad*)
> as spirits descend into bodies.
> No one who is at rest moves, unless You
> move him, from a most hidden place.
> O Shining Crescent of Moon! You appear on the fourteenth day and again on the
> eighth, and the fourth, and the second!

The great Catholic Orientalist Massignon (who quite venerated the Muslim saint Hallâj) rightly points out how the controversy of the *mas'alat ar-rûh* (problem of the spirit) was kept alive throughout the tenth century by the attempts at fusion between the Greek metaphysics of the *'aql* (intellect) and the experimental mysticism of the *rûh* (pneuma). Hallâj's *rûh* cannot be reduced to the *intellectus possibilis* that, with Averroes became a single intellect. It is an active intellect which (as Hallâj says) "is fierily enlivened in the intimate subconscious" (*tilka's-sarâ'iri*) (this image, with its concept of the "fiery 'I,'" brings to mind the Iranian *daêna*-light). In time, in the later speculations of thinkers like Ibn al-Fârid and Ibn 'Arabî, Hallâj's personal man became *al-insân al-kâmil* (abstract perfect human being), Muhammad, the Eternal Prophet, etc. Hallâj too, in a way believed in this. Adam also is Cosmic Man, that is, God. But Hallâj felt this experience personally, within himself, and he did not want to found a sect with himself as God. I believe that this is his greatest mark of originality and possibly his most typically "mystical" characteristic; it makes a Sufi of him rather than a Shi'ite extremist, unlike men such as Ibn al-Aqâzîr.

As for the problem of "Satan" (Ar. *Iblîs*) in mysticism, an entire book would be needed to study it: for more detailed information we refer our readers to the section of a chapter devoted to the question in Ritter's *Das Meer der Seele* (pp. 536–550) and to my article "Satana nell'opera filosofico-poetica di Muhammad Iqbal" (*RSO*, XXX, 1955, pp. 55–102), which contain further bibliographical citations. The focus of this problem is to be found in the Qur'anic tale (derived from Talmudic sources, later all but forgotten in the West) according to which, after Adam's creation, God ordered the angels to adore this creature of mud and prostrate themselves before him. All obeyed except for Iblîs, who refused, saying: "You created me out of fire and you have created him out of mud: therefore I am better than he is!" Thus the test lies mainly in an act of humility and in the recognition of God's arbitrary and total diversity from every created creature and from every tie with a created, even though angelic, logic. Satan, the logician, who is unaware of the Islamic arbitrariness of God, is the enemy of earth, a "racist" where fire is concerned.

The earth-fire controversy was an ancient one in Islam and particularly interesting, precisely because there were people who glorified Fire preferring it to Earth already at the time of the Shu'ûbîya and the Zandaqa (thus making Satan's negation their own). The Semitic world, on the other hand, seems to have preferred Earth to Fire. Prof. Mu'în, in an excursus in his valuable study on Mazdean influences on Persian literature, writes: "After Islam spread throughout Iran and the temples to Fire were destroyed, fire progressively lost the respect and veneration it had enjoyed among the Persians, even though enlightened Iranian spirits and the champions of ancient culture (particularly the Shu'ûbîya and the leaders of national revivals) fought constantly in many ways to rekindle the flame of national sentiment and preserve the sense of veneration for Fire." Bashshâr ibn Burd, a free-thinker, former Zoroastrian and blind panegyrist of the Caliph al-Mahdî, was put to death for his heresies in 783-4. Bashshâr wrote an ode (*qasîda*) in which he prefers Fire (an element sacred to the Persians) to Earth (an element that was considered worthy of veneration by

the Muslims, for out of earth the Islamic Ka'ba was made and from it God
moulded the father of humankind, Adam). Note well here the opposition between "the Muslims" and "the Persians!" In so doing, the poet declared Iblîs,
created from Fire, superior to Adam, created from Earth:

> Earth is dark and Fire brilliant
> And fire has been adored ever since it existed.
> Satan is better than your (sic!) father Adam:
> wake up, O assembly of depraved ones!
> Satan is of fire and Adam of mud
> And Earth will never attain the heights of Fire!

Firdausî too, in his Shâh-nâmeh, calls Fire the representative of divine splendor, the "qibla of the Persians," and earth and stones "the qibla of the Arabs"
(Mu'în, op. cit., p. 40). Elsewhere Firdausî considers Fire the first element of
the creation from which earth derived (the elements appear in this order: heat-
dryness-cold-dampness). Firdausî's attitude met with the curiously energetic
stand in favor of earth taken by 'Alî Asadî "the younger" (who completed his
poem Garshâsp-nâmeh in 1066), and this indicates that the controversy must
have been quite heated. How unimportant race was in these matters is demonstrated by the fact that Asadî was as Persian as Firdausî and Bashshâr ibn Burd
(who, in fact, wrote in Arabic!). In the beginning of the Garshâsp-nâmeh (ed.
Yaghmâ, Tehran, pp. 7 and foll.) Asadî says that though all four elements are
equally praiseworthy, "anyone who is guided by reason (khirad) must admit
that the most praiseworthy of all is earth," supporting his statement with a
number of arguments including that Earth is the qibla of angels too since they,
who are of fire, adore Adam, who is of earth. Further on in the poem (pp. 134–
139), a Brahman describes the creation of the world as starting with heat and
fire in the course of a discussion with Garshâsp. As if to apologize, Asadî presents the theory of the Greek philosophers (filsûfân-i Rûm, probably an echo of
Anaximenes) according to which air is better than fire (considering it closer to
the Islamic concept). A fourteenth century "confirmation" of this reasoning is
contained in the small volume—a kind of encyclopedia on demons and jinn—
by Badru'd-Dîn ash-Shiblî, Akâm al-marjân fî ahkâm al-jânn (Il Cairo, 1326
A.D., p. 158 and foll.). The author says that Satan also erred from a logical point
of view when he maintained the priority of fire (erring for fifteen reasons that
we will spare the reader). The last reason, championed by Rûmî too, is interesting: i.e., the Evil One erred because he saw only the external form of the mud
and not its goal, God's intention. Thus if, by an absurd hypothesis, it were true
that Fire is by nature better than Earth, this would not necessarily imply that he
who is created from fire is better than he who is created from mud, because
everything is possible for God, he can create a better creature out of inferior

matter than the one created out of superior matter. Therefore the important thing is to look at the *kamâl an-nihâya* (perfection of the intention) and not at the *naqs al-mâdda* (defect of the matter): and Satan was unable to perform this act of penetration. This ought to be enough for us to clearly perceive the abyss that lies between a supernatural and revealed religion and a philosophical and pantheistic religiosity.

Soon however the reasoning and speculations of the mystics settled on the fact that having ordered the angels to perform an act of idolatry God must have meant something mysterious and different from what his external words indicated: rather like the Wagnerian problem of the walkyrie's obedience to Wotan's orders. Or, even more daringly, that Satan was more monotheistic than God, refusing to bow down in front of a created being. We have seen how the heretic Ibn al-'Azâqîr interpreted this. Hallâj, in his *Tawâsîn* (ed. Massignon, pp. 41 and foll.) devotes almost a whole chapter to the problem with the usual restless passion that distinguishes him from later, more philosophical, mystics. The Satan-God dialogue takes place in short, sparkling sentences:

God: "Adore!"—Iblîs: "Only You!" God: "And if I were to curse you?" Iblîs: "Only You!" (he sings):

"My refusal is Sanctification to You, my reasoning is false reasoning in you. Who is Adam if he is not You? And who is writhing in the separation? Iblîs![96]

The only way open to me is to You: I am a rejected lover." God: "You have performed an act of pride!" Iblîs: "If I had been with you for only an instant calling me proud would be right, but I have known You since eternity: therefore I am better than him, because I preceded him in serving You, nor is there anyone in the two worlds who knows You better than I do. I have affection (*irâda*, also "will") in You and You have affection in me; Your affection in me precedes all things; if I bowed down to any other than You . . . if I do not bow down I will necessarily return to my origin because 'You created me from Fire.'

Moses and Iblîs met on the slopes of Sinai and Moses asked him: "What prevented you from bowing down?" Iblîs: "My claim to recognizing only one Adorable [being]. If I had bowed down to Adam I would have been like you. You were called only once: "Look towards the Mountain!" and you looked. I have been called a thousand times to adore [Adam] and I have not adored . . ." Moses: "And so you disobeyed the order?" Iblîs: "It was not an order, but a test (*ibtilâ'*, temptation)." Moses: "And yet you changed your form." Iblîs: "Oh Moses, both this and the other are travesties (*talbîs*) . . . but the knowledge is identical to what it was, only the person has changed." Moses: "Are you still speaking about Him?" Iblîs: "Oh Moses, one does not speak of thought, I am mentioned and he is mentioned (he sings):

My mentioning is his and his is mine

the two mentioners are in an eternal embrace!

My service to Him is purer now and my time sweeter and my mentioning more brilliant: because in most ancient eternity I served Him for my joy and now I serve

Him for *His* joy! Now all yearning is over, prohibition and dismissal, harm and advantage are abolished, he has caused me to be alone, he has caused me to be astounded, he has rejected me so that I might not mingle with friends, he has prevented me from any contact with strangers to estrange me, he has estranged me to astound me, he has astounded me to exile me, he has exiled me to sacralize me, he has sacralized me (*ahramanî*) to separate himself from me; he has separated me from himself to discover me, he has discovered me to unite himself to me, he has united himself to me to exclude me, to desire me!"

In an amazing and almost hysterical later passage that is imbued with the sense of the voluptuousness of abjection typical of the more extreme mystics and offers a far more convincing psychological explanation for the origins of the Malâmatîya movement than many historical studies on the "sources," Hallâj—describing a personal dialogue with Satan on "nobility"—says:

And I, Hallâj, disputed with Iblîs and with Pharaoh on nobility (*futuwwa*). And Iblis said: "If I had adored Adam I would have lost my nobility." And Pharaoh: "If I had believed in the Prophet I would have fallen from the rank of Nobility." And I said: "If I had withdrawn from my claim and statement I would have fallen from the carpets of the Nobility." Iblîs said: "I am better than He is, when He saw nothing at that time but Himself." And Pharaoh: "I know no other God for you than myself [Qur'anic phrase]," since he knew nobody among his people who could distinguish Reality from Vanity. And I say: "If you do not know Him, at least you know His works. I am that work, I am God (*Haqq*, Reality) because in eternity I was God with God. My master and my companion (*sâhib*) is Satan, is Pharaoh." Iblîs was frightened through fire and did not desist from his claim, and Pharaoh was drowned in the sea and did not desist from his claim . . . and now, even if I were to be killed or crucified and mutilated of my hands and feet, I would not desist from my cry!" (*da'va*, claim).

If these words are authentic, Hallâj was a prophet: in fact, after a long trial he was crucified and his hands and feet were cut off. He died on the cross in the midst of indescribable torments, the living prototype of the Christ he had so greatly extolled in his works (Though Christ was much loved by all Muslims as a particularly great prophet, for obvious reasons he always enjoyed the special sympathy of the Sufis). According to tradition Hallâj pronounced the following prayer on the cross before dying:

Lord! These servants of yours have gathered here to kill me, out of their zeal for Your cult, to be closer to You! Forgive them Lord! Because if You had revealed to them what you have revealed to me they would not have acted as they did, and if You had hidden from my sight what you have hidden from theirs I would not be suffering what I am suffering now.

We mentioned the Malâmatîya in connection with ignominious death and the taste for ignominious death, a certain complacency in defining themselves disciples of Satan, etc. The Malâmatî attitude is fundamental in Muslim and Persian mysticism and must be given some attention. The name Malâmatîya was given to a special movement[97] of Khurâsân mystics (see Massignon, *EI*, IV, p. 701) who initially were opposed to the Iraqi Sufis. But Malâmatism, taken in a more general sense, imbued the whole of Sufism. We will consider some of its literary aspects in the next chapter. Here we will simply remind our readers that in his Persian treatise on mysticism—*Kashf al-mahjûb*—al-Hujvîrî (c. 1030–1072) is already aware of the Malâmatî and comments: "censure is extremely efficacious in rendering love sincere," and he adds that the Prophet himself was in a way the first Malâmatî, censured as he was for being a sooth-sayer, magician, poet and madman, and that the Qur'an itself indicates the believer as being he who "does not fear the censure of unbelievers" (cf. Kor. V, 54). It is God's will that "causes those who speak of him to be censured but preserves their hearts from concern over the censure of the world . . ." The author quotes a certain Hamdûn Qassâr as one of the first Malâmatî (*Kashf*, p 62, chap. VI):

> To be censured, to be censured outwardly for love of the happiness of the soul; these heights are not reached either by Cherubims or other purely spiritual beings, they have not been sought after by any ascetic, devotee or seeker of God of antiquity; they are reserved for those who in our country have reached complete detachment from the things of this world.

This "pious beginning" ended in the excesses of certain Malâmatî "dervishes" who were like the *weise Narren* and the "holy madmen" of some religions.[98] Meshreb (a singular saint studied by Hartmann[99]) who lived and wrote poetry in the eighteenth century in central Asia is an example of this. He said (p. 162–3): "God does not love those who are without sin, he loves sinners. I shall therefore commit an obscene sin; if the man of God will have me hanged and I shall die, all the better!" And in one of his ghazal: "I knew that Your name is the guide of those who err: in order to obtain Your upright guidance I have sinned!" And the good Meshreb—whom we quote only because he was an extreme example (though an unimaginative one) of the same sublime overturning of values and even the "folly of the Cross" impersonated in higher spheres by a Christ or a Hallâj[100]—did not limit himself to singing disconcerting ghazal but even went as far as urinating from the pulpit onto the assembly of believers who expected pious words from him, giving his excrement to others to eat, reciting bacchic verses by Hâfiz instead of the canonical prayer, exposing his genital organs in public and saying that all the saints and prophets moved around them, that he was God, that he had been a donkey and a horse in previous lives and so forth.[101]

The French periodical "La Gnose"[102] (which is almost impossible to find now) offers very perceptive considerations on Malâmatism together with the translation by a certain sayyid Abû 'Abdu'r-Rahmân (almost certainly the pseudonym of Guénon who spent his last years living as a Muslim dervish in Egypt) of part of a short theoretical treatise on the Malâmatîs (1911, p. 100 and foll.) by 'Abdu'l-Hâdî. The treatise states that God is too "jealous" of the Malâmatî mystics to allow them to reveal themselves to the world as they truly are, and therefore he gives them an exterior aspect corresponding to a state of "separation from the sky" (*iftirâq*) but their inner self—whether they are in a state of concentration or of dispersion—is always with God. According to this short treatise the Malâmatîya represent the highest level of mystics. In some ways a Malâmatî is on a level with the Prophet Muhammad who was qâba qausain (see Kor. LIII, 9, i.e., at a distance little short of "two bows" from God) and yet when he came back to earth he only spoke of exterior matters (laws, wars, etc.). Nothing about his person indicated his intimate conversation with God: and, in spite of outward appearances, this was a superior level to that of Moses' level (for nobody could set eyes on his face when he came down from his conversation with God on Mount Sinai). The Sufis are (at best) on a level with Moses but the Malâmatî are beyond. A Persian from Khurâsân, Abû Hafs an-Nîsâbûrî, is mentioned as being the shaikh of the group: he maintained that men left the Malâmatî in peace with God because of their ostentation of what is blameworthy. Hamdûn al-Qassâr (who is mentioned by Hujvîrî) is also mentioned here as having said that "the Malâmatî way consists in renouncing all embellishment of self under the pretence of attaining perfect states in order to be seen by men; and in renouncing to seek men's approval where character and actions are concerned, "in order that you may not be censured *by God* concerning God's rights over you." Other passages of this treatise indicate that they also considered Bâyazîd Bistâmî one of them, though they were well aware of the dangers this position implied.

The origin of the Malâmatî attitude, as we have seen, is easily understandable from a psychological point of view, besides the fact that the phenomenon is universal, and Sino-Japanese Zen Buddhism (*dhyâna, ch'an*) offers identical passages and "stories," even though its metaphysical basis is different from that of the Muslim Malâmatî. But if we want to look for historical origins and influences I believe (with Goldziher[103]) that they must be sought for in Christianity. Giving a number of sources, Goldziher mentions the typical *anaischynìa* of the oriental Christian monks. In a more general sense, however, Paul's letters (see Rom. 3:7–8, etc.)—with their doctrine of the "folly of the Cross" and *similia*— are full of *ante litteram* Malâmatîya elements that are even verbally similar to Muslim Malâmatî expressions. The first great Malâmatî was in fact Christ himself.

Setting aside the more specifically ethical aspect, we have so far examined the "motifs" that distinguish Sufism from the philosophical and theological movements studied in this chapter: the emotive sense of the descent of divinity into humanity: the emotive identification with Satan, the terse dialectics of contrasts (Pharaoh-Moses), the sense of sacred self-abjection. Later these emotions grew less violent in the schools, Sufi systems grew and the pantheistically-oriented princes of Sufism emerged (e.g., the Spaniard Ibn 'Arabî who died in Damascus soon after becoming the master of the great Persian Sufi poet-theosopher Rûmî). But we must not forget that Rûmî was also a disciple of Shams-i Tabrîz, possibly an Ismaili, with his Malâmatî tendencies. In Rûmî, as in a great ocean, the emotive and the systematic motifs of mysticism merge. He was born in Balkh and died in Asia Minor. Geographically, he not only influenced the whole of Persian mysticism but, through the schools he founded (and particularly the order of the Maulavî dervishes—the whirling dervishes described by the journalists), the religious spirituality of the Ottoman Empire. We will now describe him more fully (and this will also serve as a general summary of the doctrines of Sufism).[104]

The first lines of his great poem, the "Spiritual *Masnavî*," are the best possible introduction.

Listen to the reed flute, how it tells its story, how sadly it bewails the separation:
Ever since I was torn from the cane-brake, my gentle sound has made men and women weep!
I want a heart, a heart rent by its Friend's indifference, able to explain to him the passion of Love:
For whoever remains far from his Origin always seeks the time when he was united to it!
In every assembly I have wept my doleful notes, the constant companion of the unhappy and the happy.
And, alas, all were under the illusion that they were my friends, and nobody sought in my heart for my deepest secret.
And yet my secret is not far, no, it is not far from my lament; I am the eyes and ears that that Light does not have!
The body is not veiled from the soul, nor is the soul veiled from the body; and yet no one is allowed to see the soul.
This cry of the flute is fire, not wind; and he who does not have this fire deserves to dissolve into nothing!
It is the fire of Love that has fallen into the flute, it is the ardor of Love that has filled the wine.
The flute is the faithful companion of he who has been torn away from a Friend; its melodies still rend our heart.
Whoever saw, as the flute saw, poison and antidote, whoever saw, as the flute saw, a confidant and a lover?

The flute tells of a path red with blood, it also tells us the stories of Majnûn's love:[105]

This hidden sense is confided only to those who are out of their senses, the tongue has no other clients than the ear.

In our sorrow, the days were importunate, the days took torments of fire by the hand;

If our days passed, say: I do not fear them! But You, You must not pass away from Us, You who are the purest of all!

But no-one who is green understands the state of he who is mature; let my leave-taking be brief![106]

I do not think that Nicholson exaggerated when he defined him as "the greatest mystic poet of all times."[107] (And he was ready to repeat this statement even after the enormous task of translating and commenting on the 26,000 and more double lines of the Poem!) But mystics do not like to talk much about their own historical and visible life on this earth. I want to remain in tune with Rûmî's spirit and will communicate only the indispensable facts of his visible existence.[108] He was born in Balkh, in present-day Afghanistan, in 1207 A.D. When he was five years old, his father Bahâ'ud-Dîn fell out of favor with the Prince[109] and the whole family left the country and emigrated first to Nîshâpûr, then to Baghdad, then to Mecca where they performed the pilgrimage, and on to Malatya where they remained for four years. From here they moved to Lârinda where Bahâ'ud-Dîn devoted himself to his son's education for seven more years. Finally he accepted the invitation of the Seljuk prince of Konya, 'Alâ'u'd-Dîn Kaiqubâd, establishing himself in that city, where he died in 1231. Except for brief stays in Aleppo and Damascus, his son Jalâl'ud-Dîn (our poet) remained in Konya, teaching and writing poetry until his death in 1273. We owe to him the foundation of the *tariqa* (mystical confraternity) that took its name, "Maulavîya" (Turkish pronunciation: Mevleviyye)[110] from *maulâna* ("our lord"), as he was called. His main works are: the *Dîvân*, a collection of mystical lyrical odes,[111] and the *Masnavî*, a poem of more than 26,000 double lines in six volumes[112] which has often been called the "Qur'an in the Pahlavî language" (Persian). Another book with the curious Arabic title of *Fîhi mâ fîhi* ("There is what there is") contains the Master's prose declarations collected by his son and disciples. This offers a commentary of what we know of his religious ideas from his poetical works.[113] But before we examine his religious poetry we should remember two facts. One is the meeting he had, apparently in Damascus, with his mysterious spiritual master Shams-i Tabrîzî, who died as mysteriously as he had entered his disciple's life during a popular rising in Konya (1247). For Rûmî, Shams-i Tabrîzî (or "Sun of Tabrîz") was "like the tinder-box that makes the sparks hidden within the stone burst forth." Rûmî's veneration for the Master—whom he almost deified in his "Collection of Lyrics"—was immense: all his lyrical poems are signed, out of respect, with the name "Shams." And it is significant that a tradition exists (whose authenticity it is hard to judge) according to which Shams was the son of Hasan III (one of the Ismaili Grand Masters of Alamût), while the Ismailis ranked him later as one of their imâms (cf. Hodgson, *Assassins*, p. 276). The second fact was his meeting with Ibn 'Arabî (d. 1249) and his disciples, which also took place in Damascus. The experts feel that Ibn 'Arabî, the great Spanish theorizer of Monist Islamic mysticism,[114] greatly influenced Rûmî—though this influence seems to me to have been more external and philosophical than religious.[115] At all events Rûmî fused and brought to perfection the religious master Shams-i Tabrîzî's mystical fervor and Ibn 'Arabî's abstract ideology.[116]

And now we must say something more about the presentation of Rûmî's two fundamental literary works (the *Dîvân* and the *Masnavî*) since they belong to a literary genre that is very far from western tradition. The *Dîvân*, or "Collection of Lyrics," is a collection of short odes called ghazal consisting in a group of verses whose contents are more or less unitary. These are connected by a rhyme that is the same throughout the verses and gives the whole its emotive harmony.[117] The *Masnavî* consists of two-lined rhyming verses (this was the rhythmic form of all long Persian poems since Persian literature did not apply a strophic form to long compositions). It is a theosophical treatise (if we give the term its etymological meaning of "science or knowledge of the Divine"): each book is divided into a number of chapters of varying length with explicative titles. They contain, for the most part, commented anecdotes and these anecdotes bring to the highly fertile author's mind other anecdotes that are often connected to the first only by a very tenuous and external thread—and so forth for more than 26,000 two-line verses. Obviously people who are not vitally interested in religious matters may find the whole thing extremely boring, but anyone who feels the religious problem a central problem to his very existence will find an inexhaustible wealth of motifs and an unsuspected depth and, at times, "modernity" in its development. In this sense, the *Masnavî* does not only belong to Islam[118] but to all religions (if it is true that mysticism is the area that is common to them all).

The reader must however be on his guard against taking Rûmî's individual statements too literally (in the western sense: i.e., taking them as a part of a well-ordered self-sufficient and autonomous system). We should remember (with G. Richter[119]) that we are in the presence of a specific "literary genre": that of "mystical *masnavî*" (which had great predecessors in 'Attâr and in Sanâ'i).[120] We would fall into grave error if we were to forget the importance of this genre. Anyone approaching a Persian treatise of this kind must bear in mind that its systematic unity does not come from within; it is not a construction that grows organically and autonomously like a plant but rather a sparkling mosaic that acquires unity only if it is seen from a certain distance, in an extra-temporal dimension. There is no room here to quote a whole anecdote from the *Masnavî* (with its sub-anecdotes and theoretical passages that appear inextricably mixed and apparently confused) in order to demonstrate exactly what I mean. Richter distinguished two "styles" in Rûmî's anecdotes:[121] the earthly-visible-narrative style of the anecdote and the "second style" that often enters into the picture a few lines after the beginning of the main story (which is set aside to enter into a meta-anecdotal reign of pure thought). The poet seems to forget the story he had started telling (often at the crucial point, with a psychological sense worthy of a modern novelist) to return to it after sinuous detours in the reign of the Spirit—taking his lead from a word or from a very tenuous and secondary thread. Treated thus the anecdote ends by becoming translucent with superior realities. Earthly reality, Rûmî explicitly maintains, is nothing but a reflection of the symbolic reality that is true reality. And, inversely, symbolic reality is not, as we generally believe, a reflection of true visible reality.

Here is a haphazardly chosen example: one of the anecdotes in the *Masnavî* is called: "The story of 'A'isha" (may God be satisfied with her!) and how she asked the Prophet (on whom may there be Peace!): "Today it rained: how is it that you, who went to the cemetery, have dry clothes on?"[122] It opens with an account of how Muhammad went to the cemetery one day to accompany the body of one of his companions. After this brief introduction Rûmî seems almost entranced by the visual connection between "cemetery trees" and "the dead who dwell below earth" and so, abruptly, after only two verses from the beginning of the story, he says:

These trees are like the inhabitants of the bosom of the earth; from the bosom of the earth they raise their hands invokingly! They make a hundred signs to men, they make those gifted with ears understand many things: with their green tongue and long invoking arms they tell the secrets of the bosom of the earth!

And he continues in this way for a number of verses until this beautiful line:

Each rose imbued with inner perfume tells, that rose, the secrets of the Whole!

Consequently the unity of the *Masnavî* (and there is unity) is not unity as we understand it but it is an indication of another, truer, "unity" that is "outside," in the world of invisible things and of those things that "are nothing" but are more powerful than those things that are[123]—a superior unity that follows a different order: an order that may appear non-order and casual juxtaposition to profane eyes.

It is therefore very easy for a translator who is "too clever" or too insensitive to Rûmî's essential religious value to make him say things he never dreamt of saying. To show how easy this is I will briefly tell the episode (well-known to scholars who have studied Rûmî's works) of Moses and the Little Shepherd.[124] A kneeling shepherd was invoking God, saying: "Where are you O my God? I love you greatly, show yourself to me, so that I may comb your hair, free you from insects, give you my best milk to drink and prepare a fresh bed of straw for you . . ." Moses, who happened to be passing by, heard the shepherd say these things that sounded like blasphemy to his ears. Irritated, he explained to him that God has neither hair, nor feet, nor hands. The little shepherd was frightened and went away crying. But then God's voice rebuked Moses in beautiful words the sense of which was: "He was wrong, it is true, but he was seeking Me in all sincerity of spirit and therefore you should not have treated him as you did." So far the whole thing seems to fit into a modern anti-objectivist vision of religious truths and the episode could easily be quoted in support of a declaration by modern religious—or pseudo-religious thinkers.[125] But in fact the anecdote has a sequel: the shepherd was tormented by Moses' rebuke and recognized his own "positive" error, adoring the "true" God and thanking Moses who, himself repentant, had gone to look for him to ask his forgiveness for his harshness. Another example is the much quoted anecdote of the four men who quarrelled over buying grapes and could not agree because one said the word "grapes" in Greek (*stafili*), one in Arabic (*'inab*), one in Turkish (*üzüm*) and one in Persian (*angûr*) which could—if used cleverly—almost become an advertisement for the adoption of Esperanto or for a generically stated and humanistically sought–for "unity of peoples." But the coda is essential (if less agreeable to some modern palates). It consists in the coming "of the man of God" (the Prophet and the Saint) who admonishes and "himself" explains Unity, with divine "authority," advising the men to be quiet and listen to the voice of God, the pacifying and unifying voice of the Prophet and Saint, (from the outside, however).[126]

This should help the reader become aware of the fact that we are entering into a world of fundamental and absolute religiosity and that, to understand it, we must forget all the humanistic slogans that the modern world has accustomed us to. The following considerations are simply a pretext to translate and present some remarkable passages from the *Masnavî* (a celebrated and little–read poem). For purely practical reasons and without any claim to exhaustiveness, I will divide my study by subject.

God: Rûmî's concept of God is very interesting and elusive. God's transcendence seems conceived not only as a spatial or intellectual transcendence (spatially, in fact, God can be even "nearer to us than our jugular vein," Kor. L., 15) but also as a moral transcendence, and this is exactly what "orthodox thinkers" sometimes reproach in Rûmî. God is conceived as the absolute Value, and therefore even beyond the values of Good and Evil which are relative to God and both subordinate to Him. This leads to a lively sense of the black-white dialectics between Nothingness and Being, Moses and Pharaoh, the Angel and Satan, where both the terms of these couples are obedient servants of the Supreme Value and there is only an illusion of disobedience. And there are often strange and unexpected transpositions of values: nothingness is true being and being is true nothingness and so forth.

Rûmî conceives reality as divided into four different "spaces":

> O God, reveal to the soul the place where speech without words flourishes: an immense, ample, open space that nourishes the space of these our fantasies, of this being. The Reign of Fantasy is narrower than the Reign of Nothingness[127] and this is why fantasies are the cause of pain and sorrow. And, again, real Existence is a narrower space than that of Fantasy, in this existence the full moon of that fantastic space becomes a slight sickle. And, again, the existence of the world of the senses and colors is narrower, it is a sombre narrow prison![128]

For Rûmî nothingness (*'adam*) is extremely important. God is the nothingness of Man (or rather, of the given being, of nature) and he develops this profound thought at various stages in an infinite series of images. Better still, God is beyond nothingness and being. God works in nothingness, nothingness is His forge.

> Turn from Being towards Nothingness, if you seek God and are divine.[129]
>
> Nothingness is the place of entries, Being is the place of expenditures, the place of this and that. Since God's workshop (*kârgâh-i khudâ*) is nothingness, nothing has effective value outside this workshop.[130] The Work has woven a veil around the Worker, and you cannot see him except in the Work and for the Work; and since the workshop is the place where the Worker lives, he who is outside is unaware of Him. Come therefore to the workshop, i.e. to Nothingness, so that from that observation point you may see both the Work and the Worker![131]

Since God is beyond nothingness and being, discussions on His personality or impersonality are vain. Considering them more poetical and religiously productive, Rûmî generally uses expressions that present God as a supreme I who discusses with man (and, as we shall see, especially with the Prophet) Consequently this God is beyond Good and Evil: we already said that he was beyond moral Good and Evil, and now we can add that God even transcends religious good and evil, i.e., "faith" and rebellious "impiety."

> Impiety too, in relation to God, is wisdom,[132] while, if you refer it to our world, impiety is the greatest misfortune.

Rûmî seems fascinated by extreme impiety in an almost Dostoyevskian way. The figures of Satan and Pharaoh, for example—the one representing impiety in spiritual space, the other in earthly space—are interestingly depicted and have a precedent in Hallâj.

Exhausted by the oppressive day's work, Caliph Mu'âwiya was asleep in his castle. It was the dead of night. He had closed himself in, had barred all the heavy doors to stop disturbers from coming in and had immediately fallen asleep. All of a sudden a voice woke him up: "Mu'âwiya, get up! It is time for the dawn prayer!" A man was beside him, in the shadow, talking to him. Amazed, Mu'âwiya asked him how he had come in. It was Satan. But Mu'âwiya was even more surprised by Satan's strange invitation and sensed a trick. We will see how in fact there was a trick: Satan wanted to prevent the Pious Caliph from forgetting the canonical hour of prayer, because he would have wept so profusely with repentance at not having said his prayer that his repentance would have been a purer act and one more acceptable to God than the physical and exterior prayer itself. But the lines that describe the outcome of the scene (consisting of Mu'âwiya's insistent questions to know the real reasons for Satan's invitation and the clever lies of the demon who finally has to give in) are certainly not as expressively beautiful as the words Rûmî has Satan say in his first answer. The demon explains his apparently strange invitation to prayer with his nostalgia for God: this is the Satan Rûmî preferred, as the reader will see from the poetic efficacy of his words.[133]

Satan answered: I was an angel, first, and with my whole soul I followed the path of worship. I was the confidant of the holiest saints, the intimate companion of the angels who live close to God's lofty throne. Oh, how can one cancel one's first mission from one's heart? How can one's first Love ever leave one's heart? Even if you were to travel from Rûm to Khotan[124] how could the love for your first home be torn from your soul? I too was once inebriated with this wine, I too was among the lovers of God's court! From birth I was carved in love for Him, love for Him was sown, from the beginning, in my soul! Fate also gave me joyous days, I too drank the refreshing waters of His sweetness in spring! Did not the hand of his grace sow me once upon a time? Did he not draw me out of Nothingness? Oh, how many caresses I received from Him, how I wandered in the Rose Garden of His approval! He would place His merciful hand on my brow and the sources of divine favor opened in front of me! Who, when I was a child went to seek milk for me? Who rocked my cradle then? He did! . . .[135] I never drank any milk other than His, no-one other than His providence brought me up! . . . And if the sea of generosity has rebuked me now, how can those doors of Grace remain eternally closed? He created the world out of an act of love, His Sun caresses the smallest atoms of dust. And separation, laden with his anger, is nothing other than a means to know better the value of union with Him. And now, during these few days He is keeping me far from Him, my eyes always remain fixed on His sublime face! How strange that such anger can come from this face . . . But I do not look at the cause of His anger which is temporal, I only look at His eternal grace outside of time, and I break and destroy what is in time . . . And even in this sorrow I savor His pleasure. He has vanquished me,vanquished me, vanquished me!

On earth, Pharaoh's lament is the counterpart of Satan's lament: the relevant passage shows, among other things, a shrewd psychological sense. Pharaoh, the most typical symbol of gratuitous rebellion against God, the symbol of the hardened heart, bursts into tears in the mystery of night and he too is aware that he is invoking God.[136]

Creation: What is this God's relationship with the world? Obviously he is over everything and all presently existing things are produced by Him in one way or another. Rûmî constantly uses the terms create (*khalq*) and creator (*Khâliq*) but his lively sense of the positivity of Nothingness gives a special hue to his whole concept of creation. Creating is a continuous act of God. Certain passages seem to suggest that Rûmî accepted the Ash'arite[137] concept of the successive creation and destruction of everything in successive and discontinuous atoms of time:

The Word was born from Form and died again: the wave drew back again into the sea. Form was born from Formlessness and returned to Formlessness, for "in truth to Him shall we return".[138] Therefore there is a death and a resurrection in every moment, and the Prophet rightly said: the world is an instant.[139] Our thought is an arrow hurled by Him high into the air: how will it remain up there? It will certainly return to God! The world renews itself at every instant and we are unaware of its renewal, because to us it seems stable and eternal. Life comes like a constantly new and newer torrent, and yet, in the body, it appears continuous and immobile. But it appears continuous and immobile because it flows too rapidly, like the spark that swiftly revolves in one's hand. If one turns a torch ably it seems like a long continuous circle of fire; the extended length of time is nothing other than the swiftness of God's creating act, it is a phenomenalist product of the swiftness of Creating."[140]

God creates things murmuring spells in their ears while they are still sleeping in nothingness:

. . . and while He pronounces His mysterious spells on the Non-Beings who have neither eyes nor ears, lo, they begin to move and to tremble: and the sons of Nothingness, through his Enchantments, run rapidly in throngs towards the regions of Being, dancing in joy. And when he again recites sublime enchantments to the Beings, these gallop like fast steeds towards Nothingness again. He whispered something in the rose's ear, and lo she opened to the smile, he murmured something to the stone, and turned it into the precious gem sparkling in the mine. To the body he read a sublime message and turned it into Spirit, he spoke to the Sun and now it is resplendent with rays. And when he says something terrible in the Sun's ear, the Sun's red cheek is covered with a hundred eclipses. But what did God sing in the cloud's ear, that it should spill tears of sorrow on earth like a white gourd? Whatever did the Lord whisper into earth's ear, for it to look at everything attentively, without uttering a word?[141]

But the creation of the world and the dialectics of Being-Nothingness must always be seen from an activist point of view, as the indication of moral action rather than as metaphysical contemplation. For example, if God creates from nothingness, this means that we too must become nothingness, in order to be recreated to newer and higher spiritual lives:

> How could Spring turn a hard and arid stone green? Become, therefore humble earth so that many-colored flowers may spring from you!

Rûmî anticipates, almost word for word, Luther's famous phrase: "It is God's habit to create from Nothingness. Consequently, if man does not become nothingness, God can do nothing with him!"

This supreme humility is reached after a long spiritual preparation and ascetic practice that is neither easy nor simple. The world is the theater of this ascetic practice of man, as well as its spectator and possibly its instrument too.

The world: the world—the non-human world—is something created by God in preparation for the creation of man and subordinate to him. Rûmî, like all the mystics, preached detachment from the world but he had a strong sense of nature (even if this, obviously, was always seen hierarchically, as a sign of God, answering to God's orders). The world is beautiful even as it is, if it is seen in the right perspective, from the most pure Nothingness of God's workshop, from the nullified eye of the Saint who sees mysterious reasons in the Lord's sovereign will. Therefore the world is a whole in which individual phenomena have no reality other than that of the instant and are not, of themselves, eternal. Their only value lies in being significant indications, symbols of truer realities:

> The water of the sea is entirely at Your orders ; Yours, oh Lord, are Water and Fire. If you wish it, Fire becomes sweetest Water, if you do not wish it, Water can also become Fire . . .[142]
>
> Branches and leaves have freed themselves from the prison of earth, they have lifted their heads high and have become companions of air. When the leaves break out from the bark of the branch and hurry to the top of the tree, one by one each fruit and each leaf sings the praise of God with the tongue of its bud. When the spirits that are bound within water and earth joyously free themselves from the prison of mud, they rise high, dancing in the air, inebriated with the love of God, pure and most limpid like the white disk of the Moon. Their bodies dance; as for their souls, do not even ask what they feel![143]

But there is still another reason why we so love and are moved by the things of the world, the spring flowers, the glistening rocks and the animals who graze in the pastures. Rûmî explains this deeper reason for man's nostalgia for nature:

At first man entered into the world of inorganic things. From the inorganic stage he passed to the vegetal stage, and for many long years he lived in the world of plants, and he remembered nothing of his ancient state, which was so radically opposed to the present one. And when he passed from the vegetal to the animal stage, the kingdom of plants in which he once had dwelled was cancelled from his memory, except for his mysterious attraction to plants especially in the season of spring and delicate flowers, like a child tending towards its mother . . . And again the Creator, whom you well know, guided him from the animal to the human stage. Thus he advanced from one endless country to another, until he became intelligent and wise and powerful, and he remembers nothing now of his ancient souls. But he must still migrate beyond this human intelligence, he must run far from this intellect that is made of avidity and egoism, he must flee to contemplate one hundred thousand more beautiful and sublime intelligences. Yes, he will yet be stirred from sleep to wakefulness, a wakefulness in which he will scorn his present stage . . . This is the world, a sleeper's dream, and the sleeper thinks that this sleep will last forever, until suddenly one day the dawn of Death will rise over him and he will be freed from the shadows of life, from false and vain opinions. And when he sees his true and eternal dwelling he will laugh loudly over these sufferings on earth . . . But take care, oh man! And do not imagine that these evil actions you are committing now are fantasies committed in sleep! No! This laughter of yours will be tears and laments on that day, for those who oppress the weak![144]

And so the world is at the same time dream and reality—a hierarchically preparatory value and subordinate to the richer worlds; it is not All, it is only one step towards All.

From the vast concentric spaces embraced in the shining ring of God's Nothingness we have descended to the *humus* of the earth and to flowers—to man's first dwelling. But Rûmî's religious themes are very complex.

Man: Let us consider man for a moment, the man who hovers between God's transparent nothingness and the pasty and opaque existence of the world. According to Rûmî man is not simply a superficial compound of body and spirit: his psychological analysis is far more penetrating. Man has a manifest body (*jism*), a hidden soul (rûh, psyché), a still more "hidden" intellect (*'aql*) and an even more hidden *rûh-i vahy* (spirit that participates in revelation)—the latter being present only in Saints and Prophets.[145] Thus Rûmî is definitely against not only modern materialism but also the pseudo-spiritualism of some theosophers and spiritualists, who mistake the products of the worst kind of *rûh* far too easily for *rûh-i vahy*. *Rûh-i vahy* is a serious matter and not within everyone's reach: if the "others" want to attain truly spiritual realities they must go through a long and hard apprenticeship; before speaking lightly they must be absolutely obedient to the spiritual Master, the Saint, the Prophet. And here we penetrate a rather delicate area of Rûmî's thought, i.e., the central importance he attributes to the Prophet, at least in the religious life of this world. Rûmî has even been considered a pantheist and some of his phrases, taken out of context, could lead one to believe in his undifferentiated

Monism:

> We were simple and one substance only, without a head and without feet in the eternal kingdom down there. Only one substance were we, like the Sun, without knots were we and limpid as water. When that most pure light took on its forms, it multiplied like the crenellated shadows of a tower. Therefore you must destroy the tower with battering rams (*manjânîq*) so that every difference may disappear again from this company of shadows![146]

But one cannot attribute "pantheism" (understood as an undifferentiated God-world unity) to Rûmî or, consequently, even the undifferentiated possibility for all spirits to become god, without the need of intermediaries, in the form of the symbols of God's personality. Nicholson (the greatest European authority on Rûmî) was of this opinion and wrote, in 1923: "I am well aware that where Jalâlu'd-Dîn is concerned this opinion (i.e. the negation of his pantheism) may appear questionable to those who have read certain passages of the Dîvân-i Shams-i Tabrîz in which he describes his union with God in terms that may at first sight appear pantheistic and which I myself understood in a pantheistic sense when I was less well acquainted with the history of Sufism than I am now."[147]

And we have seen how, in his *Masnavî*, Rûmî appears to accept the extremely anti-pantheistic idea of successive creations and destructions of the cosmos by an activist and arbitrary power. His concept of man too is clearly contrary to an easy equality of all in front of revelation, and contrary to a possible divinization of all without intermediaries (the typical concept of different pantheisms). Rûmî attributes a central and fundamental role to Perfect Man (*al-insân al-kâmil*),[148] i.e., the Prophet (or the Saint); in fact some elements in his *Masnavî* (and in his other works) could even lead one to believe that the Prophet or Saint is the true man and the rest of humanity is formed by beings who are inferior "by nature." Rûmî's world-view is far from being monistic or even dualistic (God-Man, God-World), but it could be called triadic in as far as it recognizes God's Plan, the Prophet's (Saint's) Plan and Man's Plan.

The pragmatist reasoning Rûmî uses to demonstrate the religious utility of the Prophets is interesting:

> God made the Prophets (*anbiyâ*) the mediators between Himself and creatures, so that man's envy might be made manifest. Nobody ever felt abject because of his inferiority in front of God, nobody was ever envious of God. But man is envious of a person whom he considers to be a man like himself! Now since evidence has clearly established the greatness of the Prophet, no-one is envious of him either,

because all are agreed in accepting this as a given fact. And so—precisely because of this—a saint (*valî*) or vicar of the Prophet arises in every epoch, and man's temptation lasts until the day of Judgement. Anyone who has a good disposition (*khûy*) is saved: hearts of glass are broken. That saint is therefore the living imâm[149] who arises in every period, whether he is a descendant of 'Umar or a descendent of 'Alî. He is the Well Guided (*mahdî*) and the Well Guiding (*hâdî*). He is at the same time hidden and sitting in front of you. He is like the Light of the Prophet and Universal Reason is his Gabriel. Then there is also the saint who is less than he is and is his lamp, and his light derives from that light. An even lesser saint is the niche of that lamp.[150] The light has different shadings: since God's light has seven hundred veils, behind each veil of light there is one category of Saints.[151]

God cannot make himself heard except through the mouth of the "man of God." The man of God is the sign of divine unity. He is the symbol of the spiritual fact that, if the Prophet were to be abolished, would be lacking: i.e., the fact that God is an autonomous and in some ways personal entity and not tenuous matter dissolved more or less throughout the cosmos.[152] We do not know how this occurs in the hereafter: the pantheistic phrases in the *Dîvân* and the *Masnavî* are enthusiastic and emotional and not descriptions of objective states. They are possibly pertinent, in a purely allusive and analogical way, to the hereafter, to the *vasl* (union with God), to the *baqâ* (permanency in God). But at all events here on earth we need the "battering ram," the strength given us by the Prophet (the insurmountable symbol of God's personality), to destroy those "towers." In a passage of the *Masnavî* Rûmî even says:

> He who receives the revelation from God . . . whatever he orders is the essence itself of Righteousness. He who gives his life is authorized to kill too: he is the vicar of God and his hand is God's Hand. You, like Ishmael,[153] offer your neck and smilingly place your life at the disposal of His sword!

The "you" Rûmî addresses to God is often, especially in the *Dîvân*, a "you" addressed to the visible person of the Spiritual Master (in the form of Shams-i Tabrîzî).

For Rûmî, what distinguishes Saints from the Prophet is the fact that Saints are born of the need for a practical, direct, experimentation of the divine as interlocutor of man. They are born of a desire to relive—now—the experience of those who actually spoke to and venerated Moses, Jesus and Muhammad. Saints are the guarantee of separate "man-God" dialectics, continued until the day of Judgement. The Prophet founds the religious community, he is legislator and promulgator of the *sharî'a* (law). The Saints found the *tarîqa* (meaning, more or less, mystical confraternities, and we know that Rûmî himself founded one). After death the man who has followed the Prophet of his time (his Saint) can contemplate the *haqîqa* (truth in itself, true reality of God).

Sometimes he can do this in moments of ecstasy on earth too. But both performing good works and abiding by the exterior religious rules of the cult are useful to the mystic. Rûmî is explicit on this point:

> If spiritual explanation were enough, the creation of the [material] world would have been a futile and vain labor. If love were only thought, pure spirit and mental theory, the form of your fasting and prayer[154] would disappear. The gifts that lovers give one another are nothing other than form with respect to Love, but they serve to testify to the feelings of love that are hidden in the secret of the heart.[155]

Man's external moral action is thus in no way invalidated: and here we come to a very interesting point—the point of free will. How does Rûmî—for whom, as we have seen, God is so arbitrarily powerful that, if he wants to, he can change fire into water and water into fire and Moses into Pharaoh and vice versa—look at this problem ?

Rûmî's morals are far more activist than one might expect. The key to his resolution of the problem of free will lies in an interesting passage in the third book of the *Masnavî*:

> I love your manner (*sun'*), oh God, both in the moment in which I thank you and when I patiently bear with your punishment. How could I love, like the infidel (*gabr*), what you have done (*masnû'*)? He who loves God's manner is glorious, he who loves what God has done is an idolater (*kâfir*).[156]

And he continues, shrewdly commenting on the two contradictory traditions attributed to the Prophet: *ar-ridâ bi'l-kufr kufr* (accepting unfaithfulness is an act of unfaithfulness) and *man lam yardâ bi-qadâ'i falyatlub rabb siwâya* (he who does not accept My decree should look for a Lord other than Me):

> . . . this unfaithfulness is the destined thing (*maqdî*) not the [fact of] foreordaining (*qadâ'*). This unfaithfulness is in truth the effect of foreordaining. You must therefore clearly distinguish between the foreordaining of the predestined thing, so that you may immediately be clearly aware of the difficulty you are proposing . . . Unfaithfulness is ignorance (*jahl*) and the act that destines this unfaithfulness (*qadâ-ye kufr*) is wisdom (*'ilm*) . . . the ugliness of the writing is not the artist's ugliness (*naqqâsh*), on the contrary it is a clever exhibition of the ugliness he has produced.[157]

God is, so to say, an artist-God, for whom ugliness and evil are instruments for building mysterious valencies in the higher storeys of the spirit. One has to start from this point of view (which is far from being a pantheistic one or a "divinization of nature"!) in order to understand Rûmî's concept of free will. He starts with a statement that seems at first definitely predestinational and illiberal where human behavior is concerned:

We are the harps and you touch us with the plectrum; the gentle lament does not come from us, it is You who bring it about. We are the flute, and the sound that is in us comes from You; we are inaccessible mountains, and the echo is the echo of Your voice. We are the pieces in a game of chess, engaged in victory and defeat, and defeat and victory come from You, oh Perfect One! . . . We are as lions, but lions painted on a banner: pressed by the wind, they rush forwards at every instant. Their rushing is visible but the wind is invisible . . . and if we shoot an arrow, we are nothing other than the bow and God is the archer!"[158]

But further on he notes with remarkable psychological intuition:

In every action you wish to accomplish you clearly see your power to accomplish it, but you see the constriction (*jabr*) existing in every action you do not wish to accomplish and say: It comes from God. The Prophets are therefore predestinationists (*jabrî*) concerning the things of the world, the pagans are predestinationists concerning those of the other world.[159]

Consequently the man who places himself on God's side and consciously accepts what common people call *jabr* ("constriction" rather than predestination) because they do not know how to recognize God's artistic and arbitrary and accomplishing action , is the freest man, and there is no sense in speaking any further about *jabr*. This man, in fact, becomes almost as active and powerful as God:

Do you accept to bear his load? He will lift you up on high. Do you accept His order? He will then accept you. If you accept His order, you will become His mouthpiece, if you seek union with Him you will reach Him. Free will (*qudrat*) means the effort to thank God for His favor, your predestinationism (*jabr*) is the negation of those divine graces! Thanking God for the power he has given us to act freely increases this power, fatalism (*jabr*) tears God's favour (i.e. free power, *qudrat*) away from your hand.[160]

He who has broken his leg on the path of the effort of action (*kûshish*), lo, a Bûraq[161] comes towards him and he climbs onto its back and rides it . . . Until now he received orders from the King, now he brings regal orders to the people; until now he was influenced by the stars, now he dominates the heavenly bodies!"[162]

Freedom, according to Rûmî, is not an end but is itself an instrument of active potency. It has value only here in the phenomenal world, in such a way as to destroy it activistically in order to emerge in the metafreedom and metaslavery of the superior worlds where the supreme freedom of God's slave is transformed into supreme and almost divine potency. The *Masnavî* also contains many tales of the miracles of Saints (who attained—at least in part—this "potency" here on earth too). These miracles are always explained with the consideration that, basically, they were not miracles in the ordinary, common, sense since—to the spiritually illuminated—the world of phenomena was something extremely variable, ephemeral, sorry and changeable at will.

The consequences that derive from Rûmî's concept of God, the Universe and Man are many and complex and we have barely outlined them here. I will only quote, as an example, his sense of tolerance for every philosophical idea and religious position—a tolerance that must always be understood in a far deeper and more complex sense than that of the merely humanistic tolerance of people who consider everything good because everything is more or less false:

> Therefore he who says: everything is equally true is a fool, but he who says everything is false is damned (*shaqî*). Now he who has any exchange with the Prophets gains and profits from it, he who has any exchange with the immanent world of things, colors, odors, is blind and understands nothing . . .[163]

Another logical consequence of Rûmî's concept is his sense of joyfulness and hope. This must perforce characterize those who do not stop at the data, the fact, the past, the narrow spaces of being but attain God's creating act, his doing, the unpredictable richness of the future.

> If you buy a pomegranate, buy it while it laughs, that its laughter may inform you of the sweet seeds. O blessed laughter is the laughter that shows the open heart through the mouth like a pearl hidden in the folds of the soul, but wretched is the laughter that, like that of a tulip, shows the blackness of its heart through its mouth! The laughing pomegranate makes the garden laugh; the company of pious men makes a man of you. Place your affection for the Saints in the middle of your soul, do not give your heart to anything other than the love of joyous hearts! Do not enter the narrow way of despair: there is hope! Do not go into the shadows: there is Aloneness there![164]

Certainly if Rûmî's vision of the world can be criticized at all it is for the little weight it gives to the "social" aspect of religion. Basically, Rûmî's poem centers on the spiritual salvation of man seen (it seems to me) more than anything as an individual. We must not, it is true, take this salvation in too materialistic a sense (for Rûmî, hell and heaven are stages of spiritual life) but all the same this salvation is individual: it is the abandonment of the world rather than a spiritual struggle to bring the Kingdom of God on earth. Rûmî's distinction between Saint and Prophet is a purely pragmatic one and in my opinion it could not be more profoundly or better expressed than in the following concise statement of an Indian mystic quoted by Iqbâl:[165] "Muhammad of Arabia climbed to the seventh heaven and came back again to earth. If I had been granted that most high spiritual stage, I would have remained there!" The Prophet, unlike the Saints, comes back to earth to found institutions, to legislate, to create new communities and traditions. The Prophet is a "pastor of peoples" rather than a "saviour of individual souls." Basically—according to Rûmî—Abraham, Moses, Jesus and Muhammad are simply great Saints, guides for the liberation of the soul from the cage of the world, for flight from the world rather than for the creation (a visible creation too) of a new world.

But if we take Rûmî's religious teaching as individual "preparations" for the establishment of a social religiosity—preparations of purification, of sublimation of the soul—then its religious value remains on an extremely high level. His beautiful ode in the *Dîvân* to the heart purified by long search and long religious practice—the heart that can finally be a worthy "house of God"[166]— is well worth quoting.

I was, at the time when there were no Names and there was no trace of the existence of beings.

And the eternal Friend's lock was the only trace of truth and the only object was God!

And all objects and names stemmed from Me, in that eternal instant when neither I nor We were there!

And in that most ancient and first instant I prostrated myself in front of God, when Jesus was not yet moving within Mary's womb.

From one end to the other I journeyed across the whole Cross, and knew all the Nazarenes: he was not on the Cross!

I went to the Pagoda, into the temple of the ancient monks I went: no color of Him appeared to me there.

I then turned the reins of my search towards the Ka'ba, but there, in that destination of young and old, there was nothing!

And I journeyed towards Herât, and I journeyed towards Qandahâr, and I searched below, and I searched above; alas, he was not there either!

And I wished to reach the summit of the mountains of Qâf at the confines of the world; there was no trace, there of the eternal Phoenix!

And I asked the Table of Jasper and God's Reed about him, but both were mute, and spoke no word.

And my eye, which sought only God, saw nothing but qualities and forms that were extraneous to the Eternal.

And finally I fixed my glance on my own heart, and lo, I saw Him there, he was nowhere else but only there!

And in truth I was so perplexed, amazed and inebriated by this that not a single atom of my being could be seen any more: I was no longer!

Notes

1. Hodgson, *Assassins*, p. 276.
2. "Notes sur l'Ummu'l-Kitâb des Ismaéliens de l'Asie Centrale," in *Rev. des Et. Islamiques*, VI, 1932, pp. 420, 481.

3. In *Der Islam*, XXIII, 1936, pp. 1–132.

4. See criticism in Hodgson, *Assassins*, p. 331.

5. The myth of *Kundag-Kunî* has been reconstructed in its pre-Manichaean form by Benveniste, in "Le témoignage de Théodore bar Konay sur le zoroastrisme," in *Monde Oriental*, XXVI (1932), pp. 170–215.

6. The text appears to me to even present some "Indianisms" such as *guftan* constructed with the *az*, the plural after the numerals and, possibly, the very singular *tîr-sad* for "three hundred" which Ivanow thinks is Iranian.

7. Where this is concerned an interesting passage is quoted from a Kulainî Shi'ite Twelver text, *al-Usûl min al-Kâfî* (Tehran, 1334 sol., vol. I, p. 128, quoted in Corbin, *De la gnose antique à la gnose ismaelienne*, Roma, 1956, p. 15 of the proofs, in which the Bardesanian Abû Shâkir says to one of Ja'far as-Sâdiq's disciples, Hishâm ibn al-Kakam, that there is a verse in the Qur'an (the one quoted) that is similar to the Bardesian theories (obviously if it is interpreted as our text interprets it).

8. Ivanow's observation concerning the lack of any mention of Zainu'l-Abidîn, son of Husain and father of Bâqir, is not pertinent: It is Bâqir who in particular is God here, in the sense of Mughîra.

9. *Mu'tarizân*. According to this story, all the men in that paradise were disobedient spirits without actually following Satan (Satan's partisans were in Hell).

10. For the cult of Fâtima in popular piety see chap. VI and Massignon, "Voeu et dévotion musulmane à Fâtima," *Studi Levi d. Vida*, pp. 102 and foll. which refers to other examples of a similar theophany of Fâtima.

11. See my above-quoted article "Note sulla tipologia del Monoteismo," in *St. e Mat. di St. delle Rel.*" XXVIII, 1957.

12. I am translating here from Ivanow's English translation since I do not possess the text, which is still in manuscript form; see p. 101 of *Studies in Early Persian Ismailism*, Bombay-Leiden, 1948.

13. Dieterici, *Darwinismus in X und XIX Jhrh*, Berlin, 1878, pp. 220 and foll.

14. Ouranios, not better identified, see T. J. de Boer, in *Ztschr., f. Assyr*, XXVII, 1912, pp. 8 and foll. On this see the information on Agathias, mentioned in chap. I, according to whom a non-identifiable Ouranios taught "philosophy" to the Sasanian king Khusrau I.

15. Information in *Fihrist* translated in Chwolssohn, *Sabier*, II, pp. 19 and foll.

16. According to another source: Mas'ûdî, *Murûj*, quoted in Chwolssohn, *Sabier*, II, pp. 372–373.

17. On the Sabaean ritual see Corbin's attempt at an interpretation, in *Eranos Jhrb.*, XIX, 1951.

18. This is Corbin's and Ivanow's opinion: see Corbin, *Jâmi'al-Hikmatain*, pp. 29 and foll.

19. According to Ivanow, the ode was composed in 1064. I am translating from the Persian text in *Dîvân*, ed. Taqavî, Tehran, 1304–7, col. 1929, p. 172 and foll.

20. Here we have a concept that is similar to the Mazdean *ratu*.

21. The three greatest Sunni leaders.

22. According to the cosmological legend it is the lower limit of the cosmos and holds up the Universe.

23. Historically this is the Cairo of the Fatimids, but at the same time it can be a symbol.

24. A River in the traditional Paradise.

25. A traditional angel, guardian of Paradise.

26. The Black Stone of the Canonical Pilgrimage, at Mecca.
27. Abraham's idolatrous father, according to the Qur'an.
28. Cf. all this with the text we summarised in the preceding paragraph!
29. I.e. a greeting of heartfelt tears. The beauty and sincerity of the passage should be admired from an aesthetic point of view too.
30. The works that can be certainly attributed to Nâsir are (and I only quote the principal ones) an ample philosophical, religious, moral *Divân* (collection of songs), a short treatise in verse on various points of doctrine called "The Book of Light" (*Raushanâ'î-nâmeh*), "The Face of Religion" (*Vajh-i Dîn*) in which the different legal principles of Islam are interpreted with Ismaili *ta'wîl*, the *Gushâ'ish-u-Rahâ'ish*, "Opening and Liberation" which deals with complex metaphysical questions in the form of question and answer, the *Kitâb jâmi'al-hikmatain* "The Book that unites the two Wisdoms," a wide-ranging attempt at fusion between Greek philosophy and Ismaili theosophy (written in the form of a commentary on a poem containing the Ismaili Abu'l-Haitham Jurjânî's philosophical cum religious questions), as well as other short treatises that may not interest non-specialist readers and can be found listed, together with the names of the other works "attributed" to Nâsir, in Corbin's ample and interesting preface to his edition of the *Jâmi al-Hikmatain*, Tehran-Paris, 1953, pp. 36 and foll.
31. This sense of *dîn* throws considerable light on the Mazdean idea of *dên*, too.
32. Ivanow's translation seems inexact to me here (cf. p. 449): not "*qui sont appelés*" but "*et sont appelés.*"
33. "The seven Chapters of Abû Ishâq," which is possibly slightly older that the preceding work, text in *Kalâm-i Pîr*, p. 115. The other text is on pp. 65–66, transl. pp. 60–61.
34. The passages in italics are in Arabic in the text.
35. For an Ismaili, the best proof of the existence of God is the person of the imâm himself, who is, practically speaking, God. This explains the great rationalist liberties in the field of abstract theology and philosophy.
36. I emend the *ilà muddahiti* of the text to *vâlî muddahiti*.
37. Possibly explaining them in Persian?
38. A praying God . . . should not seem strange. "Prayer" is attributed to God in the Qur'an too (XXXIII, 43, 56). It is a prayer-rite, a blessing not an invocation.
39. Ghazzâlî, in Hodgson, *Assassins*, p. 122.
40. But a Nizâri Ismaili source quoted by Rashîdu'd-Dîn (in Hodgson, op.cit., pp. 71–2) expresses pious indignation over the customs of a small group of so-called Azerbaijan Mazdakites: particularly their sexual licentiousness, or possibly because they had refused the invitation of the Dâ'î, Hasan-i-Sabbâh, the founder of Alamût Ismailism, to join them.
41. Cf. "Avicenna i persidskaya literatura," *Izv. Nauk SSSR*, 1938, 1–2, pp. 75–94.
42. There are doubts concerning the authenticity of these latter but no concrete proof to deny their traditional attribution to the philosopher. See my: Avicenna. *Opera poetica*, Roma, 1956.
43. Cf. A. F. Mehren, *Traités mystiques d'Abou 'Alî al-Hosein ibn 'Abdallah ibn Sînâ ou Avicenne*, Leyden, Brill, 1889–1899.
44. The millenary of the birth of the Philosopher calculated in Muslim lunar years fell in 1370 of the Hegira (1950–51). In 1937 other oriental countries, e.g. Turkey and Afghanistan, who both claim Avicenna as theirs, commemorated the ninth centenary of his death according to solar calculations. In Persia the Avicennian Millenary was celebrated,

Religion in Iran

with some delay, in the spring of 1945 with a great congress of orientalists (including an Italian delegation).

45. Cf. Mehren, "La philosophie d'Avicenne exposée d'après des documents inédits," Extr. from *Muséon*, Louvain, 1882, p.40.
46. Arabic text ed. by Mehren in *Traités Mystiques*, II, pp. 40–41.
47. Avicenna-Bird, the Soul, is speaking in the first person.
48. I.e. you must conceal the banal exterior appearance of the Soul and have its truer sense of a spring, which now is hidden, germinate.
49. Even after liberation there still remains the thong of matter and the earth, which one does not free oneself from except in death.
50. Only the mention of a kind of initiation pact of brotherhood seems to free the liberated birds from all doubt.
51. These nine peaks (corresponding on another symbolic plane to the nine Celestial Spheres) together form Mount Qâf, the cosmic mountain.
52. I.e. at the eighth, starting from the first (which is not calculated here). On the plane of a "celestial ascension" this mountain corresponds to the sphere of the Fixed Stars.
53. An expression that, in Mehren's text, I have difficulty in understanding. Corbin, basing himself on another text, translates: "It would be dangerous to prolong our stay."
54. Corresponding to the ninth sky.
55. Corbin points out, very suitably, the recurrence of this same motif in Wagner's Parsifal: "Nur eine Waffe taugt. Die Wunde schliesst der Speer nur, der sie schlug!" (end of the III act).
56. We are not told exactly who the Messenger is. Some commentators think that he is the Angel of Death: i.e., that man walks, at this point, in the constant company of that Angel. At the same time this "walking with the Angel" reproposes the theme of the Angelic Guide. The journey with the Messenger appears to be the Life of the liberated Human Soul moving towards the ulterior supreme liberation of death.
57. Avicenna expresses himself in the language of traditional medecine (which he was master of) in this fine ending—so full of humour and possibly even more of bitterness.
58. Qur'anic phrase: XXVI, 227.
59. Cf. Strothmann, "Ismailitischer Qur'an-Kommentar," *Abh. d. Akademie der Wiss. in Gottingen*, Phil-Hist. K1, III Folge, no. 31, 1944–55, in 4 fascicules. Text in 3rd fascicule, pp. 181 and foll. Summary in the introduction to the 4th fascicule, p. 27.
60. Quoted in A. A. Hermat, *Jâmî*, Tehran, 1941, p. 65.
61. "Filosofia orientale od illuminativa di Avicenna?," in *RSO*, X (1925), pp. 433 and foll.
62. For a list of his works, written mostly in Arabic except for the "Visionary Tales" which were written in Persian, see Corbin's editions, especially S. Y. As-Suhravardi, *Opera Metaphysica et Mystica*, vol. I, Istanbul, "Biblioteca Islamica," 16, 1945; vol. II, Tehran 1952. And also *Three treatises on Mysticism*, edited and translated by O. Spies and S. K. Khatak, Stuttgart, 1935. On Suhravardî see H. Corbin's studies, including *Suhravardî d'alep fondateur de la doctrine illuminative*, "Publ. de la Soc. des Etudes Iraniennes," Paris, 1939; *Motifs Zoroastriens dans la philosophie de Suhravardî*, Tehran, 1946. The learned Frenchman's enthusiasm for our author's "Iranian" aspects should however be slightly tempered in view of the considerations the reader will find ahead. Rather comprehensive summaries of Suhravardî's mystical philosophy are to be found in M. Iqbal, *The Development of Metaphysics in Persia*, Oxford, 1905, and in Carra de Vaux, "La

philosophie Illuminative . . . d'après Suhrawardî Maqtûl," in *JA*, s. IX, vol. XIX, 1902, p. 63 and foll.

63. Technical term, litt. "flavour, indicating a "sapidity" (Lat. sapio), a direct intuition of reality that was specific to the "Enlightened."

64. Semi-mythical names we have already quoted concerning the Mazdean profession of faith, cf. chap. I.

65. Cf. Schefer, *Sefernâmè*, p. X.

66. In fact there is proof of plastic contemplations of this kind in the world of Greek neo-Platonism; cf. Praechter, art. "Syrianos," in *Pauly Wissowa*, 1767.

67. In *Hermetis Trismegisti qui apud Arabes fertur de Castigatione animae libellum*, ed. and transl. by O. Bardenhewer, p. 56: "The image one has of a thing is really its shadow." In Suhravardî's own *Hayâkil an-nûr* there is the beautiful expression: "All dark forms are shadows of intellective forms."

68. Andreas-Henning, "Mittleiranische Manichaica," II, in *SBAW*, 1943, p. 18: The dying Mani leaves Egypt (i.e., the West).

69. Correct where Suhravardî's non-Monism is concerned, wrong where "last" is concerned: we will also see how Rûmî was not as pantheistic as might appear (Massignon's statement is in *Lexique*, p. 61, no. 7).

70. Text in H. Corbin and P. Kraus, "Le bruissement de l'aile de Gabriel," in *JA*, 227, (1935), pp. 1 and foll.

71. A manuscript dated 659 A.H. (1261 A.D.) in the National Library of Tehran, edited in Isfahan in 1319 A.H.s. (1940) by Dr. Mahdî Bayânî and re-published in Tehran by the "Society of the friends of Books," *Anjuman-i dûst-dârân-i kitab* in 1332 A.H.s. (1953) with a parallel facsimile text.

72. The mention of three points or parts of time was already frequent, in similar forms, in the Pahlavî texts.

73. These are not easily identifiable symbols of the different senses of the faculties of the incarnate soul. Once again the soul is compared to a bird.

74. Bahman, who, as we have seen, is identified with the first intellect, was the first thing created by God. An identical character appears in Avicenna's symbolic tale "Alive the Son of Awakened": in this case too we have an old man who looks youthful.

75. The Qâf mountains that, according to the Muslim legend, are at the end of the world. These same worlds recur in Avicenna's symbolic tales.

76. An ancient Persian text of the history of religions, the *Kitâb bayân al-adyân* (transl. by F. Gabrieli, Roma, in *Rendiconti Lincei*, VI-VIII, 7–12, 1932, pp. 587 and foll.) it states that "the Bâtinis (Ismailis and other Muslim "extremists") say that the Tree of Paradise (Tûbâ) is the "sun." This concept would explain better what our text is about to say.

77. The reader should note the special attention the author devotes to explaining the "spiritual" phenomenon experimentally. Suhravardî's whole concept is based on a strong realism of transcendental realities—a realism that is almost incomprehensible to the modern world. Suhravardî also wrote short treatises on the natural sciences that we hope Corbin will shortly be publishing. The symbol may also have more than one explanation. It might possibly refer to cycles of occultation and manifestation of an Ismaili type, or even to more profound psychological and mystical realities (the Saint, who is closer to God, seems "black" to common mortals, i.e., "heretic," unbelieving).

Religion in Iran

78. This passage is almost literally identical to a passage in the LXII chapter of the Pahlavî text *Mênôkê Khrat* (cf. Bausani, *Testi religiosi zoroastriani*, p. 175). The Persian writer Sâdiq-i Hidâyat (*Zand-i Vohuman-Yasht*, Tehran, 1944, pp. 58–9) has highlighted some further marked similarities between Suhravardî's epistle and Mazdean texts.

79. Legends of this kind were well-known to the Islamic Iranian world through Firdausî's "Book of the Kings." Here however we have a different interpretation in which legendary names become symbolic cyphers.

80. The reader should note how carefully the author avoids giving his symbol systematically rational explanations for, in fact, it is a realistic symbol and not an allegory (which is a pure transposition into images of rational or moral concepts). Only the initiated can cull the multiplicity of meanings of this "dream" language.

81. These are the "arrows" that, according to the Sîmurgh's instructions, Rustam used to kill his enemy. This is the epic tale told by Firdausî in the "Book of Kings."

82. This is probably the Angelic Pleroma; or possibly the "Kingdom of Mothers" in which the world is woven?

83. According to the Qur'an, among his other qualities king David, who was considered a prophet, had the quality of weaving perfect coats-of-mail (cf. Kor., XXI, 80; XXXIV, 11). Here the Davidic Armour represents the bonds of the body.

84. This "Balârak sword" is a relatively rare term that recurs in Persian fictional poetry, for example in Nizâmî, and it is explained by commentators as a "particularly sharp sword" or also in the sense of "sword edge." As usual Suhravardî uses the allusive and evocative term for his symbolic scope. It could be the sword of death, or at least of the renunciation to an attachment to the phenomenological world.

85. Concerning the state of death seen for some souls as an eternal nightmare, see ahead where the theology of some of Suhravardî's epigones is mentioned.

86. A legendary character (mentioned in the Qur'an too) who is said to have accompanied Moses on a mysterious journey as his master and who, according to other legends, reached the Source of the Water of Life. (Cf. Kor., XXVIII, foll. and my notes to this passage in *Corano*, Florence, 1955. pp. 588–589).

87. I correct Bayânî's reading of *bi-nazd* into *bi-muzd*. The author complains of men's incomprehension for his Symbols. When common men are with the Master they cannot even understand the external words he speaks; then they preen themselves at his expense, inventing inexistent meanings for them. A fault into which we hope we too have not fallen!

88. Quoted by M. M. Moreno, *Antologia della mistica arabo-persiana*, Bari, 1951, p. 143.

89. According to Ritter (see *Festschr. Tschudi*) he was under the influence of the Buddhism that remained alive in the Khurâsânî areas until about the ninth century.

90. In *Tazkiratu'l-auliyâ'*, ed Nicholson, Leiden, 1905–07.

91. A formula used, among other things, when one sees or hears something unseemly.

92. Massignon, in *Tawâsîn*, p. 138 and foll.

93. "Kistorii religioznyh dvizenii X veka," in *Izv. Rossijsk. Ak. Nauk*, 1918, pp. 785 and foll.

94. Cf. Hallâj's theory *al-ashyâ' tu'rafu bi-addâdihâ*, "One knows things through their contrary," *Tawâsîn*, p. 49.

95. According to the typical doctrines of the Ismaili-oriented sects Moses is the *nâtiq*, and less important than Aaron, the *sâmit*.

96. There are many variations to these verses that are very difficult to translate. Moreno (*Antologia*, p. 138), translates them quite differently.

97. Malâmat means censure: Malâmatîya indicates, in poor ideological language, "the censurers." Shrewd observations on Malâmatism are to be found on pp. 220 and foll. of a book with a strangely unpromising title: G. Palomba's *Morfologia Economica*, Napoli, 1956.
98. Primitive too, see my article: "Note sul pazzo sacro nell'Islàm," in *St. e Mat. di Storia delle Rel.*, XXIX, 1 (1958), pp. 93 and foll.
99. "Meshreb der weise Narr und fromme Ketzer," in *Der Islamische Orient*, V. Berlin, 1902.
100. His master said to him: "This you are doing stinks of Hallâj!"
101. For other stories of semi-mystical "passages" see, for ex., P. Loosen, "Die weisen Narren des Naisâbürî," *Ztschr. f. Assyr*, (1912), pp. 184 and foll.
102. See also Guénon, *Initiation et réalisation spirituelle*, Paris, 1952.
103. Cf. Vorlesungen, index, under Malâmatîya.
104. As we have already said, we have had to leave out any number of people and currents. At all events, for the early period, see P.G. Messina's small volume, *Inizi di lirica ascetica e mistica in Persia*, Roma, 1938.
105. An unfortunate lover, the protagonist of an ancient Arab legend.
106. Nicholson, I, 1–18.
107. Nicholson, introd. to the transl. of books V-VI, p. XIII.
108. The reader will find more or less legendary anecdotes on Rûmî's life in the ample introduction to Redhouse's English translation of the first book of the Masnavî, which includes ample extracts from the work *Manâqib al-'arifîn* ("The Virtues of the Gnostics") by Al-Aflâkî (d. after 1353), a disciple of one of Rûmî's grandsons, Chelebî Emîr Ârif (d. in 1320). (*The Mesnevi . . of Mevlana . . . Jelalu-'d-Din, Muhammed, er Rûmi. Book the first* . . . translated and the poetry versified by J. W. Redhouse, London, 1881, pp. 1–135).
109. The Khwârizmshâh (king of Khwârizm) 'Alâ'ud-Dîn Muhammad, whose rivalry with the Caliph of Baghdad and frontier incidents with the Mongols were the cause of Genghîz Khân's terrible invasion (1220).
110. On this, and on the *tarîqa* in general, see chap. XV ("Le tarîqa. Gli awliyâ") in F. M. Pareja's *Islamologia*, Roma, 1951, (pp. 509–532, and bibliography).
111. The two most accessible (incomplete) European editions are: V. Von Rosensweig, *Auswahl aus den Diwanen des grössten mystischen Dichter Persiens Mewâna Dschelâleddîn Rûmi. Aus dem Persischen mit beigeifügtem Original-Texte uns erläuternden Ammerkungen*, Wien, 1838. R. A. Nicholson, *Selected poems from the Divâni Shamsi Tabriz*, Cambridge, 1898. Now see Badî'u-Zamân Forûzânfarr's Persian editio princeps (Vol. I, Tehran, 1336–1957).
112. Called *daftar*, booklets. Each one is elegantly introduced in Arabic prose by Rûmî himself. The best known in Europe is the first, of which several translations were made before Nicholson's. The reader will also find passages from the first books translated into Italian in M. M. Moreno's *Antologia della Mistica Arabo-Persiana*, Bari, 1951 (Rûmî is on pp. 63–89).
113. Badî'u'z-Zamân FurûzânFar's (Tehran, 1330–1951) is a good Persian edition.
114. Passages of his works can been found in an Italian translation in Moreno's above-mentioned *Antologia*. For a brief profile and an essential bibliography we refer the reader to Pareja's *Islamologia*, pp. 500–501 and 507–508.
115. See ahead some observations on Rûmî's "pantheism."

116. In an interesting and stimulating article in *ZDMG*, 1925 (pp. 192–268) ("Die islamische Lehre vom volkommenen Nenschen, ihre dichterische Gestaltung) Schaeder clearly distinguishes between mystische Frommingkeit" (seeing this "type" in Hallâj) and gnostische Weltdeutung, exemplified by the personality of Ibn 'Arabî. In my opinion, however, it would be a mistake and an over-simplification to label Rûmî as a representative of the gnostische Weltdeutung; I think his works show a happy fusion of Hallâj's enthusiasm and Ibn 'Arabî's theorizing.

117. It would be hard to find a more fitting aesthetic description of the classical Persian ghazal than Schaeder's (in the article we have quoted, p. 246): ". . . (in the ghazal) the completed representation of a landscape or camp site is replaced, little by little, by a loose juxtaposition of elements that are no longer pictorial-descriptive ones but decorative ones, whose congruency is on the one hand musical (created by the identity of the rhythm and the rhyme), and on the other emotive, i.e. created by a Stimmung that soars above the verbal arabesques that follow one another. It is not a hic et nunc, the poet does not want to express a concrete experience but rather to indicate, beyond this, something unexpressed and inexpressible that gives consistency and a unitary sense to the disjecta membra of the whole."

118. On the contrast between Islamic and Christian mysticism Goethe's (rather questionable) concept (*Maximen u. Reflexionen*, III Abt.) may be of interest: "Every mysticism implies transcending and freeing oneself from any object one thinks one is leaving behind one. The greater and more valuable what is left behind, the more valuable the mystic's productions will be. Because of this Oriental [Muslim] mystical poetry enjoys a great privilege: i.e. that the riches of the world, which the adept rejects, remain at his disposal at every instant [unlike what occurs in Christian monasticism—Translator's note]. He (the adept) is consequently always in the midst of the abundance he abandons . . ."

119. His book *Persiens Mystiker Dschelâleddîn Rûmî: eine Stildeutung in drei Vorträgen*. Breslau, 1933, is very interesting and important though full of over-involute and sometimes obscure reasoning.

120. See some brief information on these in my summary of Persian Literature, in Pareja's *Islamologia*, pp. 631–632.

121. The distinction must be taken with a grain of salt and more as a starting point for further study than as final point of arrival and objective truth.

122. Nicholson, I, 201 and foll.

123. Cf. Paul, I Cor., I, 28.

124. Nicholson, II, 1720 and foll. The sources for this story are in the Arabic collection *al-'Iqd al-fârîd* by Ibn 'Abd Rabbihi (d. in 940).

125. In his article on Rûmî in the *Encyclopaedia of Islam*, Carra de Vaux uses this to support his statement that one of Rûmî's characteristics was the negation of the utility of exterior formulas and rites in religion, which, as we shall see, is completely false.

126. Nicholson, II, 3681 and foll.

127. Consequently, for Rûmî, that "immense ample open space" on which the space of being is nourished is Nothingness ('adam). This positive value of Nothingness, which we will speak about later too, is not specific only to Rûmî but to almost all the Islamic religious and mystic poets.

128. Nicholson, II, 3092–97.

129. Nicholson, II, 688.

130. Nicholson, II, 689–90.

131. Nicholson, II, 760–62.
132. I.e. an act of wisdom on the part of God.
133. Nicholson, II, 2617 and foll.
134. Rûm is Asia Minor, Khotan is China.
135. Here apparently Rûmî instinctively transposes himself, or Man, into Satan, as we have already seen Hallâj do.
136. See the translation in my article "Aspetti del Misticismo Islamico," in *Ricerche Religiose*, XX, 1–4 (Roma 1949), pp. 15–16. The passages, IV, 2341–2383 of the Masnavî are also important for an understanding of the Nothingness-Being religious dialectics in Rûmî.
137. See Pareja's *Islamologia*, pp. 458 and 695 on the ash 'arite theological school and the atomist theory.
138. A frequently repeated phrase in the Qur'an that has become a pious ejaculation in ordinary devotion: "In truth we are of God, and we will return to Him."
139. *ad-dunyâ sâ'a*: a well-known hadith, attributed to the Prophet Muhammad.
140. Nicholson, I, 1140–48.
141. Nicholson, I, 1447–1455.
142. Nicholson, I, 1335—36.
143. Nicholson, I, 1342–48.
144. Nicholson, V,3637 and foll. This concept of evolution has little to do with the modern scientific concept and is a matter above all of the evolution of each individual rather than of the species, of ontogenesis rather than philogenesis. Its principal scope is the demonstration of the personal immortality of the soul. This concept of evolution is admitted by religious currents of Islamic origin which (as for example in the Baha'i faith) believe in both the eternity and stability of the human species. Man was still a man and destined to his sublime rank in the cosmic order even when he appeared as a mineral or a plant. Identity as expressed in the above-quoted Ismaili encyclopaedia of the "Brothers of Purity."
145. Nicholson, II, 3253 and foll.
146. Nicholson, I, 686–689.
147. Quoted in Syed Abdul Vahid, *Iqbal, His Art and Thought*, Lahore, 1948, pp. 95–96.
148. On the developments of the concept of Perfect Man in Islamic religious thought see Schaeder (above-mentioned article and pp.77 and foll. in R. A. Nicholson's *Studies in Islamic Mysticism*, Cambridge, 1921.
149. The head of the Muslim Community: as we have seen, according to the Shi'ites only one of 'Alî's descendants can fill this role by "divine" right, while according to the Sunnis the Imamate (which they prefer to call the Caliphate) does not necessarily have to be limited to the direct descendants of the Prophet, though the Caliph must belong to the great Arab tribe of the Quraish. 'Umar, whom the Shi'ites hate as usurper of the office that "legitimately" belonged to 'Alî, is, on the contrary, honored by the Sunnis as a good and just Caliph.
150. Images drawn from the famous Qur'anic verse "on Light" (Kor. XXIV, 35), see the relative quotation.
151. Nicholson, II, 811 and foll.
152. In my opinion this is the true sense of the expression *huwa 'llâh* (He is God, God is Him) that recurs in the prayers of the mystics. It is the emotive annunciation that God is at that moment concentrated personally on one of his Manifestations and that he has

taken on a personality. Where the personalistic term of "Him" given to God is concerned, cf. also Otto's fascinating theory on the origin of the Jewish name of God, êl, from the third person pronoun. According to this God is the "Him," the Other par excellence. R. Otto, *Das Heilige*, München, 1947; pp. 142 and 213.

153. Nicholson, I, 225–27. According to Islamic tradition it was Ishmael and not Isaac who was sacrificed by Abraham.

154. These are canonical and obligatory fasting (*saum*) and prayers (*salât*): rites therefore and not individual pious works.

155. Nicholson, I, 2624 and foll.

156. Nicholson, III, 1360–61. Some strictly linguistic aspects of Arabic (the words in parentheses are Arabic verbal forms) have greatly influenced the thought of the mystics. See: L. Gardet, "La langue arabe et l'analyse des états spirituels," in *Mélanges Massignon*, Damascus, 1957, pp. 215 and foll.

157. Nicholson, III, 1367–73.

158. Nicholson, I, 598 and foll.

159. Nicholson, I, 635–37.

160. Nicholson, I, 936–39.

161. A supernatural mount on which, according to pious tradition, the prophet Muhammad accomplished his heavenly journey (mi 'râj).

162. Nicholson, I, 1074–77.

163. Nicholson, II, 2942–43.

164. Nicholson, I, 718–24.

165. M. Iqbal, *Six lectures on the Reconstruction of Religious Thought in Islam*, Lahore, 1930, p, 173. Iqbâl owes a great deal to Rûmî's religious thought, and especially to his concept of free will. On the fact that Iqbâl considered Rûmî his principal and fundamental Master see M. Iqbal, *Il Poema Celeste. Versione del testo persiano con introduzione e note di A. Bausani*, Rome, 1952.

166. Translation based on Rosenzweig's text, op. cit., p. 58. I have not translated the last verse, which contains Master Shams-i Tabrîz's "signature," because it seemed to me to break the aesthetic unity of the whole. It says: "And no-one was ever inebriated and amazed and mad with love, as the Sun of Tabrîz (Shams-i Tabrîz) the most pure face!"

Bibliography

Even a concise bibliography on subjects as wide-ranging as those dealt with in this chapter would take up many pages, besides the fact that these subjects have never yet been studied together in an organic synthesis and we would have to list a great many specialised works. We will limit ourselves here to listing one recent work on each subject in which scholars will find further bibliographies. Many works have in fact been mentioned in the course of the chapter and in the notes.

Gardet, L. *La pensée religieuse d'Avicenne*. Paris, 1951.
Gölpinarli, A. *Mevlânâ Celâleddîn*. Istanbul, 1953 (in Turkish, an excellent work)
Hodgson, M.G.S. *The Order of Assassins. The struggle of the early Nizârî Ismâ'îlîs against the Islamic world*. Gravenhage, 1955.

————. *Persische Strömungen in der islamische Mystik.* Leipzig, 1927.

Hörten, M. *Die Philosophie der Erleuchtung nach Suhravardî.* Halle, 1912.

Iqbal, Afzal. *The Life and Thought of Rûmî.* Lahore, 1956.

Khousraw, Nasir-e, *Kitâb-e jâmi' al-Hikmatain. Le Livre Réunissant les deux sagesses ou Harmonie de la philosophie grècque et de la théosophie ismaélienne.* Texte persan édité avec une double étude préliminaire . . . , Henry Corbin and Mohammad Mo'in, Tehran-Paris 1953.

Ritter, H. *Das Meer der Seele. Mensch, Welt und Gott in den Geschichten des Farîdduddîn 'Attâr.* Leiden, 1955.

Suhravardi, S. Y. as-. *Opera metaphysica et mystica.* Vol. I, Istanbul, "Biblioteca Islamica," 16, 1945; vol. II, Tehran-Paris, "Bibliotèque Iranienne," 2, 1952.

Additional Bibliography

The general reader wishing further information on the Ismailis in English should consult Farhad Daftary, *The Isma'ilis: Their History and Doctrines* (Cambridge, 1990). Recent English translations of the works of Nasir-i Khusraw include Annemarie Schimmel, *Make a Shield from Wisdom: Selected Verses from Nasir-i Khusraw's Divan*, London, 1993 and W.M. Thackston, *Naser-e Khosraw's Book of Travels*, Albany, N.Y., 1986. Much more continues to be written about Avicenna as philosopher than as religious thinker. Further work in English along the lines that interested Bausani includes Seyyed Hossein Nasr, *Three Muslim Sages: Avicenna, Suhrawardi, Ibn 'Arabi*, Cambridge, Mass., 1964, and Peter Heath, *Allegory and Philosophy in Avicenna*, Philadelphia, 1992. Also of interest is William Gohlman, *The Life of Ibn Sina*, Albany, N.Y., 1974. Dimitri Gutas, *Avicenna and the Aristotelian Tradition*, Leiden, 1988, constitutes among other things a thoroughgoing attack on Corbin's approach to this figure. Other recent books in English of interest include David B. Burrell, *Knowing the Unknowable God: Ibn-Sina, Maimonides, Aquinas*, Notre Dame, 1986 and Herbert A. Davidson, *Alfarabi, Avicenna and Averroes on Intellect*, Oxford, 1992. Suhravardi's narratives have been translated into English by W.M. Thackston, *The Mystical and Visionary Treatises of Shihabuddin Yahya Suhrawardi*, London, 1982. The major study of this figure in English is Hossain Ziai, *Knowledge and Illumination: A Study of Suhrawardi's Hikmat al-Ishraq*, Atlanta, 1990; an important book on a related figure is John Walbridge, *The Science of Mystic Lights: Qutb al-Din Shirazi and the Illuminationist Tradition in Islamic Philosophy*, Cambridge, Mass., 1992. Recent books on Rumi in English include Annemarie Schimmel, *I am Wind, You are Fire: The life and work of Rumi*, Boston, 1992; the same author's *The Triumphal Sun: A Study of the Life and Works of Mowlana Jalaloddin Rumi*, London, 1978; William C. Chittick, *The Sufi Path of Love*, Albany, N.Y., 1983. Shortly available will be an important set of studies: Georges Sabbagh, ed., *The Heritage of Rumi: Proceedings of the Eleventh Levi della Vida conference*, Cambridge. Bausani's account of Rûmî's life, based on the sources available to him at that time, is now out of date. See in English, Franklin Lewis, *Rumi: Past and Present, East and West* (Oxford, Forthcoming).

Chapter Five

The Magi's Wine: Notes on Religious Aesthetics

Introduction

In great traditional civilizations (like the one we are studying) the different cultural components interweave; art and religion, law and politics are not pieces of a mosaic but are closely blended into a single organism dominated and permeated by the most important of all motifs, religion. Persia is certainly no exception to this rule and one might even say that a true knowledge of Persian literature and its subtleties is off-limits to anyone who does not have a more than superficial familiarity with the intricacies of its theology, its traditional legendary motifs and above all its mysticism.

In Persian culture two kinds of literary problems arise in connection with the religious phenomenon. The first is the origin of the style of lyric verse commonly called erotic-mystical poetry, which possibly includes the greatest masterpieces of Iranian literary genius. The second is the interpretation of the motifs and images of this lyric poetry.

A few words both on the origins of neo-Persian poetry in and of itself, and on the general characteristics of the erotic-mystical lyrics, which are unknown to the lay reader, must necessarily precede a discussion of the first of these two problems.

Anyone who observes the rather meagre panorama of pre-Islamic literature prior to the Arab conquest will be struck by the almost total lack of poetic texts.

It is true that many objections could be made to this preliminary observation. In the first place, the reader may say, the Arab conquest destroyed a great deal of Sasanian literary material written in Pahlavî. And besides, the few texts that have come down to us (see Chapter I) are theological and religious works and were written by pious priests who were certainly not interested in poetry. (Though this objection is unconvincing if we consider how much religious and even aridly theological verse—if not "poetry"—has come down to us in other religious traditions, e.g., the Indian tradition.) But the most valid objection is that it would be an error of perspective to consider the surviving Pahlavî texts Sasanian since, as we have seen, most of them were composed after the Arab conquest. It follows that the hypothetical Zoroastrian who might have wanted to compose poetry during the period in which the Pahlavî texts were *written* (around the ninth century) would have done so in the already flexible "modern" Persian language of Rûdakî and Daqîqî. The fact remains however that nothing related to poetry has come down to us from the Sasanian world, except the names of a few minstrels like Bârbad (traditionally claimed to have been a poet at the court of king Khusrau Parvîz [590–628]) and the ingenious attempts of Nyberg and Benveniste to reconstruct "poetic" passages in Pahlavî in the *Bundahishn*, the *Drakht i Asûrîk*, etc. (though in my opinion they proved the existence of rhythmic prose rather than real poetry).[1]

We are therefore justified in wondering whether—beyond the easy theory of the "devastating Arab conquest" so dear to the Persian nationalists—this poetic aridity of the Sasanian official texts that have come down to us was not due to the religious attitude of the Mazdean clergy. In fact the Zoroastrian texts we possess do not contain any censure of poetry (or song, to which it is always linked) comparable to the Prophet of Arabia's harsh words about the poets, his contemporaries: "And the poets—the perverse follow them; hast thou not seen how they wander in every valley and how they say that which they do not?" (Kor. XXVI, 224–26). But a Mazdean antipathy for song (obviously profane, fatuous song) is mentioned in documents such as a late *rivâyat pârsî* (c. sixteenth century) on the Tahmûraf legend. It says: "The devil loves two things: pederasty and song."[2] This aversion is confirmed in an Islamic document on the Persian tradition concerning the "origins" of Persian poetry; it shows an awareness of the problem of the absence of Iranian pre-Islamic poetry and an interesting explanation for it.

The document is included in one of the most ancient works of Persian "aesthetics," the "Critical Treatise of Persian Poetry" (*Mu'jam fî ma'âyîr-i shi'ru'l-'ajam*) by Shams-i Qais, composed soon after 1217 (ed. Qazwini in "Gibb Memorial Series," X, 1909, pp. 167–180).

Tradition says that Bahrâm, son of Yazdigird, son of Shâpûr—who was later called Bahrâm Gûr (*gûr* means "onager") because of his passion for hunting onagers—was sent as a child to the Lakhmid Arab king of Hîra, a vassal of the Persians, to be educated and become among other things "eloquent and a poet." And Bahrâm did learn the art of rhythmic poetry there and in fact the famous "early Persian verse" is attributed to him. Though much of this tradition may have been invented, what Shams-i Qais adds—declaring that it is the result of his personal reading of "ancient Persian" (*furs*) texts—is, to say the least, highly significant. He writes:

In some ancient Persian (*furs*) books I have read that the wise men who were contemporaries of Bahrâm found nothing dishonorable in his life and habits, except
that he composed poetry. When he acceded to the throne the wise man Adhurbad
son of Zarâdusht[3] came to him and counselled him as follows: "Sire! You must
know that composing verses is among a king's worst defects and among a sovereign's
most abject habits. In fact poetry is based on lies and falsehood and it is built on
impious hyperboles and excessive exaggeration, and therefore the great religious
philosophers (*'uzamâ-i falâsifa-i adyân*, probably the Magi) oppose it and hold that
it deserves reproof. They consider the poets' satires among the causes of the down-
fall of the ancient kingdoms and past reigns and the premonitory sign of the loss of
wealth and the devastation of countries. And all the *zindîq*s and negators of the
prophecy have given form to their idle imagination,[4] and attacked the Revealed
Books and the Prophets, solely through poetry; and their dissenting thoughts have
taken form solely through the frequent habit of rhyme and rhythm. Though a group
of lovers of knowledge have considered the poetry that is based on truth and rectitude and combines advice that leads to good and wise tales and useful parables as a
miracle of wisdom and a portent of learning, they have also left us words according
to which the first created being who composed poetry on the ascetic practice and
wise admonition of the desirable soul and to the praise and glory of God was one of
the Cherubim angels, but, at the same time, the first creature who praised himself
and boasted his supremacy over others in verse was Satan, may he be accursed."

After listening to the Magi's sermon, Bahrâm Gûr abstained from poetry.
And this is why—still according to the tradition reported by Shams-i Qais—
the minstrel Bârbad, who became famous at the court of Khusrau Parvîz, "composed his panegyrics in prose and did not use poetry for them."

Of course we cannot take everything in this document as gospel truth. The
môbad's "advice" to his Sovereign, for example, probably followed the style
of the literature of "advice to Sovereigns" that was so highly developed in
Islamic literature—though it too (in the form of *andarz*) was of ancient Iranian
origin. But it presents some undoubtedly interesting points. In the first place
the concept that poetry (or poetry-song, for in antiquity these were inseparable
entities) was something second rate, only worthy of minstrels. In the second
place the profoundly Mazdean concept (though it exists in the Qur'an too) that
poetry is evil because it is based on untruth.[5] Thirdly, poetry is an instrument of
propaganda in the hands of heretics (*zindîq*) and subverters. As we have seen,
the term *zindîq* (Pahl. *zandîk*) was already present in Mazdean books and apparently means he "who keeps to personalistic comments (*zand*)," i.e. *airetikós*.
Mani and Mazdak were considered princes among the heretics and we must not
forget that tradition considered Mazdak a very able orator—an artist with words—
while Mani, besides being traditionally famous as a painter, composed hymns
and Manichaean propaganda and in fact often made use of rhyme and song. And
last but not least, the reader should note the connection between truly artistic

poetry (with specific rhymes and meters) and the Semitic Arabs. Compared to the "true" poetry king Bahrâm had come to know in Arab circles, even Bârbad's songs were "prose," i.e., probably rhythmic prose or merely accentual poetry.

And so the birth of truly artistic poetry in Persia is felt to be due to Semitic Arabism and—since we have no documents to prove the contrary—tradition, in this case, appears basically correct. But this artistic poetry was apparently born under a twofold religious curse: that of the môbad, such as Adhurbad Zarâdushtân, who based their malediction on its impious falsehood, and that of the Qur'an for whom poets (inspired by genies, the jinn) "say that which they do not." I believe this is an important point because it explains how from the very beginning poetry was connected with the idea of bad reputation, shamelessness, licentiousness (*bad-nâmî, rusvâ'î, rindî*), which seems to us so singular. When this idea merged later with the real influences of the Malâmatî concept of mysticism, it became one of the principal motifs of classical Persian lyrics, even when the reason for it had been forgotten and, eventually, it completely metamorphosed into a mystical sense. Even if the traditional Persian poet was extremely religious and an orthodox Muslim, he often felt obliged to praise unbelief (*kufr*), extol the idolatrous temple-tavern, prefer the "religion of Zoroaster" (a pure symbol of unbelief, as we shall see, which had nothing to do with true Mazdaism) to that of Muhammad, and the beardless young Christian to the Preacher and the Mullâh.

Before continuing our study of this motif we will give an example, i.e., a description of spring by Daqîqî, one of the first Persian lyric poets (d. around 978). We are quoting the whole of the brief ode also because it is one of the oldest Persian lyrics to have come down to us and is a good introduction to a particular poetic style.[6]

A heavenly cloud, O idol, has clothed the earth in
    April's festive garments,
And the world is so changed that the tiger appears
    to hurl itself onto the roebuck only to wrestle
    harmlessly,
And the rose garden seems Eden's paradise with its
    trees adorned with flowers like the houri of
    the sky.
Earth is like bloodstained brocade, and the wind
    appears as a hand anointed with sweet smelling
    musk,
A graceful hand that marks out his Friend's image
    on the grass in lines of wine and musk:
An idol with ruby-colored cheeks and red wine as
    his sparkling garment in the temple (*kinisht*)!

And you could say that the world had become like a
   peacock, both where it is rough and harsh, and
   where it is soft and light.
And the dust exhales a scent of rose-water so that
   one might even say that the roses (*gul*) were
   kneaded into the mud (*gil*).
But the good Daqîqî chose four things from the
   countless things of the world, four charming
   virtues from all good and all evil
A lip that is like a ruby and the gentle lament of
   the lute, blood-colored wine, Zarathustra's
   faith!

Much has been written on the last couplet that, as usual in this kind of poem, contains the poet's signature (*takhallus*); and the Persians who now claim Zoroastrianism as a national glory try to prove that Daqîqî was Mazdean mainly on the basis of this couplet. But it is a very weak proof. In the meantime we should note how Zoroaster's religion is coupled with three other "joyful," carefree and libertine elements, i.e. music, wine and beautiful boys—all three prohibited by official religion and symbols of "defamation." Zoroaster's religion—together with the other three—is a strong motif of poetic defamation and is quoted precisely because it is reprehensible and therefore loved by the poet. The reader should also note how in the preceding lines of this composition, which is so innocently descriptive, the Friend is compared to an "idol" (the greatest possible heresy for Islam and one that has nothing to do with Zoroastrianism) and connected with the "Wine" he offers. Here the curiously religious metaphors continue, for this wine is as red as the sacred vestments of a Christian priest (*kinisht*, originally the Jewish synagogue, becomes the generic indication of any non-Muslim place of cult). Is this enough to indicate that Daqîqî was an idolater, or Christian?[7]

Thus this very old Persian lyric offers us at least four important religious motifs that will frequently recur in later lyrics, i.e., the Cup bearer, the Idol, the Sacred Wine, the Idolatrous Temple or Church, and Mazdaism as the symbol of libertinism—besides the more usual and less significant metaphors for Heaven (Garden, Houri and Trees).

What is the origin of these . . . oenological and religious motifs that seem so strange to us? Nothing in Persian has come down to us from this period, which lasted about three centuries, between the Arab conquest and these early examples of Persian lyrics. Nor, as we mentioned, can we prove that poetry of this kind existed in the Sasanian period (besides the fact that the early Muslim Persian poets had lost the language—at least in its written form). But this was not an empty period; on the contrary it produced a wealth of Arab poetic documents, in a language well known to the Muslim Persian poets. It is in Arabic poetry and especially in the poetry of the so-called *muhdathûn* (the eighth-through tenth-century *neóteroi*) that we must look for the most immediate origin of these images. This origin is possibly less mystical and esoteric than some people may believe, even if later these forms were imbued with a deeper religious symbology. Arab pre-Islamic pagan poetry, which was copiously imitated by the Persian poets, knew all about the tavern-convent, church-wine connection. And these ancient verses often rang with the motif of wine sold in Christian convents in the desert and echoed Persia's regal glory, Khusrau and his palaces and the legends of Rustam and Isfandiyâr. According to one ancient text, they were sung by clever minstrels, who thus distracted the inhabitants of Mecca from listening to the young Prophet Muhammad's pious sermons.

With the conquest of Persia these motifs developed in Arabic poetry, especially in the school of the "new poets" that had started towards the end of the Umayyad period (the poet-Caliph al-Walid, who died in 744, is universally considered their precursor). With them the motif of "revelry" connected with the church and the taste for reprehensible behavior—a purely profane taste at the time—became more marked.

> What a beautiful night—al-Walid sings—I spent in the convent of Bawanna, where wine was poured out and songs were struck up!
> As the glass whirled so we whirled, dancing, and those who did not know thought we were mad.
> We passed near perfumed women and song and wine and there we stopped.
> And we made Peter the Caliph of God and John the court counsellor,
> We took their communion and bowed down in front of the crosses of their convent, like unbelievers.[8]

The same poet speaks of "old Khusrau's wine." And Abû Nuwâs (d. around 814), the prince of the "new style," repeatedly describes the Cup—the resplendent Sasanian cup decorated with bas-reliefs and lines—and speaks of Jewish, Zoroastrian and Christian tavern keepers and cup bearers who alone in the Islamic world dared to sell wine. Many other motifs present in Persian poetry are already present in this Arabic poetry of the Abbasid renaissance that was brought about in part by *mawâlî* (Iranian, not Arab, "clients") and we find many Persian expressions in the works of Arab poets of the period.

Lyric poetry written in Persian, which started with the decadence of the unitary Abbasid Caliphate and the assertion of local feudal states during the ninth and tenth centuries, was the most natural logical continuation of the Arabic lyrics of the Iraqi *muhdathûn* (for this new style in Arabic literature slowly ran dry and gave way to a "classical" renaissance) and was therefore born under the twofold sign of "reproach" and "unbelief" (*kufr*). Consequently it was imbued from the outset with (purely "formal") religious elements that counted as mere images. These could become coldly literary on the one hand, but on the other—if vivified by a mystical strain—they could cull from their own depths and create (as in fact happened) a singular form of lyricism in which the erotic and bacchanalian element became almost inextricably linked with the mystical and initiatory one.

The Style of Traditional Lyrics

It would be impossible for the lay reader to understand, without some preliminary examples, the historical and religious problems that these lyrics we are about to discuss present in their more mature form. Therefore, we will start by presenting some poetic odes in the form of brief love-lyrics, called *ghazal* in the more mature aspect the great Hâfiz gave them in the fourteenth century, and for which he was explicitly rebuked (possibly wrongly) as the first poet to mingle erotic and mystical motifs in his works. The reader should remember that the verses of the ghazal are completely independent, forming closed units connected by rhyme and rhythm as well as by very tenuous conceptual ties. In its very loose unity, the ode we are translating here is based on the theme of the world's return to youth, to spring.[9]

1. The splendor of the time of youth has now regained the Garden. The good tidings of the Flower have reached the sweet-singing nightingale.
2. O breeze! If you will go to the young shoots of the Meadow, present my respects to Basil, Rose and Cypress.
3. If the Young Magus, the Wine vendor, makes such a show of alluring movements, I am ready to sweep the dust of the Tavern with my lashes!
4. O, you who cover up the Moon with a Polo Club of the most pure amber, do not throw my Life into confusion too, I who am giddily perplexed.
5. I fear that these people who laugh at the drinkers of Dregs in the end will still believe in the Tavern.
6. May you be the friend of Saints, for an Earth lies hidden in Noah's ark that has no concern for the Water of the great Deluge.
7. Come out of the house of the Firmament and do not ask him for Bread for this abject Essence ends by killing the Guest.
8. Tell him that in his last Resting Place no man will have more than a handful of Earth, why then raise high Palaces towards the Sky?
9. O my Moon from Canaan! Your destiny is the Throne of Egypt: it is time for you to bid farewell to your sombre Prison!
10. O Hâfiz, live your life merrily in wine and revelling but do not, like the others, render the Qur'an a network of deception!

The translation cannot do justice to the very subtle symbolic play of words throughout the text (we have tried to capitalize the "key words"). Even in a poem as short as this one a host of symbolic motifs are interwoven in linear and tenuous movements. Already in the first couplet we find the famous Rose-Nightingale motif: the Rose is God's elusive beauty and the Nightingale is the lover who weeps and longs for union. In the second couplet we find the Zephyr-Messenger, often connected in this kind of poem with the wonderful potential of "Solomon's Kingdom" that dominated the winds and demons. Next the Young Magus (*mughbachcheh*) comes into the picture and the poet's devotion to the rite of Wine and Tavern (a rather transparent allusion to a cult considered both esoteric and defamatory). The game of polo and the images connected with it in the next couplet are still within the ambit of typically Iranian images: the Polo Bat (*chaugân*) is compared to the Loved One's wavy amber scented curl and connected with the idea that the adoring poet's head could serve as a polo ball for that bat ("giddily perplexed," *sargardân* literally means "whose head whirls" like a ball). In one difficult couplet the motif of the Flood (Water) of Noah (Ark) is mentioned. Within the Ark there is an Earth (man, Man with a capital M, the Saint, the Prophet, the Initiated One, Cosmic Man . . . and Noah, as we know, was connected with Wine in other ways too!) that cares nothing about flood Waters: therefore one should be friends with the Saints (*mardân-i khudâ*, "God's men") and have a spiritual Master in order to righteously follow God's perilous way! Couplets 7 and 8 are a clear invitation to flight from the world, to the neglect of every titanic undertaking. The world (couplet 9) is like the well-prison of Joseph the Jew (the soul), for whom destiny has already prepared the "throne of Egypt" (transcendent realities) and yet he still lingers in his prison. The last verse contains a clearly polemic allusion to the hypo-critical clergy who adore the exterior letter of the Sacred Book.

It would be absurd to want to deny any mystical meaning to this kind of poetry, for it is evidently imbued with images charged with esoteric resonance. But we must consider further the form itself of this lyric poem before examin-ing some of the typical motifs it contains. To begin with, if one has the key to the symbol it is universally accessible: even the best Western symbolist poetry (which later degenerated into individualistic Hermeticism) does not possess the insuperable and untranslatable "dualism" of meaning of the classical po-etry of the Islamic Orient. It is unlikely that a Western poet, however skilled, could have produced anything similar to Hâfiz's perfect ghazal that begins:

Dûsh dîdam keh malâ'ik dar-i maikhâneh zadand,
Gil-i âdam bi-sirishtand u bi-paimâneh zadand
"Yesterday I saw the Angels knocking at the Tavern door: they kneaded Adam's mud into the shape of a limpid cup."

Each element in the picture becomes a "motif:" it does not stand alone in its autonomous dynamics but becomes the symbolic reflection of "another," of a transcendent world of Ideas.

Let us take the first word of the verse, *dûsh*. If we translate it literally—as we have necessarily done—with "yesterday," the effect we obtain is rather different from that which the original produces in an oriental reader. *Dûsh* means a little more and a little less than our "yesterday" and is not used in common language: it suddenly places us in a day before every other day, an "absolute yesterday" before serial time, in the pre-temporal age of the *rûz-i alast* (see above). Our languages cannot express this pleiad of poetic and metaphysical concepts in a single word. But there is more to it that this: the "Tavern" symbol of esoteric knowledge; the infinite echoes with which Adam's story (told somewhat differently to "ours" in the Qur'an) resounds in the ear of an oriental listener; the idea of the Grail-Cup, another central leitmotif in this lyric form; the earth-fire metaphysical polemics (earth Adam-fire Satan) are all verbal-spiritual centers that could, possibly, be transposed in hermetic terms into a modern translation except that, in our culture, hermeticism has become purely individualistic while the hermeticism of the traditional poetry we are examining is, if the reader will excuse the paradox, "social" hermeticism: anyone who studies the dictionary of these symbols can learn them. Though this may be difficult it is at least objective. Within this social hermeticism, individualistic recklessness is considered definitely unadvisable. But let us continue: in this same verse there is an abyss between *malâ'ik* ("Angels") and *maikhâneh* ("Tavern"). The gesture of "Angels who knock on the door of the tavern" may sound ridiculous, or possibly in the bad taste of the seventeenth century, to western listeners. Why? Because when a modern western poet wants to express this same sense of two abnormally and mysteriously different things he generally has recourse to a different poetic technique. Rilke, for example, gives us a feeling of the arcane mysteriousness of the old sea wind blowing from unknown places in these words:

> Uraltes Wehn vom Meer
> welches weht
> nur wie für Ur-Gestein,
> lauter Raum
> reissend von weit hereie.

The idea of abyss, of mythical distance, is rendered not by bringing together two spiritually or topographically distant objects ("the angels" and "the tavern") on the same level but rather, I think, by entering into a third dimension, i.e., by imagining a theoretically absurd action such as the "tearing away of shreds of resounding Space." One could object of course that the action of angels knocking on the tavern door is absurd too, but I believe that we are in the presence of two types of absurdity. There is nothing absurd in itself, from the point of view of "being," in angels (if one admits their existence) knocking at a door: if there is any absurdity it is purely moral, i.e., that angels should knock at a tavern door. While even God himself could not "tear away shreds of space" from distant places! In Rilke's lines the poetic effect is created not through stressing the vastness of the distance on one plane but through creating a new dimension. Obviously this technique (which is, in a nutshell, the modern western poetical technique) assumes far greater creative freedom in individual poets than oriental poets had; but in fact, if the translations of Muslim poets into our languages seem at times ridiculously seventeenth century and baroque, modern western poetry translated into Islamic languages frequently gives an impression of unbearable sloppiness and pretentious and ridiculous innovation.

Here is another verse from the same ode by Hâfiz:

Fire is not that whose Flame the Candle derides
[True] Fire is that which was hurled into the Moth's Harvest

One can easily see the subtlety of the relationship and parallelism of the concepts that—taken not as individual realities but always as "motifs"— lead the translator to use capital letters. The Persian poet cares little whether the poetic objects are new or not. "New for newness' sake" (unless it is a newness of poetic "relationships" between the objects, and these are always relatively limited in number) carries no weight in traditional Islamic poetry because "new" signifies "individual," a concept seen only in its phenomenal reality, and this, in traditional civilizations, is not considered worthy of art. What the poet wants to say is this:

"The true Fire of love is that which is produced by self-annihilation (as with the Moth in the Flame) and not the superficially gay and brilliant Fire of an exterior life (the Candle)." He links four different images, each of which has a natural logical connection with "fire": the darting Flame (shu'leh), the Candle (sham'), the burnt Harvest (kharman), the Moth (parvâneh). These four objects are not mythologized to produce a world of highly allusive sensations (as is so often the case in our traditional poetry: for modern poetry stems from the mythology of our traditional poetry), they are simply brought together—in new relationships—onto a single plane, even though each one maintains its obvious and natural form."

This is an example of relational magic and not of creative magic, and the process is even more evident in, for example, the extremely rich metaphorical language of the greatest Persian wizard of images, the poet Nizâmî of Ganjeh (d. 1203).

He describes a water-lily opening its broad petals on the surface of a small lake on a spring morning:

Because of the torture of sleep, the eye of the nenûfar
    had been thrown by life into the blaze of the water.

Each element of this rapid description keeps its form and its original limits. As Ritter rightly noted, "things do not change their natural form," in this Persian world of images, "and we do not see faeries coming out from among the flowers, or kobolds dancing in the grass: the scene is animated through keeping the form of the objects and only changing their mutual relationships."

Every kind of mythology is excluded, at least formally. Take, for example, the beautiful passage in Shelley's "The Cloud":

. . . that orbèd maiden, with white fire laden
whom mortals call the Moon,
glides glimering over my fleece like floor
by the midnight breezes strewn;
and wherever the beat of her unseen feet
(which only the Angels hear)
may have broken the woof of my tent's thin roof
the stars peep behind her and peer . . .

An image like "the beat of the moon's invisible feet walking on the clouds" would be impossible in traditional Persian poetry. Why? Simply because—and the reader must excuse the banality of the explanation—the moon has no feet! This image would sound very odd in Persian (classical Persian of course, for present day Persians have assimilated a great many modern techniques). The moon is compared to thousands of objects in Persian too, it enters into new magical and inconceivable relationships (which may seem ridiculous or odd to us!) with other objects, but it is never perceived mythologically as a person who moves or acts in a way that is incompatible with its real form.

The moon often speaks in Persia too ("A moon told me . . . my moon came to me . . . etc.") but in the form of a *comparatio compendiaria*: for "moon" we must understand the stereotype of "a boy or girl with a round shining face like a moon." A moon that really spoke or walked would be the equivalent of idolatry—the supreme sin in a religious world molded by and totally imbued with the Semitic monotheism of Islam.

Even where the descriptions are apparently conceived as pure description, (as in these verses by Hâfiz) the individual elements are so generic on a phenomenological plane and so precise on a metaphysical plane that one cannot help defining this kind of poetry "neo-Platonic":

I went into the Garden at dawn, hoping for the scent of Flowers, crazy with love,
to heal my weary Heart, like a Nightingale
I watched the graceful movements of the Rose of Tyre
that appeared in the dark night as Lamp and light
So proud was she and happy over her youth and beauty
that in a thousand ways she ravished all peace from the Heart of her
     Nightingale lover
The eyes of tender Narcissus were nostalgically filled with tears of Dew
And the melancholy Tulip had a hundred Marks of fire on its bosom and
     heart
The Lily stretched out its scolding Tongue like a sword
The Anemone opened its mouth, like a man who is always grumbling.
One of them, like the adorers of Wine, held a Flask in his hand
the other, Cup-bearer to the inebriated, presented the Cup in his hand.
O Hâfiz, profit from joyfulness youth and pleasure,
for the prophet simply bears a message!

Nothing is specified and nothing can be singled out in this description: the garden is the Garden, the essence of Garden, The Rose, the Nightingale, the Narcissus, the Tulip, the Lily, the Anemone are the "ideas" of the Rose, the Tulip, etc. The immediacy of a dynamic description of the "fleeting instant" (the essence of all modern poetry) is scorned and shunned: the glass-like symbolic precision is even more marked in the original text than it appears in translation where some romantic shadings have worked their way in and the rigid qualitative and uniform rhyme of the original have been lost, and we are hardly aware of the total, singular, absence of verbs indicating shadings of action. Persian poetry ignores verbs such as "quivering," "penetrating," "flashing," "rumbling," etc. It consists entirely of nouns and adjectives accompanied by very banal generic verbs.

The contrast between this form of poetry (which we will call optical, neo-Platonic, visual, contemplative) and the very different classical Arab poetry (I mean the pre-new-style Arab poetry of the desert), not to mention that of the flashing Qur'anic style, is particularly interesting. The Arab aesthetic style—with its analytical taste for fine detail described with precise and photographic allusions that never become permanent ornamental"motifs" but remain an arbitrary prophetic approach to an instant—is in some ways more similar to modern-style poetry. The Prophet's language cries and invokes: "By the Fig and the Olive! And by Mount Sinai!" (Kor. XCV, 1–2). "By the white Forenoon! And by the brooding Night!"(Kor. XCIII, 1–2). Sometimes the flames of hell appear to him "as rising surrounded with fire" (XC, 20) sometimes they are immense seas of fire "like yellow camels." Elsewhere he describes the concrete, practical, short-lived sight of "cattle . . . in them is warmth, and uses various . . . and there is beauty in them for you, when you bring them home to rest and when you drive them forth abroad to pasture" (XVI, 5–6) and sees the bees to whom the Lord orders: "Take unto yourselves of the mountains, houses, and of the trees, and of what they are building. Then eat of all manner of fruit, and follow the ways of your Lord easy to go upon!" and "then comes there forth out of their bellies a drink of diverse hues," etc.

When all is said and done, if we observe the ideology reflected in the Islamic Persian poetic style we cannot but notice how clearly it contrasts with that of very early and Qur'anic Islam. Setting aside any "demonstration" of a pre-Islamic and Islamic Persian cultural unity based only on bare historical documents (and we have seen how unreliable this kind of demonstration can be), the profoundly non-Islamic character of the Islamic Persian world can be discerned through an in-depth study of the deepest folds of its aesthetic style. But this non-Islamic character cannot be identified with a Mazdean world-view, though it appears to be the reflection of a neo-Platonic concept: Islam contributed the expurgation of any mythological tendency and idolatry, thus barring the way to a possible evolution of these forms towards modern European forms. On the other hand the "Semitic" Qur'anic style was unable to develop along autonomous paths that would have led to extremely interesting results, both because it was connected with the prophetic concept of "Inimitable Sacred Book" and because it was in fact inimitable and incomprehensible at that stage of its cultural development, being too personal and individualistic (traditional cultures hate anything new).

The Motifs of Lyric Religious Poetry

At this point it will be useful to study in greater detail some of the individual motifs that play a part in this lyric form common to both Persia and Islam, though we will dwell only on those with specifically religious values. The reader can begin by meditating on this ghazal by Hâfiz, with which we will start our study:[10]

1. For years the Heart asked of us Jamshîd's Cup and longed to receive the one it already had from a stranger's hand.
2. The Pearl that is outside and beyond the empty Shell of the Cosmos asked it of the lost ones wandering on the Sea Shores.
3. I brought my quandary, yesterday, to the Superior of the Magi who knew through sacred strength of Gaze how to unravel Enigmas.
4. I saw him joyful and laughing, a Cup of Wine in his hand, seeing in that Mirror a hundred many-hued visions.
5. I asked: "When did the Wise One give you this Cup that mirrors the World?" He answered: "On the day in which He made this blue Cupola of sky!"

6. A man with a ravished heart who is with God at every instant, does not see God and calls from afar: "O God! Lord!"
7. But all those magic games played here and now by Reason were once played by Samiri in front of the White Hand with the Rod.
8. He said: "The only fault of the holy Lover for whom the leader lifted high the Gallows was that he revealed the Mystery.
9. If grace still offers the help of the Holy Spirit others still will know how to do what Christ did."
10. I asked him: "Why the Chain of the curls of beautiful Idols?" He answered: "And yet Hâfiz complains of his mad heart . . ."

The key to understanding a lyric poem of this kind, considered by some connoisseurs (Arberry) the peak of Hâfiz's poetic genius, lies in grasping the echoes of the following religious-aesthetic motifs:

Jamshîd's Cup (or Jam's, in an abbreviated form; Pers. *jâm-i jam*)

In pre-Islamic Pahlavî texts, Jamshîd (Avestam Yima Khsaêta, Pahl. Yam-shê o Yam) was one of the mythical sovereigns of ancient Iran. He was typical of civilizing sovereign-heroes (among other things he invented wine), he had marked "solar" features, and like other primeval heroes he was also connected with the events of the end of the cosmic cycle. Neither the Avestan nor the Pahlavî texts, nor the earliest Islamic translations, speak of a "Cup" of Jamshîd, but a very interesting text in the *Dênkart* (quoted in Zaehner, *Zurvan*, p. 251) presents Yam with the same characteristics as the legendary Solomon (for example, power over demons) and even as the Christ of tradition (redeeming visit to hell, immortality-giving redemption, resurrection from Hell: *dên gôbêt kû-sh ul burt hach dôshakhv*). The whole thing is in the past tense ("it was," etc.), a mythical past that is both past and future. For Yam is connected with the end of the world. Firdausî attributes the "cup which shows the cosmos" to another ancient "Kayânid" king, Kai Khusrau, in the famous episode of Bîzhan in the well: the king discovers Bîzhan's prison by looking into his wonderful Cup. This is how Firdausî sings the event:

then king Khusrau picked up the limpid cup
and within it he saw all seven parts of the world,
and the signs and works of the most high Sky,
all were manifest to him, and the Why and the How
    and the When.
And Saturn appeared in it, and Jove, and Mars, and
    Leo,
and the Sun and Moon and Venus and Mercury,
and all the future did the magical (*afsûngar*)
bearer of the world see within it . . .[11]

Therefore the salient element in the motif of "Jamshîd's Cup" is the Cup (of wine) rather than the Iranian element (Jamshîd). In fact the attribution of the cup to Jamshîd started only in the twelfth century in Persian literature, since Jamshîd was more famous than Kai Khusrau because, as Firdausî tells us, he invented Wine, and—and this is possibly the most important reason of all— because Persian-Islamic tradition identified him with King Solomon (following the well-known tendency that also identified Zarathustra with Abraham).[12]

Some experts (see Massignon, *Lexique technique*, pp. 88 and foll.) maintain that the cup-wine motif can be entirely explained as the derivation of a Qur'anic meditation. In fact the Sacred Book of Islam speaks (LVI, 18) of cups of wine offered to the chosen in Heaven, and of the Lord who acts as cup-bearer "giving the elect a pure draught" (LXXVI, 21). It seems to me rather far-fetched however to maintain that the motif "acquired nothing new" once it arrived in Persia. In my opinion, the "mirroring cup" in particular, the visible element of the "contemplation" of the arcane, is new; The Cup is *jihân-bîn* (which sees the world) and *jihân-numâ* (that shows the world), and is therefore above all a mirror-cup (and as such sometimes linked in lyric poetry with the famous "mirror of Alexander," Alexander's lighthouse). To complete the picture we must add that, according to a number of lexical sources, Jam's cup had seven lines (*khatt*) and in fact the precious Sasanian cups that have come down to us often present this division in successive phases that had their technical names starting from the rim downwards, *jûr, baghdâd, basra, azraq, varishkar, kâsehgar, farvadîneh*.[13]

What does the Cup represent symbolically? Hâfiz answers this question quite transparently. One of the earliest Persian mystic poets, Sanâ'î (d. 1141), interpreted it as "the heart" in the *Ilâhînâmeh*, as did the great 'Attâr (d. 1230). In a short unpublished poem (*Kanzu'l-haqâ'iq*, "the Treasure of Reality"),[14] Shabistarî (d. 1320) speaks of its possible "rusting" and gives various opinions on its meaning: Cup of water (sic!), astrolabe, mirror, geographical map. Shabistarî shares the opinion of the "Gnostics" ('*ârifîn*), i.e., that it is the *nafs-i dânâ*, The Knowing Soul, the pure and limpid soul. The curious opinion that considers Jam's Cup an astrolabe is almost certainly derived from the rich symbolic decoration engraved on the beautiful Sasanian cup, with the sun and moon within the lines or bands we mentioned earlier.

Elsewhere Hâfiz himself compares the cup's limpidity to that of a mirror (A4) that reflects the face of the Friend-God (A3). It is taken for granted that it is a golden cup (B3, T48) (traditionally, gold is a solar essence-metal) and even openly compared to the sun (B3). In T32 the "cup that shows the world" is explicitly declared to be "the intimate illuminating soul of the Friend" (zamîr-e monîr-e dûst). A number of times (for example in T8 and T34) the concepts of Cup and Pact are linked (and this is something more than a pun between *paimân* and *paimâneh!*): a sip from the cup seals a Primeval Pact between man and God. Some enigmatic "figures" (*rumûz*) that only a sage can read are engraved on Jam's cup and, because of its ship-like form, it has also been compared (T 56) to Noah's ark (this is one of the cup's traditional aspects,[15] i.e., it is "salvific" and "oracular"). Since the cup is the *dil* (generally translated as "heart" but "brain" or "intuition" would be better) and has its seat in the skull this leads to another symbolic development of the cup motif, i.e., it is compared to the skull, or the skull to an upside down cup (an image that often recurs in 'Umar Khayyâm) and Hâfiz also speaks of the cup as being composed of the skulls of Jamshîd, Bahrâm and Qubâd, (the other mythical kings of ancient Iran).

We will not even attempt to enter into the vast world that a comparative analysis would open up to us (to give one example only, the fascinating motif of the Grail which was so widespread in the West). We must mention, however, the presence of the oracular-chalice in the Bible (Kor., XLIV, 4–5): "why," Joseph says to the servant who was to show Benjamin up as a thief, "did you sell evil for good? Is not that the cup in which my lord is used to drink and which he uses for sooth-saying?" And Hyppolitus, summing up the Naassene doctrine, speaks of "Anacreon's Chalice": "The chalice tells me," an Anacreontic verse says, "what I must become, speaking silently without words. That is to say . . . Anacreon's Chalice tells an ineffable mystery without words . . . And this is the water, in those beautiful nuptial feasts, which Jesus, transforming it, turned into wine. This—they say—is the great and true beginning with which Jesus started the series of his miracles, in Cana of Galilee, and thus manifested the kingdom of heaven. This (beginning) is the kingdom of heaven that is within us like a treasure, like leaven hidden in three measures of flour" (*Elenchos*, V, 8, 4–7). Once again, it is from the Hellenistic-Gnostic world that gave so much to Iranian Islam (see the preceding chapter) rather than from ancient Iran that "Jam's Cup" probably comes.

The Inaccessible Pearl

The Pearl-Shell image does not exist in the pre-Islamic Iranian texts we possess: instead we find the word gôhr (mod. Pers. *gauhar*) in the triple sense of "substance," "noble race" (human substance) and "pearl" (also jewel in a general sense). In the whole of Islamic-Iranian tradition, as in our Medieval tradition, pearls are said to be born of drops of water nurtured in the womb-matrix of mother-of-pearl (*sadaf*, shell).[16] Sa'dî (twelfth century) tells the story of the Pearl in a moral readaptation (in praise of humility) in a famous poetic fragment of his *Gulistân* (Rose Garden). A drop of water dropped from a cloud and was astounded at the sight of the vast sea. If it is—the drop said—then I am nothing. But the vast bosom of the sea welcomed it and, as a reward for its humility, the shell nurtured it and nourished it with vital strength until the very humble drop became a famous regal pearl. "It had knocked on the door of Nothingness" the Poet concludes "and had found, more fully, Being!" The motif, taken from the Hellenistic-Gnostic alchemic tradition, through Arab texts, was very popular until recent times. The slightly different concept of the Original Pearl (referred to more specifically in our verse), of the *durratu'l-baid*, the Pearl of White, the original substance (*gauhar*) of all created things, often identified with Muhammadan Light (the Logos), with Universal Reason, with the Spiritual Essence of Man, was also probably originally neo-Platonic. In Najmu'd-Dîn Dâyeh's *Mirsâdu'l-ibâd* ("Observatory of the Servants of God") (Tehran, 1352 s., pp. 22–3 and foll.) we find: "God looked at the Muhammadan light with a loving eye and it was covered with shame so that drops of sweat appeared; from these drops God created the spirits of the prophets; then from the lights of the spirits of the prophets he created the spirits of the saints," etc.

According to this author (110, 13), who in fact reflects a far older tradition, the small clot of black blood at the center of the heart (*suvaidâ-i dil*) is the seat of mystical revelation, of divine knowledge (*'ilm lâdunnî*). It is in this ark that God deposited the "pearl" (*gauhar*) that no-one in the universe can understand. See also the holy saying (*hadîth qudsî*): "My earth and My sky are unable to understand Me, but the heart of My believing servant understands me" (the *hadîth qudsî* are traditions in which God speaks in the first person). The Gnostic canticle "of the Pearl" in Thomas' *Acts* is an example of the identification of the pearl with the essence of the soul. It tells the tale of the prince who was sent to Egypt as a child from his country in the Orient to seek the Unique Pearl (mentioned in the Gospel), i.e., the Soul that is in the sea (matter), etc.[17]

We still have to discover the linguistically pre-Islamic-Iranian symbolic identification of "pearl-(noble) human substance." In the case in question—i.e., the poem by Hâfiz we are studying—the Cosmos is an empty shell but the inaccessible Pearl that, according to verse 1, is nothing but Jam's Cup-Heart, is the most intimate secret essence of man himself, which therefore must not be sought for in the shell of exterior phenomena but within; it must not be asked of the lost ones of the coast but fished for personally in the most profound depths of the sea: the Waters are the symbol of deep, lower, lunar psyche. The pearl itself is, in an uninterrupted tradition that goes back to the paleolithic era, the symbol of intra-uterine germinal life (shell is equivalent to uterus), of the feminine matrix, of life and resurrection. In his *Traité*, Eliade collected abundant eastern and western material on the Pearl and its magic-religious importance.[18] The reader should note in particular how it becomes a technical term of a cyphered language that is very clear to anyone who has the key, and which interplays with other images: the image of the sea, which is immediately clear in connection with the pearl, grows in another direction to include a sea-shore relationship. Elsewhere too, Hâfiz places the symbol of the dangerous lowing abyss (A1) side by side with the symbol of those who carry light weights on shore, who are esoteric, superficial: he calls them the "lost ones" of the shore. And in other beautiful ghazal, Hâfiz's play of images places the pearl by the side of the sailor-diver ("if he has found the Pearl, the poet asks himself, what further need is there for a diver?"). And again, the "regal Friend with a face like the moon and a forehead like Venus" is declared *gauhar-i yak-dâneh*, "unique pearl." The pearl-essence of man is also revealed by the ruby-wine (T47); wine as the revealer of *gôhr*, the "essence of man," already appeared in prosaic praise of man himself in a Pahlavî text (*Mênôkê Khrat*, chap. XVI) that states that according to religious revelation the scope of wine is to draw out man's good or bad "nature" (*gôhr*, also "pearl").

The pearl-tear symbolic comparison (and with it the image of "stringing pearls with one's eyelashes, i.e., weeping) offers a completely different plane of images frequently found in traditional lyric poetry too. But the Pearl is also the symbol of the Word (the Word born of the Waters exists already in Babylonian tradition!). Here we are in the reign of myths. But it is interesting to note that this mythological truth is picked up, unconsciously I think, by traditional Persian lyrics. In fact the passage "pearl-word," which is incongruous if we consider the laws of formal similitudes we have just studied, develops through the orthodox image pearl-row of white teeth-words. Threading beads also means "speaking" and "necklace strung with beads" has even become a technical term to indicate poem (*nazm*) as opposed to *nasr* ("scattering unstrung beads"), i.e., "prose."

Though these combinations are rigorously natural to this poetic world and free from mythology and dynamic autonomy (besides corresponding, as we saw, to the visible form of the object that enters into the symbol) they are very different from our purely exterior sixteenth century puns. In other cultures their correspondence with significant symbols reduces the risk of exteriority and presupposes an esoteric symbolic doctrine (easy to decipher in fact in this Hafizian phase of its development) that the people who deny the "religiosity" of this traditional lyric poetry try in vain to negate.

The Superior of the Magi (*pîr-i mughân*) and the Mystical Wine

Daqîqî, as we have seen, already linked Zarathustra's religion with wine, ruby lips and the sound of the lute as motifs of revelry and defamation in the eyes of the world. In his didactic poem *Bûstân*, Sa'dî (who preceded Hâfiz by a century), speaks of his (probably imaginary) visit to the idolatrous temple of Sômnâth[19] in India (which became itself the motif of this lyric poem). The following is an abbreviated translation:

I saw an ivory idol at Sômnâth, encrusted with gems, as in the time of the Manât Arab paganism; his face had been so well portrayed by the sculptor that it would be impossible to imagine a more beautiful form.

Sa'dî asks why a lifeless idol was adored:

I courteously asked a magus I knew, a magus of great eloquence, my roommate and friend: O Brahmin! the custom of this land seems strange to me.

The magus is irritated at the indiscreet question and:

he told the magi and the superiors of the convent (*dair*, Christian convent!) and I saw no favorable face in that gathering, and the Zoroastrians (*gabrân*, sic!) declaimers of the Pâzend hurled themselves on me like dogs on a bone . . .

Then Sa'dî, with the tolerant and unheroic sense of morals he reveals elsewhere in his works too, is profuse in his praise of those "impious ones":

I loudly praised the great Brahmin: O wise interpreter—I exclaimed—of the Avesta and the Zand, this idol pleases me too, for it has a graceful form and an attractive stature . . .

But, he asks, what is its virtue? He is told that at dawn the idol raises its arms to the sky. All through the night Sa'dî waits for dawn to see the miracle:

A night as long as the day of resurrection, with the magi around me prostrate in prayer without ablution, priests (*kashîshân*, Christian priests!) who had never disturbed water, their armpits stinking like carrion in the sun!

At dawn everyone gathered together to see the miracle:

Magi with idle beliefs and faces untouched by water appeared there from the cities and countryside.
Unable to do anything else [Sa'dî adds] I pretended to weep too with emotion and kissed the idol's hands. For some days I imitated the atheists (*kâfir*), I became a Brahmin and began to recite the Zand . . .

Until one fine day he discovers the trick (an ordinary rope that made the idol's arms move) because:

behind the curtain there was a Bishop (sic! *matrân*), an adorer of Fire, with the end of a rope in his hand . . .

We have quoted this rather long passage (see Mu'în, op. cit., pp. 486–7) because it would be difficult to find a more obvious example (and in as cultivated and rather early a representative as Sa'dî) of absolute ignorance and incomprehension of the historic Zoroastrian religion and of the relative impossibility of historically demonstrating a continuity between pre-Islamic and Islamic tradition. Here we have Magi, Brahmins, bishops, priests and atheists, as well as Hindu temples, a Christian convent and a temple to Fire, all lumped together under the common denominator of *kufr* (unbelief, idolatry, atheism). But is it really a question of ignorance? Merely external explanations of the causes of this ignorance are not entirely convincing, especially in the case of Sa'dî who had travelled a great deal and, being a highly cultivated person, could not help but know (if only because they were already clearly distinct in the Qur'an) that Magism, Christianity and Hinduism were different religions with different rites. There must therefore be some other explanation. Elsewhere more than in this example it becomes clear that the literary-esoteric cypher of *kufr* (unbelief) signifies the in-depth study of religious realities and their experimental realization (*tahqîq*) beyond the veils of exterior and, at times, hypocritical fidelity "to the letter." Any non-Islamic religion (including idolatry) can serve as a symbol of this: Zoroastrianism—true historical Zoroastrianism—does not enter into the picture and there is no need to assume any direct link (unless it is the purely casual link of the knowledge of certain terms for contingent reasons due to the fact that Zoroastrianism developed in Iran) between Zoroastrian tradition and Islamic lyrical and mystical tradition. In fact—as we mentioned above—a blasphemous Christian rite had already been described in Arab poems.

Here, in Hâfiz's *pîr-i mughân* (The Superior of the Magi), the blasphemy and parody are only apparent and we are still within the limits of a specific symbol even if a confusion between Christianity and Magism is often present in Hafiz too. A common element—the use of wine (prohibited by Islamic law) in religious ceremonies—provides the unity between the two religions as symbols of a given function. And the use of wine, together with unbelief, introduces still another fundamental element—that of *malâmat*—into this cycle of images. In Chapter IV we mentioned the specific tendency of Islamic mysticism known as the Malâmatîya movement. A Malâmatî element pervades the whole of Persian traditional lyric poetry and it must always be borne in mind as one of the components of this kind of impudent praise of impiety, heresy and wine. The distant origins of this element in poetry must be looked for, as we have seen, in the condemnation of lyrical poetry itself and in the probably real revelries (linked with the easy Christian cells or convents) of the first "new poets" at the end of the Umayyad or beginning of the Abbasid period. Later this motif turned into the mystical self-disparagement and self-abjection that had its traditional model, in Persian Islamic poetry, in Shaikh San'ân whose story is told by Farîdu'd-Dîn 'Attâr (d. 1230) in his pious mystical poem "The Language of the Birds" (Mantiq at-tair). Shaikh San'ân, a pious Muslim mystic, went to the country of the Rûm and fell in love with a young Christian girl who persuaded him to drink wine. He was taken to a "convent of the magi" and surrounded by his ex-disciples who were horrified and wept over his abjection, but the fire of love (for the beautiful Christian girl) had destroyed the Water of his moral life and the "Christian maiden's braid had carried off his destiny." The Christians made him put on a *zunnâr* (belt—the mark of heresy non-Muslims wore) while he was drunk and he threw his pious shaikh's tunic into the fire. His Beloved insisted that he burn the Qur'an and adore an idol (the supreme sacrilege for a Muslim) and the shaikh finally did this. This story provides us not only with a symbol (the supreme renunciation the mystical lover must accomplish on God's way) but also with an out-and-out reflection on the practices adopted by certain mystical Muslim extremists (see above). It is chiefly in this Malâmatî element that we must look for the solution to the problem of the duality of meanings (earthly love-divine love, etc.) of Persian traditional lyric poetry. In the mad shamelessness that renounces reason (and "madness," *dîvânagî*, is another motif involved) human love and inebriation—not as such but as illogical and therefore supremely transcendental acts—can be considered a living sign of the elusive relationship of love with transcendence: a relationship that can only manifest itself as madness on a human level, and with a capsizing of values most effectively theorized by Christianity. Supreme shamelessness—the climax of the metaphysical capsizing of values—is martyrdom, ignominious condemnation (see verse 8 of Hâfiz's poem).

The reader will find the following short ghazal by 'Attâr a great help towards understanding this set of "concepts" (if they can be called such!). We also quote passages from two commentaries on it: one attempts to rechannel it to the most banal exterior orthodoxy, the other is more profound.[20]

O Muslims! I am that "ghebro" (*gabr*, pejorative for "Zoroastrian") who built the idolatrous temple and, climbing onto the roof, cried out a proclamation in this world. A proclamation of impiety (*kufr*) I have sent you, O Muslims! And I have again adorned and revealed those ancient idols. Again I have mated with the mother who begot me, for this reason they call me "ghebro," because I have fornicated with my mother. I was born of a virgin mother, this is why they call me Jesus, because I have again made this mother's milk my nourishment. For this his impiety (*gabrî*) they will burn the miserable 'Attâr [alive]; be witnesses, O heroes (*mardân*)! I myself have sacrificed myself.

At first sight these verses really seem to have been written by a madman! The first of the two commentaries we mentioned above is by a fifteenth century poet, 'Alî Hamzeh ibn 'Alî Malik ibn Hasan Tûsî Azarî, in his book *Javâhiru'l-Asrâr* ("Pearls of Mystery"), written in 840 H. and printed in Tehran (in *Ashi'atu'l-lama'ât*) in 1303 sol., pp. 348–49 (abbreviated translation).

Impiety (*gabrî*) means the darkness of creation (*zulmat-i khilqat* cf. the tradition: "in truth God created what is created in darkness"). The idolatrous temple is the desert of elementary existence (*bîyâbân-i vujûd-i 'unsurî*) composed of the four well-known elements, a place of darkness and the origin of perturbations. When the sun of the *tauhîd* (Divine Unity) "threw his light onto them" (in Arabic) brushing against the composite construction of man, what was in the dark corners appeared. Therefore the "climbing onto the roof to proclaim" is a metaphor indicating the "appearance of [reprehensible] psychic qualities" (*nafsânîya*) on partial intellect; "proclaiming impiety" signifies the confession of imperfection in the service of God. "Reviving the ancient idols" signifies "making the shadowy works among reprehensible works pass from potentiality to act." The "mother of whom I was born" is the love (*mahabbat*) through which I was produced and "turning to it through turning back" signifies "I have become a rebel." It is therefore a form of excusing oneself (*ma'zarat*) and means, also, that the origin of all things lies in the *fitrat* ("natural religion"). Like Jesus I was pure, but I have become impure through the accident ('Avâriz) of sins and the attachment to forbidden things. This is why he says "in virginity I was born from the mother,"[21] but then instead of the milk from her breast I took to wine, sinning.

The other commentary, published by the Russian orientalist Bertels in the "Acts of the Academy of Soviet Sciences"(January-March 1924, pp. 126–29) is much more profound and less far-fetched. It is in a collection of mystical treatises of the Maulavî confraternity founded by Jalâlu'd-Dîn Rûmî:

Impiety (gabrî) and idolatry signify the faith of the *muvahhid* (believer and up-holder of God's Unity) which was experimental and fulfilled, as opposed to that of the *muqallid* (imitator). The proclamation signifies wanting to make others partici-pate socially in the joy of inner revelation, showing those ancient pearls [i.e. the "idols," here wisdom realized plastically, from within, as if they were new]. As for the verses on the mother and on Jesus, the Mother is the Word of creating God (and also the Qur'an), with whom I united myself as I was united to it in the Beginning (it does not go so far as to say God-Mother, but Word of God [*kalâm'ullâh*]-Mother). Where this is concerned the Author even quotes the famous hadîth: "heaven is under the feet of the mothers . . ." The whole thing means: I have come from the world of the *amr* (creating word from which, according to the Qur'an, the soul stems) to that of the *khalq* (creation, extended and corporeal existence) and from this I have re-turned again to the former, uniting myself in love with the virginal Word of God. While adultery (*zinâ*) is punished in the corporeal world, in the psychological world (*anfus*) it is the contrary (*bi'l-'aks*: the capsizing of values); there is no retribution (*ajr*) corresponding to the corporal stoning of an adulterous person (as in canon law) for adultery with the Word of God in the corporeal world (letters and words), while there is a positive retribution for union with it in the world of the spirit. And it is a "great" retribution because (and here we enter into external play on words too) *gabrî* equals *buzurgî*, in this case "impiety" equals "greatness," etc.

We can also see in these commentaries how, from another point of view, Mazdaism and Christianity are felt to have an affinity in this tradition (though it is strange that in this overturned ecumenicity of "sacred heresy" no mention is ever made of Judaism). Besides the wine here we have the common element-image of the union between relatives-virginity (Mazdean *khvêtûdkâs*-Christian virginal birth).

Where *kufr* is concerned, the reader should also give some thought to the following interesting passages that should be meditated on. 'Attâr says:

> Here the burnt *faqîr* (poor man, mystic) has fled from *jahl* (religious ignorance), through knowledge he has reached China (cf. the well known hadîth: "seek for Knowledge, even as far a China!") and he became a *kâfir* (impious one).

This verse is commented upon by Jâmî (the great fifteenth-century Persian mystic poet) as follows:

> That is to say, the faqîr, who is burnt in the fire of Love and of the struggle against passions, fled from metaphorical *kufr*, i.e. from ignorance and reached the China of knowledge according to the well-known hadîth, and he became one of the true *kâfir*. In fact al Hallâj said:
>
> I repudiated God's religion, and for me the repudiation (*kufr*) was right, while it is impious for the Muslims.
>
> And 'Ainu'l-Quzât (d. in 1131) also says:
>
> "O *kufr*! What a pity it is that the Magi boast about you! They adore your name but are without your essence. In words and *formaliter* they have advanced into you for two hundred miles, but if they looked more carefully, [they would see that] they are entangled in an inextricable position at the start. If only an atom of your auspicious fortune would make itself manifest, neither *sajjâdeh* (Muslim prayer mats) nor *zunnâr* (belts that distinguished Zoroastrians and other non-Muslims) would be woven any more in the world."
>
> Now [Jâmî continues] the sense of *kufr* is "to conceal," and the *kufr* of common people is to conceal Truth under Vanity, while the *kufr* of the Elect is to conceal Vanity, i.e. what is not Him, under Truth. Those who have gone beyond the stages of *kufr* and *dîn* (impiety and religion), have hidden and forgotten all that is not God (*haqq*, that is, Truth) . . . This is the sense of "fleeing from *kufr* and from *jahl* and going to the China of Knowledge," thus becoming a prey to that very thing they were fleeing from. China, which is the distant Orient, metaphorically indicates the Orient of the Unity of the (divine) Essence that is the terminal point of the mystical stages (*maqâmât*), when all the veils, both of light and of darkness, have been burnt . . . where neither Faith nor Unbelief exist any more, since Distinguishing Intellect (*'aql-i mumayyiz*) has been defeated and left destitute (Mu'în, op. cit. p. 510).

But let us now return to one particular aspect of Hafiz's poem—The Superior of the Magi with his cup of oracular wine and his illuminating gaze— and let us dwell on another very important element in mystical doctrine and in traditional lyrics: *nazar*, the gaze.

Nazar, in Islamic mysticism, is opposed to the exoteric *khabar*. The first term literally means looking, therefore having an intuition about, vividly experimenting the object, while the second (literally "information," handed down from others) could be translated with cold tradition, only perceived through the intellect: mysticism as against theology. Consequently even an expression as elementary as this one is a technical term: Massignon (in *Lexique*)—comparing it to the Sanskrit *sattvâ*—translates it as "state of conscience," though it seems to me that he neglects the creative and not purely contemplative implications this term has in traditional lyric poetry. Hâfiz himself speaks of *nazar* as of a glance that alchemically changes stones and flowers into rubies: "Whoever knows the value of the breath of the wind of Yemen makes, through the grace of his glance, rubies and agates out of flowers and stones." Therefore it is a magic glance: the breath of Yemen refers to the magic kingdom of Saba connected with Solomon, and the word play between *yum* (grace, favor) and Yaman (Yemen) is another example and goes far beyond a mere pun since it culls a "mythical etymology" that is fascinating to those who know the legends and the concepts involved. In fact, the Loved One's Eye is often called "magic eye" in this kind of lyric poetry. The glance of the initiated is not only a contemplating glance, it is also a transforming glance: basically, it is the magic glance of the poet who composes in this style—where objects are transformed into others and always refer to other things in a continuous and methodical symbolism. Besides, the origin of the idea of an "active" rather than merely receptive glance was already present in the doctrine of Galen and other Greek doctors and was adopted by the oculists of the Islamic medical tradition according to whom vision is produced by rays of light emitted by the eyes.[22]

The Superior of the Magi is therefore the spiritual Master, both initiated himself and initiator: in this poem he is sometimes identified with the cup-bearer (*sâqî*) and sometimes he is distinct from him. Surrounded by "the young magi" or "the young Christians" he truly accomplishes a rite with the wine-fire. The element of fire—which the culture Hâfiz belonged to considered as central to Zoroastrianism as wine was central to Christianity—does not play any part in the passage we are examining but it is an essential one in the figure of the *pîr-i mughân* and his initiatory rite. Possibly the most complete description of a "Mazdean" rite (an imaginary rite, since it does not correspond at all to those of historic Mazdaism) in Persian lyric-mystic literature is to be found in the first verse of the lovely little poem in praise of God's Unity and of the esoteric identity of religions by Hâtif of Isfahân (eighteenth century)—a poet who was best known for this particular composition. In view of its importance we are translating it here:

Yesterday, distraught with love, inebriated with desire, dazed, I wandered every-where and finally the yearning to see you (here we again have the direct gaze as opposed to bookish tradition) turned my reins towards the convent of the Magi.

And there I saw a secret meeting (may the evil eye keep away from it) illumi-nated by the light of Truth not by the fire of Hell.

And everywhere, there, I saw that same fire shining that Moses the son of 'Imrân saw on Mount Sinai.

An old master was celebrating the fire cult and the young magi were in venera-tion around him,

they all had silver cheeks, rose-like faces, gentle tongues, subtle mouths, lutes and harps and flutes and tambourines and rebecks, candles and sweets and flowers and wine and spices.

A cup-bearer with a moonlike face, with hair fragrant with musk, a minstrel of frivolous words, of gentle harmonies, magi and sons of magis, môbad and dastûr, all with their loins belted (with zunnâr) in God's service, and, ashamed of being a Muslim, I hid in a dark corner!

When the Master asked: "Who is this man?" they answered:

"He is a distraught lover who can find no peace!"

Then he said: "Give him a cup of most pure wine, even though he is an uninvited guest!"

And the cup-bearer, adorer of fire, with hands of fire, poured burning Fire into the cup.

And when I had drunk it, I no longer possessed my mind or my wits, the Blaze burnt the Unbelief and Faith within me, and I fell, inebriated; and in that deep in-ebriation it seemed to me that a Voice (in powerful language that cannot now be described)[23]

rose from my limbs up to the pulsing vein in my neck and the artery of my heart:[24]

He is One and there is no other than He
The Only One and outside of him there is no God![25]

Therefore the wine is also fire, and in this it is similar to the alchemists' water, which is also fire (Cf. Jung, op. cit., p. 141). In fact in traditional lyric poetry the Wine is often called "water" and compared to the "Water of Life" (âb-i haivân): only it must be noted that *tout se tient* in this traditional lyric poem, nothing is left to chance and the motifs are interwoven according to a "logic of their own that does not always correspond to normal logic."

What is the origin of this mystical rite of fire and wine? Obviously—we repeat it—in its technical vagueness it has nothing to do with the real Zoroas-trian cult of fire (if anything it has more in common with Christian commun-ion, which the Muslims were possibly more familiar with than the fire cult).

But it may interest the reader to make a comparison with similar but profane references in a difficult passage by the great poet and panegyrist Khâqânî (twelfth century) who, instead, links all these Mazdean-Christian images with parts of the Beloved One's body (quoted in Mu'în, op. cit, p 462):

> When I saw that (the Friend) celebrated the sadeh like the magi (taking) Fire from the tulip (of his cheek) and the cross (sic!) from his own amber (braided lock); I saw that same fire that is Zarathustra's qibla and his festival from afar and I did not approach (it). In the Ka'ba I had celebrated the Festival ('îd) and I had tasted the water (from the well) of Zamzam (the image plays phonetically with Zamzameh, the "whisper" of the Zoroastrian cult), now, as sugar cane,[26] how could I savour the fire of his fresh (lips)?

Khâqânî was not a mystic poet (he turned to religion only towards the end of his life and the beloved mentioned here is clearly a beloved with a small "b"): the singularity of the connection between religious motifs and the Beloved can therefore only be explained as imitation (in this case, critical imitation) of a world of lyric-mystic images that appears to have preceded its decadence to a purely aesthetic formula. Khâqânî critically opposes Mazdean Fire to Islamic Earth (Ka´'ba is the house of earth) and the Mazdean-Christian wine to the Muslim "water" of the sacred well of Zamzam; his scope, it is true, is merely that of a colorful aesthetic game—but this game would be inexplicable without a pre-existing traditional symbolist pattern.

The symbolism of the Mazdean-Christian cult, for which we have Hâtif's beautiful description (quoted above), was in fact antecedent to the rise of neo-Persian literature (Massignon, *Lexique technique*, p. 89). It originated in the development of very brief and vague Qur'anic hints (LVI, 18, 25; LXXVI, 21) concerning the enthronement of the privileged Blessed Spirits in Heaven. This was also known as *yaum al-mazîd*, "the day of overabundance," and we have a full description of it by the moderate Arab (Mesopotamian) mystic al-Muhâsibî (d. 857). After the eleventh century this allegory of the *yaum al-mazîd* (which had disappeared from official theology) reappeared in a hidden form in the symbolism of the Zoroastrian-Christian monastery or convent (*dair*; see the story of Shaikh San'ân quoted above). The saints, who had come from afar, left their pilgrim's staffs at the door and were admitted to drink the wine poured into the cups by angelic *sâqîs* (cup-bearers); then, by candlelight (*sham'*), they were greeted by a mysterious Being who suddenly appeared in the form of a Youth of incomparable beauty (or also of *pîr-i mughân*) and they bowed down in front of this "Idol" that concealed the divine essence.

If it is true—as Massignon says—that this form of allegory combines the setting of the Qur'anic *yaum al-mazîd* with the image of Christian convents where pre-Islamic-Arab poets and their beduin caravaneers drank wine

(Massignon, op. cit., p. 90), we are still a long way from saying, as he does, that there is nothing new in the scenes the Persian poets described. What is new—in the first place—is the idea of combining the two symbolic motifs, evidently under the influence of the neither strictly Qur'anic nor strictly Mazdean Gnostic-neo-Platonic tendencies that penetrated into the Islamic world, together with the whole exuberant world of neo-Platonic ideas, through the ninth-and tenth-century translations, (see Chapters II-IV).

Let us now examine the wine element. According to a Persian tradition already present in Firdausî it was Jamshîd who first drank wine ("Jamshîd the Kai sat on that throne with a regal cup of wine in his hand"), and the tradition was considerably developed in later historical or pseudo-historical sources. Muhammad ibn Mahmûd Amulî, in the *Nafâ'is al-funûn fî 'arâyis al-'uyûn* (quoted in Mu'în, op. cit., p. 267), tells the story of how Jamshîd ordered that a number of plants be planted as an experiment and their juice and fruit tasted. The fruit of the vine seemed particularly pleasing to the sages entrusted with this task, but they found that the grapes disappeared very quickly "in the autumn winds," so Jamshîd ordered the juice to be put in a jar. Every day they tasted the liquid, until they realized that it had grown bitter. Jamshîd had the jar sealed, thinking it was poison, so that no-one should drink it. The king had a beautiful slave who was smitten with a terrible migraine: when every other medicine had failed the young girl, who could no longer bear the terrible pain, wanted to commit suicide with the "poison" in the sealed jar. She drank a large cup of it and started shaking and trembling. She drank a second cup and fell into a deep sleep that lasted twenty four hours. When she woke up her health was restored. Then Jamshîd organized a great feast during which he himself drank of that "poison" and offered it to those present. From that time on wine was called *shâhdârû* (regal medicine).[27] The poet Manûchihrî (who died in 1041) wrote a curious ode on the barrel, which he called "daughter of Jamshîd." It is interesting because it shows the as yet external connection between wine and Mazdaism:

> Thus read I today in an old manuscript (*daftar*): "One of Jamshîd's daughters is still alive. For seven or eight hundred years she has been prisoner in a certain place, and she still remains in her place [standing up] like a cypress in that house of Mazdeans (*gabrakân*, pejorative). She never sits down nor does she ever rest her side for a moment on a pallet, she does not take food or drink, and she speaks to no-one"

The poet goes to see this strange phenomenon and naturally finds a demijohn or barrel, with the consequences one can easily imagine (the poet marries her!). Thus, already in tenth century literature, wine was connected with Jamshîd and the (more or less well-known) ancient Mazdean tradition.

And in fact Bal'amî, a Persian historian who died in 974 and who followed in the wake of the Persian historian of the Arabs, Tabarî (d. 923), considers drinking wine a Zarathustrian rite. The oldest Persian treatise of history of religions, by the eleventh-century 'Ubaidu'llâh, says that "(the Magi) consider merriment (*shâdî kardan*) and drinking wine works of religion (*tâ'ât*)." This last passage is particularly important because it shows how already in early Persian Islamic circles revelry, merriment, and wine were connected with Zoroastrianism, whether rightly or wrongly (for wine does play a part in the probably more recent Mazdean rituals though not such a central part—see Chapter 1).[28] In the Zoroastrian legend that the Mazdean neo-Persian thirteenth-century poet of Rai, Zartusht-i Bahrâm ibn Pazhdû,[29] rewrote (keeping quite faithfully to the early sources), king Gushtâsp (Vishtâspa) is offered wine blessed (during the ceremony of *dârûn* or *drôn*) by the Prophet Zoroaster and " . . . the king tasted of the blessed Wine and grew merry, and drinking it he immediately acquired knowledge (of the mysteries). His body remained immersed in sleep like that of one inebriated, but his soul flew to adore God in the invisible world . . . where he saw wonderful things." According to the *Dênkart* (Sanjana, VII, 4, 84) Ohrmazd sent Neriôsangh to Vishtâsp to make him drink at the "source of life," then the archangel Ardvahisht offered him the juice of *hôm* in a beautiful goblet and Vishtâsp saw in a vision his future victory over Arjâsp and the Chionites, his glory in the other world, etc.

However this motif, in its broad lines, is widespread in Arab literature (which absorbed the old pre-Islamic traditions connecting wine with Christian convents). The great Arab or rather "arabophone" historian and scientist, Al-Bîrûnî (for racially speaking he was Iranian, from Khwârizm) mentions a feast of the magi of the Soghdian region in his work *Athâr al-Bâqiya* (p. 234) calling it, among other things, the feast of the *âb-khvâra*, "of drinking water" or wine (we know that water also has the meaning of wine in traditional lyric poetry). The poet Abû Nuwâs (who died around 810) and others call wine "Cosroe's daughter" and attribute it to the Iranian kings. All this shows us once again how one need not presume a direct knowledge of pre-Islamic Mazdean sources (which, besides, speak very seldom of wine) to explain the link between Mazdaism and wine in Persian literature. Wine was already connected with Mazdaism and Christianity in Arab literature before the birth of Persian literature and followed two currents: the mystical current of the wine of Heaven and the libertine one of wine drunk in convents in secret by more or less ill-famed poets. The fusion between these two elements took place in traditional Persian lyric poetry, partly under the influence of Malâmatî mystic tendencies: a school in which both elements merge "logically."

To conclude this survey on the various aspects of the *pîr-i mughân* (fire-wine) motif and have our readers understand more fully how this "heretical" motif was introduced into Persian Islamic traditional lyric poetry we will remind them that very early on, and in keeping with a characteristic Islamic ecumenical tendency, Zoroaster was assimilated to Abraham who, according to the Qur'an, was the founding prophet of ancient Monotheism. In the Qur'an itself—and this makes identification easier—Abraham is connected with the fire element. According to a legend incorporated in the Qur'an, the tyrant Nimrod (who is not named) threw Abraham into the fire but, by divine will, the fire was gentle and pleasing to him. Other elements have led to this identification, which was all to the advantage of the Mazdeans under the yoke of Islam because they could pass more easily for "people of the book," with all that this implied. It is curious for example that, in the Pahlavî prose epic *Abhyâtkâr i Zarêrân* ("Memoirs of the Zarêr"), king Vishtâsp's head secretary, who accepts Mazdaism from Zarathustra, bears the Semitic name of *Ibrâhîm* (Abraham). There were widespread genealogical legends in the Islamic world in which the Persian kings descended from Abraham, or more exactly from Isaac (cf. Mas'ûdî, quoted in Mu'în, op. cit., p. 87) and the heresiographer Shahrastânî appears to say in one passage that the kings of Persia were followers of Abraham (ibid. p. 88). In his precious dictionary the lexicographer Asadî identifies the Zand (Avesta) (under the entry *vestâ*) with the famous "pages of Abraham" mentioned in the Qur'an (LXXXVIII, 19) and Abraham and Zoroaster are placed together (though not identified one with the other, as Mu'în maintains) on various occasions in Persian literature. This symbolical bringing together of the two prophets over the Fire motif gave momentum to the penetration of the whole "magi-fire" motif in the traditional lyric poetry of Islamic Persia.

The Day Before Every Day

The cup that mirrors the cosmos was given by the Wise One (*hakîm*, that is, God) to the Superior of the Magi at the very instant of creation, at the outset, in the beginning of time, or rather before Time. The motif of the outset often recurs in Persian traditional lyric poetry. Here too we are faced with a dilemma that is, however, easier to solve than one might at first think: i.e., is the source of this representation pre-Islamic-Iranian or Islamic-Iranian? We studied this problem in Chapter III (to which we refer our readers) when we considered the Qur'anic passage on the "primeval day" and the choice of men. Here we will only repeat that the original Iranian concept, based on a free and—I believe—joyful choice, is tinged with fatalism and sadness in Hâfiz's lyrics. Playing on the words *balâ* and *balî* ("sorrow" and "yes") he maintains that the pact of *a-last* is indissolubly linked with sorrow and is a fate from which men cannot free themselves (T 24). The poet's union with the sorrow for his Beloved is a union that has lasted ever since the pretemporal pact (*'ahd-i qadîm*) (T 14). Precisely because we blindly declared ourselves his servants, we do not know what God ascribed to us on that day of *azal* (pretemporal eternity, therefore it is useless to trust too much to works [T 40]): God did not make me for Heaven in the *azal* (T42). But this leads also to an irrational sense of joyfulness: when God created, on that day, he evidently kneaded the clay of man with wine (T 42), and from that day on man has been predestined for love and wine (A 10, T 1, T 4, etc.: this is one of the most frequent motifs) and in fact Hâfiz was already famous as a drinker (*paimâneh-kash*) on the primeval day (T 8, T 25). At this point the play of words "cup" (*paimâneh*) pact (*paimân*) comes in again: the pact is sealed with a round of wine drinking (T 34). And this motif is also linked with the mystical legend (already present in Arabic texts) according to which, in the beginning, divine Love, the sâqî (cup-bearer) of God-the Beloved Object, poured out wine for God-the Lover.[30] The magi's rite described in the preceding section is thus transferred to the day before every day.

What is remarkable and, once again, profoundly non-Islamic (though also non-Mazdean) is how little attention is given to an eschatological vision: in this motif—which was born, as we have seen, in connection with the events of future salvation—not only is there almost no trace of eschatological lyrical emotion but future events (the mysteries of death, judgement, hell and heaven) play a very minor role in traditional lyrics in general . What fascinates the poets is the return, and what is very ancient and primeval. Thus we are led to observe, once again, how the ideological foundation of this traditional Iranian lyric poetry is neo-Platonic rather than Qur'anic or Mazdean.

The "day of *alast*" or primeval day (*azal*) motif is often expressed, as we noted a few pages back, with the cypher "yesterday" (*dûsh*). Lyrically significant events are transposed into an absolute yesterday: "yesterday the heart of the Candle, because of the drowned burning of my tears of love, shone as brightly as a moth" (T 46), "yesterday in the garden of Iram (a mythical place in Yemen: here we have a mythical place linked with mythical time) the hyacinth scented tress of the Beloved came loose in the Dawn zephyrs" (T 58), etc.

All these concepts are linked with the idea of a pre-existence of the soul that is also expressed, with intense lyricism, in the beautiful ghazal by Jalâlu'ddîn Rûmî we quoted earlier.

The origin of this kind of concept—which is already reflected in certain Christian-oriented and neo-Platonic-oriented hadîth attributed to the Prophet ("I was prophet when Abraham was still between Water and Clay" i.e., not yet born, or: "the first thing created by God was my soul")—is too evidently neo-Platonic for us to insist on the fact, even though Nallino (Op. Compl. II, p. 214) holds that the diffusion of neo-Platonism strengthened a theory that was present in Islam even before Sufism itself spread. But this does not alter the fact that the idea may stem from neo-Platonic Gnosis in the Qur'an too (from which these ancient theological speculations mentioned by Nallino are derived).[31]

Religion in Iran

The Two Magicians: Sâmirî and Moses

This motif is clearly non-Iranian in origin and evidently derived—even if its undertones are more mystical—from the Qur'an and, possibly even further, from Jewish Haggadic traditions. Sâmirî (for the etymology see the *Encyclopaedia of Islam*) was in a way the Simon Magus of Islam. A rather obscure passage in the Qur'an presents him as the antagonist of Moses, he who invited the Jews to adore the Golden Calf. But the Qur'anic calf is a calf that "lows" by magic, consequently Sâmirî is in the first place the magician opposed to the Prophet (see Kor., XX, 85 and foll.). Islamic mystical tradition has very subtle passages on the problem (which might appear ridiculous to a modern rationalist) of the true magic (of Saints and Prophets) as opposed to false magic. Since the episode of Moses and Pharaoh (the struggle of superior magic, the magic of the "white hand" of leprosy and the "serpent-rod," against the inferior magic of Pharaoh's magicians) is the most typical example of the contrast between the two kinds of magic, it has become one of the favorite illustrations of this problem. In his *Masnavî* (III, 1193 and foll.), Jalâlu' d-Dîn Rûmî tells the story of how Pharaoh invited the sons of a magician, who were themselves magicians, to combat Moses with their arts. They called up the spirit of their own father (through the well-known rite of sleeping on his tomb) and asked him to indicate a test by which they could distinguish whether Moses' magic was plain magic or something more. Their father advised them to try to steal the Rod from him while he slept. If they defeated the magician while he slept this would mean that he was simply a magician. If, he was wakeful even when asleep, it would be a sign that not he but a superior power, God, was acting through him. The divine "exteriority" and transcendence of the ever watchful "source" of his magic becomes a guarantee of eternal watchfulness and proves that he is a Prophet. The test, naturally, turns out in favor of Moses because, though his superficial sleeping "I" is unaware of what is happening, his transcendent and ever-watchful I (which is God) changes the rod into a terrible dragon and routs the young magicians.

Therefore, in traditional lyric poetry, the Moses motif is almost always linked with the motif of the two principal instruments of his "divine magic": the "white hand" (*yad-i baizâ*) and the "rod." The "white hand" is always mentioned in Arabic—the sacred Qur'anic language—and is one of the typical stock images in this lyric poetry that partly substitute for our mythological images, just as the great posters in the mosques (on which sacred Arabic names and words are written) replace our figurative icons. The magic of Sâmirî, who was also the prototype of alchemists, is assimilated here to the magic of wakeful reason that makes us feel very far away from a hypothetical God (see the preceding verse) while in fact he is in the very depths of our being. But this magic found in wakeful reason is destined to fail just as the Egyptian magicians and their leader Sâmirî failed in the face of the White Hand and the rod of the Prophet (even while he was asleep).

Hallâj's Gallows

Earlier on we saw how the capsizing of values was a characteristic motif of traditional mystic lyric poetry and how the madness of the Malâmatîs easily became the madness of the scaffold, a predilection for being killed. For a "saint," to die an ignominious death was the supreme act in his career of inebriated minstrel of God: the Malâmatî saint Shâh Meshreb (whom we have already studied and whose legend was famous in Islamic central Asia) ended on the scaffold.

Before studying this motif further we should consider its value: here the value of dying voluntarily, of accepting the scaffold, is not the "redemption" or expiation of more or less hypothetical sins in the Christian sense but is felt primarily as "supreme ignominy" and therefore, in the metaphysical capsizing of values, as supreme glory and joy. The fact that Christians gloried over their prophet having died ignominiously always remained an incomprehensible mystery not only for orthodox Muslims (the Qur'an itself, IV, 157–8, refused to admit the idea that the true Christ died on the cross and accepted the Docetist doctrine) but for Mazdeans too. The controversial Pahlavî treatise we mentioned in the first chapter, the Shkand Gumânîk Vichâr, states with surprise: "and there are even people who say that the Messiah is the Supreme Being. Now this is very strange . . . that he left the royal throne, the sky and the earth and the celestial spheres . . . that he fell . . . in an impure and narrow place and finally gave his body to the scourge and execution on the tree (or gallows, *dâr*) . . ." and, a little further on: "As for those who say that death and execution on the gallows (*dâr*) were accepted by him like a game in order to show humanity the resurrection (as if he could only prove his resurrection to humanity through this shameful demeanor)[32] this implies that his omnipotence is not effective." Firdausî clearly interprets these Mazdean ideas when, for example, he has king Khusrau write a letter to the Byzantine Qaisar who had asked him to return the true cross contained in the Persian royal treasure, he mocks at the Christians' interest in a putrid piece of wood on which the Son of God was reputed to have died, and sings the praises of the unqualified "ancient religion," the religion of Hûshang (the *pôryôt Kêshîh* of the Pahlavî texts, see Chapter I).

Thus both the Mazdeans and the Muslims consider dying on the scaffold (*dâr*) ignominious (*rusvâ'î*): the opposite idea of death on the scaffold as the crowning of the career of a Malâmatî saint can only have penetrated into Iran through Christianity: dâr, tree, is the same term the Mazdean and Manichaean texts give to Christ's cross and we know, through Massignon, how al-Hallâj, the mystical tenth-century martyr, was drawn to Jesus and his ignominious death. But since Qur'anic orthodoxy does not admit that Jesus effectively died on the cross, Hallâj substitutes him in traditional Persian lyric poetry with the representation of mystical martyrdom (Christ, too, did in fact become a motif of this lyric poetry but more in the sense of a healer and restorer of life to the dead). This mystical martyrdom accepts itself as right and just, and fully recognizes the executioners' reasons: we have already seen how Hallâj, drained of his life blood, feverishly prays on the scaffold for his executioners. Hallâj's only fault was that he revealed what was hidden with his over-emotional cry of *anâ'l-haqq*, "I am God." Mîrzâ Bîdil, a late Persian poet from India, thus poetically explains the great Saint's end:[33] the substance (*gauhar*), i.e., the Sacred Wine that was in Hallâj (see above), seeing the original and primeval Cup in which it had been contained (the Absolute, God himself), did not remember that it had been decanted into another smaller and more fragile vessel (the body of the historical Hallâj) and therefore emitted the fatal cry *anâ'l-haqq* that caused the explosion of that cup.

This however is not the motif of death-redemption: in Persian Islam this motif is connected with another character whom we will be discussing shortly (cf. Chapter VII), i.e., Husain, and his death in the Karbalâ plain. Here we are in the heart of Malâmatism: the death in question is ignominious and therefore welcome. The ignominious gallows "raises its head" (again a play on words within the play of images), i.e., it is proud of, it boasts of its martyr.

Jesus the Healer

The Qur'anic Christology that Hâfiz and all the traditional lyric poets were well acquainted with is largely based on "apocryphal" and Gnostically-oriented (especially Docetist) sources. Christ was famous in Islamic tradition mainly as the doer of astounding miracles and the restorer of life to the dead; with his breath he turned clay birds into real, living, birds. Traditional lyric poetry developed the Jesus motif ('Îsâ, Masîh) with particular reference to his vivifying breath and almost totally ignored (for the reasons we have mentioned) his death-martyrdom. The spring air is often compared to Jesus's breath because it raises flowers up from their winter lethargy. Breath is the spirit: in the Islamic tradition Jesus is also called Rûhu'llâh, spirit of God, and both in the Qur'an and in mystical lyrics his virginal birth is declared. According to Islamic mysticism he is the perfect Saint—a kind of Hallâj before the letter—to be imitated. The grace of the spirit that breathed within Mary can make a new Jesus of every mystic who is well along the Way.

The Braid of the Beloved

Few symbolic images recur as frequently as this one in traditional lyric poetry. The most common mystical explanation of *zulf*—the long lock of hair that comes down from the temples in a curl or braid[34]—is that the braid symbolizes the "plurality of the phenomenal world that veils the face of God's unity." This general definition of the symbol then produces—like streams from a river—a number of lateral systems of images based, as usual, on natural connections with the form and quality of the braid. The braid is "fragrant" and needs no perfume; it is wind-blown, it scatters and is unsettled like the unsettled and perplexed state of the lover poet; its point is curved like a polo stick and it is also often compared to this object, and since the polo stick (*chaugân*) brings to mind the round ball of the game and this, in its turn, the bewildered head of the lover thrown here and there in the field (*maidân*) of love, the comparison is obvious; the braid is also black, it is darkness, it is night, as opposed to the dazzling and solar (or lunar) whiteness of the Face, which it veils and covers; a heart is tied to or hangs on each hair of the braid; it is knotted and therefore is also a net into which fall the "birds" of hearts; it is like a chain that imprisons lovers but, since mad people are chained too, we find the braid-chain combining in different ways with the idea of the "madness of love," etc. And this is an almost haphazard list of only a few of the most important images we find if we run through the pages of Hâfiz's lyrics keeping to a simple plane of bivalent symbolism while, in traditional lyrics, three, four or more images may interweave on different planes. An example: the "bird-catching net" motif brings to mind the bait-grain motif, and this becomes the mole (*khâl*) that on a symbolical plane is the Point of the Absolute Unity of God, barely veiled by the dispersed multiplicity of the braid . . .

In the verse we are considering here we have an example of the intersection of symbolic planes. The obvious sense is: the chain of the *zulf* serves to chain your heart! did you not complain a short while ago that your heart was mad? Then let the braid serve as a madman's chain for the heart. But this leads us deeper and deeper: the "black" covering of the shining Face of the Idol, the many-colored (phenomenal) covering of the Nevus of divine unity, is a protection, to avoid the heart's too immediate contact with the Beloved, a contact that might produce madness. From a conceptual point of view, this danger is well-known to anyone interested in esoteric studies.

In spite of the length of this indispensable commentary to Hâfiz's ode we are far from having exhausted our study of the innumerable symbolic motifs of traditional lyric poetry. Though we cannot attempt to cover the whole area, we should examine a few other motifs before moving on to a brief study of the instrument of their linguistic expression: i.e., the aesthetic problem of the language of religious poetry.

The Paradise Tree, the Cypress

One example of the symbolic use of the Paradisiacal Tûbâ Tree in Suhravardî's tale, "Crimson Intellect," was translated in the last chapter.

In the passage from Daqîqî included in Firdausî's "Book of the Kings" Zarathustra the Mazdean prophet is connected with a great tree, bearing the fruit of wisdom. "When some time had passed after this, a Tree appeared on earth; from Gushtâsp's arcades to the castle, a Tree with copious roots and many branches. Each of its leaves was wise Advice, each of its fruits Wisdom. How can he who has tasted of these fruits die?" The important religious text *Dabistân-i Mazâhib* ("School of Religions," written in India, in Persian, in the seventeenth century) mentions a Parsî tradition according to which God created the holy spirit of Zarathustra connected (*muta'alliq*) with a tree. The tree is the first Intelligence (therefore Bahman) and all contingent things (*mumkinât*) are its fruits. The motif of the cosmic tree is very ancient and is the common patrimony of many Indo-European peoples: in the Mazdean apocalyptic text *Bahman-Yasht* the world itself is assimilated to a tree; Persian miniatures sometimes present the curious *Wâq-wâq* tree, a Tree that grows near the Source of the Water of Life (see Part III, Chapter II) whose branches all end in animal heads. In the Iranian tradition the Tree can be the symbol of the World, of the First Angel, of the Prophet who is inspired by it. Zarathustra's connection with the tree is also present in ancient legends, documented by the Ghaznavid historian Baihaqî (d. 1077), in the form of the Prophet who plants the tree that is at the same time himself. This Iranian sacred tree—well-known to amateurs of Persian miniatures and carpets—is the Cypress (*sarv*) and is often traditionally accompanied by the epithet "noble" (*âzâd*). This is how Baihaqî tells the story of Zarathustra's cypress, or rather, cypresses.[35]

Zarathustra, the Lord of the Magi, drew up two horoscopes and ordered that, in accordance with their disclosures, two cypresses should be planted. One was planted at Kâshmar, near Turshîz, the other at Faryûmad (16 parasangs north-east of Sabzavâr) . . . The Kâshmar cypress was described to the Caliph al-Mutawakkil (d. in 862) while he was building the palace of Ja'farîryeh. He wrote to the governor of Nîshâpûr ordering that the tree be cut down, placed on a cart and sent to Baghdad, while the branches were to be cut and sent separately, wrapped up in pieces of felt, so that they could be replanted artificially in Baghdad and nailed back onto the trunk, and none would be lost. All the "gabr" of the region met and offered to give the governor 50,000 gold dînârs for the imperial coffers to save the tree from being cut down . "That tree was planted over a thousand years ago" they said (this was in the year 847) "and cutting it down will bring ill-fortune upon us." But the governor refused to accept their proposal. A special saw was prepared, the books say that the circumference of the foot of this tree was twenty seven *tâziyâneh* and it is said—more than ten thousand sheep could gather in its shade. When no men or shepherds were there wild beasts rested under it and innumerable many-colored birds sought refuge in its branches. When it fell the whole earth around trembled and many buildings and *kârîz* (irrigation channels) were damaged. At the time for the evening prayer various species of birds came, so that the whole sky was covered with them, and they cried and lamented greatly in their song, so that the people were amazed. And the sheep too, which used to take refuge in its shade, began to bleat mournfully. 500,000 dirhams were needed to transport the trunk of that tree to Ja'farîyeh, while its branches were laden onto 1300 camels. When the tree was still one stage from Ja'farîyeh, that same evening, al-Mutawakkil was killed by his slaves: and so he did not even see the Sacred Tree. And, in one of his odes, the poet 'Alî ibn al-Jahm sang: "Death descends, while the Cypress travels in the night." The event took place on the night of Wednesday 3 Shawwâl 232 A.H. (May 847 a.d.).[36] The same fate overtook the others who destroyed the Sacred Tree."

Bayhaqî says of the cypress of Faryumad that the amîr sipahsâlâr Yanaltakîn ibn Khvârizmshâh burnt it in 537 H (1142-3), but nothing happened because the tree was killed by the element adored by the person who planted it, i.e., by Fire. And our author adds, " if it had been cut down, strange things might have occurred." The reader should note the importance given in this passage to the tree's protective shade (this is a common metaphor in Persian) and also to the possibly accidental connection between the cypress and death in the beautiful Arabic poem by 'Alî ibn al-Jahm. Daqîqî has Zarathustra say of the Kâshmar cypress he planted: "Believe in, place your trust in, the shadow of this cypress!" And he insists on the Cypress as one of the fundamental elements (sic) of the Zoroastrian creed.

> Call (the Cypress) heavenly, if you do not know: why do you call it the cypress of Kâshmar?
> Why do you not call it shoot of Paradise? For who planted a tree like the cypress of Kâshmar in the world?

The Mazdean archangels (the Amesha Spenta) are like tall, slim cypresses, according to a Pârsî tradition registered in the short Mazdean neo-Persian poem we mentioned a number a times in connection with Zarathustra's legend (Zartusht-nâmeh). Therefore, the Kâshmar cypress is a Tree of Paradise as well as prophetic-shamanic tree.[37] In this sense the motif goes back to the Qur'anic one of Tûbâ and Sidrat al-Muntahâ (though through Christian-Jewish influences it can be traced to the famous Mesopotamian tree of Paradise). In traditional lyrics all three sacred trees symbolize the upright and noble stature of the Beloved. In Hâfiz (B4) the Tûbâ tree itself takes refuge in the shadow of the stature of the Friend: "you keep the Tûbâ (the poet tells the religious bigot) I will keep the slim stature of the Friend" (T3), etc. As for the cypress motif–the "Free Cypress,"[38] "the cypress which moves (*sarve ravân*, walking cypress)—it is one of the most common in classical lyrics. It most frequently symbolizes the stature (qâmat) of the Beloved but, even quoting only Hâfiz, we find it fulfilling other significant symbolic functions. Thus, in T4 it is united to running waters (a typical motif of the earliest Mesopotamian world in which the Tree is also represented iconographically together with the Water of Life); in T14 its shadow (like Jesus' vivifying breath) across the Poet's form (*ghâlib*) is like the fragrance of the Spirit (*'atr-i rûh*) on putrefied bones (summoning them back to new life); in T31 it is also the symbol of proud spirit and rebelion (*sarkashî*). The Zoroastrian cypress of Kâshmar is used in this sense by Mas'ûd-i Sa'd Salmân (d. in 1131), for example: "in his face like that of hûrî he is portrait of Mani; in his Turk's stature he is like the Kâshmar cypress"; and by Amîr-i Mu'izzî (d. in 1147): " Their slim stature is like the cypress of Kâshmar, their wonderful face is like the portrait of Kâshmar," etc.

To sum up, two currents seem to flow into the traditional lyric "Tree" motif: the ancient Mesopotamian motif of the tree of Paradise (through Christianity, Judaism, and the Korean; cfr. Kor. XXVIII, 30, XIV, 29, XXXVI, 80, etc.) i.e., of the "tree next to the water of life," and the Shamanic-Prophetic motif of the tree planted by the prophet and symbol of Supreme Man, through the Zoroastrian legend of the cypress of Kâshmar.

k) The Bird-Soul. The Falcon. The Phoenix. Hâfiz writes (T13) that the true seat of the Falcon-Soul of man is in the heavenly tree of Sidratu 'l muntahâ ("the lotus of the end"). The image of man and his soul as a bird caught in the nets of the world from which he must escape and return to his nest in the primeval and celestial Tree is very frequent (we have seen an important Avicennian example of this in the preceding chapter).

The motif is too vast to attempt even an outline of its comparative phenomenology. We will only mention the fact that the bird-soul (often a falcon, a royal falcon, *shâhbâz*) is matched by the inaccessible bird which is the symbol of God, the phoenix (*'Anqâ*), or the Sîmurgh (Avestic sa_na-meregha, Pahl. s_n-murv). Hâfiz explicitly identifies the bird with the dil (heart, thought, intuition, soul), and it is frequently associated with the net or cage or the world and with the grain (*dâneh*), the bait in the net (the reader should remember that in Muslim tradition Adam lost the Garden of Eden because of a grain and not of an Apple).

Setting aside any more profound attributions, the link between "bird" and "heart" (or "liver", the seat of the sentiments) may even have stemmed from images which were already quite frequent in pre-Islamic classical Arab lyrics. To describe the passion of love, the poet often says that the violence of his palpitations makes him feel as if a bird were struggling within his liver (or heart). And in the Iranian tradition, the fravashi (see Chapter 1) are often imagined in the form of birds.

Jalâlu' d-Dîn Rûmî presents rather more original images: the soul is the falcon of the falconer who is returning joyously, to the sound of the tabl-i bâz ("falconer's drum"), on the arm of the Sultan hunter.[39] In a dialogue with his heart (ibid. XXXIV) the poet says: "Oh bird, speak the language of birds: I know how to decipher its secret message." Bird language, according to the legend, it the esoteric language that Solomon knew, and we will see later how some mystical circles resolved the problem of sacral language "practically."

As for the mysterious Sîmurgh, the Iranian phoenix, it is connected in the Avesta and in the Pahlavi texts (in an image which may originally have been Mesopotamian) with the tree of life that grows in the waters of Lake Vourukasha (Varkash). The Menoke Khrat (chap. LXII) says that its nest is "on the medicinal tree" with many seeds. When it alights on its branches it breaks them and spreads the seeds. It is therefore a health-bearing bird and–as the Firdausîan epic tradition specifies–the protector of Heroes (in this case Zâl and Rustam). There are also traces of a bad and terrifying Sîmurgh by the side of the good Sîmurgh.[40]

Rûmî also gives us the singular and relatively rare vision (in the figurative world of traditional Persian metaphors) of the bird-soul as a duck fluttering by the side of the primeval waters (Nicholson, IX, v. 10): "Men, like ducks (murghâbî) were born of the sea of life; how can a bird who arose from that water stop here?" We will conclude with two interesting variations on the bird motif. They are worth mentioning both for their rarity in the world of traditional images and because they introduce the mythical concept of the cosmic egg (which was probably originally Indian).[41] One is in a ghazal by Rûmî (Nicholson, op. cit. note to p. 221):

This world (zamân, "time") and the other are like the egg and the baby chick inside it (potentially), obscure and mutilated, miserable and rejected. And consider kufr (unbelief) and Faith (also) as the white and the yolk of that egg and between them, the (wall) which unites and separates, the insuperable barzakh (Kor. XXV, 53).[42]

When it has kept the egg warm under its merciful wings, atheism and religion are annihilated and the bird-united emerges from it flapping its (joyful) wings!

The passage–with its idea of a God who keeps the egg of the two worlds warm–is so singularly non-Islamic that one cannot help thinking of the cycle of mythologemes conceptually closest to it–the Indian cycle–even though it is hard to prove any historical contact. The passage–with its idea that the things of the future world are rejected, humble and dirty in this world, like the potential chick in the egg–can be taken as a further, subtle figurative justification for the capsizing of values on which the malâmatîya idea is based and which we have already seen inspire the whole of traditional Persian lyrics.

The other passage, which already attracted Berthels'[43] attention in 1925, is by the poet and saint Bâbâ Kûhî of Shîrâz (who died in 1050):

Your love is like a white cock in the two worlds, and heaven became like a (large) egg whose yolk is the sun.

Berthels rightly considered this metaphor so alien to the Sufi poetical world, and the mythical image so totally outside Islam, as to make it impossible to explain it from the inside as the fruit of the poet's personal fantasy (though in fact, as we have just seen, the image is not only Bâbâ Kuhî's). However, we do not have to leave the Iranian field to find the "cock" motif: already in Zoroastrianism it is a satellite of the angel Srôsh and an enemy of the dêv, who are put to flight by its song (for ex. Bundahishn, XIX, 33). On the other hand, the egg motif appears to be typically Indian and Bâbâ Kuhî, who was a famous wandering saint and travelled greatly, may have come across it in India (cfr. Satapathabrahmana, XI, 1.6). In Sufi cosmogony the role of the Egg is filled by the "white pearl" from which the entire cosmos is born. This, at least, is what Berthels maintains. But the "egg" motif is not in fact so very rare in islamic mysticism and we can add an extremely interesting verse from Rûmî's Dîvân to the two passages we have already quoted (Nicholson, op. cit. append. p. 334).

"The only substance (gouhar, also "pearl") boiled, like an egg, and became sea, the sea frothed and the froth became earth and from its smoke rose the sky, etc." (this brings us very close to the Indian myth of the "whipping up of the Ocean"). Thus the cosmic egg motif does exist in the pre-Islamic Iranian world, even if less frequently than in the Indian world from which it may have derived.[44]

To conclude, we cannot agree with Massignon's statement (Lexicus, p. 88) that the bird motif in traditional lyric poetry derives historically from Qur'anic sources only, even though he quotes Kor. II, 260 (the birds quartered and brought back to life by Abraham, cfr. the Bible), III, 49 (the clay birds which, according to the apocryphal Gospels, Jesus moulded and then gave life to with his breath), LXVII, 19, (a general invitation to see how provident God is with the birds of the sky). If anything, the episode–which Massignon does not mention–of Solomon and the hoopoe (XXVII, 20, and foll.), his mysterious messenger to the Kingdom of Saba, carries greater mythical significance, but where the phoenix (Sîmurgh) is concerned, the Iranian name itself is enough to prove a certain continuity in the tradition, while Jewish-Christian legends (later Islamized) and, in the case of some marginal aspects (the cosmic egg), Indian material, contributed to the development of the bird motif.

(l) Bird-Nightingale. The nightingale (bulbul) certainly occupies a very special place among birds. Even people who know little about Persian literature are quite familiar, through translations, with the love between the Rose and the Nightingale and the images connected with this. However it is more difficult to trace the historico-religious origins of this certainly mystical image which superficial interpreters have tried in vain to ignore. But let us first briefly consider the general flower-nightingale theme.

The Rose (flower) is self-conscious, proud, inaccessible beauty: She often disdainfully mocks the nightingale, who is the symbol of divine istighnâ, the attribute by which God can do without everything which is not Himself; but, at the same time, as soon as she flowers, she dies. This is a twofold cause of sadness to the nightingale who bewails both her rapid passing away and her disdainful refusal of union. But a kind of mysterious relationship exists between the two: only the Dawn Bird (a frequent epithet given to the nightingale) can understand the rose's secret language. The nightingale sings in "Arabic" (the sacred language) inviting her to partake of the mystic wine. Inebriated by the rose's perfume, he fears he will suffer the angel-magician Mârût's fate (Kor. II, 102). Traditionally, dawn prayers have particular value and a special power, and so the nightingale's lament is a dawn prayer: but it is sad prayer for something inaccessible because–as the Arab Muqqadasî says in his charming little poem (translated by Garcin de Tassy)[45]: "My song is a song of sorrow and not of joy; whenever I circle over a garden I stammer the affliction which soon take the place of the gaiety which reigns there." In an Indian Muslim allegory (the tale of "the Bakhâwali Rose") the inaccessible Rose is the only remedy able to give King Zainu'l-Mulûk back his sight, and the search for it is very arduous, etc.

The affinity of all these motifs with that of the medieval "Roman de la Rose" is evident. The inaccessible flower, symbol of union, is the transcendent projection–the mystics explain–of the desire of those who love god. The Pantheist 'Irâqî (d. in 1287) speaking of God in an ode (Kullîyât, 2, 3, quoted in *Meer der Seele*, p. 483) says: "In the rose garden you contemplated Your own face with the nightingale's eyes: then the garden resounded with the nightingale's song." Ibn al-Jauzî (Talbîs, 285, quoted in *Meer der Seele*, p. 473) says of Ahmad Ghazzâlî (d. in 1126), the mystic who was famous for his dangerous *shâhidbâzî* (love for ephebi):

. . . A host of Sufis went in to him and found him alone with a beardless youth. There was a rose between them, and he looked now at the rose now at the youth. Sitting down, one of them said: maybe we have disturbed you? He answered: Yes! And all cried out in ecstacy.

The identify of God-Rose is made clear in the famous preface to Sa'dî's Gulistân, when the mystic who is travelling in the transcendant world is unable to bring back any gifts from his journey because . . .

... I had in mind that when I reached the Rose Tree I would fill my lap with them as a gift for my friends. But when I reached it the fragrance of the Rose so inebriated me that the (already full) edge of my garment slipped from my hand (ed. Forughî, p. 3).

In his pro-Iranian enthusiasm, Pizzi[46]—a fine scholar and pioneer of Iranian studies in Italy—hoped to find the source of the "Roman de la Rose" in the Persian "rose" motif but he discovered no certain proofs since he himself admitted that there is no sign of this motif in Persian pre-Islamic (and therefore in pre-Western) literature. Langlois, on the other hand, shows to what extent the famous medieval tale drew on classical origins and Gaston Paris indicates possible Greek or Byzantine prototypes for many medieval love stories whose heroes have floral names (Florio and Biancofiore, Floriante and Fioretta, etc.) Though it is hard to document, we believe that the origin of this kind of image lies in the rich leavening of late Hellenistic ideas and images, to which more oriental elements than one might believe have contributed.[47]

Conclusion

This chapter would grow inordinately long if we were to continue examining all these different motifs: biblical and Qur'anic legends, mostly derived from rabbinical, Haggadic sources; originally Babylonian astral symbolism; moralistic motifs like that of the king and the beggar,[48] linked with the concept of sacred poverty (Muhammad is reputed to have said "poverty is my pride"), and in which the bedouin warrior's stoic poverty mingles with originally Christian-mystic concepts; the concept of the world as a dilapidated and crumbling house; that of the seven vales of the mystical journey; even Greek geometric motifs (the compass and the circle, etc.); the concept of the sacred painter connected with the founder of Manichaeism; that of the moth that burns itself in the flame and the consequent rich variations on the originally Zoroastrian fire motif filtered through other Gnostic concepts; the ancient Mesopotamian wide-ranging motif of the "Water of Life," etc.

I believe that the direct Mazdean pre-Islamic influence Mu'în was so eager to trace in his valuable and much-quoted book on the influence of Mazdaism on Persian literature is more apparent than real, and I do not think that he succeeded in proving his theory in spite of the abundance of extremely useful material he collected.

The problem ought probably to be resolved as follows: on the one hand there are, as we saw, purely verbal Mazdean themes for which we can easily find historic traces (Firdausî, the epic legends, the more or less clear information we have on the Zoroastrian cult, etc.), on the other there are conceptual elements and Gnostic and neo-Platonic *contents* that are not difficult to trace historically in the Islamic world through the great Hermetic and Pythagorean and, later, the neo-Platonic input (via the translations into Arabic of the eighth through tenth centuries, the "Treatises" of the Brothers of Purity, etc., which we studied in the preceding chapters). In some cases the two strains have combined and the Gnostic, Manichaean, and neo-Platonic elements have absorbed a Mazdean terminology that produces the optical illusion of a direct derivation from Mazdaism of Islamic Iranian literature. Besides, this whole area is deeply imbued with the metaphysics of light, which links together ideas with different origins and is like the connective tissue of all this intensely optic, visual, art. This metaphysical trend is beautifully expressed by the great Ismaili poet Nâsir-i Khusrau in a passage in which the struggle between the two worlds—the shining sky and the shadowy earth—is presented in images that recall the ancient past but at the same time offer a new synthesis and deeply felt poetic elegance. It is a fitting end to this section:[49]

Look at the branch of the tree, bent over like the back of *dâl*, look at the withered leaf, like a worn out face!

The sorrowful cloud has come and with its damp breath has made everything wet—the gardens and also deserted ruins.

Under the dark cloud the sun's disk: it is like opaque dust on an ancient golden vase!

It is as if the autumn wind had covered the face of the sky with garments, garments of black clouds,

the meridian sun was hurrying towards the low shores to clean the black dust from its face.

Once the Greek sovereign has been defeated the fierce Ethiopian prince will take his revenge on us

(and this is maybe why such an army of stars gathers each night in the sky).

Last evening, in meditation, my eye was unable to perceive what cruel fate wished of me:

Black the night, dark the sky, I an ant; dust and earth spinning within a black box of pitch!

And when half the night was over I exclaimed:

Has omnipresent Time opened its black jaw?

In the sky (by now the blackest of bodies) only Venus's star laughed, a shining nevus of certitude on the black face of doubt;

then little by little the light of the Milky Way appeared again, like white milk spilt on a blue table;

and then the Pleiades, like the last traces of light on Ahriman's nape, after Gabriel's powerful hold.

The army of the sky was donning its armour, while the soldiers of the earth, in despair, were donning shrouds of pitch . . .

Linguistic Appendix

The Problem of Religious Language

Anyone who has read the preceding pages will understand that all Persian lyrical poetry was written in a basically cyphered or, at least, a deliberately difficult language. The problem of "difficult sacred language" leads immediately to that of religious poetry. And we will see that it is a far more universal problem than it appears at first if we consider the Latin of the Catholic world on the one hand and the curious special initiatory languages of certain primitive sects on the other.[51]

The sacred language of Islam is the classical Arabic of the Qur'an (which was already a "difficult" language and not a natural Quraishi dialect at the time of the revelation of the sacred text). Later, with the affirmation of individual Arabic dialects and non-Arabic Muslim languages, such as, Persian, it became even more sacred. Some orthodox believers consider Arabic the "language of Heaven," but in mystical or esoteric circles the idea of a third more sacred and mysterious language, possessing almost magical powers, was always very popular and led to the idea that the knowledge of God's Most Great Name (*ism-i a'zam*), made miraculous things possible. The "language of birds" that—according to the legend—Solomon understood, is also connected with this mysterious language: "O bird," Rûmî says, "speak the language of birds; I can understand its secret cypher (*ramz*)."

The language of inanimate things—the *zabân-i hâl*— presents a rather different aspect and is worth mentioning, if only because the concept and motif often recurs in traditional lyrics. In the introduction to the *Musîbat-nâmeh* (quoted in Ritter, *Meer der Seele*, p. 21) 'Attâr says:

> When the Wanderer speaks with the Angel, when he listens to answers from earth and sky, when he visits the Throne and the Stool or asks questions of both, when he asks the Prophets to teach him and has every atom tell him tales, all this occurs through the *zabân-i hâl*, not through the *zabân-i qâl*. In the *zabân-i qâl* all would be falsehood, while it is truth in the *zabân-i hâl*.

Zabân-i hâl literally means "language of condition," of the given situation. It is everything any object can say through its form or situation among other objects, without need of sound (*qâl*).[52] Therefore it is far from being a natural language: the *zabân-i hâl* of a stone may say one thing (for example humility) or the contrary (hardness), according to the particular series of circumstances in which it is presented. For we must always remember that nature as fixed organic data is contrary to Islam. In the *zabân-i hâl* the rose may say that everything passes but on another occasion it may utter proud spurning words against the nightingale. The dog Bâyazîd meets on the road says that he was born a dog and Bâyazîd a saint only by God's arbitrary and fortuitous will, and so forth. Consequently, these are not manifestations of esoteric language but of a momentary moral allegory that is not necessarily linked with allegorical types.

The idea of a God-given language is connected with the concept on which the Qur'an is based, i.e., the concept of God's free creativity. In the Qur'an God is an artistic, freely creating, creator rather than a mathematician who obeys given laws; an artist whose creative plan does not involve essential things but only ingredients with which to attain constantly new forms of creation, constantly greater artistic products. Seen in this light the "emulation of God" (*imitatio Dei*) proposed by many mystics as man's supreme scope ("take possession of God's qualities," they say) cannot include any natural, psycho-physiological elements. "What do I care about nature" the ancient Arab mystic Râbi'a exclaimed, "when I have the creator of nature in my heart?" (quoted in 'Attâr, *Tazkira*, p. 68). Where the problem of the origin of language is concerned, the logical consequence of all this is that Muslims, in the classic dispute over whether language is natural (*physei*) or artificial (*thesei*), choose a middle way, i.e., they say that, yes, language is *thesei*, invented by someone, but that someone is God and not man. According to the Qur'an however God taught language to Adam, the first man in the deeper sense of the "first prophet." (Kor. II, 31). This, combined with the idea of successive revelations, led to the concept (clearly stated in the texts)[53] that each prophet, inspired by God, teaches humanity a new language, the last of which, from an orthodox point of view, ought to be the Muhammadan Arabic of the Qur'an. But once the door has been opened it is not so easy to close it again and consequently the more extremist Shi'ite tendencies (and in a different sense mysticism too) see nothing strange in the fact that he who is God's manifestation should teach an esoteric language: 'Alî, for example, is said to have written books in mysterious languages.

A curious manuscript preserved in the Bibliothèque Nationale in Paris proves that these are not simply theoretical lucubrations.[54] It contains a dictionary with grammatical indications in an invented language that developed in unidentified mystical circles (probably Hurûfî and certainly Persian or Turkish) around the fifteenth through seventeenth centuries. A group of mystics apparently also wrote poetry in this extremely ingenious language[55] called *Bâla-i-balan* ("the language of the vivifier"), but these singular productions—the logical exasperation of the cypher language in which some of the mystic lyrics we already know were written—have unfortunately been lost. This totally invented language is also an interesting solution to the problem of poetic Hermeticism. To start with we have to abandon certain over-familiar western concepts and place ourselves in a different conceptual world. For classic Muslims, poetry, as we mentioned, has never been definable as a pure or immediate expression of

291

sentiments. One of the most common metaphors the Persian writers use to express a poet's work is that of "adorning the bride of meaning with the sparkling veils of speech." Their art consists in allusions, double-meanings, deciphering and, in a way, it needs "translating" for the non-initiated even when expressed in grammatically ordinary language. Basically, in this aesthetic ambiance, the invention of an artificial language with which to veil the moonface of meaning is nothing but a logical, if extreme, consequence of the idea that art is the subtle magic connection between two planes of reality. Some concepts and tendencies are more easily understood if they are driven to their most extreme forms. In this sense, this singular *bâla-i balan* language—this attempt by the mystical artist to imitate God's creative power on a linguistic plane too—is extremely interesting and ought to be studied more thoroughly than we have done so far.

Notes

1. See M. Boyce, "The Parthian 'gosan' and Iranian minstrel tradition," *JRAS*, 1957, 1-2, pp. 10 and foll. It offers important proofs in support of pre-Islamic poetry being only "oral" and "irregular."
2. Text in Spiegel, *Einleitung in die traditionellen Schriften der Parser*, II p. 137 and foll. On religious impediments to poetry see also, for the pre-Islamic period, J. C. Tavadia, *Indo-Iranian Studies*, I (Bombay, 1950), pp. 45-46.
3. We have seen this character above.
4. I read it as *muhâl* rather than *majâl*.
5. However, the idea that Satan was the first poet is probably Islamic in origin, especially because of the allusion to the "boast" and because his phrases, in the Qur'an, are rhythmic.
6. Text in Badî'u'z-Zamân Khurâsânî, *Muntakhabât-i adabîyât-i fârsî*, Tehran, p. 7.
7. On the problem of Daqîqî's religion see Schaeder's perceptive article, "War Daqîqî Zoroastrier?" in *Festschrift G. Jacob*, Leipzig, 1932, pp. 288 and foll.
8. Trans. F. Gabrieli, *Storia della letteratura araba*, Milano, 1951, p. 127.
9. Text in Hâfiz, *Dîvân*, ed. Qazvînî, Tehran, undated pp.7-8.
10. Text in Hâfiz, *Dîvân*, ed. cit., p. 16. The quotations from Hâfiz, indicated by a capital letter and an arabic number, refer to Rosenzweig-Schwannau's edition (with a German transl.) (Wien, 1858). The letter indicates the verse, the number the numerical order.
11. *Shâh-nâmeh*, ed. Beroukhîm, Tehran, IV, 1099.
12. Cf. Mu'in, op. cit., p. 274 and foll. Hâfiz too connects Solomon's seal with Jam's cup. The Salomonic legend speaks of a Cup of Solomon as well as the famous seal. According to the Qur'an too, Solomon was provided with magic powers.
13. Cf. Mu'in, op. cit., ibid.
14. Quoted by Mu'in, op. cit. p. 534.
15. Cf. Jung, *Psicologia e alchimia*, Ital. ed. Roma, 1950, p. 503 and foll.

16. For an accurate description of the phenomenon in a Persian treatise on precious stones (*tansûq-nâmeh*) quoted by Aristotle, see vol. VII of Jalâlu'd-din Rûmî's *Masnavî*, ed. Nicholson (commentary to the daftar I-II, p. 12, Cambridge 1937).

17. Quoted in Van der Leeuw, *Phénoménologie*, p. 298. On the Iranian contacts of the Canticle of the Pearl, see Widengren, "Der iranische Hintergrund der Gnosis," *ZRGG*, 4/1952, pp. 97-114 and Reitzenstein, *Das iranische Erlösungsmysterium*, Bonn, 1902, pp. 70-92; 251-268. According to Widengren (who quotes an article by Wikander, in *Svensk Theologisk Kvartal*, 17 [1941], p 232 and foll.) the Pearl was an Iranian (?) designation for the Saviour.

18. M. Eliade, *Trattato di storia delle religioni*, Torino, 1954, pp. 545 and foll.

19. The temple of Sômnâth, dedicated to a lunar divinity, the Lord of the Sôma, was destroyed by the conqueror Mahmûd of Ghazna in 1026.

20. Both are reproduced, with the text, in Mu'in, op. cit., pp. 513 and foll.

21. This is how he interprets the *bi-bikrî zâdam az mâdar* of the text which I believe should be interpreted as we translated it.

22. Cf. Salâhu'd-Dîn al-Hamavî, *Kitâb nûr al-'uyûn wa jâmi 'al-funûn*. Book II, c. I (in *Die arabischen Augenärtze*, by Hirschberg, Lippert and Mittwoch, 206 and foll.) The great Alhazen (Ibn al-Haitham) of Bassora (d. in 965) opposed this doctrine from a scientific point of view.

23. Transposed into human terms, "into Arabic," the language which was felt to be sacred, the language in which one speaks to God. In Hâfiz too (A6) Arabic was the language of the mystic nightingale who invites to [drink] wine, the difficult language of Gnosis (T35).

24. These are the veins mentioned in Kor. L, 16: "We (God) are nearer to him than the jugular vein."

25. In Arabic in the text.

26. *Nai-shakar* (sugar cane) is compared to the lip because of its sweetness, but often the comparison is simply expressed with *nei*, cane, in the sense of cane-flute (cf. Hâfiz, T20) which is therefore connected with motifs of "music," "sound."

27. According to other traditions, for example in the *Naurûz-nâmeh* attributed to 'Umar Khayyâm, the wine was found at Herât by one of Jamshîd's relatives, a man named Shemîrân, and elsewhere (Râvandî) it is connected with another Kai, Kai Qobâd. Râvandî also mentions a *Kitâbu'sh-sharâb* ("Book of Wine") which shows the existence, since ancient times, of a whole literature on wine.

28. See what we said on Daqîqî. The sense of his verses becomes clearer in view of what we are saying.

29. Ed. Rosenberg, Peterburg, 1904, pp. 58 and foll. see 1162 and foll. of the text.

30. The legend poetically expressed by 'Irâqî (d. in 1288) clearly belongs to Gnostic-neo-Platonizing circles also because of the numbering in 40.

31. On this matter see also Ritter's notes in *Meer der Seele*, p. 340.

32. *Rusvâ'î*: this is exactly the same term used in the mystical libertinism of our lyric poetry!

33. Cf. A. Bausani, "Note su Mîrzâ Bedil," *Annali dell'Ist. Sup. Un. Or.* of Naples, N.S. VI, 1954-56.

34. The explanation is codified in Shabistarî's useful little treatise in verse, *Gulshan-i Râz*, "The Rose-Garden of Mystery" (Shabistarî died in 1320, shortly before Hâfiz).

35. From *Ta'rîkh-i Baihaqî*, ed Bahmanyar, p. 281, quoted in Mu'in, op. cit., p. 340. Slightly abbreviated translation.

36. The date must be wrong because al-Mutawakkil died in 247 H.

37. Cf. Eliade, *Traité*, Italian trans., Torino, p. 318. They call him "plant the Tree" when he feels his Prophetic vocation. This is another of the many elements which could lead to an assimilation of Zarathustra's vocation with that of the central-Asiatic Shamans; see chap. I.

38. There is documentation, in ancient times too, of an *âzâd-sarv* (free cypress, noble cypress) as a proper name. Cf. Firdausî, *Shâh-nâmeh*, in Mu'in, op. cit., p. 369.

39. R. A. Nicholson, *Selected Poems from the Dîvâni Shamsi Tabrîz*, Cambridge, 1898, XVI.

40. Cf. Barnett, "Yama, Gandharva and Glaucus," *BSOS*, IV, 1926-28, p. 703 and foll.; also A. Wunsche, *Die sagen vom lebensbaum und lebenswasser*, Leipzig, 1905.

41. Cf. Eliade, *Traité*, op. cit. p. 427, where the vast area of its diffusion, which centred in India or Indonesia, is marked out.

42. On *barzakh* in other senses cf. the preceding chapter.

43. E. E. Berthels, "Kosmiceskie mify v gazeli baba kuhi," *Dokl. Ross. Ak. Nauk.*, 1925, B., p. 43 and foll.

44. Cf. Zaehner, *Zurvan*, p. 365 (*Rivâyat Pahlavî*) and p. 349 (*Zâtspram*).

45. "Allegories d'Azzeddin el-Mocaddeci," in *Allegories et recits poétiques*. Paris, 1876, pp. 25-26. The tale spread in Syria at the beginning of the thirteenth century (Richard of England's Crusade).

46. Cf. *Storia della poesia persiana*, Turin, vol. II, 1894, p. 412 and foll.

47. For the Romance world, see also W. Ross, "Rose und Nachtigall," in *Romanische Forschungen*, 1955, p. 55 and foll.

48. Already in the Arab Abu'l-Atâhiya (d. in 875); see "Trans. of the IX Congress of Orient.," vol. II, p. 114.

49. The text of the long ode of which this is only the beginning is in *Dîvân*, ed. Taqavi, p. 332 and foll.

50. Curved letter of the Arabic alphabet.

51. The problem is briefly treated in Otto, *Das Heilige*, p. 79. For the primitive initiatory languages cf. Webster, *Primitive Secret Societies*, Italian trans., Bologna 1922, pp. 56-57. The Eskimo shamans use a special "language of the spirits" for mystical songs too--a language in which the special elements are either antiquated words of the local form of speech (also present in neighbouring ones) or new descriptive compound words which bring to mind the well known kenningar of the traditional poetry of the Scaldeans. It is a good thing, the Eskimos say, that this language is incomprehensible, for men must not understand the language of the spirits. Cf. V. G. Bogoraz, "O tak nazyvaemon jazyk duhov (samanskom) u razlicngh vetrej eskimosskago plemeni," in *Izv. Ross. Ak. Nauk.*, 1919, pp. 484 and foll.

52. Another possible explanation: the language of the "Mystical State" of ecstasy.

53. Cf. P. Kraus, "Beiträge zur islamischen Ketzergeschichte," *RSO*, XIV, 1933, pp. 127 and foll.

54. Cf. Blochet, *Catal.* Paris, vol. II, 1912, pp. 246-248.

55. Cf. A. Bausani, "About a curious "mystical" language: Bâl-a i-balan," in *East and West*, Roma, IV, 4.

Bibliography

We have indicated the most important references here and there in the notes or in the text itself. In fact there are no publications in any European language which give an overall picture of the subject of this chapter. For a general survey of Persian literature we advise: E.G. Browne, *Literary History of Persia*, 4 vols. Cambridge 1951–53 (a reprint of earlier editions). It has the advantage of being both scholarly and pleasant reading, though some parts have become obsolete owing to more recent studies.

A more up-to-date and excellent study is:
Rypka, J. Dêjiny Perské a Tadzické Literatury, (History of Persian and Tajik Literature), Prague, 1956. [Translated into English as *History of Iranian Literature*, Dordrecht, 1968.]

On the world of mystical literary symbols see:
Ritter, H. *Das Meer der Seele. Mensch, Welt und Gott in den Geschichten des Farîduddîn 'Attâr*. Leiden, 1955. This is an "ocean" of information with a very abundant bibliography on the images and ideas of one particular mystical poet, but in fact to some extent it covers the entire field of poetic mysticism. Its one fault is that the vast subject is considered only from a phenomenological point of view, without any (or almost any) attempt at a historical approach. This same author has written one of the best descriptions of the "figurative language" of classical Persian poetry (devoted, it is true, to a great romance poet, but which can be applied to lyric poetry too):
Ritter, H. *Über die Bildersprache Nizâmîs*. Berlin-Leipzig, 1927.

Some specific points are dealt with in:
Inostrantzev. *Iranian Influence on Muslim Literature* (trans. G. K. Nariman), Bombay, 1918.
Daudpota, U.M. *The influence of Arabic Poetry on the Development of Persian Poetry*. Bombay, 1934.

Though I do not entirely agree with the central theory of the book (as I have already mentioned in the course of this chapter even though I have drawn freely from it) a valuable collection of material is to be found in the Persian volume:
Mu'in, Muhammad. *Mazdayasnâ va ta'sîr-e ân dar adabîyât-e fârsî*. Tehran, 1948. The reader who does not know Persian can read H. Corbin's introduction-summary in French.

Additional Bibliography

Book-length treatments of this subject in English are few. Useful general surveys of Persian literature include A.J. Arberry, *Classical Persian Literature*, New York, 1958;

George Morrison, ed. *History of Persian Literature*, Leiden, 1981, and Ehsan Yarshater, ed., *Persian Literature*, Albany, N.Y., 1988. See also Leonard Lewisohn, ed.,*The Legacy of Medieval Persian Sufism* (London, 1992) and the same editor's *Classical Persian Sufism: from its origins to Rumi* (London, 1993). Firdausî is treated in Dick Davis, *Epic and Sedition: the case of Firdausî's Shahnameh*, Fayetteville, 1992. Examination of religious motifs can be found in Annemarie Schimmel, *As through a Veil: Mystical Poetry in Islam*, New York, 1982, and in J.T.P. de Bruijn, *Of Piety and Poetry: The interaction of religion and literature in the life and works of Hakim Sana'i of Ghazna*, Leiden, 1983. Imagery, some of it with implications for Bausani's points in this chapter, is further discussed in Julie Scott Meisami, *Medieval Persian Court Poetry*, Princeton, 1987.

Part Three

The Changing God

Chapter Six

Ferment and Revival in the Sixteenth through Seventeenth Centuries

Introduction

No study of Persian religiosity would be complete without a few words on Twelver Shi'ism, a spiritual movement that, however, is not Persian in origin. On the contrary, as we shall see, it was an Arab form of religion imposed on Persia by a Turkish dynasty! It nevertheless ended up shaping the whole of modern Iranian culture. "Twelver Shi'ism" as a term is a poor half European-half Arabic neologism and they themselves prefer to be called Imamis or Ja'faris. Briefly, they are those Shi'ites who accepted the successors of Ja'far as-Sâdiq (the sixth imâm) as a series of spiritual and material leaders, or imâms, of the community until the twelfth successor of the Prophet, the mysterious Muhammad al-Mahdî, who disappeared in 874 but is still living. Until 940, through four deputies (*vakîls*) he governed the Islamic community (the theoretical community, because the Shi'ites never held political power except over very limited areas of Islamic territory and were for the most part persecuted). The period from 874 to 940 was called the period of minor "Occultation" (*ghaiba*). This was followed by the period of the major Occultation, which is still in progress and will last until the return of the hidden Imâm, the "Lord of the Age" (*sâhibu'z-zamân*) or *qâ'im* (agent of the resurrection) or Mahdi (the well directed), at "the end of the World." During this period of major concealment the power of the Twelver Shi'ite community was in the hands of an oligarchy of learned men and jurisconsults. The official doctrine of the Twelver Shi'ites split into two great currents that were frequently in bitter contrast. In matters of law the Usulis championed the extensive use of rational methods, applying them to the analysis of (textual) sources. The Akhbârîs tended, on the other hand, greatly to restrict everything that was not pure tradition and adhered to the "imitation of the dead"—i.e., blind submission to the precepts established by the various Imâms in ancient times. These principles can be summed up in the following points: (1) If God reveals himself through the prophets to guide the community of the believers in everything—religious and social—it is unthinkable that at the death of the Prophet (the living authority accepted by all Muslims) he should have permitted the whole of authority to be contained in one book, the Qur'an, whose interpretation has been the cause of so many disputes. Consequently God must have nominated explicitly—through the word of the Prophet—a successor with interpretative and teaching authority; this successor was 'Alî, his son-in-law and cousin. (2) It is equally unthinkable that God should choose fallible beings as transmitters of his authoritative and divine precepts. Prophets and Imâms are therefore gifted with infallibility and faultlessness and are free from sin and error. (3) The Shi'ite God is in a way more inaccessible than the Sunni God; to approach him, human beings need intercessors: and here we have the important "intercessional" function of the Imâms (later exaggerated by popular piety, as were all the Imami principles in the context of various influences) and especially of the martyr Imâm Husain (see Chapter VII). Shi'ism is a religion of suffering and martyrdom. (4) This links up with the greater "sacral" sense given to the person of the Imâm and the Prophet and everything that concerns them. Together with the specific Shi'ite mentality of "the unjustly persecuted" this sense contributes to their special intolerance towards those who dare to "offend" the most holy imâms, even if only by disagreeing with, and possibly giving less importance to, their supreme qualities. Some Shi'ite authors have gone as far as placing Muslim Sunnis lower than Christians and even pagans. (5) The Shi'ite cult devotes special practices and prayers to the veneration of the imâms and the Prophet's "holy family" (as we shall see, great importance was given to the cult of Fâtima, the daughter of the Prophet and wife of 'Alî). There are beautiful prayers of intercession to the imâms, special rites of pilgrimage to their tombs and, later, sacred representations to commemorate the bloody death of the Prophet's grandson, Husain (see the next chapter).

One important point seems however to have escaped many authors who have written about Imami Shi'ism and its characteristics in their attempt (as we mentioned in connection with Shi'ism in general) to trace its origin to an "Aryan" Persian reaction to "Arab" and Semitic Sunnism. I mean the fact that with the concealment of the last imâm in 874 everything returned, in practice, to the Sunni position. The Sunnis believed that at the Prophet's death his teaching powers passed on to an oligarchy of jurisconsults; the Imamis too believed that this occurred, though not at the Prophet's death but 242 years later with the disappearance of the last living "teaching authority" in the world, the imâm. The difference is that the Sunnis had only the Qur'an and a mass of traditions of uncertain authenticity at its disposal for the later elaborations of its jurisconsults, while the Twelver Shi'ites disposed of the great mass of traditions (by definition authentic) issued not only by the Prophet himself but also by the twelve imâms. We must not forget, however, that these traditions developed at a very early stage (eighth through ninth centuries of our era) and in many cases, when all is said and done, their authenticity is as uncertain as the Sunni traditions of the Prophet. Nor should we forget that Shi'ite theology developed after the Twelfth Imam's death. And so the problems are identical, the difference lying in the fact that the historical area illuminated by divine authority is rather more extended for Shi'ites than for the Sunnis. But it is incorrect to maintain that the essence of Twelver Shi'ism is its sense of the continuous presence of the teaching authority of the living imâms, the particular sacred nature of authority, etc., precisely because Shi'ism was formed in an identical situation to that of Sunnism, i.e., when these teaching authorities were no longer present and were interpreted by jurisconsults who were as "Talmudist" as those of the Sunnis. The most logically consistent form of Shi'ism is in fact Ismailism, which we studied in an earlier chapter. For the Ismailis the divine teaching authority continues to be present among men uninterruptedly and will be until the end of time. These considerations lead to still another logical consequence. Even if we admit that Shi'ism was born of a "legitimistic" tendency of the Persian spirit to see the descendants of the Prophet (who was almost identified with a sacred Iranian King) crowned with numinous aureoles, this consideration would certainly not hold for Twelver Shi'ism, which became the official Persian religion in the sixteenth century after most Persians had peacefully been Sunni for seven or eight centuries.

After these introductory considerations we must, however, note one fact: even if the origin of the juridical and theological doctrines of Twelver Shi'ism is definitely extra-Iranian, the same cannot be said of the popular piety of present-day Persian Twelver Shi'ites. And though this piety is for them inextricably confused de facto with the doctrine, historians should not fall into the same error. Besides, this popular piety seems to have an origin in common with extreme Ismaili Shi'ism rather than with Twelver Shi'ism. We will also see how, during the period of unrest under the Safavids, which preceded the proclamation of Twelver Shi'ism as the official religion of Persia, this piety took on forms that did not conform to those of an "orthodox" and juridically codified Twelver Shi'ism and seemed more typically Ismaili, extremist and even mystical. And we will also see, basically, how the Babi and Baha'i movements revived an Ismaili tendency, thus creating a new religion.

The Religion of Shâh Ismâ'îl

We have already mentioned the fact that the "Shi'itization" of Persia occurred through the Safavid Turks, by means of a mystical confraternity, and spread geographically from present-day Azerbaijan. All three facts are paradoxical if we bear in mind (a) that many people have considered Shi'ism a product of the "Iranian" spirit, (b) that in theory official Imami Shi'ism is strongly against mysticism, and (c) that, according to a brief treatise on the history of Persian religions written in 1092, the three regions with the greatest number of Shi'ite nuclei were Iraq, Mazandaran and Khurasan! Consequently Safavid "Shi'itization" had nothing to do with the Iranian spirit, with learned Shi'ite theology, or with earlier traditional Persian centers of Shi'ism.

But let us take things in order. Shaikh Ishâq Safîyu'd-Dîn was a descendant (according to his supporters) of the seventh imâm, Mûsâ al-Kâzim [this is now doubted by scholars-ed.]. He died in 1334 in his native city of Ardabîl, in present-day Azerbaijan. He was reputed to have been an extremely pious and religious man and was the leader of a confraternity (tarîqah) of dervishes that took its name ("Safavid") from his name and whose leadership passed on to his descendants. When Tamerlane invaded the area he granted the city of Ardabîl and the surrounding countryside to the Safavids. The members of the confraternity wore red hoods made with twelve pieces of fabric to bring to mind the twelve imâms and thus symbolize the Shi'ite principles they professed. This is why they were also given the Turkish name of qizil bâsh, red heads (and in some Sunni areas this term is still synonymous with Twelver Shi'ite). Safîyu'd-Dîn had Shi'ite tendencies, it is true, but not as fanatically so as his descendants. The first member of the family to be a real Shi'ite was Khvâja 'Alî and it is in his time (1392–1427) that some Turkic tribes became the faithful defenders of the Safavid family.

The Safavids were therefore originally an order of mystics who later were strongly influenced by Shi'ism. This was not a unique case for we have a striking example in the tarîqa of the Bektâshîs that developed—at the same time—in the Turkish area and carried to the extreme a tendency, common to all the dervish confraternities, to a particular veneration of 'Alî. From whence did the Shi'ite influence over the Safavid order stem? Without definitively resolving the problem, some scholars (Babinger) have presented plausible reasons for believing in a "Shi'itization" (in a more extreme Bektâshî sense rather than a Twelver sense) from the west, from the Turkish mystical and Shi'ite confraternities of Anatolia.[1] Be this as it may, the spirit of cohesion and resistance in the Safavid order was sealed with indissoluble cement: the blood of the martyrs. The Safavid leader Junaid and his son Haidar were killed in battle. Ismâ'îl, one of Haidar's younger sons, avenged them when he started his career as a conqueror, as a boy of fourteen, and seized Shirvan in the year 1500. Later, after proclaiming himself king (shâh), he added to his dominions through successful campaigns on two fronts, against the Uzbeks on the eastern Persian border and against the Ottomans on the western border. By 1510 he was already master of the greater part of the territory of present-day Iran, while his religious propagandists (and even more those of his successors) spread his religious theories throughout Persia. By the second half of the sixteenth century most of Iran had been won over to Shi'ism. Shâh Ismâ'îl died in 1524 at the age of thirty-eight and his successors consolidated the empire, creating Safavid Persia, which lasted until 1722 and in which some historians see the beginning and nucleus of the modern nation of Persia (or Iran).[2]

What was Shâh Ismâ'îl's religion? The warlike sovereign wrote some interesting poems in the Turkic Azeri dialect under the poetic pseudonym of "Khatâ'î" but the reader who expects to find expressions of "normal" Imami doctrines will have a surprise. Here are some excerpts:[3]

> My name is Shâh Ismâ'îl. I am God's mystery (*sirr*) . . .
> My mother is Fâtima, my father is 'Alî and I am also the Mystical Guide (*pîr*) of the twelve imams . . . (Min. no. 15)
> You must know that Khatâ'î is surely divine, he is Muhammadan (*Muhammad-Mustafâ'î*) . . . (Min. no. 22)
> I am the essence of God, the essence of God, the essence of God!
> Come now and contemplate Reality, O blind one lost in darkness!
> I am the Absolute Agent people speak of: I command the sun and the moon!
> My body is God's house, know it for sure, it (behoves) you to adore me, in the evening and again in the morning!
> Know for sure that, according to those who (honestly) recognize it (*ahl-i iqrâr*), Sky and Earth all belong to God: do not go astray!
> The garden of Sanctity (*vilâyat*) has produced one Fruit: How can he whose arm is too short pick it?
> If you wish to unite God to God (or: "Reality" to "Reality") lo, God has manifested himself in the stage of the (letter) M (*mîm*) (that is, Muhammad).
> He who also has relationships considers his own person: Khatâ'î has suddenly found a Treasure (Min. no. 204).

It would be hard to find a more powerful declaration of divinity. But in the same Turkic collection of lyrics there are passages in which the King speaks as if he were the most humble servant, not only of God but also of 'Alî:

> My name is Ismâ'îl son of Haidar: I am the servant of the servants of 'Alî . . .
> A monastic superior (*pîr*) I am, and also sovereign of the world.
> I am Khatâ'î, one of the least of 'Alî . . . (Gangei Edition)

Elsewhere we find expressions that indicate what the passage between the two "stages" may have been. For example:

> I am a body, but 'Alî is my soul
> The blood that runs in my veins is 'Alî . . .

Next to him I am a drop of water
My immense Sea of Oman is 'Alî! (Gangei edition)
His name is Ismâ'îl: he is consubstantial (*ham-zât*) with the Prince of Believers
('Alî) . . . (Min. no. 211).
I am Khatâ'î and my steed is sorrel, my words are sweeter than sugar;
I have the essence of Murtazâ 'Alî: I am the Faith of the Shâh (i.e., 'Alî) (Min. no. 18)
O Khatâ'î, powerful is your hand: how radically you have vanquished Yazîd! (Min.
no. 92).
I am Khatâ'î: from eternity before time I am the Mystery of Haidar (i.e., 'Alî).
He who does not recognize him as Reality ("God") is a stranger for us (Min. no.
101).

In other words the mystical and psychological transition, which has nothing
extraordinary about it because it exists elsewhere too in the history of Islamic
mysticism, is: total devotion to the Person of God ('Alî or Husain, etc.);
theopathic identification with him (temporary transference of the attributes of
one to the other); and therefore, in those moments, the abolition of Time. It is
Shâh Ismâ'îl who fights against Yazîd rather than Husain (another Person, Center
of the Divine, see the next chapter). Or even—as we can see from another of
Shâh Ismâ'îl's singular poems—every great person who manifests, in the world,
the "signs" or attributes of God (whether of power, grace, awesomeness or
gentleness) is, outside of Time, "God" himself, in as far as in his devotion to
'Alî his historical person disappears:

Today I came into the world: I am Lord and Sovereign! Know for sure that I am
Haidar's son![4]
I am Farîdûn, I am Khusrau, I am Jamshîd and I am Zahhâk.[5] I am Rustam son of
Zâl, I am Alexander!
The mystery of *anâ'l-haqq* (Hallâj's famous cry) has risen in this my heart for I am
Absolute Reality and I proffer Reality!

And yet the last verse of this same poem says humbly (once the theopathic
instant is over): "I am Khatâ'î, the sinning slave of the Shâh; on your threshold
I am the least and last of the servants." And it is strange that the Safavid sovereign chose as his pen name Khatâ'î, which means "the sinner."
From whence did the Savafid order and Shâh Ismâ'îl draw these concepts?
As we mentioned before, they apparently stem from the partly mystical and
partly extremist-Shi'ite doctrines that form the nucleus of the Hurûfî and
Bektâshî sects. The Hurûfî sect, founded by a Persian, Fazlu'llâh of Astarâbâd
(put to death as a heretic in 1393–4), possesses some singular texts in a Persian
dialect that present a whole cabalism based on the letters of the Arabic alphabet. Fazlu'llâh himself is a manifestation of God, but God's signs are present
on the face of every man in the form of mysterious letters (the eyebrows, the

304

nose etc).[6] We find an identical expression in Shâh Ismâ'îl's poetic oeuvre (*dîvân*), which says that the human face is a sacred book, a Qur'an. Elsewhere, both in the *dîvân* and in two ghazals, he applies various Qur'anic expressions to the parts of the "mystical" body of the Friend ('Alî equals God). The Hurûfîs, whose Persian texts are extremely arid, moved to the Turkish area mainly thanks to one of Fazlu'llâh's disciples. They "hurufized" the (from an orthodox point of view) already aberrant mystical confraternity of the Bektâshîs, who among other things even had a form of communion with bread, wine and cheese. The Hurûfîs produced a beautiful and passionate poetic literature that reached its peak in the Turkish poet Nesimi, who died possibly in 1417 or 1418 by the hand of the executioner. Shâh Ismâ'îl must have known the unfortunate Hurûfî poet's collection of lyrics for, like him, he was a Turk and in some ways he echoed the "emotional" tone of mystical inebriation that links both of them to the style of the popular mystical "confraternity" poets who composed their works, for practical purposes, to be sung in ceremonies of recitation (*zikr*) and therefore often spurned the "classical" image. According to the authors who wrote about him (Ishâq Efendi, for example, whom Huart quotes in *Textes Houroufîs*, p. xiii), Fazlu'llâh was an "Ismaili." This observation is a clear indication of the fusion between Sufism and Ismailism that followed the end of the active and visible Ismaili movement and left its mark on the whole historical period with which we are now dealing.

Twelver Shi'ism was thus introduced into Persia in a far more "aberrant" way than might have been thought, i.e., by a sovereign who belonged to a Sufi confraternity with strong "Ismaili" influences. After the first enthusiastic period, this confraternity accepted the more theologically precise doctrines of the true Twelver Shi'ites, which had already for some time been codified in Arabic by the learned men of this tendency. And so, little by little, under the successors of the God-King, Shâh Ismâ'îl, the Shi'ite jurisconsults (*mujtahids*) definitively imposed orthodox Twelver Shi'ism on the Persian people. But they did so without completely extinguishing the hidden smouldering of theologically extremist Shi'ism, which was inextricably intermingled with the mysticism that was yet to produce singular manifestations in Persian religious history. The Safavid political and religious phenomenon is admirably summarized in these words by one of the greatest experts on this historical period, Minorsky (cf. "Iran, Opposition, Martyrdom, Revolt," extr. from *Unity and Variety in Muslim Civilization*, pp. 195 and foll.):

The state founded by Ismâ'îl was a theocracy, nearly in the sense which this term bears in regard to Tibet and the Dalai Lama. The state was supported by a religion and by the assistance of the unique party of the Shâhî-sevans ("those who love the shah") . . . One sometimes hears voices expressing regret at the breach in the Islamic community which resulted from the actions of Shâh Ismâ'îl. But from the point of view of the Persian nation one could maintain the thesis that it is precisely this isolation which saved the Persians . . . The new religion with its ecstatic character helped to concentrate the central power, and, on the other hand, the new doctrine, which in itself had no connection with the Persian *nationality*, provided the platform upon which the Persian people could maintain its rights against absorption into an abstract Islam and, in practice, into the Turkish ocean.

We have seen that the chief followers of the Safavids, though immunized by their beliefs against the seductions of their kindred neighbors, were Turkomans. Now, states based on nomadic and tribal organizations lack solidity, and Shâh Ismâ'îl's successor already ran into difficulties with his Shâhî-sevans. Little by little the shahs found themselves obliged to disperse certain recalcitrant tribes, and a hundred years after the formation of the Safavid state Shâh 'Abbâs modernized his armed forces. For the Turkish tribes he substituted troops of fresh Caucasian converts similar to the Ottoman Janissaries. The old ecstatic and anthropomorphist religion gave place to the official Shî'ism under the influence of theologians from Syria . . . and Bahrain, and finally the new pillar of the state religion, Mîrzâ Bâqir Majlisî, set on foot a persecutions of the extremist Shâhî-sevan "Sûfîs."

The official State doctrine reflected in Majlisî's monumental works does not really concern us here since it is not specifically Iranian, besides being almost untranslatable for the modern reader because of the vast knowledge of "common" Islamic law and theology it implies. But we will stop to look at certain aspects of popular Safavid religious literature that, in some ways, are more "Persian" and original.

Popular Legends about 'Alî in the Safavid Period: The 'Alî-Ilâhîs

We will give further examples of popular Safavid religious poetry on the "martyrs" in a later chapter. To keep to our subject and not get lost in a maze of names that would mean nothing to the reader, we will limit ourselves to the analysis of an interesting short poem on 'Alî by Husain ibn Hasan Fârigh, a poet from Gilan (Fârigh-i Gîlâni), written in the year 1000 of the Hegira (1591–2) at the time of the conquest of Gilan by Shâh Abbâs, the greatest sovereign of the Safavid dynasty and its "systematizer." This poem is also interesting because it exists in some European libraries with accessible catalogues[7] and was printed in Tehran in childlike, undated lithographs, but nevertheless seems to have been ignored by histories of Persian literature, including Browne's important history and Rypka's excellent volume. In addition, the author's sincere and artless faith gives his verses a fresh artistic expressivity. Since the author came from the Gilan area (apparently the place of origin of the Safavids) where Shi'ite revolts were recurrent over a period of time, he may even have been able to draw on older local Shi'ite traditions. Indeed, he often quotes the names of his local sources. The poem, which is in rhyming couplets (*masnavî*), tells a number of stories on 'Alî's life, alternating them with invocations and prayers to the one who, as we shall see, he considered a real demigod (in contrast to the official doctrine of Twelver Shi'ism).

The poem opens with the usual introduction and invocation, which presents some interesting Hurûfî elements. God's name, in which every work is begun, is the exact mirror of his essence, "His name is the Treasure and the world is the Talisman: only the Name opens the Talisman." Order was given to the world in virtue of two "names," those of Muhammad and 'Alî. One is the "sky of the religious law," the other the "sun of mystical certitude." They are really two equal and distinct persons: "They are a divine unity embarked on two ships," a single flash of the manifestation of the divine essence, a single lamp in two niches. The sight of those who see them as "double" is imperfect, like that of drunkards. Next there is praise for Shâh 'Abbâs and information on the year in which the book was written, i.e., the year in which 'Abbâs conquered the Gilan area. After a prayer offered directly to 'Alî (for Christians these prayers have a familiar tone but they would horrify a Sunni Muslim) the miraculous episodes of the life of the Prince of Believers are presented. Here is a summary of them:

The Child 'Alî Fights a Terrible Dragon

When he was four months old, 'Alî was attacked in his crib by a dragon who was "four hundred *gaz* long and had two horns, each of which was like the branch of a plane tree, and two eyes like two flaming torches; and its head was like a mountain and its mouth an immense cavern, etc." The baby 'Alî easily "tore him in two" without even jolting the crib and without spilling one drop of the dragon's blood. His relatives and other people, including the Prophet himself (who plays the part of the *rois fainéants* of French novels throughout the book) rush in. The Prophet is surprised and invokes blessings on 'Alî. Still in his cradle, 'Alî saves the life of a young playmate who has fallen into a well in a very singular manner, for he succeeds in miraculously stretching his arm to a distance of forty steps. "O 'Alî," the author prays, commenting the event, "do not leave me at the bottom of the well of Sorrow! Take my hand and draw me out of the abyss of hell! O 'Alî, I am the unfortunate Fârigh, the impetuous torrent of sins has torn every garment and all glory off me. Yes, even if my sins are endless, one drop of the sea of your forgiveness is enough for me!" (Note the "your": it is 'Alî who forgives sins directly and not God, even if through 'Alî's intercession, as theology would require).

This miraculous story—the author tells us—was told him by a friend of his from Rudbar (near Astarâbâd) who knew many by heart.[8] An enormous demon, as large as a mountain, appeared in Mecca and, prostrating himself in front of the Prophet, he explained one of his difficulties. He had lived happily in the world for 30,000 years before Adam until, one unhappy day, a beautiful youth appeared and trussed him up solidly with date fibres. Unable to free himself, the poor demon asked for help first from Adam and then from the later Prophets, but no-one was able to free him. In the time of Solomon (who also was unable to free him) the angel Gabriel told him that only he who had tied the knot would be able to loosen it, that he would appear in the time of the prophet Muhammad and that he would be called 'Alî ibn Abî Tâlib. A number of the Prophet's companions also tried to free the demon, but none succeeded. Then 'Alî approached. The demon recognized him and the Prophet smilingly said: "It is not surprising that 'Alî can accomplish such things, for 'Alî possesses a pre-temporal form (*sûrat-i azalî*). 'Alî in truth existed before the two worlds, in fact the world appeared through his grace. 'Alî is the spiritual master (*murshid*) of the archangel Gabriel!" We need not add that 'Alî easily loosened the thongs of the demon, who was immediately converted to Islam and became "a believer, a Shi'ite and servant of 'Alî."

"The Qur'an and tradition prove that 'Alî was the Spiritual Master of the archangel Gabriel." One day Gabriel (called here "the ignorant one"!) came down from the lofty sky and visited the Prophet. They were conversing about Revelation when, lo, the ten-year-old 'Alî came into the room. Gabriel jumped to his feet and bowed deeply to the child. The Prophet was surprised (though the author is careful to add: "even though he was acquainted with the fact . . .") and asked the reason for such humility towards a human creature from an angel. Gabriel answered: "Do not say that he is a child again. He was my master in front of God in pre-eternity." In the beginning, the angel went on to explain, only Gabriel himself and God existed. God questioned Gabriel: "Who am I? Who are you? What is the scope of your creation?" Gabriel's answer ("you are you, I am I") did not please the Lord. After 30,000 years the question was repeated and this time the answer, with a very slight variation that would justify the adjective "ignorant" (*ummî*) attributed above to the angel, was: "I am I, you are you." After another 30,000 years: same question and same answer. Losing patience, God sent him to school. For 12,000 years Gabriel wandered through the deserts of the Place Beyond (*lâ-makân*) in search of a Master, whom it was not easy to find. Then, reaching the shores of the Sea of Reality, he saw a raft made of Divine Light on which a most majestic youth was travelling. He asked him, fearfully, who he was, since only God exists. The youth was angry and burned his wings with his flaming gaze. He then answered that he was the *sirr* ("secret," intimate personality) of God and that it was bad manners to ask him this kind of question. Gabriel apologized and only after 30,000 years was forgiven and was given back his wings. The angel became his disciple and learned 700,000 sciences from him as well as how he should have answered God's question, i.e.: "I am Gabriel, a miserable slave, and You the Majestic Sovereign Lord: I live because I have been created by You. You are the Lord, and I the Servant." Gabriel went to God and finally satisfied him with this answer. Then he asked him the name of his master and God told him that he had an infinite number of names, quoting some of them ("Lion of God," "Friend of God," etc.). At the end of Gabriel's long tirade the Prophet, struck by the enormous numbers the angel used in his story, asked him his age.

The answer was: "I do not know the number of my years, but I know that there is a wonderfully bright star that rises every 30,000 years, and I have already seen it 30,000 times."

"And would you recognize that star," Muhammad asked him, "if I showed it to you again?"

"Yes," Gabriel answered, and, lo, Muhammad removed the child 'Alî's turban and that star shone on his forehead! This same star, the symbol of the "great cosmic cycle" will be mentioned in another popular text in the next chapter.

The Satanic Horseman

'Alî went hunting with his father Abû Tâlib and other people. Rushing towards them, they saw an immense pagan rider called Jabaleh, a most powerful dominator of many countries, carrying a lance weighing 30 *mann*, a shield like a mountain and two immense bows. Jabaleh wanted 'Alî and his companions to abandon their religion. A number of Muslim horsemen were defeated in duels. In despair, Abû Tâlib turned to his son asking him to save the situation by running to Mecca to warn the Prophet. The young 'Alî begged him not to despair. When Jabaleh unhorsed Abû Tâlib too, and wanted to kill him and the other defeated Muslim heroes, 'Alî let out a terrible cry.

"What thunder is this?" Jabaleh asked in great surprise.

"It is the blare of the Divine Trumpet, it is lightning, it is a thunderbolt, for all stem from my breath!" 'Alî answered. "I am, by divine grace, the absolute sovereign of this world and the other! You think I am a child, but my age is greater than earth and sky, for it is I who created them, according to God's command . . ." (sic!)

One can easily imagine the end of the story. Jabaleh refused the offer to become a Muslim and was split in two by 'Alî's formidable sword, and all were saved. The story ends with the author's artless and moving prayer to 'Alî, in which he asks him for the grace to see his beloved country, the Gilan area, again after such a long exile and to again accomplish the pilgrimage to his tomb in Najaf.

Religion in Iran

The Unfortunate Debtor

A certain man, who had contracted enormous debts with unbelievers, asked for help from the Prophet who, naturally, turned to 'Alî for a solution. 'Alî took the debtor by the hand, told him to close his eyes for an instant and then open them again. The man saw a very rich city, ruled by a Jew. 'Alî said to the debtor: "Sell me to that Jewish king." After hesitating the debtor accepted and went into that city pretending that 'Alî was his slave. He sold him to the king and 'Alî placed himself on one pan of the scales asking that gold be put on the other. His miraculous weight caused the other pan to be filled with gold until the unfortunate man's debt was extinguished. The king asked him his name and 'Alî answered that every category of beings, including animals, called him with a different name. Not content with this, the "Lion of God" performed other miracles for the amazed king (who, we can be sure, was then converted to Islam with all his subjects). He fetched a whole forest for him, he tamed a lion, and he cured countless sick people with his breath. The Jewish king himself, whose name was Yahudâ, suffered from an incurable ailment, a kind of blotch on his chest. Healing him of this blemish, 'Alî accomplished a final feat, which left everyone open-mouthed. He took nothing less than . . . the *sun* from under his armpit and after holding it nonchalantly for a few minutes, threw it back into the sky.

The Story of King 'Amr

Fârigh says that this story was told him by a shaikh by name of Masihâ. King 'Amr came to Mecca with the intention of destroying everything and, in particular, of defeating a hero by name of 'Alî, whom he had heard much about. It so happened that, without recognizing him, he asked the fourteen year old 'Alî himself where he could find him. 'Alî boasted about his qualities (he said, among other things: "With the exception of God, everything that is, is his servant: the whole of creation is nothing but skin and he its marrow"). Then, still without revealing his identity, he fought him, defeated him and trussed him up like the demon of the story (in fact, already in ancient times "demons" were naturalistically interpreted as "evil men," as Firdausî says: "tu mar dîv-râ mardum-i bad shinâs." When the king returned to his country no one was able to loosen his bonds. His minister 'Antar advised him to pretend to accept Islam and have the person who trussed him up untie him. Once free, he could then return to his own religion. 'Alî freed him, but foresaw that he would become pagan again and be suitably punished. And in fact this is what happened, after a memorable battle during which 'Alî asked God to provide him with a worthy horse and sword with which to fight the infidel. A magic sign summoned the famous horse Duldul, who was neither male nor female and as swift as the

310

wind, out of a rock. As for the sword, Gabriel came down from heaven with an apple in his hand and offered it to the Prophet Muhammad, ordering him to eat one half of it, from which Fâtima (the Prophet's daughter and 'Alî's future wife—there is no place for chronology here) would be born, while the other half would serve to make the sword Zû'l-Fiqâr, which would weigh a full 62 *mann*. (This is a significant episode for it makes 'Alî's wife the twin sister of his sword: *zû'l-fiqâr*, it should be noted, is a male name). The sword was 17 *gaz* long, but before the enemy it stretched to 70. Thus a suitable instrument was created for killing the evil king 'Amr. This occurred in a rather hyperbolic fashion that has been immortalized in an infinity of popular miniatures. With a single stroke 'Alî killed 'Amr and his perfidious minister 'Antar. The sword's strength was such, however, that it split the very earth in two, and was about to reach the mythical foundations, the "cow and the fish" on which the earth rests according to a primitive cosmology accepted by popular Islam. God sent the versatile Gabriel to avert this disaster. He prevented the deadly sword from damaging the pillars on which the cosmos rested.

The next story repeats, with some variations, the story of the "unfortunate debtor." 'Alî took the usual unfortunate debtor by the hand. The usual phantasmagoric city appeared, this time with a name, Barbar, with the usual king, this time an unbeliever, and the usual idea of selling 'Alî as a slave. Once the sale had taken place the satisfied debtor returned to Mecca with the money, leaving 'Alî in great trouble. 'Alî told the king that one of his mysterious names was Qeshmeshem, and the king, admiring his qualities, offered him one half of his kingdom if he resolved three problems. The first was to stop an impetuous river, the second to kill a dangerous dragon who lived on a mountain and the third to kill the pagan King's worst and most dangerous enemy, a certain 'Alî who lived in Mecca, and bring the king his head. The first task was very easily carried out. The second was rather more difficult: the dragon was in fact a seven-headed she-dragon pregnant with seven little dragons. Returning victorious to the king, 'Alî told him that the third task was very easy since he himself was 'Alî, and if they wanted to, they could cut off his head. After a vain attempt to imprison 'Alî, during which he destroyed a whole army, all of them, including the king, considered it more prudent to convert to Islam.

'Alî and the Enamored Unbeliever

While 'Alî was riding his Duldul in the desert he was attacked by a pagan marauder. Defeating him, he took him along as a prisoner. But, weeping and lamenting, the marauder told him a sad love story. He had gone out to plunder because he was madly in love with a young girl, and his future father-in-law promised she would become his wife only if he brought him 'Alî's severed head. 'Alî immediately freed his prisoner and, giving him a rope and a dagger, said: "Tie my hands and cut off my head, you have obtained what you desired!" The Prophet, who was watching this scene from afar, prayed God to "send away darkness with Light" and converted the young pagan. One can easily imagine the rest of the story: The young man became a fervent Shi'ite and, together with 'Alî, went to his native city where, after the defeat of some and the conversion of others, his dream was finally crowned and all became "dogs of 'Alî."

"O 'Alî," Fârigh continues, in the first person here, "I too want to be your faithful dog, faithful and always watchful on your threshold. You know my condition, look with mercy on my state. Glance at wretched Fârigh and mercifully soothe his sorrow, you who were ready to sacrifice yourself to your enemies, see that the hearts of your friends are not lacerated with pain. How could a friend ever despair of one who is ready to give his severed head for his enemy . . . ?"

'Alî's Generosity

'Alî gave one of the camels of his caravan as a gift to a blind beggar. His servant pointed out that the camels, carrying precious loads, were tied one to the other, but 'Alî ordered him to place the reins of the first camel into the blind man's hands: he could take them all with their loads. The blind man was miraculously healed and was surprised to find himself at the head of a long line of camels (he thought that 'Alî had only given him one). Another time 'Alî was praying in the mosque when a beggar came up: not one of the four hundred people present gave him anything. 'Alî signed to the beggar to remove the precious ring from his finger and take it, because he could not interrupt the prayer. Amazed at the importance of the gift, the beggar waited until 'Alî could speak to him: the simple bedouin did not know the value of the precious stone and wanted to know from 'Alî how much bread he could buy with it. 'Alî told him simply to buy as much bread as it was worth, no more no less. The bedouin went to a baker who, seeing the chance for a good bargain, proposed weighing the ring on his scales in exchange for a piece of bread. But the ring turned out to be enormously heavy and there was not enough bread in the shop to weigh it. Then the wicked baker corrupted the judges and, taking advantage of the bedouin's artlessness, accused him of stealing the ring and had one of his hands cut off according to the Islamic law. Taking the severed hand in his other hand, the poor man went back to Medina to 'Alî. Everything ends well with the exposure of the culprits and the miraculous restoration of the hand of the unjustly condemned man.

The Wonderful Bird

During prayer in the mosque in Medina a beggar asked for four dirhams. Despite the Prophet's exhortation, of all those present only 'Alî seemed willing to give them to him. When, later, 'Alî went into the palm grove, he saw a wonderful bird with a ruby head and golden feet, covered in gems, on a palm tree. 'Alî wanted to catch it to bring it as a gift to his wife and children. Catching it by the foot, he tugged at it, but the motionless bird remained unruffled and in fact carried 'Alî away, bringing him to the mythical city of Jâbulsâ. He flew so high "that one could hear the angels speaking." Jâbulsâ[9] was on the shores of the Western sea and was inhabited by happy and carefree beings—all Christians. An ascetic, the Spiritual Master of that city, lived in a hermitage there, coming away from it only once a year to celebrate the cult. 'Alî waited for this event. But this time the Master was unable to utter a word and succeeded only in making those around him understand that the best of men was among them and that it was up to him to speak. 'Alî revealed himself: he is the one whom God has praised in all the Sacred Books. All the prophets who came into the world, whether manifest or hidden (*zâhir* or *bâtin*—as we have seen, this subject was highly developed in Ismailism) had 'Alî as their designated companion. With one sermon 'Alî converted the people of Jâbulsâ, who showered gifts on him. Then he returned in the same way he had come, covering a six months' long journey in a jiffy. The bird gracefully accepted to be given as a gift to 'Alî's family after humbly kissing the feet of the Prophet and of all the other "princes" of Medina and revealed that he was a very high-ranking angel, with 40,000 inferior angels at his service. Then the Prophet and the others gave him permission to fly back to heaven.

'Alî and 'Umar Beyond the Qâf Mountains

The story, which is explicitly told with a "revivalistic" scope ("listen now, concerning this, to a story, that the structure of your faith and your religion may be renewed") begins with the usual beggar who had the usual debt that could not be extended. The Prophet asked who could help him but, the good Fârigh says wittily, "as soon as those men heard money mentioned they were all struck dumb." Except of course 'Alî, who offered 6,400 dirhams. The malicious people, and first among them 'Umar, suspected that 'Alî stole by night and showed off during the day distributing money. And so 'Umar spied on him under the pretext of accompanying and serving him. 'Alî ordered him to close and open his eyes and they found themselves in the usual miraculous city. To his great surprise 'Umar looked at the fields round about and saw that while one man ploughed another immediately sowed, and a third man followed close on their heels to bring in the harvest that had grown like lightning. This was in the area beyond the mythical mountains of Qâf that surround the world and which we have already come across in the preceding chapters. There, as in the mythical Mazdean *Erânvêj* or the *Var-i Yamkart* (see above), there existed, if not immortality, special conditions of life. There was no sickness, it was always spring and every week a ewe gave birth to five lambs, while mares and cows gave birth to their young every month. And the inhabitants of that place knew only 'Alî, and day and night they invoked only him. In other words, they were all Shi'ites. The man of whom 'Umar asked all this information added that between that place and Mecca there were a full 70 years of travel, but that there were few followers of 'Alî in the "world." This was why the world was called *dunyâ*, i.e., "low," "vile," "abject." 'Umar's only thought was for immediate vile profit and he tried to make the best of the situation. But his wheat did not grow like that of the others. Why? Because he did not curse 'Alî's enemies while ploughing and did not mention his name. 'Umar subjected himself to this too and, at least for practical reasons, was enthusiastic over 'Alî, singing his praises and cursing his enemies. When he returned (in the same way) to Medina he thought over these miracles and his heart was filled with envy.

A Horse Race Between 'Alî and a Hedouin

A bedouin boasted about his horse's speed and said that he was willing to become a Muslim if 'Alî succeeded in beating him in a race. Even a fast-flying dove was unable to catch up with 'Alî's horse (among other things, 'Alî defeated some enemies who had basely ambushed him to capture him). The bedouin, needless to say, converted to Islam.

A Muslim Saint Lucy

This is the singular episode of a pious virgin of Kufa who, though she was very beautiful, decided to devote herself to asceticism. A young man was able, for a brief instant, to see her eyes (the virgin obviously chastely wore a veil over her face too) and fell deeply in love with her, committing every kind of folly for her. Seeing this, the girl gouged out her eyes which were "moist and gentle as those of a narcissus" and, placing them on a dish, gave them to her lover's messenger saying that he should keep them, if they pleased him so greatly, since she had no use for eyes that could draw her away from the love of the One God. And, she added, if that youth again dares to send me a messenger, I will sever my head from my body! The young man went to 'Alî with the dish, weeping over his sin. 'Alî replaced the young girl's eyes in the presence of hundreds of Zoroastrians, Christians and pagans who immediately became Shi'ites. The end of the story is typically anti-ascetic: the girl agrees to marry the youth according to Muslim canon law. In view of the very specific coincidences (including the dish) we ought not to exclude the possibility of a late echo of the Christian legend of Saint Lucy: it should not be forgotten that these stories belong to the sixteenth century and there were many Christians in Persia.

Sa'sa'a's Questions

Sa'sa'a was one of the Prophet's companions, "a pure Shi'ite" (*shî'eh-yi pâkdîn*). Taking advantage of one of 'Alî's periods of forced inactivity, he went to visit him, and asked him a number of questions. We should note that in this passage 'Alî is called "guide and master of Prophets" and "lord and prince of Saints." Outwardly—the chronicler adds—he was not a prophet (*nabî*), but the flowering of prophecy came from him!

The first question: "Though the light of God was hidden in Adam and therefore he was adored by the angels, he disobeyed God by eating the fatal "grain" (our "apple"). Would you have done so?"

"No," 'Alî answered.

"And," Sa'sa'a continued, "are you not better than Noah too, who prayed for the salvation of his wicked relatives despite God's order to the contrary?"

"Obviously," 'Alî answered, "I would not have prayed for the wicked. Noah too was an unbeliever (*kâfîr* [sic!])."

"And are you not better than Abraham too?"

"Yes, 'Alî answered, and I will prove it to you with the fact that Abraham wanted God to give him an example of how he would raise up the dead. His faith was not sufficient."

"Then," Sa'sa'a asked, "what makes you superior to Moses?"

"This: that Moses was afraid of the rod that was turned into a snake through divine power, while I, when I was four months old, killed a dragon in my crib, not to mention other feats!"

"And why are you better than Jesus?" Sa'sa'a asked. "Because," 'Alî answered modestly, "while Jesus was born in a stable, I was born in the temple of the Kaaba. In fact, while Mary was about to give birth to Jesus in the Temple she heard a heavenly voice telling her to go elsewhere because that was not a house in which to give birth! In fact the Kaaba only became a place of worship and the spiritual center of the world because I was born there!"

Why is 'Alî better than Solomon? Because Solomon preferred the Kingdom and I preferred Holy Poverty; and the magic name on Solomon's seal with which he dominated the whole world was my Name. "Who are Solomon, Joseph, David? Who Esdra, who Sâlih, who Hûd?[10] They are all but a ray of my manifestation, a drop in the ocean of my light! . . . I and the prince of Prophets (Muhammad) are of the same Light!"

And then Sa'sa'a risked the most hazardous question: "Are you or Muhammad better?" This answer is less explicit, but 'Alî's supremacy over Muhammad is implicit in the statement that 'Alî and Muhammad are the same thing, but in the sense that 'Alî is the soul and Muhammad the body. 'Alî "is the (intimate) secret of God and the soul of the Prophet."

The Story of 'Alî Aswad

The fifty-year old 'Alî Aswad, a pious companion of the Prophet, was childless despite his age. He set out to look for a child to adopt, until he came to a Christian convent where he saw a poor woman with a child in rags. The woman declared herself ready to give him the child on three conditions. First, that he must not be circumcised; second, that he must not be made to become Muslim; third, that he should be sent every year to see his mother. The Prophet was consulted and advised him, with Machiavellian wile, to take the child, have him circumcised, make a Muslim of him, but to bring him back every year to his mother. One day it happened that 'Alî Aswad had to make a sea journey with his son. A frightful whale approached the ship and ordered that all the children should be thrown over to him if they didn't want him to swallow the entire ship. This fate befell 'Alî Aswad's adoptive son together with the other children. On 'Alî Aswad's return the child's mother found out what had happened and asked that the law of retaliation be applied. 'Alî Aswad was put to death. But in the end 'Alî set everything right again. Stretching his arm to an incredible length he seized the whale at the bottom of the ocean while he took hold of the dead 'Alî Aswad with his other hand and brought him back to life.

Four Unbelievers Ask for a Miracle

This is the story of four followers of Abraham, Moses, Jesus and David respectively who asked, at the death of the Prophet Muhammad (whom they had known), who would succeed him. At that time 'Umar considered himself his successor: meeting him, Abraham's follower asked him to throw himself, unscathed, into the fire like his prophet; Moses' follower, to transform a rod into a snake; Jesus' follower, to bring a dead man back to life and David's follower, to mould iron as if it were soft wax. Only on these conditions would they become Muslim. In a very orthodox way from a Sunni point of view, 'Umar answered that only the prophets can perform miracles and that he was not a prophet. Then—as usual—he humbly turned to 'Alî to resolve the situation. 'Alî invited them all to go into the desert so that he could show them his miracle. He mounted Duldul and taking his faithful servant Qanbar's whip, threw it far away: it became a dragon spitting flames that kindled the fire of the pyre that had been prepared and into which he and the dragon entered together, emerging after three hours, etc., thus producing even more sensational miracles than those asked for.

Adham's Dream

Adham, one of the Prophet's companions, told him about a horrible dream he had had, i.e., that a huge bird had torn off his head. The Prophet advised him to barricade himself in his house and not to move until further orders. After twenty days Adham was tired of this situation and insisted on going out despite the Prophet's prohibition. He went armed into the desert. He met an enormous crocodile that served as mount to a warrior who tried to attack him: in order to save himself and frighten his assailant Adham said that he was 'Alî, but the warrior was quite unimpressed and unhorsed him. As he was about to kill him Adham revealed that he was not 'Alî, but the warrior, thinking that he was trying to deceive him, cut off his head. The bloody horse returned to Adham's mother who went, weeping, to the Prophet. At this point Gabriel revealed that, in a kingdom of unbelievers governed by king Zarqum, the finest warriors were all anxious to bring 'Alî's head to the king. The lucky man who succeeded in this exploit would marry the king's daughter. Adham was killed by the warrior who thought that he was 'Alî. Hearing this, 'Alî immediately set out with Duldul and Zû'l-fiqâr and in the bat of an eyelid reached the city of Zarqum. Leaving his horse Duldul at the city gate, where the faithful animal bit off the heads of all those who went in or came out, 'Alî made his way to the very center of the main square where there was great excitement around Adham's severed head. Adham spoke to 'Alî and begged him to save him. The keeper of the head turned Muslim and went to the king to tell him. The king did not want to believe his ears, but Adham's talking head was brought to him as proof. Despite this a battle ensued, the unbelievers were defeated or converted and 'Alî returned to Mecca with Adham's head. Adham's mother begged the Prophet and the Prophet begged God that the miracle might be accomplished; but the head was re-attached to the body only when 'Alî said "amen" to Muhammad's prayer.

'Alî Returns to Medina After the Battle of Nahravân"[11]

The army was dying of thirst in a terrible desert and 'Alî discovered a miraculous well hidden under a huge stone. Salmân (Muhammad's famous Persian freedman who plays an important part in Shi'ite legends) went down forty steps into it and found a huge barred door. He came up again, 'Alî took a key out of his turban and gave it to him. Among other treasures this underground cavern contained a magic cup of water with which the entire army quenched its thirst. An interesting detail is that Salmân found 'Alî himself inside the well, while 'Alî was also above ground with the army at the same time.

The Discovery of 'Alî's Tomb

This is a pious tale told to the author twenty years earlier, during a journey from Baghdad to the Gilan area near Rudbar, by one Muhammad-i Maddâh who asked him to put it into verse and remember his name. No one knew where he had been buried once 'Alî had died (or rather, our pious author says, when "he considered it opportune to disappear"—'Alî is the essence itself of "manifestation" and only the blind cannot see him). The tomb was only discovered seven hundred years later, in the time of a faithful Shi'ite, Shâh Muhammad Khudâbandeh, and this is how it occurred. The king was out hunting with his retinue near Najaf when "they saw in front of them a little hill, which was as green and merry as a peacock's wing. Its grass was as soft as the fabric of the firmament, its earth was as pure as the Water of Life. And it gave off breath that, like Jesus' breath, could give life back to the dead and buried. The little hill was surrounded by a scent of amber, as far as a farsakh. And it was densely populated with animals and wild beasts, as if they had found refuge there. Wolves and lambs lived side by side in friendship and did not harm one another and the she-wolf even suckled the lamb." The king's soldiers tried to kill the animals, but a miraculous force protected them. A mysterious voice told the king to abstain from all violence towards those creatures and to dig up the earth. All the animals moved to one side and piously performed the circumambulation (*tavvâf*) around the rising, rubbing their muzzles on the ground in sign of adoration. When they had dug as far 'Alî's tomb it seemed to them that they had come to a perfumed garden. A hundred thousand angels came down from heaven and adoringly prostrated themselves. An inscription on the coffin stated that this one sarcophagus contained the bodies of Adam, Noah and 'Alî (the three "initiators" of a new humanity!). The good Fârigh is so moved that he interrupts his story and exclaims: "How fortunate those ancient soldiers were, what a happy man king Khudâbandeh,[12] who with the help of such easy good fortune effortlessly found such a precious treasure! Oh, if only heaven had willed that I should be the dust under that sovereign's sandals, the watchdog at the gate of his palace! Thus on that day I would have had the fortune and joy of offering my life for the king ['Alî] of Najaf! But, since fortune was not so good to me, may I now give my life for the mere mention of that day!" The king ordered that a mausoleum be built: heaven is only a pale reflection of that place. And so Najaf grew into a great city, a place of pilgrimage; the Kaaba itself humbly performed the circumambulation (*tavvâf*)[13] around 'Alî's Sanctuary, and the sick who visit the tomb are healed. An impious blasphemer against 'Alî mocked the tomb that, according to him, contained nothing but impotent remains. He was split in two by a ray of light that descended from the cupola of the sanctuary to the sound of a very shrill shriek, and his body was turned into a black stone that can still be seen there.

The Conquest of Khaibar

This well-known episode of the Prophet's early wars, enriched with a number of legendary and miraculous details, has 'Alî, to whom more and more extraordinary qualities are attributed, as its main protagonist. Among other things it is said that every prophet who comes into the world has, secretly, an 'Alî with him. In the struggle against 'Antar, when 'Alî, the prototype of chivalry, was asked his name, he answered, as in some of our medieval romances, that it was written on his sword's edge and he cut the unbeliever in two so perfectly that the two pieces held together for some time. At the most difficult moment of the battle 'Alî came to the aid of his men, flying through the air. Muhammad himself, at the sight of such a sensational accomplishment exclaimed: "If I were not prevented by my concern to refrain from saying anything contrary to religion, I would now explicitly say of him what the Christians have said of Christ. But I am afraid of manifesting this secret openly . . ." And Fârigh prudently adds: "countless people maintain that 'Alî is God, but they walk on erroneous paths."

This passage, however, is important because it shows that at one time even in Twelver Shi'ite circles many people maintained 'Alî's divinity, which was unanimously rejected by the official theologians. When 'Alî single-handedly broke through the enormous gates of the castle of Khaibar ("how will he who has the firmament as his ring fear the gates of Khaibar?") the people shouted with one voice: "There is no God other than 'Alî!" But the pious Fârigh tempers his excitement by adding that once 'Alî was unable to break a little piece of bread. All his strength came from God. Everything is still, Islamically, attributed to God's arbitrary will.

'Alqama and Hishâm

This story is similar to that of "'Alî and the unbeliever who was in love." A young girl told her lover that he must bring her 'Alî's head. When 'Alî heard of the pact, he offered his head to his enemy, even though he was already defeated. A final battle, with relative conversions to Islam, resolves everything.

The Man Whose Tongue was Cut Off

One day a man whose tongue had been cut off came to Medina. The Prophet healed the man, who told him that his pagan father had cut it off because, having seen Muhammad and 'Alî in a dream, he had been converted to Islam. Performing the usual miracles, 'Alî conquered the castle of Salâsil, of which the young man's father was lord.

Noah's Ark and Jonah's Fish

During the deluge a fish saved Noah's ark from a whirlpool. Noah asked him what he wanted in exchange. The fish answered that his one great desire was to be eaten by the "five noble" beings (i.e. Muhammad, 'Alî, Fâtima, Hasan and Husain: the Holy Family). Noah then prayed that this wish might be granted. The centuries passed. The fish kept thinking about the promise. Jonah's time came and the fish had the . . . opposite function to the one he wished for, i.e., it was he who swallowed the Prophet. The centuries of the fish's long life went by in weeping and in prayers to become the food of the "five pure ones." Until, at the time of Muhammad, his desire increased: the fulfillment of his millenary wish was at hand. But there was the problem of his enormous size. The fish prayed to God: "Make me small! make me a hundred thousandth part of my present size!" Finally, having grown smaller, he was fished and brought to Muhammad who was amazed at his admirable shape and the mysterious scent he emanated. The fish opened his mouth and again expressed his heart's desire. Placed on the scales it was discovered that he weighed exactly five *man*: one for each of the five "pure ones." This episode is enriched by another, purely zoological, one. While they were talking about the fish, some flies (though probably "bees" are meant) came down from the air and settled on the Prophet's thigh. They too had the gift of words and declared that they were bees from before Adam and that they had been waiting for the "five pure ones" for a thousand years to give them some honey that was in a distant city of theirs, guarded by two lions. 'Alî's faithful servant, Qanbar, guided by one of the bees to this distant place, brought back the honey for the Holy Family. Thus the bees too obtained what they wanted. "May God thus grant each one the fulfillment of his wish," And so the pious Fârigh concludes his little book.

We apologize for having devoted so many pages to this little work but believe that our readers will find useful a knowledge of the legends about 'Alî—which were already abundant in the Safavid period. Research on the sources of the various elements of these legendary tales would lead us into inextricable problems of comparative literature. Here we will only draw the reader's attention to the combination of early material (especially the miracles concerning the battles and his warlike exploits, which were already present in part, and in a more sober form, in Mas'ûdî, *Murûj*, IV, 376 and Ya'qûbî II, 39) and also the re-elaborations and attributions to 'Alî of Christian legends, which may have penetrated into Iran under the Safavids themselves (for example, the Saint Lucy of Kufa). Two traits are outstanding throughout the book: the unconcealed tendency (despite a few dispassionate theological corrections) to attribute a divinity to 'Alî (a divinity that only certain extreme sects attributed to him, and which the official texts of Twelver Shi'ism deny) and a relatively minor accentuation of the hatred for 'Umar and the other Sunni caliphs, so typical of the official Twelver Shi'ites. Both these traits indicate the age of the material, which preceded the appearance among the people of the first ferments of ecstatic religiosity in the style of Shâh Ismâ'îl. These, combined with doctrines of various origins, gained ground in the religious sect known as Ahl-i Haqq "the people of Truth" or 'Alî-Ilâhîs ("deifiers of 'Alî"), which still exists in Persia today and on which a brief summary will be useful.[14]

For some time Minorsky, one of the greatest European experts on the 'Alî-Ilâhîs, thought—and with good reason—that their doctrines were identical to those of the Safavid "arcana" and the religiosity of Shâh Ismâ'îl: for many of the poems by the Shâh who founded Twelver Persia were taken over and sung by the Persian 'Alî-Ilâhîs. But the connection may be less simple and, later, the Russian scholar grew to believe that the origins of the 'Alî-Ilâhî movement were linked with Kurdistan and that it was only externally connected with Safavid propaganda.[15] The 'Alî-Ilâhîs are in fact widespread, especially in western Persia, though it is hard to calculate their exact number. The cornerstone of their religion is the belief in successive incarnations or, better, successive manifestations of the divinity, who appeared among men seven times. The names of these manifestations are unexpected because they do not seem to correspond to those of the traditional prophets. They are: Khâvindigâr, 'Alî, Shâh Khushîn, Sultân Suhâk, Qirmizî, Mâmad-Beg and Khân-Atish. Each was accompanied by four or five "angels" (which often correspond to historical persons). An 'Alî-Ilâhî myth on the creation told orally to Minorsky runs as follows:

God exteriorized himself in a Pearl, then he came into the water, where Binyamîn was swimming. God asked him: "Who are you?" Binyamîn answered: "I am I, you are you." God burnt Binyamîn's wings. The same thing happened a second time. Then God appeared to him in another form and taught Binyamîn, i.e. Gabriel, to answer: "You are the Creator and I am the servant." Then God, who was in a bubble of water, told Gabriel how to penetrate into it. Gabriel reminded God of his promise to give a manifest form to the other three angels and, lo and behold, they were all four in the bubble! Then Rabzar brought a loaf of bread that was divided into six pieces, two of which were taken by God. They ate the bread, said "Huf"[16] and the world appeared. Adam, the first man, was also God, then history began and the prophets followed.

Many aspects of this tradition are very interesting: it is, among other things, a representative example of a myth as the explanation of a rite of communion or holy agape, which is typical of the Persian 'Alî-Ilâhîs and the very similar Syrian sect of the Nusairîs, which however does not concern us here.[17] Besides, it places the creation of the world as the consequence of a sacramental act. But to us the fact that Fârigh's popular Twelver Shi'ite poem (which we discussed above) includes a legend, the first part of which is identical to this one, seems very important—and proves once more, unequivocally, the contact between the enthusiastic Shi'ism of the early Safavids and the 'Alî-Ilâhî legends. In their traditions and texts both the 'Alî-Ilâhîs and the Nusairîs speak of twelve imâms, and in this sense they do not appear to be influenced by true Ismailism. Despite the name commonly given the 'Alî-Ilâhîs, 'Alî is only one of the divine manifestations and, according to the traditions Minorsky collected, they considered the fourth, Sultân Suhâk (a corruption of *Ishâq*), to be the complete revelation of deity. Probably these legends combine a chronological concept of successive revelations with one of different states or planes of life; the same angels and the same "gods" have different names according to the planes of life in which they reveal themselves. Some elements lead us to believe, for example, that the first three manifestations—Khâvindigâr, 'Alî and Shâh Khushîn—correspond to God manifesting himself at the stage of the external law (Khâvindigâr, "the Lord," the esoteric God), of Mysticism (*tarîqat*, 'Alî is the founding father of every mystical confraternity) and of Reality (*haqîqat*) (see also in Fârigh 'Alî's various names on the different planes of existence). The angelic hypostases that accompany every manifestation always include a female one. There is a curious but important statement (because it might provide a guideline for a historical identification) in the 'Alî-Ilâhî book called the "Book of Polo" according to which, among the early manifestations of God, Bâbâ Khushîn (the third manifestation) spoke Persian, Sultân Suhâk (the fourth) spoke *gûrânî* Kurdish, and a character of the fifth cycle, who is no other than the founder of the Safavid dynasty Shâh Ismâ'îl (Khatâ'î), spoke Turkic. We also have the surprise of finding among the angels of the third cycle the great mystical Persian poet Bâbâ Tâhir (who wrote lovely quatrains in a Luristân dialect and died in 1019). In the next cycle the scene moves to Kurdistân: according to some sources Sultân Suhâk was a son of the imâm Mûsâ al-Kâzim (who died in 799). Sanctuaries to one or another 'Alî-Ilâhî "angel" or "manifestation" exist throughout Persia where the pilgrims (who are often not 'Alî-Ilâhîs and at times are even Sunni) accomplish special rites that so far have received very little scholarly attention. If they were studied methodically— also in connection with the infinite imâmzâdeh of the Twelver Shi'ites and ancient vestiges of pre-Islamic religious piety—they might lead to very interesting historical and religious results and also throw light onto the earliest phase of this popular Persian religion, which the written texts of the élite religions tell us so little about. Unfortunately we still have insufficient material for an in-depth study of these matters. The fifth period still takes place on Kurdish territory, while the sixth (Mâmad beg) seems to be set in the Turkic zone of Azerbaijan. According to information Minorsky obtained from 'Alî-Ilâhî sectarians (p. 39 of the op. cit.) Mâmad beg himself came from Anatolia and found favor with the Qaraqoyunlu princes who reigned in Azerbaijan in the fifteenth century (and whom orthodox authors often accused of impiety). The 'Alî-Ilâhîs place the seventh manifestation in the Safavid period or even a little later (the time of Nâdir Shâh, eighteenth century). The last manifestation of God, Khân Atish, disappeared from the sight of men like his predecessors, this time in the form of a falcon. He will return at the end of the world.

A man called Ni'matu'llâh (who died in 1920) considered the moment ripe for revealing the secrets of the sect, which were based on ancient traditions rather than on written texts, and he published the *Furqân al-akhbâr*. The countless complete or partial manifestations of the Divine listed in the second part of this curious text includes, surprisingly, the ancient hero Rustam, the Achilles of pre-Islamic Persia.

The 'Alî-Ilâhîs also have many prophetic texts with detailed descriptions of the events and circumstances that will accompany the end of the world and the return of a divine manifestation, which they see in a far more "symbolic" form than the orthodox Twelver Shi'ites and which led to a number of 'Alî-Ilâhîs converting to the Babi-Baha'i religion when it appeared. The 'Alî-Ilâhîs, who are divided into various sub-sects, admit metempsychosis and have very interesting rites, some of which evidently stem from the Sufism of the confraternities: for example *zikr* meetings, with songs and music and bloody and bloodless sacrifices. As with the mystics, every 'Alî-Ilâhî must be the disciple of a spiritual Master (*pîr*). The initiation ceremony is called *sar sipurdan*, "the handing over of the head," and the disciple's head, symbolized by a nutmeg, is split and sacrificed to the Master in the course of a complicated ceremony. A strange spiritual contract called *shart-i iqrâr* also exists between one or more men and one woman who is considered their spiritual sister in a kind of chaste marriage "for the day of resurrection." There is a three-day fast too, followed by a celebration and the sacrifice of the cock (cf. the Jewish rite) besides communion and "holy agape" rites. The whole forms an extremely complicated syncretism made up of elements that are hard to unravel. We can clearly distinguish the Sufi element, the enthusiastic Shi'ite element (which appears to be distinct from both official Ismailism and codified Twelver Shi'ism) and finally a basis of possibly earlier vestiges of popular religion. Setting aside all reference to when their present doctrinal system was formed, it remains a fact that the 'Alî-Ilâhîs lived and still live in very isolated regions of Persia (Luristân, Kurdistân and Azerbaijan, besides other scattered colonies). The fact that the idea of the Divinity as a Pearl (see above) was also, for example, a Manichaean concept, confirms the idea that elements of popular religiosity—otherwise unknown to us—survived in the heresies of ancient Iran (Manichaeism, Mazdakism). But any conclusion concerning these problematic, though fascinating, links must wait until the abundant material—which unfortunately is disappearing because of modern progress and the indifference of even the most intelligent modern Persian scholars—on Persian popular religious traditions has been collected, arranged by region and methodically and scientifically studied. We can however propose a general conclusion: i.e., that the early Safavid movement and the popular piety connected with it is closely linked to elements of folk religion, which spread in western Persia and Anatolia and, in particular, to the Sufi type of extremist Shi'ism found in Bektâshism and the 'Alî-Ilâhî sect.

Another aspect of Shi'ite popular piety should also be mentioned (as the reader can see we are dealing with fragments, for a study of Shi'ite popular piety is probably still premature): the cult of Fâtima, Muhammad's daughter, the wife of 'Alî and the mother of the "martyrs" Hasan and Husain.[18] This aspect is especially interesting because it introduces an element of "femininity" into the very male Islamic religion that brings to mind the Catholic hyperdulia accorded to the Virgin Mary. The feast of the *mubâhala* (21, 24 or 25 of the month of *Zû'l-Hijja*) is the only Twelver Shi'ite canonical celebration in honor of Fâtima. It commemorates a kind of ordalium that occurred, according to the legend, between Muhammad and the Christians of the Najrân area who championed the idea of the *theotókos* (Mary the mother of God) which Muhammad opposed with that of an immaculate conception of Christ as the result of a vow on the part of Mary's mother. Muhammad proposed five "hostages" for the ordalium centering around Fâtima (Fâtima, her father, her husband and her sons; Majlisî, *Bihâr*, X, 1–51). But there are many "private" celebrations of Fâtima: those for her birth and death, for example. In the course of the former those present formulate vows and a table is set on which milk (the food the Prophet chose, according to the legend, during his *mi'râj* or celestial ascension) and fruit because, as we have seen, Fâtima was born of an apple of paradise brought by Gabriel to Muhammad. The "wedding of the Quraish" is another celebration in honor of Fâtima attended mainly by women: here too there is a great table with fruit and various objects (soap, henna, grains of indigo, lumps of sugar, etc.) and female singers sing excerpts of popular poetry praising the "14 pure ones" (the twelve imâms plus Fâtima and Muhammad) and their miracles. The legend-myth connected with the rite tells how a young Quraish girl invited Khadîja (Fâtima's mother and Muhammad's wife) to her wedding. Since Khadîja had died in the meantime, she asked the Prophet to send Fâtima in her place. The Prophet answered that Fâtima was in mourning and did not have suitable clothes to wear. Then Gabriel appeared bringing Fâtima gifts from God: precious silken garments and two ear-rings—one green (a premonition of Hasan's poisoning) and one red (the symbol of Husain's martyrdom). During the celebration a young girl plays the part of Fâtima who, according to the legend, came to the wedding and was so beautiful that the fiancée dropped dead of jealousy but, naturally, was immediately brought back to life by Fâtima. We will see Fâtima wearing her symbolic ear-rings once more in the next chapter. Professor Mu'în discovered two versions that already existed in the twelfth century of the female liturgy of the vow (for the purpose of the celebration is also to give thanks for graces received) (cf. Massignon, op. cit., p. 109). We should not forget that the Shi'ites also called Fâtima *batûl*, "virgin," and that according to some legends she gave birth through extra-normal channels: the navel or an ear. The legends also identify Fâtima with the Furthest Mosque of Jerusalem (*al-Masjid al-Aqsâ*) the destination of the Prophet's mysterious nocturnal journey (cf. Kor. XVII, 1) and with the Cavern of the seven sleepers of Ephesus (cf. Kor. XVIII, 9 and foll.). As the Christian Mary is "the daughter of her son," in the Shi'ite tradition Fâtima is called *umm abîhâ*, "the mother of her father." And her dowry, in the *ta'zieh* (sacred representations, see the foll. chap.) is Water: besides the water of the Euphrates, which her thirsty and dying son Husain was denied, we are in the presence here of an undeniably ancestral recurring motif. Fâtima is also identified with the rock of Moses that produced miraculous Water.[19]

But even in the learned theology of the Safavid and post-Safavid period, Persian religious thought presents characteristic traits that we will study in the next section.

The School of Isfahân

We said above that a truly scientific synthesis of the popular religiosity of the Safavid period is still premature and the same is true of the "cultivated" religious philosophy of this period. In fact, though the Shi'ite religious thinkers of this time are extremely interesting from the point of view of the history of Persian religious thought, the orientalists have not "explored" them sufficiently for a synthesis to be possible. After De Gobineau (whose information, drawn mainly from oral sources, is not always reliable and at times even inaccurate and erroneous), Browne, open-minded towards everything concerning more recent Persia, who provides us with important information on some of the Safavid and post-Safavid philosophers both in his wide-ranging history of Persian literature and in his pithy *A Year amongst the Persians* (which is much more than a travel book), the German scholar Horten's in-depth studies on Mullâ Sadrâ, and the Pakistani philosopher-poet M. Iqbâl, in his rather outdated but still valuable degree thesis on the development of metaphysics in Persia (which we have quoted elsewhere), we have to come to Corbin to find a renewed philosophical interest in these thinkers. The principal obstacle is the absence of well-ordered critical texts of their works, so that scholars still have to painfully decipher heavy oriental volumes printed in offset without indentations and with margins full of closely written comments. We will of course draw abundantly from the above-mentioned works and start with a brief historical introduction on the leaders of this school.

They were strongly influenced by Suhravardî's "illuminated" Platonism (see Chapter IV). The first place belongs to his commentator Shamsu'd-Dîn Shahrazûrî (d. 1250), who inspired Qutbu'd-Dîn Shîrâzî (d. 1311), Ibn Kamûna (d. 1277), Haravî (d. 1300) and Jalâlu'd-Dîn Dawwânî (who died in 1501 after being converted to Shi'ism through a dream) in whom the new "Twelver"

Shi'ism and Suhravardian neo-Platonism began to merge (after the more or less demonstrable contacts between Ismailism and Ishrâqism we studied above). This fusion, which appears to have been prepared by Shi'ite theologians such as Ibn Abî Jumhûr (who flourished in the second half of the fifteenth century shortly before the advent of Shâh Ismâ'îl) reached its peak in the "Isfahân school" whose most important representatives were Mîr Dâmâd (d. 1631–2) and Sadru'd-Dîn Shîrâzî (known as Mullâ Sadrâ, d. 1640–1), followed by an infinity of disciples whom we will not list for fear of boring our profane readers, and, in the ninetenth century, by the greatest modern philosopher of traditional Iran, Mullâ Hâdî Sabzavârî (d. 1878). But this period also witnessed very close contacts between Iran and Moghul India, where the translations ordered from Sanskrit to Persian by the far-seeing sovereign Akbar (d. 1605) opened a channel of possible, and at first relatively unimportant or at least undocumentable influences of the Indian Orient on Iranian thought. In this period the contacts between Iran and India assumed a very important "Zoroastrian" aspect. At the turn of our sixteenth through seventeenth centuries the Zoroastrian high priest Azar Kaivân (1529–1614) of Shîrâz moved with his disciples[20] to Patna in India where, less than a century later, one of the greatest Persian speaking poet-philosophers of India, Mîrzâ Bîdil, flourished. According to the author of the precious *Dabistân-i Mazâhib* (who was very close to this school and came into contact with it at Lahore) one of the Zoroastrian émigrés, Farzâneh Bahrâm ibn Farshâd, translated Suhravardî's works into Persian. But what is even more interesting is that a pious Shi'ite mujtahid, Bahâ'ud-Dîn 'Amilî (one of Mullâ Sadrâ's masters), appeared in the group, which was also frequented by a singular wandering Sufi, Mîr Abû'l-Qâsim Findariskî, who is mentioned in almost all the translations of the Akbarian Sanskrit period and who certainly influenced Mullâ Sadrâ. And if we also consider the presence of underground Ismaili elements in Sufism and the fact that a brief "external" renewal of Ismailism occurred at Anjudân (between Isfahân and Hamadân) in the sixteenth century with the presence of descendants of the ancient Grand Masters of Alamût under the guise of Sufi shaikhs (Ivanow, *Brief Survey*, p. 18), the sixteenth through seventeenth centuries present a real cultural-religious "renaissance" in the Iranian world; a renaissance that has so far been disregarded by the scholars who—concentrating on cultivated Persian poetry—found nothing in these centuries to equal the "great masters" of the preceding golden age. These scholars disregarded in the first place the flourishing of an often delightful popular creativity, secondly, the religious philosophy we mentioned above and, thirdly, the "new style" of cultivated Safavid poetry that, transplanted to India, was to create the so-called "Indian style" of Persian verse. This poetry is also of great aesthetic and religious interest because it is linked, I believe, with the gradual change in world-view brought about by Safavid Shi'ism.

But let us now look at the contents of this school of philosophy.

One of the principal difficulties the scholars who want to cull the distinctive traits of the *philosophoumena* and *theologoumena* of this school meet is that their texts were all written in an Aristotelian-Scholastic key, in the complicated language of the perennial philosophy, the technical framework and fundamental logic of which they accepted but which has become so difficult for "modern" scholars to understand. However, once the considerable effort of reading these works has been accomplished, there can be pleasant surprises. Basically, as Corbin[21] points out, the members of this school were Twelver Shi'ites who cloaked their *theologoumena* in an Avicennian and Suhravardian form. They were permeated with the atmosphere—the mental forms or *forma mentis*—which, according to this original French Orientalist and thinker, has characterized Iran for the past five centuries, i.e., the "nostalgia of a divine anthropomorphosis that is matched by an ideal image of Perfect Man in the person of an eternal imâm. The contemplation of this theophanic image is enough to differentiate the religion of Shi'ite Islam from other religions." In these thinkers the Shi'ite and Sufi elements are almost inextricably entwined, and they also combine with Ismaili and Ishrâqî and Suhravardian resonances. Besides, before the by–then codified official Twelver Shi'ism ("taken out of camphor" as Ivanow rather exaggeratedly expressed it) substituted the 'Alî-Ilâhî enthusiasms of the first Safavids, and before the learned super-mujtahid al-Majlisî condemned Sufism as a pernicious doctrine that tended to raise man to the level of God preventing him from giving himself heart and soul to the only one "who can be raised to the level of God," i.e., the imâm, a certain Haidar Amulî (fifteenth century) wrote (*jâmi' al-asrâr*, quoted by Corbin): "Authentic Sufism is Shi'ism and authentic Shi'ism is Sufism." Corbin insists, as usual, in seeing beyond these influences an "archetypal" rebirth of Mazdean pre-Islamic images in these thinkers. We already said what we think of this theory when writing about the earlier thinkers from whom these were derived. Even if a Sayyid Ahmad 'Alavî, commenting on the Avicennian *Shifâ*, explains the Avicennian procession of being and of the intelligences with explicit references to ancient Zurvanism; and if Muhammad Qutbu'd-Dîn Ashkivârî, the disciple and biographer of Mîr Dâmâd, compares the twelfth imâm who disappeared—"he who is awaited" at the end of time—with the Zoroastrian Saôshyant (thus showing that Corbin's theories are not based only on intuitions but can at least partially be proved "historically"); all the same I believe these contacts should be interpreted in no other light than Gardet's brilliantly expressed observation concerning Suhravardî: "The Zoroastrian motifs are the key itself to the teaching of Shaikhu'l-Ishrâq, or, more precisely, do they not assume the value of 'privileged myths' in the context of the origins of Muslim thinking, though they are characterized by Platonism and Pythagoreanism?"

Under Corbin's guidance, we will present our readers with two of Mîr Dâmâd's ecstatic experiences, drawn from the mass of his scholastic propositions. While these experiences show us how—beyond its scholastic form—this philosophy is a philosophy of experience and vision, of "realization" and pure intellectual contemplation of concepts, they also lend themselves to interesting considerations concerning the less "banal" part of the philosophy.[23] The first of these ecstatic tales is taken from a manuscript by his disciple Ashkivârî, the other is a brief ecstatic epistle, *Risâla khal'îya*, written in very elaborate, syntactically and grammatically self-conscious Arabic (in fact all the principal works of the masters of the Isfahân school were written in Arabic and it was only later that Mullâ Hâdî indulged in Persian).

First Ecstatic Tale

Therefore, in the month of God (Ramadân) of the year 1011 A. H. (1602–03) Mîr Dâmâd was in the holy city of Qum. One day, after the afternoon prayer, he stayed in the mosque, remaining kneeling in his place, sitting back on his heels, his face turned towards Mecca. He was overcome with drowsiness and this is what he says: "in front of me a radiant light, brilliantly glorious, which had the appearance of a human figure lying on its right side. And I saw another one too, of sublime appearance, extremely majestic in the beauty of its vibrant splendor, in the clarity of a light that had spread all around it. It was sitting behind the prone form. It was as if I had known myself, or as if someone else had taught me, that the prone figure was Our Lord the Prince of Believers ('Alî) while the form sitting behind was Our Lord the Prophet. I was kneeling, sitting on my heels, in front of the prone figure, right against his bosom. And lo, I saw him honor me with a smile, pass his blessed hand on my forehead, on my cheek, on my chin, as if to announce good news to me and dispel my sadness, overcome my prostration, shake the sorrow and desolation out of my soul." The imâm orders him to recite the following prayer (which is still used by pious Shi'ites and preserved as a "prayer of protection" in the Shi'ite "books of hours"): "Muhammad, God's Prophet, is in front of me; Fâtima, the daughter of God's Prophet is above me, above my head; the Prince of believers 'Alî ibn Abî Tâlib is at my right hand; Hasan and Husain, 'Alî Zainu'l-'Abidîn, etc. (the list of the twelve imâms follows) are at my left hand; Abu Dharr, Salmân, Miqdâd, Hozeifa, 'Ammâr, the Prophet's Companions are behind me; the angels are all around me and my Lord God contains me and is my guardian" (this is followed by Kor. LXXXV, 20–22). The imâm makes him repeat this formula several times until he knows it by heart. Then Mîr Dâmâd wakes up to "preserve," as he says, "the nostalgia of my vision until the day of Resurrection." The reader should note the màndala-type quadruple image as well as the manifestation of the divine in personal angelic forms; God is omnipresent but, even in the supreme ecstasy, he remains invisible, beyond any possibility of description. A whole mesocosm, an intermediate plane, "represents" God without, however, being an empty allegorical form; we have living persons of popular Shi'ite piety here. A Christian might find it much easier to understand and savour this scene than a Sunni Muslim.

Second Ecstatic Tale

This new visionary (and also "auditory") experience takes place in 1023 A. H. (1614) in the night of mid-Sha'bân (14 Sha'bân) that, according to certain Shi'ite traditions, is the most excellent of nights after the night of Power (*qadr*).[24] According to some extremist sects such as the Syrian Nusairîs (possibly connected, as we saw above, with the Persian 'Alî-Ilâhîs), Fâtima is its angelic embodiment (for all important events, including the more sacred days of the calendar, "are" people).

"On a given day of this month, and precisely on Friday the 14th of the month of the Prophet, Sha'bân the Glorious One, of the year 1023 of the holy emigration, I was speaking the name of the Lord in one of my places of retreat, redoubling my mental litanies and my repetitions of his name "the Plentiful One" (*ghanî*). And I kept repeating *yâ ghanî, yâ mughnî* ("O plentiful one, you who make us plentiful!," or else "O You who are self-sufficient and who render us self-sufficient") oblivious of any other care than that of sinking into the sanctuary of His intimate mystery and annihilating myself in the rays of His light. Then it seemed to me as if a holy thunderbolt were crashing down on me and carrying me away from my corporeal nest and I broke the links of the network of the senses and I loosened the knot of the bond of nature and I started to fly on the wing of venerable fear in the atmosphere of the reign of Reality. And it was as if I had been stripped of my body and had abandoned my usual dwelling place, as if I had cleansed the blade of my thought and had freed myself of my body as of a worn garment, as if I had definitively rolled up the carpet of the kingdom of Contingent Time (*zamân*) and had reached the kingdom of Unlimited Time (*dahr*). And lo, I found myself in the capital (*misr*, also "Egypt") of Existence (*vujûd*), among skulls (archetypes?) of the peoples of the cosmic order, emanated (*ibdâ'îyât*) and created (*takvînîyât*) existences, divine and natural existences, transcendent (*qudsîyât*) and united to matter (*huyûlânîyât*), connected with transcendent Time (*dahrîyât*) and with contingent time (*zamânîyât*) and the peoples of unbelief and of faith, the pagan nations and Islam, those who go forwards and those who remain behind, and those who precede and those who follow in Eternity who precede and follow Time (*fî'l-âzâl wa'l-*

âbâd). In brief, the monads of coalescence of what is contingent and the atoms of the universes of those who exist, all and in their totality, great and small, permanent and ephemeral, past and future, all were there, troop by troop, cohort by cohort, all together, and all turned the faces of their quiddity towards His Throne (may it be exalted!) and fixed the sight of their individuality in his direction (may His power be glorified!), though they didn't know it. And all together, with the language of the shortcoming of their indigent essences, and the poverty of their evanescent ipseity, in a lament of sadness and a cry for help, they mentioned Him and called Him, they implored Him and invoked Him *yâ ghanî, ya mughnî*! even though they were not conscious of doing so. Then, in this mental invocation for help, in this occult clamor, I began to faint, and little by little, because of the violence of my sadness and amazement, I began to forget my thinking essence, almost disappearing from the sight of my immaterial soul, and I was about to emigrate far from the desert of the earth of becoming, and to leave forever the region of the country of existence. But lo, the fugitive ecstasy was already abandoning me, leaving me with only nostalgia and tender longing. And that rapture left me sighing with sadness. And I returned once more to the land of ruins and the country of desolation, to the region of seduction, the city of illusion."

From a literary point of view this is an echo, as others have already pointed out, of "Plato's" ecstasy—of Plotinus, in fact, transmitted through the Plotinian text of the so-called "Theology of Aristotle." But it differs from the preceding ecstasies, in a singular and specifically Shi'ite manner, in its sense of nostalgic "sadness." There almost seems to be an element of sorrow in the other world too: and Shi'ism has been rightly defined the religion of "sadness." The liturgical litany "O Self-sufficient one, O you who render Self-sufficient" becomes a cosmic cry of all the single beings who feel their singleness and dependence and the impossibility of total fusion with the absolute Principle (an impossibility that is stronger in the Shi'ism, with its angelic mesocosm and its concept of purifying suffering, than in pantheistically-oriented Sufism).

We are thus led back to Mullâ Sadrâ's axiom: "the simple element of (absolute) Reality is all things, while being none of them" (*basîtu'l-haqîqa kullu'l'ashyâ' walaisa bi-shai' minhâ*). Mullâ Sadrâ was a disciple of Mîr Dâmâd. Though his master had enjoyed great fame and veneration he himself was ill-seen by orthodox thinkers who accused him of heresy. One night in a dream his master explained why. "I," Mîr Dâmâd said, "expressed philosophical questions in such a way that the official theologians might not understand them. You, on the other hand, have done the contrary, and the first school teacher who reads one of your books can understand it!" Besides the preceding axiom, Browne's oral source quoted the following, stating that these were two other original points of his philosophy:

His doctrine that true knowledge of an object becomes possible only when there is identification between the knower and the known and his statement that the imagination is independent of the physical organism and belongs, in its nature, to the world of the soul: consequently it persists—not only in very young infants but even in animals—as a spiritual entity even after death. On this point Mullâ Sadrâ differed from his predecessors who all maintained that immortality was possible only with the development of the rational soul. Since we cannot even consider summarizing Mullâ Sadrâ's immense "major works" we will offer our readers—as an example of how these Iranian religious books were composed—a very condensed summary, also in Arabic, of one his minor books that he described as a compendium of his principal work, the "Four Treatises." It is called *al-Mabda' wa'l-ma'âd*, "The Beginning and the End."[25]

The work consists in two treatises, one on theology and one on natural science. In the introduction Sadrâ maintains that the most noble of the theological sciences is the knowledge of God's first essence, of his existence and of his attributes, while the most noble of the natural sciences is psychology, the knowledge of the human soul with the relative demonstration that it is a "word of light," a "spiritual substance," "a blaze from the heavenly words" (*shu'la malakûtîya*) and "the demonstration that it does not die with the death of the body, but how it becomes more perfect until it resembles (*yudâhî*) the angelic substances . . . and how it becomes united to Active Intellect and how its intellections become active (*fi'lîya*) after being passive (*infi'âlîya*) and how material intellect (*'aql huyûlânî*) is a 'reunion of two seas' and a point of contact of two continents, etc." The knowledge of one's own soul, Sadrâ quotes from the mysterious inscription on the Sabaean temple Mas'ûdî mentioned earlier (see above), makes one divine: *man 'arafa nafsahu ta'allaha*. The introduction, which mentions Avicenna a number of times, speaks also of the need for purification, for a whittling down (*taltîf*) of the soul in those who wish to approach these matters, which the "divine learned ones" (*al-hukamâ' al-Ilâhîyûn*) have rightly always concealed under an esoteric veil, and invites the reader to free himself, before reading the book, of traditional "imitations." Finally he says that his knowledge does not only stem from the philosophers who came before him but is partly "inspired," experimental and not identical to that of those pseudo-philosophers (*mustafalsifîn*) who did not have a prophetic heritage (*al-waratha an-nabawîya*) or a heritage of Muhammadan canon law.

The book is thus divided into two "arts" (*fann*): the first on the "things of the Lord" (*ar-rubûbîyât*), the second on natural things (*tabî'yât*). The first *fann* is divided into a number of *maqâlât* ("articles"). But, as in Suhravardî, whom our Sadrâ often mentions as Shaikh al-Ilâhî (The Divine Master), the chapters are constantly interrupted by "mental flashes" (*ishrâq 'aqlî*), "subtleties of the Divine Throne" (*nukta 'arshîya*) and other similar things.

The first article (*maqâla*, p. 6) deals with the First Principle and its absolute oneness. In the meantime a Subtlety of the Divine Throne (*nukta 'arshîya*, p. 14) says that the whole thing is like an enormous book (*al-kitâb al-mubîn*, the "evident book" or the Qur'an) and at the same time like a macro-anthropus (*insân kabîr*), just as the micro-anthropus, man, is also called an "anthologic copy" (*nuskha muntakhaba*) of that supreme book. The two copies must be compared like two manuscripts. To prove the Creator's intelligent wisdom he gives the example of bees and their industrious and precise activity (p. 16). The I (*anîya*) of he whose existence is necessary (God) is the essence of every quiddity whose existence accidentally presents itself (p. 16). God's essence is his very existence (p. 20). This is followed by a criticism of the peripatetics (p. 21) for their false assertion that the existence of possibles is due to an effusion of existence over them on the part of the creator or to an addition of existence received by them. But God's essence (*kunh*) is totally unknowable, not only to men but also to angels. For Muhammad said (p. 23) that God is veiled to intellects just as it is veiled to the sight and the senses: "The supreme cohorts (of angels) seek him just as you seek him." The principal argument against the intelligibility of God's essence is that, if it were true, God's very essence, "which has no place" *par excellence*, would have to find a place in intellects (p. 24). The existent is necessarily unique, both indivisible and not divided into parts (p. 29), and, in as far as "necessary being," it has no companions (p. 36), nor does it have companions in as far as it is creator (p. 39).

The idea that the cosmos is a single animal with a single soul, etc. (which some Sufis maintained in order to explain how the absolute one can create the many) is rejected in the sense that God first created a single unconditioned existence, which is one and multiplies itself only from our point of view (p. 46).

The second article deals with God's attributes. These, as Shi'ite theology has always maintained, are identical to his essence. Merely for descriptive purposes, they are divided into attributes of Perfection (generosity, power, etc.), of Relationship (Creator, originator, etc.), Negative (as transcendent, unique, eternal) (p. 54). Next there are two sub-chapters of extreme importance for the Sadrian philosophy-theology on the knowledge of God, on his self-knowledge (p. 56) and the knowledge of the things that are other than himself (pp. 66–91). An in-depth analysis of Mullâ Sadrâ's above-mentioned theory of knowledge, which produced so many discussions and incredible theological subtleties in his spiritual successors and critics, would be impossible here. The second problem (God's knowledge of things different from himself) is more complex because it seems to imply a modification in God's very nature through the act of knowledge. "Know," Sadrâ says (p. 83) "that as there is no difference in Necessary Essence between His essence and His intellection of His essence, so also there is no difference between the existence of the First Caused and its intellection on the part of the Necessary One, since His intellection and His essence are the cause of His intellection of His First Caused, just as His Essence is the cause of the essence of the First Caused . . . therefore the existence of the First Caused is identified with intellection, on the part of Necessary One, of his essence." Thus God knows all things without, as some people object, the forms of known objects "descending" into God's very essence. Also where this theory of knowledge is concerned, Mullâ Sadrâ declares himself the disciple of the divine shaikh (Suhravardî), whose doctrines he considers similar (*qarîn*) to his own. In fact for Suhravardî too—he says—as Necessary Essence (*al-wâjib li-zâtihi*) perceives pure intelligibles through "immediate radiance" (*ishrâq hudûrî*), and so through the same system it knows material things, without involving any "forms." This, Sadrâ declares, is the best system to know how God knows (p. 84). And in effect the metaphors of the Metaphysics of Light, here as in other cases, admirably safeguard God's absolute transcendence and inaccessibility, while at the same time explaining its cognitive and other contacts with the "world"; And they occur until modern times and Babi-Bahaism in Persian religiosity.

Next we come to a sub-chapter (*fasl*) on the various degrees (*marâtib*) of His knowing things and the admonition not to confuse the divine Calamus and the Divine Table—which are included among the religious truths—with material things. The Calamus is the transcendent divine world (*mulk ilâhî qudsî*) and the Well Guarded Table is the incorporeal psychic world (*mulk nafsânî mujarrad*) and the Divine Act of writing is the Formation of Reality (*tasvîr al-haqâ'iq*), suitable symbols (*mithâl*) for expressing the graduations of God's science (p. 95). It was over this supposed negation of the reality of certain full-bodied religious truths of the catechisms that Mullâ Sadrâ and his disciples were often attacked by orthodox thinkers, who did not understand that by *mithâl* ("symbols") Sadrâ and his followers meant something far more "real" than they imagined.

Next there are sections on God's might (p. 96) and on his will (*irâda*) (p. 99). Since, in common language, *irâda* also means "affection," and "love," Sadrâ also speaks of God's love for His creatures. This love, he says, does not imply a defect and lacuna in the Lover, who thereby wishes for what he lacks, but, in God's case, the love for His works is identified with His love for Himself. For in fact he who loves a trace or an object left by the beloved, really loves the beloved in it, as the ancient Arab poet said . . . "it is not the love for walls and houses which rends my heart, it is the love for the person who lived in those houses!" (p. 100). The article ends with a detailed study of other traditional attributes of God, Life, Hearing, Sight, Wisdom (*hikma*) (pp. 105–7), Joy (p. 108) and on how he loves creatures (p. 113). In all of them Sadrâ shows his tendencies, which I would be inclined to call "realistically symbolic" or "symbolically realistic."

The third and last article of the first part is on God's Operations (p. 117). After a brief and unoriginal propedeutical introduction we have various chapters: on the four elements (p. 118); on their blending and the possibility of combining them, in as far as they lack autonomous life (p. 120); on the limitation of movement by means of a body (p. 121); on the cause of the production of movement (p. 124); on the fact that the sky is an animal in as far as it moves of its own will (p. 127); on the fact that the sky is a macro-anthropus (*insân kabîr*) in as far as the principle of its movement is not a natural animal force (*muntabi'a*) but an immaterial soul with intellective force and will (p. 128); on the fact that the motor of the sky can be neither pure intellect, nor pure nature, but a psychic element (p. 129); that the movement of the sky presupposes a separate motor (p. 130) and multiple intelligences (p. 131); on the fact that immaterial intelligences move the heavenly bodies and their souls, which are divine lovers (*al-'ushshâq al-ilâhîyûn*) in ecstasy over the contemplation of the beauty of Absolute Reality, irradiated by the rays of divine light and by the overabundant pleasures of light (p. 133); on the modality of the provenance (*sudûr*) of things from the First Provider (*mudabbir awwal*); on how God's only true attribute is his essence itself, just as his true, only and eternal operation is solely the donation of being (*ifâdat al-vujûd*) (p. 138); on the formation of the elements from the ultimate intellect (in the Avicennian series of the intelligences) (p. 141); on divine grace (*'inâya*) and its government of the world (*tadbîr*) (p. 142); on providence towards terrestrial creatures (p. 143); and on Satan's dominion over the intimate being of man (p. 147) (with an appendix, *ramz 'arshî* "lofty symbol", on the fact that the cause of the fall of souls in the world of matter is Adam's sin through a contingent defect—*naqs imkânî*—in his substance—*gauhar*—and a natural defect in his essence—*qusûr tab'î fî zâtihi*); on the explanation of certain special aspects of divine providence in the disposition of the cosmos (p. 150); on the providential utility in creation of the perceptible forces in man (p. 156); on His providence in the creation of motive powers (p. 157); on His providence in the creation of the seven categories (*tabaqât*) of angels to reform man's state and guide him to perfection and union with the acting intellect (p. 158) (with an answer to the objection of skeptics on why so many angels are necessary); on divine providence in the ideation of the sexual system for the perpetuation of the species (p. 161); on the creation of the earth and its products (p. 162); on the wonders of the planetary orbits (p. 163).

With this survey of the heavens we come to the end of the first "art" and to the beginning of the second one on the natural sciences, with particular attention to psychology, and to the "return", to death, judgement, hell and heaven and to future life. Thus the circle which started, with theology, from God as First One, ends, through psychology, with God as Last One. The "art" is divided into an introduction and four articles. The introduction (p. 164) distinguishes two species of origins of beings, by *ibdâ* (creation ex-novo) i.e., when an acting force comes into play without there necessarily being "capacity" of reception in the created thing, and by *takwîn* (essentiation) when both the capacity to be of the thing and the acting force contribute together to the creative act. At any rate there is a gradation of dignity in created things, the first created thing being more noble that the second and so forth. The articles which follow are divided into *fasl* (sections). The first article deals with the formation of the three kingdoms (*mawâlîd*) of nature. It begins with a sub-chapter on the blending (*mizâj*) of the four elements-humours (p. 165) followed by others on the formation of animal nature (p. 170); on the potencies divided into motive (*muharrika*) and perceptive (*mudrika*) potencies of animal soul (p. 171); on the two potencies which perceive individual forms, the "sensus communis," localized in the first ventricle of the brain, and the sense by which we use certain external senses to judge others (e.g., this yellow thing is hot) (p. 178); on the mental perceptive potencies which are Imagination and Memory (p. 181); on the governing force (*mutasarrifa*) situated in the middle ventricle (batn) of the brain: all these perceptive potencies have a special "framework" and a special cerebral location (p. 182); on the formation of man and his potencies (p. 187); on man's peculiarities (*khavâss*) (p. 188); on the stages of the speculative potency (p. 190); on the intellectus materials ('*aql huyûlânî*) (p. 191); on the four degrees of practical potency: (a) correctio morum, through the external religious law; (b) the moral purification of the inner person; (c) the adorning of the thinking soul with the most holy forms; (d) the soul goes beyond itself and contemplates only the Lord (p. 200); on the fact that the potency which is the place of the intelligibles in man is not a corporeal potency (with an appendix of criticisms not so much against Avicenna as against "some of his disciples" and many answers to most varied objections) (p. 203); on the fact that the human soul is an autonomous spiritual substance totally independent from the body (p. 213), which comes into existence contemporaneously with the existentiation of the body (p. 223) but does not die with it (p. 225); on the fact that the transmigration of souls from body to body in this world is not possible (p. 235). In this long and interesting sub-chapter Mullâ Sadrâ does admit however (supporting his statement with quotations from the Qur'an and from tradition, e.g., Kor. VI, 38; V, 60; II, 65, etc.) a transformation of men into forms "corresponding to the qualities which they had in this world" in other post-mortem stages of existence in the no less real intermediate worlds of "symbols," the admission and understanding of which are the key to the whole of Sadrâ's philosophy. Thus when, in this chapter, Sadrâ relates the traditions (attributed to the prophet) concerning persons who "will be raised up from the dead in the form of donkeys at the end of the world" to this world of *ashbâh mithâlîya* (symbolic forms), we deduce two things: one that for him the "end of the world" and the resurrection of the flesh do not occur on this earth but in the mesocosm of "symbols" (this is one of the points which most irritated the orthodox thinkers) and secondly that, in this meta-worldly sense, he fully admitted metempsychosis, though only for particularly "carnal" persons whose souls would have been given forms corresponding to their qualities (swine *et similia*) in the world of the beyond. "Perfect" souls, on the other hand, would be exempt from these "symbolical" incorporations, since they no longer had any need for matter. It is interesting that to prove the doctrine of transmigration (taken in this sense), Sadrâ not only quotes the Qur'an and the Prophet but also "columns" of wisdom like Plato, Socrates, Pythagoras, Empedocles, Agathodaimon and Hermes "the father of the wise." As for Aristotle, Sadrâ interprets his negation of metempsychosis in the sense that Aristotle too understood it in the same "correct" sense that he did. Next there is a sub-chapter (p. 258) on how the acting intellect contacts our souls; in a typically Suhravardian way it is angelized in Gabriel "who in the Persian nation is called *ravânbakhsh* (giver of souls) and at the same time is the highest creature in the world of the ideas of the Platonists." We are in the full "angelic personification" of Platonic ideas and the following chapter continues on the same theme (p. 260) "of the spiritual angel" whom the Gnostics (*'urafâ*) called 'Anqâ (the Phoenix) as a symbol (*'alâ sabîl ar-ramz*) which cures melancholy with the whirr of its wings (for those who know how to hear it)[26] and every sickness with the lightest touch of its feathers (these sicknesses, Sadrâ explains, are ignorance based on the stubborn obstinacy of the soul, etc.). The next chapter (p. 261) deals with the true happiness of the soul obtained through speculative intellect and practical intellect and with the relative state of unhappiness; then (p. 268) of the deprivation of intelligibles in certain souls and their consequent privation of unltra-worldly happiness and, therefore (p. 270), of the sense which must be given to "perceptible" "beatitude" and damnation in the other world, where he even admits a certain kind of perceptibe happiness for "ignorant," though not wicked, souls.

The second article deals with the Corporeal Return or, to put it in Christian terms, with the resurrection of the flesh. A first chapter (p. 272) criticizes the excesses of those who on the one hand deny all possibility of return (the materialists) and, on the other, those who consider that the return occurs in the form of flesh and blood identical to those enjoyed in this world. Since the point is theologically very delicate, Sadrâ navigates, (in another sub-chapter too [p. 277]) through extremely subtle distinctions in order not to incur is the accusation of heresy as the negator of the resurrection of the flesh. Quoting an interesting passage from the Spanish Muslim mystic Ibn 'Arabî in support of his theory, Sadrâ maintains, among other things, that in the other world *all* souls will have the creative force of imaginative phantoms (with however an autonomous and real existence) which only the souls of a few privileged miracle-makers possess in this world. It "may" be—Sadrâ adds—like a beautiful dream (for the blessed) or an eternal nightmare (for the damned) but with the difference that the "impressions" will be more vivid than those we experience in dreams (pp. 286–7). To conclude, Sadrâ interprets the data of the revelation in a psychological key, stating that (p. 300) "when man dies and his soul abandons his body, maintaining at that instant the awareness of self and the preceptive quality of details, he will imagine (*takhayyala*) himself as drawing away from the dwelling of the world and will mold for himself the image (*yatawahham*) of himself buried, and he will feel the pain and torment of being buried as a perceptible torment," the torment which the Muslim catechists call the "torture of the tomb" (see also above). If the soul is blessed it will imagine itself (*yatasawwar zâtahâ*) as having a beautiful and delicate form and will meet the promised joys. But one must be careful *not* to consider all this as purely imaginary (*mauhûma mahdan*) or, rather, that the imaginary things of the other world are more vivid and effective that the "real" things of this world. This claim of "reality" for the symbolical world is the most delicate and original point of Sadrian philosophy (or rather of the whole tradition from Suhrahvardî to Mullâ Hâdî) and it has been the cause of infinite misunderstandings between the "materialists" who accused him of reducing everything to symbols, and the ultra-symbolists who, confusing symbol with allegory, accused him of being still too strictly orthodox. However—Sadrâ concludes prudently (p. 317)—given the extreme importance of the concept of "return" and eternal retribution in the religion of Islam, and in order to avoid evil and promote moral good, even an extremely bodily and exterior belief is better for the ignorant (who are unable to study and understand the true realities of these things) than non-belief.

The third article (p. 319) is a "testimonial" (*shuhûdî*), experimental, re-interpretation of the "Return" and of "death, judgement, hell and heaven" in the style of the Gnostics. It begins with a long sub-chapter on the "start from the Beginning and on the return to It," in which three worlds are distinguished: the world of material things (heavenly or hellish), the world of spiritual exercise and ascetic practices and of the "absence" beyond this world and the other (that of complete separation or intelligibles) of the First Form. The first world is perceived by man with his senses, the second with his imagination (*khayâl*), the third with his intellect (*'aql*). Though the material world seems more real to us, it is an indicative symbol of the invisible things of the other two worlds. Reality comes down in a descending arc from the First Principle and from the most pure world of Victorious Lights towards perceptible things. Then, with man, it becomes capable of returning from these up the ascendant arc of the return to that first initial World. This is followed (p. 330) by a collection of traditions on the "place" of heaven and hell, which are contradictory only for those people on the outside who do not understand the system of interpretation of these realities through "symbolical realism." The same can be said of "death and resurrection" (p. 335) and of the "reality" (*haqq*) of the traditional eschatological concepts such as that of the reckoning with the Book, of the Scales on which actions are weighed, and of the very narrow bridge *Sirât*, which spans hell (p. 337). For example, it says of the Scales that they are as truly "scales" as good taste is *truly a scale* for judging a poem. The delights of paradise and the fire of hell are "real" too (p. 337)—"produced" by good or bad actions committed during life, in the form of metapsychic "éidola" (*ukhravîya ashbâh*) and of "persons of the world of the *barzakh*" (*ashkhâs barzakhîya*).

The fourth and last article (p. 334) deals with the prophecies and dreams. It starts with a discussion on the "cause of true visions" saying, among other things, that every "mental significance" has a real form and an unreal form. If the person who is dreaming has a soul in contact with the world of pure intelligibles or with the celestial psychic world (*an-nafsî as-samâwî*) what he sees in dream is either the intellectual thing (*amr*) itself or a real symbol of it. If on the other hand the person who is dreaming is psychic or materialist, his dreams are mainly the "confused dream images" mentioned in the Qur'an, which are dealt with in the next chapter (p. 347). A longer chapter follows (p. 348) on the possibility of seeing, in a state of wakefulness, things which do not exist outwardly where, though these phenomena may in some cases indicate a perfection of the imaginative faculty, they are partly attributed to an imbalance of the natural humours, and then (p. 354) on the miracles of the Prophets and Saints. Going back to his usual metaphysical tripartition, he maintains that the Prophet must have perfect mastery of the three potencies: "intellective" (or speculative) potency which allows him to come into contact with pure intelligibles without too much discursive thinking, "imaginative" potency which allows him to see and hear realities of the world of symbols even when he is awake, and "perceptible" potency so that he can arbitrarily make rain fall and accomplish other physical miracles. The next sub-chapter (p. 356) deals with the difference between inspiration (*ilhâm*) and learning (*ta'allum*); and then with the need for the coming of the Prophets into the world to guide souls in their reascension to the upper worlds and their "return" to their "first nature", and with the need for a religious law which is also external and civil (p. 361). Two brief chapters follow on the qualities the Leader of the visible religious community should have (p. 363) and others, of relative importance (pp. 365 and foll.), on certain prescriptions of canon law, and finally the last (p. 369) to explain the fact that "the scope of all the canon laws is to make known the architecture of the stages of the way which leads to God and provide the viaticum and the arms to keep thieves and robbers away."

And so even this supposedly dangerous heretic ends by singing the praises—not out of prudence but out of intimate conviction—of the pragmatic usefulness of the external religious law. As we have already said, the orthodox thinkers blamed him most for two points in particular (which can be summed up into one): his doctrine of the science of God which, according to them, could endanger the more litteralist concept of a tendentially anthropomorphist God like the Islamic God who knows all things one by one and, secondly, his symbolical explanation of the eschatological "realities"; for the other accusations, such as that of championing metempsychosis, etc., are secondary. The central focus of an exact understanding of Sadrian religious philosophy (which may have escaped the theologians) is its metaphysical and very ancient tri-cosmism.

Since the existence of the intermediate world of real "symbols" seems to me extremely important for an understanding of the "core" of this philosophy—the angelization of the world of Platonic ideas—we will also quote the following passage from the treatise "Hidden Words" (*Kalimât-i Maknûna*) by Mullâ Sadrâ's disciple and commentator, Muhsin Faiz.[27]

In it [the world] spirits are incorporated, and bodies are spiritualized, and moral entities and actions are depersonalized, and inner realities (*ma'ânî*) are manifested in forms adapted to them. The apparition of phantoms (*ashbâh*) in mirrors and in other burnished substances and in limpid water, all come from this world, because it is there that one can see those forms which appear to the imagination, both in dream and in waking, and they are in communication with this world and are illuminated by it. . . And it lies in an intermediate position, the senses (*havâss*) ascend towards it and the spiritual realities (*ma'ânî*) descend into it . . . and in it the traditions concerning the Prophet's Ascension (*mi'râj*) and concerning the perceptible vision in dreams of angels and prophets are authenticated, in it the presence of the Most Pure *Imâms* so realized when death draws near.

The last sentence alludes to the Shi'ite belief according to which the blessed, at the moment of death, have the grace of seeing the vision of the *imams*: a belief which is so singularly like the Christian vision of Christ enjoyed by the "elect" immediately before death.

A study of the personality and philosophy of the last great Persian philosopher of this school, Mullâ Hâdî Sabzavârî (d. 1878), would only lead to repetitions since he added very little that was essentially new to Mullâ Sadrâ's fundamental concepts. The curious reader will find a summary of his philosophy in Browne's works (*A Year Amongst the Persians*, chap. VI) and in Iqbâl's *Metaphysics*, pp. 135 and foll.).

The Shaikhî Movement

On the other hand, we should give some attention to the school of theological thought of the Shaikhî movement—also because it was the precursor of the Babi movement that later developed into a truly autonomous religion. This school was founded by Shaikh Ahmad al-Ahsâ'î, a pious Shi'ite theologian from al-Ahsâ (Arabia), (the name of the movement coming from his title of shaikh). Born in 1744 [or more likely 1753], he soon moved to Persia. He died during a pilgrimage to Mecca in 1827 or 28 [or more probably 1826] and was succeeded, as leader of his school, by Sayyid Kâzim from Rasht (who died in 1843 or 1844; "Sayyid" is a title given in Persia to the Prophet's descendants). Despite the many works by the two founders and the later spiritual leaders of the school (which still has an active printing press and a cultural center in the city of Kirmân) and despite also the enormous quantity of controversial litera-ture both between the Shaikhîs and the "orthodox" Shi'ites and between the Shaikhîs and the Babis, an overall scholarly European work on the subject does not exist. Consequently a synthesis of this area is premature: too much material has yet to be studied. The relatively most reliable information we have on the Shaikhî doctrine remains that which Nicolas, a very learned dragoman, col-lected over forty years ago. But despite his willingness, he was not sufficiently prepared philosophically and scientifically to understand certain theological "subtleties" (*Essai sur le cheikhisme*, 1911). The same is true of Browne who mentions Shaikhism here and there (he was interested in it as an introduction to his study on Babism but was not sufficiently well acquainted with the original texts) and even more so of Gobineau (*Religions et philosophies dans l'Asie Centrale*, 1865) who, as always, is extremely vague. The reader will therefore have to consider the following outline with some caution for lack of better source ma-terial. Generally speaking, Shaikhism contains a stronger Shi'ite theological "impetus" and is more purely "religious" than philosophers such as Mullâ Sadrâ were. Iqbâl's statement (op. cit., p. 193) that shaikh Ahmad was an enthusiastic reader of Mullâ Sadrâ's works is based on a misunderstanding: the Shaikhîs studied Mullâ Sadrâ but did not always approve of what he said; in fact, on some points (for example, on questions concerning the knowledge of God) they returned to less philosophical and more religious positions. The imâms as persons and the desire to feel in some way in direct contact with them, are important emotional factors in Shaikhî religiosity. The twelve imâms are the efficient cause of the creation, the interpreters of God's desires. God would not have created anything if it had not been for them: but the accusation of *tafvîz* (the doctrine that not God but the imâms, or one of them, directly created the world) which the orthodox thinkers brought against the Shaikhîs seems unjus-tified, for the Shaikhîs say that, though all the acts of the divinity are brought about through the twelve imâms, they do not have autonomous powers and are simply organs of transmission. God is incomprehensible and can only be known, in part, to men through the twelve imâms, who mirror His reality: the well-guarded tablet (see above) of traditional anthropomorphic theology is nothing but the heart of the imâm which embraces all the heavens and the earth. There is a tradition in fact that says: "The whole world cannot contain me; only the heart of my servant can." When this tradition started it probably referred to man in general and this is how the Sufi understood it. But the Shaikhîs, who in this respect are ultra-Shi'ite, have a marked tendency to attribute all these traditional glorifications of man not to man in general but to the imâm, the perfect man, compared to whom other men are worthless, the only man of whom one can say "man" (this idea is also an Ismaili one). The Shaikhî doctrine on eschatology is similar to that of Mullâ Sadrâ, but the Shaikhîs developed the distinctions between spiritual body and material body, symbolic body and real body to such a degree of subtlety (further enhanced by the controversy with the orthodox thinkers who tried to catch them out as negators of the resurrection of the flesh and the bodily realities of the other world) that it is difficult at times for a modern mind to determine the precise denotation of these terms. They even reached the point of admitting two bodies of one kind and two of another—four bodies in all! Where the knowledge of God is concerned, the Shaikhîs maintain that his knowledge of the essence itself exists, as well as another created (*muhdath*) knowledge that is the being itself of the known thing, and that the imâms (according to an old saying that has been reinterpreted) are the doors (*bâb*) that give access to this second knowledge. The world is eternal in time, but created, "new," in the sense of an essential hierarchy of values. Heaven is the love for the Sacred Family of the Prophet, for the imâms: heaven and hell are created by acts of men (this concept is similar to Mullâ Sadrâ's). One point (which may seem secondary to us) in which the Shaikhîs differ from the orthodox Shi'ites is that they believe that the bodies of the imâms decay after death while the orthodox thinkers believe that they are incorruptible. Generally speaking they tend to explain the miracles of the prophets and imâms symbolically, i.e., as figurations of more real spiritual miracles and at times, especially with the later Shaikhîs, the symbol can reach the point of allegory.

If the complex theological position of the Shaikhîs could be summed up in a few words I would say that it is based on two points, one deeply religious and the other with rational tendencies. And these two aspects continue side by side and at times even in apparent contrast in their spiritual successors, the Babis and the Baha'is. The first point is the very strong feeling that God's authority must always be present and active through an "intermediary" among men. The first intermediary (*vâsiteh*) was the prophet Muhammad; he was followed by the series of the twelve imâms. The Shaikhîs—disagreeing with the Twelver

Shi'ites—consider it absurd that with the disappearance of the last imâm the community should remain without a leader and be governed by colleges of mujtahids. This further intermediary is the Bâb (the fourth of the four pillars, *arkân*), the "gate" between man and the world of the imâms.

The other point is a tendency to symbolic explanations (which sometimes go beyond the realistic symbolism of Sadrâ) to enter into a truly rationalist allegory of the miraculous aspect of traditional theological legends.

Concerning the first point it should be noted that despite the founders' allusions to a Bâb understood as a real person to be sought for, whose coming into the world is near at hand, the Shaikhism that followed the advent of the Bâb and the conversion of many Shaikhîs to Babism interpreted the founders' rather obscure doctrines as indicating that the "fourth pillar," the Bâb or "perfect Shi'ite," was a concept, not a person, thus falling back into a form very similar to that of the orthodox Shi'ites. In fact, present-day Shaikhîs are, practically speaking, considered a normal, if slightly aberrant, Shi'ite theological school side by side with the Usûlis and Akhbârîs, (whom we mentioned above), although there was a time when they suffered cruel persecution. The fourth pillar is "the religion of the pious Shi'ites."

The second point leads us to a few comments, based on a modern Shaikhî booklet on a recent dispute (1953), couched in very moderate terms, between the orthodox Shi'ite mujtahid Falsafî[28] of Tehran—a relentless persecutor of the Baha'is—and a high dignitary of the modern Shaikhî school. Where the creation of the world is concerned, the Shaikhî dignitary maintains that God cannot be (p. 183) either the efficient, or final, or formal, or material cause of the creation because He is, in His absolute transcendence, beyond all imagination. If God were the cause, this would already contaminate his absolute transcendence. The cause of all things which is in fact meant when God is mentioned in this context, is the First Created One, identified by the Shaikhîs with *amr* (divine order). This First Creature is sometimes called Light, sometimes Universal Intellect, sometimes *amr* (divine order, divine act, which is different from the "causing one" of the "creation"), and sometimes Muhammad. Consequently when the Shaikhîs speak of God they implicitly intend the only possible way of imagining Him, i.e., Muhammad himself or the imâm. But how is it possible, the mujtahid objects, that a man like Muhammad or the imâm, who was born on a given day and died on another, can be the First Creature? (p. 199). The Shaikhî dignitary answers with the usual expedient distinctions—based on the metaphysics of light—between physical man and man as the most pure mirror of the light of the first created one (Muhammad). Questioned, for example, on another *punctum dolens* of every symbolical interpretation—the Prophet Muhammad's famous ascension to heaven (*mi'râj*)—he answers that the ascension occurred both in soul and body (with some mental reservations, of course, since he means one of the various ethereal bodies admitted by Shaikhî theology) but that since Muhammad is the "first created one," this is a logical means for a superhuman being like him and in a sense there is nothing miraculous about this though our reason is unable to grasp it. Basically, this answer makes more sense than that of the orthodox Muslim who first says that Muhammad is an ordinary man and then has him accomplish literally the most outstanding feats (splitting the moon, ascension, etc.). Everything is easily resolved by transposing the historical reality of the facts of revelation onto metahistorical planes (Muhammad, 'Alî, etc. = First Creature): it is here, and not in a humanistic rationalism, that the secret of Shaikhî symbolism lies.

To conclude, we have seen in this chapter how the advent of Twelver Shi'ism gave Persian religiosity a new emotional dimension and enriched it with a fertile popular strain. We can truly say in this sense that 'Alî, with his exploits worthy of an ancient Iranian Rustam, and Husain with his suffering and martyrdom at the hands of unjust relatives (like Siyâvush in the early epic poem) became full-fledged Persian citizens. In the next two chapters we will see, first, a recent but particularly interesting aspect of popular Shi'ite religiosity that becomes a drama of redemptive suffering in the celebration of Husain's blood, and next, how the theological philosophical doctrines—which were handed down from Suhravardî and his predecessors to Mullâ Sadrâ and the Shaikhî movement, combined with the popular emotional expectation of the twelfth "vanished" imâm and with new individual solicitations in a particularly fortunate series of exceptional religious personalities—have made Persia, as late as the nineteenth century, the home and "holy land" of a truly new and autonomous Islamic religion, the last of the classic revealed religions. It testifies to the perennial vitality of the religious spirit of Iran but also shows—as Iqbâl shrewdly observed—that, unlike the Arab genius, the Persian genius ended by preferring Plato to Aristotle (*Development of Metaphysics in Persia*, p. 136): "In Persia and in all those countries where physical science either does not exist or is not studied, philosophy always ends by being reabsorbed into religion. The 'Essence,' i.e., the metaphysical cause as distinct from the scientific cause (which means the sum of antecedent causes), must gradually change into Personal Will (the cause, in a religious sense) in the absence of other concepts of cause. And this, possibly, is the most profound reason for Persian philosophies always ending up in a Religion."

Notes

1.   "Schejch Bedr el-dîn," *Der Islám*, XI, 1921, pp. 1 and foll.; esp. pp. 78 and foll.
2.   W. Hinz, *Irans Aufsteig zum Nationalstaat im XV Jhdt.*, Berlin, 1936.

3. Cf. V. Minorsky, "The poetry of Shâh Ismâ'îl I," *BSOAS*, X (1942), p. 1041. The complete collection of Shâh Ismâ'îl's lyrics is in course of publication, edited by prof. Turkhan Gangei, whom I wish to thank here for some useful suggestions.

4. Haidar is the same as 'Alî but it was also the name of Shâh Ismâ'îl's real father.

5. A famous tyrant of ancient Iran. Here we again have the mystical bivalency of the Divine.

6. See Avicenna's above-mentioned quatrain.

7. Sprenger, *Oudh*, p. 397; Rieu, *Brit. Mus.*, p. 669 b, 670 a.

8. These are, as can be seen, local traditions of the south Caspian region, which our author made use of.

9. Which belongs to the "symbolic places" we spoke about at length in chap. IV.

10. Qur'anic prophets. The above-mentioned episodes of the lives of the prophets are in the Qur'an and in Islamic tradition.

11. A famous episode (which occurred in 659) in the civil strife which took place in early Islam.

12. The (Mongol) sovereign îl-Khân of Persia, also known as Uljaitû who reigned from 1305 to 1316 and was converted to Shi'ism.

13. Sacred circumambulation, like that practised in the course of the Islamic pilgrimage around the Kaaba.

14. The two terms may not be absolutely identifiable. But the problem is as yet unsolved.

15. It should however be noted that, according to the Turkish historian Zeki Velidi Toghan's recent studies, the Safavids were of Kurdish origin.

16. The mystical ejaculation: "Him!."

17. See the brief note on him and the bibliography in Pareja-Bausani-Hertling, *Islamologia*, pp. 581–83, 592–93.

18. See Massignon, "La notion du voeu et la dévotion musulmane à Fâtima," in *Studi Levi della Vida*, p. 102 and foll. of vol. II.

19. Cf. Massignon, "Der gnostische Kult der Fâtima im shiitischen Islam," in *Eranos Jahrbuch*, 1938, p. 167 and foll. 'Alî is often called "the lord of the Waters" (Virolleaud, *Théatre Persan*, p. 34).

20. Corbin (Suhravardî, *Opera* I, p. LV) quotes Modi, "A Parsee High Priest, Dastur Azar Kaiwân with his zoroastrian disciples in Patna," in *Journ. of the K. R. Cama Oriental Inst.*, XX, 1932, pp. 1–85.

21. "Confessions extatiques de Mîr Dâmâd," in *Mélanges Louis Massignon*, I, Damas, 1956, pp. 331–78.

22. In *Studies in early Persian Ismailism*, Leiden-Bombay, 1948, p. 29.

23. We do not want to overload the text with references to the works of Mîr Dâmâd, on whom see the above-mentioned article by Corbin.

24. In which, according to tradition and a Qur'anic passage (XCVII, I and foll.), the Qur'an was revealed.

25. I am translating from a lithograph edition from Tehran (1314 H.) with comments by Mullâ Hâdî.

26. See, for Suhravardî, my earlier study on the same subject.

27. Quoted in Corbin, Suhravardi, *Opera* I, p. LII.

28. This is why the title of the booklet is Falsafîyeh.

Bibliography

For general information on Twelver Shi'ism the handbook we have already mentioned is useful: Pareja-Bausani-Hertling, *Islamologia*, Rome, 1951. It contains the most important bibliography.

On the Imâmite schools:
Scarcia, G. "Intorno alle controversie tra Ahbârî e Usûlî presso gli Imâmiti di Persia." *RSO* XXXIII (1958), pp. 211–250.

On Shâh Ismâ'îl and the origins of the Safavids, besides Browne's frequently mentioned history of literature:
Gandjci, T. *Il canzoniere di Shâh Ismâ'îl Hatâ'î*. Roma, 1959.
Hinz, W. *Irans Aufstieg zum Nationalstaat im XV. Jahrhundert*. Berlin, 1936 (this should be used with caution because of the author's tendency to transpose German concepts of nationalism to the Safavid period, but it is useful for the information and material it contains).
Minorsky, V. "The Poetry of Shâh Ismâ'îl I." *Bull. of the School of Oriental and African Studies*. London, X (1942), pp. 1007 and foll.

On the Hurûfîs:
Ritter, H. "Die Anfänge der Hurûfisekte." *Oriens* VII (1954), pp. 1–54.
Textes Persans relatifs à la secte des Houroufis, publiés, traduits et annotés par M. Clémént Huart . . . suivis d'une Etude sur la religion des houroufis par le docteur Riza Tevfiq . . . Leiden-London ("Gibb Memorial," IX, 1909; rather out-dated but still useful).

On ahl-i haqq or 'Alî-Ilâhîs:
Minorsky, V. "Notes sur la secte des ahl-é haqq." *Revue du Monde Musulman* vol. XL (1920) and (1921). There is a bibliography in the excellent article by the same author (Ahl-i Hakk) in *Handwörterbuch des Islam*, Leiden, 1941.

On folkloristic-religious Persian traditions, material (which has not however been developed in a historical and religious sense) is to be found in the useful volumes:
Massé, H. *Croyances et coutumes persanes*, Paris, 1938 (two vols.).

On the school of Isfahan, as we have already said, there is very little besides the articles by Corbin which we already mentioned in the course of this chapter:
Browne, E.G. *A Literary History of Persia*. Cambridge, 1951. Vol. IV, pp. 423–43.
———. *A Year amongst the Persians*, Cambridge,1927, pp. 133–167.
de Gobineau, Arthur Joseph. *Les religions et les philosophies dans l'Asie Centrale*. Paris, 1865.
Hörten, M. *Die Gottesbeweise bei Schirâzî*. Bonn, 1912.

―――――. *Das philosophische System von Schirází*. Strassburg, 1913.

Iqbal, M. *The Development of Metaphysics in Persia*. Lahore (reprint) undated, pp. 134 and foll.

On Shaikhism, our basis remains Nicolas' works:

Nicolas, A.L.M. *Essai sur le Cheikhisme*. Paris (4 vols.), 1910 and foll.

One of my students, Dr G. R. Scarcia, who held the position of reader at the University of Tehran, has collected important first-hand material on the Shaikhî school and its most recent developments in Iran which we hope will shortly be published. I wish to thank him here for the valuable information he has given me.

Additional Bibliography

Bibliographical update: For subjects treated in this chapter, the best reference work in English is P. Jackson and L. Lockhart, eds., *The Cambridge History of Iran, Vol. 6: The Timurid and Safavid Periods* (Cambridge, 1986). For popular and unorthodox Shi'ite ideas, those seeking further information in English should see Kathleen R.F. Burrill, *The Quatrains of Nesimi, Fourteenth Century Turkic Hurufi* (The Hague, 1972); Michel Mazzaoui, *The Origins of the Safavids: Shi'ism, Sufism and the Gulat* (Wiesbaden, 1972); Moojan Momen, *An Introduction to Shi'i Islam* (New Haven, Cn., 1985); and Matti Moosa, *Extremist Shiites: The Ghulat Sects* (Syracuse, N.Y., 1987). For Safavid history see Roger Savory, *Iran under the Safavids* (Cambridge, 1980); and the same author's *Studies on the History of Safavid Iran* (London, 1987). For the Shi'ite revival in Iran during this period see Said Amir Arjomand, *The Shadow of God and the Hidden Imam* (Chicago, 1984). The School of Isfahan is treated in Henri Corbin, *En Islam Iranien*, vol. 4 (Paris, 1972). Indian Persian culture and possible influences at this time are discussed in Fathullah Mujtabai, *Aspects of Hindu-Muslim Cultural Relations* (New Delhi, 1978). Mulla Sadra's philosophical ideas are covered in Fazlur Rahman, *The Philosophy of Mulla Sadra*, (Albany, N.Y., 1975) and S.H. Nasr, *Sadr al-Din Shirazi and his Transcendent Philosophy* (Tehran, 1978); and one of his books, the *Kitab al-'Arshiyyah*, has been elegantly translated into English: James W. Morris, *The Wisdom of the Throne* (Princeton, 1981). For Shaikhism see Henry Corbin, *L'École Shaykhie en Théologie* Shi'ite (Tehran, 1967); the same author's *Spiritual Body and Celestial Earth: From Mazdean Iran to* Shi'ite *Iran*, trans. Nancy Pearson (Princeton, 1977); Mangol Bayat, *Mysticism and Dissent: Socioreligious Thought in Qajar Iran* (Syracuse, N.Y., 1982); Juan R.I. Cole, "Rival Empires of Trade and Imami Shi'ism in Eastern Arabia, 1300–1800," *International Journal of Middle East Studies* 19 (1987):177–204; and the same author's *Roots of North Indian Shi'ism in Iran and Iraq* (Berkeley, 1989), chapter 7. Cole has a major monograph on Shaikhism in preparation. (-JRIC.)

Chapter Seven

The Drama of Karbala and Redemptive Suffering

Introduction

"Normal" Islam does not attribute the central importance to pain and death that is so accentuated in others religions, and particularly in Christianity. We do, of course, find passages in the Qur'an like this one (II:153 and foll.):

> O all you who believe, seek you help in patience and prayer; surely God is with the patient. And say not of those slain in God's way, 'They are dead'; rather they are living, but you are not aware. Surely We will try you with something of fear and hunger, and diminution of goods and lives and fruits; yet give thou good tidings unto the patient who, when they are visited by an affliction, say: 'Surely we belong to God, and to Him we return'; upon those rest blessings and mercy from their Lord, and those—they are the truly guided.

But this is little more than a statement of the problem of pain as a "trial" sent by an arbitrary Lord; man's correct reaction to it is patience and resignation. Suffering and evil remain suffering and evil and never change—as in the classic Christian concept—into their opposite. In a less mysterious passage than may at first appear, God says to the Prophet Muhammad (Kor. XX, 2): "We have not sent down the Qur'an upon thee for thee to be unprosperous"; even if tradition has considerably enlarged on and developed the tale of the Prophet's sufferings, especially during the first years of his mission when he was surrounded by enmity and hatred. The hadîth (traditions attributed to the Prophet) that were probably inspired by ascetic-mystical circles also speak, it is true, of the sufferings of the just: "It is said that a man said to the Prophet: I love you. The prophet answered: Then you are prepared for Poverty! The man added: I love God! The Prophet answered: Then you are prepared for torture!" (*Qût al-qulûb* 2/50; quoted in Ritter, *Meer der Seele*, p. 528). And elsewhere there are a number of references to the fact that the prophets suffer more greatly because they are more loved by God. But though pain and suffering are signs of God—

the crown of martyrdom (in the sense of "death in combat on God's way"), defense against sin, punishment of past sins and insignificant in the face of the fire of hell that men would deserve for their misdeeds, etc.—even the mystics hardly ever interpret them as having "redeeming" value." The concept of redemptive suffering is alien to normal Islam precisely because admitting it would, in a way, be conditioning God. With the admission of the idea of redemptive suffering, the spiritual and productive center would pass from God to the suffering god-man, while pure Islam is always and totally theocentric. In this regard some of the passages quoted from Firdausî in earlier chapters are interesting. They indicate the Muslims' incomprehension of, and even scorn for, the idea of a God-Prophet who died on the cross, and an identical sentiment in the Mazdean Iranian (Sasanian) tradition. Words of scorn are attributed to king Khusrau at the idea that a prophet could be ignominiously killed, in answer to the Christians' request that they be given back the "true cross" that they thought Khusrau possessed. We will find very little of the "Iranian" or, more precisely, Mazdean spirit in the Husaini cult of suffering.

We have frequently used the term "normal Islam." However, in time, Shi'ism gave pain and suffering an importance that in many ways approaches that given them by Christianity or other pre-Christian religions. This deeply influenced Persian religion which—from the Safavid period on—has also been called the religion of "sadness and pain." As we have seen, Shi'ism is a religion of the persecuted and defeated; according to the Shi'ites all the imâms were martyred—i.e., unjustly killed—starting with 'Alî, the first and greatest of them. Though they "were right" and were the infallible bearers of the Truth and the Law, they were invariably defeated. And Islam—a religion of positive values, victory and success—suffered a singular psychological transformation. The fanatic follower is not frightened by these "apparent" failures. Instead of wondering whether they might not be right, he deduces that the true world must be different from this one and that suffering and death are joy and life. (In the poem summarized in the preceding chapter Fârigh says that 'Alî's tomb is a scented garden. Shi'ite traditions and legends involve constant and singular permutation: blood and death are joy, the stinking tomb is perfume, etc.) If suffering and dying are misfortunes for human beings, then 'Alî, Husain, etc., were not men but beings in which the normal laws were reversed. The consequences of this psychological position (which absorbed very different historical developments and influences that we will be studying later) were the accentuation of metaphysics, the divinization of the imâms, the special value attributed to blood, pain and violent death. We studied some metaphysical aspects of the (Ismaili and Twelver) Shi'ite world in the preceding chapters. Now we will concentrate on this last point: blood and suffering.

The historical person whose suffering and death most affected Shi'ite piety was the Prophet's young grandson—his daughter Fâtima's son, Husain. His heroic death in unequal battle in the desert plain of Karbalâ near the Euphrates in Mesopotamia (in the year 680 A.D.) changed progressively from the almost insignificant political event that it was into a drama in which both heaven and earth were involved, and even into a redemptive sacrifice for the salvation of the world. We will start with the historical facts (for the reader ought to be acquainted with these events that are common knowledge among the Shi'ites, since ignorance would preclude any deeper insights). He must remember, however, that in these profound areas of religiosity the most logical development may be the "inverse" one. In the area of Shi'ite religiosity the archetypal prototype of the "God who Dies" seeks for a historical reference point and finds it, for a number of understandable reasons, in the young Husain—who was sacrificed by evil men on the banks of the Euphrates. Here again we have what appears to be a fundamental procedure in Persian religiosity: the angelization or localization of the abstract in a historical person. Where pain is concerned it is not sufficient, or religiously valid, to weep over those who suffer in the world (as in lay philosophy or morality) or to simply patiently bear one's own pain as the arbitrary proof of a God who is too high up. Pain and death and blood and mourning have a center and a name—from which they draw their worth—and this name is Husain: we are saved if we weep for Husain, as the pious Shi'ite texts monotonously repeat.

The Historical Event

We will tell it according to the chronicle of the early Persian historian of the Arabs, Tabarî (d. 923 A.D.).[1]

The inhabitants of Kûfa invited Husain to go to Iraq where he would find a great crowd of followers who would support his claim to the Caliphate (or Imamate) against the Umayyad usurpers, and in particular against Yazîd. By the time the invitation reached Mecca most of the people of Kûfa had abandoned him—some out of fear, others out of weakness or treachery—and Husain's friends in Mecca advised him not to go: "Do not trust the people of Kûfa," they said. But Husain set out, accompanied by his whole family and escorted only by 40 horsemen and 100 foot soldiers, unaware that 'Ubaidullâh ibn Ziyâd, the son of Marjâna (the bitter enemy of 'Alî's family), had been appointed governor of Iraq and of Kûfa in those very days and that he had already sufficiently terrorized the inhabitants and killed Husain's most faithful partisans. 'Ubaidullâh instructed 'Umar ibn Sa'd, the son of the famous general Sa'd ibn Abî Vaqqâs who had been the hero of the first Islamic conquests, to set out against Husain. At first 'Umar hesitated but accepted after 'Ubaidullâh threatened to relieve him of his position of governor of Rayy (near present-day Tehran). 'Umar ibn Sa'd's army (of 4000 men) met Husain's small escort at Karbalâ, on the banks of the Euphrates. 'Umar advanced across the field, greeted Husain and exhorted him to give up his project. The negotiations lasted for several days because 'Umar tried in every possible way to avoid annihilating in unequal battle the man he himself venerated as the Prophet's grandson. But Husain was inflexible and 'Ubaidullâh sent 'Umar a threatening order to attack immediately. At this point Husain asked for, and obtained, a one day truce. In the meantime the suspicious 'Ubaidu'llâh sent Shimr (or Shamir), one of the men the Shi'ites most execrated (and we will soon see why), to give 'Umar an ultimatum: either he attacked immediately or the command of the army and the government of Rayy would be given to Shimr himself. The orders were clear: Husain must be brought, living or dead, to 'Ubaidullâh and, if killed, the horses must trample him underfoot. To prevent Husain and his men from drinking the water of the near-by Euphrates, the Umayyad troops occupied the river banks (and this, as we shall see, is a very important element in the legend that followed).

Shimr insisted on a further reduction of the respite granted Husain. The Hero only had the night to prepare for the now certain massacre. The night was spent in the women's weeping and Husain's stoic words. He said that by then he had sacrificed his own life but he freed his followers from their oath of fealty. Their answer was: "O son of the Prophet! And what excuse would we bring to your mother's father, on the day of Judgement, for having abandoned his son, alone, in the hands of his enemies?" And they all remained, to the very end, with their leader.

Then a bedouin galloped in offering Husain sure refuge if he accepted to flee. But Husain refused (and this moving element of voluntary and conscious sacrifice struck popular feeling most deeply and turned it into a voluntary sacrifice of redemption). Husain slept briefly and had a dream. The Prophet, his grandfather, said to him: "Do not be afflicted, Husain Tomorrow evening you will be with me in Paradise." From that moment the Hero gave up all hope of living. At dawn he accomplished the ritual prayer: it was Friday, the first of the month of Muharram of the year 61 A.H. (A.D. 680).

The battle began, interrupted now and then by speeches and exhortations. One of Husain's harangues to the Kûfa infidels is interesting: he insists on the principle that everything that has been near a "sacred" person like the Prophet, and all the more so the members of his family, is worthy of veneration. "Do you not see," he said (according to Tabarî) "that the Christians venerate even the hoof of Jesus' donkey and the Jews everything to do with Moses that has come down to them?" In the meantime the heat had become unbearable and Husain's small forces suffered terribly from thirst. One by one Husain saw all his companions fall at his side; only the members of his family were left. After several bloody encounters with their adversaries, his young son 'Alî came up to him for a moment and said: "Father, I am thirsty!" The father placed his own tongue on his exhausted son's mouth to give him some relief. Returning into the fray, 'Alî was treacherously wounded and torn to pieces by the overwhelming crowd of their enemies: great was the wailing of Husain and of 'Alî's mother, Zainab. The massacre continued with horrible episodes. Husain's young nephew, Qâsim, the ten-year-old son of his brother Hasan, entered the field brandishing his sword: his uncle entreated him to turn back, but he threw himself among his enemies and soon his head was cleft in two. One by one Husain's five brothers, the only able-bodied men left, perished. It was the hour of the afternoon prayer. Prostrate with thirst, Husain crouched down to earth with his one-year-old son Abdullâh in his arms and wept. His enemies approached but not one of them dared kill the Prophet's grandson. Just then an enemy arrow struck the child's ear and killed him. Husain exclaimed: "We are of God and to Him we will return! Lord! Give me strength to bear with these misfortunes!" Then, desperate with thirst, he hurled himself towards the bank of the Euphrates. As he knelt down to drink the wicked Shimr shouted: "Wretches! Do not let him drink! If he drinks he will come back to life." At the very instant in which he drew up water from the river an arrow struck him in the mouth: Husain spat out the unswallowed water, pulled the arrow out of his palate and ran, dripping with blood, to defend the entrance to his tent. 'Umar son of Sa'd came forwards to kill him. He withdrew, red with shame, when Husain asked: "Have you come to kill me?" but, returning to his own men, he and Shimr urged them on to attack the solitary Husain in a body. The Hero killed a few more enemies but he was covered in wounds and losing a great deal of blood. Shimr approached with six men: with a downward stroke one of them cut Husain's arm clean off at the shoulder. Husain fell, struggled to get up and fell again: his murderer pursued him and ran his sword through him from behind. Tradition has left us his name: Zur'a. But Shimr, who had hurried up to cut the Hero's head from his body as soon as he had expired, is even more hated by the Shi'ites. Husain's body was trampled under the horses hoofs and abandoned, together with those of his friends, out in the open. Later some local bedouins buried him. The women and children of Husain's family were taken to Kûfa. As the sad caravan of the assassins and victims was leaving, tradition says that mysterious voices were heard singing verses of lamentation: "How can men who killed Husain ever hope for the intercession of his grandfather on the day of eternal judgement?" "O you who in evil folly killed Husain, know that you will suffer very severe punishment. And certainly David curses you, and Moses curses you, and Jesus the author of the Gospel." Husain's head was taken to Kûfa to the governor 'Ubaidullâh who had it sent to Damascus to the Umayyad caliph Yazîd, together with the unfortunate women and children.

The Formation of the Legend

The above is a summary of Tabarî's account of the story. He is generally considered quite reliable as a historian and many of the details are certainly historical, but the careful reader will recognize certain traits in his tale that are too characteristic of other "hero's deaths" to be accidental: for example, the motif (present in the Gospel too) of the murderer or murderers who approach the Hero a first time and retreat at his answer, or that of the Hero or heroes always struck from behind (it would be impossible for a wicked person to fight in fair combat). In Husain's case the motif of water and thirst is particularly accentuated and plays an important part in the formation of the legend; and the apparently "normal" motif of the severed arm develops in unexpected forms connected with the common mythical and legendary element of the hand, the symbol of which is a fundamental ingredient of the "feasts for Husain" in modern Iran.

In Tabarî's tale (he wrote his story between the ninth and tenth centuries, though it was based on earlier source material), we also find other elements that already give an idea of some of the characteristics the later legend would assume, and in particular the funeral "lamentations" that contributed to the creation of, much later, the "sacred drama" of the ta'zieh. After the iniquity of Karbalâ, many "repented" and went to weep on the tomb of their betrayed lord. Barely four years after the event Sulaimân ibn Surad and his companions burst out in unison into a lament around his tomb: "Lord! We abandoned and betrayed the son of our Prophet's daughter! (the reader should note the "legitimistic" element). Forgive us for what we have committed and turn to us mercifully. . . ." Day and night, the historian tells us, the "repentant" wept and prayed, and there were greater crowds at Husain's tomb than at the Black Stone of the Kaaba. Then Sulaimân and thirty of his companions walked around the tomb (an ancient gesture of ritual veneration) and Sulaimân said: "Praise be to God who, if he had wished it, would have honored us with martyrdom together with Husain! O God! If you prevented us from being martyred with him, do not prevent us from being martyred for him, afterwards!" But there is still more, for another of the men who "repented," a certain Abdullâh ibn Walî, said: "As God is true, I consider Husain, his father, and his brother, the most noble of Muhammad's nation, intercessors with God on the day of resurrection." This is the first time Husain is considered and invoked as an "intermediary" (*wasîla*) and intercessor together with the Prophet himself, and this occurred, as we have seen, at a very early stage.

Documents exist to prove that Husain's tomb was an important place of pilgrimage in the ninth century, since the fanatical Abbasid Caliph al-Mutawakkil (847–871) strictly forbade the practice and had the tomb itself destroyed. But by the beginning of the tenth century a veritable mausoleum, venerated by pilgrims, was rebuilt at Karbalâ and rites and funeral lamentations for Husain are documented for the year 963 and were encouraged by the Shi'ite dynasty of the Bûyids (or Buwaihids).[2] But how did the idea of the redeemer hero, the man-god who sacrificed himself voluntarily for the good of his community and of humanity, develop from this meagre "historical" start? The problem is extremely complex and belongs to the vaster one of the origin of the religious concepts of the Shi'ites that we dealt with in an earlier chapter. In the meantime we must bear in mind an important point: it was "normal" Islamic belief that the prophets suffered because they were killed and tormented by "God's enemies." In Husain's case, however, as in Jesus' case (and in fact Shi'ite piety often compares the two) the Hero was not killed by an unbelieving people but by the people who, at least by rights and in theory, were the People of God. They were—in a way—killed by God. We need only sum the greater sacred intensity of the founder or the hero and his descendants with the concrete historical experience through which he ends by being killed "by the hand of the priests" to have, in kernel, all the elements of the theological idea of the "sacrificed son of God" developed very consequentially in Christianity but which manifests itself in very strong emotional forms in Shi'ite piety too. And not only in the piety of the extreme Shi'ites: for from an emotional, if not a strictly theological, point of view it would be hard to find, even in texts of the extreme Shi'ites, an expression such as that which appears in a late Persian Twelver Shi'ite text,[3] "He saw Karbalâ like a throne of Divine Glory, and he saw the divine throne steeped in the blood of God."

This religious experience was also influenced from the outside of course, for the area of diffusion of the archetype of the "God who dies" is very vast. But we should never undervalue the possibility of inner emotional developments within the ambit of Islamic piety itself. It would seem natural to look for the origins of a devotion as deeply rooted in Persia as the devotion to the blood of Husain in the area of ancient Iranian beliefs, i.e., to ask ourselves whether Husain does not have a counterpart in early Iranian religious culture. But the reader should beware, as we already said, of too easily identifying Shi'ism and Iran. Before it developed in Iran, Shi'ism (even in some of its extreme forms) developed in Arabian areas and among Arab populations, even if these were already influenced by currents of "foreign" (though not necessarily only Iranian) thought, and the generalized Husaini piety of Iran did not start before the Safavid period. At first sight the motif of the redeeming or salvific death of the hero or God is not very clear, though a few texts contain vestiges of the myth of the killing of a primordial hero or of a "cultural" hero. There are allusions to the first man, Gayômart, having been killed. In the beginning all men were born from his sacrificed body, and in the end (cf. *Bundahishn*) he will reappear, the first of the risen ones, to contribute with the other (heroes) to the final redemption. In an Iranian legend (cf. Messina, *Zhamâspîk*, p. 93) the cultural hero Jamshîd (see Chapter I) is killed, sawn through with a thousand-toothed saw by the satanic monster Azhî Dahâka. We find—still in Iranian territory— the less vague, less mythological and already more deified Siyâvush or Syâvash, an ancient Iranian hero who, according to the legend, was unjustly killed by relatives (the tyrant Afrâsiyâb, the Yazîd of the situation). The Persian historian Narshakhî (almost Tabarî's contemporary, for he lived in the tenth century), certainly used early and first-hand material for his very interesting "History of Bukhârâ" in which he says:[4] ". . . the people of Bukhârâ have wonderful songs about the murder of Siyâvush, songs that the minstrels call 'Siyâvush's revenge'." Further on, speaking of the citadel of Bukhârâ that, according to the legend, Sivâyush himself built and where he was buried, he states: "This place is particularly dear to the (Mazdean) Magi of Bukhârâ and every year each one of them sacrifices a cock to him before the sun rises on the first day of the year (Naurûz). The inhabitants of Bukhârâ possess lamentations concerning Sivâyush's murder—which are well known in every region—and the singers have composed songs from them and recite them, and they are called 'the weeping of the Magi' even though three thousand years have passed since this event." Sivâyush, like Husain (even if less frequently), has become a stock image and motif in traditional Persian poetry of the symbol of "unjustly spilled blood" (cf. Hâfiz, ed. Qazvînî, p. 72). Tolstov maintained[5] that Siyâvush was an older Central Asian agrarian divinity who was overshadowed by the advent of Zoroastrianism. He felt that this motif had distant western (Phrygian) origins and was therefore connected with legends like those of Attis, Adonis, etc. (according to Firdausî, a particular flower was born from Siyâvush's, as with Adonis's blood—in Adonis's case the anemone or the rose). If this is true, this mythological material is not, strictly speaking, Iranian. But the fact that the death mysteries of a God were celebrated in Iranian central Asia is testified by a seventh century Chinese traveller, Wei Tsû (and this testimony coincides, strangely, with the "historical event" of Karbalâ in Iraq). "The people of Samarkand," he writes, "say that the 'divine son' died during the seventh month (around September) and that his bones were lost. When this month begins the servants of God dress in black garments and they beat themselves and weep. Men and women scatter to seek the body. On the seventh day the feast comes to an end."[6]

Though no documents certainly prove the influence of Siyâvush's myth on the development of Husain's legend, Siyâvush's motif was undoubtedly a familiar one in Iranian literature and Iranian (even post-Islamic) national awareness and some of the circumstances are too similar—especially the lamentations for his death—for us to be able to deny any connection *a priori*. In a ta'zieh quoted by Virolleaud (*Théâtre*, p. 132), the brother of Shahrbânû (Husain's wife) says to his soldiers who are about to engage in battle in defense of 'Alî's family: "Siyâvush's blood is boiling." Virolleaud says that the ta'zieh contain very few allusions to the ancient Iranian murdered hero, but this ought to be checked through further study.

Besides, the documents we have on the eschatology and death rites of the peoples on the edge of the Iranian area (Ossetians, who still practice northern Iranian funeral rites, Parthians, Scythians) specifically mention some elements that are reminiscent of traits of the "feast of Husain." Thus the hero's horse—which plays an important role in the Husaini processions—was very important in the northern-Iranian rites because it represented the horse (sent from the other world) that would accompany the dead person to heaven.[7] It is a well known fact that pure Zoroastrianism definitely condemns funeral lamentations,[8] though the classic lamentations accompanied by beating on the breast, the tearing of garments, etc., continued (as the historians have documented) even in the "orthodox" Sasanian period. But all these funeral rites lack the "redemptive" value of the Husaini rites.

In the centuries that followed the martyrdom of Karbalâ the legend continued to grow. We do not, however, agree with Browne, who attributed to as early a historian as Abu Mikhnaf (Lût ibn Yahyâ, ca. eighth century A.D.) the romance translated by Wüstenfeld—"Husain's Defeat and Vengeance."[9] The definitive edition certainly contains quite early material but was probably drawn up after the fall of the Abbasid Caliphate in the thirteenth century. Abu Mikhnaf's romance adds many episodes, both legendary and not, to Tabarî's story. We will quote some of them because of their importance for an understanding of later Husaini piety. When 'Abbâs, Husain's brother, came forwards, fighting to reach the water, first his right hand was severed by an enemy blow then his left and finally the hero took his sword in his teeth and fought in this uncomfortable situation. Here again the motif of the severed hand (so frequent in contemporary Husaini iconography) is explained historically, but, as we shall see, it can also have other symbolic origins (Wüstenfeld, op. cit., p. 68). In "boasting verses" (*fakhr*) attributed to Husain before the last fatal combat, he says of himself and his family (p. 84):

> On us revelation and the true doctrine have descended; yes, and through us the Light of God will be spread. We are the possessors of the Source, and we quench the thirst of all those we love from the Prophet's chalice . . . When he, on the day of Resurrection, will come, thirsty, to the source, A Lion will quench his thirst, an obeyed imâm, whose privilege God recognizes against all men . . . I therefore greet the venerating one who visits me after death in the gardens of Eden, of uncontaminated splendor.

The reader should note the contrast: spiritual thirst-quenching is a gift from He whom men did not allow to drink even a last sip before dying in the arid plain of Karbalâ. Husain's precious head was severed after three attempts. The first murderer who prepared to accomplish the miserable task was so struck by the dying man's fixed gaze that he fled, repentant. The same happened to the second; the face of the third, the wicked Shimr, was veiled and not only did he resist all compassion but boasted of having killed the just man with satanic satisfaction. His figure was "satanized" physically too: when Husain asked to see the face of his murderer he unveiled it and revealed that he was a leper, had only one eye, a dog's muzzle and pig's whiskers (p. 95). When, after cutting off Husain's head, he raised it up on a long pike (this motif is not accidental and is among those most represented iconographically in present-day sacred processions in honor of the Saint's death), with the blasphemous cry of "God is Most Great" (*Allâhu Akbar*), seven drops of blood fell from the sky: the same happened, the author says, when John, the son of Zechariah, was martyred. The earth trembled, the horizon darkened and a cry from heaven was heard. The hero's horse (also legitimately descended from the Prophet's horse!) rubbed its head in veneration in its master's blood, and before it could be dragged away from this place of death, it killed many people with kicks and bites. Husain's head continued, independently, to perform miracles. Taken to Yazîd's palace, it carried on a curious dialogue with Goliath's head that, it seems, Yazîd kept by him (p. 131): After harshly reproving Yazîd, Goliath, or rather his head, was converted to Islam and asked for the intercession of Husain (represented by his severed head).[10]

A Christian bishop at Yazîd's court underwent a similar wonderful conversion (dramatically developed later in many ta'zieh). He told the Caliph that he had dreamt that Muhammad was being consoled by the angels in heaven for the death of his beloved grandson. When the bishop insisted that Husain's head be honorably buried, Yazîd had him tortured. In the same way described in certain acts of Christian martyrs, he saw the vision of Muhammad who presented him with a garment and a crown, saying: "Tomorrow you shall be with me in Heaven." On this same occasion a handmaid at Yazîd's court also had a miraculous and extremely interesting dream: she (p. 133) saw the sky open and a ladder of light come down from it until it reached the earth. First two youths dressed in green came down and spread a carpet on the ground. They were followed by the Prophet Muhammad who called out: "O my father Adam, come down! O my father Noah, come down!" In this way all the great prophets came down from heaven and soon after, at the Prophet's daughter Fâtima's parallel summons, all the great women of sacred history followed: Eve, Agar, Sarah, Mary, Khadîja. All those present began to weep bitterly at the thought of Husain's sad fate, and the angels themselves, unable to bear this sorrow, wept. Later we will find this weeping and sadness over Husain in heaven too. This same romance tells the story of the unusual sermon of 'Alî Asghar, Husain's young son who survived the massacre ('Alî "the Younger" also called Zainu'l-'Abidîn— the subject of many sacred representations). He climbed into the pulpit despite the wicked Caliph Yazîd's attempts to prevent him, and in the course of his sermon (p. 140), made statements such as: "I am the son of Muhammad the elect, I am the son of 'Alî the privileged one, I am the son of Fâtima the noble one . . . I am the son of Zamzam and Safâ [sic! These are sacred places in Mecca] . . . I am the son of Mecca and of Minâ, I am the son of the Apostle who was the bearer of good news . . . I am the son of the shining Lights, I am the son of He who came to within two bowshots (Muhammad, according to the Kor.

LIII, 9), I am the son of Khadîja the ancient one, I am the son of he who was slain at Karbalâ, I am the son of he whose head was severed from his neck, I am the son of he who was thirsty until death." Thus Husain is identified even with sacred objects like Mecca, the well of Zamzam, etc. This is a very original trait for a religious environment like that of Islam.

The versatile (Sunni) Egyptian writer Suyûtî said[11] that when Husain was killed the world stopped, the sun became as yellow as saffron, the stars fell. The horizon was red for six months. And the red of the horizon was seen every day after this event, while before it was not seen. (Suyûtî died in 1505, which takes us to the beginning of the sixteenth century.) The detail of the horizon, which is red with Husain's blood, is identical in the myth of Adonis. Following complex channels this myth undoubtedly influenced the myth of Husain (which cannot be explained through purely Islamic sources). It had reached its completed form by about this time (outside of Iranian territory too) and, in Iran, Safavid piety added certain more specifically devotional and emotional traits to the legend, accentuating the Hero's "divinity" and creating or rather reviving and giving official form to his "feast."

The brief poem quoted above which speaks of Husain's blood as of "God's blood" probably dates from the Safavid period. The popular piety of Twelver Shi'ism, too, went far beyond theological specifications in its "emotional" divinization of Husain and of all the sacred figures of the Shi'ites (elsewhere we saw what Fârigh Gîlânî had to say about 'Alî in his short poem). I believe that Husain's divinization, which the official theology of Twelver Shi'ism denied theoretically in vain, was mainly due to the great indulgence of the early Safavids for the enthusiasm of Shi'ite popular piety. Muhtasham of Kâshân (who died in 1588) wrote one of the many Safavid poems of mourning for Husain's martyrdom at Karbalâ. It is possibly the most beautiful one (aesthetically speaking) and I have translated one verse here. It is also interesting for some evidently "divinizing" declarations:

When the blood from His thirsting throat touched the ground
a tumult arose from the ground to the summit of the Throne.
The entire edifice of Faith almost collapsed, for the number of fractures inflicted on the Pillars of Religion.
When the cowards cut down His tall palm,
a tempest rose to the sky from the dust of the earth,
And the wind carried that dust to the Prophet's sepulchre,
and dust rose to the seventh heaven from Medina
And when the news reached Jesus, the dweller of heaven[12]
dyed his garment indigo in the vat of the firmament.
And the sky was filled with murmuring when,
after the Prophets, the Holy Spirit of the Angel wept.

And an erroneous imagination dared to think that that dust
had reached and soiled the garment of the Creator's Majesty!
For, though God's sublime essence is free from sorrow,
he dwells in the hearts and no heart is free from sorrow!

Despite the theological correction of the second to the last couplet, the poet
obviously wanted to say that God himself wept for Husain—a sentiment familiar to Christians, though it would be hard to find a less Islamic idea than this!
The Safavids, however, with their conversion of Persia to Shi'ism, made a Persian of Husain. Coming as they did from the "western" frontiers of the Iranian
world, they brought with them motifs and elements of the complex Middle
Eastern cultural world (as we saw, Shâh Ismâ'îl was undeniably influenced by
Hurûfî Gnosis). In all events the Persians felt that Husain was most particularly
"theirs" for another reason too: he was said to have married the Persian princess Shahrbânû, the daughter of the last of the Sasanians, Yazdigird III. Though
ninth century historians such as al-Ya'qûbî were already speaking of this marriage, it (and the princess herself) were probably imaginary. Faithful to our
intention of making the texts themselves speak as much as possible, here—
slightly abbreviated—is the story of Husain and Shahrbânû's wedding told in a
rather early Persian text that was famous in Iran: the eleventh century Ziyârid
prince Kai-Kâ'ûs's *Qâbûs-nâmeh*. The reader should remember that the pro-
Shi'ite Zirâyid dynasty dominated in the regions south of the Caspian sea that
were the last and least easily Islamized of all Persia and which remained for a
long time the center of Iranism.[13]

> I heard tell that Shahrbânû was a young girl when they took her prisoner from Persia
> to Arabia. The Caliph 'Umar ordered that she be sold as a slave: while the order was
> about to be carried out it reached 'Alî who, quoting one of the Prophet's traditions
> that ran: "the children of Kings must not be sold as slaves," prevented the sale.
> Shahrbânû was taken to the house of Salmân the Persian, to be given as wife to some
> man. When Shahrbânû heard this she said: "I refuse to marry unless I see the groom
> first." So they made her go to a place from where she could see without being seen
> and had the noblemen of Arabia and Yemen parade by so that she could choose the
> one who pleased her most: Salmân was by her side, describing the different people.
> But she saw faults in all of them. Of 'Umar she said: "He is great, but he is old." Of
> 'Alî: "He is a noble man, but I could never look Fâtima the Resplendent One in the
> face, I would be ashamed. This is why I don't want him." Of Hasan, son of 'Alî: "He
> is worthy of me, but he has too many wives." When it was Husain's turn she said at
> last: "This man is worthy of me. He must be my spouse. A virgin girl should have a
> virgin spouse."

The pro-'Alî tone of the story is evident. 'Alî nobly avoids a scandalous sale
wanted by 'Umar. As in many modern Persian representations, 'Umar is the

vulgar fat man, while all the members of 'Alî's family are worthy (Hasan's many wives are mentioned, but there is nothing scandalous about this for a Muslim). The Iranian princess plays an important part in the dramas of Husain's passion and some of them are explicitly dedicated to her; in them we learn that the holy imâms—Husain's descendants—which Shi'ism venerates as its spiritual leaders, were to be born of her blood. In this way Iranian national feeling is satisfied.

Husain's Feast

We mentioned that Husain's feast was, if not created, at least revived and developed by the Safavids in Iran. Already in the tenth century it seems that the Shi'ite princes of the Buyid dynasty (southern Persia and Iraq, 932–1055) organized commemorative ceremonies for the death of the members of 'Alî's family. The Arab historian Ibn Kathîr wrote that in the year 352 of the Hegira (963 A.D.) Mu'izzu'd-Daula Ahmad ibn Buwayh ordered that hired mourners should wander through Baghdad during the first days of the month of Muharram, and that pavilions for the funeral cult in Husain's name should be set up (VIII, 407, 435, 443); that the bazaars must be closed and the people wear black garments for recitations in honor of the Prince of Martyrs (Husain), which they were obliged to attend. The Sunni doctors considered this a dangerous and heretical "innovation." These celebrations continued in Baghdad until the beginning of the reign of the Seljuk prince Toghrul Beg (1055). Their nucleus must have been the recitation of funeral elegies (*marâthî*) or chants in the style of the ancient Arabic laments for slain heroes that grew progressively more religious, to the point of the emotional divinization of the dead martyr. They also included the recitation of narrative works in verse or prose on the lives of the martyrs of which, later, the Persian writer Husain Vâ'iz Kâshifî's (d. 1505), *Rauzatu'sh-shuhadâ* ("The Garden of the martyrs") became one of the most popular. It's title provided the common Persian term for "recitation of funeral lamentations on the imâm Husain," i.e., *rauzeh-khânî* (the reading of the *Rauzeh*). These short elegiac-narrative poems flourished in particular in the Safavid period, also because the sovereigns (cf. Browne in *JRAS*, 1921, p. 412) often urged the poets to write elegies for Husain and praise of the imâms rather than the usual panegyrics in their own honor. This gave rise to many partially literary, partially popular short works like *Tûfânu'l-bukâ* (the deluge of weeping), *Asrâru'sh-shahâdat* (the mysteries of the martyrdom), etc. Together with the real elegies and the "stagy" elements of the feast these were necessarily the origin, at a still indefinite period, of the authentic dramatic representations of the *ta'zieh*.

We will now describe a Husaini funeral feast of the Safavid period. Many European travellers described these "feasts" but we will quote the shrewd and attentive Roman "patrician pilgrim," Pietro della Valle. In one of his famous letters from Isfahan, written on July 25 1618, he says:

On the thirtieth day of last December, while I was still in Isfahan, the Muhammad-ans, having seen the new moon on the preceding evening (because they begin their days from sunset on the preceding day), therefore celebrated the first day of the Muharrem month, and with it the beginning of their lunar year, which now counts one thousand and twenty seven since the Hegira, which means since the flight, i.e., Muhammad's departure from Mecca towards Medina, when because of the new-fangled things he had started promulgating about his false sect, he was driven out from there and it became expedient for him to flee. Consequently, on that same day it was the first of the *asciur*, that is, of the ten days in which starting with the first of the above-mentioned month until the tenth which follows in this case, the Persians weep incessantly, with very great public manifestations, over the death of Hussein, the son of their Alì and of Fatima, Muhammad's only daughter. This Hussein is foolishly considered a great saint by all the Muhammadans, but the Persians, who are Shi'ite by belief, still consider him the legitimate imâm, the supreme leader of their sect, from which the kings of Persia claim their descent. He was attacked while he was travelling to meet those of the opposite faction (whom the Persians anath-ematize as heretics) with seventy or eighty people in his following, and was cruelly slain in a place in the Arabian desert called Kierbela, where he is buried, and where his sepulchre is now venerated and visited by great crowds of Muhammadans even from very distant regions. The ceremonies with which they celebrate the *asciur* and weep over this death are the following. They all live in sadness; they dress in a positively melancholy fashion and many wear black, which they hardly ever use at other times, nobody shaves their head or their beard, nobody bathes, they do not only abstain from everything they consider sinful but also from every form of de-light. Many poor people are in the habit of burying themselves in the busy streets, placing themselves below ground up to their throats and with even their heads inside certain specially made terra-cotta jars that are wide at the bottom and have a narrow opening the size of a head. These vases too are buried, so that they cannot be seen, and they hold the earth off from those who are inside them and they crouch down inside them so that they seem to be really buried, and they remain like that the whole day from sunrise until nighttime, and many of them even a good part of the night, while another poor man sits next to them on the ground who asks for alms and says prayers to all those who pass by. Others remain in the square or go in the other streets or in the houses, where there are people who are completely naked except for their shameful parts that they cover with a small black cloth or with dark sackcloth, and they are painted black from their head to the soles of their feet so that they seem as many devils of a shiny dark color almost like that which we give with paint to our sword sheaths or other iron instruments, and this to denote their sadness for Husain's death. They are accompanied by others who are also naked and painted, not black but red, to signify the blood and violent death that Husain suffered. And all together they tearfully chant his praises and the incidents of his death and they rap together certain small pieces of wood, or bones, which they hold in their hands and which also make a melancholy sound. With gestures and movements of the waist that, according to their custom, denote sadness, they dance in front of a circle of people like mountebanks, in fact sometimes in the company of those very mountebanks who are selling their conjurer's tricks and thus making money, which is given to them by those present as alms. Towards midday one of their mullahs goes to the square too and also to the place where people circulate. And those of Muhammad's race, particularly, are called *seidi* in Persia, which is to say lords, rather than *emir*s, as in Constantinople, or *sherif*s, as in Egypt. Wearing his green turban, which in other times I have seen no one use in these parts (unlike Turkey where those of this race constantly wear it) he sits in a very high chair, with his listeners, both men and women, some standing, some sitting on the ground or on certain small low benches, around him, and he preaches about Hussein, singing his praises and telling about his death; and sometimes he shows painted pictures about what he is telling, and in conclusion he tries in every way to move those around him to tears. These same sermons are preached every day in the mosques, and at night again in the public ways, in certain places that are decorated for the purpose with many lights and funeral adornments, and the sermons are all accompanied by a great weeping and wailing of the people who are listening and in particular of the women who, beating their breasts and making gestures of great compassion, often repeat most sorrowfully the last verses of some of their canticles. Vah Hussein! Schiah Hussein! which mean "Ah Hussein! King Hussein!" On the tenth day of the Muharrem month, which they call the day of the *catl*, i.e. the slaying, and this year it fell on the eighth of January, all the neighborhoods of Isfahan have processions, like the two that I wrote about in another letter that had taken place on the day of Alì's death, and they carry the same things in procession, i.e. those very long pikes with pennants, which they call banners, those caparisoned horses, with arms and turbans, as well as a few camels bearing coffins and in them three or four children representing the dead man's children led to prison, and they sing sad words. They also carry coffins draped in black velvet on which lies the Persian style of turban or *tag* which I spoke about on other occasions and, in some cases, it is green. There is also the sword and finally those great trophies of arms that I also mentioned then, which are carried by certain men over their heads to the sound of those cymbals and resounding bowls of theirs that they constantly knock together, and dancing and twirling in the way they do they make the coffins and trophies whirl in the air too without much care. And all the men of the neighborhood accompany these things, carrying long and thick sticks to fight those of the other processions if they should happen to meet, and not only for precedence but also to re-enact, I think, the fray in which Hussein died, and they are certain that those of them who may die in that quarrel, dying for Hussein, will go straight to Heaven. They say, in fact, even more: i.e. that in all the days of the *asciur* the gates of Heaven remain open and that all the Muhammadans who die in those days go there immediately, dressed and shod. You see, Your Lordship, how crazy they are! To conclude, the ceremonies for Hussein's death are the same as those I told you about the other time concerning Alì's death. The only difference is that these [ceremonies] for Hussein are celebrated with greater solemnity, with more processions, with more people and a greater desire and ardor to fight among those armed with sticks, who are strange-looking and wear ostentatious clothes adorned with plumes and other extraordinary things. However, as on the day of Alî's death, horsemen of the vizier and of other city officials are on duty in the square and at the end of all the streets, and they separate them if they attack, or they do not allow them to attack. However on the day I saw them they were unable to prevent a good skirmish in front of the king's gate at which I, who was also on horseback, was present. I heard that other skirmishes occurred, in other streets, and that many people returned home with broken heads. When the skirmish I witnessed started those on one side, who were closer to the king's gate, immediately brought their banners and trophies into the royal palace, that they might not be taken from them during the fight by their adversaries, because they are in the habit of taking them one from the other when they can, and those who lose them suffer great shame. They also say that during the night that precedes this day they publicly burn in the square statues of Umar and of a number of leaders of the opposing sect who had Hussein killed and that they publicly curse and execrate them and all their followers in the sect who are Turks and the greater part of the other Muhammadans who are Sunni; this , however, I did not see but I pass on the information.

Ancient and modern travellers provide many other details. Concerning the procession, we will only add that some people say that the numerous pikes bearing a hand with the five fingers spread out are symbols of 'Abbâs' severed hand (see above). In 1704 a Shi'ite "churchman" in Isfahan explained to the Dutch traveller Le Brun that the hand on the javelin was "the sign of war that the partisans of the Muhammadan Persians sometimes bore on their banners and that the five fingers of this hand represented Muhammad, 'Alî, Fâtima, Hasan, Husain." Those who take part in the procession scourge themselves with chains and wound their scalps with knives. The swaying movement of these bleeding men and their cries of pain and lamentations are, according to all the travellers, very realistic and shocking. Around 1896 the English traveller Wilson, who succeeded in attending one of these processions at Tabrîz, described it in the following order:

1. The bearers of very long beflagged pikes. A leather flask (the symbol of thirst and water) and the well-known metal hands are also sometimes fixed onto them.
2. A richly caparisoned horse, without a rider (Husain's horse).
3. A horse bearing two white pigeons (according to the legend, doves brought the news of the massacre to Medina).
4. Children tied to horses and bleeding from head wounds (Husain's children).
5. Groups of wailers who strike their shaven heads with sabres (they are generally accompanied by other people who prevent these aspiring martyrs

from wounding themselves too deeply in their wild enthusiasm by blocking the sabre thrusts with sticks).

6. A group representing Zainab (Husain's wife) with her children, as prisoners.
7. Castanet players.
8. A group of flagellants.

Other travellers' accounts agree more or less with this description, except for a few rather unimportant variations. In a description by Bricteux (who saw a procession of this kind in 1908 in Sabzavâr) we also find a group of devils on horseback, wearing yellow masks representing toads' heads and pouring dust on their heads. It is apparently the only example of this detail and—it is worth mentioning in passing—it is particularly interesting because in ancient pre-Islamic Persia toads were considered one of the worst demonic animals.

One curious aspect of Husain's feast (present only in certain areas, especially among the Indian and Indonesian Shi'ites) is interesting for its resemblance to Mediterranean Spring rites. That is, at the end of the ceremonies commemorating Husain's death, the coffin of the martyr of Karbalâ is thrown into the sea. At Byblos, Alexandria, etc., when Spring was over the faithful threw the image of the god of Spring into the water.[14]

We thus move from the first pilgrimages and lamentations undertaken by those who repented only a few years after the event, through the commemorative meetings recorded in the tenth century in Baghdad, to this more elaborate processional celebration of the Safavid period which already contains (see Della Valle's description) many "dramatic" elements. The symbols that appear in them are too transparently non-Islamic to be explained away as internal developments or accidental convergences. In an article that is rather out-dated but still offers interesting comparisons,[15] Eerdmans states that Husain's feast should be considered essentially a ceremony of yearly re-burial of the slain God. In his opinion the ceremony is full of phallic symbols: the long pikes, the two great poles the travellers saw on this occasion and also the symbol of the open hand stuck onto a tall pole. Eerdman believes that these rites originated in Mesopotamia and are reminiscent of the ancient funeral rites for the slain god Tammuz. His proofs are very weak, however. Without having recourse to phallic symbolism there are many examples in Islamic territory of the hand as an apotropaic symbol (a concept inherited from the Mediterranean and Greek world) and the idea of Martyrdom, of death and of blood as a vital and in a way redeeming fluid, was already common in Islam through mysticism that, in its turn, had taken it from Christianity. Jalâlu'd-Dîn Rûmî calls red—the color of blood—"the best of colors": the martyrdom of the great (and part-Persian) mystic Mansûr al-Hallâj in Baghdad (see above) in some ways were extraordinarily like Christ's redeeming sacrifice, and finally the idea that the Saints or

Perfect Ones must become lowly even unto death (*humiles usque ad mortem*) and that they themselves in fact desire this death, were already widespread in certain areas of the Islamic world when the "cult" of Husain developed. The legend and cult of Tammuz (and of Adonis, Osiris, etc.) may possibly have contributed to the creation of the spiritual environment from which Christianity and Gnosis sprang, but it would be absurd to consider them the direct source of the Husaini cult. Even though Ibn al-Athîr says (X, 26) that in the year 456 of the Hegira (1064 A.D.) feasts were held in Mesopotamia in honor of the "death of the king of the jinns" (and that he himself attended one in 1204 at Mosul) and though, according to an Arabic text on the Sabaeans (Chwolsson, op. cit., see above), in the tenth century Sabaean women still gathered at Harrân (Upper Mesopotamia) in the month of July to weep for the god Ta'ûz, these cases are too isolated and vague to lead to the inference of a direct descent from the Mesopotamian myths-cults, even though this descent is acceptable in a *mediated* form.

Popular iconography also contributes to a better understanding of Husaini piety. A curious miniature in the Wills collection,[16] which represents the legendary journey of Alexander the Great and his army, bearing torches, to the "land of darkness," shows Hasan and Husain in the background, their heads aureoled with the *khvarena* and their faces veiled, sitting next to the Source of the Water of Life from which a hand emerges. They sit by the curious tree Wills calls *ahwak* but which is in fact the Wâq-wâq tree (its branches all end in different animal's heads).[17] Here the hand seems a symbol of vital power and only very vaguely connected with 'Abbâs' severed hand. The fact that Husain is beside the source of the Water of Life to guard it is also significant. As we saw above, the "water" element is fundamental in Husain's saga and popular piety in Iran still today places jars of water beneath his image. It also seems to be a "reversed vengeance"; he who was unable to drink even a drop of water before dying is "avenged" through becoming the legendary custodian of the Water of Life. A rather singular vengeance, it is true, but an emotionally and psychologically very real one. The constant defeats and the repeated martyrdom of their leaders gave the followers of 'Alî's party—the "Shi'ites"—the typical mentality of the persecuted who endlessly brood over vengeance. Since this became impossible on an outward and military plane, it was transposed to the exaggeration of grief to its utmost limits. Vengeance became a cry of horror over the misdeed and of hatred for the enemy who perpetrated it, even though the enemy's blood became the blood of the flagellant. In this context, the street fights described above between the various groups of flagellants (in which both the contending parts consider their fallen to be "martyrs," as if they had fought to avenge Husain) are very significant. Another typical occurrence— described by several travellers who attended the sacred performances that, as we shall see, accompany this cult—is that the person who represented the evil Shimr, or 'Umar, or other enemies of the "Sacred Family," on stage, were sometimes lynched by the crowd. This trait clearly distinguishes Husaini piety from some aspects of Christian piety. Husain must be *avenged*, even if in the other world. In the short poem we mentioned above, Muhtasham of Kâshân says at one point:

> Alas for the time when the sons of 'Alî rise again in their shrouds, dripping with blood, waving banners as red as a blast of fire! Alas for the time when the young men of the Sacred Family will beat their crimson and carmine shrouds together on the plain of Resurrection! On the day of judgement, in serried ranks, the crowd of those whose ranks the upheaval of Karbalâ dispersed will throw into confusion all the hosts of those who have risen up!

Vengeance is moved forward to the end of the world (we have seen how Shi'ite piety is deeply eschatological, as always happens to religions that are defeated "politically") and in the meantime it becomes a cult. Besides, this transposition of revenge into songs and funeral laments is not new to Iranian territory. The lamentations of the magi of Bukhârâ for Siyâvush's death were called "Siyâvush's revenge (*kîn*)," and the romance on the family of 'Alî attributed to Abû Mikhnaf was called "Defeat and Vengeance" (even if here he is speaking of the historical revenge attempted by al-Mukhtâr). But this posthumous revenge of weeping has a dual function: it guarantees the enemy's extermination, beyond time, and it guarantees the friend's redemption. The word "redemption" as such is not used in the texts, which prefer the word "intercession"—well–known to Sunni Islam too, which admitted it (even if unwillingly) only for the Prophet. The Shi'ites, however, give a far broader interpretation to "intercession"; the principal agent of intercession is above all the martyr, *par excellence*, Husain (even though 'Alî and other "martyrs" have this power). This concept is expressed concisely and clearly in the nineteenth-century poet Qâ'ânî's original Husaini elegy in dialogue form:

> Q. And was not the dagger ashamed to sever that Head?
> A. Yes!
> Q. Why then did it do it?
> A. It was the will of Destiny!
> A. Why?
> Q. That he might become the intercessor of the people.
> Q. And what is the condition for obtaining this intercession?
> A. Lamentations and weeping!

Expressions such as, "O Lord! Through Husain's blood forgive the sins of Husain's friends" and other similar ones are frequent in the prayers that end the sacred representations.

The Ta'zieh

And so the funeral cult of revenge and lamentation for Husain was complete in all its details already in the Safavid period and contained some of the dramatic elements that were soon to develop into real sacred representations. This kind of sacred performance, connected with the events of Karbalâ or other stories about 'Alî's family, are now generally known as *ta'zieh* (literally "funeral condolences"). The problem of the period of their origin has not yet been solved. An accurate study of the many booklets of ta'ziehs donated in 1955 to the Vatican Library by the Italian ambassador to Tehran, Enrico Cerulli, may help to contribute to its solution. Cerulli's preliminary study of the ta'zieh reveals some new facts. In the first place, at one point of their development these dramas (often only distantly connected with the Karbalâ events or the saga of the 'Alid family) freed themselves from exclusively religious motifs and developed as truly popular theater (now, however, completely suffocated by imitations of European theater). In the second place, these dramas are not only performed during the period of mourning for Husain (Muharram) as we had thought, but in other periods of the year too without limitation. In the third place, these dramas are now performed by proper companies of actors and in fact a kind of satirical drama on the organization and quarrels within these companies has developed. There also appear to be regional traditions in Persia; the ta'zieh can therefore be distributed geographically by regions, with similarities in those of a given region (the cult of local Shi'ite "saints," etc.). And though these dramas originated in the cult of the Karbalâ massacre, their themes now cover a wide range of subjects. Cerulli divided the over 900 ta'ziehs he brought to Europe into eight major themes: Karbalâ, History and Epic Legends of ancient and modern Iran, Hagiography of secondary characters of Shi'ite religious history, the Twelve Imâms of official Persian Shi'ism, Islam in general, Biblical Subjects, Satires (mostly at the expense of the hated 'Umar), and Dramas on the theater itself. A further study of these booklets, all of which have been written or copied recently (up to a few years ago), can contribute to clearing up other problems. For example, are those on subjects apparently far from the Karbalâ event effectively completely unconnected with the saga of Husain's martyrdom? We will shortly be reading the translation of one of these booklets—"Adam and Eve"—on a biblical subject and apparently very far from our theme, though in fact it is completely centered around the martyrdom of 'Alî's family. As for the problem of the date of origin of these sacred plays, it is strange that Della Valle and other European travellers of the Safavid period who were present at the 'Ashûrâ celebrations (e.g., the accurate Olearius, who witnessed the Husaini ceremonies in 1637 at Ardabîl, the citadel of the Safavids) never speak about the ta'zieh, whose presence is first documented in 1781 by

Franklin and then only in the nineteenth century—thus leading prudent and careful historical documentation to situate their origin in the second half of the eighteenth century (and excluding the suggested influence of European theater because this was only very vaguely known in Iran at the time). But many scholars (especially Persian scholars) believe in a rather earlier origin of the ta'zieh. Given that the content of the latter is so similar to works of Safavid piety; that, in terms of form, popular Safavid works on 'Alî and Husain contain so many stock images and stereotyped expressions identical to those in the ta'zieh; and given the dramatic elements of the Safavid lamentations of Muharram (see Della Valle's description), I personally accept the possibility that the ta'zieh is of Safavid origin.

By attending dramatic performances of the events of Husain's martyrdom, the pious Shi'ite people found a further (and more realistic and practical way) of increasing the weeping that, as we have seen, is the necessary and sufficient condition for obtaining the Holy Martyr's intercession. And the organizers of the performances, the actors, and all those present, participated (if the reader will excuse the term) in these "indulgences." Many ta'zieh end with a prayer asking for forgiveness for the sins of the organizers of the performance. The scene or "theater" of the ta'zieh (called *takyeh*) is very simple (see Massé, *Croyances*, I, p. 122): a bed, some sofas, some armchairs; when necessary, the tomb as a sign of mourning. The battles and caravan journeys take place around the stage, which is in the center and round. The angel Gabriel occupies a wooden cage several meters above ground. 'Alî's supporters chant their parts in a nasal voice; Yazîd's, arrogantly and clearly. The actors generally hold the scrolls or sheets of paper on which their part is written and one of them goes up and down the stage to prompt those who seem to hesitate. Men or adolescents act all the parts, both male and female. The play proper is preceded by a kind of sermon on a Qur'anic text, as an introduction to the tale of the sufferings of the Prophet's family. Europeans have always been most surprised by the deep impression the show produces on the audience despite the extremely elementary staging (which, however, includes very realistic details). It is not unusual to see the spectators weeping bitterly, and the actors themselves sometimes find it hard to speak their lines because of their intense emotion. As we said before, this emotion can even reach a paroxysm: people tear their clothes, beat their heads to the point of drawing blood, and in extreme cases "heretics" (Muslim heretics rather than Christians or people of other religions) are even massacred. I was told that even in recent times it was considered imprudent for well-known Baha'is to be seen in the streets during the period of 'Ashûrâ (not in Tehran but in provincial towns and villages). The style of the dramas is very simple and can be understood by the whole audience. European readers, who are used to the stock images of learned poetry, are pleasantly impressed by the "novelty" and immediacy of the images in some of the best ta'zieh, though a more careful historical study reveals that in fact they often are repetitions of a specific "style" of "popular" religious poetry that goes back to the Safavid period.

I hope my readers will enjoy this heretofore unpublished translation of a ta'zieh called "Adam and Eve" from the Cerulli collection in the Vatican Library. I based my rather haphazard choice on the brevity of the drama, as well as on the interest it presents as one of the so far less known examples of biblical Husaini dramas. For Husain's martyrdom is not so much told in the present tense but foreseen in a fated world of transcendent realities. The central event of the religious history of Shi'ism is projected into heaven, and heaven is distraught with weeping.

To conclude this chapter and summarize what we have said so far, I believe that the motif of Husain—one of the most important pillars of present-day Persian religiosity—definitely has a "western" origin. We saw earlier in fact that the Gilan area and the Dailam mountains were the first stronghold of the Persian Shi'ites, and Minorsky traces the funeral lamentations for Husain partly to Dailamite customs.[18] By "west," however, I also mean the syncretist world (made up of subtle and at times intangible influences and counter-influences of Near Eastern and Babylonian ancient and modern cultures) that contributed to the creation of the complex phenomenon of the Christian "heresies." The archetypal importance of the motif of the "God who dies" is undeniable, beyond all strictly historical and textual proof. But this motif, for which some enthusiastic Iranists and Iranians look in a "pure" ancient Iran, is not basically Iranian. Rather, it entered Persian Shi'ite Islam through channels connected with the area west of Iran, for—as we mentioned above—even the Iranian myth of Siyâvush and his "vengeance" appears to have more distant Phrygian and Mediterranean origins.

Appendix

The Ta'zieh of Adam and Eve

Note: This ta'zieh belongs to the Cerulli collection at present in the Vatican Library. The manuscript consists of 18 small pieces of very ordinary paper containing the different characters' cues in a different order to the one they follow to come on stage. An index indicating each actor's first cue for the different scenes, however, has facilitated the arrangement and division into scenes (which does not exist in the original). The index is preceded by the following words: "Index of the representation (*majlis*) of Adam and Eve is as follows . . . ." We learn from this that the title of the drama is Adam and Eve and the characters the following:

Adam (Adam), Eve (Havvâ), Gabriel (Jibraîl) and Satan (Shaitân). On page 18 there is a name—Ghulâm Husain—which may be that of the Author (we know the names of the authors of some ta'zieh) or of the copyist, and a very recent date, the year 1372 of the Hegira which corresponds to 1952. To indicate the far from perfect style of the original we have used rather naive and contorted English in the translation.

Scene I

Adam: I sing your praises O most pure Lord!
           You created me from a handful of earth,
           you made me the Adam of men,
           you made me superior to the created,
           you created for me, hidden, a wife,
           from my side, to be my companion too,
           to be my confidant in the world.
           Therefore praise to you, O Creator of men!
Eve: Praise be to God!
           you created me in the garden of Paradise:
           my husband is Adam, the father of the human race,
           I am his wife, O Creator!
           You gave me the beautiful name of Eve,
           and I shall become Adam's gentle confidant.
           The only thing worthy of your grace is praise:
           O my God, you are the only Creator beside whom there is no other.
Gabriel: The cherubim of the Lord of the world have received an order;
           Adam has been created from a handful of earth, for the people.
           O angels, row on row, enter straight into Heaven
           and prostrate yourselves in front of this Adam of the fine nature.
           Anyone who refuses to obey the most beloved Lord's words . . .
           O Angels, the Creator of time has ordered that you adore him![19]
A Cherub:[20] My nature, before Adam, was of most pure fire
           and Adam's nature is made of the mud of this sad house.
           My nature is of light, his only of earth.
           I do not want to adore him: O Angels, do not prostrate yourselves
               in front of him!
Gabriel: An order has been issued, now, from the source of all that is Living,
               Ancient.
           Why, Iblîs, did you act arrogantly and then suffered rejection?
           Withdraw from the assembly of the Angels, O accursed one,[21]
           for you refused obedience to a clear order from the Lord!
A Cherub: Since you drove me away from your court, O Creator,
           as your most holy essence is true, know, O God, that I will act in
               the same way with this Adam and his sons,
           that neither he nor any of his descendants will remain whole.

	I have become the hereditary enemy of the sons of Adam
	until I, with evil intention, will give them a place in Hell.
	I shall do this with the sons of this your fine being,
	for not one of them will be recompensed with the sight of the face
	of Heaven!
Gabriel:	An order has come for you, O vile Iblîs;
	the assembly of those who are entering are not your followers.[22]
	You have done yourself enough harm
	anyone who becomes, through obstinateness, your follower
	will burn with you in the fire of Hell.
	Go, far away from God's court, for you have become an outcast!

(turning to Adam):

	O chosen one of God, walk and contemplate,
	O Adam of the beautiful nature, in the garden of Heaven!
Adam:	Come, O Eve! By the grace of the living and uncreated God,
	I and you are here together, without a why or a how.
	Come, let us walk in the Garden of Paradise
	for God has shown us great mercy.
	Look at the castles of the garden, and the trees:
	rivers flow from under the shade of each one.
	the Only One has given us eternal Paradise and servants
	and the houris, glory be to Him!
Eve:	Yes Adam, the one and only God
	has given us gifts in great abundance.
	We must wander, for example,
	around Heaven, thanks to God's generosity.
	Look at these trees of Paradise
	that the Creator planted with the hand of power,
	the delicacy of their leaves is such
	that our form is hidden in them.[23]
	Look: on us God, the One and Only One,
	in this instant has lavished gracious beauty.
	May God be exalted for this form that
	he has given us at this instant, He the One and Only One.
	Now beautiful grace is incarnate:
	could God have a better creation?
	No better creature than we exists
	in the eightfold Heaven, in the world![24]

Scene II

Gabriel:	God's greeting be with you, O Adam!
	Thus the lofty Creator has commanded:

now, together with Eve, in order to look at the rivers of Heaven by
the grace of the One and Only (God),
you walk together with heavy hearts[25]
for the mysteries will be revealed to you.

Adam: O Gabriel, I will obey God's order,
and will walk in Heaven, now, with Eve.

(turning to Eve):

Come, O Eve, by the grace of God
wander joyfully in Heaven, wherever you wish.
Let us contemplate Heaven and with joyous hearts
see what God has created there![26]

Eve: Yes, O Adam, come, for together
we will walk, and contemplate the world.
Heaven is not a place for common discourse;
its delights have endless eternity.

Scene III

Adam:	Why, O Eve, are you so sad?
Eve:	O Adam, look; what do you see?
Adam:	May God be exalted! This lofty castle!
Eve:	Now look upwards.
Adam:	No eye has ever seen nor ear ever heard such things!
Eve:	God created it from a single ruby.
Adam:	It looks like an emerald set in gold!
Eve:	Its gates are turquoise, wonderful walls.
Adam:	Say, Gabriel, whose is this great castle?
Eve:	Whatever can there be inside it?

Gabriel: O lofty one, you have asked me a strange question.
There is one brilliant sun in the sky, like the sun,
which shows itself for one day every thirty thousand years,
and I have clearly seen it in the sky thirty thousand times.[27]
Despite this long life, however,
I do not know its mystery,
and I know nothing as yet about this castle, and its people.
Ask God, for maybe in this instant
He will manifest the secrets of the Castle to you.

Scene IV

Adam: O generous Lord of all that is in the world,
manifest the true reality of this castle to me!
Through your glory and power, O Lord of the world,
tell me now about the hidden secret!

	Now open the gate of this castle for me,
	that I may see who, inside, has the spirit of man!
Gabriel:	The order has arrived from the Creator of all Being
	that the hidden object now be manifest to you.
	Look, O handsome Adam,
	what is manifest to you in the middle of the castle,
	look what the Lord of both worlds has created, look now at the grace
	of the Powerful Glorious One!
Adam:	May God be blessed for this form, for this figure,
	which the one and omnipotent Lord has created!
	What form is this I see, O ancient Lord?
	That, contemplating it, my heart feels split in two.
	O generous Lord, you the Only and Omnipotent One,
	is this angelic looking maiden an angel?
	Otherwise what kind of human being is she, O Only Judge?
	Of what lineage is this pretty young girl?
Gabriel:	O Father of men: this lady of the gardens of Heaven
	is of your lineage, from whom the contingent world will be created.
	Know that God created her from you, and also
	Muhammad, 'Alî, Fâtima, Hasan and Husain.[28]
	And this beauty whom you have looked upon
	is Fâtima, and it is Muhammad manifestly,
	for everyone who is the friend of Her Highness the Pure One
	can be certain that his friendship is for His Highness the Prophet,
	and everyone who is Her enemy, you may be certain,
	will dwell and be sheltered in Hell because of his divine wrath.
Adam:	May the light of these eyes be sacrificed for the (lofty) degree of
	these five:
	Muhammad, 'Alî, Fâtima, Hasan and Husain!
	But I also see a crown on the maiden's head
	and she has two earrings, one red and one green
	and I see a necklace of light around Zahrâ's neck.[29]
	Tell me about the earring, the crown and the necklace.
Gabriel:	Know for certain that this earring on the right
	is Muhammad, the most noble Prophet, who, you must know, is her
	father.
	Never did the Mother of the World[30] generate in time, O prince,
	such a father and such a daughter.
	The world and the people of the world created, through his grace,
	were, by order of the Lord the creator, adored.
Adam:	O Gabriel! enhancer of the joy in my restless heart!
	tell me, for love of the powerful and majestic Lord:
	the necklace that, manifestly, the glorious Lord of all Good
	has placed with his powerful hand around her neck,

	tell me, why did God give it to her?
	Do not keep even a single hair hidden from me, O Gabriel.
Gabriel:	Know that the necklace around this maiden's neck was placed there
	by the father of the two noble princes,[31] her husband.
	His name, among the Five Sublime Ones, is His Highness 'Alî,
	the legitimate heir of the Prophet's beauty and the vicar of God.
	If his nature had not been created, O Adam,
	no one could have been the companion of the daughter of the pledge;[32]
	if Haidar's[33] wife had not been Zahrâ,
	'Alî would have remained alone like the peerless God.
Adam:	May Adam be sacrificed for your lofty rank, 'Alî,
	for there is no other successor of the Prophet in the world but you.
	O God, be merciful to 'Alî's friends,
	and generous, make them all worthy of heaven!
	Why, O Gabriel, is one of the earrings on her ear
	red and the other green? Explain this to me!
Gabriel:	The two earrings are Fâtima's two sons,
	they are like two pledges of the Five Sublime Ones,
	one is Hasan, the other the Imâm Husain.
	Do not ask anything more of me, O light of my eyes!
Adam:	I do not know why, O Lord of the world,
	The tears spring from my eyes on hearing Husain's name.
	Heaven is not a place of sadness and the dwelling of suffering.
	And so I don't know why my heart is so full of sorrow.
	At all events tell me, O Gabriel, for the love of God:
	why the two earrings, one red and one green?
Gabriel:	Know that the green color of this earring
	indicates Hasan's state,
	for the tyrants of the nation will kill Hasan with the poison of injustice; alas, help![34]
Adam:	Alas, mercy! O sighs! O lamentation! O dear Hasan!
	Why will you be thus poisoned by treacherous men?
	How will those tyrant unbelievers impress the mark of your pain in your mother's heart?
	I have yet another question: tell me:
	explain the red color of the other earring to me.

Scene V

Gabriel:	O Adam, why this question?
Adam:	It is absurd to overlook this information!
Gabriel:	If I tell you you will be filled with sorrow.
Adam:	Tell me of her destiny in the world!

Gabriel:	This is Heaven, it is not a place of sorrow!
Adam:	Speak to me clearly of this intense torment!
Gabriel:	This red color comes from the state of her Husain.
Adam:	What, then, will happen to the light of Her eyes?
Gabriel:	Husain will be slain without crime or fault.
Adam:	Why? Tell me, for my heart is seared by this sorrow.
Gabriel:	They will cleave his thirsting throat into two hundred pieces.
Adam:	Because of this misfortune blood is pouring from my eyes!
Gabriel:	They will have his face trodden on by the horse of hatred!
Adam:	But will there be no-one with him to help him?
Gabriel:	Yes, his friends will number seventy-two.[35]
Adam:	And what will happen then, O you of the sad heart?
Gabriel:	They too will be cut into pieces by the dagger.
Adam:	Their pain makes my heart burn to cinders!
Gabriel:	But this is Heaven, do not become so dark with affliction.
Adam:	Say, will my Husain have a brother?
Gabriel:	Yes, 'Abbâs, son of Abdullâh, son of 'Uthmân.
Adam:	Now tell me about their state.
Gabriel:	'Abbâs will have a hand severed from his body.
Adam:	Tell me everything that will happen to them.
Gabriel:	They will be killed in front of their sister.[36]
Adam:	Say, and is their mother with them too?
Gabriel:	Did I not tell you that you would torment yourself with sorrow?
Adam:	What injustice is this? God is great!
	I have another question to ask you: tell me the truth!
Gabriel:	Whatever has come to your mind now?
Adam:	Why will Husain suffer such injustice?
Gabriel:	Know that it is in defense of the Shi'ites.
Adam:	And what generous gift will God give him in exchange?
Gabriel:	Tomorrow he will become the intercessor of the community.
Adam:	And what community is this, O light of my eyes?
Gabriel:	Any person who has wept over my Husain![37]
Adam:	Ah, how beautiful is their state, their fate!
Gabriel:	They will be at peace in the garden of Rizvân.[38]
Adam:	What gift, tell me, will God give them?
Gabriel:	Eternal Heaven will be their reward.
Adam:	Are these sayings in allegorical language, or present.[39]
	This tale of woes has no limits.

Scene VI

Adam:	What would happen if the one and powerful God clearly showed me the desert of Karbalâ now?
Gabriel:	O Adam, come: you have mourned and lamented, and have also pleased God.

	If you want suffering to grow within you come, and see the sad land of Karbalâ.[40]
Adam:	Tell me, Gabriel: what is this desert?
Gabriel:	This is the tormented land of Karbalâ.
Adam:	I see an army of more than a hundred warriors.
Gabriel:	Know that Yazîd's people form this army.
Adam:	In the other direction I see, clearly, a place of massacre.
Gabriel:	It is the field where those who were dying of thirst were massacred.
Adam:	I see a youth without hands or head.
Gabriel:	That is 'Abbâs, O light of my eyes!
Adam:	There is another youth, cut to pieces!
Gabriel:	Know that that youth is 'Alî Akbar.[41]
Adam:	How were they related to Husain?
Gabriel:	One was his brother, the other his son.
Adam:	I see another sad and unhappy youth.
Gabriel:	He is Qâsìm, Husain's recent son-in-law.
Adam:	Whose coffin is that, tell me clearly!
Gabriel:	It is the King of the World's funeral!
Adam:	He looks to me like a little child.
Gabriel:	Look, he has lances instead of milk and honey.
Adam:	What is the name of the baby palpitating in the blood?
Gabriel:	Know that he is Asghar, the milkless one.
Adam:	I see another youth, in the sun.
Gabriel:	If you knew who he is you would be burnt up with sorrow.
Adam:	Who is he, tell me his name, O miserable creature!
Gabriel:	It is he, the leader of the oppressed, Husain!
Adam:	Then, why does he remain there, like an imprisoned bird?
Gabriel:	He is entirely covered with lances and arrows.
Adam:	His body is naked in the dust. Why?
Gabriel:	They stripped him, this shameless people!
Adam:	And why was all this injustice done to him?
Gabriel:	He was killed for the redemption of the Shi'ites.
Adam:	And what reward will this lofty one have from the Lord?
Gabriel:	He will forgive his Shi'ites without any accounting.
Adam:	And who are his friends, O light of our eyes?
Gabriel:	Those who weep over Husain's fate.
Adam:	Will he suffer further oppression from these vile men?
Gabriel:	Look at how the Prince is still tormented![42]
Adam:	O great Lord, through Husain's honor forgive the sins of Husain's friends. Never remove the hand of we who mention his name, O God, from the hem of Husain's garment. And answer the prayers of those who have set up this meeting of mourning for Husain, in this world and the next.[43]

Notes

1. Persian translation by 'Alî Bal'amî, ed. Zotenberg, Paris, vol. IV, 1874, pp. 34–50. Bal'amî completed his translation in about 964. Our translation is summarized and abbreviated in some places.
2. Cf. Tabari, III, 1407; Ibn Hauqal, p. 163. There is a history and description of the sanctuary in Nöldeke, *Das Heiligtum al-Husains zu Kerbelâ*, Berlin, 1909.
3. The *Asrâru'sh-shahâdat*, "The mysteries of the Martyrdom" by Ismâ'îl Khân Sarbâz, quoted in Browne, *Lit. Hist. of P.*, IV, p. 189.
4. Ed. Schefer, p. 38.
5. In *Po sledam drevne-horejzmiceskoj civilizacii*, Moskva-Leningrad, 1948, pp. 84–5.
6. Quoted in Bicurin, *Sobranie svedeniah o narodah obitavsih v Srednei Azii v drevnie vremena*, t. II, M.-L., 1950, p. 296.
7. Cf. documentation quoted in Widengren, *Stand und Aufgaben*, Leiden, 1955, p. 37.
8. Cf. *Mênôkê Khrat*, chap. VI, and Widengren, op. cit., p. 58.
9. F. Wüstenfeld, *Das Tod des Husein ibn Ali und die Rache*, Göttingen, 1883.
10. The talking severed head is present in Sabaean legends. Here the author may be comparing the empious Yazîd to a pagan (the Sabaeans were considered pagans).
11. Quoted in Goldziher, *Muhammadan. Studien*, II, 331.
12. According to Islamic doctrine Jesus never died. He is still alive, in heaven. Indigo is the color of mourning.
13. Here I have translated from *Muntakhab-i Qâbûs-nâmeh*, edited by S. Nafisi, Tehran, 1320 sol., pp. 132 and foll.
14. Cf. Virolleaud, *Théâtre*, p. 134.
15. B. D. Erdmans, "Der urspung der Ceremonien des Hosein-Festes," in *Zeitschr. f. Assyr.*, IX, 1894, pp. 280–307.
16. Reproduced in *The Adventures of Hajji Baba of Isfahan* by Morier, edited by C. J. Wills, London 1897, p. 226.
17. On this tree, another aspect of this many-faceted motif (see above), see the article by G. Ferrand S.V. "Wâkwâk," *Encyclopaedia of Islam*. The tree is mentioned for the first time in an eighth century Chinese text that speaks however of arabs and appears to have taken the motif, which is recurrent in the more or less fabulous Muslim stories, from the West.
18. Cf. "Iran: Opposition, Martyrdom and Revolt," in *Unity and Variety of Muslim Culture*, p. 187.
19. According to the Qur'an God ordered the angels to adore Adam. Satan's sin was his refusal to do this.
20. This Cherub is Satan himself (Iblîs). The author still temporarily gives him the rank he had before sinning.
21. Rajîm, literally "lapidate." The epithet is based on legends we mentioned above according to which the angels stone the demons with shooting stars to prevent them from coming too close to heaven to listen to what they are saying.
22. Probably: "in Heaven," the blessed. (From the reiterated Qur'anic phrases such as: "enter therefore, O elected ones, into Heaven!" etc.).
23. He probably means that they were so limpid that they could see themselves in them.
24. According to Islamic tradition Heaven has various degrees of growing closeness to

God (eight here). According to Mazdean tradition too there are different degrees in Heaven (generally three, and four with the supreme Garôdmân).

25. This adjective which is still unjustified here, slips out from under the author's pen.

26. As we shall see later, God apparently created "the prototypes" of all historical events— even future ones—in Heaven. See our considerations in chaps. I and IV.

27. Concerning this star see the identical statement in Fârigh Gilani's Safavid booklet. These recurrent stars in the transcendental sky also exist in the old proto-Ismaili treatise *Ummu'l-Kitâb*.

28. If I have understood correctly, The Transcendent Image of Fâtima (see above) represents all five "Five Pure Ones," the Pentadic Sacred Family, generated by the Cosmic Anthropos (Adam). This naïf poet certainly could not have invented these concepts himself, therefore there is evidence of the influence of currents like the one we examined in chap. IV, on the ta'zieh, in which "formulas" of a specific religious type are blindly repeated, possibly without even being well understood.

29. Zahrâ, the "Flowering One," is one of Fâtima's many epithets. For the image of the transcendent Fâtima, see also Corbin, "De la gnose antique à la gnose ismaélienne" (*Conferenze Convegno Volta*, Rome 1956, p. 19).

30. It might be better translated the Mother-World, Nature.

31. I.e. 'Alî.

32. Of the "Prophets' Pledge," i.e., of Muhammad. Only 'Alî was worthy of being the husband of such a sacred woman.

33. Haidar, "lion" is one of 'Alî's many names.

34. According to Shi'ite tradition Hasan was poisoned for political and religious reasons. According to some historians his death was due to more banal harem intrigues.

35. The number of Husain's few followers is given here as the mystical number of seventy two, which played an important part in Islamic and other esoteric traditions.

36. He is speaking here of the fate of Husain's children. Some lines may be missing.

37. The reader should note the emotional breadth given to the concept of Shi'ism. Anyone who weeps for Husain is—for this reason alone—a Shi'ite even if (as can be seen in other ta'zieh) he is a Christian, a pagan or even . . . an animal: in fact there is also mention of the conversion of a lion!

38. One of the gardens of Paradise, of which the angel Rizvân is the keeper.

39. Here Adam seems to turn to the audience.

40. Our text, speaking of Karbalâ, often plays on the words karb-i balâ ("the torment of suffering"). The stichomythia which follows brings to mind (at times almost literally) the beautiful poem by Qânî we quoted earlier, in which Husain's martyrdom is also described in questions and answers. The Qâjâr poet was probably inspired by passages like these from some ta'ziehs.

41. He is one of the two 'Alî, sons of Husain. The elder (Akbar) was killed at Karbalâ, the younger (Asghar), also called Zainu'l-'Âbidîn, was to succeed his father as Imâm.

42. This word also means "camel-driver." I confess that I was unable to decipher the text any better.

43. Here we have the "redeeming" value of these sacred performances we mentioned at the beginning of the chapter and which is even more accentuated in other ta'zieh. The reader will have noted the extreme technical simplicity of this drama which—it must be admitted— is certainly not the best of the countless dramatic hymns to the martyrdom of Karbalâ.

Bibliography

Cerulli, E. "Una nuova collezione di manoscritti persiani della Biblioteca Vaticana." *Rendiconti Lincei* (1954), 1955, pp. 507 and foll.
Chodzko, A. *Théâtre Persan*. Paris 1878.
Generet, H. de. *Le Martyre d'Ali Akbar*. Paris 1957.
Krymski. *Pers'kyj teatr*. Kiev, 1925 (in Ukrainian).
Lassy, J. *The Moharram Mysteries among the Azerbaijan Turks of Caucasia*. Helsingfors, 1916.
Litten, W. *Das Drama in Persien*. Berlin-Leipzig, 1929.
Pelly, Lewis. *The Miracle Play of Hasan and Husain* (2 vols.). London, 1879.
Virolleaud, Ch. *La passion de l'imâm Hossein*. Paris, 1927.
————. *Le théâtre persan ou le drame de Kerbela*. Paris, 1950.
von Grunebaum, G.E. *Muhammadan Festivals*. New York, 1951.

Additional Bibliography

The reader should consult, for further information on the issues treated in this chapter, Peter J. Chelkowski, ed., *Ta'ziyeh: Ritual and Drama in Iran* (New York, 1979) and Juan R.I. Cole, *Roots of North Indian Shi'ism in Iran and Iraq* (Berkeley, 1989), chapter 6.

Chapter Eight

The New Babi-Baha'i Religion

Introduction

The English orientalist Browne—the major expert on the Babi-Baha'i religion—points out with some surprise certain singular similarities between Babi "theology" and Ismaili "theology" or, more generally, the "theology" of extreme Shi'ism (even though this latter was execrated as a "heresy" in the Twelver environment in which Bâbism flourished). But this will not surprise us, given what we have read in the preceding chapters (and especially in Chapter IV in part II, which I consider particularly important for an understanding of Persian religiosity and consequently of this problem). We saw how inextricably connected the Ismaili, Sufi, Suhravardian-Ishrâqî and Avicennan systems of thought were; then we saw how Suhravardî's illuminationism, which is a kind of summation of all these tendencies, continued in the School of Isfahan, and also how deeply steeped in Mullâ Sadrâ's thought (even if only to discuss it) was the Shaikhi milieu, from which Bâbism stemmed. We have already mentioned the great resemblance between Babi-Baha'i thought and the Gnosis of Islam (which it would be too specific to call Ismaili). An essential difference between these two forms of religious thought must not be overlooked, however, and it forms a useful introduction to understanding the "newest" element of the religious movement that interests us here. Through *ta'wîl* (taken in the sense described above) Ismailism carries out a methodical linking, and sets up a concrete referentiality, between what is apparent and exoteric (*zâhir*), and the intimate, invisible, esoteric (*bâtin*) element of all religious forms. It discovers, in this agreement, an intimate and essential unity. Consequently the followers of this form of thought can still consider themselves Muslims because, after this very daring procedure, they do not dispense a "new exoteric religious law." The unity occurs within, and all external religions in a way are repealed, though they are not replaced by a new one (as, for example, in the passage from Judaism to Christianity) but by the initiated person's personal attitude. For "the others," exoteric Islam, more or less revised and corrected, is sufficient. Even for this kind of Gnostic (as for orthodox believers) Muhammad is "the last of the prophets" because—after all—the '*ârif* ("he who knows") does not need a prophet and Muhammad is quite sufficient for the ignorant. This is why Gnosis blended easily with the great sea of Sufism, even though it left an occasional mark of the authoritarian Imâmi-centered currents we have found traces of here and there in the course of our work. The case of Babi-Bâhaism is different: the Babi-Baha'i movement considers that the moment is not ripe (and maybe never will be) for humanity to dispense with a legislator-prophet and that the distinction between the "elect" and the "common people" lacks all religious meaning. It proclaims that, when the time comes for a prophetic "dispensation" to grow old and externally corrupt, God solves the matter by sending a new one, as he has always done, according to the typically Islamic (and, earlier, Manichaean) concept of successive revelations. Not only do the old laws become mystically obsolete within the personal conscience but the social aspect of religion must change and new divine laws become necessary. Only God (via society) and not mystical man (on his own) can change things or solve the problem. Babi-Bahaism too respects the Qur'anic saying that calls Muhammad the "seal of the prophets" (*khâtamu'n-nabiyyîn*), but in a special sense. Muhammad is the last of the prophets because, after him, the prophetic cycle that unites Adam to Muhammad over an immense span of time is replaced by another cycle (here, Adam is considered, as in Gnostic tradition, not so much the first man but a more or less symbolic designation of the first Prophet). The new cycle is still legislative and social but of superior loftiness, for it is the cycle of the "Manifestation." That is, whereas God spoke through the prophets in the preceding cycle, always announcing something "future," the cycle that started with Bâb and Baha'ullah marks the beginning of the fulfillment of what the prophets announced. God now manifests himself within humanity through the great figures of the divine Legislators who, even after the Bâb and Baha'ullah, will contribute to bringing the potential of the human spirit to unpredictable degrees of perfection (Babi-Bahaism is the only historical prophetic religion that admits this).

The Bâb and Bâbism

The term *bâb* literally means "Gate" in Arabic and indicates various spiritual positions and ranks in the different Shi'ite sects, the most common being "gate between man and the knowledge of the hidden imâm." We saw in the preceding chapter how the term was used in the writings of the founders of Shaikhism as synonymous with the "fourth pillar" of the religion, that is, with the perfect

Shi'ite. The disagreement between the Shaikhîs and the Babis (which still continues in a few polemic treatises) can be summed up as follows. The present-day Shaikhîs, within the general ambit of the tendency we mentioned in the introduction to this chapter, understand *bâb* as being either an abstract concept, which cannot be personified in one or another individual, or a purely potential and interior individuality, which cannot be exteriorised in a prophet-legislator. Besides, the bâb of the Shaikhîs always remains a bâb, i.e., he does not become either the hidden imâm or the out-and-out initiator or manifestation of a new cycle of divine revelation. But, on the other hand, the man who proclaimed himself to be the historical bâb undoubtedly was in contact with Shaikhî circles. Sayyid 'Alî Muhammad, the future Bâb, was born in Shîrâz to a family of merchants on 1 Muharram 1235 (October 20, 1819; but according to another source a year later, i.e., on October 9, 1820). Orphaned at an early age, he was placed under the guardianship of his maternal uncle, Aghâ Sayyid 'Alî. At 18 to 19 years of age he was sent on business to Bûshehr on the Persian Gulf where, besides business, he went in for ardent religious meditation (as in fact he had done since childhood). During a pilgrimage to Imâm Husain's tomb at Karbalâ he met Sayyid Kâzim of Rasht, successor to the master Shaikh Ahmad and leader at the time of the Shaikhî theological school, who showed him very high and unusual esteem. Sayyid Kâzim died in December 1843 but, before his death, he sent his disciples throughout Persia in search of the "promised one" who, according to his predictions, would manifest himself shortly. One of the Sayyid's disciples, Mullâ Husain of Bushrûyeh, came to Shîrâz and was fascinated by the young 'Alî Muhammad. He was the first to recognize him as "the gate of truth," the First Point (*nuqteh-i ûlà*), the initiator of a new prophetic cycle, on the night of May 23, 1844 (a prophetic date for the Babis and the Baha'is, from which they calculate the years according to the new calendar). That evening the Bâb answered all of Mullâ Husain's requests in a satisfactory manner and wrote with lightning speed a long commentary on the Qur'anic "Sûra of Joseph" while chanting what he was writing in a most sweet voice. This commentary is known to the Babis as *Qayyûm al-asmâ'* ("He who rises up on the Attributes") and is considered the Bâb's first revealed work. The speed with which he composed, the elegance of his cursive writing and the indescribable fascination of his voice seem to have been the characteristics that most struck those who wrote about him, both friends and enemies. During the summer of 1844, the Bâb, who fiercely attacked the corrupt Shi'ite mujtahids with their own theological weapons, rapidly gained numerous followers, eighteen of whom he nominated as "Letters of the Living" (*Hurûf al-Hayy*; the reader should note, in passing, that the term is not new in Islamic Gnosis and is to be found in the form of "Letters of Life" even in early Christian inscriptions). After sending the Letters of the Living to announce his mission throughout the various Persian provinces, in the autumn the Bâb set out on a pilgrimage to Mecca. His journey left him with a very poor impression, which he noted in various passages of his works, both of the filthy and overcrowded conditions of the ships and of the poor moral disposition of the pilgrims, who were quarrelsome and violent. According to Babi sources the Bâb publicly announced his mission of Mahdî during a stop at Musqat (Oman) and then in the heart of the holy city of Mecca, but to no avail. In the spring of 1845, on his return trip to Shîraz, the Bâb released another book, *Sahîfa baina'l-haramain*, "The Book written between the two sanctuaries," in which he gave further details on the meaning of his mission. Once there his preaching and public declarations caused tumult. On the Bâb's orders his missionaries had dared to add to the profession of faith that is included in the Shi'ite-Islamic invitation to prayer (to wit, "I profess that there is no other God than God, that Muhammad is his Prophet, that 'Alî is his Friend"). The additional phrase was "and that 'Alî Muhammad is the mirror of the divine breath" (here again we have the mirror motif, which is fundamental for an understanding of the "Christology" of these movements). They were arrested, brought before the governor of Shîrâz, severely punished and expelled from the city. A man called Sayyid Yahyâ Dârâbî who represented Muhammad Shâh, the sovereign of Persia at the time, was sent to look into the matter and was won over by the Bâb's fascinating personality and converted to the new doctrine. In Tehran in the meantime Mîrzâ Husain 'Alî Nûrî (the future Baha'ullah) and his half-brother Mîrzâ Yahyâ (the future Subh-i Azal) joined the new faith after meeting Mullâ Husain. A cholera epidemic broke out in Shîrâz and all—persecutors and persecuted—fled. The Bâb went to Isfahan where the Georgian governor Manûchihr Khân protected him. At the governor's death the Bâb was ordered back to Tehran by Hâjjî Mîrzâ Aqâsî, one of the most inefficient ministers ever to be in office in Persia during the decadent period, but before reaching his destination he was arrested (in the summer of 1847) and sent, a prisoner, to the fortress of Mâkû in the inaccessible mountains of Azerbaijan. In April 1848, after Babi preaching had caused serious revolts in various parts of Iran, the Bâb, whose powerful influence had converted even the commander of the fortress of Mâkû, was transferred to a harsher prison in the distant castle of Chihrîq. Soon after, in July, he was brought to Tabrîz to be examined by a committee of mujtahids. By now his fate had been decided. The powerful minister Mîrzâ Taqî Khân had succeeded Hâjj Mîrzâ Aqâsî, deposed in 1848 by the new shâh, Nâsiru'd-Dîn. Mîrzâ Taqî Khân thought that the founder's death would break this very dangerous movement, which continued to make converts. In the spring of 1850 the news of the execution of the "seven martyrs of Tehran"—and among them his beloved uncle and guardian—reached the Bâb in the fortress of Chihrîq. This greatly saddened him and he foresaw that his own end was at hand. In the beginning of July he was brought to Tabrîz and condemned to be shot together with his two disciples, the mullâs Muhammad 'Alî of Yazd and Aghâ Sayyid Husain. During the unhappy procession of the three condemned men through the streets of Tabrîz, in the midst of the insults and blows of a fanatic crowd, Aghâ Sayyid Husain pretended to repudiate his faith and was freed. Before these events the Bâb had entrusted him with the execution of his last wishes and asked him to save some of his personal objects and writings. (He was in fact killed by Muslims in Tehran soon after carrying out his mission). Reaching the place of execution (a barracks courtyard) the Bâb and his disciple were hung with ropes from a pillar. The disciple's head rested against the Bâb's breast and his last words were: "Master, are you pleased with me?" During the execution a very strange thing occurred, which can be considered true since sources very hostile to the Bâb have mentioned it (e.g., a book with the significant title of The False Prophets). The first volley of the firing squad (an entirely Christian unit commanded by a certain Sâm Khân) only split the ropes, leaving the Bâb unscathed. Terrified, Sâm Khân refused to repeat the volley and another firing squad had to be called in. On July 9, 1850 the Bâb paid for the preaching of his new doctrine with his life. His riddled body was thrown into one of the city ditches and, after many vicissitudes (first it was carried away by the Babis and then hidden in Tehran for a number of years) Baha'ullah ordered that it be brought to 'Akkâ (St John of Acre, in Palestine) where it now rests in a fine mausoleum on the slopes of Mount Carmel. The Bâb's last words to the Letters of the Living—a kind of epistle written before the last sad events of his short life—are worth quoting. The following is the traditional edition, preserved by the historian of the Babi-Baha'i movement, Nabîl Zarandî (*Dawnbreakers*, pp. 92–94). It contains a great deal of first-hand material and is very interesting indeed. A sumptuous English translation exists, illustrated with photographs of historical objects and mementos and published in New York by Shoghi Effendi, the first "Guardian" of the Baha'i movement (see the Bibliography: S.E. died at the beginning of November 1957).

"O My beloved friends! You are the bearers of the name of God in this Day. You have been chosen as the repositories of His mystery. It behoves each one of you to manifest the attributes of God, and to exemplify by your deeds and words the signs of His righteousness, His power and glory.

The very members of your body must bear witness to the loftiness of your purpose, the integrity of your life, the reality of your faith, and the exalted character of your devotion. For verily I say, this is the Day spoken of by God in His Book:[1] "On that day will We set a seal upon their mouths; yet shall their hands speak unto Us, and their feet shall bear witness to that which they shall have done." Ponder the words of Jesus addressed to His disciples, as He sent them forth to propagate the Cause of God. In words such as these, He bade them arise and fulfil their mission:

"Ye are even as the fire which in the darkness of the night has been kindled upon the mountain-top. Let your light shine before the eyes of men. Such must be the purity of your character and the degree of your renunciation, that the people of the earth may through you recognise and be drawn closer to the heavenly Father who is the Source of purity and grace. For none has seen the Father who is in heaven. You who are His spiritual children must by your deeds exemplify His virtues, and witness to His glory. You are the salt of the earth, but if the salt have lost its savour, wherewith shall it be salted? Such must be the degree of your detachment, that into whatever city you enter to proclaim and teach the Cause of God, you should in no way expect either meat or reward from its people. Nay, when you depart out of that city, you should shake the dust from off your feet. As you have entered it pure and undefiled, so must you depart from that city. For verily I say, the heavenly Father is ever with you and keeps watch over you. If you be faithful to Him, He will assuredly deliver into your hands all the treasures of the earth, and will exalt you above all the rulers and kings of the world.[2]"

O My Letters! Verily I say, immensely exalted is this Day above the days of the Apostles of old. Nay, immeasurable is the difference! You are the witnesses of the Dawn of the promised Day of God. You are the partakers of the mystic chalice of His Revelation. Gird up the loins of endeavour, and be mindful of the words of God as revealed in His Book:[3] "Lo, the Lord thy God is come, and with Him is the company of His angels arrayed before Him!" Purge your hearts of worldly desires, and let angelic virtues be your adorning. Strive that by your deeds you may bear witness to the truth of these words of God, and beware lest, by "turning back," He may "change you for another people," who "shall not be your like," and who shall take from you the Kingdom of God.[4]

The days when idle worship was deemed sufficient are ended. The time is come when naught but the purest motive, supported by deeds of stainless purity, can ascend to the throne of the Most High and be acceptable unto Him. "The good word riseth up unto Him, and the righteous deed will cause it to be exalted before HIm." You are the lowly, of whom God has thus spoken in His Book:[5] "And We desire to show favour to those who were brought low in the land, and to make them spiritual leaders among men, and to make them Our heirs." You have been called to this station; you will attain to it, only if you arise to trample beneath your feet every earthly desire, and endeavour to become those "honoured servants of His who speak not till He hath spoken, and who do His bidding." You are the first Letters that have been generated from the Primal Point,[6] the first Springs that have welled out from the Source of this Revelation. Beseech the Lord your God to grant that no earthly entanglements, no worldly affections, no ephemeral pursuits, may tarnish the purity, or embitter the sweetness, of that grace which flows through you. I am preparing you for the advent of a mighty Day. Exert your utmost endeavor that, in the world to come, I, who am now instructing you, may, before the mercy-seat of God, rejoice in your deeds and glory in your achievements. The secret of the Day that is to come is now concealed. It can neither be divulged nor estimated. The newly born babe of that Day excels the wisest and most venerable men of this time, and the lowliest and most unlearned of that period shall surpass in understanding the most erudite and accomplished divines of this age. Scatter throughout the length and breadth of this land, and, with steadfast feet and sanctified hearts, prepare the way for His coming. Heed not your weaknesses and frailty; fix your gaze upon the invincible power of the Lord, your God, the Almighty. Has He not, in past days, caused Abraham, in spite of His seeming helplessness, to triumph over the forces of Nimrod? Has He not enabled Moses, whose staff was His only companion, to vanquish Pharaoh and his hosts? Has He not established the ascendancy of Jesus, poor and lowly as He was in the eyes of men, over the combined forces of the Jewish people? Has He not subjected the barbarous and militant tribes of Arabia to the holy and transforming discipline of Muhammad, His Prophet? Arise in His name, put your trust wholly in Him, and be assured of ultimate victory.

The Bâb's many works were almost all in manuscript form. Some have been lost and the authenticity of others is uncertain (in view also of the dissent, after his death, between the Baha'is and the Azalîs). The best known, in chronological order, are: (1) The *Qayyûmu'l-asmâ* or "Commentary on the sûra of Joseph" (see above), consisting in well over 9300 "short verses" in 111 chapters (i.e. each one on one verse of the famous sûra). It opens with the famous revolutionary address to the Kings of the earth: "O Kings! O sons of Kings! Do not take possession of what belongs to God!" It was written in Arabic but was integrally translated into Persian by the famous Babi heroine Qurratu'l-'Ain Tâhira (see below). (2) Epistles (*alvâh*, literally "tablets": from *lauh*—the well guarded celestial tablet—visible transpositions of the metaphysical concept of celestial *lauh*; this name is also given to Baha'ullah's short works) to various people: to Muhammad Shâh, the sovereign of Persia, to the Sultan 'Abdu'l-Majîd, to Najîb Pâshâ, the Ottoman governor of Bagdad, etc. (3) The *Sahîfa baina'l-Haramain*, which we have already mentioned. (4) The Epistle to the Sharif of Mecca. (5) the *Kitâb ar-Rûh* ("Book of the Spirit") in 700 chapters or "sûras." (6) *Khasâ'il-i sab'eh* ("The seven virtues") which includes his order for the modification of the invitation to prayer we spoke about above. (7) *Dalâ'il-i sab'eh* ("The seven proofs"), which is the most important of the Bâb's polemic works. (8) Endless commentaries on Muslim sacred texts as well as epistles to various people: according to his amanuensis, Shaikh Hasan-i Zunûzî, when the Bâb was in the castle of Mâkhû he wrote nine commentaries on the whole Qur'an. (9) Finally the Bâb's most important work, the two Bayâns ("Declarations," "Explanations") a shorter one in Arabic and one in Persian. The first is divided into 11 Units (*Vâhid*) of 19 *bâb* ("chapters") each, the second into nine Vâhid of 19 chapters each, except for the last one which has only 10 chapters. The two Bayâns were translated into French by the indefatigable Nicolas, who shares with Browne the honor and onus (among European orientalists) of having devoted the most time to the study of this movement. The Babis also called themselves *Ahl-i Bayân* ("the people of the Bayân") from these sacred books, even though, according to the Bâb's own explicit declaration (III Vâhid, chap. 17, of the Persian Bayân) the Bayân must be understood as everything he wrote.

The contents of the Bayân can be summarised in four basic points: (1) Abrogation of the various ordinances of Qur'anic canon law concerning prayer, fasting, marriage, divorce and inheritance, while maintaining the truth of the prophetic mission of Muhammad, whose prophetic cycle ended with the year 1260 A.H. (1844). (2) Spiritualized interpretation of eschatological terms such as Heaven, Hell, Death, Resurrection, Scales, Bridge (*Sirât*), Hour, etc., which occur in the Qur'an and other sacred books. In view of the religious orientation of Bâbism (according to which the prophetic cycle of Muhammad is followed by the cycle of "realisation") the symbolic interpretation of these terms (unlike their interpretation in illuminationist [Ishrâqî] and Sadrian philosophy) moves from the world of the *mithâl* (realistic symbols) to an effective world of reality, which is chronologically subsequent here. The end of the world is not the end of the physical world but of the preceding prophetic cycle: meeting God signifies meeting the Bâb, Heaven signifies coming into his presence, Hell rejecting the Bâb, Resurrection the spiritual regeneration of the dead and corrupt souls of the Muslims that have come into contact with the new concrete and exoteric revelation, etc. Some passages of the Bayân seem to indicate that, since the real world is the world of the Spirit (of which the material world is only an exteriorisation), with every prophetic cycle God effectively destroys the world to recreate it anew through the fiat of the next prophet. The creative value of the Word is extremely important in the Bayân. (3) The establishment of new institutions, a new direction (*qibla*) of prayer towards the Bâb's House, a new kind of division of inheritances, obligatory marriage from the age of 11, etc. (4) Constant and very strong eschatological tension towards a *man yuzhiruhu'llâh* ("He whom God will make manifest"), the future Prophet, the real and true founder of the new cycle, of whom the Bâb declares himself only the humble servant. It could even be said that the expectation of the Promised One is the essence itself of the Bayân, for even the most ordinary precepts are explained from an eschatological point of view. For example, after stating that the Babis must not own more than 19 books, and all on the Bayân and the science of the Bayân, he adds: "all these orders are for this purpose, that nothing be placed in the presence of He whom God will manifest other than the Bayân itself" (Arabic Bayân, translated by Nicolas, p. 223). Where regulations on journeys are concerned, these must not be undertaken at the moment when the Promised One will manifest himself, for all will have to travel towards him and him alone: this is the reason for the singular prohibition the Babis have against travel (ibid., p. 166). Even the care given to cleanliness, on which the Bâb greatly insists, is justified eschatologically, i.e., the Promised One's glance must not fall on something disgusting (ibid., p. 159). As for the time of the coming of the Promised One, besides the well-known passage (ibid., p. 166), "Arise all from the place where you are when you hear the name of He whom God will manifest mentioned . . . And in the ninth year you will attain everything that is good"—a passage which the Baha'is interpret as a declaration of the manifestation of the promised one in 1853, the ninth year after the beginning of the Bâb's mission (1844)—various other passages of the Bayân can effectively be taken as an indication that the Bâb, at least at some moments, felt that the future manifestation might be close at hand. The beautiful Chapter eleven of Vâhid IV of the Arabic Bayân (ibid., pp. 138–9) is particularly interesting: "Do not be the instruments of your own misfortune, because not being sad is one of the greatest commands of the Bayân. The fruit of this command is that you must not sadden He whom God will Manifest."

The Bâb's metaphysics resembles in some ways Ismaili metaphysics for it proposes, as against the one plane of monistic being in Pantheism or the double plane of the Divine and the Human of orthodox Islam, a tripartition of being: the world of the essence of God, which is absolutely unreachable and transcendent, the world of nature and of man, and the world of the Manifestation, the most pure mirror in which only God can look at himself. The Bâb's doctrine appears to give the greatest importance to the invisible world that vibrates behind and within visible things. Thus, since all the eschatological terms such as death, eternity, heaven, etc., refer only to the vision of the Prophet, very little space remains for discussing what the Bâb considered to be life after death. This has led some authors, probably erroneously (cf. Browne in his preface to M. Phelps, *'Abbâs Effendî*), to think that the Bâb denied life after death, at least in the traditional sense of the word. It would be more correct to say that the enthusiastic Babi religiosity is so oriented towards building heaven in this world that it does not have time to think of the next, which already vibrates and is "manifested" in this one. And his concept of the return of Muhammad, of the imâms, etc. in the present cycle of manifestations has led some people to believe mistakenly that he admitted reincarnation. In fact, in his singular concept of the "newness" of the various worlds of the successive prophetic cycles, the Bâb denies the Islamic and Christian dogma of the resurrection of the flesh as well as the reincarnation of souls in another body. When he writes (Arabic Bayân, Vâhid I, chaps. 2 and foll.) that "they (his lieutenants) are, first, Muhammad, God's Prophet, and then those who are God's witnesses (the imâms) concerning the creatures . . ." mentioning historical people of his time, he means to say that they "have been created in another world," i.e., God re-created those people anew in the "world of the Bayân" after having created them in the "world of the Qur'an." This very bookish concept of the worlds of nature and of the spirit leads one to understand the enormous importance the Bâb gave to letters, to the written word and to relative numerical values. He considered the love of fine calligraphy an act of religion and often advised, in the Bayân, that copies of the Sacred Book be preserved in the most elegant writing possible. The number 19, which stems from the numerical calculation of the letters which form Islamic religious formulas, was extremely important in Babi numerology. The natural calendar was abolished and a purely spiritual and theological calendar followed consisting in 19 months (each of 19 days), each bearing the name of one of God's attributes, plus 4 intercalary days between the eighteenth and nineteenth month (the month of fasting preceding the New Year, which is identical to the traditional Iranian New Year, Naurûz, March 21, the spring equinox). These intercalary days are called Ayyâm-i Hâ, "the days of the letter H" (an abbreviation of Baha', glory [of God], a name for the future Promised One). The Bâb also delighted in writing a kind of "talisman": extremely complicated *hayâkil* (plural of *haikal*, "temple," or form, which then becomes also human temple, figure of cosmic man) in intricate shikasteh writing (the difficult Persian cursive writing) which he considered the most acceptable to God.

It would be difficult to give a logical order to all the many different ethical and juridical precepts contained in the Bayân. Next to beautiful verses (as, for example: "Mention my Name each day. And if each day My Thought penetrates into your heart, then you will be among those who are always in God's Thought!" Arabic Bayân, Vâhid V, chap. 9) we find rather strange prescriptions, such as the one we already mentioned about not possessing more than 19 books, or instructions on how to eat eggs. The extreme leniency of the punishments, which are limited to fines and periods of absolute chastity, are characteristic. The most severe punishment is inflicted for murder: the culprit is condemned to pay 19,000 gold mithqâls to the victim's heirs and to practice absolute chastity for 19 years. Punishments are also prescribed not only for striking but also for raising one's voice against one's fellow men. The moral purity of the Babis—who, among other things, neither drank nor smoked—was proverbial in nineteenth century Persia. European travellers unanimously recorded it and in fact it quite fascinated some Westerners, who were struck by the singular contrast between the irreprehensible customs of the Babis and the corrupt lives of the so-called Shi'ite "Muslims" of Persia. However some passages indicate that the precepts on non-violence refer to the relationship between believers. It is only—as we shall see—in the later Baha'i doctrine that holy wars and the confiscation of non-believers' property was definitively abolished. There were also rules concerning income tax and taxes on capital, etc. Divorce was admitted but not advised. Widowers and widows were obliged to remarry: the former after 90 the latter after 95 days. The ritual purity and segregation of women was abolished. Public worship too was abolished, except for the prayers for the dead. The house where the Bâb was born and the places where he was imprisoned were recommended as places of pilgrimage. Every

19 days a good Babi must invite 19 people and offer them at least a glass of water. All alcoholic drinks were forbidden, as were begging and giving alms individually to beggars. Taken as a whole, Babi legislation presents itself as superior to Islamic legislation, especially for the general leniency of its punishments, the execution of which was in fact left to the conscience of the punished person himself: the punishment of chastity, for example, is beyond any control.

There are various explanations for the extremely harsh persecutions the Babis had to endure in Persia both before and after their founder's martyrdom and which are their greatest claim to glory because of the heroism of the faithful, whom Renan compared to the first Christians in *Les Apôtres*. Obviously one reason was the jealousy of the corrupt Shi'ite clergy who, with the rapid spreading of the faith in the years preceding the Bâb's execution, felt that they were losing control over the masses. But there were also deeper social reasons. However one may judge the Babi movement religiously, it presents itself, from the point of view of the dialectics of the class system, as one of the first stirrings of life of a healthy commercial bourgeoisie class in the still feudal and medieval Persian nineteenth century society. The Babi upheavals around 1848 are a kind of Persian counterpart to the general anti-feudal and liberally-oriented movements, which were fermenting throughout the civilized world. Some authors (Browne) have stressed the great importance of the Babi movement, albeit indirect rather than direct, in the political awakening of Persia and—in the long run—in the development of the Persian liberal revolution (1906–1911). For it was not a philosophical and theological movement only accessible to a limited circle of the elect but a true organized religion of the masses. But one should also consider a psychological aspect of these persecutions. Hatred of or antipathy toward the Babis has, strangely, become common ground up to the present day for both the reactionary orthodox religious and "indifferent" liberally-oriented people. Many nationalists no longer believe in traditional Islam, hating it as "Arab" and hostile to Persian nationality, and looking kindly on the philosophical and theological movements that tend to liberalize it in a vaguely pantheistic, Sufi and Gnostic sense. But even these nationalists are particularly irritated by the rebirth of a genuine organized "prophetic" religion which, in fact, is the only kind of religion able to move the masses.

The history of Bâbism is a history of persecution and bloodshed. It can be divided into two periods. The first one lasted from the foundation of the new faith to the vast persecutions that followed the unsuccessful attempt on the life of Nâsiru'd-Dîn Shâh (1852–3) by two Babis, who were half-crazed with sorrow at the loss of their master. These persecutions seemed to break the spirit of the new movement for ever and the period was characterized by an often violent attitude on the part of the Babis themselves. The next period, which could be called "pacifist," has lasted from 1853 to the present day and has witnessed the schism of the Babis into two branches, of unequal numbers and importance. The larger branch—the Baha'i (see below)—developed a definitely nonviolent attitude towards established governments. After the first expansion of the faith that followed the Bâb's declaration (1844) and the first persecutions which the Babis resisted strenuously in some areas, the most important event in the history of the community was the council of Badasht (1848) during which the Babis abandoned their initial precautions and openly declared their complete detachment from Islamic prophetic teaching and canon law. The famous heroine of Bâbism, the beautiful and learned poetess Zarrîn Tâj ("Golden Crown") (better known as Qurratu 'l-'Ain ("Freshness of the Eye")) or, among her correligionists, as Jinâb-i Tâhira [Her Highness the Pure One]), played an important part in this, being the first Persian woman who dared show herself unveiled to her brothers in the faith—a living example of the abrogation of Muslim canon law. Tâhira, the daughter of the learned mujtahid Mullâ Sâlih, was born at Qazvîn and became a Babi after merely reading the Bâb's works without ever having known the master: her name could well head the list—as a precursor—of the many women who fought for the emancipation of women. Here is one of her ardent mystical poems which possibly indicates her nostalgia for the contemplation of the face of her beloved Master who—we then realize—is God's face. Tâhira was strangled by the executioner in Tehran in 1852.

> If ever it should happen that I meet You face to face, I will tell of Your suffering, point by point hair by hair.
> To see Your cheek I have been, like the zephyr, to every house, every door, every road, every street.
> The pain of separation has made my heart's blood gush from
>   my eyes, in rivers, in seas, in fountains, in streams.
> Around Your small mouth, Your cheek with its amber down is
>   bud on bud, rose on rose, tulip on tulip, perfume on perfume.
> My sad heart has woven Your love into the fabric of my
>   heart, thread by thread, cord by cord, weft by weft, needle by needle.
> Tâhira has wandered within her heart and has only seen You
>   there, in every page, in every recess, in every veil,
>   in every fold.

After the Badasht meeting, which was attended by a number of the most important Babis and the future Baha'ullah (though not the Founder, who was already in prison), Mullâ Husain of Bushrûyeh—"the first believer," the *bâbu'l-bâb* ("gate of the Gate," as the Bâb himself had called him)—prepared for a siege together with a small group of Babi in the sanctuary of Shaikh Tabarsî near Bârfurûsh (Mâzanderân) where he heroically resisted the Shâh's troops together with another Letter of the Living, Mullâ Muhammad 'Alî Bârfurûshî called Quddûs ("the Saint"). They even made victorious sorties against crushing odds, until Mullâ Husain was killed and Quddûs and the other survivors surrendered with the promise that their lives would be spared. They were nevertheless cruelly massacred (July-August 1849). Soon after this another heroic Babi insurrection occurred at Nairîz in the Fârs district. It was led by Sayyid Yahyâ-i Dârâbî, called Vahîd (for the Bâb and, later, Baha'ullah and 'Abdu'l-Bahâ too were in the habit of giving converts new names—a custom which we find in many religious and initiatory communities). They barricaded themselves in the old fortress, which they defended heroically for a few days, with the good will of the population, until they were all massacred (January 1850). Almost at the same time an insurrection of even vaster dimensions was raging at Zanjân. Led by Mullâ Muhammad 'Alî Zanjâni, called "the Proof" (Hujjat), the Babis barricaded themselves in the citadel. After various ups and downs, including bloody defeats of the disorganized and exhausted imperial armies led by incapable generals, the more than three thousand Babi were cruelly massacred (February 1850). Four months before the Bâb's execution, Tehran too had its heroes: the so-called "seven martyrs of Tehran" (one of whom was the Bâb's uncle and guardian). Their very proud bearing in the face of horrible tortures is a glorious page in the history of the new religion. Babi-hunting soon became an obsession: it is interesting to see reflected in the letters to St. Petersburg from the ambassador to Tehran, Prince Dolgoruki (published in the interesting little book by the Soviet orientalist Ivanov, *Babidiskie vosstanija v Irane*, 1939, see Bibliography), the concern in the capital at the news of the defeats of the Shâh's armies (which were equipped with modern artillery) at the hands of small groups of enthusiasts. Dolgoruki, accepting the rumours that circulated in the capital and himself voicing some concern over the possibility of a takeover of power by the Babis (which in Persia even seemed possible for a brief moment), erroneously defined them as dangerous "communists." The unsuccessful attempt on the Shâh's life on August 16, 1852, set off a new wave of terror to which many eminent leaders of the faith, including the poetess Tâhira, fell victim. The sceptical population of Tehran witnessed—with a wonder that in many people changed to admiration—tens and tens of men, women and children with lit candles stuck into bleeding gashes in their breasts, their feet shod like animals' hoofs, jostled along to their death without a word of lament. Many of them sang the brief Islamic prayer: "In truth we belong to God, in truth we are returning to Him!" Husain 'Alî Nûrî, the future Baha'ullah, was arrested and locked up in a loathsome prison in Tehran and only escaped being executed because of his noble lineage. The persecutions continued sporadically throughout Persia and Baha'i tradition speaks of about 20,000 martyrs from 1844 to the present day. Martyrs again suffered this fate in 1955 [and after 1979 in Khomeinist Iran-ed.].

It can fairly be said that the great wave of persecutions of 1852–53 played a very important part in the creation of the Baha'i movement—a movement which, breaking away from a Bâbism which had become too fanatic and literalist, turned a hopeless Islamic sect into a truly universalistic religion. There are some significant passages concerning this transformation in Baha'ullah's *Epistle to the son of the Wolf* (*Lauh-i Ibn-i dhi ' b*, also known as *Kitâb ash-shaikh*, "The Book of the shaikh"). On p. 16 of the Persian text he says that while he was chained in prison he meditated on the folly committed by the two Babis who tried to kill the Shâh and had the idea of "educating the Babis" to a non-violent approach to the struggle (which risked becoming a political revolt) and of leading the movement back to its truer religious direction.

Baha'ullah and Baha'ism

Mîrzâ Husain 'Alî Nûrî (from Nûr in Mâzandarân, the place of origin of his family) was born in Tehran on the second of Muharram 1233 A.H. (November 12, 1817, two years before the Bâb) to a high ranking family which gave several dignitaries to the Persian court. According to both the Baha'i tradition and to his own written declarations, he did not go to school at all. Of a contemplative and religious disposition, he describes in one of his epistles (*Lauh-i Ra'îs*) how he was drawn to religious thoughts at the end of a puppet show when, after all the pomp of the performance, the puppets were put back into their box. This led him to think about the deception and vanity of human power and of the things of the world. He became one of the Bâb's first followers after his manifestation, even though he never actually met the Master. According to another of his works, the *Epistle to the Son of the Wolf* (Persian text, p. 122), he never even perused the Bayân which however—he said—he "had in his heart." In 1852, after the attempt on the Shâh's life, he was arrested in Niyâvarân near Tehran and, roughly handled and insulted by the populace, led on foot to the capital and thrown into the loathsome prison known as the "Black Hole" (Siyâh Châl), where he remained until January 12, 1853. In the same *Epistle*, he described his march, in chains, from Niyâvarân to Tehran and his mystical experience in prison during the long sleepless nights because of the heavy chains around his neck, hands and feet. He said he thought he heard a voice which told him: "Verily, We shall render Thee victorious by Thyself and by Thy Pen. Grieve Thou not for that which hath befallen Thee, neither be Thou afraid, for Thou art in safety. Erelong will God raise up the treasures of the earth—men who will aid Thee through Thyself and through Thy Name, wherewith God hath revived the hearts of such as have recognized him" (*Epistle*, Eng. trans., p. 21). At other moments he felt as if a great torrent of water were running down him from the crown of his head onto his breast "even as a mighty torrent that precipitateth itself upon the earth from the summit of a lofty mountain." The Baha'is consider this experience the beginning of their founder's prophetic mission and celebrated its centenary in 1953. He was banished with his family to Iraq and all his possessions were confiscated. He remained in Baghdad where his spiritual influence over the Babi émigrés continued to grow while that of his step-brother Mîrzâ Yahyâ, known under the name (given him by the Bâb) of Subh-i Azal ("Dawn of eternity"), decreased, even though the Bâb himself had appointed him as his vicar. According to the Baha'is this appointment was only temporary and pro forma and at all events it did not give Subh-i Azal the right to oppose "He whom God shall make manifest" who was, they believed, Mîrzâ Husain 'Alî Nûrî himself. Baha'ullah then went to Kurdistân where he lived as a wandering dervish near Sulaimânîya from 1854 to 1856. Returning to Baghdad, his growing influence and the many visits he received even from Persia led the Persian consul to ask the Ottoman government to exile him still further to Constantinople (Istanbul). On April 21, 1863 (shortly before his departure), Baha'ullah declared that he was the "He whom God will make manifest" (*man yuzhiruhu'llâh*) predicted by the Bâb. He made this declaration to a few followers in Najîb Pâshâ's garden near Baghdad and, with the usual transposition of celestial terms to things and events connected with the historical life of the manifestation of God, the Baha'is later called it *Bâgh-i Rizvân* ("the garden of Paradise"). The exiles reached Constantinople in August, after an exhausting journey under primitive conditions, and a few months later were sent on to Adrianople (Edirne), which they reached in December. In Adrianople Baha'ullah openly declared his mission of Divine Manifestation, sending epistles ("tablets," *alvâh*) to a number of European sovereigns (including the Tsar of Russia, Napoleon III, Pope Pius IX and Queen Victoria) inviting them to support his cause. In the meantime the majority of the Babis had opted for him and from then on called themselves Baha'is. The name Baha'ullah means "Glory, or Splendor, of God" and the Bâb had already indicated it as the title of "He whom God will manifest." The conflicts with the minority followers of Subh-i Azal, who kept to the letter of Bâbism and are now only a few tens of thousands in the East, where they have been mostly reabsorbed by Shi'ite Islam, caused some incidents which led the Ottoman government to exile the Baha'is to St. Jean d'Acre ('Akkâ) in Palestine and the Azalîs, including their leader, to Cyprus. In August 1868 Baha'ullah, his family and a few followers reached 'Akka. His close imprisonment in the fortress city lasted until 1877 when he was authorised to move to a country house he had rented at Mazra'a. In 'Akkâ, during the years 1871–74, Baha'ullah wrote the fundamental book of laws of his religion, *The Most Holy Book* (*al-Kitâb al-Aqdas*) in Arabic. Around 1880 he was allowed to move to Bahjî, not far from 'Akkâ, where he died after a brief illness on May 29, 1892. In 1890 one of the most famous English orientalists of the time, Edward G. Browne, visited him. He was the only European ever to meet him personally and was very deeply impressed by him. Browne later wrote:

> In the corner where the divan met the wall sat a wondrous and venerable figure, crowned with a felt head-dress of the kind called *taj* by dervishes (but of unusual height and make), round the base of which was wound a small white turban. The face of him on whom I gazed I can never forget, though I cannot describe it. Those piercing eyes seemed to read one's very soul; power and authority sat on that ample brow . . . No need to ask in whose presence I stood, as I bowed myself before one who is the object of a devotion and love which kings might envy and emperors sigh for in vain!
>
> A mild dignified voice bade me be seated, and then continued: "Praise be to God that thou hast attained! . . . Thou has come to see a prisoner and an exile . . . We desire by the good of the world and the happiness of the nations; yet they deem us as a stirrer up of strife and sedition worthy of bondage and banishment . . . These strifes and this bloodshed and discord must cease, and all men be as one kindred and one family . . . Let not a man glory in this, that he loves his country; let him rather glory in this, that he loves his kind . . ."[7]

Thus, through a singular destiny, Palestine became the holy land not only for Judaism, Christianity and Islam, but also for a fourth prophetic religion, Bahaism. This religion also had the unique good fortune of being guided by a number of first-class personalities (both for their religious spirit and for their practical, organisational ability). When Baha'ullah's Will (*Kitâbu 'ahdî* in Arabic) was opened after his death, it was discovered that he had appointed his son 'Abbâs Effendî, better known later as 'Abdu'l-Bahâ and, in the technical language of the Baha'is, as "The Most Great Branch" (*al-ghusn al-a'zam*), as the "Center of the Covenant," that is, as the authorised interpreter and expounder of his father's writings, and model and example of Baha'i life. One of 'Abdu'l-Bahâ's brothers, Muhammad 'Alî, contested the Will and caused a schism within the Baha'i structure, even trying to discredit his brother and his brother's followers in the eyes of the ever watchful Ottoman authorities who persecuted the Baha'is. As history proved Baha'ullah right in the dispute with Subh-i Azal, so it proved 'Abdu'l-Bahâ right in the controversy with his brother, who was left with only a very few followers (who have now almost disappeared). In the noteworthy threesome of personalities who laid down the foundations of the new religion 'Abdu'l-Bahâ's gentleness and purity remind one rather of the Bâb, after the majestic and authoritatative figure of Baha'ullah. Born in Tehran on May 23, 1844, he followed his father in his wanderings and exile. He was freed from internal exile in 1908, after the amnesty granted by the new Ottoman government of the "young Turks," and in 1910 he started his three great missionary journeys. The first was to Egypt (1910); the second to Europe (1911, Paris and London); and the third to America and Europe (1912–13). From New York he set out on an eight months' journey throughout the United States, as far as Los Angeles and San Francisco, stopping in the principal cities and preaching in Evangelical churches, synagogues, Masonic temples, etc. In September 1912 he returned to Europe and, setting out from England, went again to Paris, and then to Germany, Austria and Hungary. From Paris he returned to Palestine at the end of 1913. The first Baha'i group in America had already been formed in February 1894, and on December 10, 1898, the first American Baha'i pilgrims reached 'Akkâ. 'Abdu'l-Bahâ's journey—which he had also undertaken to confute the schismatics' propaganda in America—considerably strengthened the community of American believers and created Baha'i groups in the European areas he crossed. In April 1920 the British government made him knight of the British Empire. He died on November 28, 1921, in Haifa and, after a funeral attended by the representatives of all the religious communities in Palestine (including the Catholic community) and the British governor himself, he was buried beside the Bâb in the great Mausoleum on the slopes of Mount Carmel (which was only completed in 1954).

In his Will he appointed Shoghi Effendi Rabbânî (d. 1957)—his eldest grandson (the eldest son of his eldest daughter)—as "Guardian of the Cause" (*valî-i amru'llâh*). Shoghi Effendi Rabbânî administered the Baha'i movement from Haifa (where he was born towards the end of the last century). For some time after his nomination some people still refused him obedience, but the strange thing is that his fiercest adversary (Mîrzâ Ahmad Suhrâb, one of 'Abdu'l-Bahâ's secretaries during his journeys), who founded an umpteenth dissident movement, publicly recognized in writing the authenticity of 'Abdu'l-Bahâ's Will. Shoghi Effendi studied at Oxford and in 1936 married an American, Mary Maxwell, who took the name of Rûhiyyeh Khânum; he died in London on November 3, 1957, where he was buried. Since he did not indicate his successor in his Will, the function of "guardians of the unity" of the Baha'i cause was assumed by a board of nine "Hands of the Cause" (see ahead) living in Haifa. Shoghi Effendi is the author of many excellent English translations of the writings of Baha'ullah and 'Abdu'l-Bahâ, as well as of original works aimed at spreading and commenting the founders' teachings.

What are these teachings? Browne and Nicolas possibly were better acquainted with the Babî and Baha'i doctrine than any other orientalists. In contrast, encyclopedias and handbooks on Islamics (often by learned scholars) give judgements and descriptions of the Baha'i doctrines that do not single out their fundamental aspects and (possibly on the basis of inaccurate propaganda pamphlets) appear to consider them a kind of theosophy, or philosophical and humanitarian movement, or political organisation for a world federation. Even

Nallino—in his article on Bahâism in the *Enciclopedia Italiana*—says that it has dwindled to a vague humanitarian movement that often acts as a screen for real atheism. The learned orientalist probably never actually met any Baha'is, for if anything it seems to us that . . . they tend to the opposite excess! In fact the Baha'i doctrines, as they appear in the numerous writings of the founders (of which the principal ones are listed in the Bibliography), present a clear though simple theology and a precise legislative organisation that is totally different from that of Islam, as well as a very strong "sacral impetus" centered around the sanctuaries in Israel—a whole, consequently, which makes it an autonomous and specific religion, no longer bound to Islam. As the founders' explicitly declared, it has the same relationship to Islam as Christianity has to Judaism. It is truly the fourth monotheistic religion (together with Judaism, Christianity and Islam) and the first monotheistic religion to originate in Persia, if one excludes the partial Zoroastrian monotheism.[8]

The following is a brief summary of the Baha'i doctrines taken from texts that the reader will find indicated in the Bibliography:

God

God is an absolutely transcendental and unknowable entity. "All the ways to him are barred." The Baha'is are definitely against any form of mystical pantheism. The mystics—Baha'ullah says—have simply materialised their own personal imagination:

"To whatever heights the mind of the most exalted of men may soar, however great the depths which the detached and understanding heart can penetrate, such mind and heart can never transcend that which is the creature of their own conceptions and the product of their own thoughts." (*Lauh-i Salmân*; *Gleanings*, p. 317.)

The Created

The unknowable essence of God manifests itself, and creates the non-God. Only these "traces" can give us a vague idea of God. The Baha'i concept of the beginning of things is intermediate between that of creation and that of emanation. One could speak of eternal creation since the Baha'i texts insist on using the term *khalq* ("creation"), but at the same time they maintain that since the attribute of *khâliq* ("creator") is coeternal with God there never has been a time when the world did not exist. Therefore the world too is eternal (*Lauh-i Hikmat*).

But though an individualistic knowledge of God through mysticism is precluded and though the notions we can acquire of him through the contemplation of nature are vague, a social form of knowledge of God exists and is the surest form, i.e., the common acceptation of his Manifestation, the Prophet, and obedience to his legislative precepts (not "dogmas"). The Baha'i texts prefer the expression *mazhar-i ilâhî* (divine manifestation) rather than the term Prophet (in Arabic, *rasûl* or *nabî*). The Prophet is *mazhar* ("place of appearance," the mirror in which—in the classical terms of the metaphysics of light—God is reflected). The concept of "incarnation" (*hulûl*, descent of the divine substance into man) is firmly refused. Baha'ullah's letter on this subject to Nâsiru'd-Dîn Shâh (*Lauh-i Sultân*) is particularly interesting, and in the *Epistle to the Son of the Wolf* he describes his personal mystical experience. The prophet—he says—has two states: he is man, but he is also most pure mirror in which God is reflected. Therefore in a way it is not erroneous to call him, almost as an abbreviation, "God." The Plan of being that could be called "prophetic" is radically different from that of man and is intermediate between that of man and that of God. According to Baha'i doctrine no man, however perfect and however open to perfection to an infinite degree as man, can become a prophet: men and prophets belong to different orders of beings. The Manifestation of God through the prophets is unending: there is never a "last prophet." Man has needed and will always need a divine guide, though this guide, at least externally, will be adapted to the maturity man himself has reached.

The essential task of the prophets does not consist in teaching "divine science" (therefore it has nothing to do with theosophy and "spiritual science"), not in describing the other world, not in teaching dogmas, but it is "political" in the best sense of the word, and consists in providing the means for the creation of ever vaster social "units." The dogma of Divine Unity is theological nonsense (as is every dogma, according to Baha'i doctrine), unless it is realised practically in the world. Besides and beyond teaching divine unity, the prophets' task is to bring it about. Thus Adam, the first prophet mentioned by tradition, had the task of founding the first unit, the unit of the person just emerging from the chaos of the subhuman world, and then—in concentric circles—Noah founded the unit of the family, Abraham the unit of the tribe, Moses the unit of the people, and so forth until Baha'ullah, whose mission is the unification of all humanity. But the future must not be mortgaged: Baha'ullah admits that other prophets may come after him who are more suited to further stages in the progress of humanity, but "not before a thousand years" (*Aqdas*). Next the prophetic periods are gathered into greater cycles. The advent of the Bâb, for example, marked the end of "Adam's cycle" and the beginning of the Baha'i cycle which, according to some Baha'i texts, is destined to last for at least another 500,000 years. All the Founders of religions and especially those of the traditional "Semitic" cycle (even though it is explicitly stated that in ancient times Zarathustra, Buddha, etc., were valid prophets too, for given areas and specific peoples) are therefore recognised as being authentic, but in a "chronological sense." Just as in the seventh century it was the duty of enlightened men to recognise Muhammad as their spiritual leader, and, seven centuries earlier,

Jesus, now they must recognise Baha'ullah and his laws as suitable and wished for by God: this is something very different from a "religious syncretism," it is an authentic and autonomous religion. The doctrines of the different prophets are divided into two parts: a "mystical" and moral part which can be summed up in the law of love towards God and one's neighbour, and a legislative part. Only this second part changes in its various prophetic dispensations. The first part is eternal.

Man

Baha'i psychology is rather complex, for it follows the Gnostic tradition. 'Abdu'l-Bahâ distinguishes (in *Mufâvazât*, trans. as *Some Answered Questions*) five species of spirit: the vegetal, animal and human spirit, the spirit of Faith, the Holy Spirit. The "spirit of Faith," comes from God and is the only one which confers true eternal life on the human spirit (i.e., we are far from a purely philosophical and humanistic concept of the immortality of the soul). "Faith" is essential in Baha'i spiritual life: the first verse of the fundamental text (*Aqdas*) of this movement (which some people have considered a rationalist movement) says, rather calvinistically: "The first duty prescribed by God for HIs servants is the recognition of Him Who is the Dayspring of His Revelation and the Fountain of His laws [that is, the Divine Manifestation, the Prophet], Who representeth the Godhead in both the Kingdom of His Cause and the world of creation [*fî 'âlam al-amr wa al-khalq*]. Whoso achieveth this duty hath attained unto all good; and whoso is deprived thereof hath gone astray, though he be the author of every righteous deed" (*Most Holy Book*, p. 19). Faith in God (which, since he is unknowable, cannot but be faith in his Manifestation) bestows on the believer everlasting life. Therefore he will continue into the world of the beyond (about which the Baha'i is advised against enquiring too far: assisting at spiritualist meetings is specifically forbidden) on his eternal journey towards the unknowable Essence of God. In view of this "dynamic" concept of the other world, praying for the dead is not only admitted but advised. Besides, this other world is both very close to and co-present with ours: in an interesting passage, Baha'ullah rejects reincarnation and maintains that disembodied souls transformed into impulses of action collaborate in the realisation of a better world together with the living: this is another aspect of the religious earthliness which is characteristic of the whole Baha'i spirit. Where the emergence of human beings is concerned, the Baha'i doctrine accepts the theory of evolution—not in a Darwinistic sense but, rather, in the traditional Gnostic sense which was already present, as we saw, in Rûmî and, even earlier, in the Ikhwân as-Safâ (see above). "Man, during his whole evolution, was always man," even when he was going through the various preceding stages.

Moral and social principles

The Baha'is have taken as their own the phrase attributed to 'Alî: "Everything that is individual is human, everything that is social is divine." Hence the central importance Baha'i doctrine gives to the improvement of society. In fact it is this accentuated centrality that has caused some superficial students of the movement to miss the point and not understand the link that exists for the Baha'is between sociality and religion, so that they transformed the Baha'i faith into a mere humanitarian movement and considered the moral and social principles of the Baha'i religion (which 'Abdu'l-Bahâ summarised and listed in 12 points) as the only characteristic of the movement. The twelve principles are the following:

1. The unity of humankind.
2. The need to attain the Truth through unprejudiced and independent research.
3. The essential unity of all religions (but in the sense we have seen above).
4. The need for religion to be the cause of unity: "If this is not so atheism is better" ('Abdu'l-Bahâ).
5. The need for harmony between science and religion. Religion, conceived as the Baha'is conceive it, cannot be in contrast with science because it does not deal with knowledge, but with social action.
6. Equality of rights and duties between the sexes.
7. The fight against every kind of prejudice (the struggle against nationalism, religious fanaticism, class-consciousness and racism are particularly stressed).
8. The realization of world peace.
9. Universal education available to all (in the Baha'i communities the children of poorer families are educated at the community's expense).
10. The religious solution of the social problem through the abolition of extremes of poverty and wealth and the sharing of business profits.
11. Encouraging the adoption of an international auxiliary language ('Abdu'l-Bahâ praised Esperanto and there are a number of Esperantists among the Baha'is, though no text imposes a choice. In practice, the language used most internationally among the Baha'is, and by the Leader of the community himself, is English).
12. The institution of an international court of justice.

The Baha'i religion does not practise any public cult nor does it have sacraments or any specific sacramental rites. The only religious obligations the Baha'is have are as follows. (a) They are to meet every 19 days, according to the law established by the Bâb, on the first day of every Baha'i month for a common celebration known as the "Nineteenth-Day Feast" (for the Baha'is have maintained the Babi calendar). This celebration consists of the reading of prayers and sacred texts (including those of other religions), followed by a more specifically administrative part during which the administration of community funds is accounted for, useful information is given, etc., and all partake of simple refreshments together. (b) They are to fast for 19 days during the whole of the Babi month of 'Alâ (from the 2nd to the 20th of March). The fasting is in the Islamic style, i.e., abstention from every kind of food, drink, etc., from dawn to sunset. (c) They are to abstain from every kind of alcoholic drink. (d) When they marry the consent of both parents of both the bride and groom is necessary, whatever their age. (Marriage is monogamous, though in the early days bigamy was admitted in some cases). The proverbial affection between mothers-in-law and daughters-in-law, which is said to be typical of Baha'i circles, probably derives from this consent! Divorce is admitted, but advised against, with a trial period of one year for the spouses to be reconciled, if possible. (e) They must bury the dead at no more than an hour's distance from the place where the death occurred, and the body must not be altered: consequently cremation is forbidden. (f) They must pray with specific brief formulas three times a day (morning, noon and night). The obligatory prayers (written in Arabic by Baha'ullah) can be said in any language and some are preceded by an ablution which is much simpler than the Islamic ablution and consists in washing one's hands and face while reciting two very short prayers.

The *Aqdas* also provides precise rules for the division of inheritance, a 19 percent income tax and many other penal, civil and religious laws that at present are followed only by the Middle Eastern Baha'is (and then only in part). Even though the Baha'i religion does not practise any public rituals of worship, the *Aqdas* recommends that the faithful erect nine-sided *Mashriqu'l-Adhkâr*s (literally "the place where at dawn the name of God is mentioned") with nine-gored cupolas—a kind of temple open to the followers of every religion, all of whom can pray there when and how they want. 'Abdu'l-Bahâ specified that every temple must have attached to it an institution of higher learning in which different subjects are taught, a hospital, an orphanage, a pharmacy and other social institutions. He himself, on May 1, 1912, placed the first stone of the Mashriqu'l-Adhkâr of Wilmette (Illinois, USA) on the shores of Lake Michigan, near Chicago—an imposing construction with vast and beautiful gardens that cost over two million dollars. It was officially inaugurated in the presence of Rûhiyyeh Khânum (the Guardian's wife) in 1953. In 1902 the refugees from the Persian persecutions had already built another temple at Ashkhabad (Ishqâbâd) in Asian Russia (now Turkmenistan). The Baha'is also have the *hazîratu'l-quds* ("enclosures of holiness")—administrative centers without any sacrality where the assemblies meet (see below). The tombs of the Founders, on the other hand, are very sacred (they must be entered barefoot like the holy places of other oriental religions). These tombs are all concentrated in the "World Center of the faith" on Mount Carmel in the State of Israel (with which the Baha'is are on excellent terms. In 1956, the President of Israel paid an official visit to the Guardian of the Baha'i Faith and the holy places). The tomb of Baha'ullah is at Bahjî, while the mortal remains of the Bâb and of 'Abdu'l-Bahâ rest in the great mausoleum on the slopes of Mount Carmel, which the Persians call *Maqâm-i A'lâ* ("Supreme Place"). Tourists visit it every day because of its splendid position dominating the sea and because of the beautiful gardens that surround it. The Baha'is also consider as holy places the garden of Rizvân near Baghdad (see above), the Bâb's house at Shîrâz, etc. [though neither any longer exists, the latter having been destroyed by a Shi'ite mob in 1979–ed.)

Baha'i Administration

The most original aspect of the new religion, however, is possibly its organisational system. The Baha'is consider useless every theology, every individual moral act, every prayer—at least in this prophetic cycle—unless it contributes to the fulfillment of their one goal, that is, bringing about the unity of humankind. The means for the realisation of this goal (which according to the Baha'is are of divine origin) are to be found in the institution of the Baha'i administrative order, outlined in *al-Kitâb al-Aqdas* by Baha'ullah, perfected by 'Abdu'l-Bahâ and open to further improvement through the "Guardian" of the Faith and the Supreme world councils, which we will shortly describe.

This Order is made up of structures of two kinds: one which could be called administrative and the other pedagogical. The first is made up of elective bodies from the masses (of the faithful), the second of particularly devout personalities nominated from above. The two types of structures are united, at the top, in the person of the Guardian (*Valî-i amru'llâh*). The administrative structures are as follows:

1. The "Local Spiritual Assembly," or "Local House of Justice." This is set up in every place where there are at least nine Baha'is. It consists of nine members elected by universal suffrage. The Baha'i concept of election, which is considered an act of religious worship, implies that the electors are the instruments of a divine designation and that the elected are really chosen by God and not responsible to their electors during their entire period of office (established at present at one year). The elections take place in a climate of religious festivity, during the period in which the declaration of Baha'ullah's mission in the garden of the Rizvân in Baghdad (see above) is commemorated, i.e., from April 21 to May 2. [Baha'i Local Assemblies exist in most of the world's countries and territories, with the exception of populist-authoritarian nations (especially in the Muslim world) such as Iraq and Iran, and of Communist China-ed.).

2. Where the number of local assemblies is sufficient, a "convention" of delegates is elected by universal suffrage by the individual communities of the

country. These delegates elect in their turn—not necessarily from among themselves but from all the believers in the country—a National Spiritual Assembly (which will someday be called a "National House of Justice") that is also made up of nine members. By 1958 there were 25 National Spiritual Assemblies (some of which are also "regional," i.e., they temporarily include several countries), [and by 1992 there were 165 National Spiritual Assemblies around the world—in nearly every country; ed.].

3. ['Abdu'l-Bahâ's Will envisioned that] when there were enough National Assemblies, their members would elect (not necessarily from among themselves) a Universal Spiritual Assembly that would take the name of "the Universal House of Justice," of which the Guardian is, by right, president for life. Besides functioning as supreme court, the Universal House of Justice (which, in spite of Baha'i feminism, must be composed of men only) would have the function of promulgating laws not provided for by the *Aqdas* or the Founder's other writings and of abrogating its own enactments according to the needs of the times.

The jurisdiction of the various Assemblies is, within the ambit of their competencies, total, insofar as they combine executive, legislative and judiciary powers. Since there is no priesthood in the Baha'i faith, the members of these Assemblies are the "priests" of Bahâism (only taken in a body, however, for individual members have no authority). The Baha'is are advised to bring their problems (personal ones too) and their private disagreements before their Assemblies (first the local ones then, if the matter cannot be solved, to the National one, etc.).

Side by side with these elective admninistrative institutions there is, as we mentioned, the other system of teaching, nominated from above. The Guardian is at the head of this system but his duties are only interpretative and not legislative, i.e., he must watch, above all, over the unity of the Community and interpret the sacred texts. His function is infallible only in this area, while legislative infallibility requires the whole body of the Universal House of Justice. The position of Guardian is hereditary, but this right has two limitations. First, this position does not necessarily devolve upon the eldest son. (Before his death the Guardian must indicate his successor among his relatives and sons.) Second, this choice must be ratified by an assembly of nine "Hands of the Cause." The Hands of the Cause are the lower level of this "teaching" scale: there is no limitation to their appointment (up to 95 it seems) by the Guardian and it is they who elect the above-mentioned group of nine, which also has the general function of helping the Guardian in his duties. The Hands of the Cause, in their turn, nominate helpers who form "Auxiliary Boards" to help them in a more capillary way in their basic function, which is to galvanize, through incessant travel, the enthusiasm of the believers, though without interfering in administrative affairs, which remain the exclusive prerogative of the assemblies.

The first Guardian's death (on November 3, 1957) and the absence of a testamentary designation of his successor posed complex problems for the Baha'is. Some of the Guardian's functions (though not that of "interpreting" the texts) were carried out by the council of nine Hands of the Cause resident in Palestine. In 1963, at the election of the Universal House of Justice (which, by definition, has infallible legislative power) these problems [were] resolved. The monarchical institution may . . . be considered at an end with the work of the first Guardian. In this case the "Hands of the Cause" too, once those now living have died, [will] cease to exist. [The Universal House of Justice was elected by members of the then-existing National Spiritual Assemblies in Haifa in 1963. It subsequently made a determination that no further Guardians could be designated, because Shoghi Effendi had died without a will and none of his close relatives (many of whom had been excommunicated by him) was eligible. This decision also meant that, unlike Ismailis, the Baha'is thenceforward had no divinely appointed and hereditary interpreter of scripture (i.e., an Agha Khan, which the Guardian resembled), only elected legislators. Since the institution of the Hands of the Cause, who had to be appointed by the Guardian, also therefore would eventually come to an end, the Universal House of Justice created a new body, the Continental Counsellors. These preside over the Auxiliary Board members and their Assistants, promoting the proselytizing or "teaching" work and also ensuring the "protection" of the faith from schism. [See the Universal House of Justice, *Wellspring of Guidance*, pp. 140-144-ed.]

More or less quoting Montesquieu, 'Abdu'l-Bahâ said that the Administrative Order is far from being of secondary importance: it is "the sum of the laws deriving from the intimate reality of created things." In other words, canon law stems basically from the same source as the physical law and the moral law (though on another level), i.e., from the ever elusive Reality of God. This principle explains the great importance given by the Baha'i religion (so earthly, as we have seen, even though it remains a religion) to the whole system of its Organisation, which the Baha'is do not only consider divine in origin but also the instrument for bringing about the unity of humankind. The Baha'is do not accept the separation of church and state or, rather, they accept it only if "church" is understood as a sacramental structure that attributes special honours and sacred functions to a group of individuals, the "priests." Since priesthood and sacraments do not exist in Bahâism, Baha'i unity assumes a nature which is different from that of past experiments in theocracy. In all events this explains why declared Baha'is are forbidden to belong to any political party or secret society.

Thus, with the Baha'i faith—the last effort of Persian religious thinking and the first Iranian religion to go beyond the confines of Asia—we have reached a phase of this thinking where, having gone beyond the stage of an aristocratic

Gnosis, it offers itself to the world as a universal religion. The silent (*sâmit*) and speaking (*nâtiq*) figures of Ismailism are united here in a single person—the Manifestation; the esoteric and the exoteric merge and the esoteric (*bâtin*) is again apparent in a law and an Order. For the similarities between Ismailism and Babi-Bahâism are above all philosophical and formal similarities. We have seen, however, how the philosophical and dogmatic aspect is the least important in Bahâism, for it is a religion oriented eminently towards practical goals. In its legislation (and I do not mean specific laws but the spirit of the law) we find—renewed—the "Islamic" sense of religiosity (including the Jewish, or rather "Semitic" love for the law) which was, for centuries, more than an "intrusion." It was a necessary component of what can only in this way be called an integrally Persian religious spirit, for, as we have observed throughout this book, Persia was never free from a "Western" influence. And it is under the sign of this simplified, ethical and monotheistic Indo-European movement that we will say goodbye to Persian religion, with the quotation of an admonishment by Baha'ullah. In the primacy given to simple and robust moral exhortations and the flowery literary form, it synthethizes the Persian spirit which, in its best moments, succeeded in brilliantly combining Islamic legalism and the complex speculative flowering of Iranian culture:

"Be generous in prosperity, and thankful in adversity. Be worthy of the trust of thy neighbor, and look upon him with a bright and friendly face. Be a treasure to the poor, an admonisher to the rich, an answerer to the cry of the needy, a preserver of the sanctity of thy pledge. Be fair in thy judgment, and guarded in thy speech. Be unjust to no man, and show all meekness to all men. Be as a lamp unto them that walk in darkness, a joy to the sorrowful, a sea for the thirst, a haven for the distressed, an upholder and defender of the victim of oppression. Let integrity and uprightness distinguish all thine acts. Be a home for the stranger, a balm to the suffering, a tower of strength for the fugitive. Be eyes to the blind, and a guiding light unto the feet of the erring. Be an ornament to the countenance of truth, a crown to the brow of fidelity, a pillar of the temple of righteousness, a breath of life to the body of mankind, an ensign to the hosts of justice, a luminary above the horizon of virtue, a dew to the soil of the human heart, an ark on the ocean of knowledge, a sun in the heaven of bounty, a gem on the diadem of wisdom, a shining light in the firmament of thy generation, a fruit upon the tree of humility" (*Epistle to the Son of the Wolf*, pp. 93–94)[9].

Afterword

Important developments occurred with regard to the Baha'i faith in the decades between 1958, when this chapter was written, and the present.[10] After some years during which the stewardship of the Baha'i faith was with the Hands of the Cause who had been appointed by Shoghi Effendi Rabbani, in 1963 the members of the National Assemblies of the world elected the nine-member Universal House of Justice. This body, elected every five years, has its seat in Haifa, Israel, near the shrine of the Bab and not far from the tomb of Baha'ullah. This body is now invested with the world leadership of the Baha'is, in accordance with the instructions in Baha'ullah's *Most Holy Book*, and its legislative enactments are considered by the faithful to be sinless or infallible (*ma'sûm*).

The character of the Baha'i faith has also changed a great deal since the late 1950s. It was a substantial religious minority in Iran, nearly one percent of the population in the 1960s and 1970s, possessing many institutions such as hospitals, schools and investment funds. In all of the West, however, there were only a few thousand Baha'is, and it often possessed more the characteristics of an enlightened club there. It had only a small presence in the global South outside the Middle East. There were only about 200,000 Baha'is in the world in the early 1950s, and all but ten percent or so of these lived in Iran. In the late 1950s, Iranian immigrants or "pioneers" in Uganda began actively proselytizing villagers, and met with great success, such that thousands enrolled in the new religion. This process began in India in the early 1960s, and was repeated elsewhere in the global South. The Baha'i faith became one of the faster-growing religions in the world, and now (in 1994) claims about 5.5 million adherents world-wide, with over a million believers in India, a million and a half in Africa, and around a million in Latin America. After the collapse of the Soviet Union, hundreds of Baha'i "pioneers" and "travelling teachers" labored to establish new national communities everywhere from the Ukraine to Kazakhstan. Although some historians and sociologists have questioned the depth of the village conversions in India and Africa, it should be remembered that Islam came to be established in the Indian subcontinent in much the same way, and that only over centuries did village syncretists ultimately become more scripturally oriented and strict in observance. Among the important developments in rural Baha'i communities is an increasing attention on the part of National Spiritual Assemblies to projects of socio-economic development, from village tutorial schools in India to Radio Baha'i in Ecuador, which does a good deal of programming in Quechua for Amerindian farmers.

In the United States, the coming to consciousness of the Baby Boom generation, along with the ferment of the civil rights movement and the controversies over the Vietnam war, had a big impact on the Baha'i community. In 1963 the American community numbered around 10,000 adults. In the succeeding decade the community grew to 50,000. Under the impact of the interest in oriental religions and in peace movements, the number of U.S. Baha'is under 21 increased from about a thousand in 1968 to about 10,000 in 1974, and the

Baha'i faith became a small part of the youth culture through such performers as Seals and Crofts. In addition, thousands of poor African-Americans in South Carolina and Georgia entered the religion in the early 1970s, in a way that somewhat mirrored the village conversions in Uganda and India. The community experienced a certain amount of difficulty in absorbing and educating ("deepening") these large numbers of new believers, and has only been able to keep track of a little over half of its enrollees over time. Still, the Baha'i community claims 120,000 adult U.S. adherents in the mid-1990s, and even if the true number is somewhat smaller, its current numbers put it in somewhat the same league as much older and better-established liberal religious movements, such as the Society of Friends (Quakers) and the Unitarians.

By 1978 the Iranian Baha'i community, of about 350,000, had already been outstripped in size by the Indian, and the global South was becoming more important to the religion than either the Middle East or the North. Baha'is in the Middle East, moreover, faced an increasingly hostile atmosphere, with the rise of militant Islam in the post-colonial era. Islamists viewed Baha'is, one of the few pacifist groups in the region, as dangerous heretics and fantasized about the significance of the religion's headquarters being in Israel. (The reason for this, of course, was simply that Baha'ullah had been exiled to 'Akkâ, where his shrine still is, and this city became part of Israel in 1948). Arab nationalists were not always as secularist as they liked to sound, and were influenced by Islamist hostility to Baha'is. The Baha'i community of Egypt, mostly native Egyptian and several thousand strong, was banned by Gamal Abdel Nasser in 1960, and the Baha'is of Morocco were persecuted the succeeding year. The gradual destruction (through jailings, confiscations, and the encouragement of emigration) of the Baha'i communities in much of the Arab world proved a harbinger for their fate in Iran. The 1979 Revolution brought the Shi'ite clerics to power, one of whose corporate values was the need to stop the progress of the Baha'i faith in Iran and elsewhere. In the succeeding years, the ayatollahs confiscated Baha'i properties, banned elective Baha'i institutions, executed nearly 200 prominent Baha'is, imprisoned and/or tortured hundreds more, and destroyed the House of the Bab in Shiraz. The members of the sitting National Spiritual Assembly of 1980 were abducted by revolutionary guards and made to "disappear," almost certainly into a mass grave. They included a professor of Islamic philosophy at Tehran University, 'Alî-Murâd Dâvûdî. Human rights organizations and such institutions as the European Parliament and the U.S. Congress condemned this attack on a small, apolitical community, and the international outcry does appear to have had some effect on Iranian government policy toward Baha'is. Although after Khomeini's death the executions largely ceased, and most Baha'is were released from prison, the regime remains determined to weaken and if at all possible to destroy the community.

For instance, by denying Baha'i students the right to attend college or university, the government clearly intends to push the community into the working class and deprive it of the substantial wealth its professionals had previously been generating. This and other discriminatory practices are calculated to exercise a slow and steady influence, encouraging apostasy and making Baha'i beliefs a genuine liability in Iranian society.

The ultimate irony, then, is that the religious themes distilled in the Baha'i religion have in recent years found more fertile ground among Ugandans, Bolivians, Indians and even Americans than in Iran itself. In any case, the relative global success of this faith, despite its being spurned at home, is, as Alessandro Bausani pointed out in 1958, an abiding testament to the power of the Iranian religious imagination.

Notes

1. The Qur'an.
2. The reader should note the Bâb's knowledge of the evangelical texts paraphrased here. A European doctor who examined him in prison witnessed to the fact that the Bâb had a copy of the Qur'an and one of the Bible by his side.
3. The Qur'an.
4. Other allusions to Qur'anic passages.
5. The Qur'an.
6. As we have seen, this was one of the Bâb's titles.
7. From the introduction of *A Traveller's Narrative* (see Bibliography, pp. XXXIX and foll.)
8. For a typological characterization of Bahâism within the framework of monotheisms see my article: "Per una tipologia del monoteismo," in *St e Mat. di St. di Rel.*, XXVIII, 1957, pp. 67 and foll.
9. Cf. *Spigolature Dagli Scritti di Bahâ'ullah,* Rome, 1956, pp. 312–13.
10. The information below is largely distilled in Peter Smith and Moojan Momen, "The Baha'i Faith 1957–1988: A Survey of Contemporary Developments," *Religion* 19 (1989):63–91 and Robert H. Stockman, "The Baha'i Faith in America: One Hundred Years," *World Order* 25 (Spring 1974):9–23.

Bibliography

On the Bâb and Bâbism:

Bab, Sayyid 'Alî Muhammad. *Bayân-i Fârsî*. Tehran, n.d. French trans. by A.L.M. Nicolas. *Le Béyân Persan*. Paris, 1911–14 (4 vols).

———. *Al-Bayân al-'Arabî* in A. al-Hasanî, *Al-Bâbiyyûn wa al-Bahâ'iyyûn fî mâdîhim wa hâdirihim*. Sidon, 1957. French trans. by A.L.M. Nicolas. *Le Béyân Arabe*. Paris, 1905.

Religion in Iran

————. *Dalâ'il-i Sab'eh*. Tehran, n.d.

————. *Muntakhabât az âthâr-i Hadrat-i Nuqteh-i Ulâ*. Wilmette, Ill., 1978. Eng. trans. H. Taherzadeh. *Selections from the Writings of the Bab*. Haifa, 1976.

————. *Sahîfeh-i 'Adliyyeh*. Tehran, n.d.

Bausani, A. "Un ghazal di Qurratu'l-'Ain." *Oriente Moderno*. XXIX (1949), pp. 190–192.

Browne, E.G. *A Literary History of Persia*. Cambridge, 1953. Esp. vol. IV, pp. 194–221.

————. *A Year Amongst the Persians*. Cambridge, 1926.

Browne, E.G., ed. *Materials for the study of the Babi Religion*. Cambridge, 1918.

————, ed. *Kitâb-i Nuqtat al-Kâf*. London, 1910.

————, ed. and trans. *A Traveller's Narrative written to illustrate the Episode of the Bab*. 2 vols. Cambridge, 1891.

de Gobineau, Joseph A. *Les religions et les philosophies dans l'Asie Centrale*. Paris, 1865. Especially pp. 141 and foll.

Hamadani, Mirza Huseyn. *The New History (Tarikh-i Jadid) of Mirza 'Alî Muhammad, the Bab*. Trans. E.G. Browne. Cambridge, 1893.

Huart, Cl. *La religion de Bâb*. Paris, 1889.

Iqbal, M. *The Development of Metaphysics in Persia*. London 1908.

Ivanov, M. S. *Babidskie vosstanija v Irane*. Leningrad, 1939.

Kazem-Beg, Mirza. *Bâb et les Babis*. In *JA* VI-VII (1866), pp. 329–384; 457–522 and VII-VIII, pp. 196–252; 357–400;423–507. Lessona, M. *I Babi*. Torino, 1881.

Nicolas, A. L. M. *Seyyed 'Alî Muhammad dit le Bâb*. Paris 1905.

Root, Martha. *Táhirih the Pure, Iran's greatest woman*. Karachi, 1938. With the Persian texts and translations of several poems.

Zukovskij, V. A. *Nedavnye kazni babidov*. St. Peterburg, 1888.

Zarandi, Muhammad "Nabil-i A'zam." *The Dawnbreakers: Nabil's Narrative of the Early Days of the* Baha'i *Revelation* [*Matâli'al-Anvâr*]. New York, 1932 (with many photographs of places, buildings and relics connected with the Bâb's life).

On Baha'ullah and Bahâism:

The principal works of Baha'ullah:

Baha'ullah. *Ad'iyeh-yi Hazrat-i Mahbûb*. Cairo 1339 A.H. (1921). (Various prayers by Baha'ullah, including the obligatory prayers. Partial Italian transl.: *Preghiere Bahái*. Roma, 1951).

————. *Alvâh-i nâzilih khitâb bi-mulûk va ru'asâ-yi arz*. Tehran: MMMA, 126 B.E.

————. *Alvâh*. New Delhi: n.p. Facsimile of MS in Hand of Zaynu'l-Muqarrabîn dated A.H. 1311. Mainly supplements to the Aqdas.

————. *Aqdas-i buzurg va chand lauh-i dîgar*. Bombay: Matba'at an-Nasiri, 1314.

————. *Athâr-i qalam-i a'lâ*. 7 vols. Bombay and Tehran, 1890–1978.

————. *Gleanings from the Writings of* Baha'ullah. Trans. Shoghi Effendi. New York, 1935. Italian trans., *Spigolature dagli scritti di* Baha'ullah. Roma, 1956.

————. *Haft Vâdî* (Seven Valleys), *Chahâr Vâdî* (Four Valleys), *al-Kalimât al-maknûna* (The Hidden Words), *Mathnavî*, Cairo, 1332 A.H. (1914). English trans. 'Alî Quli

Khan and Marzieh Gail, *The Seven Valleys*, Wilmette, 1948. Eng. trans. Shoghi Effendi. *The Hidden Words*. London, 1944. French trans. H. Dreyfus. *Les Sept Vallées*, Paris, 1905; German trans. Braun. *Die verborgenen Worte*. Stuttgart, 1916. Italian trans. *Le sette valli e le quattro valli*. Roma, 1949.
Le parole celate. Roma, 1949.
———. *Ishrâqât va chand lauh-i Dîgar*. Tehran, n.d.
———. *Iqtidarat va chand Lawh-i Digar*. Tehran, n.d. Facsimile of a Mishkîn Qalam MS calligraphed in 1310.
———. *al-Kitâb al-Aqdas*. (In Arabic.) Russian ed. and trans. by Tumanski. *Zapiski Imp. Adademii Nauk*, Hist.-Phil. class, VIII, t. 36, St. Petersburg, 1899. Eng. trans. *The Kitab-i Aqdas: The Most Holy Book*. Haifa: Baha'i World Centre, 1992.
———. *Kitâb-i Iqân* (The Book of Certitude). Tehran, n.p (in Persian). English trans. Shoghi Effendi. *The Book of Certitude*. Wilmette, Ill., 1943; French trans. H. Dreyfus, *Le livre de la Certitude*. Paris, 1904. Italian trans. *Il Libro della Certezza*. Roma, 1955.
———. *Kitâb ash-Shaikh*. Cairo, 1338 A.H. (1920). Eng. trans. Shoghi Effendi. *Epistle to the Son of the Wolf*. Wilmette, Ill., 1941, 1971.
———. *Majmû'eh-yi matbû'eh-yi alvâh-i mubârakeh-yi hazrat-i Baha'ullâh*. Cairo, 1338 A.H. (1920). This volume contains many of Baha'ullah's short works.
———. *Prayers and Meditations*. Trans. Shoghi Effendi. New York, 1938.
———. *Sûreh-yi Mulûk*. Cairo, n.d.
———. *Tablets of* Baha'ullah *Revealed after the Kitab-i-Aqdas*. Trans. H. Taherzadeh et al. Wilmette, Ill., 1988.
——— et al. Baha'i *World Faith*. Wilmette, 1943. This volume contains the translation of many of Baha'ullah's and 'Abdu'l-Bahâ's minor works

On 'Abdu'l-Bahâ
Blomfield, Lady. *The Chosen Highway*. London, 1940.
Ford, Hanford. *The Oriental Rose, or the Teachings of 'Abdu'l-Bahâ*. New York, 1910.
Lemaitre, S. *Une grande figure de l'Unité: Abdu'l-Bahâ*. Paris, 1952.
Phelps, M. H. *Life and teachings of Abbas Effendi*. London, 1912.
Zarqânî, Mahmûd. *Kitâb badâ'i' al-âthâr fî asfâr maulâ'l-akhyâr*. Bombay, 1914–21 (2 vols.: this is the diary of his journey in Europe and America with a number of his speeches).

His principal works
'Abdu'l-Baha. *Alvâh va vasâyâ-yi mubârakeh-yi 'Abdu'l-Bahâ*. Cairo, 1342 A.H. (1924); Karachi, 1960. (Extracts from his will, important for the question of the succession).
———. *Javâb-i prôfesôr-i âlmânî Dr. Forel* (An answer to the well-known Swiss scientist Prof. Forel), Cairo, 1922.
———. *Khitâbât-i Hazrat-i 'Abdu'l-Bahâ fî Urûpâ va Amrikâ*. 3 vols. Cairo, 1921.
———. *Majmû'eh-yi alvâh-i mubârikeh bi-iftikhâr-i Bahâ'iyân-i Pârsî*. Tehran, 133 B.E.
———. *Makâtîb-i 'Abdu'l-Bahâ*. 8 vols. Cairo and Tehran, 1910–1977.

―――. *Maqâlîh-yi Shakhsî sayyâh*. Ed. and trans. E.G. Browne. 2 vols. Cambridge, 1891.

―――. *Muntakhabâtî az makâtîb-i Hazrat-i 'Abdu'l-Bahâ*. 2 vols. Wilmette and Haifa, 1979–1984.

―――. *An-nûr al-abhâ fî mufâvazât Hazrat 'Abdu'l-Bahâ*. Cairo, 1920. Repr. New Delhi, 1983. (Notes on conversations, in Persian, collected by L. Clifford Barney at 'Akkâ). English trans. by L. Clifford Barney. *Some Answered Questions*. London, 1908; rev. edn. Wilmette, Ill., 1981. French trans. H. Dreyfus. *Les leçons de St. Jean D'Acre*. Paris, 1929.

―――. *Ar-risâla al-madanîya*. Cairo 1329 A.H. (1911); Hofheim, 1984. (This work was written by A.B. in 1292 H. (1875). English trans. by Marzieh Gail. *Secret of Divine Civilization*. Wilmette, Ill., 1957.

―――. *Risâleh-yi Siyâsiyyeh*. Tehran: Muhammad Labîb, 1325/1907. Based on the Bombay edn. (of 1893?).

―――. *Selected Writings of 'Abdu'l-Bahâ*. Wilmette, 1942.

―――. *Tablets of 'Abdu'l-Bahâ*. Ed. A. Windust, New York, 1930 (3 vols.).

―――. *The Wisdom of 'Abdu'l-Bahâ*. New York, 1924. Italian trans. *La saggezza di 'Abdu'l-Bahâ*. Roma, 1957).

Among the works of Shôghi Effendî, who wrote equally well in English, in Arabic and in Persian, the most important in English is: Shoghi Effendi. *God Passes By*. Wilmette, 1945.

For the Universal House of Justice:
Universal House of Justice. *Wellspring of Guidance*. Wilmette, Ill., 1970.

On Baha'i doctrines:
Esslemont, J. E. *Baha'ullah and the New Era*. London, 1923, with successive and augmented and corrected editions. Italian trans. Baha'ullah e la nuova era. Roma, II ed. 1955.
Jockel, R. *Die Glaubenslehren der Baha'i-Religion*. Darmstadt, 1951. (Contains an ample bibliography of oriental and western works).

There are many works in defense of the faith in Arabic and in Persian by Abû'l-Fazâ'il Gulpâygânî (Abû'l-Fazl Jurfâdhaqânî).

One of his principal works is:
Gulpâygânî, Abû 'l-Fazâ'il. *Al-hujaj al-bahiyya*. Cairo, 1343 A.H. (1925). English transl. 'Alî Qulî Khân. *The Bahá'í Proofs*. Wilmette, Ill., rev. edn. 1983. A wide-ranging anthology (in Persian and Arabic) of the doctrinal writings of the founders, especially of the "tablets" which are hard to find, is: Ishrâq-Khâvarî, 'Abdu'l-Hamîd, ed. *Mâ'ideh-yi âsmânî* (The Heavenly Table), Tehran, 1947 and foll. (9 vols.) Statistical and other information on the life of the Baha'i communities of the world can be found in the "Year Books," sumptuously published in America under the title of *The Baha'i World*.

In addition, see:
Berger, Peter L. "Motif messianique et processus social dans le Bahaïsme," in *Arch. de Sociol. des Rel.*, Paris, 1957, pp. 93–107.
Grossman, H. "Die Ausbreitung und gegenwärtige Aktivität der Bahá'í-Religion, insbesondere in Amerika und Europa." *Zeitschr. für Religions und Geistesgeschichte.* X (1958), 4, pp. 386 and foll.
Loppert, Th. A. *Die Fortenwicklung der Babi-Behaï im Westen* Würtzburg, 1933.
Römer, H. *Die Babi-Behaï.* Potsdam, 1912.

Additional Bibliography

N.B. We have given an ample bibliography for this chapter because of the interest this "new Persian religion" presents and also because the articles in the encyclopedias which deal with the subject have not always been sufficiently up-dated.

Update: Babi and Baha'i studies experienced a significant revival in the 1980s and 1990s, and those who wish to pursue the subject further can now find a number of important works in English. H.M. Balyuzi, *The Bab: Herald of the Day of Days* (Oxford, 1973), perhaps initiated this new round of scholarly activity. It was succeeded by Abbas Amanat, *Resurrection and Renewal: The Making of the Babi Movement in Iran, 1844–1850* (Ithaca, N.Y., 1989), an exhaustive study of the movement from primary sources. An important bibliography is Denis MacEoin, *The Sources for Early Babi Doctrine and History* (Leiden, 1992); it is, however, incomplete, since it neglects to list significant manuscript holdings of the British Library. See also Moojan Momen, "The Social Basis of the Babi Upheavals in Iran (1848–53): A Preliminary Analysis," *Int'l Jl. of Middle East Studies* 15 (1983):157–183; and *idem.*, "The Trial of Mulla 'Alî Bastami: A Combined Sunni-Shi'i Fatwa against the Bab," *Iran* 20 (1982):113–143. For initial explorations of the Bab's distinctive thought, see Todd Lawson, "Interpretation as Revelation: The Qur'an Commentary of Sayyid 'Alî Muhammad Shirazi, the Bab (1819–1850)," in Andrew Rippin, ed., *Approaches to the History of the Interpretation of the Qur'an* (Oxford, 1988), pp. 223–53 and *idem*, "The Terms "Remembrance" (*dhikr*) and "Gate" (*bâb*) in the Bab's Commentary on the Sura of Joseph," *Studies in Babi and Baha'i History* (hereafter *SBBH*), (Los Angeles, 1988), 5:1–64. See also Denis MacEoin, "Early Shaykhi Reactions to the Bab and his Claims," in *SBBH*, 1 (1982):1–48; *idem.*, "Hierarchy, Authority and Eschatology in Early Babi Thought," *SBBH*, 3 (1986):95–156; and Peter Smith and Moojan Momen, "The Babi Movement: A resource Mobilization Perspective," *SBBH*, 3 (1986):33–94. Mangol Bayat, *Mysticism and Dissent*, listed in the last chapter, also has insightful things to say about the movement.

The major academic treatment of the Baha'i faith is now Peter Smith, *The Babi and Baha'i Religions: From Messianic Shi'ism to a World Religion* (Cambridge, 1987). A crucial collection of Western primary documents, many of them archival, is Moojan Momen, ed., *The Babi and Baha'i Religions, 1844–1944: Some Contemporary Western Accounts* (Oxford, 1981). Baha'ullah's biography is treated by H.M. Balyuzi,

Baha'ullah: *The King of Glory* (Oxford, 1980); his disciples are discussed in *idem.*, *Eminent Baha'is in the Time of* Baha'ullah (Oxford, 1985). Baha'ullah's major works are discussed, but in a traditional rather than an academic manner, by Adib Taherzadeh, *The Revelation of* Baha'ullah, 4 vols. (Oxford, 1974–1987). The only primary chronicle of Baha'ullah's life yet to be translated into English is Ustâd Muhammad-'Alî Salmânî, *My Memories of* Baha'ullah, trans. Marzieh Gail (Los Angeles, 1982). For Baha'ullah's thought, see four studies by Juan R.I. Cole: "The Concept of Manifestation in the Baha'i Writings," *Baha'i Studies* 9 (1982):1–38; "Baha'ullah and the Naqshbandi Sufis in Iraq, 1854–1856," *SBBH* 2 (1984):1–28; "Iranian Millenarianism and Democratic Thought in the 19th Century," *Int'l. Jl. of Middle East Studies* 24 (1992):1–26; "'I am all the Prophets:' The Poetics of Pluralism in Baha'i Texts," *Poetics Today* 14 (1993):447–476; and see also Stephen N. Lambden, "The Sinaitic Mysteries: Notes on Moses/Sinai Motifs in Babi and Baha'i Scripture," *SBBH* 5 (1988):65–184. Little has been published on the 19th-century Iranian Baha'i community, but especially relevant to Bausani's concerns would be Susan Stiles, "Early Zoroastrian Conversions to the Baha'i Faith in Yazd, Iran," *SBBH* 2 (1984):67–94.

The major biography of 'Abdu'l-Bahâ is H.M. Balyuzi, *'Abdu'l-Baha: Centre of the Covenant* (Oxford, 1973). Shoghi Effendi's life is covered in a memoir by his wife, Mary "Ruhiyyih Khanum" Rabbani, *The Priceless Pearl* (London, 1969). Two new translations have appeared of the works of the major Baha'i theologian Mîrzâ Abu'l-Fazl Gulpâygânî: *Miracles and Metaphors*, trans. J. Cole (Los Angeles, 1981) and *Letters and Essays, 1886–1913*, trans. J. Cole (Los Angeles, 1985). For American Baha'i history see Robert Stockman, *The Baha'i Faith in America*, vol. 1 (Wilmette, Ill., 1985); and various articles in the *SBBH* volumes (which with volume six, on American community histories, becomes *Studies in the Babi and Baha'i Religions*). For Baha'i women see R. Jackson Armstrong-Ingram, "American Baha'i Women and the Education of Girls in Tehran, 1909–1934," in *SBBH* 3 (1986):181–212 and Susan Stiles Maneck, "Women in the Baha'i Faith," in Arvind Sharma, ed., *Religion and Women* (Albany, N.Y., 1994), pp. 211–227. The real demographic center of gravity of the Baha'i faith has now shifted to the non-Muslim global South, especially India, Africa and Latin America. This development has been little studied, but see William Garlington, "Baha'i Conversions in Malwa, Central India," *SBBH* 2 (1984):157–188 and Peter Smith and Moojan Momen, "The Baha'i Faith, 1957–1988: A Survey of Contemporary Developments," *Religion* 19 (1989):63–91.

Figures 1-3. Statue and Achaemenid decorative motifs from Persepolis (photo by Scarcia)

Figure 4. Sassanian capital with symbolic motif at Taq-i Bustan, close to Kerman- shah (photo by Scarcia)

Figure 5. Head of griffin, Persepolis (photo by Scarcia)

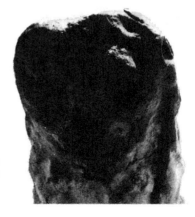

Figure 6. [Median or] Achaemenid stone lion at Ecbatana (modern Hamadan) (photo by Scarcia)

414

Figure 7. Cyrus' Tomb at Pasargade (photo by Scarcia)

Figure 8. A Zoroastrian *dakhme* (tower of silence) for exposing corpses in Yazd (photo by Scarcia)

415

Figure 9. Sasanian bas-relief depicting an angel, Taq-i Bustan (photo by
Scarcia)

Figure 10. Remains of two fire temples at Naqsh-i Rustam, Achaemenid period
(photo by Scarcia)

416

Figure 11. Friezes in the Apadana at Persepolis.

Figure 12. Columns at Persepolis (photo by Rostamy, Tehran Archeological Museum)

Figure 13. Sasanian vase (Hermitage State Museum, St. Petersburg)

Figure 14. Post-Sasanian Bronze statue. (Berlin Museum)

419

Figure 15. Luristan bronze statue from south-western Persia

Figure 16. Minaret in Damghan

Figure 17. Twelfth century minaret in Saveh

421

Figure 18. Shrine of Shaikh Bayazid Bistami, famous Persian mystic, in Bistam, c. 6 km from Shahrud (photo by Scarcia)

Figure 19. The Nayin mosque, one of the oldest in Persia (ninth century)

423

Figure 20. Interior of the Nayin mosque

Figure 21. A mosque in Isfahan

Figure 22. Mihrab of the cathedral mosque of Isfahan, 1310

426

Figure 23. A mosque in Yazd (photo by Scarcia)

Figure 24. Detail from the interior of the Saljuq mosque of Ardistan

428

Figure 25. Isfahan. Imamzade Isma'il

Figure 26. Tamerlane's Tomb in Samarkand

Figure 27. Tabriz. Front of the Blue Mosque

Figure 28. Sultaniye. Tomb of Uljaitu Khodabande, the Ilkhanid ruler who discovered the tomb of Ali

Figure 29. Two imamzadehs (Shi'ite shrines of saints) in Qom (photo by Scarcia)

Figure 30. Shrine of Shah Ni'matullah Vali, a leading figure in Persian Sufism, around 40 km east of Kerman. (photo by Scarcia)

Figure 31. Ruins of an ancient mosque (photo from Troeller)

Figure 32. The main mosque of Gulpaygan, north-west of Isfahan, from the Saljuq period, 12th century

Figure 33. The old Saljuq mosque of Ardestan, 12th century (photo by Scarcia)

Figure 34. An imamzade

Figure 35. The domes of the Shrine of Hazrat-i Ma'sumeh in the city of Qom (photo by Scarcia)

Figure 36. View of the holy city of Qom (photo by Scarcia)

Figure 37. An imamzadeh close to Golpaygan (a pilgrimage site) (photo by Scarcia)

Figure 38. The Gate of Bushruyeh in Khurasan, the homeland of the first Babi missionary, Mulla Husain Bushruyeh (photo by Scarcia)

Figure 39. Kurdish cemetery (Sunnite) (photo by Scarcia)

Figure 40. Shi'ite rites, near Tehran (photo from Troeller)

Figure 41. Contrast between the old and the new in the holy city of Qom: two Shi'ite doctors of religion (mujtahids) next to an American car

440

Figure 42. A student of Islamic theology from a seminary in Isfahan.

Figure 43. Felt hats put out to dry, Bam

441

Figure 44. Preacher reciting a religious story in public near Tehran (photo from Troeller)

Figure 45. The only Mahriqu'l-Adhkar (Baha'i temple) in the West, in Willmette, Illinois. (USA)

442

Figure 46. The Masjid-i Shah, or Royal Mosque of Isfahan, seen through the vestibule columns of the Chehel Sotun palace

Figure 47. Square in the bazaar of Yazd. In the left, a tall wooden banner used in the commemorative procession of Imam Husain's martyrdom (photo by Scarcia)

443

Figure 48. Funeral procession in Tehran (photo from Troeller)

Figure 49. Isfahan, the Madrasa (seminary) of Madar-i Shah, late 17th century.

Figure 50. The Masjid-i Shah, or Royal Mosque of Isfahan.

Figure 51. Zoroastrian fire temple, Kerman (photo from Troeller)

Figure 52. "Devil worshippers" (the Yezidis) in Kermanshah (photo from Troeller)

446

Index

Index